How Far is America From Here?

Selected Proceedings of the First World Congress of
the International American Studies Association
22-24 May 2003

Edited by

Theo D'haen, Paul Giles,
Djelal Kadir,
and Lois Parkinson Zamora

Amsterdam - New York, NY
2005

The paper on which this book is printed meets the requirements of
'ISO 9706: 1994, Information and documentation - Paper for
documents - Requirements for permanence'.

ISBN 90-420-1756-2
© Editions Rodopi B.V., Amsterdam - New York, NY 2005
Printed in The Netherlands

Acknowledgements

This volume contains a selection of papers, including most of the plenary addresses, presented at the first World Congress of the International American Studies Association in Leiden, The Netherlands, 22-24 May 2003.

The congress was organized by IASA, the International American Studies Association (http://iasa.la.psu.edu/), with the financial support, which the organizers gratefully acknowledge, of Het College van Bestuur (Board of Administrators) of Leiden University, The Mayor and the College of Aldermen of the Town of Leiden, the Royal Dutch Academy of Sciences, Leiden University Fund, The Maison Descartes in Amsterdam, The American Embassy in The Hague, The Faculty of Arts of Leiden University, PALLAS - Research Institute of the Faculty of Arts of Leiden University, Cambridge University Press, Comparative American Studies/SAGE Publications, Harvard University Press, Palgrave Macmillan, Rodopi and Routledge.

The editors of this volume particularly acknowledge the financial support of PALLAS – Research Institute of the Faculty of Arts of Leiden University in the preparation of the manuscript for the press.

Theo D'haen
Paul Giles
Djelal Kadir
Lois Parkinson Zamora

Table of Contents

American Identities

Space and Place in American Studies

American Studies from an International American Studies Perspective

Defending America against Its Devotees

My fellow Americanists, we convene at a historic moment made more momentous by history. Whenever history has been momentous, human life invariably has had to countenance at once the best and the worst of times, what the proverbial Chinese wisdom describes as 'interesting times'. We are now an integral part of profound changes in the field of American Studies, changes of an order even greater than the paradigm shift precipitated by the Vietnam War in the last century. The challenge of being an Americanist has become more challenging than ever, and a greater necessity now gives our work greater urgency. How we approach our task, how we define the subject of our investigations and objects of our scope as Americanists emerge as pressing questions. If the Vietnam War changed the focus, language, and institutional self-definition of our field, the changes taking place presently are even more momentous since the implications for American Studies are not only national but also global in their geographical, disciplinary, discursive, and ideological nature. And the global nature of the present transformations makes their re-absorption into a national(ist) project less likely. I shall be referring throughout my remarks to the underlying dynamics that inevitably precipitate these programmatic and scholarly transformations. For the moment, I shall outline what I see as the most salient changes, now in process, for and in the field of American Studies. These are key developments that serve as defining impetus for our common endeavours in the International American Studies Association (IASA):

1. From a national project, America is shifting to an international object with historical density and global signification.
2. From an object of devotion, America is becoming a subject of investigation, scientific scrutiny, and secular criticism.
3. From a generator of epistemic paradigms for its own assessment, America is emerging as a case for study through criteria and scholarly principles that do not originate in America itself.
4. From a sponsor of American Studies, America is becoming a beneficiary of human resources and intellectual capital aimed at examining America and its place in the world.
5. From a discipline in self-denial, American Studies is being revisioned as a powerfully determinative discipline and formative discourse.
6. From a continentally defined geopolitical territoriality, America is being platted onto a hemispheric, bi-continental cognitive map.
7. From its unquestionable ideological imaginary, encoded variously as 'the American dream' or as 'the American Way', America's foundational myth is becoming subject to sustainable inquiry and demystification.
8. From a gross epistemic purveyor of pedagogy in realpolitik and geopolitical assessments, America is about to become a net recipient of knowledge production about America.
9. From the tautological Americanness of American Studies, we are witnessing a reconfiguration of American Studies as an international intellectual enterprise.
10. We are about to witness a realignment in the hierarchy of disciplinary fields trained on America, with political science and international relations, economics, demographic analyses, and information technologies and media assessments moving to displace literary studies, popular culture, and ethnic studies as defined by U.S. cultural politics at the forefront of the Americanist scholarly and pedagogical agenda.
11. We shall be witnessing a strong return to the archive and to archival resources as bases for a historical revisionism in historiography on America that may or may not affect historiography in America itself.

12. The focus of national and regional American Studies associations is shifting from regarding the USA as the determinative hub to a horizontal network of alliances among Americanists, as individuals and as national or institutional affiliates, with international and multilateral alignments.

I see these shifts occurring in American Studies, ironically, at a time when the most powerful nation in America, the USA, is exerting the greatest military and economic influence in the rest of the world, and when America is no longer a hospitable and unconditional terminus ad quem of migratory intellectual and cultural transhumance but operates as terminus a quo, or origination point, of forceful dynamics with global repercussions. The very hyper-power and the quality of influence exerted by America at this historical moment may well be the ultimate cause of these shifts in American Studies. The efficient, or most immediate causes for the precipitous acceleration of these shifts at the moment, I hope, will become self-evident in the course of my remarks.

It is fitting that we should gather in the City of Leiden to countenance these issues and to explore the question we have posed for this First World Congress of IASA: 'How far is America from here?' It is apt that we should be doing so now, from this ground where the Puritan pilgrims surveyed the Western horizon for some twenty years and sailed toward it nearly four centuries ago. And the question of our congress takes on a terrible immediacy in the context of the current international situation, which has the world looking to Americanists for some elucidation of how and why the global realpolitik is where it is at this uncertain juncture. Americanists, especially those of us intellectually moulded by 'the American Dream' and formed in 'the American Way', are urgently confronted by what the majority of the world considers a wayward America that would have its way, no matter. Our most urgent task in response to this global predicament is to be sure to differentiate between America and the governing regime of the United States of America. Regimes are ephemeral events, with global repercussions, certainly. First and foremost, however, we have a special obligation to make sure that the world is reminded of the difference between the people and the state, between a country and its government, between a nation's myths and its historical reality, and between any one historical event and the continuity of history in which discrete events are embedded.

Johan Huizinga gave us a treatise most of you may know as *The Waning of the Middle Ages* (Huizinga, 1924). It is a perennially relevant meditation at the beginning of this twenty-first century, particularly for us Americanists now faced with the necessity of trying to ascertain whether we are witnesses to a waning or an ebbing, or both simultaneously, in the history of our object of study. Apogee and apotheosis have been coincident before in human history, and the religiously-inflected discourse that drives current world events before its evangelical zeal would certainly be apposite to such coincidence. It was Huizinga, who, in a twenty-year period starting with World War I, saw fit to calibrate the distance between America and Europe, between America and the rest of the world, and between America and America. In 1918, in a volume entitled *Men and Masses in America* (Huizinga, 1918), he would diagnose the significance of America's entry into the Great War and would see the rising tide of an imperial back-flow from the western to the eastern shores of the Atlantic Ocean. In 1927, Huizinga would travel to America. His sojourn would occasion yet another set of essays whose focus begins with the fin-de-siècle energy in pragmatic America's Gilded Age and its epoch of robber barons. Huizinga referred to that period as an age of the 'this, here, and soon' while Europe was self-absorbed, an epoch of transatlantic counterpoint that Theo D'haen incisively described to my graduate seminar last Fall (2002) as America's time of political energy driven by 'discursive testosterone in an age of Nietzsche'. By 1936, in near simultaneity with the founding of American Studies, after having read Whitman in juxtaposition to Nietzsche, and William James in counterpoint to Ortega y Gasset, Huizinga would wax prophetic, not only with regard to Europe's imminent Second World War, but in adumbration of its baneful 50-year Manichaean aftermath and of our own current century's New World Order. Huizinga's 1936 book was titled *In the Shadow of Tomorrow* (Huizinga, 1936). The 'tomorrow' of 1936 was not long in coming; its shadows have not been in a hurry to depart, the relentless apocalyptic impatience of our liberator messiahs notwithstanding.

It is safe but less than reassuring to say that Huizinga, despite the simultaneity of his work with the founding of the field, does not figure often or prominently in the syllabi of our American Studies curriculum in the USA, where such syllabi have historically been forged, or in the rest of the world, where they have traditionally been received. As a result of the scarcity of texts on America like Huizinga's within American Studies curricula, history devolves, time and again, upon the impatience of the present, and the present never leaves the shadows of the past. Historical life and cultural discourse, then, perpetually backslide into the facile Manichaeism of world and new world, of old order and new world order, of old Europe and new Europe, of American Studies and New American Studies.

As we gather today from over thirty different countries at this first world congress of IASA, we do so with a compelling responsibility to make sure that the Huizinga of the Netherlands and the many Huizingas from all corners of the world find their way into our investigative and pedagogical mission as Americanists working in diverse loci on the globe. America is now more than ever too terribly important to be left to itself, and American Studies is on the precipitous verge of reconfiguration. Hitherto a national US discourse has been educating the world on American Studies. Anyone wishing to know what American Studies might look like when Americanists from around the world engage America, and do so from discursive sites and criteria that emanate not from Washington DC or Omaha, Nebraska, but from wherever Americanists happen to be in the world, can get a very good idea by examining the program of our first world congress.

Within America, at those institutional sites where American Studies is practised as a serious scholarly and pedagogical field, America ceased to be merely a univocal, celebratory occasion some time ago, though neither as long ago, nor as widely as one might wish to think, especially at times of nationalist recidivism such as the present time, when critical assessment of America's actions in the world is considered by many, within and outside of the field, to be an act of sedition. Today a number of the most incisive scholars and critical voices in American Studies from America are here in transcultural colloquy with us, and we are heartened by their presence and by their solidarity in the concerns we all share with Americanists in the rest of the world at a time when official U.S. policy seeks to over-determine not only America, but the rest of the world as well. There is reason to be concerned, since historically American Studies as a discipline and as an international field, especially, has been largely defined as an extension of US international policy and what is euphemistically referred to as 'public diplomacy', now as aggressively pursued as during some of the darkest years of the Cold War, and often by the same principals. Your being here today as participants in this first world-wide assessment of our field, its past, uncertain present, and its hopeful future, is most articulate on the urgency of our concerns and of the imminent changes in the field, changes I have outlined above and that are still in the process of being defined here.

American Studies is not a given—packaged and delivered as canonical object or as historical fetish. Nor is the critical and scholarly or pedagogical discourse of and on American Studies a portable toolkit, theoretical or otherwise, manufactured and exported through official governmental organs and their professional surrogates sent on expert missions. And while such agencies and agents will always exist, they and their largesse must be taken as symptoms of the cultural milieu and historical moment from which they emanate. They must be viewed as culturally and politically symptomatic phenomena for prospective case studies that Americanists at large must consider as part and parcel of their investigative and pedagogical subject matter. In this regard, Americanists must ask, what is 'public diplomacy'? Why is it called diplomacy? To what degree is it really public and, to the degree that it is not, what private interests drive it and why? These are urgent questions for Americanists, especially at a time when an ameliorative national project that rescued Europe from the ravages of war and launched American Studies internationally, the Marshall Plan, is now being replaced by what is clearly a Martial Plan that threatens war and its depredations as the policy instrument of first resort. There is little in common other than the phonemic echo between the homonyms. While the Marshall Plan stands in history as exemplary of America's finest hour, the most recent Martial Plan outlined in the Bush Doctrine of pre-emptive war and 'full spectrum dominance', sets the United States of America against the world, and it does so in unmistakable polar contradistinction to America's momentous mid-twentieth-century eminence. While polar opposites, these two historical moments do have something in common: namely, they share the consequential power to be defining.

No historical event in recent times has done more to foreground the urgency of this historical counterpoint for Americanists than the Office of Strategic Information instituted and operated by the US Department of Defence under the direction of an ideologically-driven cabal that is headed inexorably for ignominy in posterity's ledger. The real risk lies in such self-designated saviours taking the country with them, especially in the eyes of all those who do not, or are not inclined to differentiate between an ephemeral state regime and a people with a complex history. History will, sooner or later, be the judge of veracity's vicissitudes in the professed devotions and doctrinal zeal of those driving present policy. For now (mid-April 2003 as these lines are written while the drums of war resound on the Potomac and bombs shatter people and cities on the banks of the Tigris), however, the Office of Strategic Information has, in effect, managed to put into question the very name of the Department of Defence itself. The name is clearly an oxymoron in the new offensive age of the Project for the New American Century, the zeal of the Evangelical New Right, and the racist fervour of the Neoconservative operatives in charge of the US Defence Department's preemptive international policy, all bent on preempting even the US State Department on international policy formation. The international security policy that has emerged from this tangled web is the Bush Doctrine of preemptive action and perpetual war, a policy whose recent implementation is about to change the field of American Studies even more profoundly and more globally than the powerful mendacity of the Gulf of Tonkin Resolution that launched the Vietnam War. The Office of Strategic information is a reminder that all information is, and has always been, strategic, and any correlation between information and truth is deliberate and strategically wrought. With varying degrees of subtlety, this has always been the case in the realm of the public sphere and international realpolitik. Subtlety, however, is something the current US regime cannot be accused of. This may be the regime's greatest virtue. When a state regime finds its self-justification in the barbarity of terror and war, its propensity, as with any security state in human history, is to ensure the continuity of its justification by never relinquishing the capacity to foreground and even to foment terror, persistently and systematically. The security state can only perpetuate itself through a state of insecurity and, historically, any states' foremost objective is self-perpetuation. Proverbial wisdom teaches that truth is the first casualty of war, and we now live in a presidentially decreed state of perpetual war and indispensable terror.

In his letter of resignation to Secretary of State Colin Powell dated February 27, 2003, career diplomat John Brady Kiesling, who has served in United States embassies from Tel Aviv to Casablanca to Yerevan, wrote: 'We have not seen such systematic distortion of intelligence, such systematic manipulation of American opinion, since the war in Vietnam. ... We spread disproportionate terror and confusion in the public mind, arbitrarily linking the unrelated problems of terrorism and Iraq. The result, and perhaps the motive, is to justify a vast misallocation of shrinking public wealth to the military and to weaken the safeguards that protect American citizens from the heavy hand of government .... The policies we are now asked to advance are incompatible not only with American values but also with American interests. When our friends are afraid of us rather than afraid for us, it is time to worry. And now they are afraid' (Kiesling, quoted in Barringer, 2003).

All this should remind us that we, as Americanists, need to worry about those asymmetrical frames that define our own subject agency, institutional instrumentality, discursive strategies, all of which are part and parcel of the formative complex and transformative thrust that goes by the field designation of American Studies. It is a complex system in which we perforce operate, now as agents, now symptomatically, but rarely as ostensibly in our performance and in our critical assessments as we now find ourselves obliged to work. Ostensibility is the inexorable fate of all public discourse, not as strategic alibi necessarily, at least not exclusively or overtly so, but because, as critical assessors of the public spheres in the American hemisphere, we now realize more than ever that nothing is what it seems, and it means even less what it says. In a global age of informational hyper-conductivity and even greater hegemonic hyper-power, we have come to realize that we are simultaneously spun out centrifugally and taken in by the centripetal's lure, hustled by the wizards of spin and squeezed by the buzzards of spam.

Discursive formation and the manufacture of consent have reached awful and shocking efficiency, and any analysis of public discourse inevitably begins with the realization that its operational sphere is declarative and brutally tendentious, rather than subtly ideological. The diagnostic scenarios of Marx, Gramsci, Althusser and Foucault appear tame by comparison. Their American Neohistoricist and Marxist epigonoi now come across as school children at play in a pool of sharks. In a Machiavellian world without Lorenzo di Medici or Machiavelli, realpolitik dispenses with the 'reality effect' with brutal literalness. And within this often-farcical barbarism, the American social critic, whether liberal or conservative, for the most part ends not by analysing reality nor effect, but by conjuring on the plausible fictions of media hype and academic discourse as effectively preconditioned and contained by the ceaselessly privatized public sphere. The truly critical American Studies scholar, in a field founded on and for the furtherance of democratic values, now is obliged to consider what might be at risk in broaching his or her subject in a political environment of rampant incivility and undemocratic threat to free speech and academic freedom. The international American Studies practitioner in particular cannot help but constantly anticipate the possible register of his or her professional position in the litmus test of loyalties to his or her object of study. In the globalizing hegemony of imperial right-through-might, as the official imperative in all its crudeness would have it, you are either with us, or else.

In and through the maelstrom of this spin, America has suffered an abduction at the hands of its most zealous devotees. Bushwhacked by the shrill pieties of self-righteousness and the self-serving insolence of blunt and inarticulate unilateralism, America has become reified as devotional object, shrouded in the autism of nationalist sanctimony and the gunpowder stench of bellicose and avaricious patriotism. America, historically, has been a devotional object even before it was America, as we know from *The Book of Prophecies* of Columbus and the sacralization of its territory as providential ground by its Puritan pilgrims. On this score, as the historical record proves, once the veil of the 'myth and symbol' Americanists' piety is dropped, bellicosity turns out to have been a perennial characteristic of America. The history of America is measured in aggregates of territorial expansion, whether one speaks of the ideologization of space as commensurable with Manifest Destiny in the United States, or Brazil's domestication of wilderness through its punitive and ground-clearing expeditionary bandeirantes, or Argentina's civilizing mission through European settlements ('civilizar es poblar', the mantra went in mid-nineteenth-century settler-driven Argentina). And while frontier wars between Chile and Peru decimated trans-border populations, and the genocidal War of the Chaco would ravish humanity and cultures on an unprecedented scale, none of the American nations, as it turns out, has been as consistently belligerent and invasive, within and outside the Western Hemisphere, as has the United States of America. This is why it is important that American Studies be International American Studies in this hemispheric and sea-to-shining-sea sense in addition to the US being the object of investigation and pedagogy by the international community of scholars across the disciplines.

The internationalization of the term 'America' as referent for the whole hemisphere helps us to understand what non-Americanized

Americanists, or those scholars and historians world-wide who have studied and written on America as global phenomenon have always understood: That the ideologically circumscribed reduction of America, and of American Studies, to the United States screens out history's documentary archive that could help us understand what is occurring presently on a global, that is to say, spheric, rather than just western hemispheric scale. To view America in this new light is not a reduction or a reification. It is, rather, an amplification and an elucidation of a historical phenomenon larger and more intricate than its disciplinary containers have hitherto dared to include. The West-to-East aggressive policy of regime change and occupation the US government has just embarked upon, directly rather than through surrogates as in the past, has its centuries-long adumbration in the North-to-South hemispheric history of America that American Studies must now countenance and re-map on a global scale.

The founding of IASA should serve to re-read the historical archive in a larger context than that circumscribed by the disciplinary and field parameters of US and US-formed Americanists, especially those Americanists formed by the post-World War II Marshall Plan and the Cold War. For Americanists all over the world, including a number of distinguished colleagues in the USA, who always have been attuned to historical complexity, the hitherto selectively ignored historical archive does indeed show that few nations have been as aggressively invasive in modern history as the United States of America. What the current Bush Doctrine and its implementation in the Middle East forces upon Americanists is a re-reading of the historical archive and a self-re-assessment of American Studies as a more honestly comprehensive intellectual endeavour. In this context, while this might still sound tendentious to those more accustomed to celebrating their subject than subjecting it to scientific investigation, it is no revisionary claim but part of the historical record to point out that in the past 58 years, since 1945, there has not been a single year in which the USA has not bombed and occupied another country, and frequently more than one country. In the Western Hemisphere alone, as a recent American Studies encyclopaedic compendium enumerates, the most notorious of such territorial and political incursions compute the relentless pulse of a national history with clockwork periodicity. This synoptic documentation unfolds in a recently produced handbook published under the aegis of the national American Studies Association of the USA.

I am referring to the *Encyclopedia of American Studies*, published in 2001 by Grolier Educational Publishers, 'Under the Auspices of the American Studies Association', as the title page avers. In the pages of this compendium dedicated to 'Global Relations', we read under the segment devoted to 'US-Latin American Relations' written by Philip Evanson (Evanson, 2001: 268–272) that the United States congressional legislation, recognizing all other American republics in the Hemisphere in 1822, was promptly followed by the unilateral declaration of what would be called the Monroe Doctrine one year later. Under the aegis of such unilateralism, the United States would invade and conquer half of Mexico's national territory in 1846, thereby enlarging its own by a third. As Philip Evanson records on page 270 of the *Encyclopedia*, the twentieth century would be marked by perennial incursions to ensure economic interests, regime change, and to guarantee hegemonic preeminence in the hemisphere. Following the 1898 Spanish American War and the expulsion of Spain from its last two island colonies in the Caribbean, Puerto Rico and Cuba, the United States would re-invade and occupy Cuba between 1906 and 1909, again between 1917 and 1922, and would enforce an economic blockade beginning in 1960 and still continuing today. The United States would re-invade Mexico in 1914 and in 1916; it would occupy the Dominican Republic between 1905 and 1909, and then again between 1916 and 1924; it would occupy Haiti between 1915 and 1934, Nicaragua between 1912 and 1933 and the part of Colombia that was carved up into the Panama Canal Zone between 1903 and 1999. It would intervene in Guatemala in 1954 and there sponsor a thirty-year genocidal civil war. It would intervene in the Dominican Republic again in 1965, in Chile in 1973, in Nicaragua yet again between 1981 and 1987, and in El Salvador between 1981 and 1991. This is not an exhaustive enumeration.

I cite this baneful history as narrated by Evanson because, as international Americanists, unless we re-focus American Studies into a transnational, hemispheric field, we will be missing the historical genesis and ideological morphology of what is happening today, as these lines are being written, in other parts of the world as well as in the American hemisphere still. We will miss the cultural, historical, and political significance of what Huizinga encoded for us in 1936 as 'the shadow of tomorrow' (Huizinga, 1936). The bellicose litany I have just reviewed from the historical record in the context of an international reconsideration of American history is the shadow the United States has cast in its neighbourhood. We are at the daybreak of a new tomorrow whose shadow extends around the globe. In an era of globalization, then, we have no choice, as international Americanists, but to read the Bush Doctrine, as laid out in *The National Security Strategy of the United States of America, September 2002*, as the twenty-first century's Monroe Doctrine on a global scale. In a global village of unipolar hegemony, the most powerful neighbour in the village, as history demonstrates, is rather bipolar. This duality has long been remarked, perhaps even before Abraham Lincoln's 1863 'Gettysburg Address'. Lincoln, the paradigmatic figure of 'the American Way', at Gettysburg remarks the disjunction between the Enlightenment-derived seminal 'proposition that all men are created equal' and the internecine war he is witnessing as a contestatory occasion that confronts that very 'proposition'. As a result of a similar realization, the generation of American Studies practitioners that became the field's command cohort in 1976 after the Vietnam War was obliged to re-visualize American Studies as it had been practised to that point. We are now obliged to embark on yet another revisionary self-examination as a field, only we must do so not just as a national project but on a global scale and as an international field. This is a profound paradigm shift that finds us, and IASA, on the frontline of examining what these changes mean and articulating their implications for our curricular and investigative endeavours.

George Bush, then, is not a pathological aberration in the annals of American history. He certainly is no aberration. Preemptive action and 'full spectrum dominance' are not the ex-nihilo invention of the now infamous National Defence Board and its notorious slate of candidates for trial by the International Criminal Court, which the United States predictably enough refuses to recognize. And such frighteningly radical programs as the Project for the New American Century, whose basic tenets were instituted by the White House in September of 2002 as *The National Security Strategy of the United States of America*, otherwise known as the Bush Doctrine and reiterated in Bush's 2003 State of the Union Address, have little that is new about them. They are, in William Carlos Williams's phrase, 'in the American grain' (Williams, 1925). What is different today is the scale of systematic legitimation of violence on the part of the state through extra-judicial killings and terror under the guise of counter-terrorism and in the name of democracy, the unprecedented technological facility for planetary destruction, and the global, not just hemispheric, reach of simultaneous intervention. Sadly for the great nation of Jefferson and Lincoln, the global arena of US policy today mirrors Palestine's West Bank and Gaza, where occupation is divinely sanctioned and any dissent is viewed as defiance and as grounds for preemptive action. And such practices as house demolitions, mass detention, collective punishment, and targeted extra-judicial assassinations will more than likely find their way into Iraq and the rest of the world, if indeed those who devised the blueprint for the invasion of Iraq do have their way. This is not a coincidence, nor is the invocation of the linkage between today's American Studies and the Middle East gratuitous.

Just as America and American Studies were defined by the Marshall Plan in Europe at the end of World War II, America and American Studies are being defined even as we speak by the martial role the current US regime has scripted for itself as its political raison d'être in the Middle East and in the rest of the world. These are not speculative or suppositional conjectures, and the governmental actions themselves, not the fact that they are being remarked, should cause chagrin and alarm. Indeed, it is our professional obligation and ethical duty to remark them. And unless we are willing to become complicit in the banishment of historical facts and the masking of the positivity of deeds, the factual record is unmistakable in showing that among the principal architects of the Bush Doctrine are Likud Party operatives including Richard Perle, Paul Wolfowitz, and Douglas Feith, all former apparatchiks of Israel's Netanyahu government. The 1996 'white paper' authored by these same operatives for the Netanyahu regime, 'A Clean Break: A New Strategy for Securing the Realm' (Perle, 1996), on 'clearing the ground' now reads like a blueprint for the strategy these same men have ominously named 'shock and awe' presently being implemented in Iraq, not only for Iraqis but as example for all of the Middle East and for the rest of the world. No doubt, the political scientists and international relations analysts among us will find the overlaps here interesting indeed. It is precisely the mounting archive of such key documentary tracts that will finally bring political science and international relations to their deserved eminence among American Studies practitioners, a position from which these disciplines have generally been screened out, and for tactically understandable reasons that can no longer go unexamined and unchallenged by those working in the field of American Studies.

It was an ominous sign in this 'seamless' connection of the Americas to the Middle East, particularly for Americanists who have studied the Western Hemisphere, when Elliot Abrams, Undersecretary for the Americas in the Reagan regime and an avowed Zionist, who was indicted for lying to Congress in the Iran–Nicaraguan Contra Affair, was put in charge of Middle Eastern policy in George W. Bush's National Security Council—one assumes on the basis of his expertise on Iran. The mounting body-count in Palestine, Israel, Afghanistan, and Iraq, and the unveiled threats against Cuba, Syria, and Iran, and anyone else who would dare cross the regime's policies, continue to bear out those portentous signs. The world, as the Bush Doctrine makes explicit, must be ruled by force and intimidation, what the text of the September 2002 *National Security Strategy* refers to as 'full-spectrum dominance'. What the nations of the Western Hemisphere and Latin American Studies scholars have known all along, the rest of the world and American Studies in general are now learning as well. Any country that would contemplate crossing the US and its interests, as envisioned in this doctrine, cannot claim innocence about the consequences that await their temerity. And, just in case there should be any doubt, all one has to do is put a 'Google' search on the likes of John R. Bolton, the US Undersecretary of State for international security, to read the unveiled threats to the international community of nations about the lessons Iraq should hold for them. On Wednesday 16 April 2003, speaking to a seminar on governance sponsored by the Conference Board, former US president Bill Clinton would observe, though, some might say, with convenient historical amnesia: 'Our paradigm now seems to be: something terrible happened to us on September 11, and that gives us the right to interpret all future events in a way that everyone else in the world must agree with ... And if they don't, they can go straight to hell'. And, the former president muses, '[i]f you got an interdependent world, and you cannot kill, jail or occupy all your adversaries, sooner or later you have to make a deal' (Clinton, 2003).

And so, the global repercussiveness of America makes it imperative for us Americanists to be international Americanists, to look at and examine America not only on a national scale, and not only on a hemi-spheric and transnational scale, but also on a global scale. Failing this, we risk entrapment in a nationalist cocoon, serving as unwitting instruments of nationalist unilateralism, exceptionalism, and incomparability. We risk being little more than echo chambers for the delusionary self-privilege of a corporate-run state apparatus that arrogates to itself the perennial American status of a Providential nation with Providential election, fronted to the world through the Office of Strategic Information and its corporate devotees and ideological zealots. The America we have to investigate, historicize, and teach today, then, is certainly hemispheric, global, transnational, transoceanic, intercontinental, omnipotent, and ubiquitous. Which is to say that the America we are obliged to deal with is claustrophobically not very far off at all, no matter where we are on the face of the planet. Thus, in today's world, the International American Studies Association is not only timely, it is an unavoidable necessity.

Today, the farthest one finds America, in fact, is from the America we have all been taught as Americanists, in the nationalist-conditioned history of our discipline. In this regard, and despite academic arguments among US academics on this score, American Studies is, indeed, very much a *discipline* in the strongest Foucauldian sense of governmentality. It is so to the point of having disciplined the practitioners of American Studies to deny that their practices form and are formed by a discipline. The United States of America, then, to the extent that one can identify a nation with its government at the moment, has turned away through its governmental policy from all that we have been taught to value as the best of that America. Now, at the other polar end of America's bipolarity, through such legislative instruments as the Patriot Act of 2001, we witness the violation of liberty in the name of liberty, the relentless privatization of democracy in the name of 'free' markets, the flouting of justice in the name of justice, the curtailment of civil rights in the name of protecting civil society, the attenuation of constitutional principles in the name of the Constitution, and the breach of international law by unilateral self-exemption to an exceptional status answerable only to what the regime deems a higher law of its own. And lest we succumb to the belief that this is an aberration, now more than ever before, we come to realize, just as post-Vietnam Americanists in the 1970s discovered with regard to the inequities in America's racial, ethnic, economic, and gender history, that at the international, global level, too, there is a profound inconsistency between the ideal and the real, the proclaimed and the practised, despite what American Studies has been teaching the international community for the past half century.

In the face of the disciplinary shifts that ensued in the USA from the experience of Vietnam, there has been a decided asymmetry between the national and the international teachings of American Studies. We are now forced to countenance these discrepancies, incongruities, and self-contradictions as integral and historically consistent parts of 'the American Way'. It is this realization that makes a revisioning of American Studies as an international field imperative, and our professional and pedagogical practices will obviously have to follow suit. Clearly, this readjustment stands to rattle a number of institutions, associations, and individual scholars who have hitherto derived their disciplinary sanction and material support on grounds that are precipitously becoming the status quo ante. As a result, IASA itself may be perceived as auguring the inevitable changes necessary and may well be looked upon by some with a jaundiced eye. Defaulting reflexively to casting the blame on the messenger rather than examining the message and its genesis tends to come naturally. In the face of such reflexes, however, professional steadfastness, intellectual honesty, and scholarly rigour remain the best course for the new Association and its members—individual, institutional, and national.

I emphasize that the discrepancies and ambiguities I have referred to here are part of 'the American Way'—not exclusively so, but a historically consistent part, as the archive shows, despite the best intentions of those who would anxiously disambiguate history for whatever reasons of their own. And I reiterate that, urgent as the predicament foisted on us at this historical moment might be, we must not forget the other America, the one we have been taught. Thus, we would do well to recall Walt Whitman, who is also America in all his contradictions, especially the Whitman who embodies his country's ambiguities. I would like to remind us of Whitman's roaring peroration in his 1871 *Democratic Vistas*: 'In vain do we march with unprecedented strides to empire so colossal, outvying the antique, beyond Alexander's, beyond the proudest sway of Rome. In vain have we annex'd Texas, California, Alaska, and reach north for Canada and south for Cuba. It is as if we were somehow being endow'd with a vast and more thoroughly-appointed body, and then left with little or no soul' (Whitman, 1982: 938).

In matters of the soul, which must be of special concern to us now, when the domestic politics and international realpolitik of the United States function as an emanation from a convergence of evangelical zeal and patriotic rapacity, no American philosopher may be more apt than William James. And I would like for us to remember that William James himself—the James of both New England and (just as much) of Agassis' ethno-racist Brazilian expedition—is also America. Few American thinkers have meditated as intensely as has James on the intricacies of the convergence of religion and politics in public life and civil society. In his treatise *Varieties of Religious Experience* (James, 1902) he worried about America's capacity for transmuting all human experience to religious experience as pragmatic expedient and at political convenience. We would do well to recall, as Americanists who come after the ravages of the twentieth century, especially its Second World War, the perils that ensue when such messianic nationalist spirituality converges with Roman imperial republicanism. In the last century, the yield of such convergence was the Third Reich. Now, we need to be ever-vigilant to what it might mean for the crusading Pentecostal Evangelism of today's messianic fervour to have conflated its apocalyptics with Zionism. Yet, also, the structural, systemic, and perennial anti-Semitism, that inheres in such eschatological programs as 'universal conversion', as prelude to the Second Coming, are frightening indeed. One shudders to think of the irresponsible, historical myopia among today's Hobbesian disciples of Leo Strauss, ostensible liberals-turned-Neoconservative 'chickenhawks', and their amnesia toward what ensued the last time the fate of a people was yoked to a systemically anti-Semitic, messianic regime's post-historical agenda. Huizinga's 1936 essay, *In the Shadow of Tomorrow* may be not only timely, it may be frighteningly apt. And it is in this terrifying context that I wish to remind us of William James and the historic tendency in 'the American Way' to countenance crusade and jihadic obsession, especially when the ethical and moral quotient is emptied out of religion, leaving only what Alexis de Tocqueville had already diagnosed in his *Democracy in America* as 'virtuous materiality'. Here, then, is William James:

> [A]n attitude might be called religious, though no touch were left in it of sacrifice or submission, no tendency to flexion, no bowing of the head. [Any] habitual and regulated admiration [...] is worthy to be called a religion [... therefore] our Music, our Science, and our so-called "Civilization", as these things are now organized and admiringly believed in, form the more genuine religions of our time. Certainly the unhesitating and unreasoning way in which we feel that we must inflict our civilization upon "lower" races, by means of Hotchkiss guns, etc., reminds one of nothing so much as of the early spirit of Islam spreading its religion by the sword .... (James, 1902: 77)

Not being a member of the National Rifle Association, and cursed with the aversion of a pacifist and conscientious objector to all armaments, I don't know what a 'Hotchkiss gun' is. But the United States of America is certainly at no loss for nation-shattering armaments and clever bombs of transcontinental global reach, 'swords' so smart and so lethal that before them the swords of jihadic Islam, yet another aberration of a people's true religion, devolve into little more than suicidal curiosities of deadly children's tales.

I compose these remarks in mid-April, 2003, as bombs fall on Iraq and as Iraq's National Museum, along with the record of our common civilization, are being looted under the watchful eye of the American military that has, by contrast, diligently ensured the security of Iraq's Oil Ministry. As I write, across my desk comes a disconcerted essay from the German novelist Günter Grass. Grass is alarmed because he remembers well the history he has lived and the histories he has read. The essay is dated 10 April 2003, entitled 'The Moral Decline of a Superpower: Preemptive War' and published in the *International Herald Tribune*. I shall cite a brief passage from it. I will do so because Günter Grass's unease is one we cannot help but share as Americanists who dedicate our professional life and intellectual efforts to America, because we consider America a worthy subject and, now, more than ever, a necessary burden we must bear for the sake of both the world and the well-being of humanity, both now in peril, as is every Americanist who might dare interrogate his object of inquiry with any critical scrutiny. Here is Grass:

> Disturbed and powerless, but also filled with anger, we are witnessing the moral decline of the world's only superpower, burdened by the knowledge that only one consequence of this organized madness is certain: motivation for more terrorism is being provided, for more violence and counter violence. Is this really the United States of America, the country we fondly remember? The generous benefactor of the Marshall Plan? The forbearing instructor in the lessons of democracy? The candid self-critic? The country that once made use of the teachings of the European Enlightenment to throw off its colonial masters and to provide itself with an exemplary constitution? Is this the country that made freedom of speech an incontrovertible human right?
>
> It is not just foreigners who cringe as this ideal pales to the point where it is now a caricature of itself. There are many

Americans who love their country too, people who are horrified by the betrayal of their founding values and by the hubris of those holding the power. I stand with them. By their side, I declare myself pro-American. I protest with them against the brutalities brought about by the injustice of the mighty, against all restrictions of the freedom of expression, against information control reminiscent of the practices of totalitarian states and against the cynical equations that make the deaths of so many innocents acceptable so long as economic and political interests are protected.

No, it is not anti-Americanism that is damaging the image of the United States; nor do the dictator Saddam Hussein and his extensively disarmed country endanger the most powerful country in the world. It is President Bush and his government that are diminishing democratic values, bringing sure disaster to their own country, ignoring the United Nations, and that are now terrifying the world with a war in violation of international law. (Grass, 2003)

In solidarity with Günter Grass's 'pro-American' protestations, our response to his questions has to be in the affirmative. Yes, indeed, this is the same America. We are startled by it only because we now see the obverse side of its historically bipolar character on a global scale. However, as scholars of America we cannot afford, we never could, to focus exclusively on one side of this polarity. And it becomes imperative for us to teach and write on the face of America that is now turned away from us, as we must on the America we, along with the rest of the world, are now being forced to countenance. The essentialist idealization of America as devotional object packaged by the celebrants of 'the American Way' should not be replaced by the equally essentialist reification of a dark side of America as compensation for our chagrin at demystification and disenchantment. Those who have made themselves vulnerable to disappointment must not substitute one flat, univocal essentialism by another. As scholars and teachers, we cannot afford to neglect either the America Günter Grass laments, or the America that elicits his lamentation. The America of George Bush is also the America of Thomas Jefferson, of Herman Melville, of Walt Whitman, of Mark Twain, of William James, and of William Carlos Williams. If our professional commitments are to be truly international, exogenous, scientific, intellectually rigorous, and pedagogically honest, our task challenges us to hold the contradictions in play and the ambiguities of history in counterpoint. All pressures within and outside the institutional establishments of America and of American Studies notwithstanding, we must resist all coercion and any temptation to disambiguate history and to resolve contradictions. Otherwise, we run the danger of becoming complicit in the kind of compartmentalization that normalizes the most atrocious acts human beings are capable of inflicting on the rest of humanity. We owe this steadfastness to America, to our students, and to future generations around the world, who may yet be 'in the shadow of tomorrow'. Our task is obviously more complex than the essentialist self-reductions of our subject matter, and our labours more arduous than the self-serving exertions of a world power. Together, we must live with its contradictions, and together stay the course. It is our hope that the International American Studies Association will continue to serve as congenial and enabling locus for our diverse concerns and common responsibility for many years to come.

Djelal Kadir

References

Barringer, Felicity (2003) 'US Diplomat Resigns, Protesting 'Our Fervent Pursuit of War'", *New York Times* 27 February 2003, rpt. as 'US Diplomat John Brady Kiesling: Letter of Resignation, to Secretary of State Colin L. Powell', Athens, 27 February 2003 http://www.truthout.org/cgi-bin/artman/exec/view.cgi?archive=1&num=61 (accessed January 9, 2004)

Clinton, William (2003) 'Clinton Blasts US Foreing Policy', Agence France-Presse, April 16. http://truthout.org/docs_03/041803A.shtml (accessed January 9, 2004).

Evanson, Philip (2001) 'US-Latin American Relations', *Encyclopedia of American Studies*. Edited by George T. Kulian et. al. New York: Grolier Educational Publishers, pp. 268-272.

Grass, Günter (2003) 'The Moral Decline of a Superpower: Preemptive War', 11 April, *International Herald Tribune*10 April, rpt. at Tribune Media Services International, 11 April 2003 http://www.iht.com/ihtsearch.php?id=92876&owner=(Tribune%20Media%20Services%20International)&date=20030413151821 http://www.iht.com/ihtsearch.php?id=92876&owner=%28Tribune%20Media%20Services%20International%29&date=20030413151821 (accessed January 9, 2004)

Huizinga, Johan (1918) *Mensch en menigte in Amerika*, rpt. as *America: a Dutch historian's vision, from afar and near*. Translated, with an introduction and notes, by Herbert H. Rowen. New York: Harper and Row, 1972.

Huizinga, Johan (1924) *The Waning of the Middle Ages: a study of the forms of life, thought, and art in France and the Netherlands in the fourteenth and fifteenth centuries*. Translated by F. Hopman. London: Edward Arnold, 1924.

Huizinga, Johan (1936) *In the Shadow of To-morrow: A Diagnosis of the Spiritual Distemper of Our Time*. Translated by J. H. Huizinga. London: Heinemann, 1936.

James, William (1902) *Varieties of Religious Experience*. Rpt. Harmondsworth: Penguin, 1982.

Lincoln, Abraham (1929) *The Addresses of Abraham Lincoln*. Kingsport, TN: Kingsport Press.

The National Security Strategy of the United States, 2002, http://www.whitehouse.gov/nsc/nss.html (accessed January 9, 2004)

Perle, Richard, et al. (1996) 'A Clean Break: A New Strategy for Securing the Realm' (June) http://www.israeleconomy.org/strat1.htm (accessed January 9, 2004).

Tocqueville, Alexis de (1838) *Democracy in America.* Translated by Henry Reeve; with an original preface and notes by John C. Spencer. New York: G. Dearborn.

Whitman, Walt (1982) *Whitman: Poetry and Prose.* New York: Viking Press, 1982.

Williams, William Carlos (1925) *In the American Grain.* New York: A. & C. Boni.

The Tenacious Grasp of American Exceptionalism:

A Response to Djelal Kadir, "Defending America against Its Devotees"

I am honoured to represent the American Studies Association at this important inaugural meeting of the International American Studies Association. On behalf of the ASA, I welcome this opportunity to initiate new conversations, exchanges, and debates about our common interest in the project of internationalizing the study of America. Professor Kadir has eloquently described and prescribed the global contours and multiple dimensions of this project and the urgent intellectual and political issues at stake at this historic moment.

I applaud Professor Kadir's courage and passion in insisting that the project of internationalizing American studies has become more than a new academic trend, but rather a project that must address the current international crisis. While the United States marshals unprecedented military force around the world under the doctrine of preemption, it shows little interest in learning about others and refuses to see itself through the eyes of the world it seeks to dominate. The Bush administration is committed to shoring up its own national boundaries, through juridical, covert, and discursive means, at the same time that it violates international law and turns the rest of the world into a space of porous and violable borders for its own exercise of power. This division between the United States and the world can be seen in the embrace of two new terms in U.S. public discourse, which have become predominant since September 11, 2001: the Empire and the Homeland. In a dramatic turn away from the disavowal of its own imperial history, the embrace of Empire across the political spectrum celebrates and normalizes U.S. global dominance as an inevitable process. The notion of the Homeland, with its nativist connotations, works to protect a sense of domestic insularity, always under attack yet cordoned off from the threatening outside world.

While mainstream discourse places the homeland and the empire in separate spheres, Kadir shows us, on the contrary, that isolationism and internationalism in US policy today are two sides of the same imperial coin. He importantly places the current crisis in a longer sweep of imperial history that links U.S. intervention in the Americas from the early nineteenth century to the current interventions in the Middle East. And he situates the development of American studies as a field within the broader historical moments of the Marshall Plan, the Cold War and the Vietnam War. He urges what would be a welcome shift for American studies—to go beyond its cultural turn to include international relations, political economy and public policy, the workings of the state. And he insists that we study America in its multiple hemispheric dimensions, to challenge the U.S. appropriation of the name to itself. These shifts, he argues, require both new collaborative efforts of international networks of scholars, and the emergence of new archives to remap the terrain of the object of study.

The international initiative represented by this conference goes against the current grain of imperial internationalism The yoking of violent intervention and willed ignorance creates the urgent need for a critical international American studies; as Kadir puts it, 'America is now more than ever too terribly important to be left to itself'. This centralized global power can be decentred, he believes, by analysing America from 'non-American points of view' and 'non-American national agendas', from the vantage of what Dr. Kousar Azam calls 'critical cosmopolitanism'.[1] I would add that the project of international American studies has the potential to undo the tenacious paradigm of American exceptionalism, the paradoxical claim of the United States to uniqueness and universality at the same time.

---

[1] See Kousar J. Azam, "Resisting Terror, Resisting Empire: The Evolving Ethos of American Studies," in this volume, p. ?

While endorsing the need for critical international American studies, I would like to point out some of the risks and blind spots in the way this project could be formulated. Dividing international from national perspectives may, paradoxically, recuperate a national paradigm that this conference is committed to undoing. Stressing the difference between American and non-American practitioners of the field risks resurrecting the rigid binary divisions between inside and outside, between the foreign and the domestic. A critical cosmopolitanism should be dedicated to analyzing and breaking down these conceptual and geographic boundaries. We can see such a division emerge, for example, in Kadir's use of 'we' and 'them' in his welcoming of U.S. based scholars to the conference in Leiden, 'we are heartened by their presence'. Who belongs to this 'we' and who to 'their presence'? There's a danger that geographical location could become reified as the a priori source of knowledge and that the politics of location could turn into the politics of identity. It is as important to be aware of the differences, power relations and unequal access to resources among international scholars, as it is between U.S. and non-U.S. scholars. Just as scholars across the disciplines have worked to undo the essentialism of national identity, it is equally important not to essentialize an international identity—with its hint of exoticism—and to assume that critical perspectives naturally emerge by virtue of being located outside the U.S. The production of knowledge circulates too globally, unevenly, and circuitously to fit neatly into this inside / outside model: 'from discursive sites and criteria that emanate not from Washington DC or Omaha Nebraska, but from wherever Americanists happen to be in the world'. There's a risk here of homogenizing both 'the world' and the U.S.

Furthermore, if one posits the possibility of viewing the United States from a purely external vantage, one risks recuperating a vision of the nation as a monolithic, cohesive, and unitary whole, even from a critical perspective. American studies scholars around the world have worked hard to destabilize this totality by showing the necessity of remapping America not only from outside its borders, but more importantly from transnational movements and geographies that traverse and challenge those borders. International American studies ought to build on these transnational configurations, such as the borderlands, the Pacific Rim, the Black Atlantic, and multiple diasporas. Paying attention to new archives and international collaborative work also has the potential to articulate new transnational sites for the production of knowledge that challenge the cohesive borders of a mythical America. Kadir's pointing to the historical nexus of the United States, Latin America and the Middle East is a case in point.

If the United States can be recuperated as a spatial whole, though, there is a similar danger of reinstating a teleological linear narrative of historical continuity, of viewing American history, even in its imperial dimensions, as a singular march from Columbus to the Puritans to the Monroe Doctrine to twentieth-century military interventions to the Bush doctrine—and practice—of preemptive strikes. The turn to new spatial configurations—or the recovery of old spaces repressed by nationalist paradigms—such as the circum-Atlantic, or the Americas, has provided a way of reconceiving alternative modernities that break from the linear progressive sense of history, one propelled from an imperial centre outwards over time as well as space.

In Professor Kadir's exhilarating call for a momentous paradigm shift, traditional paradigms of American studies curiously reemerge. For one, he resuscitates a Euro-American white male canon, even for those he calls upon as critics and outsiders. Johan Huizinga and Günter Grass, eloquent as they may be, are by no means outsiders lacking authority in the American academy. Walt Whitman and William James have been staples of American Studies since its inception, and their criticism of America places them squarely in the American grain. When Kadir gestures to alternative visions of America to the one offered by George Bush, he only names traditional authors—Melville, Twain, Williams—and statesmen, Jefferson and Lincoln. He shockingly does not mention any minorities or women, and or anyone from the Caribbean or Latin America, Africa or Asia. This blind spot may relate in part to his claim that the fields of 'political science and international relations, economics, demographic analyses' are moving to 'displace literary studies, popular cultural and ethnic studies'. Why relegate ethnic studies to the 'cultural' and exclude it from the political and the international? The most important work in ethnic studies today shows that culture and politics, the national and international are inseparable from one another.

Furthermore, why call for a new disciplinary hierarchy, which revives an old dichotomy of 'hard' political science and 'soft' cultural studies, or base and superstructure, with its gendered connotations. Leading work in American studies internationally has been committed to bringing together these arenas and breaking down that disciplinary hierarchy. Political scientists and historians of foreign relations have demonstrated that race, gender, ethnicity and sexuality are central to the operation of global politics and international economics. If in the fields of culture and politics, Kadir invokes a traditional canon, he has a similar approach to contemporary politics, where he singles out individual policy makers, statesmen, and inner cabals. International American studies, in its commitment to interdisciplinarity, has the potential to situate these individual operators in broader and richer cultural, historical and political contexts.

While international American studies can provide crucial grounds on which to contest American exceptionalism, this tenacious paradigm reemerges in Kadir's address. Glossing Günter Grass's eloquent critique, Kadir reenacts a kind of jeremiad, which chastises America for not living up to its own ideals. Condemning the United States for failing to measure up to its own highest standards may have some strategic value in public debates, but this approach is both insular and exceptionalist, as it implicitly makes the United States the bearer of universal values. This approach also reduces the complexity of U.S. engagement with the world to a Manichean conflict between a good and a bad America. Kadir writes, for example, 'Sadly for the great nation of Jefferson and Lincoln, the global arena of U.S. policy today mirrors Palestine's West Bank and Gaza, where occupation is divinely sanctioned'. This formulation renders U.S. imperial policy an imitation of others, something external to its own foundational history. Does Jefferson's 'Empire for Liberty' need to learn from Israel, or does it have its own historical models for the divinely sanctioned occupation of native lands? Was Lincoln purely a voice for freedom and liberation from slavery? In other words, we ought not defend ourselves from the charges of anti-Americanism or 'American haters' (as *The New Republic* would have it [Wolfe, 2003: 25]) by pledging allegiance to America's ideal self images. Instead we should hold the United States to international, local and cosmopolitan values, still in the making.

In a similar vein, Kadir's U.S. critics of imperialism should be understood as more implicated in the imperial project than he allows. The anti-imperial Whitman he quotes was once an ardent supporter of the U.S. war against Mexico in 1846 and the poet who penned 'A Passage to India'. Although William James was an adamant spokesman for anti-imperialism, scholars have seen imperial dimensions of his pragmatism, and in the passage quoted, he uses Islam as a measure of barba-rism—albeit as an ironic barb at the United States. My point is not to turn Kadir's good Americans into bad ones, but to note that all of the figures he names had ambivalent and complex relations to American imperialism, as participants, products and critics. And it is imperative that an international American studies go beyond viewing American policy and culture through the lenses of a white male hegemony.

A quick rereading of two examples from Professor Kadir's address might suggest alternative approaches to international American studies that point beyond the exceptionalist paradigm. Let's start with the Puritans, one of the powerful origin myths on which exceptionalism relies, where Kadir starts somewhat ironically because of the location of the conference in Leiden. An international approach to the Puritans would contextualize this small community of migrants in the context of world trade, commerce and competing imperial projects in the seventeenth century. At the same time that some Pilgrims were looking toward the new world from Leiden, the Dutch West India company was chartered in the Hague to have a trade monopoly, which included parts of West Africa, 'the gold coast', islands in the Caribbean, the Americas on the Atlantic and Pacific coasts, Portuguese possessions in Brazil, and part of the Atlantic slave trade. To place the Puritan mission in this wider context of mercantilism, colonialism and the slave trade among the British, Dutch, Portuguese and Spanish empires would invite a truly international effort that could decentre the United States as the teleological object of study, even during the colonial period. This approach would follow in the footsteps of earlier transnational thinkers, by scholars such as W.E.B. Du Bois, Eric Williams and C.L.R. James. They wrote of developments in the American empire, such as the suppression of the slave trade and the Louisiana Purchase, not in terms of a self-propelled engine of the 'errand into the wilderness' or 'manifest destiny', but as complex responses to the upheavals of antislavery and anticolonial revolts in the Caribbean.

Another example: in discussing James, Kadir quotes what seems to be an obscure reference to the Hotchkiss gun. Tracing the history of this artifact of destruction can also lead us through transnational routes that would be key to an international American studies. These early rapid fire guns were invented by an American and produced in France in the 1860s. Hotchkiss guns first achieved notoriety when the U.S. army used them to massacre Lakota Sioux at Wounded Knee in 1890. A decade later they were deployed in the brutal US war to occupy the Philippines, the war to which James refers, at the same time that the British deployed them in the Boer War. An international approach in this case, would trace the trajectories of weaponry and colonial policy circulating among outposts of different empires across the globe. Such an approach, which traverses imperial battlegrounds in the Philippines, Native America, and South Africa, would also include other international sites, such as the St. Louis World's Fair of 1904, which celebrated the Louisiana Purchase by bringing together colonized people from all over the world as spectacles for domestic consumption. These are the kinds of connections we could learn about from Leslie Marmon Silko's *Almanac of the Dead* Silko, 1991), where she writes powerfully about the movements of native peoples against colonial violence across the national boundaries of the Americas. Both these examples point to a broader need for international American studies to be involved in collaborative comparatives studies of empires and their legacies, so that even the study of the American empire doesn't simply reproduce an imperial insularity. Professor Kadir's call for a critical international American studies is all the more urgent, when we realize that international perspectives on the U.S. can be mobilized for very different political ends. In his popular book whitewashing the history of the British Empire, for example, Niall Ferguson (2003) concludes by urging the current Administration to take up the White Man's Burden that Rudyard Kipling urged upon the USA in an 1899 poem, subtitled 'The United States and the Philippine Islands', over a century ago (Kipling 1899 [1994]: 343-44).

Professor Kadir's call for a international American studies is indeed critical in both senses of the word: it is vital to the integrity of our intellectual pursuits during these troubled times; and for the same reasons, it must continually question itself.

Amy Kaplan

References

Ferguson, Niall. 2003. *Empire: the Rise and Demise of the British World Order and the Lessons for Global Power.* New York: Basic Books.

Kipling, Rudyard. 1899. *The Works of Rudyard Kipling.* Ware: The Wordsworth Poetry Library, 1994, pp. 323-324.

Silko, Leslie Marmon. 1991. *Almanac of the Dead.* New York: Simon and Schuster.

Wolfe, Alan. 2003. 'Anti-American Studies', *The New Republic*, 10 Feb.: 25.

Resisting Terror, Resisting Empire:
The Evolving Ethos of American Studies

The Changing Nature of American Studies

The internationalization of American Studies is now an accomplished fact, as is evident from the emergence of so many international organizations devoted to American Studies. Apart from traditional, regional associations affiliated to the American Studies Association (ASA), the birth of new bodies such as International Forum for US Studies at Iowa (IFUSS), the International American Studies Association (IASA) and other allied bodies such as MELUS, the Society for Multi-Ethnic Studies of Europe and America (MESEA) and the Collegium for African American Research (CAAR) all, taken together, suggest the growing internationalization of American Studies. The focus is therefore shifting on the changing nature of the discipline itself and the consequences that it might have for its survival in an age of globalization.[1] With increasing internationalization it has lost some aspects of its traditional disciplinarity. The concerns that engaged American Studies scholars, such as American exceptionalism, national consciousness, identity, freedom, democracy, the literary canon,

---

[1]   For a recent critical summary, see Ickstadt (2002: 543-562) and Lenz (2002: 96-119).

etc., have acquired a multi-cultural, transnational character. This amounts to a gradual moving beyond a geographically-determined national space, a coming out from an ontological provincialism and parochialism. It is true that some of the newer paradigms of transnational American Studies are not free from regionalism, by failing to extend beyond Europe, Latin America or the Americas and almost excluding Asia, Africa and other parts of the world. The discipline is, however, moving, as Heinz Ickstadt points out, towards 'an impossible redefinition of American Studies as an at once locally decentralized and globally comprehensive field' (Ickstadt, 2002: 553).

This growing circulation and consequent loss of a traditional 'disciplinarity' is a cause of concern for some scholars. It may promote 'academic dilettantism' as Ickstadt points out (p. 554), or it can lead to 'sanctioned ignorance' (p.554) in the name of globality or hybridity, as Gayatri Spivak suggests. Yet, despite such apprehensions, American Studies is increasingly engaging with concerns which traditionally fall in the field of International Relations, such as migration, diaspora, transnational and transcultural exchange of labour, capital and goods, multiple identities, security, cultural contacts and identity formations beyond borders, so that it almost appears to be evolving into a subdiscipline of International Relations. As America and Americans move out of the cold war paradigm to cope with a rapidly shifting, newer paradigm of a globalizing world, they are forced to constantly redefine their new role in international affairs. Similarly Americanists engaged with the transnational are getting into newer discourses that seldom, if at all, used to concern them. The process does lead to a certain ambivalence, for how does one engage with the transnational or with the postnational while problematizing the national? The two presuppose the national. Nevertheless American Studies scholars are moving towards the global as the location of the discourse. This shift towards the global throws the discipline into engagement with what might be described as the welter of globalization—both as a process and as a discourse (Ickstadt, 2002; Lenz, 2002).

American Studies and Globalization

The increasing implication of the global in the local marks the course of the new American Studies wherever they are pursued. What shape it will take is hard to discern at the moment, because we are at the beginning of the process and must wait for some time to see its consequences. The enlargement of the discipline has, however, opened up possibilities which can take it beyond some of the ontological parochialism and provincialism of 'the national' into the cosmopolitan but contentious space of the global. It would appear to be a logical evolution, considering the way that American Studies, which originated in the anxieties of the 'national', is gradually evolving into a larger discourse that involves other states, other societies, other cultures.

Some aspects of this shift have been elaborated by Gunther H. Lenz, though his conflation of American Studies into American Culture Studies tends to restrict the applicability of that paradigm. It excludes the whole range of social, political and economic issues that follow the internationalization of American Studies. His emphasis on a genuinely dialogic notion of cultural critique, his thesis that cultures are always 'hybridized and hybridizing multi and intercultural' and 'work through debates, controversies, and negotiations,' and his suggestion that 'American Culture Studies in the future have to investigate the changing modes and public representations of cultures to explore these complex and often contested "cultural flows" (Ulf Hannerz) from different locations and in different post colonial discourses' all open up the field for newer perspectives in the theory and practice of American Studies (Lenz, 2002: 98). We have to reconceive American Studies, as Lenz proposes, 'in terms of the notions of interculturality, cultural translation, hybridization, creolization and diaspora as they have been elaborated in the "border discourses" of minority cultures, cultures of difference, including feminist critiques, and cultural anthropology' (p. 98). However, he rightly cautions that this exercise has to go beyond the restrictive practices visible in current scholarship. To quote him again: "Envisioning American Studies in a truly international perspective means enacting the transnational intercultural discourses in real dialogues and debates among scholars from different parts of the world" (p. 98).

By identifying Cultural Studies as the core of new American Studies, Lenz appears to overlook the many ramifications of the global that the new paradigm of American Studies is expected to negotiate. His understanding of the global is conditioned by his own location as a European committed to North American Studies. Lenz does not take into account the fact that globalization is often associated in the popular imagination with the process of Americanization. More often it is associated with the impact that American popular culture and media have on cultural practices elsewhere in the world. Serious aspects of globalization, such as the implications it has for the nature and practices of the state, and the autonomy and sovereignty of systems, governance, law, justice, security and international order do not engage scholars rooted in the humanistic paradigms of the cultural and the aesthetic. The dominant role that America plays in the process of globalization and the influence that it exerts on some of the regulatory mechanisms of globalization, such as the World Bank, the International Monetary Fund and the World Trade Organization, makes it a logical target of anti-globalization protest. The unchallenged status of the new post-Cold War America as the only existing super power, when taken in alliance with forces of globalization, seems to destabilize the existing order in most parts of the world. The 'new exceptionalism' of America, as Mary Caldor points out, is rooted in the American belief that

> America is a cause, not a nation with a mission to convert the rest of the world to the American dream and get rid the world of the terrorists and tyrants. For them sovereignty is conditional for other states, but unconditional for the United States because the United States represents 'good'. Hence the United States can act unilaterally, it can reject treaties like the Climate Change Protocol, the Land-mines Convention, the Biological Weapons' Convention, and above all the International Criminal Court because America is right, but others do not have the same option. (Kaldor, 2003: 12)

Coping with Global Anti-Americanism

The sometimes enticing sometimes threatening presence of America as the doppelganger of modernity engenders many variants of anti-Americanism which appear as the eternally agonistic 'other' in the discourses of the contemporary.[2]

---

[2] See a special section on Anti-Americanism in *The New Criterion* 21.3 (November) 4-34. The section includes articles by Roger Kimball, Gerald Frost, Paul Hollander, David Pryce-Jones and others. For another perspective on the same problem see the special issue of *Partisan Review*, 'Our Country our Culture', 69.4 (Fall 2002).

The concerns of American Studies in the most recent scholarship appear to be shaped by the political debates, mostly of the left, that inform particular societies and vary from one part of the world to another. They do not have a center but circulate according to the circulation of American power which is not only economic, political or military, but practically encompasses all aspects of social life, in some form or the other everywhere in the world. It is no longer America alone contending with the other world, it is America the other world is increasingly contending with. The parameters of this contention are as complex as the complexities of the modem world itself. They have complex and multiple ontologies and move into more than one telos.

While anti-Americanism has, in one form or the other, been part of the modem western tradition, it has acquired the character of an ideology in the new world order of globalization. It has a local dimension as well as a global one, with several regional variations, defined by geography and history. As an essential part of the American tradition of liberal non-conformism, it engages both the Left and the Right. The global engagements of US produce global anti-Americanisms.

American Studies, rooted as it is traditionally in liberal non-conformism, has always reflected a degree of anti-Americanism, though the content of this phenomenon has varied from one paradigm to another. In fact as Paul Hollander puts it: 'There is anti-Americanism on the Left as well as on the Right. Instant anti-Americanism sometimes makes the extreme Right and the extreme Left hard to distinguish from one another' (Hollander, 20002: 14).

While some kind of anti-Americanism has been a part of America's growth as a historical entity, America has not ceased to exercise a fatal attraction for the multitudes of mankind from different parts of the world. It has also been the chosen destination of political, cultural and religious exiles. The slogan 'Yankee go home' has often been accompanied by the tag 'and take me along'.

However, the recent wave of anti-Americanism is an entirely different phenomenon. In it 'the United States and all things Americans are identified with a religiously defined transcendent Evil and not merely with social injustice, moral corruption, economic exploitation or the abuse of power as used to be the case until recently' (Hollander, 2002: 16). Anti-Americanism is widespread not only outside the US, but as Norman Podhoretz puts it, 'until September 11, 2001 most American writers and intellectuals were infected with an attitude towards their own country that ranged from distaste to outright hatred' (Podhoretz, 2002: 510). Anti-Americanism is thus an integral part of the modern intellectual tradition of critique and a phenomenon American Studies scholars have to come to terms with. It appears as a theoretical constant in new American Studies, though its tenor varies according to the personal or ideological predilections of the scholars or scholar communities in different parts of the world, including the USA. How does one practice American Studies in a world where America is perceived as the new evil empire by large sections of humanity?

Given the increasing internationalization of American Studies, it devolves upon the practitioners of American Studies to convince local policy makers that it is a serious discourse to understand the complexities of the modern world in which the US is a key player. They have to do it even if it has to be done in the form of anti-Americanism. However anti-Americanism, because of 'its adverse moralism', tends 'to short circuit self-criticism' and prohibits 'just and effective criticism' (Kimball, 2002: 7). It tends to detract from the local in the name of the global or the transnational. In fact anti-Americanism is a response to global concerns and anxieties, as they impinge upon a world no longer protected by traditional sanctities, securities and values. Global anxieties and aspirations have a local dimension though the reverse is not always true. The price of hogs in Iowa or corn in South Carolina have a local relevance which may not obtain in a global context. It will be pertinent therefore to reflect on the impact that globalization is likely to have on the practice of American Studies.

Globalization and American Studies

In most of the world globalization is perceived as a form of Americaniza-tion. The economic preeminence of the US and the control that the US exercises through other regulatory mechanisms on global money, trade and finance flows seems to sustain that perception. However none of these figure in American Studies as a discipline. The impact that globalization has had on the practice of knowledge and the institutions of knowledge has not received the kind of critical attention that it should have. Immediate concerns over funding and the declining number of opportuni-ties in the traditionally structured institutions of knowledge such as

Universities and colleges have prevented scholars from looking at the transformative possibilities opened up by the process of globalization. Globalization has forced academics to refix their priorities and to relocate them by effecting structural changes within the traditional structures. It has accelerated the process of redrawing the boundaries consistent with the principles of free circulation of knowledge. Whilst scholars attribute the decline of scholarship in Humanities and Social Sciences to globalization, they fail to see the enormous opportunities opened up by the emergence of the post-human for all branches of knowledge, radically altering the universe of knowledge. The new order of science and technology most visible in bio-technology, cybernetics, and computers has opened up new frontiers of knowledge for scholars to pursue.

The wider implications of the new knowledge are yet to be absorbed in our knowledge systems. As Edward Rothstein has pointed out:

> The excavations of the human genome, advances in computing power, early ventures in creating artificial life and intelligence and the possibility of disruptive innovations in unexpected areas of research, all have an impact on how we think about what it means to be distinctively human, how we think. about the just organizations of societies and how we debate current policies on everything from cloning research to missile defense systems. (Rothstein, 2002: 543)

The challenge of the post-human in knowledge is immediate and real. Have we thought enough in the Humanities and Social Sciences about the radical possibilities of the post-human and the impact it is likely to have on our moral, ethical and aesthetic assumptions? Not only are we expected to cope with 'scenarios which invent with technologies of the future' (Kurzweil, 2002: 543), we are also confronted with the enormous responsibility of defining our essential and distinct humanity. The historical moment for the confluence of the 'two cultures' in a single discipline is now. It is time that Americanists, instead of talking about the futures of American Studies talked about it as a discipline of the future which 'will open us up', as William Connolly puts it, to how 'the play of possibility in the present ...[may] incite critical responses to unnecessary violence and injuries surreptitiously imposed upon life by the insistence that prevailing forms are natural, rational, universal or necessary' (Connolly, 1995: 34).

The new knowledge is contributing significantly to the process of globalization. Unfortunately, the traditional university is in most cases is not able to absorb the changes ushered in by the emerging globalism. While there is a tendency among scholars to attribute the decline of the Humanities and Social Sciences to globalization, the proliferation of newer forms of knowledge in trade, business, communication, biology, chemistry, medicine has hardly come under the critical gaze of these disciplines. At a time when the state itself is going through a crisis of identity it is unrealistic to expect the university to retain its traditional character. The newer developments in the economic and political organization of societies are asking the same old questions about value, legitimacy and desirability that have resided at the core of the traditional humanities and social sciences. The tendency to see the aesthetic and the ethical exclusively belonging to the humanities have inhibited scholars from looking for their presence in other spheres of life and other cultures of academia.

The increasing convergence in various disciplines belonging to different frontiers such as technology or science, or trade or commerce, of issues related to the aesthetic or the ethical reemphasizes their place in the new areas of knowledge. American Studies scholars should open up to these possibilities because people everywhere in the world are interested in knowing globalization through the agency of the US and its many cultures. The new globalism is creating conditions for a reorientation and relocation of traditional forms of knowledge. With its interdisciplinarity and radical reorientation American Studies is the right discipline to take up this challenge.

However, as Ickstadt has pointed out, 'institutionally speaking American Studies in a strict sense has almost disappeared in the US' (Ickstadt, 2002: 551). The fragmentation of whatever was once single, its movement into many parallel disciplines, has deprived it of much of its power and influence. Even its expansion into some areas of the transnational does not go beyond its geographical periphery—Canada, Latin America and the Caribbean. Large parts of the world, particularly what is called the third world still remain excluded in the new geographical space of American Studies. The need of the hour is to integrate local American Studies with a global perspective and to discover the vast network of relationships that connect America with the world and the world with America.

One positive move in this direction was the Iowa project on Reciprocal American Studies initiated by Jane Desmond and Virginia Dominguez at the International Forum for US Studies. It opened up the possibility of not only bringing together disciplines such as African American Studies, Ethnic Studies and Feminist Studies, that have moved away from American Studies but also collaborating with diverse disciplines across faculties and across the globe on a reciprocal basis. The movement has the potential to globalize American Studies not merely in a geographical sense, but also in the sense of a broad disciplinarity that will cope with the new globalism. In fact coping with the new globalism in which Americanization and anti-Americanism playa crucial role will remain on top of the agenda of all those bodies, such as this one, which are seeking global coalition of American Studies scholars and communities.

American Studies and the Challenge of the Transnational

How far is American Studies ready to grapple with the issues confronting a transnational, post-national, post-colonial borderless world that is visible in some recent scholarship? The breakthrough that have been made in this area by scholars in International Relations theory has not yet filtered into American Studies. Instead of opening up to the challenges of new globality, many American Studies scholars are agitated about the possibility of shrinking space of multiculturalism, about reduced funding and academic space, about the neo-liberal, neo-imperial designs of the US and a sad reiteration of the already essentialized discourses of race, ethnicity, gender, language, etc.[3] American Studies should now strive to locate itself in the expanding globality of knowledge that is also emerging as a new frontier in human history. To achieve that it must liberate itself from the vestiges of the past paradigms and the legacy of canon and culture wars that were fought and won or lost depending upon which side you belonged, without making any significant changes for the situation on the ground. One negative fallout of that academic intervention was the erosion of popular belief in the power of the intellectuals to alter radically reality, and an increasing unwillingness of the funding agencies to support programs which produced rhetoric and no results. The storm over the University was, for once, real.

---

[3]   See Palumbo-Liu (2002): 109-127.

American Studies and the Regime of Terror

The situation has been further complicated by the events following 9/11. The conflation of all discourses into the discourse of terror and the tendency to suspect terrorist threat in all aspects of human activity has made security a primary concern of all societies. Terror in conjunction with globalization seems to have subsumed all other discourses.[4]

While organized societies have always felt the threat of subversion in one form or the other the new regime of terror is exceptional in its reach and its capacity for violence and disruption. Like many other modem phenomena it is globalized and has adopted perfectly the techniques of globalization: a dot.com venture located everywhere and nowhere, a mobile network of intractable connections that are immediate and remote at the same time. It has radically altered the security environment in the sense that old insecurities have acquired a new potency and a post-human character. It has engendered what has been called ontological insecurity, a fear of loss of the fundamentals of any given society.

Terrorism is only one of the many non-traditional security threats facing societies all over the world. There are others, such as ethnic and sectarian conflict, unrestricted migration of people across borders, environmental degradation due to unethical exploitation of natural resources, illegal transfers of money, insurgency, the growing political influence of drug cartels and arms smugglers and finally crimes committed in cyberspace. In all these activities there is a combination of crime and conflict that does not reckon any boundaries. The scale and volume of these activities and the money involved in them goes beyond the total resources of many states.

Apart from the transnational crime syndicates there are those legitimate transnational organizations that seem to threaten the legitimate regimes by their reach and influence. As Robert Hall and Carl Fox point out 'control is now directed more by way of financial markets than any precise geopolitical structures and disruption is created by the same route. It is perhaps not surprising therefore that traditional state mechanisms based on ideas of frontiers and order, monarchies, public

---

[4]   See Rasmussen (2002): 323-349. See also the special issue of *Radical History Review* on 'Terrorism', 95 (2003) for other nuanced views on terrorism.

establishments of power-appear under threat' (Hall and Fox, 2001-02: 8).

Everywhere systems appear to be incapable of coping with threats posed by these forces, which have shown a greater capacity to absorb the destructive capability of new technologies, free as they are from the slow procedure-ridden bureaucracies. Real power seems to be operating beyond the control of traditional institutions of power management. To quote Hall and Cox again 'the pervasive and pernicious nature of the new security challenges is universal in effect. Transnational assaults have transnational victims' (p. 8).

Since terror operates beyond systemic boundaries it emerges as the ultimate threat to the order of states as it avails now. The problems of the new regimes of terror are 'simply too politically intractable, too thematically interconnected and too economically costly' (p. 11). Resisting terror thus appears as the ultimate concern of all humankind at the moment. The challenges it poses to the identity and legitimacy of the state makes it imperative that we radically revise our notion of existing world order and network of institutions that makes it possible. It demands real foundational changes. The confounding of all existing ideologies, systems and traditional belief systems in the new phenomenon of terrorism thwarts any attempts at clarity or universally acceptable answers.

Like any other force, terror also percolates in the constitution and practice of knowledge. It creates an environment of doubt and suspicion in which free thinking and freedom of expression yield ground to intolerance or tactical silence. How does one pursue knowledge and truth in such an environment? The task is further complicated for those who are involved in the pursuit of American Studies by the fact that America is perceived by many, within and outside the US, as one visible source of global terrorism. There is much in America's history to substantiate that perception.[5]

By joining hands with forces of discontent and disenchantment and by borrowing the rhetoric of the protest and reform, terrorism has acquired the appeal of a revolutionary ideology that appeals to the poor, the dispossessed, and the marginalized everywhere in the world. The moral untenability of the terrorist acts and the increasing vulnerability of innocent civilians do not move those who advocate violence as an

---

[5]   See Blum (2001).

acceptable mode of protest. How does one resist terror when it is practiced in the name of the very forces that provide the primary bonds of social cohesion, such as community, tribe, religion, caste, language and culture and finally the nation.

One way to comprehend the contemporary phenomenon of terrorism is to go back to history and to let people traverse the many trajectories that have led to the creation of modernity. The recent 'We the People' project of National Endowment of Humanities recognizes the role history plays in the lives of a people. The project, according to the new chairman Mr. Bruce Cole, will help Americans 'recover from their collective amnesia'. It was introduced to convey the lessons of history to all Americans because 'democracy demands wisdom'. The pursuit of history was consistent with the goals of national security. The terrorist attacks 'were an assault on our heritage of freedom, our history and our culture', he argued and therefore 'To defend our country we must first understand it. A knowledgeable citizenry is essential to homeland defence' (Cole cited by Borrego, 2002: 4-24). How far the new project will go to spur interest in American history will depend upon the kinds of histories Americanists will pursue. However, there is a promise of a renewal in the new project that should engage American Studies scholars.

American Studies and the Return of the Empire

The ethos of enlightenment that went into the foundational principles of USA and promised mankind 'an empire of liberty' is seldom reflected in US policies. The fractured discourses of American exceptionalism do not even promise that empire.

On the contrary, the US evokes the chimera of the return of empire that threatens to negate the notion of liberty and destroy in the process the very idea of sovereignty that makes liberty the basis of all civilized existence. The return of empire in recent world affairs where the US is a key player demands serious considerations from those who are interested in American Studies. In their controversial yet influential book, *Empire*, Michael Hardt and Antonio Negri have tried to draw our attention to the shift that is taking place the euro-centered Westphalian model of world order is yielding to what they call empire. According to them: 'What used to be conflict or competition among several imperialist powers has in important respects been replaced by the idea of a single power that over determines them all, structures them in a unitary way and treats them under one common notion of right that is decidedly post-colonial and post-imperialist (Hardt and Negri, 2002: 9). Hardt and Negri see empire 'as an impersonal network that can not be equated with any state, however apparently powerful' and while they do not specifically mention US, they seem to suggest that a transnational state dominated by the US and monitored through its many agencies is slowly emerging. More specifically their notion of empire hinges on a 'new global form of sovereignty' which is 'composed of a series of national and supranational organisms united under single logic of rule' (Hardt and Negri, 2002: xii).

Resisting Empire

While some weaknesses of Hardt and Negri's empire thesis have been exposed after the post Iraq realities of America (such as the USA's inability to have UN sanction for the war against Iraq, the belligerence of North Korea, and the failure of US to secure international approval of its policies) the ground realities of international politics, the presence of US as the lone superpower, its unilateral ism, its new doctrine of preemptive action and its overwhelming presence in the regulatory mechanisms of international politics do vouch for its global dominance. An understanding of the many networks that give US its power is a must for those who are interested in transnational American Studies. Since empire manages 'hybrid identities flexible hierarchies and plural exchanges through modulating networks of command' (Hardt and Negri, 2000: xii-xiii), it will be good intellectual strategy to enter the terrain of this empire and understand 'its homogenizing and hydrogenising flows in all their complexity' (Hardt and Negri, 2000: 42). Whether one likes it or not one has to reckon with the unrestricted circularity of the power of this empire. Like terrorism it has enormous capacity for unmediated violence. Resisting empire in its unrestrained circularity is another task before intellectuals to undertake.

The increasing concern with the transnational in recent American Studies has opened up new possibilities for exploration. At a time when democratic aspirations of a world looking for the proper recognition of diversity and difference are increasingly threatened by the specter of one-dimensional society, seeking to impose its own disciplinarity on the world, it becomes the moral responsibility of intellectuals to resist such forces and create conditions for a just and humane world order. The new ethos of American Studies should be located in that space of critical cosmopolitanism the goal of which is "not to disseminate one world view but rather to build consensus that leaves room for diversity and difference while being sufficiently substantial to provide the basis for the validity of norms' (Ellis, 2002: 274).[6]

American Studies scholars should focus on those forces within American experience that help create that cosmopolitan space: its multiple new world ontology, the confluence of many languages, cultures and traditions in its people, its commitment to the enlightenment values of individual dignity and freedom, its openness to the culture of science and technology, and finally its eternally restless multitudes, always eager to embrace the new and different, despite temporary deviations. Its very presence in global affairs, both positive and negative, forces others to meditate on subjects of global ethical concerns such as International Law, diplomacy, violence, justice, human rights, the environment, the status of women, refugees migration. Can American Studies engender that critical cosmopolitanism that will remind America's policy planners of the foundational principles that promote 'life, liberty and pursuit of happiness', to 'have a new world' for a new Adam?

It is apparent that there is a vast gap between here and there. The US has not yet reflected enough on its own transnationality, the global role that it has played and continues to play in the constitution of identities and transformation of geographic spaces and the ethics of those transformations. Though pursuing a globalism through 'Davos Culture' and 'Toyotaism', it seems to be unaware of the ethical obligations of that globalism. Under the regime of terror, America's policy planners have made Seneca's words, 'odarint dum metuant' ('Let them hate us so long as they fear us') the motto of their global policy. As America and American Studies move into the seamless space of the transnational, both need a new ethos rooted in critical cosmopolitanism with room for both difference and diversity.

Kousar J. Azam

---

[6]   See also Franceschat (2002): 347-357.

References

Blum, William. 2001. *Rogue State: A Guide to the World's Only Superpower*, London: Zed Books.

Borrego, Ann Marie. 2002. 'A New Emphasis for Humanities Endowment', *Chronicle of Higher Education*, (December): A4-A24.

Connolly, William. 1995. *The Ethos of Pluralization*, Minneapolis: University of Minnesota Press.

Ellis, Jaye. 2002. International Regimes and Legitimacy of Rules: A Discourse Ethical Approach', *Alternatives* 27(3): 273-300.

Franceschat, Antonio. 2002. 'Moral Principles and Political Institutions: Perspectives on Ethics and International Affairs', *Millennium: Journal of International Studies* 31(2): 347-357.

Hall, Robert and Carl Fox. 2001-2002. 'Rethinking Security', *NATO Review* 49(4): 8-12.

Hardt, Michael and Antonio Negri. 2000. *Empire*, Cambridge, MA: Harvard University Press.

Hollander, Paul. 2002. 'The Politics of Envy', *The New Criterion* 21(3): 14-19.

Ickstadt, Heinz. 2002. 'American Studies in an Age of Globalization', *American Quarterly*, 54(4): 543-562.

Kaldor, Mary. 2003. 'American Power: From Compellance to Cosmopolitanism', *International Affairs* 79(1): 1-22.

Kimball, Roger. 2002. 'Failures of Nerve', *The New Criterion* 21(3): 4-8.

Kurzweil, Ray. 2002. 'The Ascendance of Science and Technology (Panel Discussion)', *Partisan Review* 69 (Fall): 542-73.

Lenz, Gunther H. 2002. 'Transculturations: American Studies in a Globalizing world', in *American Studies (Heidelberg)*, 47(1): 96-119.

Paulmbo-Liu, David. 2002. 'Multiculturalism Now: Civilization, National Identity and Difference Before and After September 11th', *boundary 2* 29(2): 109-27.

Podhoretz, Norman. 2002. 'Intellectuals and Writers – Then and Now', *Partisan Review* 69 (Fall): 510ff.

Ramesh, Jairam. 1999. "'Yankee Go Home, but Take Me with You'": Yet another Perspective on Indo-American Relations," *Economic and Political Weekly* (11 Dec.): 3532-44.

Rasmussen, Mikkel Vedby. 2002. 'A Parallel Globalization of Terror: 9/11, Security and Globalization', *Cooperation and Conflict: Journal of Nordic International Studies Association*, 37(3): 323-349.

Rothstein, Edward. 2002. 'The Ascendance of Science and Technology (Panel Discussion)', *Partisan Review* 69 (Fall): 542-73.

How far from America is America?

> The heart of American studies is
> the pursuit of what constitutes
> democratic culture.
> —Alice Kessler-Harris

— I —

The question raised in the title of the first IASA conference, "How far is America from here?" is quite intriguing, reminiscent in a postmodern way of the old French Academy questions. Trying to answer it one is almost compelled to say, it depends on where "here" is ("¿Dónde es aquí?" as a Mexican conference speaker rephrased the question) and how one defines "America" ("America Is Here" is the title of a conference paper--about Brazil; or "NOT HERE." the title of a Bulgarian talk at this IASA.) Assuming that Leiden is "here," we may answer the question literally: the closest point of the American continent is about 3000 nautical miles or 5550 km away from here. That is, in fact, what my daughter advised me I should entitle my paper, "3000 Miles." But perhaps the question is metaphoric; and which tool is better equipped than the world wide web to help answer metaphoric questions? Google locates, for example, Aleksandra Sladjana Milosevic, a singer from former Yugoslavia whose CD *Animal tested* contains a song with the title "How Far is America?" (which comes right after another track entitled "Sexy drama"). Unfortunately, this song is not readily available; there is, however, another undated North Italian musical answer to our question "AMERICA LONTANA E BELLA." Here is the second stanza of the song in which America gets double-edged praise as a large land, with rivers and mountains, where with the help of our Italians we built up country and city; America is far and beautiful, and all call her "sister":

> E l'America è lunga e larga
> e circondata di fiumi e montagne
> e con l'aiuto dei nostri italiani
> abbiamo fatto paesi e città.
>   America lontana e bella
> tutti la chiamano l'America sorella.

Perhaps this somewhat enigmatic song will make sense in the context of the panel on "The Space of America in Contemporary Italian Literature."

Another Google hit is "The King of Sitges," a gay love story set in Spain in which a wealthy American suitor attempts to persuade his love interest, a Spanish hustler, to go to America with him. Here is a relevant sample of the dialogue.

> "How far is America?"
> "Around the corner."
> "I don't like feeling a kept man, you know that."
> "Don't feel so."
> "Let's try?"
> "To do what?"
> "To go to Boston. To work together at your business. To really love each other, above all."
> "Let's try."

Is this perhaps a case in point of "Mapping "America" as a Sign of Liberation through Eroticised Consumption"?

Then there are numerous Mommy joke websites with versions of that venerable old one that goes: "Mommy, Mommy!! how far is America?" "Shut up son and keep rowing" (or, alternatively, "keep swimming"). No real answer there, though "Shut up and keep swimming" might also have made for a good title of a paper at this conference. But so far one cannot say that the Google answers were truly enlightening.

So I started thinking more about Leiden and America. There are, of course, the Pilgrims, that band of about a hundred Calvinist separatists who in 1609 sought refuge in Leiden from English religious persecution. William Bradford described their anxiety about going to Holland memorably in his history *Of Plimoth Plantation*:

> But to go into a country they knew not but by hearsay, where they must learn a new language and get their livings they knew not how, it being a dear place and subject to the miseries of war, it was by many thought an adventure almost desperate; a case intolerable and a misery worse than death. Especially seeing they were not acquainted with trades nor traffic (by which that country doth subsist) but had only been used to a plain country life and the innocent trade of husbandry.

The "new language" was what increased the perception of distance between England and Holland. It is telling that Holland is referred to as "new world." But among the dissenters' greatest worries was the fear that their children might be going Dutch:

> [O]f all sorrows most heavy to be borne, was that many of their children, by . . . the great licentiousness of youth in that country, and the manifold temptations of the place, were drawn away by evil examples into extravagant and dangerous courses, getting the reins off their necks and departing from their parents. Some became soldiers, others took upon them far voyages by sea, and others some worse courses tending to dissoluteness and the danger of their souls, to the great grief of their parents and dishonour of God. So that they saw their posterity would be in danger to degenerate and be corrupted.

(The editor's note to this passage informs us that Nathaniel Morton and Edward Winslow also voiced the Pilgrims' fear that their children might lose their language and nationality in Holland.) By contrast, America held the promise of not requiring any linguistic or moral assimilation by the English protestants: and their children would surely not become soldiers, sailors, or worse.

Even though Bradford referred to the New World as "those remote parts of the world" and Cotton Mather would later on view the America to which the English protestants were going as "the ends of the earth" (after Psalms 19:4, in a passage Djelal Kadir once examined with great rigor), to Bradford, America still seemed inviting: "The place they had thoughts on was some of those vast and unpeopled countries of America, which are fruitful and fit for habitation, being devoid of all civil inhabitants, where there are only savage and brutish men which range up and down, little otherwise than the wild beasts of the same." The promise of an English-language continuity seemed to shorten the geographic distance.

Perhaps half of the Pilgrims did leave Leiden, but because they were once here, Leiden is now also a site of proto-American history. Joke Kardux and Eduard van de Bilt have fully explored the Pilgrims' history in Leiden. The traces the Pilgrims left here are not particularly prominent. There are a few markers, and there is a little memorial room at Beschuitsteeg 9, run by the historian Jeremy Dupertuis Bangs who also put together an informative pamphlet. And there is a recent dispute, in which Bangs played the part of the preservationist against the Leiden city planners. Bangs would like to save such remnants as "the Aalmarkt area where Capt. Myles Standish was treated in the 1571 St. Catherine's Hospital for his wounds." A Leiden alderman rejected the notion that the Aalmarkt should be preserved because a Pilgrim was once a patient in the hospital. "I consider it pedantic of those Americans that they are getting in the way because of that one Pilgrim. As a governor of Leiden I had to weigh that interest off against the interests of thousands of Leiden's modern-day residents."

This issue may take on more virulence because the current US president is a descendent (through his father and his mother, a geneaological link Kardux and de Bilt have analyzed at some detail). All of this goes to show only that America need not be 3000 miles away from Leiden. No matter where you are there is also something that can be called "American" even if it is as invisible as Myles Standish's ghost at the site of the former Leiden hospital—as if to illustrate the response to our conference question given by Jean Baudrillard in the motto to his book *Amérique*. It is the phrase inscribed on American convex rear-view mirrors: "Caution: objects in this mirror may be closer than they appear!"

What if the "here" in our question stood for Canada (as the conference paper "Figuring North (of) America" suggests)? How far is America from Canada? Of course, one assumes that Canada, which also is "America" in the geographic sense of term, would symbolize great closeness to the United States. Yet immediate geographic vicinity may mean a greater need to differentiate oneself so as not to be mistaken for what one is close to. Such differentiation need not be an opportunistic gesture. Take, for example, William John Rose (1885-1968) who was born on a poor Manitoba farm, went on to be a classics student, and was in Prague in 1914 in connection with the Student Christian Movement. When World War I broke out, he and his wife were in Ligotka, a small town in the province of Teschen, in Austrian Silesia. After Britain declared war on Germany and Austria, the Roses' situation became more delicate—as Canadians, they were British subjects, hence enemy aliens. Rose writes in his memoirs:

> [W]hen I ventured to go to the County Office in Teschen . . . to enquire whether we could get permission to move to Vienna with a view of taking up some kind of Red Cross work, I discovered that the officials in charge thought of Canada as belonging to the United States! The answer I got was, 'Why, of course; Americans are free to go where they like.'

One might think that Rose would have let things stand at this mistake and gone on to Vienna, but even in this complex situation this Canadian apparently could not tolerate the idea of being mistaken for an American. His memoir continues:

> When, however, I explained the error, the prefect (who was a fine example of aristocratic Pole attached to the Austrian Civil Service) made a long face. His final advice was that we were to stay quietly where we were, not attract unnecessary attention to ourselves, and not think about getting back to our home in Prague, where anti-Austrian feeling was running high. (25)

As a result of Rose's candor, the Canadian couple ends up sequestered in Ligotka for the entire duration of the war. Rose made the best of this experience, learned Czech and Polish, and later became a Professor of Slavic languages.

I was reminded of Rose's book when I read a "Letter to America" last month (*Nation*, April 14, 2003), authored by the Canadian writer Margaret Atwood (who is also the subject of two papers here). Atwood's letter addresses the question of our conference explicitly, and in the context of the war on Iraq and the Patriot Acts. "We've always been close, you and us," she writes, emphasizing her Canadian location. "History, that old entangler, has twisted us together since the early seventeenth century. Some of us used to be you; some of us want to be you; some of you used to be us. You are not only our neighbors: In many cases—mine, for instance—you are also our blood relations, our colleagues, and our personal friends. But although we've had a ringside seat, we've never understood you completely, up here north of the 49th parallel. We're like Romanized Gauls—look like Romans, dress like Romans, but aren't Romans—peering over the wall at the real Romans. What are they doing? Why? What are they doing now?"

Having established a position of well-wishing closeness, Atwood briefly expresses her view that the Iraq war was "an ill-advised adventure," but soon focuses on what Americans are doing to themselves at this moment: "You're gutting your Constitution. Already your home can be entered without your knowledge or permission, you can be snatched away and incarcerated without cause, your mail can be spied on, your private records searched. Why isn't this a recipe for widespread business theft, political intimidation and fraud? I know you've been told that all this is for your own safety and protection, but think about it for a minute. Anyway, when did you get so scared? You didn't used to be easily frightened." After taking on the other damages, the US national deficit and the economy, she concludes with the myth of King Arthur sleeping in a cave, but ready to return in Britain's hour of greatest peril: "You too have great spirits of the past you may call upon: men and women of courage, of conscience, of prescience. Summon them now, to stand with you, to inspire you, to defend the best in you. You need them."

Atwood juxtaposes two Americas, both embedded in European myths: one is the United States as empire, the new Rome, and the other the America embodied by domestic equivalents to Arthurian spirits of the past. In her admonition to one America to summon the spirit of the other, her careful balancing of Canadian closeness and distance, intimate knowledge and lack of comprehension, Atwood is rather restrained when compared to the following excerpts. Please be prepared now for stronger language.

— II —

"This American government,--what is it but a tradition, though a recent one, endeavoring to transmit itself unimpaired to posterity, but each instant losing some of its integrity," a well-known author comments famously at a time of a war, a war this writer describes as "the work of comparatively few individuals, using the standard government as their tool; for, in the outset, the people would not have consented to this measure."

Another author comments on "too-young and too-new America, lusty because it is lonely, aggressive because it is afraid," a country that "insists upon seeing the world in terms of good and bad, the holy and the evil, the high and the low, the white and the black." America is "frightened by fact, by history, by process, by necessity. It hugs the easy way of damning those it does not understand, of excluding those who look different; and it salves its conscience with a self-draped cloak of righteousness."

Yet another literary figure voiced the hypothesis that the conservatives in the American government "have come to the conclusion that the only way they can save America and get it off its present downslope is to become a regime with a greater military presence and drive toward empire." He adds: "My fear is that Americans might lose their democracy in the process."

No, these are not Old Europe's critics of the present moment, they are not Canadian, Mexican, South American, African or Asian skeptics; these are not anti-American but all-American voices. I quoted Henry David Thoreau (the subject of Albena Bakratcheva's paper here) confronted by the Mexican war; and Richard Wright thinking about the relationship of political and racial dualism—perhaps these two are among Atwood's Arthurian spirits of "Old America"; and last, the eighty-year-old Norman Mailer commenting on the present crisis, which has provoked rich reactions in the literary world. Adrienne Rich and Stanley Kunitz and were among many well-known American poets who have recently raised their voices against current US foreign and military policy. Maxine Hong Kingston has just finished *The Fifth Book of Peace*, with an epilogue that includes an account of her protest against the war on Iraq and her arrest in Washington DC on International Women's Day:

Never before had I experienced such nonviolence. Thousands of women tried to send our good feelings and protection all the way to the Iraqi children. The police carefully arrested two dozen women, including me and my sister writers - Rachel Bagby, Susan Griffin, Alice Walker, and Terry Tempest Williams. The charge: "Stationary demo in a restricted zone (White House sidewalk)." But first, the police arrested the journalists - Kirsten Michel, a filmmaker, and Amy Goodman of Pacifica Radio - and took away their camera and audio equipment, and cell phones. We had been talking live via cell phone on independent radio stations all over the country. Amy said, "If an event - an arrest - is not witnessed and photographed by the media, it did not happen."

Arthur Miller asks, "HAS the essence of America, its very nature, changed from benign democracy to imperium? Why do such majorities across the water fear and despise this administration? Too much piety, triumphal arrogance? We are being blasted by issues raised by an unprecedented American position at the top of the world. The meanings of words have changed; is it really a cause for unalloyed boasting that we can fight two wars at the same time, or is this to be lamented as the failure of America's creation: the United Nations and the system of collective security? One has to wonder sometimes if the art of giving things their right names is being surrendered." The 88-year-old playwright Miller also finds strange echoes in contemporary political rhetoric to that of the 1950s, a rhetoric that reminded Miller then of the Puritan witchhunts. "Almost 50 years ago now,' he writes, "I felt compelled to write in a speech for Judge Danforth in *The Crucible*: 'You must understand, sir, a person is either with this court or he must be counted against it, there be no road between. This is a sharp time, now, a precise time -- we live no longer in the dusky afternoon when evil mixed itself with good and befuddled the world. Now, by God's grace, the shining sun is up, and them that fear not light will surely praise it. I hope you will be one of those.' How many times do we have to indulge the same idiocies for which we must later be ashamed?"

Edward Albee states that he remains "appalled by the curtailment of civil rights and human rights that these Republicans think they can get away with as a result of the attack on the US" and that he is "not convinced" "that there is any justification for an attack on Iraq."

A few days after the beginning of the war on Iraq, Jonathan Franzen wrote a political allegory, entitled "When the Wing Broke Away from the Old Mansion: A Short Story about Europe and America" (*Guardian*, March 25, 2003), in which America is cast as the biblical Joseph and Europe as his older brothers. Joseph, after eight years of partying with a great beauty from Arkansas whom his brothers adore, wants to settle down. He intends to marry his "good, sensible friend Albertine" who, however, is not sexy, and so he spends a night of fun in an SUV with Georgina whose parents and five lawyers later force Joseph to marry her. He complains in vain: "But I don't even like her! . . . She's spoiled and stupid and mean." Georgina invites her parents and her parents' lawyers into the mansion and is rude to Joseph's older brothers. It looks as though the marriage would be brief. "But then, one night, a bully from a poor neighborhood threw a rock through the window of Joseph's study, scaring Joseph badly. When he went to his brothers, he found that he'd forfeited their sympathy by marrying Georgina. They said they were sorry about the rock, but a broken window was nothing compared to what they'd suffered, over the years, in the old wing of the mansion." And this is how the story ends:

> Although Georgina was too stupid and spoiled to think for herself, her parents were shrewd opportunists. They hoped to use Joseph's momentary fright to gain control of the entire mansion. They went to Joseph and said: "This is the logic of war. You're the head of the family, Georgina is your wife now, and only her parents can defend this house. You must learn to hate your useless brothers and trust us."
> The brothers were enraged when they heard this. They went to Joseph and said: "This is the logic of peace. Your wife is a bitch and a whore. As long as she's in this house, you're no brother of ours."
> And the rich little brother clutched his head and wept.

Kurt Vonnegut, now eighty years old, writes that he feels the United States "might as well have been invaded by Martians and body snatchers. Sometimes I wish it had been. What has happened, though, is that it has been taken over by means of the sleaziest, low-comedy, Keystone Cops-style coup d'état imaginable. And those now in charge of the federal government are upper-crust C-students who know no history or geography, plus not-so-closeted white supremacists, aka 'Christians,' and plus, most frighteningly, psychopathic personalities."

In the poem "We Speak Not of Osama," Calvin Trillin satirizes the thrust of the war against terrorism:

> We said we'd pound him once he's found
> so flat that he'd cry for his momma.
> Forget that jive, that "dead or alive."
> 'Cause we speak not of Osama.
> He's not even in the axis.
> No, his evil did not make the grade.
> For the thing he mostly lacks is
> A country that we can invade.

And the poet Nikki Giovanni focuses her comment on Condoleezza Rice:

> "I think there's something seriously wrong with a girl born in Birmingham, who went to Notre Dame on affirmative action, who went to Stanford on affirmative action; who got her job because of demonstrations against Stanford, so they had to hire somebody black; and who all of a sudden is advising for war and against affirmative action. Something is really wrong with that."

Could it be that at moments of crisis, of which the present time certainly is one, America as idea, as democratic promise, as literature, as guardian spirit of the past, is at the greatest possible remove from itself, from the United States as present political practice?

American literature has certainly had its famous oppositional moments. There is thus a long American tradition of dissent articulated freely (but not risk-free) by some of the most well-known writers, and the present moment is no exception to this legacy of saying "No in thunder." Perhaps what characterizes our time, however, is the general indifference to what writers are saying about politics. (I must confess that I, a teacher of American literature, was not aware of many such comments before I started searching for them in pursuit of answers to our conference question.) Unlike in some earlier times, artists may no longer be the "conscience of the nation" who scandalize general readers and the politically powerful. What happens at the Oscar ceremonies, the quick gestures of popular culture celebrities, may nowadays be more important for visually dominated news media than are the literary statements, be they carefully reasoned or simply cantankerous, that are tucked away in OpEd pieces or on such web pages as Poets Against the War. Of course, the awarding of an Oscar to Michael Moore's *Bowling for Columbine* as the best documentary of the year constitutes an important continuation of this oppositional tradition as well. Gary Trudeau's Doonesbury has been running a sustained satirical and partly prophetic comment on the Iraq War in the press, while David Rees's comic strip *Get Your War On* is web-based. And Bruce Springsteen has revived the old Edwin Starr song "War" for opening his concerts. Perhaps some of you have registered more examples of American writers and artists articulating their critique. But the few passages I have cited may suggest the extent of alienation, the depth of the rift between America and America.

Paradoxically, closeness—no, identity, sameness!—may make for the greatest distance. How far from America is America? The Chinese slogan, vis-à-vis China's completely capitalist parts like Hong Kong, goes: "One country, two systems." Is there perhaps an American equivalent, one country, two Americas?

III.

How has American Studies, the heart of which is "the pursuit of democratic culture," addressed this question? Going back to Google, many citations prompted by the question "How far is America?" actually refer to our International American Studies Association conference and its topic, and perhaps the fullest answer to the general question and to my modification of it will be given by this conference itself.

Perhaps inspired by the often memorable pronouncements made by American writers and artists, our discipline of American Studies also has had a respectable past history of often spirited engagement for democracy that included implicit and explicit ways of addressing the question. As probably all of you know, American Studies was established in the United States in 1937, not only in order to permit interdisciplinary work between the disciplines of English and History at a time when disciplinary boundaries were very jealously guarded but also in order to develop in scholarship, and to convey to students, a fuller understanding of democratic cultural practice against the prevailing international threats of fascism and communism, in the midst of a deep crisis of capitalism.

Leo Marx, a practitioner of the first hour, has recently published a memoir in which he characterizes the contexts out of which his dissertation emerged, the dissertation that became also his first book and a landmark study in the field: "The tenor of *The Machine in the Garden* is in part traceable to the left-wing political ferment—especially the student movement—of the late 1930s. Taken together, a set of converging developments—the financial collapse and mass unemployment of the Great Depression; the sense that capitalism might be doomed; the military build-up of the Franco, Hitler, Mussolini, and Stalin dictatorships; the all-but-certain imminence of a war for service in which we students would be conscripted—had intensified the social conscience of my college generation" (186) His teachers, virtually all of them "leftists of one stripe or another" (F. O. Matthiessen and Paul Sweezy most notable among them) (187) strengthened the feeling of this generational location. The dissertation that emerged was premised on the assumption that capitalist-driven industrialization was "the central event in American history" and on the conviction that accomplished artists and writers would be likely to have the "most sensitive, critically telling responses to such complex transformative processes" (confirming the truth of the Poundian maxim, "Artists are the antennae of the race").

Marx's scholarship provided new contexts for familiar texts like Hawthorne's short story "Ethan Brand" which were examined in close readings, but readings placed in the history of industrialization. Here is Marx's retrospective summary: "For the setting [of "Ethan Brand"], Hawthorne drew extensively upon observations he recently made during a walking tour of the Berkshires. Factories with modern machinery recently had been built there, and he was struck by the picturesque impression they made in the midst of wild scenery. He noted the melancholy women workers staring out of factory windows, and a man whose hand had been cut off by a machine. In composing the story, however, Hawthorne omitted almost all explicit references to the factories, the new artifacts, or their disturbing implications. Yet when we read the published story with his notebook observations in view, it is obvious that the protagonist's alienation was prompted by his dubious reaction to oncoming industrialism" (189). The method, one could paraphrase, was one of demonstrating a partly hidden political context for Hawthorne's short story that made more explicit the social critique it embodied. Throughout his work, Marx delineated a specific ideology, that of the pastoral ideal of a middle landscape in the face of industrialization. Marx noted that, like "many people on the Left in the 1930s," he "found it difficult to reconcile" his "political and aesthetic preferences." He aimed for an integration of close reading and historicization, yet he ended his book with the resonant statement expressing hope for a social transformation that would effectively bridge the two Americas: "To change the situation we require new symbols of possibility, and although the creation of those symbols is in some measure the responsibility of artists, it is in greater measure the responsibility of society. The machine's sudden entrance into the garden presents a problem that ultimately belongs not to art but to politics." How far America was from America became a progressive question and encouraged a critique of capitalism.

Let me take another more explicit example from that period (though it was not institutionally a product of American Studies and though its author was not an American but a Swede), Gunnar Myrdal's *An American Dilemma: The Negro Problem and Modern Democracy* (1944), which casts the distance between the two Americas differently. The author chose the title in order to redefine the issues of racial injustice, disfranchisement, and segregation that were then commonly discussed as "the Negro problem." Invoking John Dewey's *Freedom and Culture*, Myrdal argues: "The 'American Dilemma,' referred to in the title of this book, is the ever-raging conflict between, on the one hand, the valuations preserved on the general plane which we shall call the 'American Creed,' where the American thinks, talks, and acts under the influence of high national and Christian precepts, and, on the other hand, the valuations on specific planes of individual and group living, where personal and local interests; economic, social, and sexual jealousies; considerations of community prestige and conformity; group prejudice against particular persons or types of people; and all sorts of miscellaneous wants, impulses, and habits dominate his outlook" (xlvii). From that premise Myrdal proceeded to demand a large-scale program of racial equalization as little more than an overdue adjustment of the status quo to long-cherished American ideals: "From the point of view of the American Creed the status accorded the Negro in America represents nothing more and nothing less than a century-long lag of public morals. In principle the Negro problem was settled long ago; in practice the solution is not effectuated. The Negro in America has not yet been given the elemental civil and political rights of formal democracy, including a fair opportunity to earn his living, upon which the general accord was already won when the American Creed was first taking form. And this anachronism constitutes the contemporary 'problem' both to Negroes and to whites" (24). Addressing a pressing social problem meant closing the gap, bridging the distance, between two Americas by changing American racial practices so as to fulfill the American ideal. "How far is America from America?" could have been the question that would help energize the struggle for racial equality, in the manner of Langston Hughes's famous poem,

> Let America be America again.
> Let it be the dream it used to be.
> Let it be the pioneer on the plain
> Seeking a home where he himself is free.
> (America never was America to me.)
> ....
> And yet I swear this oath—America will be.

Myrdal never forgets that his delineation of the "American Creed" is no "American monopoly," as he puts it, but, "with minor variations" it is "the common democratic creed." It goes back to the philosophy of Enlightenment with such postulates as "the essential diginity of man," "confidence in the value of the consent of the governed" or "the value of decisions arrived at by common counsel rather than by violence and brutality." Myrdal therefore stresses that the "American Creed is older and wider than America itself."

I think these examples suffice to sketch a moment. The dichotomies between pastoral ideology and capitalist industrialization were different, of course, from those between human rights Creed and racist prejudice and practice. But one can sense in either case how the distance between two Americas was established in the service of proposing change toward more democratic structures.

After the institutional proliferation of American Studies and the general expansion of scholarship on the United States both at home and abroad, there came a challenge to such approaches in the 1960s, at the time of the Vietnam war and the international student movement, and in much scholarship of the following decade, beginning with Bruce Kuklick's famous critique of the "myth-and-symbol school." You are probably quite familiar with these critiques and with the resulting proliferation of particularizing studies in the growing number of disciplines that were joining the field. Women's Studies, Black Studies, Ethnic Studies,

Cultural Studies and Theory became in many ways more active areas than any overarching "American Studies" out of which they had in many cases emerged. The field opened its doors to areas of inquiry that had been invisible as long as generalizations about America had been made on the basis of small dominant groups and major literary works. "Relevance" became a new slogan; much was introduced—and much dismissed—in its name. American literary anthologies began to change the authors and texts included; and in a field that lacked a long-standing historical consensus about great works, the "canon" underwent many changes. If American Studies emerged in the course of World War II and found its highest moment of development in the Cold War, then it was reshaped in the wake of the antiwar sentiment that the Vietnam war generated among intellectuals in the United States. As Heinz Ickstadt put it, the so-called "Myth-and-Symbol-School" "came under heavy critical fire by a younger generation of American studies scholars who suspected that even a critical focusing on mythic structures implied ideological complicity." Or to put it differently: The older generation instilled democratic principles so successfully that the 1960s generation extended the suspicion toward the older Americanists themselves.

In recent accounts of this time, there is a tendency to note continuities rather than only the obvious ruptures between the Old American Studies and the new, post-1960s approaches. Leo Marx himself observed that the rhetoric he had analyzed in *The Machine in the Garden* had a surprising resilience among 1960s radicals. Thus he mentioned that Berkeley Campus radical Mario Savio used Thoreauvian rhetoric in exhorting students to stop the military supply trains bound for Vietnam: "You've got to put your bodies upon the [machine] and make it stop." Thoreau had said in "Civil Disobedience," "Let your life be a counter friction to stop the machine." Marx saw in this echo "the mere surface expression of a much deeper ideological continuity between 19th-century pastoralism and the New Left radical Movement (or counter-culture) of the 1960s." Were the critics of the Old American Studies similarly dependent on the patterns established by their predecessors, whom they often criticized?

In his essay "The Deforming Mirror of Truth." the African American historian and American Studies scholar Nathan Huggins described the situation in 1989, after twenty years of Black Studies, in a manner that showed that the hopefulness of *An American Dilemma* had evaporated.

Huggins highlights that "being counted in" could only be a first step in a much more complicated process of making previously excluded groups, African-Americans, women, Hispanic-Americans, Asian-Americans, white ethnics, and Native Americans part of an American historical narrative that would have to change radically in the process. Stressing that blacks were on American soil "before the Mayflower" and could therefore be legitimated as "founders" constituted a merited claim for a birthright, but it did not resolve the deeper problem, namely that it left the essential structure of the narrative intact.

If the problem were merely one of exclusion and lack of recognition, the response could be to work for inclusion and appreciation of the black contribution to American history. The end-product would be an "integrated" history in which the African-American role—ordeals, contributions, great men and women, achievements, etc.—complements what has been a powerful white male-dominated story.

What Huggins terms "nationalistic" scholarship, valuable studies focused on African Americans alone, while helpfully increasing general knowledge, also would not challenge the patterns of historical imagination. But how could a cultural narrative look that would take seriously, for example, the recognition forced upon its readers by Edmund Morgan's *American Slavery, American Freedom* (1975) that American history may not have been the story of the creation of "free and democratic institutions" in which slavery and racism remained "anachronistic" aberrations, but rather the other way around, that "racial slavery created among white men a kind of equality," in short, that "American freedom itself" was the "creation of slavery."

> The paradox of American slavery and American freedom, however, challenges the master narrative itself... It goes, rather, against the ideological and conceptual basis of conventional history, exposing it as unsound.. . .The challenge of the paradox is that there can be no white history that does not begin to comprehend that slavery and freedom, white and black, are joined at the hip.

How would American cultural history have to be reconceived if it were to understand slavery no longer as an anachronistic exception and aberration in a free country, as a temporary detour on the road to universal suffrage and democracy, but rather as intimately and frighteningly connected with the rise of liberty (a question Orlando Patterson has pursued in depth, and in a broad comparative perspective)? What would this mean for historical narratives? Would they still look like Bunyan's *Pilgrim's Progress* or more like Sartre's *No Exit*, Huggins asks. The deforming mirror of truth would have to change the forms of historical imagination. Similar questions have been asked from the point of view of other ethnic histories and of women's studies. Was the image of two Americas distant from each other, an America of racial slavery and an America of freedom, nothing but an illusion, an ideological by-product of the belief in progress?

In the field of canonical American literature, Sacvan Bercovitch has made the case for an at least equally deep impasse. Bercovitch occasionally presents himself as a Canadian outsider, an agnostic alien to the myth of America, the American dream, or the American Creed. He writes: "When I first came to the United States, I knew virtually nothing about America." (1) "America," in quotation marks, as the land of the dream and the myth has thus been differentiated from the country on the map. What strikes Bercovitch most are the impressively varied ways in which modes of dissent could be transformed into rituals of assent, with the help of a rhetoric he traces back to the concept of the "errand into the wilderness" of the 17th-century Protestants. As was Leo Marx, Bercovitch is particularly struck by the fact that even the 1960s radicals continued in forms of the consensus mode.

When I first encountered the ritual of American consensus, in the mid-1960s, it took the form of protest and despair: the Jewish anarchist Paul Goodman berating the country for abandoning its promise; the descendant of American slaves, Martin Luther King, Jr., denouncing the injustice a violation of the American Way; an interminable debate about national destiny, full of rage and faith, conservatives scavenging for un-Americans, New Left historians recalling the country to its sacred mission. (29)

The quintessentially liberal program for change that linked Elizabeth Cady Stanton to Gloria Steinem encompassed, blurred, and eventually eliminated other feminist alternatives (those which did not focus on America).... This form of cultural work joined Jefferson to Thoreau and both to Martin Luther King, Jr., in an omnivorous oppositionalism that ingested all competing modes of radicalism—from the Fourierists to Herbert Marcuse and Noam Chomsky—in the course of redefining injustice as un-American, revolution as the legacy of '76, and inequities of class, race, and gender as disparities between the theory and the practice of American-ness. (19)

Bercovitch particularly deplores the lack of a recognition of internationally available political and intellectual alternatives, which he attempts to sketch in giving new historical-political contexts to the American literary tradition. Bercovitch reads Hawthorne's campaign biography for Franklin Pierce in which Hawthorne "defends Pierce's support of the Fugitive Slave Act" alongside Hawthorne's fiction. And he is skeptical of the whole tradition of dissent: "Melville's greatest No-in-thunder comes in an essay extolling America's destiny." The lure of what he calls "The Music of America" simply seems irresistible, permeating even what appears to be its critique.

Bercovitch stresses how dissent may inadvertently support and even strengthen consensus, for, "in this country, the unmediated relation between social structure and social ideal has made the very exposure of social flaws part of a ritual of socialization—a sort of liminal interior dialogue that in effect reinforces the mainstream culture." Or: "American liberalism privileged dissent." Hence the Puritans' legacy was "their success in making a dissenting faith the cornerstone of a community."

Bercovitch's views on American Studies are similarly pessimistic. He finds that American Studies in the United States, "as it had developed from the Forties through the Cold War decades," seems "a method designed not to explore its subject." (And abroad, "it took the form of an academic Marshall Plan.") He asks why new Americanists were "so intent on demonstrating the subversiveness of authors who for the most part had either openly endorsed the American Way, or else had lamented American corruption as the failure of New Eden." And he comments specifically on the recent history of American Studies as an indication of the "alliance between radicalism and upward mobility:"

Surely, it is no accident that, of all academic specialties, this field has been the most hospitable from the start to new waves of immigration from the other America into the profession. Nor is it by accident that, in spite of its very name, American Studies (as in United States), has gravitated toward a denial of cohesion, that this rhetoric of denial has presented itself in protests against exclusion (i.e., for integration), that the protest has taken the form of hyphenated ethnicity—Italian-American, Irish-American, and Jewish-American hand in hand with African-

American, Asian-American, and Hispanic-American—and that the result has been an adversarial form of interpretation which roots subversion in institutions of culture. It makes for a paradox that could obtain, in the old immigrant myth, only in America: a school of subversion geared toward the harmony of politicl activism and the good life, and directed (under the aegis of American literary studies) toward a fusion of personal, professional, and national identity.

Marx noted the ideological continuities of old American paradigms and New Left; Huggins insisted on the fact that the American Creed had included both liberty and slavery since American liberty was founded upon racial slavery. In a Bercovitchian view, the ritual of consensus seems able to absorb and coopt all alternatives, both those offered by American writers and those advocated by scholarly Americanists. Sacvan Bercovitch sent me a special comment on our conference topic:

> I would say that in a crucial way America has always been elsewhere for Americans. In 1801 John Adams wrote that "there are no Americans in America"; Emerson talked about America as a nation of individuals that was yet to exist, there's also his "new yet unapproachable America we have found in the West"; doesn't King imply that America hasn't yet really happened in his Dream speech?—that's a tradition implied, usually indirectly but often enough directly, in the equation of America as the land of futurity—or for that matter in American nostalgia—and sometimes as part of the jeremiad mode ("Let America be America again"). . . . —I believe that the appeal to America as a form of cultural revitalization has always required that dissociation of America from the United States.

Are the American war critics I cited earlier part of a ritual of consensus? Is their differentiation of current American practices from an earlier, better America just Arthurian myth-making (as Atwood proposed) or part of the legacy of the jeremiad with its two-part structure of critique leading the way only to a rededication toward the mission of a new errand into the wilderness? Is even the question how far America is from America, far from freeing the potential for democratic struggle, part of the very process of containment Bercovitch has analyzed? What does Bercovitch's diagnosis of this "institutionalization of dissent" mean for American studies, for an International American Studies Association, for us?

— IV —

This is exactly the kind of conference at which local perceptions of America, be it too close or too far, can be examined comparatively and from different vantage points. The Association that is here giving its public debut, is in part the living result of a debate around the issue of internationalization that has been going on in American Studies for a long time (as the journal American Studies International will demonstrate), but with particular intensity since 1996 when Jane C. Desmond and Virginia R. Domínguez published their manifesto toward internationalism in the *American Quarterly*. Are there differences between between US-based and foreign approaches to American literature and history (the disciplines most likely to dominate any international association). Does academic location, does the citizenship of a given critic matter? To rephrase my question once again: How far is the non-US Americanists' America from the US-based Americanists' America? The outsiders' from the insiders' views? The present conference is likely to provide answers to these questions as well as to the general question that guides all our proceedings.

Perhaps we'll be moving into the direction of the "poetics of the diverse" that Edouard Glissant has proposed, placing American literature into new global contexts, for, as he has stated: "to write in the presence of all the world's languages does not mean to know all the world's languages. It means that in the present context of multiple literatures and of the relation of poetics with the chaos-world, I can no longer write in a monolingual manner." This approach is present here in Hana Wirth-Nesher's panel "How Far Is English from Here?" and Armin Paul Frank's session on "How Far is English America from There?"

Or we might, as Kousar J. Azam has suggested, think of a writer like Khaleel Gibran in the context of his long-lasting US residence and see this as an opening for a fuller examination of Islamic people in the United States and for "expanding the discourse of American Studies to the excluded actors and their discourses, by widening the canvass of American Studies to include other faiths, other civilisations and other cultures."

Or we might imagine various forms of a hemispheric focus—the context of the Caribbean, Mexico and Latin America for American literature that Anna Brickhouse, for example, has so compellingly established for major mid-nineteenth-century American writers in her forthcoming book *Transamerican Renaissance: The Hemispheric Genealogies of U.S. Literature, 1826-1865*, a work that brings major American writers and intellectuals like Hawthorne and Melville, William Cullen Bryant and Frederick Douglass, into dialogue with texts from Cuba, Mexico, and the francophone Caribbean.

The political relations with the British Canada could also be very fruitfully brought to bear on American transcendentalists, as Paul Giles has recently shown in his historicization of the political significance of "Maine" and "Oregon" in Thoreau.

Or we could think of transpacific cultural relations that Xiaohuang Yin has pursued in his pioneering study *Chinese American Literature since the 1850s* (2000) which examines writing in English and in Chinese. Yin also extends his work to examine Asian-American international relations.

Or we could deepen the various Atlantic approaches that colonial historians have been pursuing for some time (Leiden and the two Plymouths became part of one transatlantic world) that are also the subject of Ralph Bauer's two panels here. Such approaches have recently, since Paul Gilroy's *Black Atlantic*, flourished especially in African American studies. One only has to think of Allison Blakely, Anita Patterson, and the whole Boston University school of internationalizing Black Studies. Younger scholars have also picked up this thread: thus Brent Edwards' *The Practice of Diaspora: Literature, Translation, and the Rise of Black Internationalism* (2003) analyzes René Maran, Alain Locke, Jessie Fauset, the Nardal sisters, Claude McKay, W. E. B. Du Bois, and Nancy Cunard's Negro through a meticulous focus on interactions in and outside the francophone world, and Kate A. Baldwin, *Beyond the Color Line and the Iron Curtain: Reading Encounters between Black and Red, 1922-1963* (2002) examines the Soviet travels of Hughes, Du Bois, McKay, and Robeson through the new lens of many Russian sources.

In many of these cases, however, what seems to me to be at stake in each case is proposing new contexts for American literature,--a method not unlike the one that Leo Marx chose in suggesting a new context for reading "Ethan Brand," or the one that Sacvan Bercovitch employed when he showed how readings of Hawthorne's campaign biography of Franklin Pierce can help understand the "centrist" strategy Hawthorne brings to *The Scarlet Letter*.

What internationalization might imply for the study of American literature is that it would also strengthen the understanding of literature as a system that keeps defying the boundaries within which we are again and again tempted to pin it down. American Studies is thus always in need of cooperation with Comparative Literature, with interdisciplinary approaches to literature, visual arts, photography, music, and film. The act of crossing many borders, of coming to a fuller understanding of deterritorializing processes enveloping American culture, might therefore also bring back to the foreground of international Americanists the issue of aesthetics that Heinz Ickstadt has argued is "a discourse not separate from or against American studies as cultural studies but very much within it."Whatever routes we will be taking, the internationalization of American Studies will provide many opportunities for Americanists from all nations, for insiders and outsiders, newcomers and expatriates, to exchange ideas and information. Robert K. Merton (who passed away earlier this year) deplored in his classic essay "Insiders and Outsiders: A Chapter in the Sociology of Knowledge" (1972) that the terms of this dichotomy had hardly been sufficiently examined. His essay which surveys the insider and the outsider doctrine, as well as examples of "insiders as 'outsiders'" remains the fullest conceptual contribution to an issue that has great relevance for the International American Studies Association. I shall therefore conclude with Merton's manifesto-like ending, which I think deserves to be adopted as IASA motto: "Insiders and Outsiders in the domain of knowledge, unite. You have nothing to lose but your claims. You have a world of understanding to win."

Werner Sollors

Bibliography and Webliography

I.

Aleksandra Sladjana Milosevic. *Animal tested.* www.gerila.com/cd/katalog/149c.htm

"America lontana e bella". http://scuolaworld.provincia.padova.it/pendola/ipertxt/p6l3!a1.htm

Matt & Andrej Koymasky. "The King of Sitges". www.http://andrejkoymasky.com/sc6/051/sitg16.html

William Bradford. 1963. *Of Plymouth Plantation: 1620-1647.* Ed. Samuel Eliot Morrison. New York: Knopf.

Joke Kardux and Eduard van de Bilt. 2002. *Newcomers in an Old City: The American Pilgrims in Leiden, 1609-1620.* Leiden: Uitgeverij Burgersdijk & Niermans, 2nd. ed.

Djelal Kadir. 1992. *Columbus and the Ends of the Earth: Europe's Prophetic Rhetoric As Conquering Ideology.* Berkeley: U of California Press.

Jeremy Dupertuis Bangs. 1997. *Pilgrim Life in Leiden: Texts and Images from the Leiden American Pilgrim Museum.* Leiden.

Jean Baudrillard. 1988. *Amérique.* Paris: Poche.

The Polish Memoirs of William John Rose. Ed. Daniel Stone. Toronto and Buffalo: Univ. of Toronto Press, 1975.

II.

Edward Albee., "On the Playwright's Role"
http://www.commonground.ca/iss/0302139/edward_albee.shtml

Margaret Atwood. 2003. "Letter to America" *Nation* (April 14, 2003): 22
(letter electronically circulated under title "What Happened To America? A Letter, A Lament")

Jonathan Franzen. 2003. "When the new wing broke away from the old mansion: A short story about Europe and America," The Guardian (March 25, 2003)
http://www.guardian.co.uk/g2/story/0,3604,921240,00.html

Nikki Giovanni. 2003. http://www.tribnet.com (April 15, 2003)

Maxine Hong Kingston. 2003. *The Fifth Book of Peace.* New York: Knopf.

Norman Mailer. "Gaining an empire, losing democracy?" http://www.iht.com/articles/87763.html

Arthur Miller in "Miller backs people's peace power"
http://news.bbc.uk/go/pr/fr/-/1/hi/entertainment/arts/2779879.stm

Michael Moore. 2002. *Bowling for Columbine.*

David Rees. "Get Your War On". www.mnftiu.cc/mmftiu.cc/war.html

Calvin Trillin. 2003. "We Speak Not of Osama," *Nation* (March 3, 2003): 6.

Gary Trudeau. "Doonesbury" http://images.ucomics.com/comics/db/2003/db030307.gif

Poets Against the War http://www.poetsagainstthewar.org

Kurt Vonnegut Vs. the !*!@ http://www.alternet.org

Richard Wright. 1961. "The Man Who Went to Chicago." *Eight Men.* New York.

III.

Leo Marx. 1999. "Writing *The Machine in the Garden*: A Contribution to the Geneaology of 'Technology and Culture' Studies." In *Predecessors: Intellectual Lineages in American Studies*, ed. Rob Kroes. Amsterdam: VU Press.

Gunnar Myrdal. 1944. *An American Dilemma: The Negro Problem and Modern Democracy.* New York: Harper & Brothers.

Nathan Huggins. 1995. *Revelations: American History, American Myths.* New York: Oxford UP.

Sacvan Bercovitch. 1993. *The Rites of Assent: Transformations in the Symbolic Construction of America.* New York: Routledge.

IV.

Kousar J. Azam. 2002. "Globalisation of American Studies after 9/11: Some Ruminations." *Transit Circle # 1* (2002): 8-17.

Edouard Glissant. 1999. "Introduction to a Poetics of the Diverse," *Boundary 2*, 26.1 (Spring 1999): 19-121.

Heinz Ickstadt. 2002. American Studies in an Age of Globalization. *American Quarterly* 54.4 (2002) 543-562.

Robert K. Merton. 1972. "Insiders and Outsiders: A Chapter in the Sociology of Knowledge" (1972). In *Theories of Ethnicity: A Classical Reader*. New York: NYU Press, 1996.

INTERNATIONAL, TRANSNATIONAL, HEMISPHERIC AMERICA

Through the Fun House Mirror:

The Fulbright Teaching Experience in Germany

When it came time to title this essay, I was not sure which of two titles to choose. The first—which I discarded—was "Connecting the Dots." As will be apparent from what follows, the title is apt. Repeatedly during my Fulbright year in 1992-93, I was connecting the dots of my experiences, trying to make sense of the country that produced both my students and my great-grandparents, a higher education system strikingly different from the one that educated me, and the country from which I came. The alternative title was the one I chose: "Through the Fun-House Mirror." In selecting that title, I opted to begin with my conclusion. My teaching experience in Germany can best be described as the experience of looking into one of those distorting mirrors that lets you see yourself and what is behind you in new ways, sometimes humorous and sometimes frightening. Those insights shape how I view my Fulbright year, how I have experienced the intervening decade, and even how I have explored possible research topics for the future.

By selecting that title, I have also indulged myself in hoping that, by knowing the ending, the reader will be tolerant in letting me present some of the dots to be connected.

Dot 1: Spring Semester, my course in African American History

Mid-semester. The class of thirty-five has been engaged with the topic, but never surprised by the content . The previous spring in an US History survey class at Case Western Reserve University, I had been involved in a lengthy discussion with students who felt that our newly revised course paid too much attention to issues of race and of social history more generally. By focusing on such topics, they argued, I, and the others who designed the course and readings, were subtly undermining America. The contrast between my American students and my German students was sharp. The latter took for granted that America was a racist country. Readings that either surprised or angered American students are readily accepted here.

Borrowing from my own research, I provide a set of readings about Freedom Summer in Chicago (1966) and illustrate them with the *Eyes on the Prize* episode, "Two Societies." The students sit attentively through the shots of the slums of Lawndale and the obscene threats against open housing marchers. Then, as the protesters near Marquette Park, an audible gasp comes from the audience. It takes me a minute to understand the response, as it was not associated with the scene that always causes me to wince—when Martin Luther King, Jr. is attacked with a piece of rubble. Finally, I realize that, there on the screen, are uniformed members of the American Nazi Party, wearing and brandishing signs adorned with swastikas.

Dot 2: November 1992

The newspapers report an arson attack in Moelln in which three Turks are killed. Before my *Herald-Tribune* arrives so I can read the details in English, I receive an e-mail from a colleague in the United States asking how I can bear to live in such a racist country.

Dot 3: Spring 1993

In response to the increasing number of attacks on Turks and other foreigners, Bremen, like other German cities, organizes a candlelight protest against Ausländerfeindlichkeit and Rechtsextremismus. Hundreds of people line up on both sides of the Weser River with their candles. Initially, people are silent or quietly talking among themselves. Then, someone starts to sing and others join in. The song? We Shall Overcome—in English. Amazed, I inquire of several people, "Warum singen Sie das?" The response is that it is the only civil rights song they know. Only later do I learn that some of the local schools actually teach the song.

Dot 4: Early Fall Semester

Talking to Fulbrighters with school-age children, I learn about the religious /ethical instruction requirement in the schools. With classes just beginning, many find it a quaint German custom. As Americans, we are used to the rather fierce separation of church and state. The idea that they should have to choose among Protestant, Catholic, or general ethics classes for their children seems peculiar.

Dot 5: Inauguration Day, 1993

German broadcast news covers the inauguration festivities for Bill Clinton. Having watched the election from a distance (and, rejecting my Chicago resident status, voting on only one of the two absentee ballots I received from the Cook County Board of Election Commissioners), I was eager to participate in the Democratic celebration, even if only vicariously. Parts were difficult to follow. While the speeches in English played quietly in the background, near-simultaneous German translations were overlaid on them. What was easy to understand, however, was the ongoing commentary by the German newscasters. One of the recurring themes was their surprise at the regular references to God and to America as the beneficiary of his gifts. Why, they wondered out loud, was a nation that so prided itself on the division between church and state so public in religious profession at such an important state event?

Dot 6: Sometime in 1968

My first year in college, I'm sitting in a beginning German class when a light goes on. The signs at protests I've attended and passed by seem to play with different spellings of America. AmeriKKKa is obvious. The reference to the Klan is unmistakable, especially since this spelling is most likely to appear at civil rights demonstrations. More puzzling to me was the spelling Amerika, with a K. Only there in German class did the reference hit me. Amerika with a K was a reference to Germany, where they spelled it that way. My generation had grown up with stories of German militarism, Nazis as the consummate bad guys. By spelling Amerika with a K, protesters were attributing those very same characteristics to the United States in its policies toward Vietnam.

Dot 7: the Second Session of My Course in American Popular Culture

One semester of teaching in Germany had opened my eyes to the importance of language. Words, even in the same language, did not always mean the same thing across cultural boundaries. Drawing on my experience of the previous semester, I had organized the course so that the class (some 75 Germans, 10 Americans, and 3 British citizens) could better appreciate some key words in American culture. One of those words was patriotism. As I had done the previous week, I opened the floor to ask for definitions. German students began the discussion and each of their definitions had a negative connotation. Patriotism involved compromising one's own principles for those of the state. It implied an irrational confidence in a government. Only after five or six such definitions did one of the American students weigh in. Patriotism meant being proud of your country. Several other negative definitions made their way to the blackboard. Then one of the American students suggested that patriotism meant trying to change your country when it was doing something wrong. The response was quick: "You come from the most militaristic country in the world. You don't even know when your country is doing wrong."

From my vantage point in the front of the room, the students' reactions encapsulated two views of the post-World-War-II and post Cold-War worlds. Almost every German student was nodding in assent. Almost every American and British student looked stunned.

Dot 8: Several Weeks Later in Downtown Glasgow

A college-age man stops me and says something to me in Glaswegian. I am totally mystified, chuckling (I thought to myself) about the fact that I had come to a country that spoke English and I seem to understand even less than I do in Germany. When he looks angry, I apologize and explain that I didn't understand. He responds, this time in Oxbridge English that I cannot fail to understand, that I'm a typical American. He is passing out materials protesting America's military involvement in Somalia and I seem not to be able to assess the damage my country inflicts on the rest of the world.

Dot 9: The First Session of the American Popular Culture Class

I ask the students to submit a piece of paper on which they offer one definition, one practice, or one cultural mode that best represents American popular culture. The responses cover a wide range. Some are predictable—McDonald's and Mickey Mouse. Others are far less so—cosmetic surgery. The influence of Hollywood is strong. As a Midwesterner (this was before I moved to Los Angeles), I was troubled by the easy equation of America and California, although I realized when I interviewed German students applying for Fulbright fellowships that they saw America in terms of the two coasts. By this point in the year, I am not surprised that most cultural signifiers in response to this pedagogical exercise carry a negative connotation. My single favorite answer was "American popular culture is like Coca-Cola. It tastes good but it rots your teeth."

Dot 10: Sightseeing in Paris, Bastille Day, 1993

On previous trips to the city, I had concluded that being an American in Paris at least occasionally provoked a certain disdain. This time I went wearing German shoes, carrying a German jacket, and thumbing through a German guidebook to the city. Watching the display of French military equipment, I overheard several comments about the Germans. To one seemingly outspoken man nearby (my French is atrocious), I found myself responding, "Je suis une Américaine." Then change in his attitude was notable in his offer to show me around Paris. As I walked through Paris, I became aware—for the first time—of the plaques appearing on numerous buildings remembering soldiers who died fighting German invaders in World War II. When I ask my German friends about this on my return, they tell me they have experienced hostility in many European countries.

Dot 11: Waiting for the Tram after Doing Laundry

It is about 9:00 at night. Parked near the tram stop is a taxi bearing a sign that reads: "Wir sind alle Ausländer." I think little of it; the sign is ubiquitous in the campaign against anti-immigrant sentiment and violence. Three skinhead-types walk down the street, see the sign, and start to kick in the door. I consider, fleetingly, saying something. I had had my own moment of moral bravery earlier on another tram when two men grabbed two African men on the tram. I jumped up and, losing all of my German vocabulary, asked them what they thought they were doing. They responded: "Wir sind Polizei. Diese Männer sind unter Anhalten." Grateful that my language had identified me as an American, I left that tram and walked the rest of the way.

Standing there in front of the laundry, however, I was afraid that if I said anything I might become a target of their violence. I knew from past experience that if I said nothing my parents' and grandparents' genes would guarantee that I could be taken as German. I also knew from past experience that if I spoke, even in German, I would be identified as a foreigner. So I simply waited for them to move on.

Connecting the Dots

Coming back to the United States, I felt a desperate need to put the dots together. Moving to Los Angeles exacerbated that need. In many respects, Germany felt more familiar to me—a child of a German American family who grew up in a predominantly German American town before moving to Chicago with its long German American legacy—than did Los Angeles. The car culture of Los Angeles seemed at odds with my public transportation-oriented world in both Chicago and Europe. Moreover, I shared some of my students' prejudices about LA—La-La Land in the words of well-known Chicago columnist. From the first movie premier I stumbled upon walking home one night to the student who offered the excuse that her paper was late because all the streets in Beverly Hills were blocked off in anticipation of the Academy Awards, I knew I was now a part of that American culture my German students knew most about.

At the same time, in their assumptions about American history, many of my UCLA students were far more similar to my Bremen students than to my Cleveland students. Interestingly, I was learning that lesson in a huge lecture class on America since 1945, a course that I had significantly reorganized since I had taught it before going to Germany. The year in Germany had caused me to rethink the course in small and significant ways. The 1945-1989 chronology I had used earlier as representing Cold War America now made sense to me as chronology that tied America and Germany together in profound ways. The end of World War II marked the beginning of the class, the fall of the Berlin Wall the end. Its construction fired American policy makers' fears of communism. Our occupation of and, from the American perspective, our rebuilding of Germany provided a model for thinking about what might be done in Vietnam. Most important, however, was that I could no longer teach American history from a perspective that saw the United States as being the only center of the story.

In an effort to learn more about my own experiences in Germany and to translate the implications of that last realization for my students, I started reading *Der Spiegel*. The exercise was extraordinarily revealing. One example may suffice. Incidents like the lunch-counter sit-ins that I had used in my lectures to illustrate the growing demand for civil rights appeared on the foreign news pages of *Der Spiegel* right next to examples of the growing strength of apartheid in South Africa.

Through the Fun House Mirror

As I read through week after week, focusing particularly on the 1960s and early 1970s, the dots began to form a pattern. I started to understand why teachers at a workshop in which I participated seemed so amazed—and angry—when a German SDSer, a former liaison to the Black Panther Party, suggested that certain Panthers were guilty of criminal behavior. I could see why my German friends of my age were far more familiar with artists from the Black Arts Movement than were my American friends of comparable age. And, I could see why the Vietnam War looked so different from Germany than it did in the United States.

As I looked back on some of my experiences during my Fulbright year, I also began to wonder if America and Germany did not serve each other in a very different way during those tumultuous years of the 1960s. For many of the Americans who did not spell it with a K, the horrors of World War II showed America's basic goodness. The mass exterminations of the Holocaust provided a context for slavery and, according to scholars and citizens alike, a spur to solve America's ongoing racial injustices. The "just war" against Hitler seemed to ensure that America's goals in Vietnam were equally just. The correctness of the "American Way of Life" was verified by Germany's economic miracle.

At the same time, America in the 1960s—with its violence against civil rights activists and its expanding war in Southeast Asia—provided Germans, particularly younger Germans, with a way to address their own country's past. War and militarism were not necessarily good—even when an elaborate geopolitical explanation tried to make it so. In embracing the culture and causes of America's oppressed populations, there was the possibility of understanding the oppression that had tried to wipe out one of Germany's rich cultures. At the same time, by embracing that culture, Germans could reject the mainstream American culture that was spreading throughout the world. Perhaps I was letting too much of my own distorted reflection enter into my reading of what I saw in the fun house mirror when I speculated that—in sheer numbers if nothing else—that mainstream American culture was more German than anything else.

A Postscript

The possibility of investigating these questions as a serious research topic still intrigues me. I have become an assiduous reader of related materials in the United States, Germany, and other countries. When I do—or when I accidentally run across some appropriate primary source—I am convinced I should try to connect those dots more systematically. Then I back away, realizing that the best funhouses involve multiple mirrors and the scholarly task of understanding German history and culture well enough to appreciate the reflections of reflections is probably beyond my capabilities. Yet, especially as I watched the events leading up to the war against Iraq unfold, I could not help but wonder whether trying to do so might not provide some lessons. At least one stands out, based on the personally expanding experience I had as a Fulbright professor teaching in Germany. The United States government might find richer financing of the Fulbright program to encourage more Americans to live abroad to be a better investment in the war on terror than developing a new nuclear "bunker buster" bomb.

Janice L. Reiff

American Diplomats in South Africa and the Emergence of Apartheid, 1948-1953

1. Introduction

Until the Second World War South Africa was regarded by the United States of America (US) as essentially part of the Commonwealth, on the one hand, and part of Africa, on the other. In that ambiguity it had limited political value for the Americans. But after 1945 both the expansion of communism and a new awareness of racial discrimination in South Africa forced upon the US a greater degree of involvement, an involvement that continued to be characterized by ambivalence and uncertainty for the largest part of the twentieth century.

Relations between the two countries in the nineteenth and early twentieth century were largely of an economic nature. Initial interest in South Africa by the Americans was awakened by the discovery of diamonds in the 1860s and 1870s. Since then they remained interested in developments in the country, despite an aggressive protectionist policy by Britain during the second decade of the twentieth century, which temporarily drove the Americans out of colonial markets. Trade with South Africa grew, and by 1948 the favorable trade balance of the US with South Africa was $300 million per year. The spadework for attracting American tourists to South Africa had been done in the 1920s and 1930s and more

American tourists were visiting South Africa by the late 1940s than previously. Diplomatic relations followed suit: already in 1926 South Africa appointed a consul in the US, and three years later a Legation was opened in Washington, which attained Embassy status in 1949. An office of the South African Bureau of Information was established in New York in 1942, and in 1949 the US Legation in South Africa also became an Embassy. The staff of both Embassies expanded during the following years.

Studies on US-South African relations have shown significant similarities between the two countries, but also marked differences. Both had experienced British colonialism and were emancipated from it, though at different stages of their development. The natural advantages which the US had over South Africa in the process of growth in terms of climate, ports and navigable rivers, as well as its economic policies which stimulated entrepreneurship, were decisive. The US, contrary to South Africa, developed into an economic giant that attracted immigrants from Europe.

Studies on race relations in the two countries show some similarities but also significant differences. The same Christian-heathen dichotomy that characterized viewpoints on race in South Africa was present in the US. There was institutionalized racial discrimination in the American South and the Boer Republics and there were efforts in both countries to legitimize segregation through scientific racism. The importation of slaves to the US affected race relations to such an extent that a situation developed which could be compared to black-white relations in South Africa. The differences were also decisive. For instance, the numerical ratios of black-white and the composition of the population of the two countries always differed vastly. It was precisely that huge numerical preponderance of whites in the US which largely explains why acculturation could take place without white fears. Self-preservation was never a serious issue for white Americans as was the case with white Afrikaners. In the course of time differences grew more significantly, especially after the Union of South Africa had adopted a constitution in 1910 which practically denied political rights to Africans, whereas the US by adopting the Fourteenth and Fifteenth Constitutional Amendments gradually moved away from institutionalized race discrimination. By the middle of the twentieth century, when the National Party government in South Africa was transforming segregation into apartheid—a much more rigid form of control and domination—race discrimination in the US, though not rooted out, had come under increasing pressure.

The Second World War produced a profound change in international relations. The US government had to adapt to a threefold challenge: to curb communist expansion, to address racial inequality in the US itself, and to come to terms with the growing anti-colonial sentiments in Third World countries. The three issues were interrelated. President Harry Truman, after 1945, needed as much internal and external support as he possibly could muster in his Cold War battle against the USSR. This support would have to come in the first place from the US's traditional Western allies which had the resources and military capacity to withstand the communist onslaught. These allies would include colonial and white minority governments such as the South African, which were practising racial discrimination.

North of the Limpopo the US, for strategic purposes, was mainly interested in the Belgian Congo as a source of minerals, particularly uranium and the air force base in the Portuguese Azores, which was secured in exchange for recognition of Portuguese authority in Angola and Mozambique. South Africa's value lay in its strategic position with regard to the Cape sea route and its possession of minerals such as manganese, diamonds, platinum and especially uranium. And, perhaps more important, its outspoken anticommunist stand turned it into a more than valued ally for the US.

On the negative side, the US must have read the signs of the times. South Africa, even before the National Party came to power, had been moving in the opposite direction of world opinion as far as race relations were concerned. The country had become a microcosm of the postwar world, but, as a CIA report on South Africa in January 1949 stated: "The issues which unite white South Africans are among those which divide the world." Black politics in the country had become more militant than ever before and the first signs of an international conflict with the UN on South West Africa and the treatment of South African Indians were on the horizon. Although the Americans did not regard the local communists in South Africa as an immediate danger, the latter were beginning to exploit the discriminatory race policies of the NP government. In the US the Council on African Affairs (CAA), which had ties with black nationalist organizations in Africa. and particularly South Africa, had expressed itself on numerous occasions against racial discrimination in colonial

Africa. It also had the benefit of a sympathetic ear in the Unite Nations. The US, in order to expand its influence, could not afford to overlook the anti-colonial attitudes of the Third World, whose peoples mostly found themselves at the receiving end of racial discrimination. The Americans' concern about communism left Africans and other Third World countries cold. Yet, support for the Eastern Bloc by the latter would be extremely detrimental to the cause of the anticommunist forces. The increasing dilemma the US faced was that it needed the support of anticommunist countries with unacceptable race policies, while attempting not to alienate Third World countries that vehemently opposed such race policies. The gnawing dilemma for the US was that all was not well at home as far as race relations were concerned. Despite Truman's commitment to combat racial discrimination in the US and the fact that the country hosted the United Nations (UN), there were glaring examples by the end of the 1940s of racial discrimination in the US, particularly in the Southern states. Embarrassing racial incidents during and after the Second World War occurred from time to time and black protests were regularly registered by organizations such as the National Negro Congress and the National Association for the Advancement of Colored People (NAACP). These incidents were also reported by the South African legation in Washington, and provided useful ammunition for South African diplomats and politicians when confronted by Americans about racial discrimination in South Africa. A "sweep before your own door" attitude was often adopted, also by the South African Ambassador in Washington, Gerhardt Jooste, even toward Americans with whom he was on good terms. And although comparisons were embarrassing to Americans, especially where racial discrimination in their own country was involved, these comparisons were often unavoidable. US officials themselves drew comparisons. Referring to repression of blacks, Robert McGregor, the US consul in Durban, on one occasion—perhaps inadvertently—expressed the opinion to the State Department that Americans would possibly have acted in a similar way if they had to govern over black people outnumbering whites by five to one.

Concerning the particular scope of this study the most informative and comprehensive work is Thomas Borstelmann's, apartheid's reluctant uncle. The author has shown convincingly that the main concern for the US in the early Cold War was Soviet expansionism; thus, to counteract the USSR and its surrogates, Washington would sacrifice moral issues such as basic human rights and longer term benefits of lasting ties with the Third World readily in favour of potential strategic support from countries which practised racial discrimination. Borstelmann's work focuses primarily on US policy towards South Africa, and although the author utilized US diplomatic reports as a source of information, analysing these reports was not his primary concern. A closer look at these reports reveals more than just general dismay with South African racial attitudes and policies. Apart from showing an awareness of nuances in South African racial attitudes, they also point to diversity of opinion among American diplomats about the imminent danger of racial conflict in the country. These subtle differences might well have strengthened presupposed beliefs about the South African situation among the major policy makers of the State Department in Washington, as will be explained at the end of this article.

Considering the above-mentioned, this article offers a more comprehensive examination of American perspectives on the embryo phases of the emerging apartheid policy of the Malan government. It also examines South African attitudes towards the State Department, a dimension which is not present in Borstelmann's study because he did not undertake research in South Africa.

2. The postwar US legation in South Africa

If racial matters in Africa did not attract serious official attention in the US, particularly in the context of the global Cold War, the Americans in official capacity in South Africa were not unaware of growing tensions in that country since 1945. Contrary to their South African counterparts in Washington, the Americans had a strong legation in South Africa. Apart from the embassy in Pretoria there were consulates in Johannesburg, Cape Town, Durban, and Port Elizabeth. In 1948 the total body of diplomatic staff amounted to 29 (including an agricultural, commercial, minerals, and labour attaché, as well as five military attachés), 11 other military personnel and 59 administrative people (including clerks, messengers and chauffeurs). The South African contingent in Washington by 1954 consisted of 17 (including two military, an agricultural, press and scientific attaché, plus two other trade officials). On the administrative side there were 13 employees.

The ambassadors in the period under discussion were all over sixty years of age when they were in South Africa, except for Gallman, who was in his early fifties. Their experience prior to South Africa was primarily limited to first world countries, mostly in Europe. They were career diplomats and none of them had any record of promoting civil rights; no-one was specially equipped for dealing with complex race relations. This lack of first-hand contact with social calamities also seemed to apply for the rest of the legation, with the exception of Joseph Sweeney, a 37-year-old former social worker who possessed a Ph D in Political Science. He was sent to Pretoria in 1950 with the specific assignment to study race relations in the troubled South Africa.

With sufficient staff available, it was possible for the Americans to scrutinize the South African newspapers and tap other possible sources of information, written or oral, to compile their dispatches for the State Department. Attachés with special knowledge of particular subjects assisted in presenting accounts of various aspects of South African life. Quite impressive were the embassy's untiring efforts to understand political and social issues concerning Afrikaners. In order to facilitate such understanding they had the major Afrikaans newspapers translated. Even Afrikaans cartoons were studied. They fully realized that the country's racial situation could hardly be understood without a thorough background of the Afrikaner's psyche. However, their efforts to penetrate black politics had little success, as I will be pointing out shortly.

3. Encountering structural apartheid

Thomas Holcomb, who was US Minister in South Africa up to 30 May 1948, had no doubts that General J. C. Smuts was essentially a white supremacist. The legation was displeased with the way the Smuts government handled the African mineworkers' strike in 1946 and it was also well-informed about the adverse circumstances in the black reserves. Holcomb, nevertheless, preferred a United Party government to be in power rather than a National Party one despite the shortcomings in Smuts's race policies. In Holcomb's view international tensions would result in whites opting for the man with international stature, and that they would therefore rally behind Smuts. In fact, he was quite hopeful, by the end of 1947, that Smuts would win the 1948 general election.

Holcomb, of course, misread the mind of white South Africans. After 26 May the apartheid government came to power and stayed in power for the next forty-six years.

The Nats' electoral victory surprised the American diplomats as much as it shocked the English-speaking South Africans, particularly those in Natal. The opinion was expressed that the new government might be careful not to go to extremes at first when applying its apartheid policies and Ambassador North Winship reported in October 1948 that there were signs of insecurity in government attitude, particularly with regard to the question of urban blacks. This was, however, nothing but wishful thinking because Winship had to admit shortly afterwards that the NP government had already during their first parliamentary session in power made some inroads into the rights of blacks and other people of colour. Racial incidents in the course of 1949 on the Rand convinced the Ambassador that racial tensions were on the increase and that the Malan government was responsible for ill feelings between race groups.

If the Americans were still sceptical about the practical implementation of a systematic policy of apartheid, they were in for a surprise. The battery of apartheid legislation starting in 1949 and proliferating in the 1950s must have convinced them of the sincerity and single-mindedness of the new government. Embassy personnel periodically commented on legislation in process, such as the Group Areas Bill (June 1950) and the labour bill in September 1952 which aimed at setting up conciliatory machinery for black workers. Bernard C. Connelly, Chargé d'Affaires, thought that the sudden enforcement of the Group Areas Bill in the Cape Town area would be a "national catastrophe" and lamented that no provision was made for compensation for the dispossessed. Besides, the colored people who were involved were never consulted. Third Secretary Morris Dembo concluded that the labor legislation in view, avoided the crucial issue, namely to provide for a proper foundation for a black trade union movement. In turn, this would contribute to the existing frustration of black people.

Pass regulations were also mentioned, and after a police raid on the offices of the African National Congress (ANC) in August 1951, Attaché Joseph Sweeney reported that "[a]ll authorities on urban Native Affairs with whom Embassy officers have come in contact in the past few months, have stressed that Native anger is mounting more sharply [sic] than at any time in their memory." And Sweeney's colleague, Henri LaTendresse had personal experience at the Pretoria Embassy of the cumbersome process a black man had to endure in order to obtain a pass, when the Embassy attempted to obtain the services of one Mathapo as a gardener for that Embassy.

Settlement of blacks in the reserves, which would be eventually evolved into the homeland policy, was questioned. The enquiring eyes of Sweeney did not miss a *Cape Times* interview with Dr. Edith Walton in April 1951 in which she disclosed some of the findings of the National Council for Social Research. Walton said that the reserves had nothing to offer the black population and had become "rural slums." Economic rehabilitation was out of the question. Both Sweeney and Consul General Marselis Parsons thought that the industrialization of the country was not possible without an increasing flow of black labor to the urban areas; thus, the government's policy to transfer more blacks to the reserves did not make economic sense. To make things worse, in urban regions numerous restrictions were placed on black people and shortages of houses had reached epidemic proportions.

Opinion among US diplomats on the ordeal of black people in South Africa under apartheid was not unanimous, however. Though the Consul General in Johannesburg, Sydney Redecker, was also sensitive to the adverse social conditions of blacks in the townships around Johannesburg and was concerned about what he perceived as their extreme vulnerability against communist propaganda, he was nevertheless convinced that South African black people were better off under apartheid in South Africa than blacks elsewhere in Africa.

4. Observing South African attitudes towards race relations

To the American embassy staff, as was the case with other observant visitors to the country, South Africa was a deeply divided society. The policies of segregation and apartheid had embedded such cleavages, and under apartheid, relations between black and white had deteriorated to an unequalled low point. Ambassadors North Winship, John Erhardt (who died in Cape Town after only ten months' service in South Africa), and Waldemar Gallman all noticed increased racial tensions and disintegrating relations between whites and blacks.

The Embassy reacted to various instances of black (and Indian) protest in the early 1950s to demonstrate that the views of the majority of whites and those of blacks and other people of colour had become so divergent that the settlement of conflicting issues had become almost impossible. Commenting on an editorial by the United Party-supporting Bloemfontein paper, *The Friend*, in which the standpoints on race relations by Gerhardt Jooste, South African Ambassador in New York, and Manilal Gandhi (second son of Mahatma Gandhi) were compared, Dembo had no doubt that apartheid was the culprit, that it was "driving the non-Europeans further and further away from the European people, that all hope of bridging the gap and finding a via media [sic] is receding at a rate that fills all reasonable people with gloom and alarm." This estrangement, due to government policies, was echoed by Sweeney on several occasions.

To what extent did the NP government's policies reflect the views of ordinary white South Africans? Sweeney, after the May Day riots of 1950, speculated on this question and concluded that the attitude of the man in the street would depend on his color and in the case of a white person, also the political party he belonged to. Sweeney quoted a "prominent Transvaal attorney," Pierre Roux, who had told him that "this is a white country and we are going to keep it white if we have to kill all of the others." Only white liberals, Sweeney thought, really had an idea what black people thought and wanted. These liberals were truly prepared to get to the bottom of the racial tensions and to improve the situation of black people. A few months before his death Ambassador Erhardt expressed similar views, saying that for the exponents of white supremacy black opinion was of no importance.

White "ignorance" of black sentiments was, however, partly explained by the American Embassy staff themselves. More than once diplomats mentioned how difficult it was to obtain the viewpoints of black people and that few "non-black" people really had significant contacts in the black community. The Americans were nevertheless convinced that blacks disliked whites and especially Afrikaners. Racial feelings had become so politicized that Erhardt remarked in 1950 that South African blacks were opposed to the country's participation in the Korean War, because they regarded it as a racial war. According to Connelly, blacks had become increasingly sympathetic towards the North-Koreans, merely because the latter were referred to as "Gooks" (natives of Asia). Often the real issues, Connelly concluded (from a Western perspective), were less important.

It has been pointed out that Washington needed South African support to counteract communism in Africa and South Africa, but ironically the agent to propel the anticommunist drive, the Malan government, was according to diplomatic dispatches driving blacks into the arms of the communists because of its repressive racial policies. Very soon the Americans discovered that whites, and particularly Afrikaners, regularly blamed the communists for black unrest. Black protest and communism were thus linked by white South Africans (especially Afrikaners) as well as by the US diplomats, but for different reasons.

According to the CIA report in early 1949, the communists' influence on blacks had gained ground and Ambassador Winship rightly remarked that Sam Kahn's huge victory in the parliamentary election for Native Representatives had confirmed black aversion to racial discrimination. To what extent the Communist Party of South Africa had really penetrated the black communities in South Africa was not easy for embassy staff to determine, but Erhardt was convinced that the handful of white communists had much more contact with blacks and their frustrations than white liberals had.

White liberals indeed seemed to be of peripheral value to the US diplomats. Apart from a typed list of "Organisations in the U.S.A. concerned with race relations and kindred matters" and a few references to the US in general, the documents of the South African Institute of Race Relations do not reveal significant contact between the Institute and the American Embassy. On an individual level, liberals such as Julius Lewin of the University of the Witwatersrand and Leo Marquard commanded great respect. Sweeney in his memoirs described Marquard as the "finest man" he met in South Africa. But the collective efforts of liberals (whether in party or other organizational capacity) did not instill much confidence of success. The findings of Quinton Whyte, for instance, in a pamphlet "Behind the Racial Tensions in South Africa" (Johannesburg, SAIRR, 1953), which appeared shortly before the Nationalists were returned with an increased majority in 1953, were seriously questioned by Wm. M. Johnson, Second Secretary in Pretoria, because it "overestimates the force of liberalism" in South Africa.

Clearly the political powerlessness of South African white liberals in the late 1940s and 1950s was fully realized by the American men on the spot. However, that hardly explains why virtually no contact was made with these liberals, people who certainly shared the values and ideological sentiments of most of the American diplomats. The only possible explanation for this lack of communication seems to be that the

Americans deliberately avoided encounters with white South Africans about racial discrimination, because their own position was vulnerable on that issue. In fact, the State Department in a policy statement in 1948 discouraged its officials to be drawn into discussions about South Africa's racial policies.

5. On the possibilities of a black uprising

The chance of a successful black uprising was a topic quite often raised by the American diplomats, even if the discourse was conducted at a speculative level. Their experience of black protest in the apartheid era started early in 1949. Responding to the Durban riots, when blacks attacked Indians, Robert McGregor expressed his surprise about the rapid spread of violence and the degree of disturbance unarmed black people could cause. But Ambassador Winship was more surprised about the circumspection of the rioters. He noted that although no evidence could be found that these blacks were controlled by an external force, care had been taken not to harm whites or their property. In his memoir about his South African career Ambassador Gallman also recalled the "widespread, disciplined response" of the ANC and its allies during the Defiance Campaign, and at the time thought the blacks would be able to disrupt the South African economy within the next ten years. Two decades later (by1971) he nevertheless remarked that "effective countrywide organization of the native is still in the making."

Police brutality also did not pass unnoticed. The Consul General in Johannesburg, Marselis Parsons, who reported the arrest of Solly Sachs in 1952, mentioned that the police hit women and blacks indiscriminately and it appeared to him as if the government intended to provoke violent action. His colleague in Pretoria, Henri LaTendresse, observed that many policemen were inexperienced and irresponsible. They were apparently determined to impress blacks with a show of force.

Of all the US diplomats of the late 1940s and early1950s Joseph Sweeney was the most apprehensive of a racial clash between white and black. Within a few months after his arrival in the country in January 1950, he was convinced that violent conflict between the black and white races was lurking around the corner. May Day protest actions by blacks in 1950 and 1951 and the hostilities between protesters and the police enforced his belief that race relations had deteriorated to such an extent that a bloodbath was imminent. The future of the country would be determined by limited choices: a compromise, further black riots or a police state. And the latter seemed most likely to him, because the government had no intention of compromising on race issues.

It should be considered, of course, that there was a considerable build-up of mass organization by the ANC and its allies during Sweeney's term of office. And Sweeney was perceptive to observe that "the pace of Non-European movements is now being set by the masses rather than the leaders," which was contrary to the belief by many white South Africans that the "African National Congress leaders are a group of trouble-making intellectuals who command no support." A few months before the Defiance Campaign was launched, Sweeney prepared a report (which was approved by Connelly) for the Ambassador assessing the chances of a successful uprising by blacks. He dealt with three different schools of thought about an uprising, and concluded that none of these opinions was really superior to the other and that a prediction about an uprising was almost impossible. He had to admit, though, that the government had sufficient capacity to curb any uprising that would not get out of hand, an opinion shared by Ambassador Gallman. However, privately Sweeney was much more perturbed. In his memoirs he recalled:

> In November 1951 I became so concerned about Native unrest that I thought something should be done, but again I experienced that hopeless feeling that comes when you see tragedy approaching and can get no one to help avert it. I couldn't interest anyone in the imminence of this holocaust.

Though Sweeney's colleagues were certainly in no way naive as far as racial tensions in South Africa were concerned, they demonstrated less anxiety. Possibly they perceived the real situation more hardheaded than Sweeney, who tended to overreact to incidents. A keen observer and apparently sensitive person, Sweeney was honest enough to articulate his fears for the wrath of blacks on whites by describing how he and his wife Adelaide late one night had to walk to a nearby farmhouse when his car broke down "...all the stories of what happened to Europeans in such circumstances running through our minds, and the joy with which we saw a farm house [sic] lights in the distance as we passed Africans who stared at us hostilely because by our skins we were the enemy..."

Henri LaTendresse had a different view. His observations, supported by some interviews with South Africans, including white farmers, were that discontent among blacks was not as widespread as was believed overseas. He nevertheless qualified his point by saying that he did not suggest that there was no black unrest in the country. In one of his reports to the State Department he wrote:

> Here as elsewhere, it is the educated vocal few who set up the clamor. It is easy to hear in this loud small voice the cries of the multitude, and thus create for oneself false views and a false assessment of the news. In the African masses are restless centers, but also are there large peripheral groups which, lethargic and somnolent, are unaware of the hubbub raised in their name.

La Tendresse thus differed markedly from Sweeney about the masses being setting the pace of protest. Even amidst the Defiance Campaign, LaTendresse doubted the capability of its leaders to achieve much. In the third week of the campaign he reported: "Unless the non-European leaders of the Defiance Campaign are assumed to be stupid and inept, a plan that lands volunteers in jail in wholesale lots with a minimum of trouble to the police and no inconvenience at all to the White population cannot be taken at face value."

6. Assessing the Malan cabinet

Since 1948 the aims of the US diplomatic mission in South Africa became more ambivalent. The one part of its objective, to inform the State Department back home about the country, was not as complicated. But the other, to establish a relationship with the host country, was no plain sailing. South Africa had to be placated as a Cold War partner despite its racial policies that had become an increasing embarrassment to the US. Surely the State Department had no clear intention to reprimand the Malan administration. But the situation remained uneasy, and especially diplomats such as Connelly and Sweeney found it increasingly difficult to report anything positive about the South African government.

Ambassador Gallman was nevertheless convinced that friendly persuasion was the only possible approach towards the Malan administration. In April 1952, when the South African government was heavily criticized by India for its racial policies, the American Ambassador told the Secretary of State that "a word of caution" and "some suggestions" would be the appropriate way to deal with apartheid. In any case, he found the members of Malan's cabinet "daily more approachable, open and friendly." Gallman, though realizing the need for some kind of political reform and the improvement of the social conditions of black people, was a gradualist who did not believe in granting universal voting rights to blacks in South Africa because it could result in turmoil which might be exploited by "irresponsible elements or by Communists."

Gallman's "suggestions," by his own admission, did not bear much fruit. That does not mean that he did not try. After the general election of 1953 he tactfully hinted to Malan that in the light of the NP government's strong position it might be wise to consult with recognized black leaders in a series of round-table discussions. Malan listened patiently but replied that opportunities for those black leaders to communicate with the government already existed via the Department of Native Affairs. Upon the Ambassador's counter-argument that such discussions had to be conducted on a higher level, the aging Prime Minister indicated that he would give it a thought. Needless to say, nothing came of that in Gallman's period of office in South Africa, or in the ensuing years of service of many of his colleagues.

Diplomatic reports reflected Americans' astonishment about the contradictions that existed in white South African society regarding apartheid. A number of Afrikaners and Nats were highly rated; and yet, to the US diplomats it was incomprehensible how these capable people could adhere to an illogical policy such as apartheid. There was no doubt in the mind of Joseph Sweeney about H. F. Verwoerd's abilities and intellect. "Verwoerd," he reported, "was far and away the ablest and most energetic man any South African Government had placed in charge of Native Affairs. Compared to a buffoon like Piet van der Bijl, Smuts' personally appointed Minister of Native Affairs, he represented high intelligence indeed." Though industrialization of the reserves was an imaginative idea and might raise the living standards of black people, it was no solution to the race problem, Sweeney thought. Verwoerd's approach not to consult black leaders on policy matters and his determination to apply policy only within the apartheid framework were wrong and would ensure further estrangement between the races.

Both Sweeney and Bernard Connelly, the Chargé d'Affaires in Cape Town in the early 1950s, were most impressed with Dr. Eben Dönges, whom they thought was brilliant, with exceptional abilities as a debater. Others scored fewer points. Connelly thought J. G. Strijdom to be tough and uncompromising; Eric Louw blunt, untactful yet sincere and somewhat able; Paul Sauer jovial and the most friendly cabinet minister towards the Americans.

7. Analysing the mind of the Afrikaner

To dissect Afrikaner thinking as far as race attitudes were concerned had become a standing diplomatic exercise for the Americans in South Africa. In sharp contrast with Ambassador Gallman's fond recollections, Sweeney and Connelly were far less sympathetic. When Sweeney left South Africa, some of his most outstanding memories of the Afrikaner were the latter's denial that blacks had owned the country before the advent of the whites. In addition, Afrikaners believed that concessions towards equality with blacks would undeniably result in "their own submergement." He also commented on the Afrikaner's (to him) strange obsession with race association. He claimed to have seen the genealogies of some of the most respected Afrikaner families and had noticed that "the tar brush has made itself felt". Yet, Afrikaners seemed to disregard this fact and made association the acid test: if you lived with Cape coloureds you were coloured and if you lived with whites you were white. Apart from the moral injustice of apartheid, Sweeney thought it was politically stupid, because Afrikanerdom succeeded, inadvertently, to do what blacks themselves could not achieve, namely to unite all "non-whites" by introducing apartheid.

In his memoir Sweeney hinted at the benefits Afrikaners would have obtained from visiting the US, despite the imperfections of that society. Sweeney had a high opinion of the intellect and knowledge of E. A. Malga, political correspondent of *Die Burger* and although he regarded Malga a true Afrikaner nationalist who believed in white supremacy, he cherished the ambitious thought that Malga was the type of person who might interpret the spirit and values of the US to the rural Afrikaner farmers. Bernard Connelly, Sweeney's senior, who occasionally acted as head of the legation, shared most of these views, adding in a sarcastic tone that Afrikaners did not believe any foreigner could understand the country's race problems unless that person had been living in South Africa for half a century or, alternatively, had agreed with the policy of apartheid.

Yet, despite the despondency about Afrikaners' inclination to review their stand on racial issues, the same Connelly signed a report to the Secretary of State after the 1950 May Day riots, indicating that there were voices, although perhaps isolated, that asked for introspection. He specifically referred to Dr. William Nicol, then Administrator of the Transvaal and former Dutch Reformed Church minister. Nicol had told an Afrikaner audience in Johannesburg in May 1950 that the days were over when blacks would be considered as the enemies of whites, and that it was time to work towards the achievement of goodwill from black people.

The US embassy in those years had a special interest in two Afrikaans institutions, SABRA (South African Bureau of Racial Affairs) and the Dutch Reformed Church (DRC). SABRA, an organization whose membership included some very prominent Afrikaner intellectuals, supported the concept of total separation and vigorous development of the black reserves. Henri LaTendresse, attaché in the Pretoria Embassy, was convinced that SABRA "cannot be dismissed as an organization of crackpots, dreamers and theorists." Responding to a SABRA pamphlet entitled "Integration or Separate Development?" in July 1952, he doubted whether the SABRA idea could be fully implemented and feared that dislocation of black people would strain race relations even further. "To the Embassy," he wrote, "the most curious feature of total apartheid is the ability of some people to believe in it."

David Robertson, First Secretary of the Embassy in Pretoria, attended an informal dinner in Johannesburg in the same month, which was attended by a number of prominent people including Edwin G. Arnold of the Ford Foundation. Also present was A. F. Weich, national organizer of SABRA. The main theme of the discussion was whether the whites in South Africa could remain in control indefinitely on the basis of apartheid or whether economic forces would prove too powerful for the sustenance of such a policy. The SABRA spokesman was convinced that there was no immediate threat to the security of the country, but did not completely rule out conflict between white and black in the future. He could see no reason why 13 million black people could not make a living in the reserves if a policy of active industrialization was pursued. Robertson's private comment was that Weich had not "carefully considered the practical implications involved in his 'apartheid dream.'" What was more, Robertson did not believe that government leaders would "sponsor a very costly program designed primarily to benefit the Bantu at the expense of the White population."

If the American diplomats rejected SABRA's idealism, they still had a degree of hope for the country in the form of the Dutch Reformed Church (DRC). Connelly, Sweeney and Dembo had no illusions about the "official" viewpoint of the church, the vast majority of its clergy and members. A congress of all the Dutch Reformed churches in April 1950 in Bloemfontein affirmed a policy of complete racial segregation. Sweeney thought that the Dutch Reformed Church represented a view on racial separation that was even more extreme than that of the government itself; thus, a different attitude from the church would influence the government and also the Afrikaner public. Particularly encouraging for Sweeney was the viewpoints of a theologian like Dr. (later Professor) Ben Marais regarding the conference of the World Council of Churches. Marais had, inter alia, referred to the struggle between democracy and communism and had indicated that racial discrimination would drive the blacks into the arms of communism. Likewise racial discrimination would be to the advantage of the Roman Catholic Church because that church did not follow such a practice.

Marais was not the only DRC theologian who had reservations about apartheid. Connelly also reported that the influential Dr. (later Professor) B. B. Keet of Stellenbosch by the end of 1949 had disagreed with a synodal commission report that stated that the Bible supported apartheid. Though the majority of whites in South Africa would not budge from the white supremacy stand, Connelly noticed, "twinges of conscience [which] are causing many individuals to reconsider the basic relationship between the races."

Some three years later, by the beginning of 1953, the Americans still showed interest in the DRC as a possible facilitator of change. Morris Dembo sent a report to the State Department referring to a conversation Ambassador Gallman had had with officials of the State Department during a recent visit to Washington obviously on the DRC and racial policies in South Africa. Dembo reiterated the Embassy's conviction that the official view of the DRC on racial issues did not reflect the view of all members of the church and that the "Embassy has gathered enough evidence to show that important groups within these churches are conscious of their prophetic role as the 'conscience' of the State." These people were conscious of the dilemma of Afrikaner nationalism versus the Christian principles of unity, brotherhood, and equality. Dembo believed the US could play a role in encouraging the articulation of thoughts of these DRC members. They were not really liberal Afrikaners, but they were outspoken. He mentioned the names of Professors B. B. Keet and L. Pistorius, Dr. Ben Marais, the Revds. J. Reyneke, J. L. Reyneke, J. Alex van Wyk, A. A. Odendaal, R. S. van Niekerk, and J. A. Lombard, as well as the compiler of the NGK year book, Norval Geldenhuys (who had studied at Princeton), and two Moderators of the Church, Rev. C. B. Brink and Dr. A. J. van der Merwe. Various organisations in the US which had shown interest in the race problems in South Africa, such as the Hazen Foundation, Phelps-Stokes Foundation, Carnegie Corporation, Ford Foundation and the Divinity Schools of Yale and Princeton were mentioned and the suggestion expressed that the existing ties be expanded. Progress, Dembo warned, might be very slow and the "isolationist streak in South African Calvinism can all too easy [sic] be inflamed." Yet, the influence of the churches on government and the people was so decisive that it ought to be guided. His optimistic prognosis was: "If the Churches recommend a change in racial policy, the whole Afrikaner people will follow."

The churches, of course, did not recommend a change in racial policy. Marais and Keet, who openly questioned the scriptural grounds for apartheid, remained voices in the desert. And after H. F. Verwoerd, Die Kerkbode, and the Afrikaner Broederbond launched a concerted effort to discredit those Dutch Reformed delegates to the Cottesloe Council (December 1960), the DRC never questioned apartheid again until the mid-1980s.

8. Did Washington listen? The effects of diplomatic reports

In the period of President Truman's second term diplomatic reports from the US diplomatic staff in South Africa to the State Department reflected a realistic picture of increasing apartheid legislation and resistance by the people on the receiving end of it. Opinions and interpretations about the extent of deterioration of race relations and the danger of an anti-apartheid uprising showed some variation, but not a single diplomat denied the existence of a racial problem in South Africa. However, if the South African contingent of the State Department had thoughts of changing the minds of the higher authorities in Washington DC, they were mistaken. Despite the conscientious studies and carefully compiled reports on the racial climate in South Africa, pointing to an imminent dilemma for the US, if it would continue to ignore the racial policies of the South African government, the State Department had no intentions of modifying its relationship with the Malan administration.

There were occasional voices of concern within the Department about the effects of events in South Africa such as the Defiance Campaign and the constitutional crisis. It was suggested that racial tensions in the Union might stir up unrest in other African countries and that the credibility of the Western powers might be in danger if they would longer be associated with South Africa. But no evidence could be found that any of the dozens of diplomatic dispatches from South Africa dealing with the racial situation in the country was referred to either the US congress or cabinet for discussion. The State Department was the terminal point, and as Joseph Sweeney observed, "No one in the Department of State paid any serious attention to South Africa except as a source of strategic minerals. Our country had no policy toward South Africa and vaguely wanted 'no trouble'[sic]. In those days we consistently avoided indicating where we stood on the racial issue."

Ambassador Erhardt, during his short term in the country, approached Sweeney in January 1950 to compile a draft statement of proposed US policy on South Africa. In a flattering tone (according to Sweeney) the Ambassador made Sweeney understand that he wished to utilize intellectuals (such as Sweeney) to strengthen his case. The junior diplomat suggested that the US "were losing Africa," but Erhardt tactfully reminded him that the State Department would never buy that line of thought. Eventually the two agreed on a statement of objectives written in "a tone acceptable to the Department." Considering Sweeney's liberal views on race relations, the final product was thus not extreme by any standards.

The six objectives formulated confirmed the value of South African support to the West, including its supply of raw materials. In addition, South Africa's participation in the United Nations Organization should be maintained and its membership of the British Commonwealth encouraged "without opposing the Afrikaner ideal of a republic." The two points touching upon group and race relations were devoid of any radical transformation. It envisaged American influence "toward broadening the outlook of Afrikaner nationalism" in order to lessen "parochial national-ism", to improve relations between the two language groups, to bring policy towards blacks more in line with Western democracies, and to help South African leadership in Africa to become "a positive force". American influence, Sweeney thought, could also be exerted upon African national-ism in South Africa in order to facilitate harmonious co-existence between black and white, to lessen anti-white feelings and to curb communist influence. The memorandum was sent off, but they never received any response from the State Department.

9. Conclusion

How did South Africa then fit into the grand scheme of US foreign policy? Why would the leading Western power to emerge from the ravages of the Second World War persist with condoning the racial policies of a small country on an underdeveloped continent if such practices were potentially devastating for future US policy? With the benefit of hindsight, modern scholars have readily criticized the US lack of foresight in its dealings with apartheid South Africa. Without exception these scholars have also mooted South Africa's own perception of its supposed value to the US and the West. There are various examples to illustrate this: military assistance to the US in the Korean War (1950-51), when South Africa provided an air force squadron and later also ground troops, added to existing expectations by South Africa that their strong anti-communist stand should be rewarded. It expressed its desire to be included in the uranium program launched by Britain and the US, and it also asked for military aid in the form of weapons from the Americans. Whereas the US was somewhat hesitant to meet with the request, the confirmation of South African supply of uranium according to contract in 1951, plus its staunch support in Korea opened the door for the Truman administration to facilitate military aid. An additional reward was secured in the form of increased US loans since 1951.

South Africa also assumed US support in the increasingly hostile UN. That support was afforded where the South West Africa issue, as well as apartheid in general were on the UN agenda. Although there was not mutual consensus within the State Department on the US viewpoint regarding the debate in 1952 on apartheid, the US abstained from voting on a resolution which would provide for a UN commission to study apartheid. It voted in favour of a vague resolution that supported racial equality, without mentioning South Africa in particular. This evoked a response of indignation from the Malan government.

South Africa's strategic position to the West concerning the Cold War would therefore provide vindication for a US policy of condoning of unacceptable racial policies. That does not necessarily mean that the country was of special importance to the US. In the late 1940s and early 1950s Europe, and to a lesser extent the Middle East, were America's top priority, not Africa. And in the State Department South Africa fell under the Office of British Commonwealth and Northern European Affairs, which was a section of the Bureau of European Affairs. It was regarded neither an African country, nor one associated with European or Commonwealth matters. And although trade between the two countries had expanded in the 1940s, US investments in South Africa in the Truman period still only represented approximately one percent of US capital invested abroad. The bulging volumes of documents in the National Archives in College Park (US) and those in the Truman Library pertaining to the period of Acheson's office as Secretary of State contain scant evidence of US-South African matters. And the scattered references to South Africa in Acheson's book on his most crucial years in the Truman administration, *Present at the Creation: My Years in the State Department* (London, Hamish Hamilton, 1969) do not fill a full page when put together. But even though South Africa was of little concern to Acheson, he was certainly not negatively disposed towards the country. When he was appointed Secretary of State in 1949, the South African ambassador in Washington, H. T. Andrews, reported: "I have found Mr. Acheson better informed on Commonwealth Affairs than perhaps any other official in the State Department, whilst as regards South Africa his knowledge and friendship is perhaps second only to that of his feelings for Canada."

Then there was the question of priorities for the State Department. In Acheson and George Kennan (Director of the Policy Planning Staff in the office of the Under Secretary of State until December 1949) the State

Department had two leading lights who showed little sympathy for the freedom ideals of Third World countries. For the focus of this study Acheson in particular was a determining factor. During and after World War II he established a considerable reputation as formulator of US foreign policy. He was not merely anti-communist but also unsympathetic towards anti-colonialism, and thought black people of Africa was incapable of achieving independence without external support, by definition the Soviet Union. In addition, they were incapable of establishing stable and economically viable democracies once they obtained independence. Acheson consistently backed Portugal in its attempts to maintain political control over the black majority in its southern African colonies, Angola and Mozambique, and in the process became involved in a fierce conflict with the "Africanists" in the State Department, particularly G. Mennen Williams, Adlai Stevenson, and John K. Galbraith. In direct opposition to the US position, he wholeheartedly sympathized with the Smith regime in Rhodesia (now Zimbabwe) after its unilateral declaration of independence in October 1965. Acheson's view was that the racial policies of Rhodesia and South Africa, two sovereign states, were a domestic issue and that the UN had no right to interfere. All the US would achieve by punishing Rhodesia was to endanger its access to strategic minerals in the region. Besides, he thought that the white minority governments in southern Africa were important buffers against communism.

How strong pro-South African sentiments in the State Department were, is of course debatable. The South African consul in Elizabethville recorded that E. H. Bourgerie, whom he met in early March 1950 and who had just been appointed Joint Director of the Bureau of African and Middle East Affairs, was outspoken in his criticism of South Africa's racial policies and told him bluntly that apartheid had no chance of success. Forsyth recalled that Bourgerie had served as US Commercial Attaché in South Africa previously, and added that his opinions "are similar to those held by many Americans." Significantly Forsyth added: "I am inclined to doubt whether his [Bourgerie's] views will necessarily carry great weight in the State Department." At least one other important official in the State Department, G. Hayden Raynor, who was Director of the Office of British Commonwealth and Northern European Affairs and also adviser to the US delegation to the UN, was on friendly terms with South Africa. Informing the acting Secretary for External Affairs in

Pretoria of Raynor's intended visit to South Africa in May-June 1953, Ambassador Jooste described him as "an important and reliable friend." (translated from Afrikaans).

With a man of Acheson's stature (and his ideological beliefs) in command of the State Department, US diplomats had little chance of changing the mind of the State Department about their attitude towards racial discrimination in South Africa. Besides, it should not be forgotten that Acheson also heard versions of the situation in South Africa that differed from the views of Sweeney and Connelly. The opinions espoused by people like Gallman, Redecker, and LaTendresse were less condemning and reflected more sympathy with the sentiments of Afrikaners. The Secretary of State must also have received a positive image of South Africa from the Assistant Secretary of State for Near East, South Asian and African Affairs, George C. McGhee, who on the initiative of the South African Department of External Affairs paid a six-day visit to South Africa in March 1950, meeting Prime Minister Malan, senior cabinet members and a few departmental secretaries, as well as General Smuts. McGhee was received warmly and treated like a real VIP, for which he showed abundant appreciation. Although McGhee in his later reminiscences expressed serious doubt whether South Africa was on the right track with its racial policies, he certainly made different noises shortly after his visit, telling Jooste in Washington that the country had made good progress in developing the black people and that he, as a Texan, well understood South Africa's racial dilemma.

These views and those of some of the diplomats in South Africa without doubt were more in line with Acheson's own thoughts. Perhaps that contributed most to Acheson's opinion that American businessmen in South Africa through their influence would achieve much in cultivating better race relations in that country. And it possibly explains best why Sweeney and some of his other colleagues' cries of distress hardly moved the Department. The diagnosis made in the Sweeney memorandum was accurate but the recommendations, though moderate, were obviously too radical as far as the State Department was concerned. The issue was clearly decided: constructive engagement regarding South Africa would be the road to follow, but not on the terms suggested in the Sweeney memorandum.

Assessing the value of the dispatches by diplomats in South Africa, it should be acknowledged that they were informative and authoritative to a large degree. If not succeeding in swaying the opinion of the policy makers in Washington, they at least presented a credible picture to the State Department of race relations in South Africa. And importantly, the reports convincingly refuted the allegations, often made by South Africans, that the US was ill-informed about the racial situation in South Africa.

Seen from a broader perspective, the dispatches from South Africa during the early Cold War years reveal a policy of profound continuity that only changed in the mid-1980s. The fluctuations that occurred were sporadic. Certainly, the creation of the Bureau of African Affairs within the State Department in 1958 provided for a sharper focus on Africa and consequently generated some hope for anti-apartheid groups that the US government would accelerate pressure on the South African government to demolish apartheid. When John F. Kennedy took office, expectations rose for such action, but the "Africanists" in the State Department were unable to manage more than vocal condemnation of apartheid.

Some ten years later, when the Portuguese withdrew from Africa, the US was forced to re-evaluate the position of a beleaguered South Africa in the southern African region. But the changed situation made the appeal by the CIA and Pentagon to cherish South Africa as an ally against the growing Soviet penetration of the area even more compelling. None less than the Carter administration, supported enthusiastically by anti-apartheid lobbyists, and with officials that expressed commitment to ending racial discrimination and undemocratic rule everywhere in the world, eventually stopped short of advocating sanctions against the country.

As long as political stability in South Africa prevailed, as long as there was no crisis, the US would not intervene, despite the mounting international campaign against apartheid. It was only in the mid-1980s, when the P. W. Botha government declared a state of emergency following the insurrection of 1984-86, that the US Senate could be persuaded to recommend comprehensive sanctions against South Africa, without, of course, the approval of the CIA, the Pentagon, and President Ronald Reagan himself. Ironically, this came at a time when Assistant Secretary of State for African Affairs, Chester Crocker, was on the verge of making a significant breakthrough to end the conflict in southern Africa by involving South Africa in a regional plan. But the state of emergency of 1985 made an end to "constructive engagement," the term used to describe the US approach towards South Africa in the early 1980s. The time, so it seemed, had arrived for the US to act, because South Africa was now finding itself in a crisis. It became almost impossible for the State Department to fend off any longer the concerted efforts in the US to bring South Africa to its senses through punitive measures. The acceptance of sanctions legislation therefore signified the end of an era full of ambiguity in US foreign policy towards its dubious Cold War partner on the southern tip of Africa.

J.P. Brits

Archival Sources

Department of External Affairs (hereafter DEA), BTS, 1/33/13 , vol 1, H.T. Andrews - Secretary for External Affairs, 27 June 1947; *Ibid*, W.D. van Schalkwyk - Secretary for External Affairs, 15 Dec 1948; "Memorandum on racial discrimination in the United States, 5 Feb 1952 and 19 Mar 1952; BTS, 1/33/13, vol 8, "Memorandum on race relations in the United States", 18 Apr 1952; 72/1/1, vol 7, "Personnel of United States Government Offices on the Union of South Africa, March 8, 1948, pp 1-7; S 4/5/16 (7), Washington, Record of service of the Embassy of South Africa; "Biographical entry from the Register of the Department of State relating to North Winship"; vol 8, "Biographical data - John George Erhardt"; vol 9, "Biographic data" (W.J. Gallman); 72/1/1, vol 8, "Biographical sketch of Joseph H. Sweeney".

United States State Department, Central Files, Correspondence members of US Embassy in South Africa - United States Department of State, 1946-1953.

Harry S. Truman Library, Papers of Harry S. Truman, President's Secretary's Files, Central Intelligence Agency, *The political situation in the Union of South Africa,* ORE 1-49, 31 January 1949, p. 1; Central Intelligence Agency, *The political situation in the Union of South Africa* (31 Jan 1949), p. 13; General Historical Documents Collection, W J Gallman "Some thoughts on foreign affairs" [1971], pp 82-83; Papers of Joseph Sweeney, South Africa: 1950-52 , p. 3.

William Cullen Library, University of the Witwatersrand, SAIRR, B5.14.

Bibliography

Bissell, R. E. 1982. *South Africa and the United States: The erotion of an influence relationship* (New York, 1982).

Borstelmann, T.1993. *Apartheid's reluctant uncle: The United States and Southern Africa in the early Cold War* (New York, 1993).

Brinkley, D. 1992. *Dean Acheson: The Cold War years 1953-71* (New Haven and London: Yale University Press).

Cell, J. W. 1982. *The highest stage of white supremacy: The origins of segregation in South Africa and the American south* (Cambridge/New York: Cambridge University Press).

Fredrickson, G. M. 1981. *White supremacy: A comparative study on American and South African History* (New York: Oxford University Press).

Geldenhuys, D. 1984. *The diplomacy of isolation: South African foreign policy making* (Johannesburg).

Greenberg, S. B. 1980. *Race and state in capitalist development: South Africa in comparative perspective* (Johannesburg: Ravan Press).

Jooste, G. 1977. *Diensherinneringe* (Johannesburg: Perskor-uitgewery).

Kapp, P.H. and Olivier, G.C. (eds). 1987. *United States/South Africa relations: Past, present and future* (Cape Town).

Lake, A. 1974. *Caution and concern: The making of American policy toward South Africa 1946-1971* (Ph D thesis, Princeton University).

Lamar, H. and Thompson, L. 1981. *The frontier in history: North America and Southern Africa compared* (New Haven: Yale University Press).

Lynch, H. R. 1978. *Black American radicals and the liberation of Africa: The Council on African Affairs 1937-1955* (Africana Studies and Research Center, Monograph Series no 5, Cornell University).

Martin, H.P. 1974. *American views on South Africa, 1948-1972* (Ph D thesis Louisiana State University).

McGhee, G. 1983. *Envoy to the Middle World: Adventures in diplomacy* (New York: Harper & Row).

Massie, R. K. 1987. *Loosing the bonds: the United States and South Africa in the apartheid years* (New York: Nan A. Talese Doubleday).

Mokoena, K. (ed.). 1993. *South Africa and the United States: The declassified history* (New York).

Noer, T.J. 1985. *Cold War and black liberation: The United States and white rule in Africa, 1948-1968* (Columbia).

O'Meara, D. 1996. *Forty lost years: The apartheid state and the politics of the National Party 1948-1994* (Randburg: Ravan Press).

Schraeder, P. J. 1994. *United States foreign policy towards South Africa: Incrementalism, crisis and change* (Cambridge).

Spooner, W.A. 1979. *United States policy towards South Africa 1919-1941: Political and economic aspects* (Ph D thesis, St Johns University, New York).

Wolf, J. B. 1991. "A grand tour: South Africa and American tourists between the wars", *Journal of Popular Culture*, vol 25, 1991, pp 99-114.

The Quest for Cultural Identity in the African Diaspora in the Americas and Europe in the Early Twentieth Century

The main line of thought that I wish to pursue is that in the engagement with questions of cultural identity in the African Diaspora in the Americas and Europe in the early twentieth century there was an unresolved tension between the striving for ethnic identity and the asserting a universality of all humankind. These at times contradictory strivings can be seen within both cultural nationalist movements and within international communism, with all its ideals of equality and social justice. Some individuals tried both. For those involved in the latter, the problematic is compounded by the fact that the contradiction between nationalism and universalism was also manifest within Soviet Communism. This quest for self-fulfilment moved simultaneously on two levels: one was the aspiration for civil rights, the other the deeper search for cultural identity. I will present brief examples of both these levels of activity.

Going Abroad and Becoming Whole:
The Americas and Africa to Europe and Back

One of the most striking aspects of this quest for cultural identity is the extent to which those seeking it traveled abroad in their quest. It is more than coincidental that the titles of Langston Hughes's and Claude McKay's respective autobiographies are *I Wonder as I Wander* and *A Long Ways from Home*. In this era travel for self-fulfillment was most prominent among artists from the United States. Here I need only mention in passing the well-known sojourns in France of African American artists such as Josephine Baker and Sidney Bechet. As evidence that this circuit was Europe-wide, let me mention the less known fact that even on Europe's eastern border in Russia direct exposure to African-American culture actually began at the very beginning of the twentieth century. An example can be seen in the career of Coretta Arli-Titz, formerly Coretta Alfred, whose career in Russia spanned the tsarist and Soviet periods. Eventually a graduate from the Leningrad and Moscow Conservatories of Music, who in the 1930s married a noted professor of music, she had actually originally come to Russia in 1904 as a member of a vaudeville troupe of seven Negro women called "The Louisiana Amazon Guards." She stayed through the Revolution and became one of the most popular concert singers in Moscow, performing in four languages, and a successful movie actress. On a tour in the 1930s, Marian Anderson visited Arli-Titz (Poston, Smith 36-38).

The attraction to these artists attests to the growing popularity of African-American culture in Russia, especially jazz music, despite the official Communist attitude, summed up in the writer Maxim Gorky's description of it as "degenerate, bourgeois music" (Gorky 4, and Starr). The avant-garde theatre director Vsevelod Meyerhold staged a full jazz band in some of his productions in the early 1920s, comprised entirely of Russians. Although Communist ideological strictures required that jazz represent decadence in Meyerhold's plots, the irresistible appeal of the music can be seen in the steady stream of artists touring the Soviet Union, such as the Leland Drayton revue, for six months in 1925, and Sam Wooding and His Chocolate Kiddies, featuring thirty-three black American jazz musicians, dancers, and singers, for three months in 1926. Benny Peyton's seven-piece New Orleans Jazz Band also visited Russia that year, including the legendary saxophonist Sidney Bechet. Jazz enjoyed ever growing popularity. The Soviet government also paid special tribute to American Negroes during this period through special awards such as the selection of the novelist Arna Bontemps for the Pushkin Prize in 1926. Others were elected honorary members of the Moscow City Council; and a mountain was eventually named after Paul Robeson, who first visited Russia in 1934 (Duberman).

Of the hundreds of black Americans who visited Soviet Russia during its early decades in search of opportunities for self-fulfilment, only several dozen actually settled there. Some left in disillusionment with Soviet life, others simply out of homesickness, or because material conditions had improved in the United States (Smith). The Soviet government capitalized on propaganda gems such as the notorious Scottsboro Case by expelling from the country two white American workers at the Stalingrad automotive factory who had attacked Robert Robinson, a black Jamaican and former Ford Motor Co. ball bearing maker working there. They had thrown him out of the factory cafeteria in an effort to impose American segregation practices. In addition to several individuals like Robinson, there was also a group of eleven black American agricultural scientists who worked in Central Asia during the 1930s (*Pravda Vostoka*). Some stayed for several years, a few permanently. A closer look at the experience of one of them, John Sutton, may be instructive. Sutton joined the enterprise, and in 1932 sent what was apparently his second letter from Russia to George Washington Carver, his mentor:

Dear Professor:
The last time you heard from me I was simply a physiologist working in the cotton fields of Central Asia. Now I am a research chemist following in the footsteps of my illustrious teacher, Professor G.W. Carver.
I have been lately appointed manager of a newly organized laboratory of Technology in the Soviet Rice Institute. My main function is to discover some methods of utilizing to better advantage the rice plant. Particularly do we hope to utilize the rice straw, which until now goes completely unused in Russia. The Japanese utilize it for the weaving of bags and allied material, and as they are secretive in their various processes we have no way of knowing what they do. In the first place I expect to work on and solve this problem. Next in order of importance is the possibility of developing or rather making building material from rice straw. Wall board of they[sic] type of "Beaver Board" is our objective in that direction. This of course offers greater mechanical difficulties than the fiber problem as it must involve presses and such related problems. But never-the-less [sic] I will try that too. As my example and guide in this pioneer experimental work, I have you. From nothing at all, as a beginning you made undying history thru[sic] your application to the "study of

things." I firmly believe that I can and will make world famous discoveries in the field in which I am working. They are giving me the opportunity here and I shall do my best to justify their belief in me. It is a rare, rare thing that a Negro gets such an opportunity as this so I will have to work hard and make the most of it...(Carver)....

Sutton was born in San Antonio, Texas, the eldest in a family of 15 children. The youngest was Percy Sutton, who would one day become borough president of Manhattan, and owner of the Apollo Theatre and radio stations. Carver had recommended John Sutton to the Soviet government after he himself declined an offer of a huge sum of money to come to the Soviet Union and work in agricultural research. Sutton went in 1931 and worked in Uzbekistan until 1938 (Sutton, and Fax 132-34). This was a uniquely positive experience for these scientists, whose college degrees would have at best garnered them teaching jobs in secondary or elementary schools at home.

The Allure of Socialism

The attraction of African Americans to socialism merits prominent mention here because it actually preceded the better known Pan-Africanist movement and the various twentieth-century forms of Black nationalism. For example, W.E.B. Du Bois, who was later to organize five Pan-African Congresses, extending into the second half of the century, was much earlier drawn to socialism. He became interested already in the early 1890s while studying in Germany, publicly expressed socialist sympathies in the first decade of the twentieth century, and later reflected some Marxian analytical framework in his historical writing, especially in *Black Reconstruction* in the 1930s, but also earlier in articles. He was urged on in this direction by friends such as New York reformer Mary White Ovington, a moderate socialist and co-founder of the NAACP. Du Bois is so well known that I will give no more than passing mention of him here, dwelling rather on figures less well known.

One such figure is Otto Huiswood, a very interesting but still obscure actor from the Dutch empire in South America. The grandson of a slave, Huiswood was born in 1893 in Suriname. In 1912, following a pattern that would be characteristic for many West Indian and South

American black intellectuals in the twentieth century, he moved to the United States. There he was working as a trader in tropical products, and later as a printer in Harlem, when he became involved with American socialist and Negro organizations. One was a group surrounding *The Messenger*, originally a socialist monthly established by A. Philip Randolph and Chandler Owen that ran from 1917 to 1928 (Kornweibel). Another was the African Blood Brotherhood, a nationalist organization founded in 1919 by Cyril Briggs and Richard B. Moore, a group that advocated the establishment of an independent Negro nation in the western or northwestern United States, South America, the Caribbean, or Africa (Draper 324-26). By 1920 Huiswood was reputed to be the first black member of the Communist Party USA. In 1922 he was a member of the American delegation to the Fourth Congress of the Communist International (Comintern). While there he was elected an honorary member of the Moscow City Council and had a rare audience with Lenin, who was already mortally ill. In 1927 he studied at the Lenin School in Moscow, one of the political institutions founded to train elite communist leaders. At the meeting of the Sixth Comintern Congress in 1928 he was one of several black delegates who helped shape the official policy on nationalism, which urged creation of independent Black Soviet republics in the Southern United States ("Self-determination in the Black Belt") and in Southern Africa (Blakely 84-85, Haywood 256-68).

Two years later Huiswood openly challenged this position in an article entitled "World Aspects of the Negro Question."

> Our approach to the Negro question has not only been largely sectional rather than international, but our concept and interpretation of the Negro question was narrow and incorrect. The old Social Democratic notion that the Negro question is only a class question, prevailed with us for a considerable time. We are only now beginning to realize that the Negro question is not only a class question but also a race question. [...] The situation of the Negro masses varies in different countries and therefore requires investigation and analysis. [...] It is essential that we distinguish the situation of the Negro masses in the colonies—Africa and the West Indies; the semi-colonies—Haiti and Liberia, who suffer from colonial exploitation, from that of the Negro in America, a racial minority, subjected to racial persecution and exploitation. We must take into consideration the National-colonial character of the Negro question in Africa

and the West Indies and the racial character of this question in the United States (Huiswood 132-33, Haywood 321-25).

Thus, even within the Communist movement, the Black thinkers asserted the importance of race in contradiction to the official Party line (Huiswood 138). Huiswood became a veritable authority on conditions in the Caribbean region because he was assigned by Comintern to be the primary organizer there. He also succeeded the Trinidadian George Padmore as editor of the Comintern monthly the *Negro Worker*. Padmore, who earlier was the Party's main liaison with Black Africa, had been expelled from the Communist Party for his failing to toe the Party line, which temporarily downplayed opposition to colonialism (Blakely 92). This monthly had been based in Hamburg; but flight from the Nazis prompted moves to Copenhagen and then Paris from 1936 to 1938. Huiswood and his British-Guianese wife, H.A. Dumont, travelled through Europe. In 1935 they were in the Netherlands; then in 1938 they moved back to New York, and in 1941 returned to Suriname. Upon their arrival in Paramaribo in January, however, the authorities arrested him without charges and detained him for 22 months in an internment camp whose mixed population of Nazis, Jewish refugees, and anti-fascists reflected the political uncertainty common to a number of European colonies during the war. After the War he and his wife moved finally to the Netherlands, where for years he served as president of the nationalistic association *Ons Suriname* (Our Suriname). In collaboration with the two other main like-minded groups, *Wie Eegie Sanie* (Our Own Things) and the *Surinaamse Studenten Vereniging* (The Surinamer Students Union), *Ons Suriname* promoted cultural pride and spoke out against colonialism and racial discrimination in various parts of the world, including the Dutch empire (Oostindie 63-64 and 77-85).

The founding of political schools "to promote universal Communist brotherhood" brought a coterie of blacks to Russia. The KUTV (Communist University of the Toilers of the East) had been founded in 1921 under Stalin's Commissariat for Nationalities Affairs, for East and South Asians, Arabs, Jews, Turks, etc. However, when the Nationalities Commissariat was replaced in governmental restructuring in 1923, the government placed the school under the Communist International (Comintern), which added Africans and black Americans (10 places set aside for 1925/1926, including 2 for women, though none came that early).

The more prestigious International Lenin School was founded in Moscow in 1926; and several dozen Blacks from the West Indies and Africa attended between then and 1938. The students took classes at both schools: Political Economics, Comintern History, Leninism, Historical Materialism, Party Building (the most hours), military science, current politics, and English.

Artists Made Political: Claude Mc Kay and Wayland Rudd as Examples

A closer look at the illustrative listing of touring artists I mentioned above reveals a number of artists who found themselves increasingly drawn into radical politics. The poet Claude McKay was the first prominent Black to visit the Soviet Union on his own, without party affiliation. When he arrived in 1922 he was welcomed as a poet, not a politician. However, because the one black American delegate to the fourth Communist International Congress was the very light complex-ioned Otto Huiswood, the Soviet leaders wanted McKay, who was very dark, to represent the American Negro to the Russian public. He was, therefore, photographed with the leaders of the Communist International, introduced to other such luminaries as the poet V. Mayakovsky, to Leon Trotsky, and to Lenin's wife Krupskaya, who was representing her ill husband. He was also made an honorary member of the Moscow City Council, and was treated to a brief airplane ride while on an inspection of the Red Army (McKay). During several months' stay in Russia, Mc Kay wrote both articles and poetry, including one reverent homage to Moscow and Lenin entitled "Moscow:"

> Moscow for many loving her was dead...
> And yet I saw a bright Byzantine fair,
> Of jewelled buildings, pillars, domes and spires
> Of hues prismatic dazzling to the sight;
> A glory painted on the Eastern air,
> Of amorous sounding tones like passionate lyres;
> All colours laughing richly their delight
> And reigning over all the colour red.
>
> My memory bears engraved the high-walled Kremlin,
> Of halls symbolic of the tiger will,
> Of Czarist instruments of mindless law...

And often now my nerves throb with the thrill
When, in that gilded place, I felt and saw
The presence and the simple voice of Lenin.

The intensity of the (at least temporary) appeal of the Soviet dream can be better gauged if one contrasts that mood to the one expressed in his poem "If We Must Die," a shrill cry of outrage against lynching in America.

If we must die, let it not be like hogs
Hunted and penned in an inglorious spot,
While round us bark the mad and hungry dogs,
Making their mock at our accursed lot.
If we must die, O let us nobly die,
So that our precious blood may not be shed
In vain; then even the monsters we defy
Shall be constrained to honor us though dead!
O kinsmen! We must meet the common foe!
Though far outnumbered let us show us brave,
And for their thousand blows deal one deathblow!
What though before us lies the open grave?
Like men we'll face the murderous, cowardly pack,
Pressed to the wall, dying, but fighting back!

(McKay 1981 36 and 83)

Even the usually mild-mannered, good-humored Langston Hughes was inspired to some rather stern rhetoric by the Soviet ideals. See, for example, "Goodbye Christ," composed during his travels in Russia in 1932.

Listen, Christ,
You did alright in your day, I reckon –
But that day's gone now.
They ghosted you up a swell story, too,
Called it Bible –
But it's dead now,
The popes and the preachers've
Made too much money from it.
They've sold you to too many
Kings, generals, robbers, and killers –
Even to the Tzar and the Cossacks,
Even to Rockefeller's Church,

Even to THE SATURDAY EVENING POST.
You ain't no good no more.
They've pawned you
Till you've done wore out.

Goodbye,
Christ Jesus Lord God Jehova,
Beat it on away from here now.
Make way for a new guy with no religion at all –
A real guy named
Marx Communist Lenin Peasant Stalin Worker ME –
I said, ME!

Go ahead on now,
You're getting in the way of things, Lord.
And please take Saint Ghandi with you when you go,
And Saint Pope Pius,
And Saint Aimee McPherson,
And big black Saint Becton
Of the Consecrated Dime.
And step on the gas, Christ!
Move!

Don't be so slow about movin'!
The world is mine from now on –
And nobody'd gonna sell ME
To a king, or a general,
Or a millionaire   (Rampersad 228-29).

Among other little-known artists who moved to Russia during this period
was Wayland Rudd, who originally went to work on an abortive Soviet
propaganda film project (which is detailed in Langston Hughes's autobiography, *I Wonder as I Wander*). He later earned true celebrity status
in the Soviet Union, winning wide popularity with Soviet audiences for
roles in such films as "Tom Sawyer," a George Grebner adaptation of
Jules Verne's "Fifteen-Year-Old Captain," and many others. Rudd, no less
than Paul Robeson, consistently made favourable pronouncements about
the Soviet Union. However, in stark contrast to their optimistic assessment of Soviet achievements, the world knows that the 1930's also had a
much darker side in the Soviet Union. I need only mention Stalin's
purges. Moreover, recently available archival materials also show that all

was not well even within the Soviet Union with regard to racial attitudes toward Blacks, and that other Blacks on hand in Russia were reporting observations which directly contradicted optimistic accounts. Dramatic evidence of this is a report on an African and Afro-American student protest against racism in artistic productions and against Soviet practices they were experiencing while resident at the political schools (McClellan). This inconsistency between theory and practice was true not only within Russia, but also within the American Communist Party, as recounted by the American writer Richard Wright in his essay titled "American Hunger" (Wright).

These contradictions confronting black performing artists, writers, and scientists who visited Soviet Russia in the 1920s and 1930s illustrate the depth of their dilemma. The Soviet experiment fell far short of its promises on racial equality; and yet any black Americans showing sympathy for that society were subject to ruin at home, as shown especially by the career of Paul Robeson. However, despite the disappointment of the African American adventurers over Soviet duplicity, there is a sense in which the rapprochement between the United States and the Soviet Union did advance their cause. This foreshadowed a symbiotic relationship between the international Communist movement and the Civil Rights movement in the United States during the Cold War. A case can be made for the proposition that even if the Soviet posture against racism was not genuine, it put positive pressure on the United States to live up to its own ideals in the rivalry for the allegiance of the so-called developing world. Thus the black Americans involved in these contacts with both superpowers, though suffering the fate inherent in such a role, were useful gadflies, reminding both of their unfulfilled promises.

Engaging the Philosophy and Psychology of Wholeness:
Du Bois, Senghor, Césaire, Damas

Further illustrating the point that the search for self-fulfilment and cultural identity in the African Diaspora was characterized by travel abroad, the celebrated *Négritude* movement originated by African and Caribbean intellectuals in the 1930s emerged in Europe, rather than in their homelands. A good place to focus a more in-depth discussion of the fusion of the realms of art, politics, and cultural identity in the African

Diaspora during this era are the contributions of Leopold Senghor, a celebrated poet and eventually the first President of independent Senegal; Aimée Césaire, also a poet and writer, and later a deputy in the French Assembly representing the Communist Party from his native Martinique; and Leon Damas, another fellow student and poet who, originally from French Guyana, had been a schoolmate and friend of Césaire's in Martinique. It was during their university studies in France in the early 1930s that Césaire first articulated the concept *Négritude*, a concept first published in a collection of poems by Damas entitled *Pigments*, and was to be most fully developed by Senghor. W.E.B. Du Bois's articulation at the turn of the century of the peculiar form of alienation experienced by Blacks in America might first have appeared to refer only to the United States with its unique black-white dichotomy in the definition of race and collor (Blight and Gooding-Williams 38). However, examination of the concept of *Négritude* and comparable ideas emergent in the Diaspora in Africa, Europe, and the Americas during the first half of the twentieth century reveals that what Du Bois had posited as "two-ness" was an experience common throughout the African Diaspora. Moreover, what is also evident is that these thinkers who are often portrayed as asserting Black cultural superiority or nationalism were nearly all stressing instead the need for a universality and cultural unity over ethnic or racial particularity. Senghor, Césaire, and Fanon all wanted to invent a new identity encompassing all of humanity. This resonated well with the aspirations of North Americans such as Paul Robeson, who had an extensive career in Western Europe as well as Russia and his native America, was constantly trumpeting universality as a solution, and even had a theory concerning a universal music scale that he hoped to derive from comparison of the broad spectrum of world folk music he performed.

While there was a common desire for a kind of universality in the different regions of the Diaspora, this goal was complicated by the fact that the types of "two-ness" were themselves not identical, due to differences among the colonial powers regarding their attitudes towards those they subjugated. The British, for example, seemed to wish mainly to impose social inferiority, and not encourage assimilation. By contrast, the French appeared to wish to make their colonial subjects "French," as in the public school history primers which read, "...our forefathers the Gauls," but inferior French. They used such concepts as assimilation, integration, and association, but were essentially just bent on indoctrination (Abbot). Senghor recalled reading in the French schools of the history of what he was encouraged to accept as his "ancestors," described as "men tall, robust, with skin white as milk, blue eyes, and long blonde or red hair which they let hang on their shoulders," while in fact he did not even enjoy full French citizenship, because only Africans from certain very limited, designated metropolitan commune areas in the colonies were even given that status. In independent Senegal, Senghor would attempt to replace this sort of education with an African-centered curriculum (Senghor and Sadjii).

Like Du Bois, whose formal education, pursued at Fisk, Harvard, and in Europe had been grounded in Western civilization and culture, these Afro-French intellectuals too drew readily from that influence and made something new. Senghor, for example, found his inspiration to write poetry from reading Maurice Barrès, whose novel *Les déracines* is about provincial children defying the "civilizing" education offered to them by a group of Parisian schoolteachers. He thus felt an affinity for the French common folk experience. He later found himself drawn to the works of Baudelaire, whose mixed-blood West Indian mistress had inspired him to write about contrasting cultures, and to those of Rimbaud. Senghor also was personally acquainted with leftists such as George Pompidou, later President of France, as well as another future statesman, Pierre Mendès France. Prior to his own cultural initiatives, he was also exposed to earlier black consciousness efforts in France, such as the *Revue du Monde noir*, published by the Antillean community of Paris. Senghor also was influenced by the example of fellow countryman and politician Blaise Diagne, whom he met at a young age, and who in his career demonstrated that assimilation and pragmatic collaboration was a workable approach to cope with the European establishment.

Senghor was proud to consider *Négritude* to be both Black and universal, and acknowledged direct inspiration from the Harlem Renaissance. He in particular acknowledged influence from W.E.B. Du Bois's writings all the way back to the beginning of the century, and Langston Hughes's 1926 article in *The Nation,* where he declared that "we younger Negro artists, who create now, intend to express our individual dark-skinned selves without fear or shame." A conscious linking to traditional Western culture can also be seen in Senghor's comparison of *Négritude* to the German concept of *Weltanschauung* in some of his writings. Nevertheless, he did assert that there is a distinctive Negro contribution, a Negro rhythm expressed in all the arts, through presence and absence of parallel structure, accentuation, atonality, asymmetry. Courting controversy, he goes on to explain the emergence of the special qualities of African civilization in environmental terms similar to some of the language used by racists to reach quite opposite conclusions about the consequences of the warmer climate. Césaire noted that he and Senghor read the writings of Joseph-Arthur de Gobineau. While this was mainly in order to refute him, Senghor found that he liked some of de Gobineau's ideas, such as an assertion he made that "Art is black." In America a similar sort of flirtation with incompatible ideologies during that era was Marcus Garvey's bizarre association with the Ku Klux Klan (Lewis 79-81). Jean Paul Sartre in his essay "Black Orpheus" called *Négritude* an anti-racist racism that represented a phase along a dialectical progression moving toward a synthesis of recognition of a common humanity in a race-less society. In his view it was thus intended eventually to self-destruct. Senghor concluded that it makes Africans more sensitive, more open to all around them, more likely to feel before they see, in general more intuitive; thus, the Negro African ontology is not only unitary, it is existential. Senghor also believed that understanding the language and aesthetics of the people is crucial to promoting revolution, which he believed could be fomented more easily through art and poetry than through oratory (Vaillant).

It was Senghor who first turned Césaire's attention toward Africa in a positive way. Césaire later was drawn to the work of the anthropologist Leo Frobenius, who wrote positive views of African cultures in *Histoire de la civilization africaine* (1936). Like Senghor, Césaire also read Langston Hughes, Claude Mc Kay, and other North American writers. Césaire recalled Mc Kay's "Banjo" as the first work he had read dignifying Blacks in literature. Césaire and Senghor joined with Leon Damas to publish for their informal self-educational group a short-lived newspaper called *L'Etudiant noir* (1935-1936). It was this activity that directly fostered the *Négritude* movement. In addition to Césaire and Damas, Senghor was instrumental in bringing together the Africans and West Indians in general, a fact noted later by Claude Mc Kay and Frantz Fanon. There was earlier an attitude among West Indians that Africans were barbarians. The activities of Black North Americans visiting Paris, including publication of *La Revue du Monde noir* in 1931, also had a direct influence on initiation of the *Négritude* movement.

Aimée Césaire brought to the group yet another form of universalism, in that he was a devout Marxist who believed part of the solution was the elimination of capitalism. In his view, a formula where colonization equalled objectification explained how it was always Whites whose perspective defined Blacks as objects, rather than people, and as commodities in a world economic system (Césaire). Thus, even in a concept called *Négritude* there was an underlying recognition of universality apart from collor. If time permitted here, examples of Black intellectuals from other European colonial areas could demonstrate this further, for example, C.L.R. James, the versatile, black writer and socialist from the British realm, with his Hegelian as well as Marxian moorings. His Hegelian bent is shown best in the posthumously published *American Civilization,* that was actually written early in the century. Or looking at the Harlem Renaissance, Alain Locke saw the New Negro movement as providing a better basis for a world of cultural pluralism, not separatism. It is also important to note that the *Négritude* movement represented different emphases during different time periods, beginning as more universalist, later becoming more cultural-nationalistic, and later anti-colonialist. The evolution of the journal *Présence Africaine*, founded in the late 1940s, mirrored the evolutionary phases of *Négritude*. In its pages Africa was at first viewed as the antithesis to Europe, in a universalist framework; but later that continent was seen as being unique and complex in its own right. This trend was reflected in thinking among visual artists as well as writers. A number of writers have noted that the conscious coupling of *Négritude* to the Western classical tradition can be seen not only in Sartre's 1948 essay "Black Orpheus," but also in other crossover artistic works such as some of Romare Beardon's in the 1940s and Ralph Ellison's somewhat Homeric novel *Invisible Man* (1952).

The writings of Frantz Fanon are the most articulate projection of this same tradition of psychological, philosophical and political tradition into the second half of the twentieth century. His favourite formative readings also were Western standards, including Nietzsche, Jaspers, Kierkegaard, Hegel, and later Sartre, Husserl, and Heidegger. His full sense of his identity as black came when he came to realize that he was viewed as a detestable object irrationally hated by seemingly a whole race, and it was all the worse because he realized it was so deeply rooted that it was not even conscious; his inferiority was considered a given. In the West Indies, including Martinique, he saw the French and natives in an all-out effort at being French, with the middle class avoiding speaking Creole even at home - hence his description of native behaviour as donning a white mask (Fanon). This of course also resonates with Du Bois's "two-ness" and Ellison's "invisibility." Yet, what Fanon strove for as well was more a form of universalism, racial equality, rather than ethnic identities. Fanon's analysis would best articulate this dynamic of the colonial world. In his interpretation, the subjugated engage in psychological over-valuation of their native culture to compensate for guilt for having lost it. Thus, racism, a Western weapon, can be used against the West, just as liberalism and nationalism in general were.

Conclusions

This is a study in its very preliminary stages. A number of intriguing additional issues need to be considered before real conclusions may be proposed. For instance, to what extent should "two-ness" be considered as an asset, rather than a liability? To Du Bois's notion that it arms one with special sight, and Senghor's about special feeling, might be added the observations of one Afro-Dutch intellectual, the sociologist R.A.J. van Lier, a Surinamer of African and Jewish descent who came to Holland early in the twentieth century, and whose most famous book is the classic study on Suriname entitled *Frontier Society*. In an interview in the 1980s he reflected:

> I reminisce over my school class...full of Negroes, Chinese, every type was there. I found it delightful. You didn't think about that difference. It was there... I have had the privilege of being born on the edge of groups and civilizations. I proceed upon the assumption that an intellectual is marginal by definition. If he is not he is not an intellectual, for his intellect places him on the edge and outside the group. And I was *born there*—between civilizations. What a privilege! (Vuijsje)

Another interesting question is, why are West Indians so prominent among the leading voices in this quest for identity? And how does the engagement with issues of cultural identity and self-fulfillment in the African Diaspora in the post-colonial world compare with that in the first half of the twentieth century? Also, besides Europe, the other main destination of Black migrants in the second half of the twentieth century was the United States. The engagement over cultural identity in the African Diaspora in the United States makes for very interesting comparison with that in Europe. On the one hand, it too features migration from both the Caribbean and Africa, while on the other, involvement with these issues among the native African Americans there manifests strikingly similar patterns, even though they are not migrants.

The most striking characteristics of the black community in the United States in the period since World War II, and especially the past two decades, are its growing diversity, and its divided nature (Fears). This new composition of African-American society, which is more akin to that of the existing Asian-American and Latino communities, represents a shift away from the more artificially fashioned black-white configuration of American society fostered by the legacy of slavery. In Miami, the West Indian population that now constitutes 48% of the total black community is expected within this decade to outnumber the native-born. One third of New York city's black population is foreign-born; one third of the population of the New England state of Massachusetts, where I live, is foreign-born; that in Washington DC where I also live, has jumped from 1% in 1970 to 8% today. Thus the diversification of the black population mirrors what American society in general is undergoing. Now a brown-skinned man or woman on the street could just as easily be Haitian, Jamaican, Senegalese, or Nigerian as native-born. In Boston the person might be a Cape Verdean; and in Washington Ethiopian, Eritrean, or Somali. Since most of the new populations arrived after the passing of the 1965 Immigration Act, they lack the sense of identity forged earlier by the common experience of slavery, Jim Crow, and the Civil Rights and Black Power movements in the United States. Also, these cultures have clearer knowledge of their ancestral roots and cultural traditions. This leads at times to denigration of each other from both sides: with the West Indians, for example, saying of their black hosts such things as: "they are violent, they don't respect their elders, they have no sense of family, and they don't want to work and they prefer to depend on welfare"; while the black North Americans say of the newcomers that "they're here to take our jobs, they'll work for nothing, they're cliquish, they smell, they eat dogs, and they think they're better than us." There is not even much intermarriage between the groups.

Part of the conflict arises because of the differing definitions of "blackness" and attitudes towards that. There is, of course, the possibility that a given person may prefer not to be lumped into one large category, rather than being described in terms of his or her own ethnic group; but there can be no doubt that there is also stigma attached to "blackness." Otherwise the distinction would not be given such great importance: whereas in the United States one who is not quite white is considered black, in Brazil one who is not quite black is considered white. Among Latinos nearly 48% in the 2000 census self-identified as white, and another 42% listed a category of a race other than black; only 2% were willing to be called black. Nevertheless, those with conspicuous darker complexion are treated as black in American society. This remains consequential, as a survey in 2001 found 37% of blacks having been unfairly stopped by the police because of race or ethnic background, 20% of Hispanics, 11% of Asians, and a mere 4% of Whites. Over 40% of Blacks and Latinos had experienced some type of racial discrimination during the past 10 years (Morin and Cottman). Meanwhile, other studies show a sharp divergence between the views of Blacks and Whites concerning the amount of attention given to racial issues. Some 52% of whites think too much is being made of the racial problems, while 64% of African Americans say too little attention is being given. Forty-one percent of Latinos agree with them, and 33% of Asians. Interestingly, in this survey 31% of Latinos and 28% of Asians thought that just about the right amount is being given it. The same sample showed 71% of whites believing that African Americans have more or about the same opportunities in life as whites, but with only 24% of African Americans agreeing (Morin).

Just as populations within Africa and the Caribbean first moved to local regions more industrially active and with more jobs, the two major regions they moved to abroad with the ending of colonialism, Europe and the United States, are the world's leading industrial areas. The predominance of the nation state as the basic form of social organization in the course of the Industrial Revolution, which also inspired cultural nationalism, now finds its counterpart in the aspiration of migrants for either total integration into a viable host society, or strong consciousness and organization along ethnic lines in order to survive and prosper, in a world that seems driven by competition for basic resources. How all of this might affect the still continuing search for cultural identity within the African Diaspora remains an open question.

Allison Blakely

Works Cited

Abbot, Sarah. "Black and French identities in the Colonial Empire and France: Encounters with French Culture in the lives of Léopold Sédar Senghor, Aimée Césaire and Frantz Fanon" [unpublished Boston University HI 481 research paper, 2002].

Blakely, Allison. 1986. *Russia and the Negro.* Washington, DC: Howard University Press.

Blight, David and Robert Gooding-Williams, eds. 1997. *Souls of Black Folk.* New York: Bedford Books. Originally published 1903.

Césaire, Aimée. 1955. *Discours sur le colonialisme* .Présence Africaine: Paris.

Draper, Theodore. 1960. *American Communism and Soviet Russia.* New York: Octogon Books.

Duberman, Martin. 1988. *Paul Robeson.* New York: Alfred A. Knopf.

Fax, Elton. 1974. *Through Black Eyes: Journey of a Black Artist to East Africa and Russia.* New York: Dodd, Mead.

Fanon, Frantz. 1952. *Peau noire, masques blancs.* Paris: Editions de Seuil.

Fears, Darryl. 2002. "A Diverse – and divided - Black Community: As Foreign-born Population Grows, Nationality Trumps Skin Color." *The Washington Post* 24 February 2002.

Gorky, M.1928. "O muzyke tolstykh (Degenerate Music)." *Pravda* 18 April 1928.

Haywood, Harry. 1978. *Black Bolshevik.* Chicago: Liberator Press.

Huiswood, Otto E. 1930. "World Aspects of the Negro Question." *The Communist* (February 1930): 132-47.

Kornweibel, Theodore. 1975. *No Crystal Stair: Black Life and the Messenger, 1917-1928.* Westport, Conn.: Greenwood Press.

Lewis, David Levering. 2000. *W.E.B. Du Bois: the Fight for Equality and the American Century 1919-1963.* New York: Henry Holt.

McClellan, Woodford. 1993. "Africans and Black Americans in the Comintern Schools, 1925-1934." *International Journal of African Historical Studies* 26 (1993): 371-91.

McKay, Claude. 1981. *Selected Poems of Claude McKay.* New York: Harcourt Brace [originally by Bookman Associates, 1953].

————. 1924. "Soviet Russia and the Negro," *The Crisis,* December 1923, 61-64; January, 1924, 117.

Morin, Richard. 2001. "Misperceptions Cloud Whites' view of Blacks." *The Washington Post* 11 July 2001.

Morin, Richard and Michael H. Cottman. 2001. "Discrimination's Lingering Sting: Minorities Tell of Profiling, Other Bias." *The Washington Post* 22 June 2001.

Oostindie, Gert. "Kondreman in Bakrakondre," in Oostindie and Maduro, *In het land van de overheerser.*

Poston, Ted. "Negroes in New York" Collection, New York City Works Projects Administration Federal Writers Project Records.

Pravda Vostoka, 19 January 1932.

Rampersad, Arnold, ed. 2001. *The Collected Works of Langston Hughes,* vol. 1. Columbia, MO: University of Missouri Press.

Senghor, Léopold, and Abdoulaye Sadji. 1953. *La belle histoire de Leuk-le-Lièvre [Cours élémentaire des écoles d'Afrique Noir]* Illustrated by Marcel Jeanjean. Paris: Classiques Hachette.

Smith, Homer. 1964. *Black Man in Red Russia.* Chicago: Johnson Publishing Company.

Starr, S. Frederick. 1983. *Red & Hot: the Fate of Jazz in the Soviet Union.* New York: Oxford University Press.

Sutton, John to George Washington Carver, July 1, 1932. Carver Archives, Hollis Burke Frissell Library, Tuskegee University.

————. Interview with author 2 February 1978. *Black Dispatch,* 4 June, 1938.

Vaillant, Janet G. 1990. *Black, French, and Africain: A Life of Leeopold Sédar Senghor.* Cambridge, MA: Harvard University Press.

Vuijsje, Herman. 1986. *"Met discriminatie moeten we net zo omgaan als met onze agressiviteit en seksualiteit'* – R.A.J. van Lier, *...over zijn Surinaamse achtergrond en zijn studie..."* NRC *Handelsblad* 23 January 1986, 3.

Wright, Richard. 1944. *American Hunger.* New York: Harper & Row, 1977.

Notes on Border(land)s and Transculturation in the "Damp and Hungry Interstices" of the Americas

This essay examines how T. C. Boyle, Dionne Brand, Leslie Marmon Silko, and James Welch problematise migration and the resultant ethnic and cultural interaction within and across regional and national borders. Taking the border and the borderland—a shifting geographic, psychological, and cultural space—as a point of departure, it theorizes their value as cultural indicators and conceptual tools in connection with the critical paradigm of transculturation—the mediator of the disruptive in-between zone of inter- and intracultural relations. In the process, it explores the following questions: How is it possible to analyze the fractal reality of cultural forms within and across borders? How do we measure the dynamics of (characters dwelling in) in-between-ness and the inherent issue of cultural difference? How do we map the rhizomic flows of people from one point to the next, and the effect of this movement in terms of subjectivity and identity formation?

In *The Tortilla Curtain* (1995), T. C. Boyle foregrounds the shifting geographical and cultural border separating and uniting Mexicans and North Americans in California. By juxtaposing and intersecting the lives of Mexican illegals América and Cándido and Los Angeles liberals Delaney and Kyra, Boyle renders an up-to-date version of the American Dream as a living myth distorted by a self-serving dynamic of othering that affirms Anglo-American identity. América and Cándido's vision of the American Dream, their struggle for work, food, and a place of their own, collide with a mental border determined by Anglo-American monoculturalism, a xenophobic nationalism shot through with ethnoracial and classist prejudice that affirms a racially coded image of Americanism.[1] For Jack Jardine, resident of a newly gated hilltop community, "this society isn't what it was" because it does not control its borders. He does not blame so much the *"legal* immigrants ... with skills, money" and "education" as the illegal ones, the illiterate "peasants" without "resources" and "skills," who have nothing to offer but their "strong backs" (101). For Kyra, a realtor, these illegal immigrants pose a threat to the community by "ruining the schools, gutting property values and freeloading on welfare .... They were like the barbarians outside the gates of Rome, only they were already inside, polluting the creek and crapping in the woods" (311). "Barbarians," however, whose "invasion from the South had been good for business to this point because it had driven the entire white middle-class out of Los Angeles" and into neighbouring areas up the coast (158-59). Unable to continue their flight, the inhabitants of these hilltop communities decide to wall themselves in. Boyle's novel is a telling example of a heightened policing of the border by the dominant culture. In this novel, the border(land) is a war zone where two seemingly incompatible conceptualizations of culture and nationalism grapple with each other: the notion of culture and nation as organic and homogeneous entities based on static, ethnically marked identities and bound to a fixed territory and one language; and the concept of culture and nation as heterogeneous entities characterized by shifting, permeable boundaries between ethnic groups and different cultural codes.

In Boyle's novel the border between Mexico and the United States moves north. Those who make it across the heavily militarized U.S.-Mexico border soon recognize that the chain link fences and steel walls, what Leslie Silko (115-23) has memorably termed "the border patrol

---

[1]   This new form of racial prejudice is discussed by Etienne Balibar. It is a racism that is against the abolition of frontiers since different lifestyles and traditions make for cultural incompatibility (21).

state," multiply north of the border.[2] What Boyle ultimately emphasizes is the contradiction between neoliberal border-free trade and border militarization underlying the economic integration of the North American Free Trade Area. Conceived as an economic space without borders to increase the mobility of capital and goods, NAFTA applies a different regime in terms of labour mobility. In the United States, this regime, as the novel illustrates, is characterized by a double dynamic: an increased border control to keep immigrants and refugees out and a semiofficial tolerance and exploitation of illegal low-wage workers. The neoliberal border-free market economy, as the novel's social-realist passages illustrate, uses the migrants' mobility for its own benefits without allowing them access to the legal and political realm of American society. Deterritorialized, exploited and kept on the move, América and Cándido are denied citizenship by both Mexico and the United States. Within NAFTA, which makes virtually no provisions for the free movement of people across its borders, they are walled in, "pinched like ... bug[s] between two granite rocks, and how long before [they were] squashed?" (278)[3] Read another way, the novel denounces the deterritorialized state of NAFTA labour chasing an illusory American Dream stripped of its moral principle. What grapples with each other in this border zone, then, is a manifest destiny as nostalgic desire for that which time itself has defeated and a manifest necessity (in the Marxian sense) continuously recreating this desire as hopeful future that is yet to be.[4]

---

[2]   This border resembles the division of North and South Korea, which the U.S. government regards as a major hindrance to freedom and democracy. For a detailed analysis of the militarization of the U.S.-Mexico border, see Dunn.

[3]   Boyle's novel, then, illustrates the opposite of border erosion celebrated in a June 11, 2001 special issue of *Time* entitled "Welcome to America" and subtitled "The border is vanishing before our eyes, creating a new world for all of us." It reveals and problematizes the maintenance of borders responsible for what Ralph Ellison, in his seminal speech "Going to the Territory," has pointed out as the gap between North American "principles," the nation's "social structure" and the nation-people's "conduct" as well as the inherent misconception of the nation's "cultural identity" (129, 125).

[4]   While both manifest destiny and manifest necessity clash throughout the novel, they seem to converge in the final passage of the book. Departing from a very asymmetrical relation of power this meeting half way of Anglo destiny and Mexican necessity – symbolized by Cándido's taking hold of Delaney's hand – seems rather problematic since the narrative conveys the message that Anglo culture is unwilling to make that move.

In her short story "Sketches in transit ... going home," Dionne Brand probes the psyche of her characters to lay bare the effects of living in between borders separating and uniting Canada and the Caribbean. Loaded with consumer goods, the very "reason for emigrating in the first place," Caribbean migrant workers at Toronto Airport board a vacation flight back home. Being low-wage, sweat-job immigrants in Toronto who wear masks of rags-to-riches emigrants in their island homeplaces, they are described as being "half here and half there." Pushed out by dismal economic conditions in the Caribbean and forced into a subaltern subject position in Toronto, these migrants are as much pulled by nostalgia and family relations as by the internalized desire to play the master figure in a game in which successful emigration is supposed to mean a change of "class ... station" and colour—the elevation from "nigger" status to "brown-skin status."[5] Nowhere at home, torn between places, they do not only live in an interstitial space but they have internalized its boundaries, that is, their subjectivities and identities refract the in-betweenness of this space. Going 'home' for a couple of weeks per year, these in-between migrants have an ambiguous relation to their home places, a "[l]ove which was not love because it could not centre itself on a shape, a piece of land. Love which only recollected gesture and not movement, event and not time." Toronto, the other end of the migratory axis, means a life characterized by "starvation," exploitation, cultural alienation and fragmentation—a space where the Caribbean migrant feels out of place (Brand, "Sketches" 133, 134, 142, 132). Unable to see and comprehend themselves fully, they stumble in and through a cultural limbo driven by an anxious longing for place and determined by global designs of neoliberal economics.[6] Theirs is a deterritorialization characterized by a constantly deferred reterritorialization, a continuous leaving without arrival: they "had been grown for export, like sugar cane and arrowroot, to go away, to have distaste for staying" (134).

Dionne Brand, like T. C. Boyle, highlights that border crossings are not necessarily acts of liberation. They neither disrupt historically

---

[5]   Here I am drawing on the "push-pull" thesis of migration described by Stephen Castles and Mark J. Miller (19-22).

[6]   Whose rules they accept. Spivak (96) has aptly described the migrants' willingness to play the game of neoliberal economics as their "common interest with dominant global capital."

established hierarchical structures and systems of exploitation nor eliminate borders per se. On the contrary, as her short story tellingly dramatizes, border crossings may lead to a multiplication of borders as mental states. In this story, as well as in her two novels, *In Another Place, Not Here* (1986) and *At the Full and Change of the Moon* (1999), Caribbean diaspora borderization, rooted in the "nonhistory" of slavery (Glissant 62), does not imply borderless borderlands where liberation and healing take place and new visions and possibilities facilitate practices and forms of desubalternization.[7] Here the borderlands, what Brand calls the "damp and hungry interstices" of the world (*At the Full* 167), far from being "the privileged locus of hope for a better world" (Michaelsen and Johnson 3), are characterized by the fragmented experiences of individuals unable to re(-)member the pieces of their shattered identities. As I have illustrated elsewhere, the imposed nomadism of Brand's characters does not mean fluidity without borders but rather an acute awareness of the shifting multiplicity of boundaries (Walter 173-95). Like Boyle, Brand adds to Houston Baker's useful statement that "[f]ixity is a function of power" (*Blues* 202) that the imposed and internalized mobility of the "placeless" is also a function of power. Thus, borders and the spaces in between constitute the terrain upon which relations of power determine the manifold ways border crossers act out their identities-in-process through both a transcultural exchange and clash of values and meanings—a process that transforms and/or multiplies, mines, deconstructs and reconstructs these borders and in-between spaces.

Boyle's novel and Brand's short story are telling narrativizations of inter-American border(land)s that denounce the violence inherent in "the new world order of mobility" and "rootless histories" (Clifford, *Routes* 1). Migrations, seen as a planetary cultural phenomenon, create "contact zones," as Mary Louise Pratt (6-7) has argued, where questions of identity involving negotiations of borders that separate and unite the self and the other are historically structured in containment and resistance. It is my contention that these questions are specifically pertinent to the Americas since different forms of mobility such as slavery, indenture, deportation, migration and immigration constitute key factors in the historical

---

[7]   Both writers, then, deconstruct the valorization of border crossings, mobility, and hybridity celebrated in borderlands theory by Gloria Anzaldúa, Renato Rosaldo, Emily Hicks, José David Saldívar, Juan Flores and George Yúdice, and Sonia Saldívar-Hull, among others.

development of the continent. What links Boyle and Brand in their difference is the insight that in the Americas boundaries between cultures and ethnic groups cannot be seen as fixed and stable limits but, given the historical process of migration and transculturation, as dynamic, fluid and porous ones. Their writings recall questions asked by Henry James in 1907: "Who and what is an alien ... in a country [a continent]... peopled, that is, by migrations at once extremely recent, perfectly traceable and urgently required. ... Which is the American, by these scant measures? Which is not the alien ... and where does one put a finger on the dividing line?" (James 124). By delineating characters unable to cope with their postnational borderized existence—their otherness within as well as "soi-même comme un autre," as Paul Ricoeur put it—both writers, contrary to Walter Mignolo, suggest that "[t]he 'frontier of civilization' in the late nineteenth-century"—the dividing line between civilization and barbarism—has not simply "become the 'borderland' of the end of the twentieth century ... where a new consciousness, a border gnosis, emerges from the repression subjected by the civilizing mission" (Mignolo 299) but rather continues within the borderlands.

It is precisely this multidimensional frontier as dividing line between "civilization" and "barbarism" and its impact on the minds and agency of individuals that Boyle and Brand, among others, try to reveal and deconstruct. In the process, they implicitly revise Frederick Jackson Turner's frontier thesis. For Turner, at the end of the 19th century, the ever-expanding frontier did not enclose space as in Europe but opened it up. It was a "consolidating agent" (15) to the nation-state, a space of freedom where "immigrants were Americanized, liberated and fused into a mixed race ..." (23). Boyle and Brand, however, cast this frontier myth in significantly different light: as a strategy of global empire building based on violent dislocation and dispossession involving both spatial and psychological deracination of place, language, identity, tradition, ethos and world view. While the forms of exploitation and subalternization have changed during the various phases of this empire building, the hierarchically structured relations of power enacted within and through the frontier system continue to pit oppressors against oppressed in the borderlands separating and linking Mexico and the United States as well as the Caribbean and Canada. Rather than realms of amalgamation, these border(land)s are realms of exile in which migrants are neither insiders nor outsiders (and yet both), fluctuating in between intersecting territories and patterns, condemned to an identity-in-process and in search of cultural roots. Whereas in Boyle the encounter between Mexicans and Americans on the border renders intercultural relations as a clash of values and meanings, in Brand the cultural exchange between Canadians and the people of the Caribbean is basically a one-way "deculturation."[8]

Leslie Marmon Silko's *Gardens in the Dunes* (1999) renders a different picture of borders and transculturation. Set in the 1890s, the novel features a protagonist, Indigo, who struggles to reconcile two worlds that are diametrically opposed. Forcefully ripped from her tribe, the Sand Lizard people, by white soldiers, placed in a government school to learn the ways of white America, and rescued by a couple of scientists, Hattie and Edward, Indigo selects and invents from the order of knowledge transmitted to her by both cultures. While she cannot readily control what emanates from the two cultural forces in her life, she does determine what she absorbs into her own, and what she uses it for. In terms of my discussion, it is important to note that Indigo appropriates the materials transmitted to her by the dominant culture—a process that influences (and transforms) not only her own tribal culture but also white culture.[9] During the journey with her adoptive parents from California to Europe and back to the desert of Southwest America, Indigo receives "gifts of packets of seeds and corns" from like-minded white people and takes notes on how to "perform the pollination process for hybrids" (303). Back in her place of birth, the Sand Lizard gardens in the dunes, Indigo plants these seeds and hybridizes flowers. This transcultural move nourishes her kin and, in view of the fact that she uses the flowers as "peace offering" to their Christian neighbours (439, 475-76), builds cross-cultural bridges. Indigo's use of botanical knowledge should be seen as a transcultural procedure since it is a two-way, multi-level cultural inter-

---

[8] Ortiz defines transculturation as follows: "I am of the opinion that the word *transculturation* better expresses the different phases of the process of transition from one culture to another because this does not consist merely in acquiring another culture, which is what the English word *acculturation* really implies, but the process also necessarily involves the loss or uprooting of a previous culture, which could be defined as a *deculturation*. In addition it carries the idea of the consequent creation of new cultural phenomena, which could be called *neoculturation*." Fernando Ortiz, *Cuban Counterpoint*, 102-03.

[9] Note, for example, Hattie's development throughout the narrative.

change based on borrowings, displacements and recreations. Here, hybridity in a transcultural process does not signify a break with but rather a revision of traditional practices. In accord with Betonie's explanation in *Ceremony* that ceremonies have to change if they are to be effectively used in the present (126), Indigo's consciousness and identity change while yet remaining the same. In short, Indigo's identity, similar to many of Vizenor's characters, is both based on *tribal* membership and committed to a *transtribal / transnational* community of people. Indigo, then, actively redraws borders in the interethnic contact zone of North America. These borders, unlike those in Linda Hogan's *Power*, are fluid, porous, and inclusive. Whereas Hogan categorizes earth defenders as Indian and earth destroyers as white people, Silko, as Hattie's example demonstrates, suggests that white people are capable of learning. In other words, to make reference to the most important historical and cultural event in *Gardens*, the Ghost Dance Silko envisions is not for Indians only but calls both Native and non-Native people to join together in the struggle for justice and peaceful coexistence.[10]

Whereas Indigo goes home in order to construct her identity, Charging Elk, in James Welch's *The Heartsong of Charging Elk* (2000), continues to be Lakota far away from the Black Hills of South Dakota. The novel tells the story of an Oglala Sioux who witnesses his people's annihilation of Custer's Seventh Cavalry at Little Big Horn and their change to reservation life; as a young man, he joins Buffalo Bill's Wild West Show, travelling all over Europe. Left behind after an accident in Marseille, Charging Elk is involved in a series of events, including a murder, that changes his life and fosters his decision to stay and live in France. Here Welch describes an identity shaped through a transcultural process. Plagued by the shock of cultural distance from tribal life—initiated by the colonial imposition of reservation life in the United States and aggravated by racial ostracism in France—and driven by the need to survive, Charging Elk's outward appearance changes as he gradually grows into a French working-class life. This does not mean, however, that he stops being Lakota. In fact, he does survive the most difficult situations by drawing strength from his Lakota identity. Furthermore, his

---

[10] According to Krupat's categorization (109-15), Indigo is a "cosmopolitan" character. I would add that Indigo's cosmopolitanism is characterized by the process of transculturation.

irrevocable Lakota ties are stressed through his dreams. Thus, not living in the old way as he had vowed to do during a Sun Dance ceremony, Charging Elk translates his original identity into a transcultural one, a different identity bearing both original and new characteristics. That his Lakota roots have not been cut but are on the move in a transcultural process is confirmed by a Lakota near the end of the novel: " 'I can see you are still one of us, yet you are different. ... You are not a stranger. You are Lakota wherever you might go. You are one of us always' " (431, 435-36).

While this transcultural process is rooted in colonialism, it does not reconcile opposites in synthesis. In both Silko and Welch, transculturation functions as a liminal cultural contact zone, not without marks of violence and loss, but where the subaltern may recuperate the necessary space to actively shape his/her subject position and identity without sublating original identities. Against Alberto Moreiras (234), who regards the reconciliatory synthesis underlying transcultural processes as a complicit ideological practice of Western metaphysics since it sublates "cultural heterogeneity," I want to argue that both *Gardens* and *Heartsong* demonstrate that the process of transculturation is not exclusively characterized by synthesis, but also involves rupture and symbiosis, that is, exchanging and overlapping cultural interactions that do not issue in a synthetic sublation of cultural differences, yet which prevent them from being outside of one another. Although Indigo and Charging Elk change through intercultural contact, they are confirmed in their Indian identity-in-process. Thus, both Silko and Welch, against Turner's frontier thesis of ethnic amalgamation—the formation of new hybrid identities through acculturation—affirm transcultural *agency* in the process of identity re-construction. Moving within and across the in-between minefields of a dividing cultural and racial borderline, their characters enact what Houston Baker (*Modernism* 49) has termed "the *deformation of mastery*" based on a transcultural process in which neoculturation as a result of the interplay between synthesis and symbiosis is forever deferred in the making. In other words, the *trans* in this type of transculturation signifies the *trans* of the transitory performative process of transtribal identity formation.

The above-mentioned writers illustrate in different and yet related ways the arbitrariness, what Said calls the "fictional reality" of bound-aries. If boundaries are *fixed* in the mind by "social, ethnic and cultural" (54) anticipations, then they *move* according to changing epistemes and relations of power. In terms of cultural interaction, borders are both lines and spaces where contradictory tendencies supplement each other. As dividing lines of spatiotemporal and cultural differentiation, borders distance the inner from the outer of the other, and as shared spaces in between they link both to each other. Furthermore, they establish hierarchies not only between the inside and the outside, but also within the inside. They are created to contain cultural and ethno racial difference and reproduced to subvert this control. Borders and borderlands, then, are the terrain where identities are acted out in the tension-laden and contradictory interplay of cultural stasis (definitions as other) and cultural transgression (definitions as self). Thus, borders connote cultural stasis by channelling cultural identity into nationally identified epistemes (orders of knowledge) whereas the transgression of these borders reveals interstitial spaces (borderlands) mediating cultural differences. Borders and borderlands thus are actual material entities and symbols that constitute sites of both repressive (normalizing) state power and trans-gressive transnational functions and practices.

I contend that this double-voiced border discourse involves a complex transcultural exchange. In other words, this double nature of the border, as is suggested in the analysed texts, corresponds to a double nature of the transcultural contact zone. The hybrid vibrations of intercultural contact in this zone involve both fusion and separation, coalescence and antagonism. In the interstices between domination and resistance, continuity and rupture, the disjunctive in-between space becomes a border zone of conflictive exchanges characterized by "pro-cesses of appropriation, compromise, subversion, masking, invention, and revival" (Clifford, *Predicament* 338). Thus, transculturation should be understood as a multivalent mode and paradigm encompassing an uneasy dialogue between synthesis and symbiosis, continuity and rupture, coherence and fragmentation, utopia and dystopia, consensus and incommensurability, deconstruction and reconstruction. A dialogue, that is, between hegemonic and counter hegemonic forces, practices, gestures, acts, and strategies. As such, it is a critical paradigm enabling us to trace the ways transmission occurs within and between different cultures, regions, nations, ethnic groups and communities, and languages, parti-cularly those in unequal relations of power rooted and routed in slavery, (neo)colonialism, migration, and/or diasporization. Furthermore, and perhaps most important, as such a negotiator of the disruptive in-between zone of inter- and intracultural disjunctures and conjunctures—the place where diverse histories, customs, values, beliefs, and cognitive systems are contested and interwoven without their different representations being dissolved into each other—transculturation accounts for the local and global production and interplay of difference and sameness.

Both difference and sameness are inevitably linked to the politics of domination, subalternization, and resistance. Since identity is not an inherent state of being or condition but rather a meaning effect produced by an intricately interwoven relationship between symbolic representation and specific political, economic, and sociocultural policies, and furthermore, since identity is always posited in a differential relation with another, the desubalternization of subaltern identity, for instance, in order to materialize and begin its counter agency, implies a critical appropriation of the dominant discourse. Only an understanding of the negative image of subalternity facilitates the re-creation of an alter-image. If the subaltern cannot be thought without the dominant subject, both implicated in a hegemonic structure based on diverse forms of sociocultural inequality, and if the politics of subalternization and desubalternization are implicated in transcultural processes of appropriation and reappropriation, I would venture that it does not make much sense to pose the study of subalternity as an alternative model of cultural interpretation to transculturation, as is suggested by Moreiras. Transculturation, seen as a multivalent mode and paradigm, maps the (in)communicability inherent in the subaltern/dominant split in the in-between zone. Consequently, we should relate questions of subalternity and transculturation so as to map the dynamic forces that produce, limit, prolong, and transform dissimilar identity positions in specific inter- and intracultural contact zones.

Borders and borderlands. Connection and division. Transculturation and hybridity. Synthesis and symbiosis. Home places and homeless spaces. Location, dislocation and relocation. Being deeply embedded in the network of power and knowledge and the hierarchical structures of class, sexuality, gender, race, ethnicity, and collor, borders and the spaces in between refer to the construction of difference. As a place/metaphor of crossing and cross-cultural contact they serve as a useful point of departure for the analysis of both the stratifications within and between ethnic groups or nations and the interstitial spaces and places between the past and the present, (pre)modernity and postmodernity, colonialism and neo/postcolonialism, orality and writing. In other words, the critical view from the border(land)s allows us to map the structures, forces and practices of (trans)national/ethnic homogenization and heterogenization, subalternization and desubalternization, that is to say, the complex transcultural processes that mark intercultural relations and transnational identities in between the local and the global. Since border crossers, located on the interlocking hyphen between cultures, always translate and thereby mediate different cultural codes, they could be seen as transcultural mediators of the tension-laden bonds holding cultural differences in relationship. The issue of the border and the borderland (the stories, myths and ideologies created within and between them) is always a question of alterity—the 'I' crosscut by the other(s). If we are in a transnational moment when time and space are "out of joint" (Derrida 83), when culture is seen as a hybrid matrix-in-process[11] with subjects involved in continuous re-naming and re(-)membering and characterized by what Boyce Davies calls "migratory subjectivity"—a subjectivity "which turns on migration, mobility, movement, departure, return, re-departure ... and transformation" (36, 47)—then borders, borderlands, and transculturation are useful conceptual tools and critical paradigms to examine hybrid identities within and across national boundaries. In light of the envisioned Free Trade Area of the Americas, they are indispensable indicators of cultural, linguistic, ethnic, political and economic encounters.

Roland Walter

---

11   I am indebted to Houston Baker's delineation of the matrix as "a womb, a network ... a point of ceaseless input and output, a web of intersecting, crisscrossing impulses always in productive transit" (*Blues* 3).

Works Cited

Anzaldúa, Gloria. 1987. *Borderlands/La Frontera: The New Mestiza.* San Francisco: Spinsters/Aunt Lute.

Baker, Houston A., Jr. 1987. *Blues, Ideology, and Afro-American Literature.* Chicago: The University of Chicago Press.

—————. 1987. *Modernism and the Harlem Renaissance.* Chicago: The University of Chicago Press.

Balibar, Etienne. 1991. "Is There a 'Neo-Racism'?" *Race, Nation, Class: Ambiguous Identities.* Etienne Balibar and Immanuel Wallerstein. London: Verso, 17-28.

Bhabha, Homi. 1994. *The Location of Culture.* London: Routledge.

Boyce Davies, Carole. 1994. *Black Women, Writing and Identity.* New York: Routledge.

Boyle, T. Coraghessan. 1996. *The Tortilla Curtain.* New York: Penguin Books.

Brand, Dionne. 1989. *Sans Souci and Other Stories.* Ithaca: Firebrand Books.

—————. 1996. *In Another Place, Not Here.* New York: Grove Press.

—————. 1999. *At the Full and Change of the Moon.* New York: Groove Press.

Castles, Stephen, and Mark J. Miller. 1993. *The Age of Migration: International Population Movements in the Modern World.* London: Macmillan.

Churchill, Ward. 1992. "The Earth is Our Mother: Struggles for American Indian Land and Liberation in the Contemporary United States." *The State of Native America: Genocide, Colonization, and Resistance.* Ed. M. Annette Jaimes. Boston: South End Press,139-188.

Clifford, James. 1988. *The Predicament of Culture: Twentieth Century Ethnography, Literature, and Art.* Cambridge: University Press.

—————. 1997. *Routes: Travel and Translation in the Late Twentieth Century.* Cambridge: Harvard University Press.

Derrida, Jacques. 1994. *Spectres of Marx: The State of Debt, the Work of Mourning and the New International.* Trans. Peggy Kamuf. New York: Routledge.

Dunn, Timothy. 1996. *The Militarization of the U.S.-Mexico Border, 1978-1992.* Austin: CMAS Books.

Ellison, Ralph. 1995. *Going to the Territory.* New York: Vintage Books.

Flores, Juan, and George Yúdice. 1990. "Living Borders/Buscando America: Languages of Latino Self-Formation." *Social Text* 24 (1990): 57-84.

Glissant, Edouard. 1992. *Caribbean Discourse.* Trans. J. Michael Dash. Charlottesville: University Press of Virginia.

Hicks, D. Emily. 1991. *Border Writing.* Minneapolis: University of Minnesota Press.

Hogan, Linda. 1998. *Power.* New York: Norton.

James, Henry. 1968. *The American Scene.* Bloomington: Indiana University Press.

Krupat, Arnold. 2001. *Red Matters: Native American Studies.* Philadelphia: University of Pennsylvania Press.

Michaelsen, Scott and David E. Johnson. 1997. "Border Secrets: An Introduction." *Border Theory: the Limits of Cultural Politics.* Eds. Scott Michaelsen and David E. Johnson. Minneapolis: University of Minnesota Press, 1-39.

Mignolo, Walter D. 2000. *Local Histories/Global Designs: Coloniality, Subaltern Knowledges, and Border Thinking.* Princeton: Princeton University Press.

Moreiras, Alberto. 2001. *A exaustão da diferença: A política dos estudos culturais latino-americanos.* Trans. Eliana Lourenço de Lima Reis and Gláucia Renate Gonçalves. Belo Horizonte: Editora UFMG.

Ortiz, Fernando. 1947. *Cuban Counterpoint: Tobacco and Sugar.* Trans. Harriet de Onis. New York: Alfred A. Knopf.

Pratt, Mary Louise. 1992. *Imperial Eyes: Travel Writing and Transculturation.* London: Routledge.

Ricoeur, Paul. 1990. *Soi-même comme un autre.* Paris: Seuil.

Rosaldo, Renato. 1993. *Culture and Truth. The Remaking of Social Analysis.* Boston: Beacon Press.

Said, Edward. 1979. *Orientalism.* New York: Vintage.

Saldívar, José David. 1997. *Border Matters. Remapping American Cultural Studies.* Berkeley: University of California Press.

Saldívar-Hull, Sonia. 2000. *Feminism on the Border: Chicana Gender Politics and Literature.* Berkeley: University of California Press.

Silko, Leslie Marmon. 1986. *Ceremony.* New York: Penguin.

——. 1997. *Yellow Woman and a Beauty of the Spirit.* New York: Touchstone.

——. 2000. *Gardens in the Dunes.* New York: Scribner.

Spivak, Gayatri Ch. 1995. "In the New World Order: A Speech." *Marxism in the Postmodern Age: Confronting the New World Order.* Eds. Antonio Callari, Stephen Cullenberg and Carole Biewener. New York: The Guilford Press, 89-97.

Time Special Issue, "Welcome to America" (June 11, 2001).

Turner, Frederick J. 1956. *The Significance of the Frontier in American History.* Ithaca: Cornell UP.

Walter, Roland. 2003. *Narrative Identities: (Inter)Cultural In-Betweenness in the Americas.* Frankfurt/New York: Peter Lang.

Welch, James. 2000. *The Heartsong of Charging Elk.* New York: Doubleday.

Antropofagismo and the "Cannibal Logic" of
Hemispheric American Studies

As we embark on American studies from a hemispheric perspective, we should be aware of a few potential roadblocks. First, there is nothing exceptional about any single nation or community in the Americas, certainly nothing that would warrant exclusion from a hemispheric purview. Yet, and this is my second caveat, hemispheric Americanism does not necessarily have to be an *inclusionary* practice—by which I mean to say that it should not be thought of as a means of achieving integration between communities, nations, states, peoples, etc., on a hemispheric level. This integrationist approach may be politically favorable to the majority of scholars working in the humanities, above all in the United States, where ethical aspirations seem directed to a utopic realm of happy, seamless multiculturalism. However, there can be little doubt that hemispheric Americanism has only become a possibility in the humanities because of the passage of NAFTA, and soon the Free Trade Agreement of the Americas (FTAA). Despite humanists' protests of the capitalist machine, it is this very capitalist machine which seems to have *provoked*, and which will soon *promote* (through direct monetary contribution), the long-awaited advent of a viable inter-American studies. Whatever one's opinion of Corporate Americanism (my own are none too favorable), we must remember that economic and political integration of the Americas does not imply conceptual integration, or intellectual integration, especially along the lines favored in that nation with the most concentrated academic capital.

My third and final caveat is that hemispheric Americanism is *not* a comparative practice, despite our immediate assumptions. Perhaps *any* American study is a comparative study even if one treats only a single nation or city or community. But beyond this obvious fact, hemispheric Americanism is a *theoretical* problem that touches on any experience in the Americas; that touches on the study of cultural production, economic production, politics, public policy, marketing, etc.; and that may or may not mandate comparative research on "primary" texts. The question is not whether we can compare George Washington to Simón Bolívar; if you really need to know the answer, I can tell you right now: *we can*. The more interesting question is whether, at some point in near future, we will really need another Deleuzian reading of the rhizomatic mechanism binding the Washington-machine to the Bolívar-machine. Or whether we will need another Bhabha-esque inquiry into how Washington is almost the same as Bolívar, but not quite. Or whether, following Judith Butler, Bolívar merely reiterates the prohibition imposed by Washington and at the same time works, indeed, exploits that prohibition for the possibilities of its repetition and subversion. If you still do not get what I'm saying here, the question is not, "Is it comparable?" The question is, "What's your approach?" And that is the question for two reasons: A) Because hemispheric Americanism cannot merely be fed into the loop of whatever theoretical horizon happens to be in vogue in a particular place; hemispheric Americanism must already *be* a theoretical horizon, such that we would find it counter-productive to limit ourselves only to, say, Deleuze, or any of the French post-Structuralists. And B) Because I would make the fantastic proposition to Americanists that we divine our theories from the problems and facts peculiar to the Americas, or at least to have some dynamic relation between theory and practice. Metaphorically speaking, it makes more sense to feed Deleuze into the loop of the Americas, rather than the other way on.

A broad-based theory of Americanism would have to allow us to do several things, given the sociological peculiarites of the region and its historical relation to the "other" hemisphere. First, our theory must offer us a means to confront the social-migratory forces at play in the Americas, including the encounter or clashes between these forces, and also the distinct configurations of migratory forces in different parts of the hemisphere.[1] The definitive "fact" of any American experience is the encounter between migrant groups—whether a violent encounter, a forced encounter, or a disencounter—and the inevitable mixing of cultural practices between those groups. Second, because migration implies a movement from a *here* to a *there*, or as it were from a *there* to a *here*, our theory would have to allow for a creative engagement with history, its relations to the movement of peoples over time and space, *and therefore*, the constant *re-configuration* of history given fluctuating patterns of migration. In other words, we need always to find what is contemporary or "NEW" about the "New World," specifically in relation to how that contemporaneity has been formulated historically. Last, given that social groups migrate between *here* and *there*, our theory would have to be able to distinguish those two places—to distinguish "American" as a distinct quantity—while still understanding the ways that Americans continue to participate in the cultures they define as their "origin." For example, we could look to the ways Brazil is distinguishable from its former colonizers—the Dutch—while still understanding the ways in which (certain) Brazilians continue to participate in the Europomorphic, or should I say, "Occidental," world. Essentially, we are looking to unhinge the duality between original and copy, between *here* and *there*, without undoing this duality: to find what is *originally* American by uncovering the history of its *translations* from prior sets of originals.

Now this theory, according to the parameters I've just listed, would obviously have to perform some fairly complicated tasks. Just as we find it difficult to speak of "America" except in terms of a plural "Americas," we may find it increasingly difficult to speak of anything but "theories" (in the plural), or a theory of theories. Here I am *not* suggesting that Americanists cease to explore post-Structuralism, or neo-Liberalism, or any particular theoretical perspective they choose; in fact, I'm urging you to choose whatever perspective you wish, only with the understanding that this perspective will necessarily become fragmented and re-defined given the particularities of American experiences. Or should I say, your theory will necessarily become *masticated* by America, for the "theory of

---

[1]   By „forces" I mean to imply both a sense of migratory „groups" and the historical, economic, and political causes for their migration.

theories" that I'm outlining may be found in Brazilian *Antropofagismo*. In my current research, I am exploring *Antropofagismo* (or Anthropophagism, Cannibalism) not at it was originally formulated as a *modernista* aesthetic movment in the 1920s and 30s, but rather as it has developed over the past 70 years as a model for Brazilian nationalism, in order to foster its potential as a hemispheric theory. We must bear in mind that concepts, metaphors, and theories are never static, but develop in both scope and specificity in their usage over time.[2] Nevertheless, I'd like to return to the roots of Cannibalism, in the famous opening lines to Oswald de Andrade's original "Manifesto Antropófago" ["Cannibal Manifesto"] of 1928:

> Só o antropofagismo nos une. Socialmente. Economicamente. Filosoficamente. Única lei do mundo. Expressão mascarada de todos os individualismos, de todos coletivismos. De todas religiões. De todos os tratados de paz.
> Tupi or not tupi, that is the question.[3]

> [Cannibalism alone unites us. Socially. Economically. Philosophically. Singular law of the world. Masked expression of all individualism, of all collectivism. Of all religions. Of all peace treaties.
> Tupi or not tupi that is the question.]

With these words, Oswald was attempting to re-valorize the Tupi-Guarani[4] "savage" as a national paradigm for *modern* Brazilian civilization. That is, Oswald sought to reverse the flow of European dominance over the Americas, placing emphasis on that subject conquered by the European, that subject through which the very notion of a European "civilization" had been based: not the "noble savage" upon which Romantic philosophers would determine the "universal" rights of man, but rather the "bad savage." Moreover, it would seem that this promotion of the cannibal gives way to a potent image-metaphor for the sociology of

---

[2]   *Antropofagismo*, that is, has been studies and employed by a great many people over time, to a great many ends, such that we are now far from its "original" significance.

[3]   Oswald de Andrade. „Manifesto Antropófago." *A Utopia Antropofágica*. São Paulo: Editora Globo, 1990. 47. My translation.

[4]   Tupi-Guarani being the indigenous culture to the region now known as Brazil.

migration; as the cannibal, this radical "other," himself ingests others, the cannibal is also ingesting other cultures, masticating their practices, norms, and forms so that the ingested culture is still recognizable, but thoroughly *trans*formed. While Oswald here seems to be promoting national unity (cannibalism alone *unites* the nation, cannibalism as that which *unifies* an "us"), this unity is already impossibly differential from the start: Brazilian civilization, that is, is henceforth to be unified through that activity that is by definition barbaric and uncivilized—anti-civilized. By doing so, Oswald may have arrived (*avant la lettre*) at an un-deconstructible space for the nation, since the deconstruction of the Brazilian nation has *already* been encoded into its own construction.

With the final lines of the passage, then, we will discover *in nuce* everything I have been saying so far: "Tupi or not tupi that is the question." For Brazilians or Brazilianists, this line has been so often quoted and discussed that it must by now seems trite. Nonetheless it is quite effective, and its effectivity stems primarily from its migration between different linguistic codes. Because the line is surrounded by Portuguese in a text we already know to be Brazilian prior to reading it, the English seems oddly Lusophone even though there really isn't any Portuguese in it. Partly this is because we have a proper-name ("Tupi" in the Latinized spelling of both Portuguese and English) that we associate with the geographic space now occupied by Brazil. Yet what is more, we already recognize an *original* text from Shakespeare lurking rather transparently below the surface of "Tupi or not tupi"; the impact of the line stems from the fact that we already know Shakespeare himself had no idea of the chance phonetic proximity of "to be" and "Tupi," nor would he have had any idea that "Tupi" could be held as a metonymic marker for a nation Shakespeare, living as hie did in Shakespearean England, could not have imagined existing. In other words, the line not only migrates between *here* and *there*, but also between *now* and *then*, between twentieth-century Brazil and sixteenth-century England. Bear in mind that these spatial and temporal dualities remain in full-effect, even as the line ineluctably con-fuses them. Let me phrase this simultaneous maintenance and collapse of dualities another way: semantically, the line migrates between the original written in Shakespeare's English, and an original written in Oswald's English—a non-native speaker speaking through the foreign words of a long-dead native speaker. As you can see by my own diction, it becomes difficult to discern exactly who is the native speaker in this line. The native speaker may be Shakespeare, even though the line plays with, and thus veers into, the native Portuguese of Oswald. And let us not by any means discount the only "native" present in the line, the Tupi—strangely present yet absent (note the total lack of actual Tupi-Guarani language)—whose absence allows us to remember that both Shakespeare and Oswald speak languages that are "foreign" to the Americas. By having the Tupi become the model for the Brazilian, Oswald operates in the binary logic of "us *versus* them," but only in order to show that "us *is* them."

In this sense, Oswald attempts to write a NEW history of Brazilian identity, through the re-valorization of the cannibal. In essence, Oswald has uncovered a secret history of cannibalism just under the surface of the Brazilian national psyche – and he's uncovered this history simply by inventing it. In Oswald's model, we might might think of *brasilianidade* as a poignant "pseudo-history" or "pseudo-etymology," as history remains a real, shaping force, even though this history is nothing less than a contemporary invention. Just briefly, it must be noted that as *Antropofagismo* has been taken up by subsequent artists and critics, such as the Noigandres group of concrete poets, it has sparked the re-discovery of "forgotten" figures of the tradition along such "pseudo-historical" lines: Oswald himself in large part owes his continued survival to Haroldo de Campos' efforts in the 1950s to resuscitate him as amjor figure of *modernismo*; and we have the exemplary case of the nineteenth-century poet, Sousândrade, forgotten for a century until he became central to the work of Augusto de Campos. In these cases, the *concretistas* were mining a tradition for any prior voice that might have justified the arrival of *concretismo* itself as a national aesthetic. As with the "Manifesto Antropófago," what has been produced is not properly *historicization*, although nor is it that *dehistoricization* follows from the lack of proper historicity. If we need a motto, let us just say, "Re-historicize everything!"

Now we have only so far been outlining *Antropofagismo* as a theory of Brazilianism, but my purported intent all along has been to outline *hemispheric* Americanism, not just one of its particular facets. Clearly I intend to broaden Cannibalism beyond the borders of Brazil. And so, if I am correct that Cannibalism provides us the "logic" of all Americanism (and not just its Brazilian side), it stands to reason that we should be able to recover (i.e., to *invent*) a secret history of cannibalism lurking behind myriad cultural manifestations of non-Brazilian American cultures. And here I do not mean that we should limit ourselves to *actual* practices of cannibalism such as the Donner Party, but rather that we locate (again, *invent*) certain subconscious, social-psychic cannibalistic drives underpinning the very existence of culture. Such work would obviously demand much more time and space then we have available here; but what we do have time for is a sort of super-rapid, machine-gun excursion through United States culture, just to spark our minds.

Our first example arrives to us from a text that has not already generated too many interpretations and revisions; perhaps you have heard of it: Herman Melville's *Moby Dick*. One almost hates to add yet another allegorical reading to the seemingly interminable body of allegorical readings of this allegory of allegories, until one comes across one of Ishmael's first descriptions of Queequeg:

> Whether it was, too, that his head being shave, his forehead was drawn out in freer and brighter relief, and looked more expansive than it otherwise would, this I will not venture to decide; but certain it was his head was phrenologically an excellent one. It may seem ridiculous, but it reminded me of George Washington's head, as seen in the popular busts of him. It had the same long regularly graded retreating slope from above the brows, which were likewise very projecting, like two long promontories thickly wooded on top. Queequeg was George Washington cannibalistically developed.[5]

I scarcely think I have to explain my selection of this quotation. Quite clearly, at a foundational moment, in a foundational text, of U.S.-American literature, we find this binding-by-resemblance of the cannibal to the Founding Father of the nation. On the surface, it seems that Queequeg may actually be more "advanced" or "developed" than Melville's audience might have assumed. Yet such questions of relative cultural "development" or "advancement" should not really merit our attention, especially since Ishmael (or Melville) never specifies from which culture, exactly, Queequeg has come. What is in fact interesting, however, is that the Founding Father is re-founded as a cannibal; it is *George Washington* that Mellville re-uncovers as nearly "pre-human," with his "regularly

---

[5]   Herman Melville. *Moby Dick*.
Culled from an online edition of the text: www.princton.edu/~batke/moby/moby_010.html.

graded retreating slope" in the brows. As a result, we don't really get an image of Queequeg, so much as we are left with a portrait of George Washington, corresponding precisely to the phrenological traits assigned to "savages." This is not to say that "savage" or "pre-human" are verifiable categories, or particularly useful. But within the context of Melville's presentation, we nonetheless find that the civilizing father of the nation *is* uncivilizing, as uncivilizing as the highly civilized language, based on faulty pseudo-science, Melville uses to represent him.

This con-fusion of civilized/uncivilized is paralleled in another aesthetic creation: "You're the Top!" by Cole Porter, a song that was first published in 1934 for Porter's Broadway musical, *Anything Goes*, later peaking at #4 on the Hit Parade as the A-side to a record with "I Get a Kick Out of You" on the flip-side. Now if we had time (or technology), we would now hear the original cast-recording performance with Ethel Merman and William Graxton, or perhaps show the original film performance with Merman and Bing Crosby, or even hear the famous Ella Fitzgerald rendition from her recordings of the Cole Porter song book in the 1950s (widely considered the standard). I'll leave you to search out these versions, or at least to track down Porter's lyrics.[6] Given present constraints, I'll merely provide a few short examples to start; the second verse:

> You're the top! You're the Colosseum!
> You're the top! You're the Louvre Museum!
> You're a melody from a symphony by Strauss,
> You're a Bendel bonnet, a Shakespeare sonnet,
> You're Mickey Mouse.
> You're the Nile, You're the Tow'r of Pisa,
> You're the smile on the Mona Lisa.
> I'm a worthless check, a total wreck, a flop,
> But if, Baby, I'm the bottom, You're the top!

And the sixth verse:

> You're the top! You're an Arrow collar.
> You're the top! You're a Coolidge dollar.
> You're the nimble tread of the feet of Fred Astaire,

---

[6]   The most readily available version of those cited is that of Ella Fitzgerald, in "Ella Fitzgerald Sings the Cole Porter Song Book" (Verve 314537 257-2), 1997 [originally released 1956]. All lyrics cited in the present essay were found on a single website of Porter's lyrics (of which there are many): www.thepeaches.com/music/composers/cole/YoureTheTop.html.

You're an O'Neill drama, You're Whistler's mama,
You're Camembert.
You're a rose, You're Inferno's Dante,
You're the nose, of the great Durante.
I'm just in the way, as the French would say, "De trop,"
But if, Baby, I'm the bottom, You're the top!

These verses should be sufficient evidence of how Porter effectively "chews" through citations to various cultural bodies. That is, Porter's lyrics are really a litany, or better a *catalogue* or *anthology*, of references to "high" European culture (at various points, Strauss, Shakespeare, the Tower of Pisa, Mona Lisa) juxtaposed to references to "popular" U.S. culture (e.g., Mickey Mouse, Jimmy Durante, Arrow shirts, and later Waldorf salad, Pepsodent, Ovaltine.)

Such juxtapositions of "high" and "low" culture are acts of gleeful barbarity—in the sense of "savage wit," "¡Qué bárbaro!" or "Que barbaridade!" And this barbarity stems from the subtle contradictions elicited by the performance. On one hand, "You're the Top!" accomplishes a "flattening" of high and low culture.[7] Essentially, the song catalogues *superlative* examples of culture in ways that are nonetheless "value-neutral." For example, "You're a melody from a symphony by Strauss, / You're a Bendel bonnet, a Shakespeare sonnet, / You're Mickey Mouse." Or in verse 8, "You're a Boticelli, You're Keats, You're Shelley, / You're Ovaltine." To hammer home the point, by rhyming "Strauss" and "Mickey Mouse," "Fred Astaire" and "Camembert," Porter effectively synthesizes or equalizes in some sense their relative cultural values, solidifying all as "great." Yet there's also a barbarous "flip-side" to this endeavour. The flattening of Richard Strauss and Mickey Mouse also represents a radical *deformation* of Strauss. Indeed, as the song continues, the references to "high" culture become stranger and stranger. Whistler's "Portrait of the Painter's Mother" becomes "Whistler's mama"; Dante's *Inferno* is re-inscribed as "Inferno's Dante," and this only so that it will rhyme with "the nose of the great Durante." By the end of the song, language itself is deformed: "divine" is sung as "diveen" so as to rhyme with "Ovaltine"; in the final verse, we find an approximation of a various New York City accents,

---

[7] If we are good post-modern critics (and let me assure you we are NOT), this flattening is somewhat old hat, yet I persist.

"You're my thoist, You're a Drumstick Lipstick, / You're da foist in da Irish svipstick." That is to say, we have in this *masterful* song some very *bad* spelling, *bad* usage of European language and writing-systems—so as to seem *colloquial*. In reality, the flattening of high and low does not flatten, but rather exacerbates the gap between high and low, American and European. The humour of Porter's lyrics lies precisely in the fact that we *know* Boticelli and Ovaltine do not carry equal cultural and historical value even though the song implies that they do. The song rigorously maintains value-differences between its references, even as it insists on equalizing them.

This "contradiction," by the way, is mapped onto scales of socioeconomic class, and to understand this aspect we must return to the original context of *Anything Goes*. Now there are various story-lines to the musical depending upon which version or staging you see, but in most of the versions, Reno Sweeney (originally played by Ethel Merman) is a former evangelist turned nightclub performer who has secret cush on up-and-coming Wall Street executive, Billy Crocker (originally played by William Graxton). In some versions, Billy follows Reno onto a cruise ship to say goodbye to her, stays too long on board as the ship sets sail, and unwittingly stows away; in most others, Reno follows Billy onto the ship and impetuously decides to stay there without paying fare. Either way, as Reno and Billy begin to sing "You're the Top!" as a duet, one of the two is a destitute stow-away stealing their way into a world of luxury. They are professing their admiration for one another with the song, as if to say, "I myself and really nothing much, but, Baby, you're the *top!*" The use of colloquial slang ("the top") is no accident, as both Reno and Billy are upwardly-mobile New Yorkers originally from the lower end of the socioecomic scale—certainly not part of the British aristocracy inhabiting the cruise ship. As characters, then, Reno and Billy are allowed to participate in the world of the European landed gentry, even as the song itself lands them somewhere apart from that very world. We recognize the two characters as rather uncouth, uncivilized stow-aways on a ship bound from New York to Britain, destined for a place that is at once familiar and entirely foreign to them—and "You're the Top!" is the key moment at which their Americanism come to full fore, the point at which they are identified as lower-class and as American even though they have somehow managed to pass themselves off as coevals of aristocratic Europeans—again, the collapse of differential, yet still effective, dualities, all caught in a moment of translation between *here* and *there*. And one last bit of information... The cruise ship is none other than the *S.S. American*.

Now these two cases, *Moby Dick* and *Anything Goes*, are rather easy, I suppose, especially for literary critics trained to find interesting proofs of their theories in creative texts. But bear in mind that the "Manifesto Antropófago" also directs us to the *economic* implications of cannibalism ("Socialmente. Economicamente. Filosoficamente"). Here we may find the "secret" cannibalistic history of the U.S. that I have been uncovering (i.e., inventing) to be more complex than strictly *symbolic* or *allegorical* renderings of culture and class. Our final test-case, then, is a document that I dare say no one reading or listening to my thoughts has ever seen, or even thought to look for. In fact, it's a document that fell into my lap entirely by accident, the details of which I will not describe. The document in question is a speech given by Steven Heyer, President and Chief Operating Officer of the Coca-Cola Company (TCCC), presented to upper-level advertising and media executives on February 5, 2003 in Hollywood, CA. The address was then re-printed the next day in the online edition of *Advertising Age* magazine under the title, "Steven Heyer's Manifesto for a New Age of Marketing." This title is not, I believe, fortuitous; in fact, as near as I can tell, it is an indirect, subconscious reference to the "Manifesto Antropófago," a document I assume Mr. Heyer nor anyone at *AdAge* has ever seen.

In *his* Manifesto, Heyer locates TCCC in a historical predicament: he plainly see that with the proliferation of media channels (through print, satellite, cable, and internet), that mass media will begin to disintegrate into increasingly fragmented substrata, fragmented audiences, and inevitably, the fragmentation of corporate consolidation of ownership. As a result, mass markets as such will likewise begin to erode. From a marketing standpoint, this erosion means trouble, since it will soon become impossible to "broadcast" a commercial message to targeted demographic groups at once. When, for instance, TCCC buys ad space for Coke on even the largest television network, with less and leess viewers tuning in to those mass channels it becomes less and less likely that the message will, in significant way (i.e., profitable way), reach the eyes TCCC wanted to reach. Heyer's response is, for the cultural critic at least, nothing less than astounding:

It's that simple and that tough. We must creat more value for consumers, audiences, and customers.

How?

...Through working together to create something for our brands that matters more on Main Street and ultimately Wall Street. For TCCC, that's value around the bottle that's at least as great as the value in the bottle. (Use bottle as prop).

Why do we believe that this is possible?

Because creating value around this bottle is the secret formula of Coca-Cola's success. Coca-Cola isn't black water with a little sugar and a lot of fizz any more than one of your movies is celluloid digital bits and bytes, or one of your songs is a random collection of words and notes. Coca-Cola isn't a drink. It's an idea. Like great movies, like great music. Coca-Cola is a feeling.

Coca-Cola is refreshment and connection. Always has been... always will be.

That's a timeless proposition...[8]

In essence, Heyer is giving us the visible proof of Marx's theory of the commodity fetish: Coke isn't a drink, Coke is an incorporeal sensation generated "around the bottle." The critical difference from Marx, of course, is that Heyer is *not* using the commodity fetish as a mode of social critique, but rather as a marketing practice at the service of the very forces Marxism opposes. Once Heyer has thus de-substantiated ("de-territorialized" we might say) Coke from its physical "being," he is free to make Coke "become" whatever he needs that this particular historical juncture. And his desire is to make Coca-Cola into a *network* capable of interacting with other market and social networks. That is, Coca-Cola is already omnipresent throughout the global environment, such that literally billions of eyes will catch sight of Coca-Cola iconography every day – and not just in traditional advertisements, but also in restaurants, vending machines, clothing, and so forth. So why does Coca-Cola need a television network to advertise itself, when Coke itself will soon be (if not already) a much larger advertising medium for itself than any television network could ever imagine? Heyer thus sees the day when Coca-Cola will

---

[8]   Steve Heyer. „Steve Heyer's Manifesto for a New Age of Marketing: Madison & Vine Explained as Coca-Cola's Master Plan." *AdAge.com* (http://www.adage.com/ news.cms? newsId=37076), February 6, 2003.

be integrated into other advertising channels to promote other products, for a nominal fee, of course, paid directly to TCCC. In other words, Heyer foresees the day when the media industry will pay *him* to advertise its movies and CDs and TV programs, instead of TCCC having to pay the media industry to "place" TCCC's products.

Here, then, is where the historical-philosophical underpinning of *Antropofagismo* allows us to gauge Heyer's intentions. The traditional corporate model has always been to invent a product, find a way of producing that product, and then finding a way of bringing that product to market so that it actually sells. Heyer's Manifesto represents a move toward the kind of "flow reversal" of differential dualities that is spelled out in the "Manifesto Antropófago." We still have a concept of what is *in* the bottle and the packaging *around* it, between *inside* and *outside*, and, in this way, between *here* and *there*. Only now the values of *inside* and *outside* are finally recognized to be thoroughly embedded in one another. As a result, whereas production used to give way to marketing, marketing will now give way to production; or as Heyer puts it, "In a networked economy, ideas, concepts, and images are the items of real value – you know, marketing. Demand creation and demand fulfilment."[9] To be sure, there is still some (at least conceptual) division between production and marketing (manufacturing and advertising), but now only insofar as the marketing side intends to consume and ingest the production side so that it becomes difficult to tell who is a producer and who a marketer. In *this* new world, the producer has no need to take his product to media networks, since the product already *is* its own advertising, and in fact its own media network capable of bringing other products to market, capable indeed of advertising the traditional media networks themselves. And this will only happen once it is recognized that Coke is *not* a thing, but rather a social-historical culture that consumes demographically-identified subjects (consumers) migrating "around the bottle." Call this not the *doxa* of Coke, but rather the *paradoxa* of Coke.

Is this good? Is this bad? That's not the point. *Antropofagismo* does not direct us to a UTOPIC AMERICAN HEMISPHERE. My point is that *Antropofagismo* provides us the correct theoretical lens to see the EMPIRICAL REALITIES OF THE AMERICAN HEMISPHERE. I'll leave you to sort

---

[9]   Ibid.

out the ethical implications of this for yourselves. I only bring up these examples for something else: that is entirely possible to recover (perhaps for the first time) a history, or general zeitgeist perhaps, of cannibalistic thought that has coursed just under the surface of U.S. culture throughout its history. "Cannibal logic" will bubble up in nineteenth-century transcendentalism, twentieth-century Broadway musicals, and twenty-first-century corporate culture. And of course, this history is not available to us until we construct it ("transcreate" it to be technical) *a posteriori*—a scholarly move that is decidedly "barbaric," but that nevertheless produces some elegant consequences. And to return to the real point here, such *a posteriori* historical understandings of Coca-Cola and the U.S.-American mind would not be possible without a firm grasp of Brazilian, and indeed Latin American, intellectual history—without, that is, a firm grounding in hemispheric Americanism.

Cannibalism is, after all, never more than a practice of consumption.

Dedicated to Jim Meskauskas

Justin Read

AMERICAN SOCIAL, ETHICAL, AND RELIGIOUS MENTALITIES

Is Truth Defunct ?

There is one thing a professor can be absolutely certain of; almost every student entering the university believes, or says he believes, that truth is relative.

— Allan Bloom, *The Closing of the American Mind*

If truth is no more than relative, truth is defunct since truth is nothing but a moving target. Worse, if truth is but a moving target, but we can never see if anyone hits it or not, even science and mathematics are on the hit or miss list. Indeed, most of my students think beyond Nietzsche's heart-wrenching question, "Why rather truth than untruth?" They typically think they believe that there is no truth. How they can recognize this one truth, i.e. that there is no truth, must remain a mystery. They may have derived this postulate from the axiom that there is no falsity. All express their own opinions and free individuals are each right for themselves. Or, alternatively, each culture, each community, each cult determines its own truths, which leads to the conclusion that there are many truths, no touchstone for evaluating them, and, thus, again no truth in particular since all is true. In fact, cultural and social "truths" may

conflict as they do on the question of female genital mutilation or beauti-
fication or the pro-life/pro-choice debate on abortion. The sophisticated
among us recognize the fundamental position of so-called post-modernity
in the above. My task today shall be to describe the two-fold theory of
truth that dominates, although does not control, the scene in the United
States today. Following that description, I shall provide some prophecies
as to the possible directions for future intellectual history.

I. Description of the Natural World of American Public Education, Including Some Hip Universities

Stephen Satris has argued that the relativism that reigns in American
colleges and universities is not to be confused with the positions of
cultural relativism, subjective relativism, etc. Rather, Satris believes that
student relativism is a defense against holding to any position whatso-
ever. He thinks that student relativism is

> primarily a method of protection....'Who's to say?' is not an
> expression of one's own intellectual humility, broadmindedness,
> or unwillingness to condemn others. Rather, it is an expression
> of the idea that no one step forward and judge (and possibly
> criticize) one's own opinions. (PoE, p.50)

Americans have long been schooled in the impropriety of discussing
views on politics or religion in social settings. However, without discussion of opinions, they have no opportunities to form or reform their
opinions. Thus, they give lip service to the proposition that "What is right
to you may be wrong to me or vice versa." Not only does such a proposition lead to a moral mess, which relies on politics and laws for determina-
tions of the default position, but also to an eventual skepticism concerning
all questions of truth. In the States,

> Many people come out of a public school background having
> learned that "value judgment' or 'controversial issue' simply
> means a judgment or issue with respect to which there is no
> right response or answer and about which (since it's all a matter
> of personal opinion and not of scientific fact) we may all
> conveniently believe as we wish while remaining error-free....
> (PoE, p.52)

Americans, by and large, don't think they think that there is truth. The products of the American public school system have been indoctrinated in the position that all knowledge claims reduce to expressions of opinion. We live, after all, in a democracy in which any opinion is as valuable as any other. Hip intellectuals hold basically the same view except that they would claim that no opinion is worth much, perhaps adding modestly that some stories may be more interesting. The politicians believe, or say they believe, that they have the truth, but Americans don't generally trust politicians, as our voting apathy demonstrates. Also, as we have recently witnessed, Americans are susceptible to old-style, oft-repeated big lie propaganda. The failure of Americans to think critically is the result of inadequate education, as we have seen above. Since this deficiency in training in thinking harms no one but the hoi polloi, no serious efforts towards educational renewal are being made. The present batch of educational "reforms," includes, for example, unfunded, mandatory yearly testing for children throughout their schooling. The aim seems to be greater assurance that American children are learning the basic skills they need to contribute to the economy.

Americans, despite their schooling, nevertheless take for granted that there are truths in their lived lives. When pushed, my students, for instance, will agree that they know when it is raining, but the concession doesn't come easily. The difficulty, of course, has to do with the puzzle about where little truths come from, if there is no big truth. They seem to have a fuzzy intuition that they are on dangerous ground so they especially don't like to think about the necessary roundness of circles or bachelorhood of the unmarried.

II. The American Version of the Two-fold Theory of Truth

Round circles and unmarried bachelors acquire their problematic aspects from seeming to be objective truths, which nevertheless have their source of verification in subjective intuitions. Most of us can recall working on a problem in math or physics until the moment that we finally "got it." For the Modern, and many Americans are still Modern, science, despite its own glory in its hypothetical, provisional character, yields objectivity (i.e., facts), while indubitable intuitions are subjective (and therefore suspect). Also characteristically, the Modern natural sciences and philosophy have no need of the past. Modern philosophy begins with Descartes and ends with a metaphysics of primary and secondary qualities that writes all subjects, including both scientists and philosophers, out of the story. And, history belongs to no one and, thus, can have no meaning. Max Horkheimer (one of the founders of the Frankfort School) described the fundamental error of dichotomizing rationality in this way,

> For just like the absolute dualism of spirit and nature, that of subjective and objective reason is merely an appearance, although a necessary appearance. The two concepts are interlaced, in the sense that the consequence of each not only dissolves the other but also leads back to it. The element of untruth lies not simply in the essence of each of the two concepts, but in the hypostatization of either one as against the other. (EoR, p.173)

Subjective reason soon becomes reduced to subjective relativism: David Hume's assertion that moral judgments report the speaker's feelings or attitudes results in moral skepticism. "'Tis nothing good nor bad but thinking make it so." Thus, relativism trumps both liberal and conservative politics and ethics; relativism reduces all beliefs to dogma and dogma to repression. Too often, liberals and conservatives view each other, but not themselves, as repressive. Science, writing in numbers, becomes the bastion of objectivity, yet philosophers (the likes of Francis Bacon, David Hume, Emmanuel Kant and Edmund Husserl) have argued that the inductive method of the modern natural sciences cannot lead beyond probabilities to truth. Hume showed that the scientifically operative notion of causality cannot itself be demonstrated empirically, thereby showing that a purely empirical epistemology was incoherent. The predictive power of science gets its clout from a future that cannot be known. If the future only reveals itself as a presence-yet-to-come, it is possible that our cherished scientific theories go the way of ether of flogeston. All of this occurred well before Thomas Kuhn's stunning critique of science in the twentieth century. Science then becomes history of science that chronicles its shifting paradigms.

Kant preached the necessity of the subject for any knowledge. The Kantian subject can achieve intuition of Universal Law, since its experience "captures" a noumenal realm, thing-in-itself. Husserl recognized that Kant's unknowable thing-in-itself, the foundation of a priori intuitions, can never be known. When it is known, the noumenal appears as phenomenal. Husserl does not reject Kant's Copernican Revolution. Perspective makes a difference, not so great, however, as to preclude the meaning, objectivity. Yet, Husserl found the cause of the crisis of civilization that he was observing at the dawn of the Second World War in the blind belief in the empirical method of the modern sciences as the avenue to truth. In any case, at their best, the results of the natural sciences will not answer questions about the meaning of life.

Martin Heidegger and the critique of technology that he initiated condemn the modern reliance on calculative reason that excludes, in Pascal's great phrase "the reasons of the heart." To which Horkheimer adds, "[p]aranoia, the madness that builds logically constructed theories of persecution, is not merely a parody of reason, but is somehow present in any form of reason that consists in the mere pursuit of aims" (EoR, p.176). To explain the contemporary American version of the two-fold theory of truth further, we look to Martin Heidegger's distinction between calculative and meditative thinking. These two senses of Reason have foundations in very different metaphysical systems.

Calculative reason is based on the mathematical objectifying of the modern natural sciences and the metaphysics of the naturalism or materialism that they entail. In this view, nature is but a standing resource and Dasein but a human resource. Meditative thinking listens. Meditative thinking discovers; it controls only theoretically and not always theoretically. Edith Stein, St. Teresa Benedicta, adds that the emotions disclose others who we can discover and let live. This is no afterthought, Stein's emphases on emotions and empathy restore and enhance the Classical idea of Reason.

Plato was a poetic philosopher who evoked his insights in receptive readers throughout the centuries. Even the more prosaic Aristotle taught that the great-souled man felt the goodness of what he believed to be true. Human maturity amounts to an integrity that is the unity of the heart and the mind. The person must become conversant.

Meditative thinking is despised by the fundamentalists who head the government, the military, the corporate world, the religious right, and so forth. Those who espouse the path of calculative reason must have in mind a fathomable goal, if not a telos. Usually, the goal is wealth, although power is an oft-desired by-product of wealth. Less frequently perhaps, desire is for honor. All of these, Aristotle points out, are not within our control. The bursting of the bubble of the fraud of the nineties shows how ephemeral the value of wealth can be for those who count on it alone. All of this striving is rooted in naturalistic materialism, even the mathematical method used to calculate one's worth by one's assets. The complexities and contradictions in modern beliefs continue to constitute most persons' lived lives, but not all.

The two-fold theory of truth popular in the United States presently could be summed up as follows: (1) there is no truth in particular, i. e. truth is defunct, although science blithely makes true statements, and (2) the metaphysics of naturalism/materialism that are the presupposed grounds of the modern natural sciences and of American political debate. "It's the economy, stupid," is a phrase that sticks. This metaphysics generates leaders who seek desire's fulfillment in the world, not heroes who seek self-realization in desire's transcendence into meaning.

III. Reason's relation to truth

Essential truths, eternal verities are for the gods alone, Socrates proposed. Twenty-five hundred years or so later, we have no reason to doubt the proposition. Yet, Socrates did not believe the contemporary corollary that humans could not know anything. Most academic philosophers in the United States ignore the prevailing wisdom in order to ascribe to Truth, as the *telos* of their endeavors. With an unexpected tacit cunning many philosophers seem to sense that without truth, they are totally out of a job rather than merely useless, as philosophers have been most of the time since Plato first attributed the condition to his experience that nobody uses philosophers. Philosophers are not alone in a rear guard defense of Truth as the rational ideal. Mathematicians recognize the function of self-evident insight in their demonstrations, although fuzzy set theory provides interesting developments. Musicians sing on key, even when the music is not harmonious. Physicists believe that science is the endless task of seeking knowledge and what is really real is best captured by a probability smear. As Plato also pointed out, all knowledge is true (or it would not be knowledge), but still we must ask, what is truth? And, even if we can imagine what truth may be, how could we know it?

The problem of knowledge has its beginnings in Plato and Aristotle. For Plato, essences, i.e. universal concepts that convey what an entity must be to be what it is, help us make sense of our experience. For instance, the ideas "masculine" and "feminine" admit of many interpretations. Yet, most people in the United States readily understand the distinction between masculine and feminine gift wrap, say. Thus, according to Plato, we use essences to make sense of the world, although an essence is not itself another thing in the world. Aristotle thought that everything existed as the unity of matter and form. Ideas informed matter to generate things, but form could not exist in separation from things. Or, this is what nominalists, who hold to the position that words are names which we apply to things, took Aristotle to imply.

With William of Ockham, the nominalist position carried the day on the battlefield of the history of philosophy. This tradition, in various of its aspects, dominates Western philosophy, still. Eventually, Americans figured out (with help from John Locke, et al.) that if essences were just names for different existents, then there was no human essence. So, most Americans believe that each person is totally different, *mutatis mutandis*, each of our cultures, representing most cultures on the planet, is totally different. Since the line our educators pass on as diversity is "every opinion is fine," the blow to Brotherhood that reason suggests does not strike most American students. My classes, made up primarily of first generation college students, including many minorities, figure that, although we condemn slavery now, it was okay in the 19th-century South. They are then at a loss to explain why Dr. Martin Luther King, Jr. was a hero, not a criminal. So, some philosophy instructors try to sell the idea of Truth. To lament: this situation seems wildly unfair since proper solutions to math problems can be determined by its method and thus does not have to justify the possibility of a dichotomy between right and wrong answers, as philosophy does.

One can recognize philosophizing in the active assumption of the logos tradition that began with the Greeks, but need not have dead-ended in the end of philosophy in the late twentieth century. Tradition in philosophy can never be in a straightforward acceptance of dogma. The philosophic tradition, above all, involves the historical effort to make sense of the activity of philosophizing through rigorous questioning. The past of philosophy can only be inherited through its intellectual acquisition which means, as Husserl explained, that each philosopher must piece together a history of philosophy which tells the story of human efforts at sense-making in the face of the inscrutability of life. This style of philosophy is not the current fashion of relativizing, trivializing, and ignoring the possibilities that philosophy enjoyed in the past. Let the fashion stand condemned by the sweep and the "high seriousness" of thinkers who still seek for Truth, standing on the shoulders of Giants.

Existence and reason are dialectical poles that require one another; neither is possible without the other. Surely, a contention such as this is the faith of philosophy and the other sciences, as well. The practical tasks of reason include seeing to the satisfaction of the needs of existence and to the establishment of the conventions and taboos of culture. These practical concerns give way to language, which carries and conveys the machinations of spirit so that the mysterious aspects of human life become intelligible (if never fully understood) as integral parts of the spiritual in human being. Unlike what the culture of high modernity preached through the materialistic capitalism that established its existential foundation, spirit unmasks itself in the miraculous mundanity of speech, if we can but hear.

IV. The Default Position: Unreason of Relativism

For my conclusion, I would now like to submit some sanguine prophecies concerning the future of intellectual history, perhaps even in the United States. People who do not think that it is possible to know anything often believe that they should act according to their own feelings. Yet, perhaps the technological advances that feel disgusting to us probably are. For instance, most people express revulsion at the prospect of human cloning. The idea feels repugnant, monstrous, indecent, somehow. Philosophy can respond with an ethics which, although not a variety of subjective emotivism, takes feelings seriously. Edmund Husserl, in the phenomeno-logical tradition, holds that emotions may be harbingers of objective value.[1] Edith Stein, his first assistant, goes so far as to claim that the emotions are organs for evaluating the world since emotions grasp value immediately.

Many people seem to be feeling an openness to the other and to letting the other be, recognizing the other's right to be. Against the

---

[1] Ullrich Melle, "Husserl's Ethics," *A Handbook of Phenomenological Ethics*, edited by John Drummond and Lester Embree, Kluwer Academic Publishers, 2002.

fundamentalisms of all stripes, feelings of brotherhood and reverence seem to be spreading. Simultaneously, some American philosophers, too, have begun to utter the word, Love. This attitudinal switch promotes the ascendance of the value of "a perfected humanity," in Edith Stein's phrase, a family of humankind, all wishing each other well, each taking the other's good as if it were his own.

In Stein's work we can see suggestions for a phenomenology that breaks free of modernity and encourages, "a restoration of the convictions that animated ancient and medieval philosophy. Like premodern philosophy, phenomenology understands reason as ordered to truth."[2] Also according to Robert Sokolowski, phenomenology neither rejects modernity nor rebels against the perennial tradition in philosophy. Rather, phenomenology may provide a means to "a recovery of the true philosophical life, in a manner appropriate to our philosophical situation."[3]

Briefly to rehearse the history of philosophy in the West, The Pre-Socratics were monists and materialists. Socrates' turn towards the truth that a person sees with inner intuition introduced a radically new method and hence a radically new direction for philosophy. Since then, philosophers have followed Socrates lead and guide themselves by the motto engraved on the Temple of Delphi. Philosophers still seek to follow Socrates by learning to know themselves. In the process, philosophers often recognize Emperors Who Have No Clothes. Seeking back before what a people takes for granted, reason leads past the altars of many false gods to the irrationality that must be the well-spring of any intelligibility. Intelligibility is a function of proper ordering, of prudentially taking the good of persons as the highest good we can achieve. Love becomes valorized, not only for its own sake, but also because love allows the deepest grasp of the other in the otherness that is necessary to serve him properly.

All of these conclusions seem to follow after skepticism, initially Socratic Irony, next Augustinian Doubt, followed by the bi-polar Cartesian Cogito and, most recently, phenomenological reduction of all experience to its source in consciousness. The necessary post-modern

---

[2]   Robert Sokolowski, *Introduction to Phenomenology*, (Cambridge University Press, 2000), p. 202.

[3]   Ibid, p. 203.

failure of theory and subsequent substitution of power for Truth results in a rational conundrum. The Will to Power, in any of its manifestations except self-control, asserts itself beyond the good for each. Will to power denies the intuition that we are all in this together. Truth must be the arbitrator of which will to bless. Heidegger claims that aletheia, the word we translate from the Greek as truth, more properly refers to Unconcealedness, Unhiddenness. Reason, the path of thinking that leads to the source of truth, can be shared by all those interested in dialogue, in reciprocal communication, in speaking the truth in love.

Kathleen Haney

Works Cited

Max Horkheimer. 1974. *Eclipse of Reason*, New York: Seabury Press (1947).

Ullrich Melle. 2002. "Husserl's Ethics." *A Handbook of Phenomenological Ethics.* Ed. John Drummond and Lester Embre. Kluwer Academic Publishers.

Stephen A. Satris. 1998. "Student Relativism" in *Perspectives on Ethics.* 2nd Edition. Ed. by Judith Boss. New York: McGraw Hill, p. 49-52.

Robert Sokolowski. 2000. *Introduction to Phenomenology.* Cambridge University Press.

True Ethics: American Morality in (Post-)Modern Times

I. Introduction

On March 16, 2003, announcing his decision to send American troops into Iraqi territory, the President of the United States, George W. Bush, put forward a programmatic statement: "This is a moment of truth for the world." The following considerations will try to line out that such presidential insights may be indicative of a permanent addiction to truth within American culture. And what is even more relevant, the truth in question is not centred on any complex form of epistemological texture concerning human knowledge and anthropological problems of knowing; rather, this truth implies human action and decision-making. This is an issue central to Occidental culture, ever since Enlightenment authors and their followers subscribed to the freedom of human will. It is the truth of ethics.

All kinds of ethical considerations converge on one simple sentence, which the German philosopher Immanuel Kant formulated in a famous passage from his *Logik*: "What shall I do?" Bearing the consequences and accompanying aspects of this question in mind, the subsequent discussion will present a short survey of Occidental ethical thinking and its typical formation within American culture; at the same time, it will concentrate on the de-ontological tone, fascinatingly relevant within American ethical discourses, spreading out in an enormous variety of different subject matters. Developing some rough idea of an ethical orientational background structure by taking a look at eminent examples of nineteenth-century American literature, the critical awareness will turn to contemporary ethical problems, searching for systematic patterns heuristically sufficient to understand basic issues within contemporary discussions—and some of the more important statements of the American President.

One of the results of this 'mixed' approach, including literature, cinema and politics, will be to discover a surprising persistence of America's cultural adherence to Kantian ethics—though the relevancy of such a de-ontological variant of morality seems to be centred on public presentations in critical situations. Nevertheless, these "de-ontological exhibitions," singular as they may seem with their repetitive reference to notions like "duty," "reason," and "truth" are highly resonant in American everyday culture, even in popular films. On the other hand, the acceptance of utilitarian ethics in America is remarkably lower; what remains, though, is its considerable impact on daily procedures of orientation, as long as they are localized in "off-stage" sites, confined to private or semi-private situations.

II. Nineteenth-Century Ethics:
European Groundwork and American Literature

1. The Twofold Rationality of Occidental Ethics

Highlighting typical developmental stages of Occidental ethics in a kind of tour de force may yield main points of a simple matrix, appropriate for discussing typical ethical trends in contemporary culture. A starting point, of course, is Plato's objective idealism, which regards ethical action as integrated into a pattern of correct social positioning, adapted to modes of cosmological harmony. In Plato's view, ethics have to be modelled on the standards of a pre-structured world-order, framed by a horizon of pre-stabilized perfection existing only in the world of abstraction and idealization. According to his philosophy, ethics have to rely on a perfect and divine world-order, while trying to adapt human imperfection to this cosmological harmony. Such a systematic pre-determination of acceptable constellations and structural variants leaves no room for subjective autonomy and personal decisions. Though reason, in this ideology, is a basic category, it is constitutively fixed to the world and not to the subject.

Bringing about a sea change in this scenario, modern ethics turns this external authority outside in. Modern times, heavily relying on Descartes' ideas, start with the ultimate radicalization of the reasonable subject's inner authority, which no longer depends on any kind of external backing or control. Installing this change within the realm of epistemology and knowledge, Descartes leaves the task to Jeremy Bentham and John Stuart Mill on the one hand, and Immanuel Kant on the other, to conceptualize a subjectified rational ethics within the scope of modern world making. The outcome is the well- known polarization between two rationalistic versions of European ethical standards: British utilitarianism, based on the rational analysis of "that property in any object, whereby it tends to produce benefit, advantage, pleasure, good, or happiness ... to the party whose interest is considered"[1]; and Kant's deontological ethics, culminating in the categorical imperative and its foundation of all ethical actions in subjective legitimate generalizations: "... I am never to act otherwise than so that I could also will that my maxim should become a universal law." [2]

Lying—in Kant's opinion the act of undermining the credibility of reason by reason—becomes the touchstone of these radically subjectified versions of rationally constructed ethics. Immanuel Kant's still famous example marks a centre of the discussion, whenever the problem of white lies comes to the fore: The police are knocking on my door, looking for a friend of mine, suspected of murder. Being convinced of his innocence I have given him shelter under the roof of my house. Am I allowed to lie, when the policeman asks: "Is your friend in this house?" Kant's answer is fascinatingly unambiguous: White lies, as tolerated forms of ignoring the truth in favour of a positive social outcome, constitute an immanent self-contradiction of reason, thus destabilizing the whole system of truths and lies and—finally—ethics. We have to trust in truth and the persistence of

---

[1] Jeremy Bentham, *The Principles of Morals and Legislation* (1781; Amherst: Prometheus Books, 1988), 2.

[2] Immanuel Kant, *Fundamental Principles of the Metaphysics of Morals*, tr. T. K. Abbott (1785; Amherst: Prometheus Books, 1988), 27.

true statements and actions in the long run; any episodic and recurring tendency to make the strict laws of duty "more accordant with our wishes and inclinations, that is to say, to corrupt them at their very source" (Kant 1988: 30) will subvert the reasonableness of all human standards. Utilitarians, like Bentham and Mill, to the contrary, support a positive evaluation of human lies as long as they lead to positive consequences. If such infringements of truth enlarge the total sum of pleasure in a given community, such lies may be considered as ethically correct.

What is especially interesting about long-term developments in American culture is the influential overlap between these two versions of Occidental ethics, both founded on basic considerations concerning the reasonableness of human beings and their endeavour to support their individual ways of world making by making use of generalizing schemas. The 'polarized convergence' of both concepts has played a major role in America throughout the periods ranging from the age of colonialism to contemporary culture. The following considerations will try to elucidate to what degree these two interfering concepts have led to a typical American way of making ethical statements and convictions, and furthermore, how these statements and convictions become pivotal points for judging one's own procedures of composing a coherently subjective world view.

2. In the Wake of Kant:
Ethical Foundations in American Nineteenth-Century Prose

In order to avoid the plausible critique of using marginal material for illustrating a central idea, the 'lions' of American nineteenth-century literature will move into the fore of the following considerations. Thus, the ethical background of authors like Hawthorne and Melville will be of primary interest, without entering a discussion about the aesthetic aspects of their works.

A cursory look into Hawthorne's *The Scarlet Letter*[3] will lay bare some of the main influential components within American culture that make the autonomous subject a leading figure in ethical considerations. Most impressive about this novel is the overt influence of Calvinist ideals and, simultaneously, the explicit undermining of any introverted

---

[3]   Nathaniel Hawthorne, *The Scarlet Letter* (1850; New York: Penguin, 1986)

Protestant model of self-evaluation. Being accused of adultery, the novel's heroine, Hester Prynne, strictly refuses to unveil the name of her child's father, thus, indeed, covering up for her lover, the minister Dimmesdale. Though suffering enormous pressure, this woman withstands all attacks on her ethical ideal of subjective autonomy and personal decision.

Hester Prynne's enlightened ideology represents a modern model of radical autonomy and thus she is never going to submit to anything but generalizing rationales, built on principles of reason. Nor will she allow them to bend to considerations concerning the results of thoughts, feelings or actions. This rigid ideal is a direct descendant of the Kantian credo that only rationality, installed in the realm of subjectivity, may be taken as a general basis for ethics. And only rationality, in its self-relying and self-oriented referentiality, dares to ignore the consequences of a well-considered action. Such a form of ethical world making, culminating in Kant's categorical imperative, fosters the hope that reason reflects some kind of divine groundwork, implicit in rationality and its practical trans-formations. Hester, this 'categorical' woman, enters the literary scene like a Jean d'Arc of American culture and ethics. She is never going to bend under the weight of any kind of utilitarian striving for the majority's optimum pleasure in a given social system. For her, being good means acting according to well-founded principles, autonomously grounded and competently applied in every subject's own mind. Responsibility for oneself, without any submission to outer authority, coerces the modern subject into a position of deciding independently, without constraints. This is modernity's positive result, assigning everybody the role of an autonomous decision maker, accompanied by the enormous gravity of being personally responsible, without support from any outer authority or emotional backing. Within the realm of Kant's ethics, there is no help from (or for) my friends that might be ethically relevant.

Another radical variant of making the subject a rationally introverted subject, always testing his/her intentions on the touchstone of reason's internal consistency—and disregarding all unpleasant consequences—may be found in Melville's *Billy Budd, Sailor*[4], another famous version of American ethical world making in nineteenth century. Here we have an almost ideal young person, untouched by society's inner

---

[4]   Herman Melville, *Billy Budd, Sailor* (1924; London: Penguin, 1995)

strategies of achieving the best results for a person's life, trying to lead a life of perfect innocence, or—in Kant's words—the life of an angel. And like Kant's angels, Billy Budd, the sailor, does not need any explicit rules to arrive at a categorical imperative. According to the German philosopher, such a strict corset is only indispensable for ordinary human beings, because of a permanent anthropomorphic affliction arising from inclinations and non-rational preferences. Billy Budd knows right action from the bottom of his mind: he never falters, nor does he need to reconsider his decisions. When he is finally confronted with another man's blatant and outrageous attack on truth, he is carried away by a fit of uncontrolled fury and kills the man spontaneously with one terrible blow. At once he determines to accept the adequate punishment for this deed, i.e. death.

Billy Budd knows that reasonable persons are never allowed to kill one another because of the self-contradictory consequences implied by such a deed: rationality would eliminate itself in such an act. And though his own death penalty counts among such forbidden self-contradictions of rationality, Billy Budd takes his punishment as an individual and personal decision, implying no role models for others. In perfect accordance with Billy's position it should be remembered that Kant does not accept good examples as blueprints to be copied in the realm of ethics because such grounding—and this is his argument—would be totally empirical. But ethical principles are *a priori*, being automatically connected to the capability of being rational and reasonable. Examples, like Billy Budd's self-inflicted death sentence, simply strengthen the tendency to act according to one's own reasonableness; they take over the task of an intellectually helpful and contouring device, never approaching the level of constitutive relevancy. Or, in Kant's words: "Imitation finds no place at all in morality, and examples serve only for encouragement ... but they can never authorize us to set aside the true original which lies in reason ..." (Kant 1988: 36).

Condensing the aforementioned observations into a simple summary, it has to be underlined that considerable areas of American nineteenth-century literature are ethically impregnated with deontological ideas, partly in sheer contrast to the quantifying reductionism of many utilitarian perspectives. English Literature of this period—as examples, George Eliot's *Silas Marner* and Charles Dickens' *Hard Times* may be named here—is predominantly marked by the leading influence of utilitarianism, regularly demonstrating to the reader that pure continental ethics à la Kant will not result in a satisfactorily structured realm of intersubjective and social activities, mainly governed by considerations implying best results for the majority of a given people. During the nineteenth century, an ethical gap between American and British culture opens up: American culture starts to oscillate between ethical reasoning, strongly addicted to deontological principles, and utilitarian considerations that, in any commercially based and capitalistically structured society, have to be taken into account, in order to secure the economical texture of a running system. These 'categorical' considerations smoothly fit into the ethical horizon of the Sermon on the Mount, uncovering a tight connection to the New Testament and the basic ethical backgrounds of Calvinist ideology. Demonstrating this connection, almost reduced to a secondary footnote, Kant implements the basics of Christian ethics into his deontological system: "It is in this [deontological] manner, undoubtedly, that we are to understand those passages of Scripture also in which we are commanded to love our neighbour, even our enemy. For love, as an affection, cannot be commanded ..." (Kant 1988: 24).

III. Mainstream Ethics in Twentieth-Century American Culture

Leaving the primary terrain of nineteenth-century ethics, i.e. literature aside, to enter those forums of contemporary culture which seem to be as dominant as literature was in 19th century, some recent and outstanding examples from film and presidential politics will be analysed. The aim is to illustrate the persistent relevancy of the above hypothesis, which can neither be confined to the realm of literature nor to the specificity of nineteenth-century ideologies. Taking these 'spectacular' levels as exemplary modes of implementing ethical discourse into the sphere of cultural development and communication, the idea is to demonstrate the permanent contrast between the ethical positions of Kantian universal deontology and utilitarianism—both addicted in different ways to rationality and truth—in American contemporary culture.

1. Violence and Ethics: American Black Cinema

Films like Spike Lee's *Do the Right Thing* (1989), John Singleton's *Boyz N the Hood* (1991) and Allen and Albert Hughes' *Menace II Society* (1993) are outstanding examples of the New American Black Cinema. They involve a decidedly precise confrontation with different and contrasting forms of modern ethics within the dominant visual medium of contemporary culture. The intention here is not to give an appropriate introduction into the narrative and formal structure of these films but rather to demonstrate the relevancy of the above considerations by looking at the ethical structure of one of these films in more detail.

Menace II Society is a film about the black adolescent involvement into the Los Angeles drug scene, forcing the moviegoer to follow a story of bloodshed and murder between rivalling gangs and ethnic groups. At first glance, the spectator feels that he/she is forced to follow a simple and violent demonstration of almost all Occidental ethical standards being jettisoned. Degraded to moving bodies, human lives can be taken out of their social orbits by a weapon whenever such an intention comes to the mind of another human being. But in the course of this film, we realize that the whole story is built around ethical patterns and ethical modes of world making, installing brutality and violence as simple means of keeping specifically-ambitioned types of audiences in their cinema seats. *Menace II Society* is a film about the influence of different variants of Occidental ethics—classical virtue-ethics, Kantian ethics, utilitarianism—in the social milieu of a specific African American way of surviving under the pressures of late-capitalism. What is structurally given in this film is a systematic confrontation between these different ethical positions, incorporated by different characters and thus presenting to the audience a simple way of identifying or refraining from doing so.

To understand the ethics and ethos of this film, the easiest way is to look at its ending and make a death count, or better: survival count. Caine, the adolescent black protagonist of the film, who is drawn into heavy crime by the influence of his even younger friend O'Dog, dies in the end. Though he is on his way to personal and social amelioration, intending to start the life of a family man and to leave Los Angeles' South Central, he gets killed in the final scene by a rival black gang. Yet his totally anarchic and 'spontaneously' criminal younger friend O'Dog survives. Putting these simple facts together, the message of this film appears to be devastatingly counteractive to any form of ethical evaluation in the grain of classical Occidental approaches. But, taking a closer look at the reasons for Caine's death, the whole accent of the story changes. Caine, breaking up with a girl several months earlier, took ethical decisions, not being aware of their full implications. When she talked to him about her pregnancy and asked him on the phone if he would take over the role of a father for this child, which could be his, he denied any responsibility for this child, being sure of having used safe forms of contraception. He harshly breaks with this girl only a moment after she put the decisive ethical question on the phone: "If you can take away other people's lives so easily, couldn't you just, for once in your life, take over the responsibility for a new life?"

Getting killed in the end, Caine dies a pre-modern death, dominated by the idea of "an eye for an eye, a tooth for a tooth." He loses his life as a result of revenge for an innocent unborn life that could have been spared if he had been led by the principle of "caring for others" in the sense of "caring for human beings." Though already under the influence of generalizing ethical principles, Caine still leads part of his personal life according to utilitarian principles. Becoming a good person, in his opinion, is still connected with simple conceptions of personal pleasure. To a certain extent, he is an involuntary and almost absurd Billy Budd, on whom death is inflicted from outside because he could not work out the concrete modes of a deontological position. Acting according to rational principles and not to utilitarian leitmotifs—and this seems to be the central message of *Menace II* Society—is the abstract duty of an American mind. Only in the final pictures of the film, showing the last impressions and thoughts of a dying consciousness, Caine achieves the ethical perfection of a Hester Prynne, putting him in a position to understand the fact that the maturing of rationality and reason may come too late.

Fascinating about this film is its radical ethical colouring and theoretical consistency. While Caine represents different evolutionary stages on the way from a utilitarian to a Kantian position, even in its most radical version, O'Dog lives outside any real ethical framework, aside from his solidarity with his friends. His 'ethics' are the 'ethics' of a depraved child: he acts, kills, loves, survives like a child, not being mature enough to submit to the strict rules of deontology. And even Caine's grandfather, taking over a father's role for the orphaned boy, represents a precisely definable version of Occidental ethical standards: he enacts the classical position of a religious virtue-ethical evaluation of one's own and other people's life. The fact that he does not succeed in reaching his grandson's emotional position underlines another radical hiatus in Occidental culture, the deep abyss between antique and modern ethics. The value systems of classical times (and pre-modern Occidental religions) are dominated by outer authority and external criteria of perfection, while modern ethics emanate from the inner autonomy of a reasonable subject. The contrast between both concepts remains unbridgeable, leaving grandfather and grandson in a position of deep and grave misunderstanding. In the American cosmos, an ethical foundation with religious pillars appears to be hopelessly inadequate. Offering some kind of ideological panacea, Kant's idea of modernizing the subject's moral status by fixing it self-referentially in its own sphere of rationality, becomes one of the last asylums of a universal ethics.

2. American Presidential Culture: Moments of Truth for America
On March 16, 2003, in his ultimate address to Saddam, announcing the American decision, to put a martial end to the tyranny in Iraq, George Bush said: "This is not a question of authority. It is a question of will." In a fascinating way, Bush combines statements about the authority of leadership with the ethical question of human will. And doing so, he follows the basic Occidental issue between outer authority and inner autonomy ("will"), putting them together in one breath, though in two sentences. Taking the role of the autonomous modern subject, Bush presents a decision in the wake of subjective autonomy, presupposing a rationally found and founded solution and assuming that this "will" is ultimately "good'." Thus, two days after giving a clear task to the world—"This is a moment of truth for the world"—Bush overtly enters the terrain of Kantian good will, never to be undermined by any considerations that might presumably be untrue. In Bush's (as in Kant's world) those who are acting in accordance with truth can never go wrong.

Interesting to note that there is no utilitarian component in Bush's argumentation. At best, he is looking for examples that might be taken as illustrations for the general relevance of his position, as supporting evidence for the rational foundation of his version of reality and how to cope with it on a solid basis of truth, where the difference between right or wrong can be discerned easily. Declaring war on Iraq implied, according to Bush's ideology, a war against 'evil' and a principal reaction to the subversion of rationality (which, in Kant's ethics, can never be reasonable when human beings are under attack: this would imply a self-elimination of rationality in a primary, i.e. formal sense). But it does not seem to irritate the American President very much that his "rational" ethics endangers the lives of many people. Here, we have a paradoxical, almost clandestine change to utilitarian standards: Bush's argumentation concerns the threats to mankind in future times, which, in his opinion, are supposed to be enormously bigger than the casualties of an immediate war. But such an open utilitarian line of reasoning achieves only secondary rhetorical importance. It has to be derived from the President's detailed examples that such an argument may be among his reasons for legitimating the war.

All in all, Bush's argumentation is predominantly deontological (that is based on rational self-coercions of the subject, called duty) and not utilitarian – adding a more Prussian than British tone to his groundwork of ethical reasoning. Fascinating to note that such forms of bringing a presidential decision into the public have long since been the basis of the White House's public politics, and have even been turned against it in times of presidential turmoil. Nixon's Watergate scandal may be mentioned here and—to refer to another example from America's recent history—the Lewinsky-Clinton affair. Though many Americans disapproved of Bill Clinton's sexual relationship with Monica Lewinsky, the main reason for a public attack on the President was the assumption that he had been lying. Lying to the public and the democratic institutions of the American people. In a utilitarian light, this would not have posed any real problem, taken for granted that no real damage was done by Clinton's inclination to tell stories that were blatantly incongruent with the standards of truth. But this was not the central point in accusing the President. A whole nation was interested in finding out if their President had told the truth or not. But telling the truth, without taking the consequences of such a truthfulness into regard, is—within a modern world—a question of being *consistently* rational or not. And being rational implies a universally applicable ethical logic: no consequently reasonable man can ever be evil. This, again, is the Kantian position.

So, whether in offense or defence, an American President, as the eminent representative of good Americans, will generally be judged by the rules of consistent rationality. Though other arguments may be helpful in the background—economic, commercial, utilitarian—America's implicitly standardized version of good and bad has to stand the test of Kantian good will, where the union of a non-contradictory rationality with personal autonomy becomes the touchstone of ethical consistency. In this sense, every President of the United States has to act according to the standards of Kant's categorical imperative: Your actions should always be compatible with "the conception of law in itself" (Kant 1988: 26) and never be self-contradictory (Kant 1988: 66).

IV. Conclusion

The argument of this short aperçu on American ethics has put the main focus on the relevancy of Kantian ideas within American culture. Constructing a scenario of diverse examples, the aforementioned considerations have tried to comment in detail on some of the varieties of American ethical Kantianism. One of the results of this discourse may be reduced to the simple statement that we observe, even today, a considerably higher quotient of Kantian thinking within American cultural and political developments compared to the significantly weaker influence of 'classical' Anglo-Saxon, i.e. utilitarian, concepts. There can be no doubt about the fact that a considerable number of these deontological enactments may be counted among sheer habitual and rhetorical gestures. But this somewhat devaluing dictum does not subvert the basic truth of the presented argument. On the opposite: if truth comes along in degraded versions, reduced to a polished facade of truth, this ethical Potemkin-(dis)course underlines the fact that, even in times of moral decline, there is a consistently high, perhaps growing, demand for the idea of rationally based ethics. Which reminds us of Kant's conviction that there is no alternative to reason as a universal (and thus: global) basis of ethics or, to quote it in the beautifully oscillating style of Immanuel Kant: "Nothing can possibly be conceived in the world, or even out of it, which can be called good without qualification, except a Good Will" (Kant 1988: 17).

Bernd Klähn

"In All People I See Myself": The New American Spirituality and the Paradoxes of Cultural Pluralism

Next fall, for the first time, I'll be teaching a course called "American Spiritualities." Not American *Religions*. American *Spiritualities*. Its title is taken from Catherine Albanese's recently published reader of the same title. In her introduction, Albanese tries to locate interest in spirituality as a moment in the history of American religion. She notes that initial definitions of spirituality explicitly linked it with institutional religion, and indeed makes a case for contemporary notions of spirituality in part flowing from Catholic devotional practice of the 1950s. But citing several late twentieth century sociologists of religion, she explains how "religion" and "spirituality" have increasingly become separate in the minds of many Americans in the last third of the twentieth century. Indeed Albanese dedicates her book to her sister Lucille, "who is spiritual but not religious."[1]

In this paper I want to ask some questions about spirituality as a phenomenon in the United States today. Among whom is there contemporary interest in spirituality as something *apart from* religion? Adopting for a moment Richard Rorty's pragmatist suggestion that "truth is simply

---

[1] Catherine Albanese, "Introduction," *American Spiritualities: A Reader* (Bloomington: Indiana University Press, 2001), 1-15.

a compliment paid to sentences that seem to be paying their way," I also want to ask how the concept of spirituality provides a pragmatic way for (some) people to deal with some of the fundamental questions of existence in a way that may differ from that of organized religion.[2] And finally, I want to begin to explore some possible reasons why interest in spirituality in the United States is on the rise in the United States, along with some reckless speculation about its possible implications for the way (some) Americans view the rest of the world. What does it mean to live in a Whitmanesque world whose cardinal assumption is "Ian all people I see myself, none more and not one a barleycorn less"?[3]

I. "I Tramp a Perpetual Journey":
Among Whom is There Contemporary Interest in Spirituality?

If spirituality originally referred to that which belonged to the clergy, by the last part of the twentieth century, those interested in a redefined notion of spirituality were often precisely those most sceptical about the clergy.[4] Sociologists of religion Wade Clark Roof and Robert Wuthnow make compelling cases that the quest for spirituality developed in the United States among a post-World-War II generation who had generally become alienated from institutions.[5] Seeking a personal connection with

---

[2]   Richard Rorty, quoted in *New York Times Magazine*, Feb. 12, 1990.

[3]   Walt Whitman, "Song of Myself," *Complete Poetry and Collected Prose* (New York: Library of America, 1982), 45. All additional quotations from Whitman taken from this poem, this edition.

[4]   See Albanese, 3, on *Webster's Third New International Dictionary*.
       See also the *Oxford English Dictionary*
       <http://dictionary.oed.com/cgi/entry/00233694?single=1&query_type=word&queryword=spiritua
       lity&edition=2e&first=1&max_to_show=10>, whose first two definitions make reference to
       ecclesiastical or concerns. Clearly the use of "spirituality" in reference to things pertaining to the
       spirit has been a relatively late developing definition culturally.

[5]   Wade Clark Roof, *Spiritual Marketplace: Baby Boomers and the Remaking of American Religion*
       (Princeton: Princeton University Press, 1999); Roof, *A Generation of Seekers: The Spiritual
       Journeys of the Baby Boom Generation* (New York: Harper Collins, 1993); Robert Wuthnow, *The
       Restructuring of American Religion: Society and Faith Since World War II* (Princeton: Princeton
       University Press, 1988); Wuthnow, *After Heaven: Spirituality in America Since the 1950s* (Berkeley:
       University of California Press, 1998); and "Forum: American Spirituality," with contributions by

the transcendent and a tangible sense of connectedness, increasing numbers of Americans who might in early times have identified them-selves with liberal or mainstream religious groups began to describe themselves as "spiritual," often in contradistinction to "religious."[6]

The religious right has made its presence known as a political and institutional force over the past two decades, and sometimes these days in the United States that group seems to be cornering the market on religious discourse. One of the reasons may be that many would-be liberals, once a part of American religious dialogue, have fled institutional religion altogether. Like the nineteenth-century intellectual Ralph Waldo Emerson, whom some have seen as the precursor of American spirituality as a movement, they see the individual soul as "the perceiver and revealer of truth."[7] Institutional mediation is not only unnecessary; it can hinder the development of spirituality. Because it tends to be private, the non-institutional variety of spirituality is far less visible than the institu-tional. In 1995, two-thirds of those American adults surveyed said that religion was playing a diminished role in public life, but two-thirds also said that spirituality was playing a larger role in their private lives. "What this means," writes sociologist Wuthnow, "is that the monopoly of spirituality by the religion industry has been broken."[8]

What precisely is this "spirituality"? Scholars who work in the area of contemporary American religion describe a sea change in American religious experience in the second half of the twentieth century. And *spirituality* is a word they summon frequently to help describe it. A 1986 study of spirituality links the word with the notion of individual commu-

Wade Clark Roof, Anne E. Patrick, Ronald L. Grimes, and Bill J. Leonard, *Religion and American Culture* 9 (Summer 1999): 131-158.

[6] See, for example, the conclusions of Conrad Cherry, Betty A. DeBerg, Amanda Porterfield, *Religion on Campus* (Chapel Hill: University of North Carolina Press, 2001), 275-276.

[7] Ralph Waldo Emerson, "The Over-Soul," *The Collected Works of Ralph Waldo Emerson*, II (Cambridge MA: The Belknap Press of Harvard University Press), 166.

[8] Robert Wuthnow, "From Religion to Spirituality," in Robert Royal, ed., *Reinventing the American People: Unity and Diversity Today* (Washington DC: Ethics and Public Policy Centre, 1995), 200.

nion with the divine, bordering on or akin to mysticism.[9] Spirituality may be defined as "personal relationships to the sacred," or alternatively, as "that which animates the mind and body, giving meaning, purpose, and context to thought, word, and action."[10] Spiritual culture is a sense of the whole; spiritual development, "an internal process of seeking personal authenticity, genuineness, and wholeness as an aspect of identity development"; spiritual quest, "a normal developmental process in which a person negotiates questions and concerns regarding personal destiny, happiness, God, the ethical implications of one's behaviour, suffering, and death," a process which may or may not be tied to a particular religious community."[11] Spirituality, in short, deals with individual persons and their relationships to ultimate meaning. It may or may not involve either formal religious commitment or belonging to a religious community.

It is not that *spirituality* has altogether superceded religion as a way of exploring the ways in which (some) Americans make or find meaning in their lives. Rather, religion and spirituality exist in a curious relationship where not everything that is religious is spiritual; not everything that is spiritual is religious; and some ways of approaching the world can be seen as both religious and spiritual. Robert Wuthnow, long one of the most perceptive students of religion in the United States, describes what I might call the "newer" emanations of spirituality as ways of relating to the sacred that are characterized by an eclectic *seeking*. Life is a journey, and seekers pragmatically sift through the variety of sacred forms, images, metaphors, and practices humans have generated to find what works for them as private individuals. Hence, spirituality for

---

[9]   "Preface," *The Study of Spirituality*, ed. Cheslyn Jones, Geoffrey Wainwright, and Edward Yarnold (New York: Oxford University Press, 1986), xxi-xxvi.

[10]   Robert Wuthnow, *After Heaven: Spirituality in American Since 1945*, vii; Peter Laurence and Victor H. Kazanjian, Jr., "The Education as Transformation Project," in *Transforming Campus Life: Reflections on Spirituality and Religious Pluralism* (New York: Peter Lang, 2001), 69.

[11]   John K. Roth, *Private Needs, Public Selves: Talk About Religion in America* (Urbana: University of Illinois Press, 1997), 1-2; P. Love and D. Talbot, "Defining Spiritual Development: A Missing Consideration for Student Affairs," *NASPA Journal* 37 (1999): 361-375, quoted in Margaret A. Jablonski, Ed., *The Implications of Student Spirituality for Student Affairs Practice* (San Francisco: Jossey-Bass, 2001), 1; Andres G. Nino, "Spiritual Quest Among young Adults," in *Education as Transformation: Religious Pluralism, Spirituality, and a New Vision for Higher Education in America*, ed. Victor H. Kazanjian, Jr. (New York: Peter Lang, 2000), 46.

seekers is a process of negotiation. In contrast, more traditional forms of spirituality—those we might call organized religion—emphasize *dwelling* as a metaphor. Dwellers encounter the sacred in places that are sharply bounded and set apart—in houses of God, as it were. "God occupies a definite place in the universe and creates a sacred space in which humans too can dwell," Wuthnow writes. The dominant metaphor he uses for this type of spirituality is habitation.[12]

For a certain segment of the American population born since World War II, there is a lot more seeking than dwelling, and skepticism about institutions is easy to come by. Robert D. Putnam's jeremiad on the decline of American institutional involvement, *Bowling Alone* (2000), meticulously documents the decline of civic engagement among the Baby Boomers and their children. It is not only religious participation that is declining, he shows. It is also political participation and voting, membership in social and philanthropic organizations, and civic participation in virtually all its forms. Just as we often bowl alone now, if we bowl at all, many of us also pray alone—if we pray at all.[13] The explanations for this shift away from institutional affiliation are various, and none completely satisfying. The Vietnam War and Watergate destroyed our trust in leaders and in institutions. Commercial entertainment is more readily available than ever, and much of it (e.g., television, listening to music on a Walkman) involves things individuals can do alone. Patterns of marriage and family life have changed. (The family dinner is rapidly becoming a thing of the past.) Greater geographic mobility has eroded community and familial ties.

Whatever the causes—and doubtless they are multiple—a large number of Americans now live lives that the historian of religion Martin Marty has described as valuing

> ... the personal, private, and autonomous at the expense of the communal, the public, and the derivative; the accent on meaning at the expense of inherited patterns of belonging; concentration on the local and particular more than the

---

[12]   Wuthnow, *After Heaven*, 3. Wuthnow develops his metaphors of contrasting types of spirituality in 1-18.

[13]   Robert D. Putnam, *Bowling Alone: The Collapse and Revival of American Community* (New York: Simon & Schuster, 2000).

cosmopolitan or ecumenical; concern for practical and affective life accompanied by less devotional and intellectual expressions....[14]

Any shift in values and practices is a mixed blessing. Some—most notably Putnam, but also to a degree Wuthnow, Marty, and others—have emphasized the loss that has occurred with the contemporary American preoccupation with the private and the personal. Without structure or community to sustain them, my experiences of the sacred are likely to be spontaneous and intense when they come, but also sporadic, unpredictable, episodic, and disconnected. The good news is, there is no time and place set aside to experience the sacred in ways that are communally prescribed. Any time and place can be sacred if approached in the right way. Formal structure or community is no longer a necessary condition for encountering the sacred.

II. "I Hear the Chorus. ... It is a Grand Opera" : Pluralism, Diversity, and the New Spirituality

In the last decade or so, the notion of spirituality has begun to work its way into institutional discourse in that bastion of secular humanism, the academy. Gradually, public conversation in a number of areas, particularly those concerned with human relations, has begun to explore spirituality as a concept that can allow for serious talk about religion as a factor in human experience (1) without privileging any religion in particular, and (2) without seeming to reduce it to an epiphenomenon of something else.

Permit me first to illustrate the rise of the concept in scholarly work. A quick check of my local library catalogue tells the tale. Miami University, my home institution, is a public liberal arts institution of about 18,000, with a small number of graduate programs. Sherlock, our on-line catalogue, shows that of the 1051 books written in English held by the library that contain the key word *spirituality* somewhere in the title,

---

[14] Martin E. Marty, "Where the Energies Go," *Annals of the American Academy of Political and Social Science* 527 (May 1993): 11-26.

subject, series, or notes, 1016 (or almost 97%) were published since 1970. Fully 820 (or about 78%) have been published since 1990. Contrast a similar search of the word *religion*: of 17,173 entries, 9436 (or about 55%) have been published since 1970, and 6167 (or about 36%) since 1990. Clearly something is going on.

But what? It might be worthwhile to look a little deeper to see what trends appear in these books that deal with spirituality. My survey is cursory, based only on what the titles of the books listed can tell me about their content. But even that little bit of information seems telling. There are 246 books with a publication date of 2000 or later.

1. 36 of these (14.6%) explicitly relate to psychotherapy or to counselling.
2. 32 of these (13%) deal explicitly with women's issues or take clear feminist stances.
3. 24 (9.7%) focus on issues related to health and wellness, illness, healing, medicine, or care giving. A number of these explicitly relate to nursing—a profession dominated by women.
4. 12 relate to education.
5. 11 have as a strong component an emphasis on ethnic or cultural identity that is *not* primarily religious in definition (e.g., African American, Latino/a, gay).
6. 9 deal with aging or dying as a process.
7. 8 deal with issues of social change, social ethics, or social work.
8. 4 address issues of sexuality.

Some works fall into more than one of these categories.

Of the books listed in our catalogue that utilize *spirituality* as a keyword and that have been published in the year 2000 or later, 139 (or considerably more than half) fall into one of these topic areas, associated largely with women, cultural outsiders, or the so-called "helping" professions.[15] How to account for the particular interest of these groups in using the new discourse in a scholarly setting? One hypothesis might be that these groups until recently have largely dealt with their questions and concerns outside the "public marketplace" of ideas, because they had relatively little access to it. But I'll leave a fuller exploration of that

---

[15] Marty, "Where the Energies Go,"whom I quoted earlier, goes on in the same article to note that contemporary American religion in general is shifting toward "the feminist as opposed to the male dominated.."

question for another day, for now simply noting that the trend exists.

Instead, in order to illustrate how this discourse about the private self is becoming public, I'd like to examine briefly one area where talk about spirituality has increased markedly in the last half decade or so as a legitimate topic for discussion—the literature on religion and education.

Look into the topic as recently as five years ago and you will find very little. In fact, the sole major publication, Warren A. Nord's *Religion and American Education: Rethinking a National Dilemma* (1995) doesn't mention spirituality at all in its title.[16] Rather, it deals with how religion is to be taught and discussed in schools. In a powerfully argued book, Nord claims that "the conceptual maps we provide students in our public schools and universities continue to chart a world without religion," and such a world map is misleading and deceptive.[17] In our efforts to insure religious neutrality, we have created an environment where religion cannot play a serious and legitimate part in public discourse though it plays a serious part in many individual lives. It becomes instead a matter of private taste or preference.

Nord, along with Diana L. Eck, a prominent scholar in the field of religious studies, pioneered a conversation about religion in American life that attempts to shift the tone of religious discussion from one focussed on diversity of experience to one focussed on pluralism of belief and practice.[18] The difference? Emphasizing religious diversity as the condition of American religious life frequently assumes a kind of exclusivity and particularity: no common ground among differing belief traditions is sought, and little is found. Different traditions live side by side, sometimes with mutual respect and sometimes not. Pluralism, in contrast, begins from the premise that diversity of belief can contribute

---

[16] Warren A. Nord, *Religion and American Education: Rethinking a National Dilemma* (Chapel Hill: University of North Carolina Press, 1995).

[17] *Ibid.*, 1.

[18] Diana L. Eck, *Encountering God: A Spiritual Journey from Bozeman to Banaras* (Boston: Beacon Press, 1993). See also Richard E. Wentz, *The Culture of Religious Pluralism* (Boulder CO: Westview Press, 1998), and "Final Report of the Ninety-Sixth American Assembly, on Religion in Public Life," March 23-26, 2000, in *Religion in American Public Life: Living with Our Deepest Differences* (New York: W.W. Norton, 1001), 159-177. Eck's Pluralism Project, centred at Harvard University, was first funded in 1990. Its focus was on the growing presence and influence of non-Judeo-Christian religions in the United States. See <http://www.pluralism.org/about/index.php.>

richness to a common culture and is something to be desired rather than tolerated. Pluralism (according to Diana Eck) "goes beyond mere plurality or diversity to active engagement with that plurality."[19]

Must such a culture of religious pluralism be produced through self-conscious effort, or does it already exist *de facto*? Some scholars, most notably Wade Clark Roof, maintain that many Americans already live in a state of religious heteroglossia. Where pluralism is the standard operating procedure in other cultural areas, religious traditions hardly ever exist in pure forms. Roof cites figures to suggest that in 1999, nearly half of all Americans believed that all religions are equally good and true.[20] Not that all religions have a right to exist, but that all on some level, all have equal value. This is pluralism at its most relativistic.

Yet, if Roof is right in his figures, that still leaves a good half of the American populace who *don't* believe that all religions are equally good and true. In other words, Americans are split down the middle as to whether they consider themselves particularists or pluralists in religious terms.[21] For particularists, pluralists may seem lax in their approach to things spiritual—something less than committed to the good and the true. For pluralists, particularists may seem narrow-minded bigots, who, in their own zealous belief that they have the truth, pose a danger to the rest of civil society.

What to do? The answer, increasingly among the pluralists, is to engage in self-conscious dialogue that looks for commonalities while

---

[19] Diana L. Eck, "A New Religious America: Managing Religious Diversity in a Democracy: Challenges and Prospects for the 21st Century Kuala Lumpur, Malaysia." Keynote address at MAAS International Conference on Religious Pluralism in Democratic Societies, Kuala Lumpur, Malaysia, August 20-21, 2002. Http://www.usembassymalaysia.org.my/eck/htm.

[20] Wade Clark Roof, 36, 84. Van A. Harvey, "On the Intellectual Marginality of American Theology," in Michael J. Lacey, ed., *Religion and Twentieth-Century American Intellectual Life* (Cambridge: Woodrow Wilson International Centre for Scholars and Cambridge University Press, 1989), 172-192, suggests that theology became intellectually marginal in the late twentieth century because of the pluralization of social worlds.

[21] Wuthnow, *The Restructuring of American Religion*, identifies these two perspectives as "liberal civil religion" and "conservative civil religion" and sees them as relatively distinct versions of civil religion (247-255).

respecting differences.[22] To do so is to make religion once again a part of public culture—to combat the aura of privatization that has come to surround religion as something that is personal, not meant to be talked about in public by polite audiences. By exiling religion from the public arena, these pluralists argue, we have impoverished ourselves. We have lost an important way of talking about collective morality and group sentiment.

One academic area where this concept has caught fire in recent years is in the literature on student affairs. I want to talk for just a few minutes about how the notion of spirituality gets played out in this literature, and then go on to speculate a little about some possible implications of this way of thinking about beliefs and values.

III. "I Am Large ... I Contain Multitudes": Spirituality and Notions of Selfhood

In 1998, more than 800 educators came together at Wellesley College for a two-day meeting entitled "Education as Transformation: Religious Pluralism, Spirituality and Higher Education." The group included representatives from over 250 universities and college and 28 university presidents and had been in the works since 1996. Its goals were twofold:

1. to explore the impact of religious diversity on higher education and the potential of religious pluralism as a strategy to address the dramatic growth of religious diversity in American colleges and universities; and

2. to consider the role of spirituality at colleges and universities and particularly its relationship to: teaching and learning pedagogy, the cultivation of values, moral and ethical development, and the development of global learning communities and responsible global citizens.[23]

---

[22] Robert Wuthnow, *Producing the Sacred: An Essay on Public Religion* (Urbana and Chicago: University of Illinois Press, 1994); "Final Report of the Ninety-Sixth American Assembly, on Religion in Public Life"; Roth, *Private Needs, Public Selves*.

[23] http://www.wellesley.edu/RelLife/transformation/gathering/part_one.htm#r_a. See also the volume of conference papers, *Education as Transformation: Religious Pluralism , Spirituality, and a New Vision for Higher Education in America*, ed. Victor H. Kazanjian, Jr., and Peter L. Laurence (New

At the same time (1997-2000), the Lilly Foundation funded a series of annual seminars on religion and higher education.[24] These two events opened the floodgates to a series of conferences, articles, books, and web sites dealing with the how institutions of higher education ought to handle issues of religious pluralism. Nearly always, the common denominator that was invoked as a way of bridging gaps and negotiating differences was the concept of spirituality.[25]

Scholars of spirituality and higher education today generally take one or more of three tacks in making the case for attention to issues of the sacred in colleges and universities today.

1———. Because the United States is a nation comprised of diversity, we must confront and engage with diversity in religious perspective along with every other kind of diversity. Toleration is not enough, for it

---

York: Peter Lang, 2000), and Peter Laurence, "Can Religious and Spirituality Find a Place in Higher Education?" *About Campus* 4 (November-December1999), 11-16.

[24] Robert J. Nash, *Religious Pluralism in the Academy: Opening the Dialogue* (New York: Peter Lang, 2001), 10.

[25] Victor H. Kazanjian, Jr., "Moments of Meaning: Religious Pluralism, Spirituality and Higher Education," *Connection: New England's Journal of Higher Education and Economic Development* 13 (Fall 1998):37-39; Robert J. Nash, *Faith, Hype, and Clarity: Teaching About Religion in American Schools and Colleges* (New York: Teacher College Press, 1999); Patrick Love and Donna Talbot, "Defining Spiritual Development: A Missing Consideration for Student Affairs," *NASPA Journal* 37 (1999): 361-375; *The Heart of Leadership: Spirituality in Education*, ed. Steven Glazer (New York: Jeremy B. Tarcher/Putnam, 1999); Martin E. Marty with Jonathan Moore, *Education, Religion, and the Common Good: Advancing a Distinctly American Conversation About Religion's Role in Our Shared Life* (San Francisco: Jossey-Bass, 2000); Courtney T. Goto, "At the Edge of the Future: Projects in Spirituality and Religious Pluralism in Higher Education," World Council of Churches, http://www.wccc-coe.org/wcc/what/interreligious/cd36-02.htm; Cherry, DeBerg, and Porterfield, *Religion on Campus*; Margaret A. Jablonski, ed., *The Implications of Student Spirituality for Student Affairs Practice*. New Directions for Student Services, 95. (San Francisco: Jossey-Bass, 2001); Nash, *Religious Pluralism* (2001); *Transforming Campus Life: Reflections on Spirituality and Religious Pluralism*, ed. Vachel W. Miller and Merle M. Ryan (New York: Peter Lang, 2001); Arthur Schwartz, "Growing Spiritually During the College Years," *Liberal Education* (Fall 2001): 30-35; Alan Wolfe, "Faith and Diversity in American Religion," *Chronicle of Higher Education* 48, #22 (8 February 2002): B7; Arthur Zajonc, "Spirituality in Higher Education: Overcoming the Divide," *Liberal Education* 889 (Winter 2003): 50-58. Major conferences included "Spirituality and Learning: Religion, Meaning, Value, and Inclusion in Higher Education," co-sponsored by the California Institute of Integral Studies, the National Association of Student Personnel Administrators, and the Association of American Colleges and Universities, San Francisco, April 2002; and "Spirituality on Campus: Reflection & Practice," National Association of Student Personnel Administrators, New Orleans, December 5-7, 2002. A list (by no means exhaustive) of web sites related to the topic of campus spirituality can be found at http://www.wellesley.edu/RelLife/transformation/Links.htm.

amounts to nothing more than a polite marginalization of religion as irrelevant to educated conversation. "I know in my own seminars," writes Robert J. Nash, a professor of education at the University of Vermont,

> that whenever the occasional Muslin, Buddhist, Hindu, or neo-Pagan talk about their beliefs publicly, my majoritarian Christian believers, along with disenchanted ex-Christians—in the interests of civility and for fear of offending—will either remain silent, or else respond in an overly polite, but banal manner. Although well-intended in their attempts to show empathy and respect for religious differences, often these students unwittingly send a clear message to the more articulate (and passionate) adherents of other faiths: They do not take them seriously enough to engage them in probing and extensive conversation about their religious and spiritual convictions.[26]

And so too with the majoritarian students in other settings. The secular academy has its own code of speech, and in that code, serious mention of religion as anything other than historical artifact is often seen as impolite at best, benighted at worst. Advocates of this perspective urge a broadening of the codes of secular conversation so that religious belief is taken seriously as a contributing factor to the belief structure of individuals. No one, the argument goes, is exempt from bias—including the presumably value-neutral discourse of secular humanism.

To deal with the full range of human difference and to leave religion our constitutes a serious oversight.

2.—— Because education exists as much to build character and create civic consciousness as to provide job skills or fill vocational needs, explicit talk about spiritual needs and growth helps to provide for the education of the whole person, not just for the future worker. Inclusion of attention to spirituality in the college experience counteracts the cultural tendency to focus on vocational preparation. "The primary goal of a college education," assert some of the participants in the Self-Exploration Symposium Movement centred at Duke University, "should not be the

---

[26]   Nash, *Religious Pluralism*, 12.

imparting of facts, but the transforming of people."[27] Such arguments provide rhetoric reminiscent of more traditional arguments that the central purpose of a liberal education is to build civic character. But not surprisingly, in a culture with strong anti-institutional overtones and privatizing tendencies, the focus now is on individual growth and well being rather than on the commonweal.

3.—— The scientific approach to knowledge of Enlightenment objectivism is in itself a world view that leaves out other forms of knowledge important to learners. Ironically, perhaps, what higher education in the past has seen as neutrality some critics now see as a separate orthodoxy. Skepticism about the absolute value of objectivism has been fed by post-modernism's emphasis on the role of the subject or perceiver in the construction of knowledge. This "epistemological challenge"—the demand for "a plausible basis for knowledge that can extend beyond a reductionist, materialistic ontology to one that is inclusive of contemplative and spiritual experience"—emphasizes the value of synthetic and holistic approaches to knowledge *in addition to* rational analysis.[28] The orthodoxy of higher education "insists that we can know the world only by distancing ourselves from it, by separating our inner lives from the external objects we want to know," writes Parker Palmer, whose *To Know as We Are Known: A Spirituality of Education* called for a more integrative epistemology as early as 1983. Such a way of knowing pushes holistic knowledge to the edge of human experience.[29]

4.—— How should higher education deal fairly and sensitively with issues of religious pluralism and of spirituality? The answer is different, depending on whether one conceives mainly of meeting public or private sphere needs. Of those seeing the need for students to engage the reality of religious belief in connection with public issues—mainly scholars of

---

[27] Mary Alice Scott, Georg Buehler, and Kenny Felder, "I Do and I Understand: The Self Knowledge Symposium Model for Spiritual Education on Campus," in Miller and Ryan, eds., *Transforming Campus Life*, 98. On this movement, see also http://www.selfknowledge.org/home/ and Megan Rooney, "Spiritualism at What Cost?" *Chronicle of Higher Education* (10 January 2003): A31-A32.

[28] Zajonc, 54-55.

[29] Parker L. Palmer, "A Vision of Education as Transformation," in Kazanjian and Laurence, eds., *Education as Transformation*, 17. See also Palmer, *To Know as We Are Known: A Spirituality of Education* (San Francisco, Harper & Row, 1983).

religion—approaches of choice include specifically addressing differing religious perspectives on issues in the classroom; engaging in public discussions on the impact of religious belief on public life; and simply removing the taboo in the classroom on offering religious-based perspectives on public issues.[30] The goal is to provide a space in public discourse to acknowledge that one's spiritual platform makes a difference in how one thinks about important public issues. Another group, mainly student affairs professionals, advocate encouraging dialogue among those of different spiritual orientations and faith traditions that focuses on personal narrative.[31] In this model spirituality is seen as a central factor in individual growth and well-being. Students now more than ever are flooding counselling centres, battling substance addictions, dealing with severe stress and depression, suffering from eating disorders. Focussing through personal narrative on the meanings and values central to one's own life can prepare students better to deal with the problems of life.[32] Or as John Roth puts it in his *Private Needs, Public Selves*, "*the primary venue for talking about religion in public can be found whenever and wherever people are willing to share and receive the narrative of their lives.*"[33]

In fact, some now maintain, spiritual development is an essential part of young adulthood, and its character often ends up being defined in quasi-therapeutic language.[34] What is spiritual development? Patrick

---

[30] For some examples of scholars who advocate a renewed discussion of religion's impact on public culture, see Robert Wuthnow, *Producing the Sacred: An Essay on Public Religion* (Urbana and Chicago: University of Illinois Press, 1994); Nord, *Religion and American Education*; Marty, *Education, Religion, and the Common Good*; Nash, *Religious Pluralism in the Academy*.

[31] See especially Victor H. Kazanjian, Jr., and the Students of the Wellesley College Multi-faith Council, "Beyond Tolerance: From Mono-religious to Multi-religious Life at Wellesley College," in Kazanjian and Laurence, eds., *Education as Transformation*, 213-230. See also Sarah Stockton, "Private Conversations about Public Spirituality," in Miller and Ryan, *Transforming Campus Life*, 145-160.

[32] Judy Raper, "'Losing Our Religion': Are Students Struggling in Silence?" in Miller and Ryan, *Transforming Campus Life*, 17-18.

[33] John K. Roth, *Private Needs, Public Selves: Talk About Religion in America* (Urbana: University of Illinois Press, 1997), 16. Italics in the original.

[34] Nino, "Spiritual Quest Among Young Adults," 45-57.

Love and Donna Talbot, student affairs professionals, attempt a five-pronged definition:

1. Spiritual development involves an internal process of seeking personal authenticity, genuineness, and wholeness as an aspect of identity development.
2. Spiritual development involves the process of continually transcending one's current locus of centricity.
3. Spiritual development involves developing a greater connectedness to self and others through relationships and union with community.
4. Spiritual development involves deriving meaning, purpose, and direction in one's life.
5. Spiritual development involves increasing openness to exploring a relationship with an intangible pervasive power or essence that exists beyond human existence and rational human knowing.[35]

Thus, how one approaches the task of integrating spirituality into higher education depends on whether one thinks of the issue mainly as a public discourse problem or a problem in the private realm. Ironically, this split duplicates American confusion about what to do with religion in a pluralist culture: to what degree are religion and spirituality mainly personal issues, and to what degree are they—and ought they to be—legitimate in public talk about institutional goals and objectives?

IV. "Very Well Then .... I Contradict Myself": Implications

Pragmatically, the new emphasis on spirituality in the United States is a phenomenon that allows some Americans to begin to grapple with two important contemporary dilemmas in American culture today: cultural pluralism and the challenge of individual identity definition. Liberal emphasis on cultural pluralism (as opposed to cultural assimilation) values the richness that a diversity of beliefs, values, and traditions can bring to a culture. At the same time, cultural pluralists struggle with the question of whether and how new common cultural elements can emerge

---

[35] Love and Talbot, "Defining Spiritual Development," 364.

within the pluralist stew to give diverse groups some common identity. It is not an easy problem.

Similarly, the erosion of some older communal ties and the rise in individual mobility has led to issues of identity and self-definition culturally. If I can move from community to community and culture to culture without much external impediment, is there any essential self I carry from situation to situation? Or does self simply change to mould to the requirements of each new situation?

Spirituality provides a functional way of addressing both dilemmas at once. Individuals can maintain their own particular beliefs, values, and traditions—mainly on a pick-and-choose basis—while at the same time affirming a common spiritual kinship with others who may choose different concrete expressions of spirituality. By positing a common human underpinning to all spiritual expression, the concept of spirituality attempts to maintain cultural distinctiveness on one level, yet dissolve it on another. We are not all the same, and that's OK, because on some level we *are* all the same. We each of us develop a spiritual identity, adaptable yet constant, that we carry with us from place to place. We are who we are, yet we can remain open at the same time to a variety of other sorts of cultural expression, affirming that all forms of spiritual identity are finally compatible. "I am large," as Walt Whitman might say; "I contain multitudes."

In some ways, spirituality as a concept promises to be the Esperanto of religions. The catch is that the belief that a culture *ought* to include a variety of opinions and beliefs springs from a cultural system that is at base capitalist to begin with. In such a culture, individual freedom of belief is important, because individuals are cut loose from traditional communal ties to participate more efficiently in the mechanisms of the market. Cultural pluralism is a necessity, since finally citizens have their status as workers and consumers, not as perpetuators of communal traditions or mores. To buy into the cultural pluralism model is in some ways to buy into the communal and individual models, and the models of cultural power, that it supports. Not every country, not every culture, structures itself in this way – or wishes to.

Consider.

If the world were a village of 1000 people, who would we be religiously? 329 Christians, 174 Muslims, 131 Hindus, 61 Buddhists, 52 Animists, 3 Jews, members of 34 other religions, with 216 claiming no religious affiliation. 564 of us would be Asian, 210 European, 86 African, 80 South American, 60 North American. 60 would own half the income, 600 would live in a shanty town, 500 would be hungry at all times, 700 would be illiterate. How would all these people conceive of the relation between religion and spirituality? How would they feel about cultural pluralism? "Revealingly," Robert Nash tells us, "the vast majority of the 'have nots' would be the most religiously zealous as well as the most angry; while the 'haves' would be content simply to assume a stance of benign, bourgeois neutrality toward religion."[36] In other words, poverty and economic disadvantage tend not to coexist well with the search for common values characteristic of cultural pluralism. One might speculate that there is simply too much evidence on a day-to-day basis of real difference to concern oneself overly with the question of commonality.

Nevertheless, the notion of spirituality provides those of us living in late capitalist culture with ways of grappling with some of its most emotionally debilitating features. If we are all homeless now in an existential sense, we meet the necessity by finding ways of considering anyplace home. If we are constantly challenged with a welter of new and strange cultural impression of which we must make sense, we find ways of turning them into the prerequisites for personal growth.

And if we find ourselves in the midst of a perpetual journey without clear destination, we universalize our experience, making it the metaphor for the human condition at large.

Mary Kupiec Clayton

---

[36] Nash, *Religious Pluralism in the Academy*, 36. The statistics are taken from Nash, 35-36.

References

Albanese, Catherine, ed. 2001. *American Spiritualities: A Reader.* Bloomington: Indiana University Press.

Cherry, Conrad, Betty A. DeBerg, Amanda Porterfield. 2001. *Religion on Campus.* Chapel Hill: University of North Carolina Press.

Eck, Diana L. 1993. *Encountering God: A Spiritual Journey from Bozeman to Banaras.* Boston: Beacon Press.

—————. 2002. "A New Religious America: Managing Religious Diversity in a Democracy: Challenges and Prospects for the 21st Century Kuala Lumpur, Malaysia." Keynote address at MAAS International Conference on Religious Pluralism in Democratic Societies, Kuala Lumpur, Malaysia, August 20-21, 2002. Http://www.usembassymalaysia.org.my/eck/htm.

Emerson, Ralph Waldo. 1979. "The Over-Soul." *The Collected Works of Ralph Waldo Emerson*, II. Cambridge MA: The Belknap Press of Harvard University Press, 157-176.

"Final Report of the Ninety-Sixth American Assembly, on Religion in Public Life." March 23-26, 2000, in *Religion in American Public Life: Living with Our Deepest Differences.* New York: W.W. Norton, 2001, 159-177.

Glazer, Steven, ed. 1999. *The Heart of Leadership: Spirituality in Education.* New York:Jeremy B. Tarcher/Putnam.

Goto, Courtney T. "At the Edge of the Future: Projects in Spirituality and Religious Pluralism in Higher Education." World Council of Churches, http://www.wccc-coe.org/wcc/what/interreligious/cd36-02.htm.

Harvey,Van A. 1989. "On the Intellectual Marginality of American Theology." In Michael J. Lacey, ed., *Religion and Twentieth-Century American Intellectual Life.* Cambridge: Woodrow Wilson International Center for Scholars and Cambridge University Press, 172-192.

Jablonski, Margaret A., ed. 2001. *The Implications of Student Spirituality for Student Affairs Practice.* San Francisco: Jossey-Bass.

Jones, Cheslyn, Geoffrey Wainwright, and Edward Yarnold, eds. 1986. *The Study of Spirituality.* New York: Oxford University Press.

Kazanjian, Victor H., Jr. 1998. "Moments of Meaning: Religious Pluralism, Spirituality and Higher Education." *Connection: New England's Journal of Higher Education and Economic Development* 13 (Fall 1998): 37-39.

Kazanjian, Victor H., Jr., and the Students of the Wellesley College Multi-faith Council. "Beyond Tolerance: From Mono-religious to Multi-religious Life at Wellesley College." In Kazanjian and Laurence, eds., *Education as Transformation*, 213- 230.

Laurence, Peter. 1999. "Can Religious and Spirituality Find a Place in Higher Education?"*About Campus* 4 (November-December1999), 11-16.

Laurence, Peter, and Victor H. Kazanjian, Jr. 2001. "The Education as Transformation Project." In *Transforming Campus Life: Reflections on Spirituality and Religious Pluralism* . New York: Peter Lang, 57-72.

Love, Patrick, and Donna Talbot. 1999. "Defining Spiritual Development: A Missing Consideration for Student Affairs." *NASPA Journal* 37 (1999): 361-375.

Marty, Martin E. 1993. "Where the Energies Go." *Annals of the American Academy of Political and Social Science* 527 (May 1993): 11-26.

Marty, Martin E., with Jonathan Moore. 2000. *Education, Religion, and the Common Good: Advancing a Distinctly American Conversation About Religion's Role in Our Shared Life.* San Francisco: Jossey-Bass.

Miller, Vachel W., and Merle M. Ryan, eds.1999. *Transforming Campus Life: Reflections on Spirituality and Religious Pluralism.* New York: Peter Lang.

Nash, Robert J. 1999. *Faith, Hype, and Clarity: Teaching About Religion in American Schools and Colleges.* New York: Teacher College Press.

Nash, Robert J. 2001. *Religious Pluralism in the Academy: Opening the Dialogue.* New York: Peter Lang.

Nino, Andres G. 2000. "Spiritual Quest Among Young Adults." In *Education as Transformation: Religious Pluralism, Spirituality, and a New Vision for Higher Education in America*, ed. Victor H. Kazanjian, Jr. New York: Peter Lang, 45-58.

Nord, Warren A. 1995. *Religion and American Education: Rethinking a National Dilemma* Chapel Hill: University of North Carolina Press.

Palmer, Parker L. "A Vision of Education as Transformation." In Kazanjian and Laurence, eds., *Education as Transformation*, 17-22.

————. 1983. *To Know as We Are Known: A Spirituality of Education*. San Francisco: Harper & Row.

Putnam, Robert D. 2000. *Bowling Alone: The Collapse and Revival of American Community*. New York: Simon & Schuster.

Raper, Judy. "'Losing Our Religion': Are Students Struggling in Silence?" In Miller and Ryan, *Transforming Campus Life*, 13-32.

Roof, Wade Clark. 1993. *A Generation of Seekers: The Spiritual Journeys of the Baby Boom Generation*. New York: HarperCollins.

————. 1999. *Spiritual Marketplace: Baby Boomers and the Remaking of American Religion*. Princeton: Princeton University Press.

Roof, Wade Clark, Anne E. Patrick, Ronald L. Grimes, and Bill J. Leonard. 1999. "Forum: American Spirituality." *Religion and American Culture* 9 (Summer 1999): 131- 158.

Rooney, Megan. 2003. "Spiritualism at What Cost?" *Chronicle of Higher Education* (10 January 2003): A31-A32.

Roth, John K. 1997. *Private Needs, Public Selves: Talk About Religion in America* . Urbana: University of Illinois Press.

Schwartz, Arthur. 2001. "Growing Spiritually During the College Years." *Liberal Education* (Fall 2001): 30-35.

Scott, Mary Alice, Georg Buehler, and Kenny Felder. "I Do and I Understand: The Self Knowledge Symposium Model for Spiritual Education on Campus." In Miller and Ryan, eds., *Transforming Campus Life*, 97-114.

Stockton, Sarah. "Private Conversations about Public Spirituality." In Miller and Ryan, *Transforming Campus Life*, 145-160.

Wentz, Richard E. 1998. *The Culture of Religious Pluralism*. Boulder CO: Westview Press, 1998.

Whitman, Walt. "Song of Myself." *Complete Poetry and Collected Prose*. New York: Library of America, 1982.

Wolfe, Alan. 2002. "Faith and Diversity in American Religion." *Chronicle of Higher Education* 48, #22 (8 February 2002): B7.

Wuthnow, Robert. 1998. *After Heaven: Spirituality in America Since the 1950s.* Berkeley: University of California Press.

————. 1995. "From Religion to Spirituality." In Robert Royal, ed., *Reinventing the American People: Unity and Diversity Today.* Washington DC: Ethics and Public Policy Center, 191-202.

————. 1994. *Producing the Sacred: An Essay on Public Religion.* Urbana and Chicago:University of Illinois Press.

————. 1988. *The Restructuring of American Religion: Society and Faith Since World War II.* Princeton: Princeton University Press.

Zajonc, Arthur. 2003. "Spirituality in Higher Education: Overcoming the Divide." *Liberal Education* 889 (Winter 2003): 50-58.

COMPARATIVE PERSPECTIVES, LITERARY COUNTERPOINTS

The End of History?
Contemporary World Fiction and the Testing of
American Ideologemes

In his widely discussed study of teleology in modern world history, *The End of History and the Last Man* (1992), Francis Fukuyama suggests that a "worldwide liberal revolution" has realized an incontrovertible success. And to be clear, Fukuyama does not advance the obviously implausible view that "history" as a skein of often unpredictable events has ended, but rather "History" as a "single, coherent, evolutionary process" has come to an end, and that there will be "no further progress in the development of underlying principles and institutions, because all the really big questions (have) been settled" (xii). While this claim appears to have significant validity, it is hardly universally accepted or globally evident and, indeed, the world today, more than a decade after the book's publication, is not quite the same place it was in the early 90s after the collapse of European communism. (One might cite Samuel Huntington's "clash of civilizations" thesis [1996] and the cultural conflicts that it accurately predicted as telling challenges to Fukuyama's sanguine pronouncements.)

In what follows, I will briefly consider the cogency of Fukuyama's now signature claim that liberalism and its associated ideologemes—civil rights, separation of the public and private spheres, universal suffrage, market economics, consumerism, technophilia—now provide an exemplary model for global political, economic, and social arrangements. I will focus in particular on a cluster of recently published novels drawn from world literature that interrogate, though in highly disparate ways, various tenets and consequences of contemporary liberalism. The works I have in mind are Walter Abish's *Eclipse Fever* (1993), Hanif Kureishi's *The Black Album* (1995), Hong Ying's *Summer of Betrayal* (1997), and Michelle Houellebecq's award-winning *The Elementary Particles* (1998). Each of these novels provides a critical engagement of American values and "American-ness" in the late twentieth century from highly nuanced geopolitical perspectives: Mexico (Abish), France (Houellebecq), China (Hong), and multicultural London (Kureishi). Given America's relative intellectual insularity, its economic dominance, and its growing inclination towards unilateralism as the world's sole remaining superpower, it is of utmost importance that we examine "constructions" of America "from afar," in order to understand more fully the effects of American hegemony on the world today. Let me first turn here to Hong Ying's evocative Summer of Betrayal which was inspired by the dark events in the spring of 1989 in her native China.

— 1 —

First some background. On April 15, 1989, Hu Yaobang, Politburo member, and former Secretary-General of the Chinese Communist Party died of a heart attack. While the passing of a prominent politician is always a circumstance of some note, national or even global in some instances, no one could have envisioned the series of events that his death would trigger, but then again Hu Yaobang was not a typical member of the ruling gerontocracy of the day. He was a man of (relatively stated) liberal sensibilities, who two years earlier had been forced out of his position as Secretary General when he was found guilty of the ultimate apostasy for a Chinese leader; he was tolerant of the values of " bourgeois liberalism."

On April 18, four thousand students gathered in Tiananmen Square to place a banner that anointed Hu as the "Soul of China." A few days later, fifty thousand students defied a government ban and camped out overnight in the Square in preparation for Hu's funeral. Chinese television and the *People's Daily* denounced the students' actions as conspiratorial counter-revolutionary attempts to overthrow the government. In the weeks that followed, protesters and government leaders incrementally raised the stakes, each side refusing to make any accommodation. One thousand journalists demanded freedom of the press; students demanded an end to censorship, with hundreds of them initiating a hunger strike in Tiananmen Square. A million people marched in Beijing and disturbances occurred throughout the country. Premier Li Peng called on students to end their protest and, rebuffed, declared martial law over areas of the city while thousands of students continued to hold Tiananmen Square. Late on the evening of June 3, students and the army clashed in the Square. When the population blocked troop movements in the city, soldiers opened fire. At 2 a.m. on June 4, soldiers reached Tiananmen Square and began to forcibly clear it. Some 2,600 people were killed in the ensuing violence.

This is the historical context of *Summer of Betrayal*, a novel written by a young (now expatriate) writer, Hong Ying, who was a student at Beijing's Lu Xun Writers' Academy in 1989. *Summer of Betrayal* tells a double story. One deals with the democracy movement in China and is manifestly macro political; the second takes up matters of gender and sexual liberalization, and is micro political. These two narratives do, however, irrespective of their different inflections, advocate Americo-Western style liberties. Ernesto Laclau and Chantal Mouffe make a useful distinction between two types of subject positions or positions of political agency. The "popular subject position" refers to a position "that is constituted on the basis of dividing the political space into two antagonistic camps," i.e., the "people" and the "regime" (131). The "democratic subject position" refers to "the locus of a clearly delimited antagonism which does not divide society in that way" (131). When an entire citizenry is seeking its freedom from a totalitarian government, "a single clearly defined enemy" creates a single axis of antagonism. Alternatively, in democratic countries such as the United States, antagonisms proliferate between any number of social constituencies and are diverse, rather than singular, in nature. The multiplication of political antagonisms advanced by the agendas of various "identity politics" groups illustrates the formation of plural democratic subject positions.

In *Summer of Betrayal*, each of the positions of antagonism has its own figurations. The popular subject position is represented through, predictably, descriptions of mayhem and violence in and around Tiananmen Square where, we recall, protesting students erected their large makeshift model of the Statue of Liberty during their action. For its part, the specific democratic subject position—built around a quest for gender equality and especially equality of opportunity for sexual expression—is captured through depictions of the female body, whether in body painting or dance or cinematic erotica/pornography. The novel's protagonist, a young poetess, Lin Ying, occupies both subject positions, the popular and the democratic. As a writer, her desire for free artistic expression is frustrated by the dictatorial state-sanctioned aesthetics of the day which permits only socialist-realist narratives of the "boy-meets-tractor" kind and highly sentimental, de-politicized folkish literature. Avantgardism is the lamentable product of the "dark rain of individualism" (66). Literary criticism utilizing Western approaches such as deconstruction and psychoanalytical methods is denounced as immoral (61-62). In addition to freedom of expression, others related to that of assembly, movement, and association are similarly proscribed. External organs such as the Chinese Voice of America and BBC Radio are the only (quasi-)reliable sources of information about evolving events. (30, 33). The economic reforms initiated by Deng Xiaoping during the period of his "Open Door" policy (1978-1989)—now viewed as "capitalist-class liberalization"—have not been matched by political liberalization and the tragedy of Tiananmen ensues (61). The separation of the public and private spheres is limited to elements of economic life, but is elsewhere absent. The news industry must now undergo a state-mandated "rectification" (103), and those students seeking liberal reforms have become counter-revolutionary "hooligans" to be imprisoned or shot.

As a woman in a male-dominated society, Lin Ying is reified, disrespected at birth by her father because she is female and hence a "disappointment," and later as an adult relegated to the status of a mere sexual plaything for males. She feels profound shame that her life is "so manipulated by men," e.g., lovers, editors, professors, fellow writers, and fellow students. In the words of Lin Ying's friend, Hua Hua:

> Men divide women into three types: wives, witches, and whores. The tiring work goes to wives, the evil work goes to witches, the dirty work goes to whores—only men are allowed to be great and wise. (84)

In a country where only male members of the governing class are allowed such liberties, the otherwise banal act of viewing pornography becomes a profound political gesture for Lin Ying and her friends (86). And Lin Ying laments that Chinese history in the twentieth century has lacked the directionality that Fukuyama sees as normative:

> This is a crazy century, a train that has jumped its tracks and gone amok. ... If each person could decide his own way of doing things, choose the most appropriate methods, perhaps we could bring the train back on track.
> ... Since the beginning of this century, every new generation, hot blood pounding in its veins, has wanted to do something ... each attempt has caused China to move backward. (132)

At the end of the novel, with all prospects of liberal reform gone in the post-Tiananmen repression, Lin Ying is left to make a symbolic gesture using the only instruments of freedom available to her, her body and her spirit (163). At a party, she engages in a naked "freedom dance," that leads to a brief liberatory love-in before the police arrive. Invoking the Martial Law Edict, the police lead her away to prison for "indecent behaviour" (181).

— 2 —

Citizen of a totalitarian country, caught up in the repression and horror of the Tiananmen affair, Lin Ying bears eloquent testimony to the appeal of fundamental American-style liberal freedoms and values. Still, there are other legacies of American liberalism, not all of which merit approbation. In the three other novels under consideration here, there is considerable concern about the materialism and compulsive consumerism that economic liberalism gives rise to.

Walter Abish's *Eclipse Fever* revolves around eclipse-chasing by wealthy Americans which leads them to Mexico. Yet this innocent, if indulgent, act of eco-tourism comes to symbolize the predatory nature of American capitalism with its elevation of the private sphere. Not content with simply viewing unobtrusively a natural event in Mexico, various Americans, in an odious display of "gringoism," seek to colonize the country commercially.

Preston Hollier, an American entrepreneur, wants to colonize Mexico, or at least parts of its pre-Columbian historical legacy. Like Disney Corporation's attempt a few years ago to commercialize American Civil War history—ultimately unsuccessful—by erecting a theme park near a Civil War battlefield in Virginia, Hollier wishes to build a $200-million retirement community for Americans beside the Aztec Pyramid of the Sun, outside Mexico City, as an alternative to Arizona. For Mexico "to develop to its full capacity," its national heritage "will of necessity have to be connected to a U.S. infrastructure" (96). In a telling illustration of how Arjun Appadurai's "ethnoscapes" function, Americans and Mexicans offer conflicting constructions of what constitutes "Mexico." For Hollier, "Mexico" must be shaped and branded, adhering to a restricted, idealized view—and his firm is called Eden Enterprises—while Mexicans see their national identity as fluid, overtly multicultural, and deeply embedded in national history. Guided by perfectionist notions of possibility, and tied to an "eternal present," a "carefree Now," the American entrepreneur uses the mechanisms of the free market to fashion a Mexico that is more succinctly, more essentially "Mexican" than anything that Mexico and the epic sweep of its history can possibly conjure up (231). And all in the service of that most American of ideologemes, the constructed matrix of needs called consumerism. Where Mexico is for enterprising Americans a blank slate on which to sketch visions of corporate empire, America is for Mexicans a place of infinite possibility, offering prospects of perfectability. As one Mexican says in the novel:

> What draws us [Mexicans] to America is not the superabundance of their malls but the underlying promise . . . The Walt Disney virtual reality of life dominates . . . It's a kind of Edenic promise of an extended childhood—a Nintendo existence: I'm a child, therefore I am! (249)

Venture capital in hand, bought politicians in his pocket, the American entrepreneur moves boldly to make Mexico more Mexican for Americans and Mexicans alike.

In *The End of History and the Last Man*, Fukuyama takes up the matter of recognition at some length. Building on earlier discussions by Plato in The Republic of "thymos" and by Hegel on humankind's fundamental yearning for recognition, Fukuyama provides a serviceable taxonomy of recognition in contemporary civil society. For him, Plato's thymos is akin to what we might today call "self-esteem" (165). And, further, it suggests "something like an innate human sense of justice: people believe that they have a certain worth, and when other people act as if they are worth less—when they do not recognize their worth at its correct value—then they become angry" (165). Some people embrace "megalothymia," the "desire to be recognized as superior to other people" (182). Alternatively, there are those that endorse what Fukuyama calls "isothymia," "the desire to be recognized the equal of other people" (182). In the distinctly illiberal society of China as portrayed by Hong Ying, but also interestingly in the apparently liberal United States as represented by Abish, oligarchies and individuals assume megalothymic postures in an effort to subordinate others to their will and to their material interests.

By advancing the interests of the few, at the expense of the many, individuals undermine a society's sense of the collectivity and of the public sphere, and therein diminish liberalism's attempts to arrive at a functional synthesis between individual and group/social rights and liberties. The last two novels upon which I will briefly touch here provide case studies in the collapse of a sense of community under the pressure of mindless consumption, petty narcissism, and unreflective tolerance, each of which is a by-product of liberally sanctioned economic self-determinism and the politics of self.

Hanif Kureishi's *The Black Album*, a novel-of-ideas set in multicultural London of the early 90s, portrays a series of conflicts set amid a group of young Londoners. There is the book-burning Islamic fundamentalist demagogue who takes advantage of Americo-British liberal freedoms of speech and conscience to undermine those same freedoms for others. An immigrant from Pakistan seeks to become more American than Americans as he indulges in a lifestyle full of American name-brands—Ray-Bans, Marlboros, Jack Daniels, Calvin Klein, and on—and African-American behavioural tics. An old-style British socialist slowly talks his way into the dustbin of history. And, finally, we find the protagonist, a liberal's liberal, who embraces by novel's end contingency and multiple subjectivity, overcoming the rancorous proselytizing of others that a liberal society defines as a sacred rite even as it threatens the very foundations of that society.

In some respects, Michel Houellebecq's *The Elementary Particles* poses the stiffest challenge to the view that American-style liberalism has achieved a "final victory" in the modern wars of ideology, and that that victory is not only indeed final but also, quite as importantly, fit and good. Espousing a misanthropic vision suggestive of Céline, Houellebecq has unalloyed contempt for the complacent materialism, reflexive promiscuity, and technophilia promoted by contemporary American liberalism. The co-protagonists of the novel, two step-brothers, Michel, a scientist, and Bruno, a burned-out dipsomaniac, move through life aimlessly, oscillating between moments of ennui and open despair. As authorial persona, the narrator dismisses the claims that the "sexual revolution" will lead to "communal utopia," seeing in it rather just "another stage in the historical rise of individualism" (96). The apotheosis of individualism and individual freedoms is embraced equally, by "(a)ctionists, beatniks, hippies, and serial killers . . . all pure libertarians who affirmed the rights of the individual against social norms and against what they believe to be the hypocrisy of morality, sentiment, justice, and pity" (175). Social atomization has become normative. The Elementary Particles is indeed a very dark lament on the anti-social consequences of unbridled freedoms. The solution that it proposes is equally distasteful. In a flash forward at the end of the novel, scientists in the year 2011 contemplate the distinctly dystopian prospect of altering the genetic code of humans in order to delete elements of human individuality. In this way, it is hoped, a "sense of community, of permanence, and of the sacred" might be restored (262). One can of course only cringe at the prospective communitarian nightmare that would ensue in such a context.

Still, community—its maintenance and nurturing—remains a profound challenge for contemporary liberal societies and certainly for the United States. As Fukuyama observes in the conclusion of *The End of History*, "The decline of community life suggests that in the future, we risk becoming secure and self-absorbed last men, devoid of thymotic striving for higher goals in our pursuit of private comforts" (328). Profoundly unequal distributions of economic shares, structural poverty, the lack of universal health care, corporate misgovernance and corruption on an epic scale—all of these suggest a seriously eroded commitment to the communal in contemporary America and, at the same time, call into question the ethos of individualism, the most enduring and formative American ideologeme of them all, though the most alluring as well for many of those who view America "from afar."

Jerry A. Varsava

Works Cited

Abish, Walter. 1993. *Eclipse Fever.* Boston: David R. Godine (1995).

DeLillo, Don. 2003. *Cosmopolis.* New York: Scribner.

Fukuyama, Francis. 1992. *The End of History and the Last Man.* New York: Avon.

Hong, Ying. 1997. *Summer of Betrayal.* Trans. Martha Avery. New York: Grove (1999).

Houellebecq, Michel. 1998. *The Elementary Particles.* Trans. Frank Wynne. New York: Vintage (2000).

Huntington, Samuel. 1996. *The Clash of Civilizations and the Remaking of the World Order.* New York: Touchstone (1997).

Kureishi, Hanif. 1995. *The Black Album.* New York: Scribner.

Laclau, Ernesto, and Chantal Mouffe. 1985. *Hegemony and Socialist Strategy: Towards a Radical Democratic Politics.* Trans. Winston Moore and Paul Cammack. New York: Verso.

Excentric Positionalities: Mimicry and Changing
Constructions of the Centre in the Americas

My paper will focus on various constructions of centres and eccentricity in three works of fiction from different parts of the Americas in the second half of the twentieth century. I am interested in the complex positionality of fictional characters who are profoundly aware of being situated on the margins of global power structures and institutions and who express their feeling of eccentricity in various ways depending on race, ethnicity, class and location. Particularly significant is the emphasis on the specifically inter-American context of the peripheral subjectivities examined. This hemispheric context progressively displaces, over the four decades separating the date of publication of the first example from that of the last, the predominantly colonial Atlantic connections represented in the earliest of the three narratives. These three examples illustrate very different responses to marginality.

V.S. Naipaul's Trinidadian novel *The Mimic Men* (1967) exemplifies, in a somewhat caricatural fashion, the more traditional colonial attitude of the local elite toward the metropolitan (European) centre, which could be found in varying degrees in all former British colonies. The myth of the promised land so prevalent in white settler societies, especially in the Americas, had little relevance in the plantation societies of the Caribbean, whose predominantly non-European inhabitants could seldom identify with the collective project of building a new civilization based on unlimited progress and material wealth and comfort in the New World. In the second half of the 20th century, the mythical colonial centre was still very present in the more privileged circles of the hybridized island societies of the Caribbean, in which the descendants of African slaves and indentured Asian labourers have often severed all ties to the homelands of their ancestors and where strong ties to the Commonwealth remain. My second example of eccentric positionality is Manlio Argueta's narrative *Un día en la vida* (One day in the life; 1980), which illustrates the profound sense of marginality of poor Salvadorians with respect to the new centre of world power, the United States. Not only has the mythical centre moved North, but it is constructed in quite different terms as part of a new neocolonial power structure. Finally, Émile Ollivier's Haitian exiles in a Canadian circus ("Regarde, regarde les lions;" [Look, look at the lions]; 2001) represent an eccentric positionality with respect to the country in which they are living, which is not one usually associated with an imaginary centre of any kind. But they also illustrate a dissolution of the geographic boundaries of the North-South economic divide in new global structures of privilege and exclusion where the Third World enters the first as a perpetual Fourth world within its borders. In these three works of fiction, constructions of and responses to eccentricity vary, and not only in terms of language (English, Spanish and French). They exemplify the profound changes that have affected the Americas since their conquest by Europe.

The subjects involved in the European colonial enterprise generally saw themselves as situated within the outer reaches of a centre/periphery construction in which a vaguely defined and expanding territory was opposed to the metropolitan Paris, London or Madrid. The explorers, administrators, travellers, soldiers and sojourners often felt like exiles in a foreign and generally hostile land. In the history of the Americas, there are many accounts of Europeans' dismay at the "emptiness" of the continent, its lack of history and cultural institutions, its environmental rigours and "barbarous" natives. Many members of the upper middle classes in the newly independent nations also expressed a profound sense of exile and undertook the inevitable pilgrimage to what they considered to be the centre of culture and civilization. This is the case with all settler colonies (the Americas, Australia, New Zealand), since European institutions largely replaced indigenous ones on a permanent basis. As for the colonized (non-European) subjects aspiring to recognition and power in the colonial society, they often adopted metropolitan paradigms and manners in what Homi Bhabha has named "mimicry" (Bhabha 85-92).

My first example, Naipaul's *The Mimic Men*, falls largely within this category—that of the non-European colonized subject. But although Bhabha uses this novel as an illustration of his theory of mimicry, it represents a far more extreme case of both mimicry and eccentricity than the discourses analysed by Bhabha in his discussion of colonial mimicry in India, which is the main focus of his article. Ralph Singh, the protagonist of South Asian origin in Naipaul's novel, shares a profound sense of living on the margins of the world with his white cosmopolitan friends in the fictional Isabella, a thinly disguised Trinidad. His situation is not quite like that of South Asians in colonial India, since he is a descendant of the indenture diaspora and therefore cannot locate his cultural roots on the island of his birth. Neither is he like white settlers in a foreign land, since his ethnic origins situate him within the ambivalent category which Bhabha describes as an Other that is "almost the same, but not quite" (86): "[...] to be Anglicized is *emphatically* not to be English" (87; emphasis in the original). Race, exilic consciousness and the feeling of peripherality combine in Singh, leading to an extreme sense of eccentricity and rootlessness.

Although he was born on the island, he considers himself an exile, just like his European immigrant friends, who feel a "collective sadness" (Naipaul 66). Within this small group of expatriates, to which Singh thus belongs in an ambivalent way, "nothing was prized so much as the visitor from countries reasonably far away" who brings a breath of the real world to the "narrowness of island life" (66). Even Deschampsneufs, the descendant of an old French land-holding family and thus not a recent expatriate, dreams of life elsewhere: not of France, the country of his ancestors, but of Quebec, which he describes as "French and marvellous" (143) and where, he claims, art is appreciated. Singh's schoolteacher, although embarrassed at his education in an "obscure" Canadian university (145), dreams about skiing in the (Quebec) Laurentians and arouses in his pupil a strong desire for the "slopes of white, uninhabited snow" (146). Further on he refers to his "longing for different landscapes, a different world, where a child's first memory of school was of taking an apple to the teacher and where, in essays at least, days were spent on temperate farms" (212). As a child, Singh has heroic fantasies about Aryan knights

(98) in an imaginary filiation with obvious racial connotations.

It is interesting that these dreams of elsewhere are not limited to the former colonial centre. Although the novel generally emphasizes the mythic aura of London for the islanders of South Asian origin, the scattered references to the far North of the Americas foreshadows a displacement of the centre in the later fiction of Argueta and Ollivier. The oblique allusions to race in these passages are also particularly significant. The "white" snow, the "temperate" climate (associated with Europe and parts of anglophone North America) and especially the "Aryan knights" conjure up a racial fantasy that is partially actualized by Singh's marriage to a white Englishwoman.

Accompanying the idealization of the outside world by the community of expatriates and islanders such as Singh is a thorough contempt for everything associated with Isabella, described by Singh's English wife Sandra as "the most inferior place in the world," with "inferior natives, inferior expats" (69). The couple's house seems empty, and in no way a real home, since Sandra and Singh had "never succeeded in colonizing it" (71). It is an obvious metaphor for their attitude toward the island, which the more privileged and educated islanders have never appropriated symbolically and populated with pleasant childhood memories, in spite of their being born there. Isabella is a place of exile, instead of an imagined community with which islanders such as Singh can identify. It is not simply a question of disliking Isabella, but one of a total lack of belonging, as if Singh were actually an exile. He has no sense of rootedness or connection to place, as his subjectivity is constituted through a strong "disidentification" with the society of less privileged and uneducated islanders, especially those in menial jobs and rural surroundings. The imagined community is elsewhere—in white settler societies, and especially in England.

An essential element in this gap between the more privileged islanders' everyday experience and the culture with which they identify is the colonial education system. Singh explains that everyday life is considered as something inferior by the schoolchildren, who express their contempt (and at the same time their self-hatred, since their families are not always educated) through scornful laughter: "The laughter denied our knowledge of these things to which after the hours of school we were to return. We denied the landscape and the people we could see out of open doors and windows [...]" (95). On a drive through the island's rural region, he describes the island as "unbearable," and this desolate portrayal of the countryside echoes his deep despondency at having to live in what he considers as the edge of the world: "We were in the area of swamps. Sodden thatched huts, set in mud, lined the road. It was a rainy day, grey, the sky low and oppressive, the water in the ditches thick and black, people everywhere semi-naked, working barefooted in the mud which discoloured their bodies and faces and their working rags" (98). On a trip to the beach, he sees the island as "a place still awaiting Columbus and discovery" and himself as a "shipwrecked chieftain on an unknown shore, awaiting rescue" from a "distant island, [...] lost and deserted" (111). His gaze resembles that of the white European contemplating what he considers to be primitive natives totally lacking in civilization. He shows no empathy toward his compatriots, partly because of class differences, but also because of his negative view of island culture in general. Like the Black inhabitant of the Caribbean whose subject formation Fanon analysed in his psychoanalytic studies on race and who is described as profoundly affected by the pejorative white gaze (Fanon 1952), Naipaul's narrator has a problematic relation with his community through his appropriation of pejorative discourses on and attitudes toward the non-European and his construction of the metropolitan Other as his ideal. He differs from Fanon' Black subject, however, in the particular type of mimicry in which he engages, to which I will return.

Singh's profound "disidentification" with island life leads to the inevitable decision to leave the island for the "real world," the "reality which lay elsewhere," after which everything around him becomes "temporary and unimportant" (118): "Fresh air! Escape! [...] Good-bye to this encircling, tainted sea!" (179) is all he can think of before moving to London, which represents the mythical and almost sacred centre of civilization to Singh. Isabella, instead of signifying home, has become a dystopia, and even a form of heterotopia, defined by Foucault as an "other place" set apart from normal public spaces: "Places of this kind are outside of all places, even though it may be possible to indicate their location in reality" (Foucault 24). Even though Singh's Isabella does not correspond precisely to Foucault's concept, which designates enclosed spaces such as prisons, libraries, museums and rest homes, it does suggest certain parallels (the island as a prison, cut off from the outside; the island as a space considered as absolutely Other with respect to the "real" world). Unlike Foucault's heterotopia, however, the gaze comes both from inside the marginalised space (Singh was born on the island and speaks from within), and from the outside, since his cultural references displace his gaze to a position depicted as metropolitan (the outsider within). Isabella is also a heterochrony, to borrow another of Foucault's concepts (26), since the island is constructed by Singh as situated outside modern time, waiting for discovery by Columbus.

While Isabella is outside contemporary time and real space in its dystopian backwardness, London as the sacred utopian space rapidly dissolves on closer contact. Singh's "feeling of being adrift" (27), his "placelessness" continues to haunt him in the "real world," as well as a "sense of captivity and lurking external threat," as the red brick houses of London become "interchangeable" with the houses back on the island (154). He sees his experience in London as an "even greater shipwreck" than his past in Isabella (180). The dilapidated rooming-house in which he first lives, the grey roofs, the brown smoke rising from "ugly chimney-pots," and the visible bombsites quickly make the "magic of the city go away" and replace it with "forlornness" (7): "So quickly had London gone sour on me. The great city, centre of the world, in which, fleeing disorder, I had hoped to find the beginning of order" (18). He realizes that the city had always been an idea, a god vainly pursued, and that it is in reality a "conglomeration of private cells" (18), empty factories and warehouses, empty streets, and "rotting wooden fences" (19).

In his restlessness, Singh moves from dingy room to dingy room, has "unrelated adventures and encounters" (28), takes trains "for no reason except that of movement" (30), travels to the provinces and the Continent, only ending up exhausted and "oppressed by a feeling of waste and helplessness" (41). The contrast between his experience as an expatriate and the image of England abroad is absolute, as he sits dejectedly with Sandra at a plastic-topped table covered with crumbs and luke-warm tea in the canteen of the radio service that, "when picked up in remote countries, was the very voice of metropolitan authority and romance, bringing to mind images, from the cinema and magazines, of canyons of concrete, brick and glass, motorcars in streams, lines of lights, busyness, crowded theatre foyers, the world where everything was possible" (46). He eventually escapes back to his island, feeling like a tourist in front of a "desired object of pilgrimage" that leaves him cold (31). On his return to Isabella with his English wife, the exotic myth of the island paradise conjured up by the film *The Black Swan* disappears as fast as the colonial myth of London nourished on the island during his childhood.

The idealization of an absent centre often leads to an effort to imitate the behaviour of the representatives of the colonial metropolis. But mimicry, as Bhabha has pointed out, is not just the hiding of a supposedly "real" identity, as in Fanon's *Black Skin, White Masks,* in which Black Caribbeans still have a strong sense of identification with their community. In colonial mimicry, the mask is all there is: "Mimicry conceals no presence or identity behind its mask" (Bhabha 88). A profound sense of exile on his island has led Singh and his compatriots not only to strive to become "almost the same [as the English] but not quite," to use Bhabha's oft-quoted expression (86), but also to forego any sense of identification with his land of birth. Since the "real world" is felt to be elsewhere, Singh knows nothing about the fauna of Isabella, for example (146-7). Bhabha's category of "mimic men" is defined in Macaulay's words as "a class of persons Indian in blood and colour, but English in taste, in opinions, in morals and in intellect" (Bhabha 87). Although Bhabha draws his examples from discourses on India (except for his reference to Naipaul), his mimic man who lacks any sense of identification with his place of birth is particularly relevant to the educated classes of South Asian diasporic societies.

In an ironic deconstruction of the supposed "authenticity" of well-assimilated Englishness, the caricatural mimic man, Ralph Singh, ironically copies the behaviour of foreigners in London, like Mr. Shylock, whom he admires for his suits and mistress (5). He is not the only mimic man/woman in the novel. Lieni, the Maltese immigrant and indigent single mother, tries hard to act the role of the "smart London girl" (11). As for Singh, he plays the "dandy, the extravagant colonial" (20). However, mimicry is not just the imitation of manners, speech and gestures or the creation of a simulacrum of identity in the expatriate community of London. Every activity is transformed into the acting of roles, both in London and on the island. Play-acting is found in all spheres of colonial and postcolonial island life—everything is a game in the unreal place of Isabella. Back home after his first stay in London, accompanied by his English wife Sandra, Singh becomes a politician, but "politics remained little more than a game" (38). Their friends are also "acting, overdoing domesticity and the small details, over-stressing the fullness of their own lives" (63).

Already as a child, Singh and his friend Hok had walked through the streets, acting out the role of "disrespectful tourists" (96), and Hok also lives in an elaborate private world of fantasy, far from Isabella. Since the "true, pure world" is Liège in a traffic jam or the snowy slopes of the Laurentians—any world but Isabella—life on the island can only be unreal: "We pretended to be real, to be learning, to be preparing ourselves for life, we mimic men of the New World, one unknown corner of it, with all its reminders of the corruption that came so quickly to the new" (146). This "playacting" (184) is not just the desire of the mimic man to imitate the gestures of metropolitan society. Departing from the depiction of colonial subject-formation as a personal predicament, Naipaul brings up the question of colonial power (Bhabha defines mimicry as "one of the most illusive and effective strategies of colonial power and knowledge;" 85) and attributes the prevalent feeling that acting, especially in the public sphere, is playacting, largely owing to the situation of colonial dependence, which ensures that local politics remains a "joke" (190). He asks: "Did we then act? Or were we acted upon?" (190). This hardly changes after independence, because of the island's continuing neocolonial ties and the resulting perpetuation of eccentricity; the new rulers of Isabella only lose the dignity of colonial service and become "totally ridiculous" (191). The moment of success, when "playacting turns out to be serious" (200) only leads to despair and a lack of purpose, as the new politicians become prisoners of their roles (203). There are no common interests, no "link between man and landscape", no "true internal source of power"—the only real power lies outside (206)—in the colonial centre before independence and in the new globalized power structures in which Isabella continues to be linked to the outside in a relation of neocolonial dependency that dictates the conditions of economic development (or rather, the pillaging of national resources).

The emphasis on mimicry in Naipaul's novel echoes the cliché, frequently criticized by Latin Americans condemning the colonial mentality of many of their countrymen, of the colonial as an imperfect copy, a pale imitation of the metropolis, a rapidly degenerating transplant of civilization contaminated by barbarism. But it also situates the novel in the second half of the 20th century, with its awareness of the hopeless situation of a perpetually dependent society remaining on the margins of seemingly immutable global power structures. The deconstruction of the mythical centre once Singh arrives in London, and the disenchantment with optimistic dreams of autonomy and progress, illustrate a position quite different from that of Domingo Faustino Sarmiento, for example, the nineteenth-century Argentine president who idolized the United States and advocated immigration from northern Europe to lead his country to prosperity and civilization. No longer the utopian centre that it was for many nineteenth-century Latin American politicians, the United States have become a neocolonial threat, at least since the critical essays of the Cuban essayist, poet and revolutionary José Martí in the last two decades of that century.

Naipaul's depiction of the displaced, deterritorialized identification with the colonial centre, leading to a total "disidentification" with the society of his birth and childhood, stands in salient contrast to Manlio Argueta's sympathetic representation of the central American peasants, torn between the misery of exploitation and abuse of power by the corrupt landholding elite and brutal armed forces on the one hand, and collaboration with United States-trained special forces that transforms them into their countrymen's tormentors and exploiters. According to the critic Fernando Alegría, Argueta "idealizes" the peasants (417). The Salvadorian author presents a very different type of eccentric positionality in his short 1980 novel, in which the protagonists are not members of an educated elite dreaming about a mythical colonial centre and desperately seeking escape. His characters are situated within a new neocolonial structure in which the former colonizer has been totally replaced by the colossus to the North. Argueta dwells on the miserable conditions of his country's peasants, who live in utmost poverty, have no medical care or adequate education, and are afflicted with the daily tragedy of a high rate of infant mortality. He strongly identifies with his poor countrymen through the voice of his female protagonist/narrator, condemning the exploitation of labourers by the landowners in league with the Church and the brutal repression of any form of resistance by the military (arbitrary arrest, execution, torture, destruction of houses) in league with United States military experts.

The first-person monologue of Guadalupe, who struggles to survive and care for her children in these extreme conditions, and who has lost several family members to governmental repression, illustrates a subject-position far removed from that of Ralph Singh in Naipaul's novel, who feels like an exile in his country and venerates European culture. Although she is certainly a marginalised subject within her own society,

Guadalupe does not fall within the paradigm of the "mimic (wo)man."

A certain parallel between the two novels can, however, be found in Argueta's description of the"special forces" of the military, who are trained by United States experts in ways of dealing with popular resistance and revolt. In a recurring monologue (alternating with that of Guadalupe), a special forces soldier, who has left behind poverty to enter the training school, rapidly "disidentifies" with the popular classes, not only because of the privileges enjoyed by the soldiers and the specialized knowledge acquired in the school (nutricious food and advanced training in military techniques, including martial arts and psychological torture), but also because of the constantly repeated lessons that the worst enemy of the country, and of democracy, is "the people" (*el pueblo*—the popular classes; 97). Profoundly influenced by the negative portrayal of Latin America by the foreign instructors, whose knowledge he admires, the narrator of the monologue describes his countrymen as ignorant, lazy, illiterate, and indelibly marked by their unfortunate Hispanic heritage: "We had the misfortune to be conquered by Spaniards who were nothing but heavy drinkers, whereas up there, in the North, came the English, who are great workers. On top of that, the English finished off the Indians, while the Spaniards didn't" (98).

Although he initially had great difficulty getting used to North American food, the special forces soldier quickly despises his own, informing his interlocutor that corn is only fed to pigs and horses (99). As for religion, he ends up claiming that the "real Christ" came to the United States with the Jehovah's witnesses and Mormons, whereas the Catholic church, "poisoned with pure communism" (99), brought only syphilis. The academy has also inculcated him with a hatred of his own race, a mixture of white and indigenous blood; in the United States, he adds, they would be taken for Blacks (99). His association with the gringos has profoundly changed his self-perception: "[...] I belong to God's armies, because we are saving civilization, not with damned ideas from books, but with daily practice, using the procedures of the most civilized nation on earth" (100). Profoundly aware of belonging to an underdeveloped country, he sees himself on the margins of a hemispheric power structure in which the centre—civilization, military power, economic might—is situated in the North.

His is the position of the stereotypical colonial or neocolonial middleman, who derives a certain power by repressing his own people and adopting the attitudes of the foreign (or foreign-influenced) authority. The parallel with Naipaul's protagonist, however, is only partial. While the educated Singh sees himself as belonging to a cosmopolitan cultural elite whose imagined community is not the society in which he was born, the special forces soldier continues to identify with the poor rural inhabitants of his country. He is perfectly at ease drinking in a tavern with his poor and illiterate countrymen, speaking their own language, and is impressed and awed by the educated Northerners (including the Chinese instructor who belongs to the American team of experts), whom he sees as his betters, very different from himself in every way, and thus certainly not as members of his own community. While Ralph Singh perfectly illustrates the concept of colonial mimicry in which no sense of identification with one's country lies beneath the mask, the soldier identifies with his country and wants to render it service, albeit in the misguided ways the narrative describes.

Furthermore, many of his values are those of his exploited countrymen, in spite of his partial assimilation of United States customs, food and ideas. Although he praises the "real" Protestant Christ of the North, he is very worried about the consequences of betraying his Catholic religion. And in spite of his ostentatious exhibition of power and privilege in front of his drinking companion, he is worried about the man's perception of him, insisting on paying for drinks and denying that he is brainwashed. In no way does he feel like an exile in his own country, totally alienated from his surroundings and dreaming of elsewhere. Instead of having a totally displaced subjectivity with respect to his society, like Naipaul's narrator, Argueta's soldier is a partially split subject who identifies with his countrymen but considers himself as different and superior because of his privileged contact with the representatives of neocolonial power. Underneath the transparent mask of the middleman, he maintains a strong identity forged by two centuries of independence from the Spanish colonial power and his links to a much older indigenous culture, which has been hybridized with Spanish transplants.

In Émile Ollivier's short narrative, "Regarde, regarde les lions" ("Look, look at the Lions;" 2001), the eccentric positionality of the protagonist is not that of the colonial or postcolonial subject identifying with the metropolis and feeling like an exile at home, like Ralph Singh, or that of the Salvadorian soldier admiring the strength and know-how of the gringos, even though he feels a strong affinity with his own culture. It is that of the political exile or economic refugee living on the margins of his northern host country, namely, French-speaking Canada. For the Haitian refugee Manès, the centre has moved even further north, partly owing to the affinities of French creole-speaking Haitians with Quebec. But strong emotional and cultural ties keep his Haitian past very present in the refugee's thoughts. Although Quebec is seen as belonging to the First World, it in no way resembles the mythical metropolis of England, or the United States centre of American military and economic power. The eccentricity of Ollivier's black protagonist is that of the Caribbean immigrant, who fails to feel part of the new society even if he appears to be fully integrated.

Although this experience is shared to a certain extent by all immigrants, exiles and refugees, Ollivier's narrative offers a particular twist to the alienation of the newcomer that must be situated within the entire structure of the colonial/postcolonial imaginary. When Manès, the black Haitian protagonist of his short story "Regarde, regarde, les lions" arrives in Montreal, he accepts a job as a costumed lion impersonator in a circus, prodded by the whip and boots of the visibly foreign lion tamer to perform stunts with another human lion (also a Haitian, who terrifies Manès because the latter does not know that the second lion is not real either). Instead of the mimicry of metropolitan customs, Ollivier depicts the mimicry of the opposite—an animal associated with wildness, blackness and the primitive. Bhabha's colonial mimic man who becomes "almost [white and civilized] but not quite" is here replaced by a third-world subject forced to act out the old European fantasy of the primitive Other.

The narrative representation of the spatial configuration of the circus ring and bleachers strongly emphasizes the inequality between the observers (the spectators on the darkened bleachers) and the observed (the terrified Haitians parading as wild animals in the brightly lit ring). A metaphor for the colonial gaze as well as the semiotic construction of non-Europeans as non-humans fit only for amusement or observation, the representation of space situates the protagonist at the physical centre (the focus of the gaze in the ring), and at the same time in a strongly eccentric position not only as an immigrant accepting a degrading job in a building at the edge of the city, but also as an exile from the poorest nation in the Americas. In other narratives, Ollivier describes Haiti as a dumping ground for hazardous American waste, and as a perpetual place of chaos, corruption and misery, which he explicitly attributes to the legacy of colonization. The circus is a heterotopia of illusion (Foucault 27), whose function is to represent the "real" society outside in an exaggerated form. The power structures within the circus and the role played by the two Haitian lion impersonators depicts the globalized division between the privileged and the indigent. The neocolonial peripherality of Argueta's peasants has given way in Ollivier's short story of the beginning of the 21st century to the excluded subjects of a diffused border inside as well as outside modern industrialized society. The centre has lost its clear definition, specific location and mythical qualities as it is transformed into the privileged spaces surrounding the inter-American pockets of poverty and exploitation.

Three different eccentric positionalities are thus presented by the three authors discussed—that of the colony/ex-colony still connected to Great Britain in a profoundly unequal power structure (Naipaul), that of the inter-American South dependent on the North for the maintenance of a repressive internal regime (Argueta), and that of the immigrant of colour from an acutely underdeveloped society who is situated on the margins of power and privilege whether he remains in his country of origin, or immigrates to the prosperous North. In all cases, there is an absence of hope in the protagonists, who do not see themselves as inhabitants of a promised land, as founders and builders of nations, or as the elect who are finally allowed to enter a mythical centre. Eccentricity is not only the marginal position of the colonized or formerly colonized, but that of the permanently excluded subjects struggling to survive on the edges of a new global Empire—that of power and wealth—that will always remain unattainable. Colonial east-west dependency (Naipaul, 1967) has given way to neocolonial inter-American peripherality (Argueta, 1980), and finally to the permanent exclusion in a North-South divide of changing borders (Ollivier, 2001). Although Naipaul's novel already refers to the new global market that will condemn peripheral societies such as Trinidad to perpetual marginality and dependency, and Ollivier presents colonial stereotypes of the native, the three narratives illustrate different manifestations of eccentricity linked to particular stages of the increasing globalization of the world.

Amaryll Chanady

Bibliography

Alegría, Fernando. 1986. *Nueva historia de la novela hispanoamericana.* Hanover, NH: Ediciones del Norte.

Argueta, Manlio. 1987. *Un día en la vida.* San José, Costa Rica: EDUCA [1980].

Bhabha, Homi K. 1994. *The Location of Culture.* London and NY: Routledge.

Fanon, Frantz. 1952. *Peau noire masques blancs.* Paris: Seuil.

Foucault, Michel. 1986. "Of Other Spaces." *Diacritics: A Review of Contemporary Criticism* 16.1 (Spring 1986): 22-7.

Naipaul, V.S. 1969. *The Mimic Men.* London: Penguin [1967].

Ollivier, Émile. 2001. "Regarde, regarde les lions." *Regarde, regarde les lions. Nouvelles.* Paris: Albin Michel, 41-64.

Approaches to Margaret Atwood's *The Edible Woman*

The Edible Woman was Margaret Atwood's first novel, published in 1969. The outline of the story and the main context explicitly respond to the 'second wave' feminist issues. Many critics have regarded it as a comic satire. The theme is about the female protagonist's search for identity with an emphasis on her inner mental journey in the modern world of consumption and materialism. It specifically deals with the relation of the sexes in a consumer society where men view women as commodities or as properties to enhance their social status.

Marian McAlpin, a woman in her mid-twenties, is an ordinary, capable young college graduate who works for a market research company. She is engaged to a handsome young lawyer named Peter Wolander, whose hobbies are hunting and photography. In contrast, Ainsley Tewce, Marian's roommate, is a superficial feminist, who insists that motherhood will fulfill her feminine mystique. She is determined not to marry, but ends up hunting for a man to father her unborn child and finally "settles down." Other stereotyped female characters are portrayed in Clara Bates, Emmy, Lucy, and Millie. Clara Bates' marriage is depicted as conventional. It has made her become submissive and passive. Marian thinks that Clara's role as a wife and mother has made her life empty and wasteful, and it makes her apprehensive about her own marriage. Apart from Clara, the "office virgins" are presented as typical young women who are conscious about their looks and their femininity. They are preoccupied with beauty, and their goal in life is to get married and raise children. As the story develops, we experience the intensity of Marian's inner struggle to free herself from being captured by Peter. Since Marian becomes increasingly oppressed by her status as a victim and commodity, consumed by all around her, she gradually identifies herself with food. She is fully aware of being used and exploited by everyone around her, so she finds it difficult to eat. The story reaches a climax when Marian makes a second attempt to escape Peter while he is busy gathering party guests for a group photo. Marian reunites briefly with Duncan, who has returned to save her after they have an affair. Eventually, Marian has regained her energy and is able to confront Peter by inviting him to her apartment and offering him a woman made out of cake for tea. Marian wants to use the cake as a symbolic explanation for her escape, but, as it turns out, Peter refuses the cake and leaves. The story ends with Marian's self-discovery, and her rejection of marriage as a social norm for success. She is able to eat and maintain her balance in life with identity and self-esteem.

The Edible Woman explicitly incorporates the key issues of the women's liberation movement as they became established around the 1960s. Marian's confusion about her identity, and the nature of her oppression in its resistance to social myths of femininity, are visible in Betty Friedan's *The Feminine Mystique*. In this novel, Atwood portrays the protagonist's journey to self-discovery, and how she finds her identity through her struggle against stereotypes and confrontations with dominant males. Marian has two choices: to conform to the social standard or to reject it and maintain her own identity.

At the outset, we immediately see the contrast between Marian and her roommate, Ainsley Tewce, in their choice of outfits:

> Ainsley says I choose clothes as though they're a camouflage or a protective colouration, though I can't see anything wrong with that. She herself goes in for neon pink...Ainsley would sit and look innocent, something she can do very well when she wants to—she has a pink-and-white blunt baby's face. (Atwood 13-15)

Atwood intentionally symbolizes Ainsley's acceptance of her feminine role through the choice of her make-up and outfit. The colour "pink" conventionally signifies "femininity." Ainsley is also portrayed as a hypocrite, who tries to be liberal. She even comes up with the idea of becoming a single parent just to fulfill her "fruitful" feminine role. She chooses to live without a man to demonstrate her superficial notion of liberation, and her conventional definition of her independence, which we can see through her conversation with Marian:

> "All right," I said. " Granted. But why do you want a baby, Ainsley? What are you going to do with it?"
> She gave me a disgusted look. "Every woman should have at least one baby." She sounded like a voice on the radio saying that every woman should have at least one electric hair-dryer. "It's even more important than sex. It fulfills your deepest femininity." (Atwood 40-41)

Although Marian objects to Ainsley's desire to be a single parent, she is equally critical of Clara's role as a wife and mother after her marriage. Clara becomes passive and submissive. In fact, Marian sees her old friend's role as a stereotyped mother, helpless and empty. We can see this according to Marian's observation when she and Ainsley make their visit:

> We walked the length of the house, which was arranged in the way such houses usually are–living-room in front, then dining-room with doors that can be slid shut, then kitchen–stepping over some of the scattered obstacles and around the others. We negotiated the stairs of the back porch, which were overgrown with empty bottles of all kinds, beer bottles, milk bottles, wine and scotch bottles, the baby bottles, and found Clara in the garden, sitting in a round wicker basket-chair with metal legs. She had her feet up on another chair and was holding her latest baby somewhere in the vicinity of what had once been her lap. Clara's body is so thick that her pregnancies are always bulgingly obvious and now in her seventh month she looked like a boa-constrictor that has swallowed a watermelon. Her head, with its aureole of pale hair, was made to seem smaller and even more fragile by the contrast. (Atwood 31)

From what Marian has described above, Clara is seen as disorganized. She has obviously become a victim of her growing family. In this sense, Clara is also being consumed as is humorously reflected by the statement: "she looked like a boa-constrictor." Through Marian's observation, we can understand Atwood's satire on the absurdities of social conventions. Coral Ann Howells points out that *The Edible Woman* is an imaginative transformation of a social problem into comic satire as one young woman rebels against her feminine destiny.[1]

The nature of Marian's frustration and depression can be classified into three major categories: resistance against social myths of femininity, her depression about consumer society, and finally her depression about male dominance. Throughout the story, Marian is portrayed as sceptical which, to a certain extent, reflects the problem of her maturation. She is sceptical about her job, about her role as a woman and about her marriage. Her critical attitudes and her friends' attempts to fulfill their femininity are seen through her comments about Ainsley and Clara, and in references to the "office virgins" (a comic reference to Marian's co-workers, Lucy, Emmy, and Millie). They are being caricatured as typical stereotyped women who are competitive and conscious only about their appearance. The following is a scene at Peter's party:

> The first to arrive were the three office virgins, Lucy alone, Emmy, and Millie almost simultaneously five minutes later. They were evidently not expecting to see each other there: each seemed annoyed that the others had been invited...Each glanced at herself in the mirror, preening and straightening, before going out to the living room. Lucy refrosted her mouth and Emmy scratched hurriedly at her scalp.
>
> They lowered themselves carefully into the Danish-modern furniture and Peter got them drinks. Lucy was in purple velvet, with silver eyelids and false lashes; Emmy was in Pink chiffon, faintly suggestive of high-school formals. Her hair had been sprayed into stiff wisps and her slip was showing. Millie was engaged in pale blue satin which bulged in odd places; she had a tiny sequin-covered evening-bag, and sounded the most nervous of the three. (Atwood 232-233)

Atwood's subtle satire of the office virgins is very similar to Betty Friedan's attack on the media and advertisements that feed females' illusions about their perfect femininity:

> The image of woman that emerges from this big, pretty maga-zine is young and frivolous, almost child-like; fluffy and feminine; passive; gaily content in a world of bedroom and

---

[1]   Coral Ann Howells, *Modern Novelists: Margaret Atwood* (New York: St. Martin's Press, 1995) 30.

kitchen, sex, babies and home. The magazine surely does not leave out sex; the only goal a woman is permitted is the pursuit of a man. It is crammed full of food, clothing, cosmetics, furniture and the physical bodies of young women, but where is the world of thought and ideas, the life of the mind and spirit?[2]

We see the difference between Marian and the office virgins, as Atwood intentionally equates Marian's oppression with her feminine destiny because she is a university graduate seeking her own identity. Unlike the office virgins who are totally victimized by the media and social convention, Marian is sceptical.

Marian's depression about consumer society is seen throughout the text. As discussed earlier, Marian sees Clara as being consumed by her growing family. She also sees herself as being consumed by all the people around her. Ainsley consumes her energy for domestic work, her company consumes her labour, and Peter and Duncan consume her femininity. The physical consumption is conveyed through eating and drinking and display of food which has a symbolic meaning. In *The Edible Woman*, we find a lot of eating activities that illustrate the world of production and capitalism, and the protagonist's struggle over it. This is quite relevant to the issues of the women's movement. In *Hidden from History*, Sheila Rowbotham concludes that:

> Reforms from above or on behalf of the oppressed can actually serve to rationale capitalist production. It is much harder to contain people's persistent resistance to conditions of production and cultural definition which separate them from their own sense of themselves. We are involved in a continuing struggle to claim our bodies and our labour power which social relationships of domination have removed from our control.[3]

Marian's consciousness about the material consumption of the world around her is actually an awakening. Her resistance to it is seen through her rejection of food while having dinner with Peter:

> She set down her knife and fork. She felt that she had turned rather pale, and hoped that Peter wouldn't notice. "This is

---

[2]   Betty Friedan, *The Feminine Mystique* (New York: Dell Publishing, 1963) 30.

[3]   Sheila Rowbotham, *Hidden from History; 300 Years of Women's Oppression and the Fight Against It* (London: Pluto Press, 1973) 168.

> ridiculous," she lectured herself. "Everyone eats a cow, it's natural; you have to eat to stay alive, meat is good for you, it has lots of proteins and minerals." She picked up her fork, speared a piece, lifted it, and set it down again. (Atwood 152)

As the story develops, the symptoms of Marian's eating disorder are intensified. It is an unconscious revolt. Even she herself does not know what is really wrong. She becomes irritated with all kinds of meat products:

> The day after the filet, she had been unable to eat a pork chop, and since then, for several weeks, she had been making experiments. She had discovered that not only were things too obviously cut from the Planned Cow inedible for her, but that the Planned Pig and the Planned Sheep were similarly forbidden. Whatever it was that had been making these decisions, not her mind certainly, rejected anything that had an indication of bone or tendon or fibre. (Atwood 152)

Marian's obsession with the dangers of consumerism and consuming is deeply rooted in her fear of marriage. In *Margaret Atwood: A Biography*, Nathalie Cooke states that:

> Curiously, Marian McAlpin seems to be even more on "the cutting edge" than Atwood herself was. Like Atwood (and so many young women of that era), Marian is profoundly ambivalent about marriage; unlike Atwood, she develops a severe eating disorder. It is the outward, physical manifestation of her turmoil.[4]

The above is obviously connected with the cannibalism motif reflecting Marian's unconscious fear of becoming an object of consumption herself. Marian's depression increases even after her engagement to Peter. At this point, her conflict is clear. She has to choose between being an adorable but submissive wife, and maintaining her freedom. Here, sexual politics is at work. Cooke states that: "Although Atwood was not actively voicing her political concerns, she was certainly looking very closely at what was happening around her and turning it to its political significance" (Cooke, 116).

---

[4]   Nathalie Cooke, *Margaret Atwood: A Biography* (Toronto: ECW Press, 1998) 117.

This is precisely related with Kate Millett's view in *Sexual Politics* when she points out that the male-female relationship is the paradigm for all power relationships. With Marian, this division signals two powers of agency within herself. Her consciousness and her instinct have confused her. Coral Ann Howells argues that Marian's troubled relationship with food can be seen as political:

> In this early feminist text the personal is fused with the political as Marian's body speaks its language of rebellion against the socialized feminine identity that she appears to have accepted. Marian can quote the received 1960s wisdom about the influence of the subconscious on behaviour (Howells, 47): 'It was my subconscious getting ahead of my conscious self, and the subconscious has its own logic.' (Atwood 101)

Marian's first escape from Peter is also inspired by her instinct:

> I was running along the sidewalk. After the first minute, I was surprised to find my feet moving, wondering how they had begun, but I didn't stop.
> The rest of them were so astonished they didn't do anything at all for a moment. Then Peter yelled, "Marian! Where the hell do you think you're going?"
> I could hear the fury in his voice: this was the unforgivable sin, because it was public. I didn't answer, but I looked back over my shoulder as I ran. Both Peter and Len had started to run after me. Then they both stopped and I heard Peter call, "I'll go get the car and head her off, you try to keep her out of the main drag,"...
> I felt myself caught, set down and shaken." (Atwood 74)

The hunting image is powerful here. Howells demonstrates that:

> It is not insignificant that Peter represents the law-giver and the hunter in Marian's scenarios of violence, whereas she is the escape artist identified with the spaces of the wilderness...that attempt is fuelled by Marian's subconscious identification with the disembowelled rabbit in Peter's story and then confirmed by the description of her recapture. (Howells, 48)

Men's stereotyped attitudes toward women are presented in different situations in the novel. One obvious example is Len's view about women when he talks to Peter about his experience and his job in England:

> "I had a good job going for me and some other good things too.
> But you've got to watch these women when they start pursuing
> you. They're always after you to *marry* them. You've got to hit
> and run. Get them before they get you and get out." He smiled,
> showing his brilliantly polished white teeth. (Atwood 66)

The above reflects not only Len's conventional attitude, but also his sense
of superiority. He sounds like a libertine, who enjoys flirting with women
and does not want to have any responsibility or obligation. Peter's
instinctive pride in his hunting confirms his traditional sense of manhood
that inspires Marian to make her first escape:

> "One shot, right through the heart...I picked it up and Trigger
> said, 'You know how to gut them'... So I whipped out my knife,
> good knife, German steel, and slit the belly and took her by the
> hind legs and gave her one hell of a crack, like a whip you see,
> and the next thing you know there was blood and guts all over
> the place." (Atwood 69)

Here we can see Peter's pride in his masculine strength, his cruelty, and
his vicious instinct in hunting.

Marian's physical submission to the feminine mystique is complete
after she follows Peter's suggestion to change her hair style and buy a
new dress for his final party. Peter seems to be very pleased:

> "Darling, you look absolutely marvellous," he had said as soon
> as he had come up through the stairwell. The implication had
> been that it would be most pleasant if she could arrange to look
> like that all the time. He had made her turn around so that he
> could see her back, and he had liked that too. Now she won-
> dered whether or not she did look absolutely marvellous.
> (Atwood, 228)

Atwood portrays Peter's party as a miniature of society that is split into the
consumers and the consumed. Everyone is engaged in the activity of consuming. Against this highly symbolic setting, Marian has a chance to explore
Peter's true nature through his room, his taste for clothes, his lifestyle, and his
hobbies. She now sees the core of her problem. She suddenly realizes her great
fear of Peter's authority and dominance, and makes a second attempt to escape.
At this point, the story reaches its climax, which Atwood intends to make into
an anti-comedy, as she explained in an interview:

Gibson: Let's pause here. What do you mean by an anti-comedy? *The Edible Woman* is an anti-comedy?

Atwood: In your standard 18th-century comedy you have a young couple faced with difficulty in the form of somebody who embodies the restrictive forces of society and they trick or overcome this difficulty and end up getting married. The same thing happens in *The Edible Woman* except the wrong person gets married. And the person who embodies the restrictive forces of society is in fact the person Marian gets engaged to. In a standard comedy, he would be the defiant hero. As it is, he and the restrictive society are blended into one, and the comedy solution would be a tragic solution for Marian.[5]

Up to this point, the anti-comedy is presented through Marian's escape, Ainsley's public announcement of her pregnancy, and Joe's perspectives on femininity. Here, "the wrong person" (Atwood means Ainsley), who eventually can trap Fischer Smythe into marrying her, has fulfilled her biological role that conforms to social convention.

Sexual politics plays its role in different ways. Joe, Clara's husband, reveals his perspective on femininity through his experience with Clara:

"Her feminine role and her core are really in opposition, her feminine role demands passivity from her..."
"So she allows her core to get taken over by the husband. And when the kids come, she wakes up one morning and discovers she doesn't have anything left inside, she's hollow, she doesn't know who she is any more; her core has been destroyed."
(Atwood 235-236)

Joe, then, is very critical of the feminine mystique. He sees it as the source of the destruction of Clara's life. After their marriage, she leads her life based on social expectations. Toward the end of the novel, Atwood twists the viewpoint in terms of sexual politics. That is, despite their limitations, Marian, Ainsley, and Clara manage to survive better than the men. Marian eventually gains her integrity and develops her self-esteem after her escape. She can cope with Duncan, who tries to dominate her. She can confront Peter by inviting him for tea and offering him a cake in the shape

---

[5]   Earl G Ingersoll, ed, *Margaret Atwood: Conversations* (Ontario: Ontario Review Press, 1990) 12.

of a woman, hoping it to be a symbolic explanation for her escape. Now that she has gained her strength, she can cope with Peter calmly:

> She went into the kitchen and returned bearing the platter in front of her, carefully and with reverence, as though she was carrying something sacred in a procession, an icon or the crown on a cushion in a play. She knelt, setting the platter on the coffee-table in front of Peter.
> "You've been trying to destroy me, haven't you?" she said. "You've been trying to assimilate me. But I've made you a substitute, something you'll like much better. This is what you really wanted all along, isn't it? I'll get you a fork," she added somewhat prosaically. (Atwood 271)

This is neatly done as Peter is shocked to know that Marian apparently is not silly after all, and he immediately leaves her without feeling guilty about his actions.

Oates particularly admires Atwood's manipulation of the absurd:

> Oates: Your sense of the absurd – and of the essential playfulness of the absurd – is one of the elements in your writing that I particularly admire. What inspired your novel *The Edible Woman* – especially that surreal scene – and *Lady Oracle*?
> Atwood: *The Edible Woman* was written in 1965, before the Women's Liberation Movement had begun. It was still very much the model pattern, in Canada anyway, to take a crummy job and then marry to get away from it. I was writing about an object of consumption (namely, my bright but otherwise ordinary girl) in a consumer society. Approximately, she works for a market research company. Even in 1969, when the book was finally published, some critics saw the view as essentially "young" or "neurotic." I would mature, they felt, and things (i.e. marriage and kids) would fall into place.
> About the cake in the shape of a woman – all I can tell you is that I used to be a very good cake decorator and was often asked to reproduce various objects in pastry and icing. Also, in my walks past pastry stores, I always wondered why people made replicas of things – brides and grooms, for instance, or Mickey Mice – and then ate them. It seems a mysterious thing to do. But for my heroine to make a false image of herself and then consume it was entirely appropriate, given the story – don't you think? (Ingersoll, 75)

It is clear that Marian has discovered herself and realized that the image she has previously presented was false. Therefore, she can resume her normal life and is able to eat again. This even shocks Ainsley:

> Ainsley's mouth opened and closed, fishlike, as though she was trying to gulp down the full implication of what she saw. "Marian!" she exclaimed at last, with horror. "You're rejecting your femininity!" (Atwood 272)

By this time we can see that Ainsley is too conventional to understand that what Marian is rejecting is Peter's dominance and the male-influenced idea of femininity, in order to become free and independent.

A male who ironically submits to feminine dominance in terms of sexual politics is Leonard Slank, who has a nervous breakdown and is looked after by Clara as if he were one of her children. Clara makes an excuse to bring him to Peter's party:

> "As you can see, he's in piss-poor shape. He turned up just after the baby sitter got there and he looked really awful, he'd obviously had a lot...We both feel so sorry for him, what he needs is some nice home-loving type who'll take care of him, he doesn't seem to be able to cope at all..." (Atwood 234)

Ainsley's hunt for a husband has ruined Len's life. Viewed in this light, Len is a victim dominated by Ainsley, who is soulless, cold, and self-centred.

Among all the characters in *The Edible Woman*, Duncan is the most mysterious character. Sherrill Grace sees him as:

> The self-indulgent English graduate student, more important and enigmatic, and in every way the antithesis of Peter – sloppy, ineffectual, childish...Duncan is most successful as a symbol of Marian's inner life or subconsciousness; he represent her fantasia, her attempts to escape, as well as her sensible return to consumer reality.[6]

---

[6] Sherrill E Grace, "Versions of Reality" in Sherrill E. Grace and Ken Norris, eds, *Violent Duality: A Study of Margaret Atwood*, (Montréal: McClelland & Stewart, 1980) 87.

For Eleonora Rao, "Duncan functions as Marian's projection, her alter ego."[7] However, D.J. Dooley's comment is perhaps the most accurate:

> This man is anything but ordinary ... His response to the world of commerce ... is gamesmanship ... The difference between him and most other people is that he is quite aware that he is playing a role, whereas they are falling into roles without knowing it. Just as he is capable of looking at his own situation objectively, he is capable of analysing his society. He prefers a literal wasteland to the wasteland of the modern commercial world ... In other words, his response to being as it is defined in the modern mercantile world – fitting into the cycle of production and consumption, making one kind of garbage into another – is to come as close as possible to not-being.[8]

Duncan is apparently a great consumer who can detach himself from the outside world. He leaves Peter's party immediately after his arrival as he finds it noisy. In Marian's flight from Peter to seek his protection, he addresses her as "the scarlet woman herself" (Atwood 274). This can be a pun as Marian is wearing a red dress, or it may be an allusion to Hester Prynne, a heroine in Hawthorne's *The Scarlet Letter*, who commits adultery while her husband is away. After spending a night with Duncan, Marian is shocked to find him indifferent to her problem when she pleads:

> "Duncan," she said, "please don't go."
> "Why? Is there more?"
> "I can't go back."
> "No," he said , ... I'd have to start worrying about you and all that, I haven't time for it" (Atwood 257-258)

Marian finds herself at a dead-end. She has to take action: "She had been so thoroughly taken in. She should have known. But after she had thought about it for a few minutes, gazing up at the blank sky, it didn't make that much difference"(Atwood 264). This moment can be regarded as her "epiphany." Marian has discovered herself. After Peter's disappear-

---

7   Eleonora Rao, *Strategies for Identity: The Fiction of Margaret Atwood* (New York: Peter Lang, 1993) 50.

8   D.J Dooley, "In Margaret Atwood's Zoology Lab." *Moral Vision in the Canadian Novel* (Toronto: Clarke, 1979) 137-147.

ance, Duncan appears at her apartment. When she tells him what has happened, to her surprise, Duncan says:

> "That's ridiculous," he said gravely. "Peter wasn't trying to destroy you. That's just something you made up. Actually you were trying to destroy him."
> I had a sinking feeling. "Is that true?" I asked.
> "Search your soul," he said, gazing hypnotically at me from behind his hair. He drank some coffee and paused to give me time, then added, "But the real truth is that it wasn't Peter at all. It was me. I was trying to destroy you." (Atwood 280-281)

Everyone is either a victim or being victimized in our own social conventions. In the end, Marian can turn back to her normal life. She is able to eat the cake. Many critics say the manner in which she consumes the cake is symbolic:

> Suddenly she was hungry. Extremely hungry. The cake after all was only a cake. She picked up the platter, carried it to the kitchen table and located a fork. "I'll start with the feet," she decided...
> Marian looked back at her platter. The woman lay there, still smiling glassily, her legs gone. "Nonsense," she said. "It's only a cake." She plunged her fork into the carcass, neatly severing the body from the head. (Atwood 271-273)

Marian's transformation to her normal life is illustrated here. Instead of being submissive, she is now taking action. She can manipulate and direct her life. She now acts with authority. Marian's consumption of the cake is symbolic. Because the cake represents food and the cake woman represents the whole notion of femininity and her victimized self, Marian, by eating it, is destroying the masks of femininity and announcing to herself and others that she is not a consumable product. She has truly discovered herself. Marian can turn towards a normal life, as she is now independent, and free to direct her own destiny. In this light, this passage tallies with the narrative structure of the story that begins and ends with the first-person narrator, while the middle part is narrated in the third-person. Linda Hutcheon points out that: "In *The Edible Woman*, the change in narrative voice from the first-person to third, and then back to first, explicitly reflects the psychological changes of the heroine."[9] That is, in the first part, Marian is trapped within the social system. We hear the story from her sceptical, limited point of view. In part two of the novel the narrator is not "I" but "She" – the third-person, as it represents Marian as really two people: the surface and the real one. Catherine McLay argues that, "the change from "I" as teller to "She" as character marks her altered perception of herself and others. Her vision is distorted."[10]

The exploration of *The Edible Woman* through the female protagonist's observation, participation, and interaction in life, explicitly demonstrates Atwood's concern about gender issues. Many interviews and critics confirm that the characters in *The Edible Woman* are drawn from Atwood's real life experiences, so as to make a large narrative point. Cooke notes that: "Atwood's critics have made a convincing argument that the 'point' of *The Edible Woman* is, most obviously, a feminist one." The point is that our society is full of absurdities that are made conventional, and that trap men and women into behaving the way they do, while taking for granted that this behaviour is normal. In order to escape patriarchy, to maintain our sanity, we have to quest for our own identity. Then we can direct our destiny and fulfil our goal in life. Otherwise, we will be consumed or become victimized, as the modern world is the world of consumption and production. And Atwood's point is very well reflected through Marian's search for her identity, no matter whether she claims herself to be a feminist or not.

Amporn Srisermbhok

---

9   Linda Hutcheon, "From Poetic to Narrative Structures: The Novels of Margaret Atwood" in Sherrill E. Grace and Ken Norris, eds, *Margaret Atwood: Language, Text, and System* (Vancouver: The University of British Columbia Press, 1983) 22-23.

10   Catherine McLay, "The Dark Voyage: *The Edible Woman* as Romance" in Arnold E. Davidson and Cathy N. Davidson, eds, *The Art of Margaret Atwood: Essays in Criticism* (Toronto: House of Anansi Press, 1981) 131.

Bibliography

Betty Friedan. 1963. *The Feminine Mystique*, New York: Dell Publishing.

Coral Ann Howells. 1995. *Modern Novelists: Margaret Atwood* ,New York: St. Martin's Press.

Catherine McLay. 1981. "The Dark Voyage: *The Edible Woman* as Romance" in Arnold E. Davidson and Cathy N. Davidson, eds, *The Art of Margaret Atwood: Essays in Criticism*, Toronto: House of Anansi Press.

D.J Dooley. 1979. "In Margaret Atwood's Zoology Lab." *Moral Vision in the Canadian Novel*, Toronto: Clarke.

Earl G. Ingersoll, ed. 1990. *Margaret Atwood: Conversations*, Ontario: Ontario Review Press.

Eleonora Rao. 1993. *Strategies for Identity: The Fiction of Margaret Atwood*, New York: Peter Lang.

Linda Hutcheon. 1983. "From Poetic to Narrative Structures: The Novels of Margaret Atwood" in Sherrill E. Grace and Ken Norris, eds., *Margaret Atwood: Language, Text, and System*, Vancouver: The University of British Columbia Press, 1983.

Nathalie Cooke. 1998. *Margaret Atwood: A Biography*, Toronto: ECW Press.

Sheila Rowbotham. 1973. *Hidden from History; 300 Years of Women's Oppression and the Fight Against It* , London: Pluto Press.

Sherrill E Grace. 1980. "Versions of Reality" in Sherrill E. Grace and Ken Norris, eds, *Violent Duality: A Study of Margaret Atwood*, Montréal: McClelland & Stewart.

How Far is Modernity From Here?
Brazil, Portugal: Two Novels in Portuguese

In this paper, I examine two novels from the Lusophone tradition—a Brazilian one (*Lavoura Arcaica*, 1975, by Raduan Nassar) and a Portuguese one (*Árvore das Palavras*, 1997, by Teolinda Gersão)—in order to try to show how each of them explores the question of "modernity", felt as a problem that needs to be addressed. The first point to stress is that the concept of modernity is not at all easy to define here: both novels display a consciousness of the inevitability of being modern in a modern world—and yet their plots reveal an awareness of the difficulties of weaving this modernity into a social fabric that draws strongly upon non-modern roots. This is why I speak of it as a "problem": it is not that modernity is denied or refused, but rather that issues are involved that are generally considered to have been resolved at the onset. This is definitely not the case, as we shall see.

My basic point arises out of the conviction that, as Michel de Certeau[1] clearly states, there is no "newness" that does not imply a "re-use" (*réemploi*), and nothing clear-cut that does not presuppose at least some form of continuity. Indeed, it is this "dialectic of progress", as De

---

[1]   Michel De Certeau, *L'ètranger ou l'Union dans la Différence*, Paris, Desclée de Brouwer, 1991 (1969), pp. 58/9.

Certeau terms it, that is the very condition of history. Consequently, the fact that the two cases analysed here mostly stress their problematic relationship to "modernity" may perhaps be understood as the very foundation of their historical awareness, of their being historical.

I will then try to show how, in both novels , forms of modernity and forms related to the archaic are conceived as interconnected, rather than as mere oppositions. But first I must point out that I am not referring to "modernity" in a literary or period sense, but rather indicating an historical perspective that roughly distinguishes it from an "ancien régime" view of the world. This is especially relevant, as we shall see, in the case of the Portuguese novel, where we basically have two sets of space, rural Portugal in the '50s, and Mozambique at the end of the colonial period in the '60s, before the beginning of the colonial war. But modernity also comes to have a wider meaning here (especially as regards Raduan Nassar's novel) in its apparently radical separation from mythical, archaic or pre-modern elements. In my use of *archaic* , I do not want to imply "primitive"—this now discredited adjective presupposes a historic condition considered mainly from an (erroneous) evolutionary perspective: rather, I am referring basically to an anthropological condition, set in history but conceived of as pre-historic, which then configures itself as trans-historic. The archaic, from this point of view, survives as a silent force throughout the ages, even when it has seemed for a while to be completely doomed. It surfaces in our modern world mainly within smaller social units: small-scale societies, such as insular or endogamous families or small groups, or "tribes"—kinship groups who act, on a small scale, as paradigmatic social units. We could perhaps point out that, in this view, a pre-modern conception of history such as that described in these two novels (despite the fact that they are strongly historical, once again!) will tend to stress elements such as nomadism, orality, a magical conception of the universe (with a strong presence of rituals and of the sacred), and forms of extasis felt both as a threat and as a sublime invitation. All these elements are to be found particularly in the novel by Nassar, as we shall soon see.

The concepts of "ancient/traditional", on the one hand, and "modern/innovative", on the other thus no longer appear as a dichotomy but rather to converge. This shift in perspective is in both novels used as a way of thinking about the place of subjects, families, and nations in the context of a "modern world". In fact, in both works, the stories take place in the second half of the 20 th century in countries (Portugal and Brazil) that are felt to be situated, for different reasons, on the precarious border between the centre and the periphery; between old and new; between pre-modern and post-industrial modes of living. And both novels take as their point of departure the family, where happenings are felt to symbolise things taking place in society at large. What comes to pass within these families is a kind of duel between lights and shadows; and if any kind of "progress" is achieved, it is a "progress" of the type Michel de Certeau described, quoted above. Finally, both novels depict nations afflicted by some kind of doubt, insecurity or aggression: Brazil, Portugal and Mozambique, between the 1950s and the 1970s. How far (or how close) modernity is from here consequently becomes a very pertinent question.

The book by Gersão roughly spans a period corresponding to the childhood and youth of a young woman in Mozambique, the daughter of a white Mozambican. It also tells of Amélia, her mother, a Portuguese woman who, in the late forties/early fifties, goes to Mozambique to be married and thus (she hopes) to escape a constrained future. Africa seems to be the land of the future, of possibility, of social elevation, and of escape from an ambiguous past and present, as she is an illegitimate child by a man who has never recognized her as his daughter. There is then, in Amélia, a strong inner revolt, which fuels a desire for order and restraint, in feelings, in the keeping of the house, in the daily routine, and in the upbringing of her only child. The capital of Mozambique, then Lourenço Marques, is the geographical symbol of all this: an open space offering virtually everything but also pointing to the tacit but constantly present danger of a reversal, a revolution. The two houses "Casa Branca" and "Casa Preta", the two "mothers", the white one (Amélia) and the black one (Lóia), and the two "cities" within Lourenço Marques (the white, geometrical city and the black convoluted one, of "Caniço", where white people lose their way) represent then this strange alliance between the desire for newness and the permanence of the old—an alliance built upon a latent conflict that the ambiguous position of the female protagonist will illustrate.

The same conflicting alliance connects the European and the African country, because Portugal also seems to share in this same condition. It was, in the late fifties, a country where time seemed to have stood still, where personal relations between individuals were still regulated by immutable conventions, and where modernity appeared an almost alien concept.

The three symbolic moments that constitute the three parts of this novel, all situated in Mozambique, therefore represent three very special moments in the conflicting alliance between a sense of the archaic (the African roots), the presence of a static old (the shadow of an apparently frozen Portugal) and the awareness of a future that has to emerge out of this connection. The first part, concerning the early childhood of the girl, narrated in the first person and constituted of fragments of personal memory, basically rediscovers Africa, Mozambique and the mythical and symbolic roots of the affections—the houses, the smells, a daily lifestyle whose rhythms are determined by contact with the bush, the wilderness, the open spaces, the animals, the people. The second part, on the other hand, presents a flashback narrated in the third person and centring on the character of Amélia. It is still the same Africa (or is it?), now seen as a place of utter frustration, manifested in the way the controlled geometry of the modern city is unable to triumph over the meanderings and the complexity of the black city: a place where no Vichiçoise or vol-au-vent will ever find a proper setting! It is also the site of social exclusion—classes that set themselves apart from others (with apartheid, of course), as if modernity consisted only of the ability to deny the other, the archaic, the black. Finally, in the third part, still set in the same city of Lourenço Marques, the narration is once again returned to the first person: the girl has now grown up, and her seventeenth birthday coincides with the discovery of sexuality and the body, but also of deceit and of ambiguities. The beginning of the colonial war also marks this political and symbolic change: nothing will ever be the same again. But has modernity triumphed over the pre-modern? Hardly.

In the end, this novel also seems to be a family tale, and involves the coincidence between different sorts of triangles that shape the various encounters and non-encounters: between father, mother (or mothers, as we have seen) and daughter; between daughter and both mothers; between father and the two wives that will bear him children—the white European one, who is always trying to speak "correct" Portuguese, and the black Mozambican one, with her chaotic use of this language; and also between the three figures of "motherhood"—the biological mother (Amélia), the chosen mother (Lóia), and the stepmother (Rosário)—none of whom is able to completely fulfil the role of parent, for very different reasons.

If in Gersão's novel the family tale is presented as the symbolic site where the tensions between modern and pre-modern take shape, this is even more pronounced in the case of Raduan Nassar's novel, *Lavoura Arcaica* . The general framework of this story clearly resonates with the biblical parable of the prodigal son: the first chapter opens the door for an elder son who has come in search of his younger brother, who has inexplicably left home (secrets and guilt are lurking in the shadows, of course, but the narrator quietly tries to evade them). The boy's exile and nomadic flight clearly affect the entire family, and in this context, the biblical parallels might lead us to expect that the return of this prodigal son might in the end bring prosperity, peace and progress to his family.

Soon we come to realize that this is not to be, that it cannot be. The world to which the son returns rests upon a social and symbolic order based upon apparently unshakeable exclusions and frontiers: the frozen patriarchal authority of the father, with its discourse of prescriptions and bans, to which the eldest son adheres; the surreptitiously affective order of the matriarchal world, full of secret words, understandings and touches, represented by the mother and the sisters; and in the midst of all this the memory of a sensitive young boy, torn between a fervent religious faith and a body that aches, expects and feels much more than he himself is capable of recognizing and accepting.

I have already mentioned the biblical resonances, which are of course quite visible. But no less evident are the classical echoes in this fable: everything happens within the apparently ordained, but oh so tragic, inner space of a family, where curses cannot be avoided, only lived (I might as well say performed). The core problem (although by no means the only one) is the existence of incest, or rather, of incestuous desire that is not overcome by any form of flight but merely delayed (prolonged?). The narrator describes his sisters, his "dark Mediterranean" sisters, several times as if they were a tragic chorus, like the Erinyes, who will not be transformed this time into the Eumenides—this would be a supreme form of irony, if we recall that these primitive archaic goddesses, born from the drops of blood coming from Ouranos' mutilation, were specifically linked to the avenging of crimes against family order. But if we take into consideration that they are also frequently depicted in contexts involving dancing, feasting and libations, specifically wine drinking, it is not hard to recognize in them the surge of chaotic and anarchic desires and violence that the priestesses of the cult of Bacchus both propitiated and ritualised. So, we are clearly supposed to feel the primitive breath that sweeps through this novel, and maybe even recognize the weight of ancient traditions in the political authority (patriarchal power), religious education, and mythical and symbolic echoes that resonate throughout society.

But we are never allowed to forget that this is also "an American story", set in a land that has very specific characteristics, and which draws upon disparate and mingled European roots (Nassar himself is second-generation Lebanese) in order to carve a place for itself at the forefront of modernity. America, then, as a continent, is inscribed into Brazilian reality as a problem, an identity to be created out of the tension between Europe, North America and, yes, South America. What happens inside this family, in the novel, has to be seen in this context: it is a way of exploring how Brazil will be able to shape its own pathway into modernity out of "archaic labour" ("lavoura arcaica"). But this is a modernity that does not contradict the ancient roots and traditions. On the contrary, what we have here is once again the extensive non-opposition between tradition and modernity in our contemporary societies, rather like threads which are woven together and which create internal channels. Only by investigating the ways in which the archaic still survives today will we be able to get an accurate view of the future—in this particular case, the Brazilian future. For from this very basic social unit, the family, and its transformations, emerges the pathway into modernity.

I would also like to point out the dialectics between inner and outer space, particularly between home and the exterior. It is through this tension that ideology takes shape in this novel, for symbolically, the exchanges between "in" and "out" are one of the anthropological movements that enable societies to regulate their own ability to survive, through change. It is significant that, in this novel, everything takes place within the family, although outer spaces interfere with the "home" where this family lives: the parable of the prodigal son might then be understood in a new light, as an indication that departure and transformation are indeed a condition of permanence.

Modernity thus resonates with the ancient. Moreover, the modern novel is what it is because it coalesces many things and brings together various forms of writing, in which we do not always immediately recognize modernity: nevertheless, it is there, especially as a problem, our problem. It is basically this set of problems that is addressed in the two novels considered, for in a certain sense both tell us stories in which silent voices from distant pasts find a way to leap into the present and implicate themselves in the future. This is indeed a way to recognize that modernity is and is not far from here: and this paradoxical condition, perhaps more immediately understood in cases such as Brazil (in what regards America) and Portugal (in what regards Europe), would perhaps gain to be thought of as a paradigm of other conditions, apparently more homogeneous. I am sure a more complex picture of "modernity" would emerge from that.

Helena Carvalhão Buescu

How Far is T.S. Eliot From Here? The Young Poet's Imagined World of Polynesian Matahiva

[W]e know that the discovery of Shakespeare's laundry bills would not be of much use to us; but we must always reserve final judgment as to the futility of the research which has discovered them. (T.S. Eliot, 1923)

We are apt to expect of youth only a fragmentary view of life; we incline to see youth as exaggerating the world as did Chicken Licken. But occasionally the intensity of the vision ... may give to a juvenile work a universality which is beyond the author's knowledge of life to give, and to which mature men and women can respond. (T.S. Eliot, Nov. 13, 1930)

For a long time we have believed in nothing but the values arising in a mechanized, commercialized, urbanized way of life: it would be as well for us to face the permanent conditions upon which God allows us to live upon this planet. And without sentimentalizing the life of the savage, we might practice the humility to observe, in some of the societies upon which we look down as primitive backward, the operation of a social-artistic-religious complex which we should emulate upon a higher plane. (T.S. Eliot, 1945)

It is difficult to prophesy that Eliot's criticism will prove to be of permanent value, but perhaps we need to await the arrival of a generation neither formed by him, or rebelling against him, before we justly can place him. (Harold Bloom, 1985)

1. "A Savage Beating a Drum"

In 1932, when Eliot was just beginning to get international fame, he received an invitation from his alma mater, Harvard University. In the last of a series of lectures he gave on that occasion, the poet said: "Poetry begins, I dare say, with a savage beating a drum in a jungle and it retains that essential of percussion and rhythm: hyperbolically one might say that the poet is older than human beings...." (T. S. Eliot, *The Use of Poetry and Use of Criticism*, p. 155).

I suspect the ordinary reaction to this passage would be like this: Because Eliot read at Harvard some early anthropological writings by Lévy-Bruhl, James Frazer and others, he must have been only quoting from anthropology and not necessarily expressing his own idea . However, I shall argue that he was not borrowing bookish knowledge but primarily expressing the valuable idea of his own. More specifically, w hen he spoke of the "savage beating a drum in a jungle," he was recalling his own experience, particularly, what he witnessed on the fairgrounds of the Louisiana Purchase Exposition that was held in 1904 in the city of St. Louis in which he was born and raised.

All critics like John Vickery (1973) and William Harmon (1976) before them share the view that it was during his Harvard graduate student years that Eliot started a serious discussion concerning what I call cross-culturality for lack of better terminology. To be sure, the outcome of academic thinking done during his attendance, for example, to Josiah Royce's seminar is manifestly too important to ignore. However, I have to point out that it was as early as his St. Louis period that the poet's concern with cross-culturality took definite shape .

2. A New Approach to the "The Man Who Was King"

In 1905, the young Eliot wrote three short stories and three poems (see Table 1). The most marvellous of the six pieces is "The Man Who Was King" published in the school magazine *Smith Academy Record*.

Table 1: Three Short Stories and Three Poems Written in 1905
"The Birds of Prey" (a short story)
"A Fable for Feasters" (a poem)
"A Tale of a Whale" (a short story)
"A Lyric" (a poem)
"The Man Who Was King" (a short story)
"At Graduation, 1905" (a poem)

(1) About this short story, I argue first that it is in essence an elegy—an elegy lamenting the dying out of an unspoiled, healthy, indigenous society once thriving in the South Pacific.
(2) After such an internal discussion of the story and others, I shall proceed to think about how one would be able to relate the story to new external, factual evidence.

"The Man Who Was King," set in Polynesia, starts with a shipwreck of a man named Magruder. The people of an island called Matahiva in the Paumota Group found him asleep on their seashore to which Magruder was washed up. Judging from the way he was strangely dressed and moreover "of a whitish collor," islanders straightway concluded that "the gods had dropped him down for the purpose of ruling over them." On their way to the village, they formed a procession while beating their percussion instruments called "bghgongs." In the village, they inaugurated Magruder as king. Several months later, however, islanders, after finding him not only too incompetent in comparison with the former king but also despicable as a human being, succeeded in achieving his virtual expulsion from their society.

This story is manifest evidence showing how deeply the young Eliot conducted his thought extensively about the relation between indigenousness and civilization. It is particularly interesting that he concluded the story in favor of health of the islanders and to the detriment of Magruder. Despite the backwardness on the surface, islanders seem to have never lost the health of society. Contrary to Western expectations, Matahiva islanders appear to be armed with wisdom and ingenuity.

In such a society a sinister aftermath set in. After Magruder left, what is described as the "French" came in to rule. They built a post and educated the natives to wear clothes and go to church. While their efforts helped the islanders emerge from backwardness, there is no hint in the short story of rejoicing in the new practices brought from the West. Rather, the civilizing effects are bitterly lamented as attested to by the passage running as follows: "Not long after the captain was there the French got hold of it and built a post there, they educated the natives to wear clothes on Sunday and go to church, so that now they are quite civilized and uninteresting." (T.S. Eliot, "The Man Who Was King").

Nothing is described in the story about the particular way in which the "French" got hold of the island. But we can deduce from the expulsion of Magruder that islanders exerted every effort but to no avail. In contrast to Magruder, who was almost naked and deprived from any products of modern civilization, the "French," as is construed from the above-quoted passage, came not individually but in great numbers, complete with systematization of warfare . When a man from the West appeared alone, without any weapons, they showed their communal strength. But confronted with the systematic assault, they were acutely vulnerable.

In the post-Magruder period, we are told, the islanders came to be "quite civilized" but are at the same time "uninteresting." At first glance this would simply mean that to the eyes of an observer/narrator the islanders are too westernized to gratify curiosity. But judging from the context delineated above, it should be evident that the passage contains in it a n in-depth lamentation that the indigenous, unique culture of the South Pacific was devastated. The integral culture was lost for good; it was replaced by standardized civilization.

In such a sense "The Man Who Was King" is an elegy on the fall of Matahiva. And importantly, in so portraying the imagined world of Matahiva, the young author was manifesting for us the high intellectual stage to which he was culminating . He assigned to Matahiva islanders undeniable capability to accomplish sustained reasoning and judgment and, at the same time, the capability to achieve self-government. In perhaps sharp contrast to such an interpretation of ours, Lyndall Gordon the eminent Eliot scholar, says, "Eliot made proud use of sailing jargon" (Gordon, *Early Years*, p.12). T his was all she had to say. In light of the definitive portrait drawn about our poet, this should not be surprising.

3. Eliot and the World's Fair of St. Louis

Over four decades ago (1965), Herbert Howarth, one of the contemporary leading Eliot scholars published one of the decisive cornerstones of Eliot scholarship, *Notes on Some Figures behind T.S. Eliot*. This research is decisive in the sense that up till then no definitive systematic biographical study on the poet had been conducted. In those days what was then called New Criticism, a type of formalist literary criticism, was flourishing. New Critics actually dominated the study and discussion of literature . They proposed that a work of literary art should be regarded as autonomous and declared that they should focus attention on literature itself, emphasizing explication, or "close reading," of "the work itself." As a result, virtually any biographical approach to literature was rejected as external to the work . Besides, since one of the main founders of the old New Criticism school was considered to be T.S. Eliot, a large portion of the Eliot scholars were faithful practitioners of New Criticism.

In his book, Howarth made use of Henry Ware Eliot, Sr. Scrapbooks, which are preserved in the Missouri Historical Museum archives. Created by the poet's father, the Scrapbooks consist of 18 volumes, covering more than a decade . The Scrapbooks contain mainly newspaper clippings, clippings garnered from those local papers like the *St. Louis Post-Dispatch* and the *St. Louis Globe Democrat*. They have a very, very low percentage of biographical material.

When Eliot was just a young man, aged sixteen, the World's Fair came to St. Louis. Much to our surprise, so far Eliot scholarship displayed no intention of casting light on th is greatest event St. Louis ever held in context of the whole world. Indeed, no Eliot critic whosoever seems to have ventured into exploring something new relating to the future poet's possible World Fair visits. Moreover, throughout his life the poet never mentioned the event, much less his own visit s to the fair.

When I was investigating the Scrapbooks, I found an entirely new piece cf biographical evidence, which escaped the watchful eye of Herbert Howarth. According to this new evidence, it is an undeniable fact that the future poet visited the 1904 World's F air of St. Louis, for several reasons. (1) The evidence I have discovered is a "Stockholder's Coupon Ticket," a ticket published by the Louisiana Purchase Exposition Company to its stockholder, "Thomas S. Eliot." This is pasted somewhat firmly on the pasteboard of the Scrapbooks. If you flip open t he cover of the ticket at the upper portion, you find a n identification photograph of the bearer attached. This bearer is no other than our young Eliot in his mid-teens. Adjacent to this "Stockholder's Coupon Ticket" pasted is his father's Stockholder's Coupon Ticket.

(2) Around the time of the World's F air Eliot's father, Henry Ware Eliot, Sr. was serving on the Washington University board. It is important in this relation to note that situated almost immediately adjacent to the fairgrounds is the newly built Washington University in St. Louis, the university Eliot's grandfather built; and the Exposition Company rented the campus and used it as its administrative department. We may point out that the Eliot family actually committed themselves to the Exposition event.

(3) Certain evidence clearly shows that the young Eliot visited the Philippine Exposition, held as a part of the World's Fair of St. Louis. The Igorot Village gained popularity because of its "gangsa" ring dance performed on the fairgrounds. The dancers used the gangsa percussion instruments, which correspond to what the young Eliot depicts in his short story as the "bghgongs," a coinage by the young author, which is given a parenthetical explanation "a cross between tin pan and gong."

(4) Henry, Eliot ' s father appears to have been an ardent admirer of the Philippine Exposition, in particular the Igorot Village. In his Scrapbooks he preserved, for example, a clipping of the newspaper item "Modern Conquest of the Orient as Viewed from the Philippines." He pasted in another pamphlet significantly entitled "The Igorot: A Souvenir."

With these new pieces of evidence at hand, I will proceed to argue by relating them to the internally significant plot of the short story. The main question underlying my argument is: What made it possible for the young author to unfold such remarkable thinking as we have seen? I think that it was made possible primarily by the young Eliot's exploring of the Philippine Exposition fairgrounds, including the Igorot Village. He must have been well aware of the way the Philipinos were exposed to the Western civilization on the fairgrounds; they underwent rapid changes and they *were* westernized. In the short story "The Man Who Was King," we are told: "They [the French] educated the natives to wear clothes on Sunday and go to church, so that now they are quite civilized and uninteresting." In so making the judgment, the young author most likely was not satisfied with, rather he deplored the westernization and standardization with which the Philippine people were involved during the fairground life.

When, years later, Eliot referred to the "savage beating a drum in a jungle" as a source of imagination, he must have had in mind the Igorot gangsa dance and the bghgongs dance. His "gangsa" dance experiences of the early American period have been so firmly embedded in his own mind as to seem almost natural and inherent. When occasion arose, part of the experiences resurfaced years later in 1932.

4. The Young Eliot Aged Ten Years as a Spanish-American War "Correspondent"

Several years earlier, in 1899, when the US invaded the Philippines, the precocious future poet at age ten virtually visited the Philippines as a newspaper "correspondent." As editor for the home-made "Fireside" magazine Eliot dispatched things Philippine, mentioning the rise of the independence leader Emilio Aguinaldo (1869-1964). In another "Editorial" section of the magazine, a picture is drawn by pencil of the Philippine flag streaming in the wind. The picture is given the caption "The Philippine flag looks like this." Eliot was a virtual correspondent and also an illustrator reporting the new war developments from the Philippines to the US.

The Spanish-American war broke out in 1898. On April 25, the US announced the state war had been waged against Spain since April 21. On May 1, 1898, Commodore Dewey totally defeated the Spanish navy in the renowned battle of Manila Bay. On August 13, the Spanish forces made the point of surrendering to the Americans and not to the native Filipinos. In accordance with the agreement, the US troops marched into the Manila Wall to occupy the City in August . The US and Spain put an end to the war by signing the Paris treaty on December 10 of that year. On December 21, President William McKinley (1897-1901) proclaimed the acquisition of the Philippines.

Meanwhile, hostilities were developing between the US and the Philippines since the Americans marched into Manila City in August without allowing any Filipinos to take part in the march. When the US and Spain were negotiating a formal end to the war, President McKinley refused to meet with a representative from Aguinaldo' s government. The hostilities took a decisive turn when the Paris treaty was signed between the US and Spain without any representation from the Philippines.

Emilio Aguinaldo, resenting all this, was changing his basically pro-American policy. By the end of 1898 he turned antagonistic toward the US. In Januar 1899, he announce d the independence of the Philippines; the Philippine Republic was born at Malolos. On February 4, war broke out. On the following day, Aguinaldo declared war. However, by March 4, when Jacob G. Schurman, president of Cornell, arrived at Manila to form the Schurman Committee, the US had established its rule. Aguinaldo was forced to retreat to Tarlac. After Tarlac was captured in November, Aguinaldo switched to guerilla warfare . On March 23, 1901, he was captured and nearly all of his generals surrendered within a few weeks.

In connection with the future poet, we should focus attention on the fact that after the announcement of Philippine independence in January, when Aguinaldo was forced to start a resistance campaign against the US occupation, the then ten-year old Eliot was doing the editing of his homemade magazine, the "Fireside." At the end of January 1899, the Fall semester was over. Starting with the second day of the holidays, which lasted from January 28 through January 30, the young Eliot brought out the eight numbers of the "Fireside." (The remaining three extant copies, numbers 9, 13, and 14 are dated February 11, 18 and 19 respectively.) During the early part of 1899, the famous discussion called "The White Man's Burden" flared up. Significantly, in the "Editorial" of number 14, dated February 19, we read: "There have been many parodys [sic.] on 'The White Man's Burden'." At age ten, then, Eliot, as "virtual war correspondent," dispatched reports on Aguinaldo and the Philippine flag, and, as an "editor," tackled the "White Man's Burden," laving little doubt about the relation between indigenousness and civilizing power.

W hen the Philippine Exposition came to St. Louis several years later in 1904, the young Eliot was naturally attracted to the Exposition. At sixteen, more intellectually equipped, he must have done intensive thinking on the relation between indigenousness and civilization. Most importantly, he must have reflected much on the fate of Igorot Village people exhibited on the fairgrounds in the civilized world of St. Louis. Thus, at seventeen, in June 1905, he published "The Man Who Was King," creating the imagined world of interaction between Matahiva and the West. In an important sense, the short story could be read as yet another virtual, well-wrought "dispatch" from the "on-site" Philippine world in St. Louis. The young T.S. Eliot, as "ethnographic reporter" may not be far from those of us "here," still confronting cross-cultural problems today .

5. A Major Shift Prior to his Entrance to Harvard

Ezra Pound once extolled the young Eliot, then in his early twenties, with much of enthusiasm for a certain ability he perceived in him. Pound wrote: "He is the only American I know of who has made what I can call adequate preparation for writing. He has actually trained himself *and* modernized himself *on his own.* The rest of the *promising young* have done one or the other but never both (most of the swine have done neither). It is such a comfort to meet a man not to tell him to wash his face, wipe his feet, and remember the date (1914) on the calendar" (Pound, *The Selected Letters*, p.4 0; italics in the original).

How could Eliot really train and modernize himself on his own? The usual answer would customarily be given in connection with the studies, anthropological or French-symbolism-related, that comprised the poet's schooling during his Harvard years. But in view of "The Man Who Was King," we may focus attention in two directions. One of these is concerned with the inter-culturality issues embodied in the Philippines conflict already discussed . The other is a fairly extensive critique of Christianity as presented from a Unitarian perspectives.

Unitarianism was the religion the Eliot family embraced. The family members were all assured that the youngest boy was to "achieve greatness" (Powell, "Notes," p. 4) like William Greenleaf Eliot before him, the greatest Unitarian pastor of the day, whom Whitman called the saint of the West.

"The Man Who Was King" displays the initial signs of what will emerge as an ever-growing conflict with Unitarianism. Suggestively, we find the central Christian dogma 's critical depiction in the story as follows:

> "The captain of course did not understand all this, but learned it afterwards. It appears that the king had just died, and that while they [islanders] were casting about for a new one, somebody discovered the captain asleep on the shore. As he was strangely dressed and moreover, of a whitish color, they straightway concluded that the gods had dropped him down for the purpose of ruling over them, and were now triumphantly bearing him to the village to inaugurate him."

Within a year, Eliot seems to have turned away from the once deeply cherished Unitarianism. Frederick May Eliot, a first cousin of Eliot's and also one of the important playmates, testifies that

> "by the time Eliot got to Harvard in 1906, he had become completely indifferent to Unitarianism." (Powell, p.4)

In the short story, the author shows signs that he had been raised and trained in the intellectual milieu of Unitarianism. However, judging from the testimony of Frederick May Eliot, the then-president of American Unitarian Association, the would-be poet was very soon to have severe conflicts with his Unitarian heritage that led to his being "completely indifferent to Unitarianism."

It would appear that Eliot was fostering a world of his own during the time when he, as a young man, was passing through the tumultuous period of adolescence. The poet's Unitarian formation and the intercultural experiences of the St. Louis World's Fair found their way into the imagined world of Matahiva and would be significant in illuminating the nature of Eliot's American days.

Tatsushi Narita

Bibliography

Bennitt, Mark. ed. 1976. *History of the Louisiana Purchase Exposition* (1905). New York: Arno Press.

Bush, Ronald. 1995. "The Presence of the Past: Ethnographic Thinking/Literary Politics." *Prehistories of the Future: The Primitivist Project and the Culture of Modernism* . Ed. Elazar Barkan and Ronald Bush. Stanford: Stanford University Press, 1995, pp. 23-41. [This article gives a detailed account of T. Narita's new discoveries.]

Bush, Ronald. 1989. "[A review of] The Savage and the City in the Work of T. S. Eliot." *Modern Philology,* 86 (1989), 104-106. [This review refers to T. Narita's new findings.]

Crawford, Robert. 1987. *The Savage and the City in the Work of T.S. Eliot* . Oxford: Oxford University Clarendon Press.

Eliot, T.S. 1905. "The Man Who Was King." *Smith Academy Record,* June, 1905.

Eliot, T.S. 1933. *The Use of Poetry and the Use of Criticism* . London: Faber and Faber (1967).

Gordon, Lyndall. 1977. *Eliot' s Early Years* . Oxford: Oxford University Press.

Harmon, William. 1976. "T.S.Eliot, Anthropologist and Primitive." *American Anthropologist.* 78(1976), 792-811.

Howarth, Herbert. 1965. *Notes on Some Figures behind T.S.Eliot* . London: Chatto and Windus.

Jain, Manju. 1992. *T.S.Eliot and American Philosophy.* Cambridge: Cambridge University Press.

Narita, Tatsushi. 2002. *American Cultural Studies: An Attempt.* Nagoya: Kougaku Press [original in Japanese].

Narita, Tatsushi. 1999. *T.S.Eliot and Cross-Cultural Interactions: His Early American Years* . Preface by Professor Peter Milward. Nagoya: Kougaku Press.

Narita, Tatsushi. 1996. *A Study of T.S.Eliot: Perspectives of Comparative Culture* . Nagoya: Kohgaku Press [original in Japanese].

Narita, Tatsushi. 1994. "The Young T.S.Eliot and Alien Cultures: His Philippine Interactions." *The Review of English Studies* (Oxford University Press), New Series, v. 45, no. 180 (1994), 523-525.

Narita, Tatsushi. 1992. "Fiction and Fact in T.S.Eliot's 'The Man Who Was King.'" *Notes and Queries* (Pembroke College, Oxford University), v. 39, no. 2 (1992), 191-192.

Pound, Ezra. 1971. *The Selected Letters of Ezra Pound: 1907-1941*. Ed. D. D. Page. New York: New Directions, 1971.

Powell, Hartford William Hare, Jr. 1954. "Notes on the Life of T. S. Eliot, 1888-1910." MA Thesis, Brown University.

Report of the Philippine Exposition in the United States for the Louisiana Purchase Exposition. [Washington, D. C.:] Bureau of Insular Affairs, War Department, 1905.

Soldo, John J.D. 1972. "The Tempering of T.S.Eliot, 1888-1919." Ph.D. Dissertation, Harvard University.

Cities in Ruins: The Recuperation of the Baroque in T.S. Eliot and Octavio Paz

The etymology of "barroco," of Portuguese origin, points to something extravagant or bizarre, a pearl with an irregular shape.[1] The "pérola barroca" is the product of the Portuguese commerce with pearls in the East, a result of their explorations in the early sixteenth century. In a headlong dive, searching for irregular pearls in the traditional corpus of enigmatic conceits and paradoxical images, Octavio Paz and T.S. Eliot immerse themselves in the poetic and critical endeavour of recuperating the seventeenth-century Spanish Baroque and the English Metaphysical poets respectively. I will analyse T.S. Eliot's critical and aesthetic ties to the English Metaphysical poet, John Donne's influential *The First Anniversary,* and Paz's homage to, and rewriting of Francisco de Queve-do's sonnet "Amor constante más allá de la muerte" ["Love Constant

---

[1]   Helmut Hatzfeld gives a detailed description of how the "pérola barroca," a pearl with an irregular shape, comes from the commerce of pearls by the Portuguese in early sixteen hundreds. At first the term had pejorative connotations of fraud since it was a cheaper, less valuable type of pearl. But the word "barroco" evolved and the nineteenth century acquired its modern significance as something characterized by bizarreness and artificiality. *Estudios sobre el Barroco.* Madrid: Gredos, 1964. p.418 The etymological meaning of baroque as an irregular pearl is also suggested in Corominas, J., and Pascual, J.A., *Diccionario Crítico Etimológico Castellano e Hispánico.* Madrid: Gredos, 1980. p.529

beyond Death"]. Both Paz and Eliot use the Baroque tradition in a "historical sense" as an "objective correlative" to rethink questions of death and decay, ruinous bodies and ruined cities in post-war Europe and America. I want to discuss how they balance their desire for modern formal innovations in a "tradition against itself," using Paz's terminology, and the inter-textual dialogue they establish with the Baroque and the Metaphysical poets, shown in Eliot's *The Waste Land* and "Whispers of Immortality," and Paz's *Homenaje y profanaciones*.

The connections between the Spanish Baroque poets and the English Metaphysicals are various and multilayered. Helmut Hatzfeld argues that the Spanish Baroque had an immense influence over all the European poetry of the seventeenth century, and especially in England: "With regard to English literature, it seems difficult to understand how is it possible that a Protestant and an Anglo-Saxon country could adopt for half a century spiritual elements from another country, which was precisely its political and religious adversary."[2] Although he suggests that the Metaphysicals were more Mannerist than Baroque, he emphasizes the influence of the Spanish Baroque in Donne: "A poet like John Donne with his Catholic education and his trip to Spain (1596) knows Spain well—its word plays and its ingenious conceits."[3] In an essay on Donne, Paz encourages a comparative study between the English poet and Quevedo. Like Hatzfeld, Paz indicates that aesthetic movements like the Baroque are never national enterprises.[4] Since I cannot devote much time to the

---

[2] Helmut Hatzfeld, p. 445

[3] Ibid., p.448

[4] Paz underlines that Donne's poetry is closely linked to the Spanish conceptualist trend, and he quotes Donne when he writes to Buckingham, who was in Madrid in 1623: "I can thus make myself believe that I am where your lordship is, in Spain that in my poor library, where indeed I am, I can turn my eye towards no shelf, in any profession, from the mistress of my youth, Poetry, to the wife of mine age, Divinity, but that I meet more authors of that nation than any others."" It is significant to note the hint of irony, not noticed by Paz, when Donne alludes to the great proliferation of poets and priests in Spain, not necessarily commenting on the quality of poets like Quevedo, Góngora and Lope de Vega, among others. However, Paz makes a relevant point on the "transnational" facet of the Baroque and Metaphysical poets: "Las afinidades entre los "metafísicos" ingleses y los poetas españoles es uno de tantos temas apenas tocados por la crítica... Aquí subrayo que los estilos nunca son nacionales..." ("The affinities between the English Metaphysical poets and the Spanish poets is one of the many subjects that have been neglected by the academic critics... I underline that styles are never conditioned by their nationality...") ("Un poema de John Donne," (1958, 1965). *Obras Completas, Excursiones / Incusiones*. Vol.2, México: Fondo de Cultura Económica, 1994. p.96)

literary links between the Metaphysical poets and the Spanish Baroque poets here, I will focus instead on how and why Eliot and Paz recover Donne and Quevedo in their search for the irregular pearls of their respective literary canons.

Eliot and Paz are American poets who seek the presence of the past in the European literary tradition. Their essays and poems about the Baroque and the Metaphysical poets reveal their desire to find new connections with the Old World that will legitimize and enrich their own poetic practices. Eliot elucidates: "Tradition... cannot be inherited, and if you want it, you must obtain it with great labour. It involves, in the first place, the historical sense, which we may call nearly indispensable to anyone who would continue to be a poet beyond his twenty-fifth year... (it) involves a perception, not only of the pastness of the past, but of its presence..."[5] Tradition, in particular for American writers, is not "inherited" but acquired and manufactured. Adriana Méndez Rodenas asserts that "Both Eliot and Paz gloss a temporal concept of tradition, (and) since then poetics have as points of departure the influence of past literary models and simultaneously the imperative of formal experimentation."[6]

However, unlike Eliot's, Paz's search for cultural origins leads him to the past buried in Aztec ruins and modern ruins, where the Pre-Columbian and the European traditions coincide: "México buscaba el presente afuera y lo encontró adentro, enterrado pero vivo. La búsqueda de la modernidad nos llevó a descubrir nuestra antigüedad... era un descenso a los orígenes." ("Mexico looked for the present outside and found it inside, buried but alive. The search of modernity drove us to discover our own antiquity... it was a descent to the origins.")[7] In *Homenaje y profanaciones*, the allusions to Itálica and Uxmal exemplify the conjunction of both heritages through their cities in ruins. In his essay "La búsqueda del presente," ("In search of the present") Paz places

---

[5]   T.S.Eliot. "Tradition and the Individual Talent," *The Sacred Wood*. London: Methuen, 1972. p.49

[6]   Adriana Méndez Rodenas. "Tradition and Women's Writing: Toward a Poetics of Difference." *Engendering the Word*. Ed. Berg, T.; Elfenbein, A.S.; Larsen, J., and Sparks, E.K. Chicago: University of Illinois Press, 1989. p.36

[7]   Paz. "La búsqueda del presente," "In search for the present". *Revista Canadiense de Estudios Hispánicos*. 16, núm.3 (1992 Primavera) p.389

himself in the tradition of Lope and Quevedo, yet maintains that Mexicans have an ambiguous relation to this tradition: "Somos y no somos europeos." ("We are and we are not Europeans.") This quest for the lost origins in both the European and the indigenous heritage ties Paz's work to a Neobaroque poetics, and I would suggest that Eliot is also part of a Neo Baroque poetics.[8] Eliot was particularly enthralled by the Metaphysicals, privileging the English over the French or the Spanish seventeenth-century poets, and he considered himself more a part of the European literary tradition than the American canon. On the other hand, Paz defines himself as a Mexican poet, in between modernity and antiquity, the Americas and Europe. As he states in relation to the Baroque poets of New Spain like Sor Juana Inés de la Cruz, "Respiraban con naturalidad en el mundo de la extrañeza porque ellos mismos eran y se sabían extraños." ("They breathed comfortably in the world of bizarreness because they were and they recognized themselves as bizarre.")[9] Paz hints that the irregular beauty of the Baroque pearl is represented by the New World itself. Defining the American Baroque as the epitome of what is bizarre is also a way of essentializing those "origins" as unique and eccentric.

The strange curves and the bizarre imagery of Eliot's *The Waste Land* prompted Paz to compare it to a Cubist painting or a collage, although he focussed on elements that we also associate with Baroque aesthetics. In an essay about Eliot's influence in his work, "La vuelta de los días, T.S. Eliot," ("The return of the days, T.S. Eliot") Paz explains in detail how *The Waste Land* fascinated him when he first read the translation by Enrique Munguía in 1930: "El imán que me atrajo fue la excelencia del poema, el rigor de su construcción... también su novedad, su extrañeza... el carácter fragmentario de cada parte y la manera aparentemente desordenada en que se enlazan." ("The magnet that attracted me was the excellence of the poem, the rigor of its construction... also its novelty, its bizarreness... the fragmentary character of

---

[8]   Lois Parkinson Zamora proposes that Carpentier's and Paz's recovery of the Baroque poets is comparable to Eliot's revival of the English Baroque, the Metaphysical poets (in contrast to the American Transcendentalists' connections with the Romantics). *The Usable Past*. Cambridge: Cambridge University Press, 1997. p.208

[9]   Octavio Paz, "Manierismo, barroquismo, criollismo." *Revista Canadiense de Estudios Hispánicos* 1, no.1, 1976. p.14

each part and the apparently disorderly manner in which everything is tied.")[10] Indeed, Paz's comments on Eliot in turn echo Eliot's praise of John Donne's abilities to maintain poetic order while integrating diverse moods and feelings, "rapid alterations and antithesis."[11]

Paz continues his homage to Eliot by stressing that *The Waste Land*'s main literary contribution resides in its incorporation of history and history-making: "La novedad de *The Waste Land* está tanto en su forma cuanto en la aparición de la historia humana como (con /in)stancia del poema. La poesía regresa a la épica. Como toda épica, ese poema cuenta una historia transfigurada en un mito." ("The novelty of *The Waste Land* is both in its form and in the presence of human history like a con/instant of the poem. Poetry returns to the epic. But like every epic, this poem tells a history transfigured in myth.")[12] The historical context of World War I is deeply embedded in *The Waste Land*'s cities in ruins, but Paz is referring to a human history of continuous destruction. Eliot's poem also reflects upon a wider historical interpretation: the social and cultural decay of Western civilization. As Northrop Frye declares, Eliot believed that "the disintegration of Europe began soon after Dante's time," and that "history since represents the degeneration of the (this) ideal" of a European community with shared values.[13] Paz finally points to the political differences between him and Eliot, and considers that as a self-confessed "rebel" what ultimately united him to the more conservative poet was their mutual anguish at modernity's ruins and disasters.[14]

---

[10] Octavio Paz. "La vuelta de los días, T.S. Eliot," "The return of the days, T.S. Eliot." *Vuelta 142.* (Sept. 1988). p.40

[11] T.S. Eliot. "John Donne." *The Nation and Atheneum,* 33, (April-Sept. 1923) p.331

[12] Paz, "La vuelta de los días, T.S. Eliot." p.41

[13] Northop Frye. *T.S. Eliot.* Edinburgh and London: Oliver and Boyd, 1963. p.8

[14] Paz indicates that: "Toda visión de la historia... contiene un metahistoria. La que anima a *The Waste Land* estaba y está en abierta oposición a mis ideas y creencias... Pero la fascinación persistía, ¿Qué me unía a *The Waste Land*? El horror al mundo moderno. Ante los desastres de la modernidad, el conservador y el rebelde comparten la misma angustia." ("Every vision of history... contains a metahistory. What moves *The Waste Land* was and is opposed to my ideas and beliefs... But the fascination persisted, what united me to *The Waste Land*? The horror to the modern world. In the face of modernity's disasters, the conservative and the rebel share the same anguish.") "La vuelta de los días, T.S. Eliot." p.41

Eliot's disturbed view of the modern city as a wasted, barren space is full of literary allusions. His critical and poetic readings of Donne will shed light on the gloomy, fractured, or dead bodies that become symptomatic of a world in ruins. Eliot's fascination with Donne's aesthetics is substantiated by two of his essays "The Metaphysical Poets" (1921) and "John Donne" (1923), where he underlines Donne's complex unity of different emotions and moods: "with Donne... (it is) impossible to isolate his ecstasy, his sensuality and his cynicism."[15]

Eliot's "Whispers of Immortality" (written between 1917 and 1918) is a poetic revaluation of the Metaphysicals—not just a reaction to the current affairs of World War I but also an intrinsic part of his exploration of a spiritual and poetic strain within the English tradition. The poem is divided into two parts, each composed of four stanzas. The first four stanzas revolve around questions of death and the body, explicitly referring to the Jacobean playwright John Webster (1580-1625?) and John Donne (1572-1631). In contrast, the final four stanzas distill exuberance and desire, provoked by the mysterious Grishkin, the exotic emblem of the Russian woman who surpasses a Brazilian jaguar's feline qualities. Richard Bradford offers an accurate explanation that connects the erotic aspects of the second part with Eliot's ruminations on the Metaphysicals: "Donne's and Webster's treatment of sex has an odour of death about it—Eliot's point is that in their poetry, love and physical attraction are continually and relentlessly attended by a morbid anxiety."[16]

The representation of the body in the first part of the poem suggests that morbid anxiety with the "skull," "the breastless creatures," the "lipless grin," "the dead limbs," the "skeleton" and its bones. The powerful image of nature taking over the remnants of our bodies strikes me as a modern homage to the paradoxical conceits of the Metaphysics: "Daffodil bulbs instead of balls/ Stared from the sockets of the eyes!" The

---

[15] T.S. Eliot. "John Donne," *The Nation and Atheneum,* 33, (April-Sept. 1923) p.332 Eliot continues to write about Donne in the thirties, but I will discuss primarily his critical and poetic meditations from the early twenties period. In an essay that commemorates the tercentenary of Donne's death in 1931, Eliot distances himself from his earlier commentaries on Donne, signalling his lack of organization. T.S. Eliot. "Donne in Our Time," *A Garland for John Donne (1631-1931).* Ed. Theodore Spencer, copyright 1931. Gloucester, Mass.: Meter Smith, 1958.

[16] Richard Bradford. "Richard Lovelace and Eliot's 'Whispers of Immortality.'" *Trivium* 22 (Summer 1987) p. 106

daffodil and the bulb share a particular brightness, a yellow that unites the natural and the artificial. The flowers replace the gaze of the dead by invading the hollow sockets of their eyes. As in the Baroque topos of ruins, when nature "takes over" the remnants of the city, here nature occupies the skeletons of the dead bodies. In her essay, "Eliot Re-Donne," Aileen Shafer highlights the imagistic similarities between Eliot's "Love Song of Alfred Prufrock" and Donne's "Valediction: Forbidding Mourning," sustaining that "In view of the seventeenth century use of dying as a sexual metaphor, it seems logical that the characteristics ascribed to the act of death, natural and sacred as opposed to clinical and analytical, be extended to the emotion of love in each poem."[17] In the image of the "daffodil bulbs," Eliot integrates the Metaphysicals' use of natural metaphors with the modern "clinical and analytical" metaphors, the mechanized versions of death.

For Eliot's Webster, thought seems to be a repressive force, aiming to control the body, and at the same time, depending upon the body: "He knew that thought clings round dead limbs/ Tightening its lusts and luxuries." As for Donne, thought seems to equal experience:

> Donne, I suppose, was such another
> Who found no substitute for sense,
> To seize and clutch and penetrate;
> Expert beyond experience.

Perhaps Eliot incorporates the colloquial "I suppose" as a way of recognizing Donne's revolutionary use of "natural conversational diction instead of a conventional tone."[18] In another article about Eliot's Donne, Peter Carpenter comments on these verses and suggests that the polysemic word "sense" evokes both sex and understanding.[19] The sexual

---

[17] Aileen Shafer. "Eliot Re-Donne: The Prufrockian Spheres." *Yeats Eliot Review*. Vol.5, No.2, (1978) p.40

[18] Eliot. "Donne in Our Time," p. 14

[19] Peter Carpenter. "Taking Liberties: Eliot's Donne," *Critical Survey* 5, no.3 (1993) p.280

connotations of "to seize" and "penetrate" are also projected in "sense."[20] Nevertheless, Donne is characterized by Eliot as an "Expert beyond experience," a subtle parody of his lack of actual, physical, material experience. Eliot remarks in his essay "The Metaphysical Poets" that: "A thought to Donne was an experience; it modified his sensibility. When a poet's mind is perfectly equipped for its work, it is constantly amalgamating disparate experience..."[21] The fourth stanza describes Donne's ability to penetrate metaphorically to the core of things, reaching the "anguish of the marrow." Yet, the only possibility of relieving the morbid anguish, "the fever of the bone," is to have no contact with flesh, to stay in the realm of "sense" as understanding and of thought as experience.[22]

The second part of "Whispers of Immortality" is devoted to a feminine symbol of modern eroticism, Grishkin. Her Russian eye and her "uncorseted bust" offer a promise of sexual pleasure and availability. The comparison of Grishkin to a jaguar depicts her as both "wild" and in control of her space: her maisonnette and her drawing room. But for my argument, the most revealing verses are the final ones:

And even the Abstract Entities
Circumambulate her charm;
But our lot crawls between dry ribs
To keep our metaphysics warm.

Grishkin's charm seems to be especially powerful, a magnet for both abstractions and real bodies. However, the final verses show that "our lot," probably referring to modern poets like Eliot himself and Ezra Pound, who helped in the editing of this poem, instead of falling for her

---

[20] Quevedo also exploits this double meaning of sense and it becomes particularly revealing in relation to Donne's *First Anniversary* if we consider love as a destructive force, of ruinous power: "Amor me ocupa el seso y los sentidos... Todo soy ruinas, todo soy destrozos..." ("Love inhabits my sense and my senses... I am all ruins, I am all shredded pieces...") (Soneto 109). Francisco de Quevedo. *Poemas escogidos*. Edición de José Manuel Blecua. Madrid: Castalia, 1989. p.183

[21] T.S. Eliot. "The Metaphysical Poets," (1921) *Selected Prose*. London: Penguin Books, 1953. p.117

[22] Northrop Frye clarifies that "In the age of Donne what Eliot calls sensibility was called wit, and what he calls objective correlative was called conceit, or something conceived. "Wit" has more intellectual sound than "sensibility" or "emotion," and indicates why poetry of Donne's school is called "Metaphysical." Its "metaphysical" quality is actually a technique of fusing images and ideas which is deliberately strained and forced. Hence there is a latent irony in its conceits, a suggestion of the grotesque which seems conscious, and so intellectual." p.31

seductive body, opt for "dry ribs" and empty skeletons. These poets move through poetry like a jaguar. They "crawl" into a dead, desiccated body to keep the "Metaphysical poets" warm, alive, valuable in the literary canon—whispering words of immortality.

I will not analyze in detail the presence of Webster and Donne in *The Waste Land*. Nonetheless, I want to review some of the most obvious connections. Remember the striking verses in "The Burial of the Dead": That corpse you planted last year in your garden,

> Has it begun to sprout? Will it bloom this year?
> Or has a sudden frost disturbed its bed?"
> O keep the Dog far hence, that's friend to men,
> Or with his nails he'll dig it up again!

In Eliot's notes, where he revealed some of the literary allusions of the poem, he affirms that "O keep the Dog far hence..." is a reference to Webster's *White Devil*.[23] I would again point to "Whispers of Immortality" and the image of the daffodils blooming out of the skeleton's eye sockets. The imagery of the Metaphysicals is both buried and revealed. These verses assign the reader with the duties of the dog, who will dig out those corpses from the ruins of the modern city.

The desert zone of Eliot's poem strikes me as being especially in touch with Donne's *First Anniversary*, where the world is represented in a lethargic, convalescent state since the death of the speaker's beloved mistress. Donne's apostrophe to the world exposes the morbid anguish evoked in "Whispers of Immortality": "Sick world, yea dead, yea putrefied, since she/ Thy intrinsic balm, and thy preservative,/ Can never be renewed thou never live." The analogy of the dead female body as a symptom of a decayed, ill world is not explicitly developed in *The Waste Land*. But the reflection on death and the disillusionment with the idea of progress in the world is made manifest in similar images in both Donne and Eliot.

---

[23] S.A. Cowan offers a hypothetical reading of the dog as an echo of Donne's work: "Associating the dog with blight and death is consistent with the decay and extinction of spirit that is the most prominent theme of *The Waste Land*... Had Eliot wished to clarify his allusion to the Dog Star as a symbol of blight and death, he could have cited a precedent in John Donne's "Devotions upon Emergent Occasions." Although I have found no evidence that Eliot had read the *Devotions* by the time he had composed *The Waste Land*." Cowan. "Echoes of Donne, Herrick and Southwell in Eliot's *The Waste Land*." *Yeats Eliot Review*. Vol.8, no.1 and 2, (1986) p.97.

The "tumbled graves," the falling towers and the ruined cities in "What the Thunder Said" portray a similar landscape to Donne's apocalyptic vision of the future, where "This world, in that great earthquake languished." Donne's poem is an elegy to his mistress; its ultimate goal is to pay homage to her memory and his pain. *The Waste Land*'s final verses "These fragments I have shored against my ruins" allude to all the voices and the literary fragments that compose its intricate nest. In a few verses earlier in the poem, he quotes the famous Provençal poet Arnaut Daniel in *Purgatory 26* telling Dante to remember his pain. Eliot's work also traces his own pain, his own modern anguish. Paz shares Eliot's disenchantment and modern sense of distress.[24] When Paz compares Quevedo and Donne's works, he also points to their consciousness of the fractured self as strikingly modern:

> Quevedo... nos muestra la visión de la caída de la conciencia en sí misma, una caída que revela nuestra fractura interior... el primer poema realmente moderno de la literatura española es *Lágrimas de un penitente*... Y si pienso en la poesía europea de esa época, sólo encuentro en Donne una premonición semejante, en un pasaje de *The First Anniversary, An Anatomy of the World*.

"Quevedo... shows us the vision of the fall of conscience into itself, a fall that reveals us our fractured self... the first really modern poem is *Lágrimas de un penitente* [*Tears of a Penitent*]... And if I think of the European poetry of that era, I only find in Donne a similar premonition, in a segment of *The First Anniversary, An Anatomy of the World*."[25]

Paz indicates how the Metaphysicals and the Spanish Conceptualist poets share a consciousness of conscience, although there is a poignant difference between them in their representation of the universe. Donne

---

[24] In the interviews and writings in which Paz discusses Eliot's legacy, he stresses Eliot's insertion of his poetry into *history*, responding to both the cultural and political context of the twenties, and to a very modern sense of anguish. Among other interviews: Roberto González Echevarría's "Interview to Octavio Paz," (*Diacritics* 2, no.3, 1972), and Manuel Ulacia's "Octavio Paz: poesía, pintura, música, etcetera. Conversación con Octavio Paz," ("Octavio Paz: poetry, painting, music, etc... A conversation with Octavio Paz") (*Revista Iberoamericana* 55, no. 148-149, July-Dec. 1989).

[25] Octavio Paz. "Reflejos: réplicas. Diálogos con Quevedo." (Reflections: Replies. In dialogue with Quevedo") (1996) *Obras Completas, Miscelánea II*. Vol.14. México: Fondo de Cultura Económica, 2000. p.74-75

meditates on the decay and the fragmentation of the universe, incorporating the scientific revolutionary theories of his time, while for Paz, Quevedo does not venture into reflections about the universe. "Homenaje y profanaciones" is Paz's ultimate poetic reading of Quevedo's famous poem "Amor constante más allá de la muerte" ["Love Constant beyond Death"], in which he pays homage, and at the same time parodies Quevedo's sonnet. Paz's title underscores that paradoxical double intention. Paz's "Homenaje y profanaciones" does not really parody Quevedo's poem, although it does expose a more pessimistic, more sceptical view of death and the remains of the body. The poem is divided into three parts, which reflect the structure of the sonnet. "Aspiración" ("Aspiration") stands for the first quatrain, and in Paz's words, it expresses "inhalación, afirmación y homenaje" ("inhalation, affirmation and homage"); "Espiración" ("Respiration") stands for the second quatrain, and it implies "interrogación, negación y profanación" ("interrogation, negation and profanation"); and "Lauda" ("Tomb") stands for the two tercets and finally it points to a sense of beyond, "más allá de la afirmación o la negación, la eternidad o muerte." ("beyond affrimation or negation, eternity or death.")[26] In an essay on Donne and Quevedo, González Fernández de Sevilla discusses "Amor constante más allá de la muerte," affirming that the sonnet shows the common antitheses of temporality and eternity, body and soul, prevalent in all Metaphysical poetry.[27] Paz's poem plays with these dichotomies, but especially in the final strophe, he desires to transcend them with the enumeration of all the senses and all the temporal adverbs.

"Homenaje y profanaciones" has been compared by Manuel Ulacia to a collage or a deformation of Quevedo's sonnet, parallel to Picasso's parody of Velázquez's *Las Meninas*, in the context of the revalorization of Baroque aesthetics in twentieth century poetry.[28] In this sense, it reminds me of Eliot's "Whispers of Immortality." Memory and imagination are the

[26] Paz. "Reflejos: réplicas. Diálogos con Francisco de Quevedo." (1996). p.78-79

[27] José Manuel González Fernández de Sevilla. "La poesía metafísica de John Donne y Francisco de Quevedo." ("The metaphysical poetry of John Donne and Francisco de Quevedo.") *Neophilologus* 95, (1991). p.556

[28] Manuel Ulacia, "Francisco de Quevedo and Pablo Picasso en "Homenaje y profanaciones," *El árbol milenario, Un recorrido por la obra de Octavio Paz*. Barcelona: Galaxia Gutenberg, 1994.

creative sources of the poem. The poem can be read as a metaphor of how to write a poem, a sonnet about sonnets, and that is why the whiteness of the first strophes resembles the whiteness of the blank page: "Yo no veo nada sino lo blanco... el alma desatada del ansia y de la hora," ("I see/ nothing but white:/ white hour, soul unchained.")[29] The whiteness of the page evokes the blinding light of Quevedo's "blanco día," ("white day") as well as the multiple possibilities of poetic recreation, without time as a limitation. Using Quevedo's paradox of memory: "nadar sabe mi llama el agua fría," ("my fire can swim through the frigid water.") Paz makes memory swim against nihilism, holding on to the belief in the immortality of the soul: "nada contra corriente y mandamiento/ nada contra la nada." ("swims against the current and commands / swims against nothing.") Memory paradoxically fuses fire and water, defying the river of forgetfulness. Along with memory, imagination is the other source of creativity in "Aspiración," with the verses "pensar que transfigura la memoria/ el resto es un manojo de centellas," ("thought recasting memory itself/ The rest is a handful of flares.") The poetic imagination is the power that transforms memory and gives it a particular energy or brightness.

In contrast, "Espiración" presents us with real doubts about the immortality of the soul and the power of memory to survive: "Tiempo de luz: memoria, torre hendida... la ciudad se desprende de sí misma..." ("Time of light: memory, tower cracked,/ the city shakes loose from itself.") Eliot's cities in ruins may be evoked by these verses, which illustrate that literary memory is a fragile construction. But a more poignant question deals with "immortality," will the work survive the author: "Vana conversación del esqueleto/ con el fuego insensato y con el agua/ que no tiene memoria... y con la tierra/ que se calla y se come sus palabras." ("The skeleton's futile conversation/ with senseless fire and water/ that has no memory/ ...and earth/ that keeps still and eats its words.") This skeleton does not bloom with nature like the ones in "Whispers of Immortality" and *The Waste Land*. The disintegration of the body, portrayed in Quevedo's sonnet as reanimated by love's power, is actually recalled later on as "polvo de los sentidos sin sentido/ ceniza lo sentido y el sentido." ("dust of unaware awareness/ ash the cared and

---

[29] I refer to Eliot Weinberger's translation, *Homage and Desecrations*. New York: Red Ozier Press, 1987.

cares.")[30] Like in Donne and Quevedo's poems, these verses play with the double meaning of sense or "sentido." Quevedo's famous "serán ceniza, mas tendrá sentido;/ polvo serán, mas polvo enamorado" ("ash they'll be, yet still aware;/ they will be dust, but dust in love.") are truly "profaned" when sense and sensibility become mere ashes.

The third part of "Espiración" discloses Paz's intention to achieve a burlesque tone with a strophe full of wordplay and empty conceits like "Los laúdes del láudano de loas/ dilapidadas lápidas y laudos," ("The Lauds of laudanum of praise/ gravestones decayed stones the graves.") But this part of the poem raises a much more remarkable issue, the temporality and a-temporality of death. His eyes have to imagine, see the invisible: "lo que miraron sin mirarlo nunca," ("what they saw without looking.") They saw, in past sense, making the act of imagining one of remembrance. In one of his essays on Quevedo, Paz emphasizes that the imagination is a historical construction.[31] With "El entierro es barroco todavía/ en México," ("Burial is still baroque/ in Mexico,") he is upholding that the burial of the dead—our ways of imagining, remembering or paying homage to our dead, is a historical and cultural endeavor, with temporal and spatial particularities. However, the only "universal" certainty, without temporal or spatial particularities, is death itself: "Morir es todavía/ morir a cualquier hora en cualquier parte," ("To die is still/ to die some hour somewhere.") The final part of the poem disrupts all notions of temporality, eternity, and death, by fusing the lovers' bodies and their memories: "los cuerpos abolidos en el cuerpo/ memorias desmemorias de haber sido/ antes después ahora nunca siempre," ("bodies abolished in the body/ memories that can't remember having been/ before after now never forever.") The lack of conjunctions and commas re-enacts the breathlessness of this collage of paradoxes.

"Whispers of Immortality" and *Homenaje y profanaciones* evoke the conventional Baroque dichotomies of the eternal and the temporal, *eros* and *tanatos*, in experimental and original ways. Eliot and Paz insert

---

[30] In *La Llama doble,* Paz analyzes closely Quevedo's "Amor constante más allá de la muerte," ("Love Constant Beyond Death") and he underlines that the final verses enact the "Derrota del cuerpo: ese polvo está animado y siente." ("The defeat of the body: the dust is always animated and it feels.") Barcelona: Seix Barral, 1993. p. 67.

[31] Paz. "Quevedo, Heráclito y algunos sonetos." (1981) *Obras Completas 3, Fundación y disidencia.* México: Fondo de Cultura Económica, 1994. p.132

themselves in the tradition of Donne and Quevedo, and they recover the seventeenth-century poets' fame, their "immortality," while securing their own. Eliot's and Paz's recuperation is an essential step for the conceptualization of Neobaroque poetry in the twentieth century. Their conscience of the "presence of the past," the meeting point of modernity and antiquity, lead Eliot and Paz into the making of new and irregular poetic pearls.

Cecilia Enjuto Rangel

An "American Venture":
Self-Representation and Self-Orientalization in Turkish-American Selma Ekrem's *Unveiled*

This article introduces and discusses a twentieth-century Turkish-American woman's autobiographical text, *Unveiled: The Autobiography of A Turkish Girl* (1930)[1] by Selma Ekrem (1902-1986). Born in Istanbul as a Turk,[2] Ekrem moved to the US while still in her twenties, eventually became a US citizen, and died in Massachusetts. Penned in English,[3] and published in the US, *Unveiled* was a relative best-seller in its day, and attracted quite some attention when it first came out, with articles about it published in the *Chicago Tribune, Current Literature, Philadelphia Enquirer, Philadelphia Public Ledger* and *New York Herald Tribune* (see Ekrem, *Peçeye İsyan*, 6). It is an account of Ekrem's life until she was

---

[1]   The next edition of the work was published in the UK as *Unveiled* (1931), with *The Autobiography of A Turkish Girl* part of the title left out. Ekrem will later publish two other books in the US: *Turkey Old and New* (1947); and *Turkish Fairy Tales* collected by Selma Ekrem (1964).

[2]   As Ekrem relates in *Unveiled*, ethnically, her maternal grandfather was Albanian and his wife, her maternal grandmother, was Greek.

[3]   The text was subsequently translated into Turkish as *Peçeye İsyan: Namık Kemal'in Torununun Anıları* (Rebellion Against the Veil: Memoirs of Namık Kemal's Granddaughter, 1998).

twenty-one, and was written when she was twenty-eight, while the events she relates were still fresh in her mind. Coming from a prominent Ottoman family, Ekrem was able to witness first-hand what turned out to be the dying days of the Ottoman empire, a dramatic period which she recounts with disarming candour and a child's starry-eyed bewilderment—a stance that sometimes works against her, as it prevents her from distinguishing between natural calamities such as cyclones and the gravity of some of the political developments that had major repercussions in world history.[4] She also relates her days at an American school in Istanbul that instilled in her the sense of freedom that eventually led to her emigration to America. In many ways, her autobiography resembles Edward Said's book of memoirs, *Out Of Place* (1999), as it parallels his rendering of experiences, prior to his move to the US, which include his days in an American school in Cairo (one of a number of English-medium institutions he frequented while still in Egypt). Ekrem also felt "out of place," it turns out, in her birthplace, but for very different reasons—that had to do with the issue of gender she had to cope with. In both texts, the *expérience vécue* that is translated on paper, and that stops when the memorialist is still very young, has been lived outside of America, and on similar ground: the Levant, as the region used to be called before the Ottoman empire was dismantled and the "Middle East" created. While Ekrem writes about the Moslem aristocracy, Said writes about the non-Moslem well-to-do merchant class, both reflecting a *Weltanschaung* that is totally alien if not inimical to the American mind set.

It must be noted that Ekrem's belonging to a prominent Ottoman family marks her personal history. She was the granddaughter of the celebrated poet Namık Kemal (1840-1888), champion of freedom and democracy[5] during Sultan Abdülhamid II's (1842-1918)[6] reign (1876-1909),

---

[4]   For a more insightful memoir, also in English and reflecting the same period, see Adıvar.

[5]   He was one of the founders of the "Young Turks," who were militating against what they saw as the despotism of Sultan Abdülhamid II; but as a poet, novelist and dramatist treating of social and political issues, he is also one of the major figures of the 19th century Tanzimat (read Western-type) literature.

[6]   The last great Ottoman emperor, he ruled with an iron hand. The absolute power he exercised led him to be called the "Red" sultan, but it is during his reign that the first ever two constitutions were proclaimed and the first ever two parliaments convened. After the Unionists, as the Young Turks came to be called, deposed him, the Ottoman empire quickly disintegrated, retrospectively

reputed for its terror. Persecuted and imprisoned for his political views, and self-exiled for a time in Paris and London, N. Kemal is today one of the dead white males towering over the canon every Turkish schoolchild is made to memorize. His son, Ekrem's father Ali Ekrem Bolayır (1867-1937), was employed at the palace by the same Sultan Abdülhamid II, more for control than as a favour, but later also held the jobs of governor general of Jerusalem (i.e. was the viceroy of Palestine), and later that of the Archipelago (read Aegean) islands[7] that belonged at the time to the Ottoman state. Ekrem is very much aware of her social standing, and expresses herself accordingly. In a way, she self-consciously *represents* what and who she is, rather than merely render on paper the specificities of her individual experience. As a result, Ekrem's text is formal and impersonal—there is no mention of personal feelings or sensations. To illustrate this, when at the end of the volume she briefly describes her life in the US, she fails to give any information about the "friend" with whom she shares an apartment in the US—let alone her feelings for the said friend; although reading between the lines, one has the impression there exists an affective bond between them, that is of a lesbian nature.

The impersonality in question does not mean, however, that this life writing by a woman lacks a female voice. There is much pondering of gender roles and the position of women, both in Turkey (during the last years of the Ottoman reign, as well as during the republican period) and in the US Ekrem is adamant she does not want to wear the veil and/or experience what she sees as the traditional lack of freedom of Turkish women. It is nevertheless a female voice that belongs to the public sphere. Rebelling against the veil becomes a public gesture, as much as it is lived individually in a specific household. She takes care thus not to disclose any private attribute, or divulge any private misdemeanour, as lesbianism would be considered in 1930, anywhere in the world. The "confessional" text becomes in effect a public autobiography, and what it

---

justifying his absolutism, however anachronistic that may have appeared to be for the twentieth century. Abdülhamid II is also known for having refused to sell Theodor Herzl, whom he received in audience, the province of Palestine in return for cash.

[7] A job that sent him and his family first to Rhodes; then to Lesbos, during which governorship the island was occupied by the Greeks, for what turned out to be for good. A poet and dramatist in his own right, who also taught literature both at secondary-school and university levels, Bolayır wrote his memoirs as well.

represents of public significance. The autobiography gives Ekrem the opportunity to problematise a national history in her own manner, as it allows her to come to terms publicly with the solution she found to the turn this history took, i.e. emigrating to the US and becoming an American citizen.

And all the while, between the lines and unwittingly, she lays bare the personal drama that, I believe, was at the heart of her objection to the veil: her rejection of the gender designated for her, by birth and in society. Yet nowhere is this made explicit—or ever consciously formulated.

I would like to argue that the main concern of the author is not so much to portray an existence that was *sui generis*, or perhaps not at all to do so; but to offer to the American reader, using American lenses, a reflection of an event that was very much public—the demise of the Ottoman state and its society's transformation into a republican "community" (as in Benedict Anderson's "imagined communities"), within a context based on female parameters. I advance that this is a complicated endeavour, since she positions herself as both subject and object. Writing from the premise of the tongue of the Americans, i.e., the English language, Ekrem perforce rejects a mono-cultural Turkish/Eastern perspective—naturally absent from the paradigm afforded by the English language-medium, yet that would have been just as natural, and inevitable, for the content of her tale. She adopts instead an American/Western female voice, interpellating basically the American reader, and seeing as Other[8] the focus of her text, producing thus a testimony of a unique transcultural nature. In so doing, she fails to perceive, however, that what she takes to be a universalist impulse constitutes in effect an exercise in orientalization. Accordingly, I propose to label "self-orientalization" the perspective from which the events recounted in the text are narrated, and I engage the autobiographical text from that angle. By "self-orientalization," I designate the internalization, in native self-images, of cultural representations of what has come to be summarized as *Orientalism* since Said's seminal volume of that title (1978). Discussing that work, Meyda Yeğenoğlu, author of *Colonial Fantasies: Towards A Feminist Reading of Orientalism* (1998) points out that "Said's analysis

---

[8]   Ania Loomba indicates that colonial discourse distinguishes between the West's "other"s, as: one, "those who were constructed as savage (such as the inhabitants of America and Africa)"; and two, "barbarous infidels" who may be "degenerate" (Turks, Russians, Eastern people) (108).

demonstrates that what is at stake in the constitution of the Oriental other is the West's desire to set boundaries for itself as a self-sustaining, autonomous and sovereign subject" (14), and I take this proposition as the basis of the theoretical framework of my discussion of *Unveiled*. I also have recourse to the ideas of various feminist critics, starting with Yeğenoğlu, to argue that through self-orientalization, by representing her life story as Americans would represent it, Ekrem is attempting to attain the identity of the "self-sustaining, autonomous and sovereign subject" which she could not attain otherwise.

Orientalist Fantasies

Numerous scholars and critics (e.g. Amin) have pointed out how the Westerner shaped "self-images of modernity" by construing putative "Others who were to be marginalised in a Eurocentric historiography—if not excluded from it altogether" (Dirlik 20). As Arif Dirlik puts it,

> modernity defined itself with reference to the Other conceived to be pre- or non-modern, by rendering the whole project of modernity into an internal European affair ... The Others were brought into this history only ... to underline European particularity—and, as a by-product, European supremacy. (21-22)

One significant aspect of self-orientalization is the internalization of the Western modernity—Eastern pre-modernity binarism by the Easterners themselves. A number of postcolonial critics of Indian extraction, Partha Chatterjee among them, have argued that, for example, the emergence of nationalism and the establishment of independence in India have meant the duplication, so to speak, of Western Eurocentric thought and practice (*Nationalist Thought and the Colonial World: A Derivative Discourse?*; and *The Nation and Its Fragments: Colonial and Postcolonial Histories*). The elites who acceded to power as leaders not only behaved towards the "subalterns" the way the British colonial administrators had behaved towards *their* subalterns, the Indians, elites and all (for the concept of "subaltern," see e.g. Spivak). These leaders also retained the Orientalist, imperialist binarism even as they wished to move from one end of it to the other. They acknowledged the existence of a distinct and fixed demarcation between the values of Western "modernity," such as those of the Enlightenment, which they wanted to implant in their society, and those of the "traditions" of that society which they considered to be backward.[9] Chatterjee believes that this attempt at reaching modernity betrayed subjugation to the very Western hegemony that it proclaimed precisely to oppose and fight.

Yeğenoğlu contends that the same thing happened in Turkey, as a moribund "Eastern" empire was transmuted into a republic upholding Western principles of governance. The nationalist project valorized the "ideals of humanism and Enlightenment," she writes (128), "[p]rogress was identified with breaking away from Ottoman backwardness" (131), and "the construction of modern Turkish identity" was opposed to "backward Ottoman identity" (132). Mustafa Kemal (later Atatürk), the military leader who fought back the occupying armies and became the first president of the Turkish republic, "adhered strongly to the premises of European Enlightenment thought," with the "Orientalist divide between the East/West," one of the basic traits of his reforms, specifies Yeğenoğlu (132, 133). She points out that M. Kemal was later to mark the "unveiling" of woman and her entry into the public sphere in republican Turkey as a manifestation that the Turk had become enlightened. "Woman thus became a convenient signifier[10]" (129), she notes, in debates concerning tradition vs. modernity or nationalism vs. colonialism/ imperialism.

In effect, many critics, from Ania Loomba to Julie Marcus, to name but a few, have indicated that a major dimension of the Western "imperial gaze," to use Mary Louise Pratt's term, has been its treatment of gender (which almost all accuse Said of having bypassed in *Orientalism*). "From the beginning of the colonial period till its end (and beyond), female bodies symbolize[d] the conquered land" (Loomba, 152), with "sexual and colonial relationships becom[ing] analogous to each other," as Loomba puts it (151), and with, "in the language of colonialism, non-Europeans occu-

---

[9] For a discussion of the conceptualization of Eastern traditions as "backward," see, *inter alia*, Pultar.

[10] ""Woman thus became a convenient signifier," not only for the proponents of the "Anatolian revolution," as it is sometimes called, but for the opponents of the latter as well, the conservatives and/or reactionaries who saw in the liberation of woman, which they resented, "the representation of the moral decay caused by 'excessive' Westernization" (Yeğenoğlu 129).

py[ing] the same symbolic place as women," as Helen Carr, explains (qtd. in Loomba 159). Loomba relates how, as the next step in the colonizing project, a process took place by which women became emblems of their culture and nationality (168), and woman, a metaphor for indigenous culture (169). The West vs. East binary was converted into the male vs. female opposition in which the West was the superior, strong, omnipotent, rational, civilized, modern, masculine element, and the East the inferior, weak, helpless, barbaric, pre-modern, feminine Other, devoid of rationality but exotic. This has also meant that the Eastern/ethnic woman came to represent the Other both as exotic and as inferior. As women became the metaphor for indigenous culture, the Eastern/ethnic woman's predicament came to represent the reality of the culture itself. Marcus explains at length how the West visualized the Ottoman Turks as oppressive because their women lived in the harem, which the West chose to interpret as a prison, however gilded.

That the Eastern woman came to represent the East itself led further to another development. The Western woman who, within Western society, was the Other of the Western man, inferior to him in status, saw herself vis-à-vis the Eastern woman as the superior "masculine." This allowed her, the Western woman positioned in the "West," both to distance herself from the "Oriental" woman and what she stood for; and to obtain, as she thought, what she lacked in the West vis-à-vis the Western man. As the superior, masculine Westerner, the Western woman acquired power over the Eastern woman. And in her craving for mastery over the Eastern woman and aspiration to reach the "level" of men, the Western woman collaborated, inadvertently or not, with Western imperialist interests.

It is this complicity that both forged and fortified the feminist position of the Western woman, which ineluctably acquired a colonial/imperialist tenor. This is the stance, I argue, Ekrem espoused as she composed her life story; the way Ekrem the scribe writing on the East Coast behaved towards Ekrem the rebellious teenager on the Bosporus. The veil[11] in this instance becomes a trope for traditionalism and pre-modernity, as well as the lack of freedom that inhere to these, alongside

---

[11]   For current discussions on the issue of the veil, in Turkey and elsewhere, see Ahmed; Göle; Kandiyoti; Mernissi, Olson; and Özdalga.

the chains that the lack of freedom entails; while being *unveiled* represents both acceding to freedom and the adoption of the persona of an American woman, unquestioningly and firmly ensconced within a Western feminist tenor.

To be or not to be veiled—and wear a hat

Roughly spanning the years 1902-1923, that is to say the period between the author's birth and the proclamation of the Turkish Republic that signalled the formal end of the Ottoman state, *Unveiled* is at surface level the reminiscences of a not so dutiful daughter. It begins with a postcard-picture description of the Ottoman capital where she spent her childhood:

> Winter has come, the horses slip and slide, children muffled to their ears throw snowballs at passers by, cheeks red as apples, eyes glowing ... (1)

Yet it immediately continues with "Constantinople has donned her bridal dress, she is all curves and softness except for the tall minarets that stretch dreamily to the sky while the snow falls ... mysteriously" (1). Istanbul, as the city would have been called in Turkey by 1930 when the book was published, is called Constantinople, thereby establishing the Western perspective from page one, a stance that foreshadows the self-orientalization that will permeate the volume. The city is feminized by the "curves and softness," *is* in fact a "bride" waiting to be ravished, with the phallic symbols, those "tall minarets," not far away, intimating, in spite of the season, a scene of Eastern sensuality that is a common feature of Western fantasy concerning the East. The clichéd phrase, "tall minarets that stretch dreamily to the sky," firmly introduces an element of exoticism that leaves no doubt about the orientalization.

Ekrem then describes her childhood home. This is a typical Ottoman upper-class home with the head of family a high official at the imperial court, and the household comprising a multitude of servants from various ethnic elements that make up the Ottoman melting pot: Greeks, Armenians, Tatars, etc. ... Upstairs and downstairs live in complete harmony. The little girl, it must be said, spends more time with the downstairs group than she does with the upstairs members, as her nurse sleeps in her room, is the one to tell her bedtime stories, etc. Thus

the most important news item to report is the rivalry between the old
nurse and the new one who has just been hired to look after the new-born
baby (Ekrem's younger sister); and the only incident worth mentioning is
when Isaac, grandfather N. Kemal's Armenian retainer become in his old
age a regular guest at N. Kemal's son's home, complains that Maria the
Greek maidservant has pinched his newly bought handkerchiefs; or when
he resents the new French governess's posing as French while in reality
being Armenian,[12] or again when the old Turkish nurse of the eldest girl
(Ekrem's oldest sister, whom she calls *Abla*—older sister) resents having
her position in the girl's life now taken over by the governess.[13] Life
includes traditional "bath days"—"the house permeated with the smell of
soap, clean towels and lavender ... the big Turkish bath ... lit all afternoon," where Ekrem's nurse would soap her (29)—extra-ordinary days
that persons who are still alive today would remember with nostalgia,
unable to represent the sensation to anyone used to having access to hot
water twenty-four hours a day.

But of course this is not an ordinary upper-class home. As
mentioned earlier, the head of the family is the son of Namık Kemal the
infamous intellectual; and before long, sensing, as a close friend of his
falls into disgrace, that he is going to be sent away from his palace job, he

---

[12] Ekrem relates in the following manner Armenian style "passing":
"Isaac, this is mademoiselle Lucy, our new governess," explained mother.
"Hum," grunted Isaac. "And do you know Turkish?"
"Yes," put in Mlle Lucy, "I have learned how to speak it."
"But she is 'Frenque,'" a term applied to all ... foreigners, added mother laughing to herself.
"Haide djanim, hanoum effendi [Come on, madam], whom will she fool? She is a sweet waters
Frenque born and bred here." Turning to Mlle Lucy, he broke into glib Armenian.
But Mlle Lucy shook her head and answered in Turkish:
"I do not speak Armenian, I am a Catholic."
"Catholic, Catholic, and what is that?" burst out Isaac. "You are Armenian as I am; to whom are
you telling all these tales?"
In Constantinople there are a great many Armenians who are Catholics [unlike the Orthodox
majority, to which Isaac must have belonged]; these deny that they are Armenian or that they can
even speak the language. They talk French and call themselves Catholics. Mlle Lucy, being one of
these, was furious with Isaac.
"How impolite he is," she said in French.
"Now, now, don't use your Frenque words on me," retorted Isaac. "I have lived too long in this house
not to understand your French."
My mother was laughing to herself and trying to smother her smiles. (25-6)

[13] "She gives herself airs because she can speak French. Let us see if she can take as good care of you
as I did" (23).

pulls strings to be appointed governor general of Jerusalem. The description of that city and of her family's life there, Ekrem executes in the same manner as she did her native city and their life there; in other words, as mentioned earlier, domestic happenings turn out to be just as important, if not even more so, than political developments taking place outside of the family home, and natural phenomena, such as cyclones, as in the chapter entitled "Cyclone in Rhodes" (129-41), are treated with the same awe and dramatic scope as war and occupation, as in the chapters entitled "War," "Prisoners," and "In the Enemy's Land" (179-219).

While Ekrem commiserates, for example, with her father because multiethnic, multicultural, and especially multi-devotional Jerusalem is "not an easy city to handle. One had to pacify a thousand hatreds and jealousies" (50-1),[14] she explains in almost greater detail her infant sister's nurse Ferhounde dadi (nanny)'s search for unadulterated milk,[15] and the cook Varbet's request for a cooking stove, missing in the kitchen of their residence in Jerusalem.

One important item that attracts her attention is clothes, especially those worn by women; not unnaturally, in view of the title of the volume. This is how she describes the various accoutrements of the women of the household as they prepare to leave Constantinople for Jerusalem: Her mother is wearing a tcharshaf, as "[e]very Turkish woman had to wear

---

[14]   "It is a city where races have come and gone, where many hatreds are still burning, where Christians look at each other with deep-rooted suspicion, where they swear at Jews and Jews swear at Christians. It is here that religion is marred with battle. Head bowed meekly in prayer are raised fiercely, the worshippers and priests of the different sects of the Christian religion spring at one another's throats. Knives are flashed, blood flows, and people lie dead until the Turkish soldiers come to restore peace" (52).
Later, Ekrem will quote her father saying, "They [the members of the various Christian sects] will murder each other with a vengeance; all that pent-up rage will burst open like a boil" (70). Interesting to note that there is no mention of any violence on the part of the Moslems, nor any animosity between Jews and Moslems; these are phenomena that the British who occupied the city when they snatched it from the Ottomans succeeded in generating, even before the proclamation of the state of Israel.

[15]   "Ferhounde dadi had come like a dragon raised in fury. There was no [decent] milk in this forsaken hole of a place" (50).
What Ekrem then writes becomes interesting for very different reasons—the perception of the Americans by Easterners:
[Then s]omeone told us about the American colony where one could get good milk ... We were then told in whispers that those Americans were not decent at all. They walked in groups over the city, climbed hills like goats, and they even danced! All Jerusalem turned its back on them. Such wild behaviour, it was enough to raise the saints from their graves" (50).

this costume"; Ferhounde dadi has put on "her tcharshaf, a long loose skirt that swept the floor as she walked, a pelerine covering her arms and shoulders, and a thick black veil now thrown over head. Not a bit of hair showing—that was considered a sin. ... in the streets ... [her face] would be covered too with the veil and she would become a black bundle"; Mlle Lucy is wearing "a big black hat and was immaculate in her ... clothes"; and Ekrem's Armenian nurse is "dressed in a black coat," with "a black silk handkerchief ... tied over her hair. Nurse never wore a hat, as all the other Christians did; she said she was too old-fashioned for it" (40). As to Ekrem herself, "Nurse had made me wear my blue woolen sailor suit and woolen sailor cap with two black ribbons hanging down my back. ... I loved my sailor suit ... and I was proud of my cap" (39-40).

The issue of women's outfit gains in importance for Ekrem on the family's return to Constantinople about three years later (after a brief stint in Beyrouth) when her older sister is "veiled." Ekrem recounts thus the introduction of the veil into an Ottoman household:

> From my room I heard peals of laughter and familiar voices, and ... I dashed out to the big hall that ran all the length of the house. In the middle of it I saw Abla and around her a group of gesticulating people. Abla was wrapped in her first tcharshaf with a black veil floating from the back of her head. The tcharshaf was of black heavy silk with a skirt that fell to her ankles, a pelerine ●hat covered her head and her arms, and a heavy veil that she was throwing over her face to see how it looked. ... A stranger to me now, a slim black bundle whose dark veilings cast over me a shadow, a shadow that seemed to grow mammoth and extend its clutches over my life. I felt cold with fear and anger. I did not want to see Abla in this black prison of a tcsharshaf. But she looked happy, once her veil was thrown back, and her lips were smiling. How could she smile from this black prison that cut the air and sunshine from her and the glint of her beautiful hair from us? (153-54)

"Your Abla is grown up now," explains the mother proudly, unable to hold back tears of pride; while a woman relative eagerly informs Selma, "You too will wear one soon," and promises that she will make Selma's first tcharshaf.

"I don't want to wear a tcharshaf, I will not cover my face, I cried out in fear" (154); "But the black-robed relatives were over me, crowding me with the dark wings of their tcharshafs that seemed to float over me and stifle me."

Ekrem then ponders:

For the first time I found myself fighting alone a battle of dread and grief. Up to now we had all clustered together to stand against all our fears and sorrows. Apparently this covering of one's face was not a vital question to mother or to Abla.[16] But I knew it would be different for me. I felt my rising horror of veils that covered faces and long skirts that entangled legs. How could I run and play with the tight cords of this misery binding me from hand to foot? ... The tcharshaf had entered my life brutally and from now on would hang over my childhood. I could not wrench the idea from my head, and the dread of it was worse than any fear I had known. One escaped sultans and cyclones,[17] but not the tcharshaf. Millions of women had worn it before me. And to my eyes came these women in thick clusters, wrapped in blackness, their faces covered. These millions of black bundles of resignation smothered me. The storm closed over my head, but I rose above it, lifting my face wildly. I would fight, I would tear these shadows from me, the million bundles could sneer at me and revile me, but I would not be a bundle. I wanted to feel the wind and the air on my face for ever, I wanted to dip like a sea-gull in the freedom of life. Those voluminous folds of depression could not cling to me. What was the law or the will of my elders to me? I would stand against them with the recklessness of youth. (155)

Note that this lamentation has all the accents of a soliloquy by a heroine of a Greek tragedy.

On this important occasion of the eldest daughter's donning the veil for the first time, evidently a rite of initiation on the path to female adulthood in Ottoman society, the mother and her three daughters go to visit Ekrem's great-grandmother: "Abla was to show off her first tcharshaf." So, Ekrem gets ready to go out: "I put on my hat defiantly ... I was defying the world with my hat" (155-56).

As can be observed, the hat becomes juxtaposed as the second element in a binary opposition. It is the hat versus the tcharshaf. Ekrem relates an incident, among many others, when "Big Aunt," a member of

---

[16] Later, it will not be for the youngest, Beraet, either (249).

[17] Allusions to calamities her family had encountered she has recounted earlier.

the household of her maternal grandfather, Djelal pasha,[18] in whose home the family is residing at the time,[19] took her and her younger sister "to visit one of her numerous Egyptian Princess friends. ... Beraet and I were wearing our best dresses and hats while Big Aunt[20] was wrapped in her long silk tcharshaf." As they are reaching the stop where they are to catch a ferry boat and travel along the Bosporus, people, both men and women, come upon them, bar their way and remonstrate that it is a sin for children not to be "covered," and to wear "hats as the Christians do" (167-68). The incident attains such proportions that the party is obliged to retreat and return home, when this time a very much annoyed Big Aunt, in reality not at all a pious person, remonstrates with the girls' mother. A few pages later Ekrem remarks: "Our hats were being noticed more and more, and the people were grumbling" (176). One constant remark people make as they see these girls with hats, e.g. blue sailor hats, is to surmise they are not Turkish.

---

[18]   "I stood in awe of grandfather and his ways. He was a tall, erect man, and every inch of him shouted his life in the army... . He kept his eye everywhere in the house ... Often I heard him say in his deep masterful French, 'L'œil du maitre engraisse le cheval.'
    "Grandfather, Djelal pasha, had had an interesting life, and the aroma of it still clung to him, setting him above us and making him a mysterious person whom we children wondered about. His father belonged to a rich family from Cavalla [in Albania, which made him ethnically Albanian] who had gone to live in Egypt, then under Turkish rule. The great Mehmed Ali pasha [the Ottoman viceroy of Egypt, also of Albanian origin, who rebelled against the Sublime Porte and founded the kingdom of Egypt, becoming its first king] gave his adopted daughter in marriage."
    Ekrem then recounts that the young Djelal and his brother were sent to France to study:
    "In France the brothers were educated at St. Cyr, the famous military school, and became well-known with their handsome faces and the jingle of their gold. Days of fame spread before them, the full glory of the court of Napoleon III... . Grandfather was nicknamed 'Le Beau Djelal' and was a great favourite of the emperor and of the flirtatious empress, Eugénie. Then grandfather came to Turkey as the aide-de-camp of Sultan Aziz, and rose in power. A general in the army under Sultan Hamid, his glittering uniform and decorations were the joy of our hearts" (104-5).

[19]   "And now grandfather had retired from the army and lived surrounded by his numerous relatives in his great house perched on a hill. We had come to live here, too. But did matter? There were so many rooms to spare! Days of wonder and joy mixed sometimes with the agitation of the outer world.
    "Every morning I woke up with the summer shining in my room. Nurse dressed me and I ran out in the big hall crowded with people. The huge oak table was covered with snow-white linen and on it there were many cups and plates... . A ravenous group, noisy and hilarious, gathered round the table... ." (106).

[20]   She was the "first widow" (i.e. had been the first wife) of Djelal Pasha's deceased brother, and when her husband had died, had come with the "second widow," whom Ekrem calls "Little Aunt," to live in her brother-in-law's home.

The alternative for these girls not old enough to get into the tcharshaf would have been to wear a head scarf—"bash urti" as Ekrem erroneously spells the *başörtü*—which Big Aunt suggests, but the patrician mother doesn't have the heart to make them do it, seeing the head scarf as "that white rag *others* tie over their children's heads" (169, emphasis added). They then try putting on Arab head-dresses they had become familiar with in Jerusalem, the "big silk cover with tassels at the edge and two coloured cords" called *kufie*. But they are made fun of as "Arab girl, Arab girl with the kufie," by street urchins, which, in Ottoman society, is the equivalent of being called "nigger" in the US So, "[a]fter weeks of these humiliating scenes we laid aside the kufies. That day I felt ... that I could look people in the eyes again." They also undertake wearing headdresses with ribbons: "It was something like a child's bonnet," and when the ribbons are tied under her chin, Ekrem felt "as if a heavy load had been put on my head. This was even worse than the kufie." And, "out in the streets my hatred increased. People still stared at us, laughter still pursued us and the mob scowled, for these ribbons resembled hats" (177).

Ekrem concludes:

> Nothing could please that mob, with its head narrowed with fanaticism. We were open to the anger of their savage ridicule. And now that vast net of prejudice and ignorance was over my life, and each day the cords were drawn tighter. These people, whom I had seen with snarling faces, they could not be appeased with kufies and ribbons. I too must become one of them, a bundle of resignation, to add to the millions that had come and gone. I, too, must be stamped with the same seal, and shut from my life the sunshine of freedom. The mob had neither pity nor reasoning. It would rise against anything that was not in its own world. But I would fight. Not the tcharshaf for me, not the bowing before the stupendous force of fanaticism. I would rise above these waves that came crashing over the boat of my life. (177-78).

The fact is that in the meantime Sultan Abdühamid is gone, but those who have deposed him, the members of the Union and Progress party that has acceded to power, turn out to be even more despotic. As Ekrem relates:

I had long fights over the tcharshaf question. Not that my parents were narrow-minded, they did not care whether I wore a hat or not. But one could not play with the Unionists. One day my father might be thrust into prison for our hats. ... Now I had grown older and the restrictions piled on the Turkish women irritated me. Women could not go anywhere. ... [T]he police had arrested [two girls] for wearing hats and appearing in a public place. ...
"The Turkish women should rise," I shouted. "Why do they accept this tyranny? ..."
To think that in the tram-cars an ugly red curtain separated the Turkish women from the men. That small place was jammed with women and they could not step out of it even if they suffocated. Women could not work, if they belonged to the higher classes, women could not enjoy themselves, women could not live. Their fate was to sit behind lattices and curtains and peer at life with a sigh. It was time someone should stand up for their rights. And with this spirit of defiance I wore my hat. (231-2).

"Born again to a land of freedom"

Another alternative, the one Ekrem will eventually resort to, is to leave the country altogether and go—to America.

On their return from Lesbos, Ekrem has been put in the American Preparatory School.[21] The country is at war; there is a shortage of almost everything, leading the family to make do with "Black Bread and Paper Dresses," as the chapter describing their life in war-stricken Constantinople is entitled. The school becomes a place of refuge for Ekrem, "the only consolation" (234) she had; where, she writes, "in its four walls I put everything else out of my mind. There the horror of war and death had to be forgotten with books. There I did not hear ... the moans of poverty ...

---

[21] Later called the Istanbul American College for Girls, it was part of Robert College, an American missionary school that opened in 1863, the first of its kind outside of the US. It merged in 1972 with Robert Academy, its counterpart for boys, and became the co-educational Istanbul Robert Lycée, today considered one of the best secondary-school institutions in the country. For the fascinating history of Robert College, see Freely; Greenwood; and Kuran.

and the criticisms that my hat roused" (233-4). Yet, the school gives
something else, too: "Also I became bolder. Now I had read and heard
about the American women and admired them for their courage. They
seemed as free as the wind to me who was shackled and bound"[22] (234).

There is worse to come: Constantinople is occupied by the British
troops in the name of the Allied forces, and the Turkish population of the
city is obliged to go through humiliating times. When at last the treaty of
Lausanne is signed, and the Allies evacuate the city, "we felt weak in the
knees," she writes, as "exciting events [had] followed each other with
breathtaking rapidity" (248). She finds that "during the Allied occupation
and our days of sorrow the college had been my haven. ... And in these
days of oppression, the college was one place where I felt free. There the
clutches of the allies did not reach, and there I could wear my hat in peace
and dream of better days" (248).

Thus the "dream of better days" becomes inexorably coupled with
the American school, and obliquely with the dream of America itself.[23]
Ekrem explains:

> I wanted freedom now. This load of oppression was stifling me.
> The country was bound, the Turkish women were shackled, and
> the more I thirsted for freedom. I heard tales from my American
> teachers: all that American women had done during the war
> and since the war had increased my respect for that country. I
> felt drawn to America irresistibly. In that country I would find
> a solution for my life that had been one long struggle against
> tyranny. America was a goal to which I was creeping by inches.
> The very air of Stamboul crushed and strangled me. I had
> enough of fighting and struggling, I had enough of running
> away like a criminal and silencing all the thoughts that sprang
> into me. Freedom I wished to have at all cost and America,
> remote and alluring, seemed to draw me to her.
> ...
> I would go to America. The thought came upon me suddenly,

---

[22] See Demetra Vaka's novel *In the Shadow of Islam* (1911) for a fictional comparison between "free"
American women and "caged" Turkish women. See also Postma for an intelligent reading of that
novel.

[23] At this point, one exercise would be to compare this autobiographical text with other American
autobiographies such as that of Mary Antin's *Promised Land* (1912), where again life in the country
that is left behind is shown as having lacked in freedom for the memorialist.

and would not let me go. ... I felt chained by tradition, my country, and even members of my own family. I had no work and no opportunity in Turkey. The heavy hand of fatalism and the dust of centuries were choking me. I wanted a new land where the air was young and people with fiery desires and tongue could breathe. (249-50)

"... for my life ... had been one long struggle against tyranny..." It becomes clear that the "tcharshaf versus hat" binary opposition encodes a vaster scheme, and woman and veil represent larger forces. Thus, if the struggle enacted in this autobiographical text is not merely one to shed the veil and obtain the permission to put on a hat, but one that is conducted against tyranny, then the whole text needs a rereading.

Fair enough, the first chapter is entitled "The Shadow of Fear," and the second, "Fear Knocks at the Door." Sultan Abdülhamid's tyranny not only imprisoned the paternal grandfather and caused his death at an early age—a fact that is not made explicit in the volume but which the author seems to expect the reader to be familiar with; the family at the beginning of the volume are afraid that the same tyranny will persecute their father. They believe that his every step is being espied by the Sultan's men; and, whenever he is late in the evenings, the whole household is terrorized with the possibility of his having been apprehended. Then what they dread does take place, although not in such dismal conditions. The sultan wants Ali Ekrem out—because of the presumed disloyalty of a close friend of his, but the reader senses that this is a pretext and that the Sultan would have found something else if need be—and so the trip to Jerusalem imposes itself. That job is no bed of roses—it was not meant to be, and even the usually not so discerning Ekrem, in the various quotations she makes of her father's words, some of which have been cited above, is cognizant of the fact. The subsequent stay in the island of Lesbos is a disaster: Greek forces invade the island, and the governor general and his family become prisoners of war. They are sent to Piraeus in Greece, leaving behind all their belongings, which they are never able to recuperate; and only later are they allowed to travel to Constantinople, all of which constitutes a dramatic experience that could have proven fatal ("The Greeks will murder us all" [201] is the fear), and that obviously marks the impressionable adolescent. Yet, on their return to Istanbul, war catches up with them as the Unionists side with the Germans: "One day we woke up to the horror of war" (223).

However, as already stated above, even worse is to come with the occupation of Constantinople: "The allied police had taken charge of Stamboul" (244). Not only do British soldiers terrorize the streets, and the British occupying forces, in their blind fervour to establish authority, proclaim rules that expressly go against the customary lifestyle of the inhabitants of the city, but the family, who have sought refuge in Djelal pasha's house (which is not so wonderful anymore now that he is dead, and all the aunts and other relatives making up the extended family have departed) run the risk of becoming homeless:

> Every big house in the city was in danger of falling into the hands of the Allies. They [the British officers] came to the houses and ordered the people out.... . If the people resisted, the soldiers threw them out ... Many houses were thus occupied and people were left homeless. (243)

An English general not at all versed in the refinements of Ottoman manners does indeed appear one day at their door on such an errand, at a time when Ekrem's father is out, but is met with such resistance by Beraet the youngest daughter that he leaves.

To sum up, Ekrem directly or indirectly suffers tyranny, through the lived experience of her paternal grandfather, is in fact born to it; then through that of her father, an experience that she shares as a child; then at the hands of the Greeks and the British, as well as the Unionists. Becoming "unveiled" is her semiotic manner of expressing her shedding the identity of a victim of tyranny. More than anywhere else, this narrative of liberation from "shackles" uses woman as a symbol for nation, and the veil as a symbol for her shackles. In the chapter "My American Venture," recounting her arrival to the New World, she explains that she had travelled "those hazardous miles ... *to be able to wear a hat in peace*" (251, emphasis added).

After contrasting life in the US with (certain positive yet different aspects[24] of) life as she had known it in Turkey, and somewhat shocked at the Americans' lack of knowledge concerning Turks and Turkey, both propositions that afford Ekrem the opportunity to express some of the disappointment she feels once on American soil, she decides that, all in

---

[24]   "We in the East sip life leisurely ..." (267).

all, she is now "free" as she was not before; "free to wear a hat and to have my personal freedom" (266-7):

> Free from neighbours, free from gossip, free from the hat question and the dread of prison. I was born again to a land of freedom. No longer would I peer at life behind the stifling lattices of prejudices that were reared in Turkey, but I, too, would be free to walk over the peaks of life and set my sail over the shoreless sea of my freedom. (262)

I believe nevertheless that when Ekrem writes that the "very air of Stamboul crushed and strangled me. I had enough of fighting and struggling, I had enough of running away like a criminal and silencing all the thoughts that sprang into me," she has more in mind than mere political oppression. After all, she never really fought or struggled except over the issue of the hat vs. the veil; and, when wearing the hat, has never really "run away like a criminal," nor "silenced the thoughts that sprang" into her as she has been quite vocal at home concerning both the veil and Turkish women's freedom in general. I suggest that these last assertions become intelligible only if comprehended at a third level (after "the hat question and the dread of prison") as alluding to Ekrem's lesbianism. Except for the mention of an unnamed friend with whom she shares a flat—a fact of which she informs the reader in the last chapter entitled "Turn to the East and Turn to the West," with cryptic sentences such as "I watched my friend leaving for work each morning, and after she had gone ..." (266), there is no other indication concerning her lesbianism. Yet it looms throughout the volume, especially once one is alerted to the fact. Nonetheless, because there is such scant material to go by there is not much to discuss. Perhaps the title "unveiled" should be read as "coming out of the closet." I argue that the reason she was adamant not to don the veil is because she just did not want to acquire a female persona. The veil is for Ekrem an ambiguous signifier for the gender she has rejected, as well as for her ambivalent feelings concerning the nation she has left behind.

Conclusion, or how to be lost in self-orientalization/self-representation

As stated earlier, *Unveiled* possesses features that are similar to Said's *Out of Place*, both works by hyphenated Americans written from US ports of call, which are nevertheless transnational in character. Yet it must be owned that this autobiography of a poor little rich girl is evidently no ordinary life writing. It is neither within the tradition of Saint Augustine (I was a bad boy in my youth but saw the light and became a good Christian, reader let this text guide you to do the same); nor that of Jean-Jacques Rousseau, trying to justify his acts and clear himself in the eyes of society, magnifying/distorting facts if necessary to be interesting; or that of the aged *picaro* writing about the events that he left behind, aware, as he is composing, of what he was not as a raw youth, while explaining that it was not so much him who was rotten but the times that were. There is no awareness and no maturity reached at the end. What is reached is the tangible goal of acceding to the coveted land of freedom—the recounting of which is, however, couched in a discourse that is devoid of the edifying "city upon a hill" perspective of the early American diarists. Had she really been able to do self-searching and/or confessed to her sexual preference and come out of the closet, Ekrem's memoirs would have had some similarities with the Protestant diary, but as it is, the work is lacking too much in any introspection or self-reproach; and contains throughout too mundane a viewpoint, to fit.

As a woman's autobiographical text,[25] neither is it the kind that Marie Baskirtsheff and Anaïs Nin, who combined *élans* for amorous inclination and artistic creation alike in spontaneous outbursts, have accustomed readers to expect. It cannot really be compared to Mary Antin's *The Promised Land* (1912) either, as there is not much about life in the "promised land" itself. The same reason prevents comparison with American immigrant life writing such as Eva Hoffman's *Lost in Translation* (1989), or for that matter Richard Rodriguez's *Hunger of Memory* (1983), or Ilan Stavans's *On Borrowed Words* (2001), although for all these, Americanization, as in Ekrem's instance, has been essentially through language. In fact, seen from the point of view of American culture, WASP and First World, this text is by, and relates the story of, a "gendered subaltern," as Gayatri Spivak terms it. In other words, we need the frame of reference that feminist postcolonial theorists and critics have elaborated in order to make sense of the posture of this multicultural/postcolonial work *avant la lettre*.

---

[25] For women's autobiographical texts, especially American ones, see Benstock; Brodzki and Schenck; Cosslett, Lury and Summerfield; Culley; Demirtürk; Ellerby; Gammel; Gilmore; Hagaman; Jelinek; Polkey; Siegel; Smith; and Smith and Watson (1992; and 1998).

Trinh T. Minh-ha writes that it is "as if everywhere we [the non-Western women] go, we become Someone's private zoo" (82). In other words, explains Leela Ghandi, wherever she goes, the "'native woman' is required to exhibit her ineluctable 'difference' from the primary referent of Western feminism" (85): From the little that the reader is informed of in *Unveiled* about Ekrem's life in the US, one knows that during the first years she gave talks about Turkey, and got paid for it. So *Unveiled* is the written form, so to speak, of the exhibition of the "zoo creature," with all due respect, exhibiting herself. Ekrem needed to orientalize herself, as she was required, in order to get published, to be worth the "spectacle"—she does it grandly, of course, as the granddaughter of a celebrated poet become a household name, and of a general having flirted with Empress Eugénie and married into the Egyptian royal family, but it is still from the perspective of the "primary referent." That referent was nevertheless necessary for Ekrem, as her predicament required that as a white Caucasian, she side with that referent rather than with Native Americans, Blacks and other ethnicities whose existence, in the "land of freedom" that has become her new *patria*, she does not acknowledge—and, being the patrician that she is, would not wish to identify with.[26] As Chandra Talpade Mohanty advances, "the composite 'Othering' of the third-world woman' becomes a self-consolidating project for Western feminism. Echoing Loomba and Yeğenoğlu, Talpade Mohanty reaffirms that the representation of the third-world woman as "ignorant, poor, uneducated, tradition-bound, domesticated, family-oriented, victimized," facilitates and privileges the self-representation of Western women as "educated, modern, as having control over their own bodies and 'sexualities,' and the 'freedom' to make their own decisions" (qtd. in Gandhi 86). Or, as Ghandi explains, "the implied cultural lack of the 'third-world woman' fortifies the redemptive ideological/political plenitude of Western feminism." For Ghandi, Trinh's and Talpade Mohanty's critiques of liberal-feminist imperialism draw upon Said's understanding of colonial discourse as the cultural privilege of representing the "subjugated Other": "Both Said's orientalist offenders and ... Talpade Mohanty's feminist opportunists seem to speak to the third world through

---

[26] That being one more reason why her autobiography cannot be compared either to such ethnic women's life writings as Mary Brave Bird's *Lakota Woman* (1990).

a shared vocabulary which insists: they cannot represent themselves; they must be represented" (86).

It is rare that the culturally privileged offending voice should self-represent herself as the subjugated Other, as in the case of Selma Ekrem in her *Unveiled*.

Gönül Pultar

Works Cited

Adıvar, Halidé Edib. 1926. *The Memoirs of Halidé Edib.* New York and London: The Century Co.

Ahmed, Leila. 1992. *Women and Gender in Islam: Historical Roots of a Modern Debate.* New Haven: Yale University Press.

Amin, Samir. 1988. *L'Eurocentrisme: Critique d'une Idéologie.* Paris: Anthropos.

—————. 1989. *Eurocentrism.* Trans. Russell Moore. New York: Monthly Review Press

Anderson, Benedict. 1983. *Imagined Communities: Reflections on the Origin and Spread of Nationalism.* London: Verso.

Antin, Mary. 1912. *The Promised Land.* Boston and New York: Houghton Mifflin Co.

Benstock, Shari, ed. 1988. *The Private Self: Theory and Practice of Women's Autobiographical Writings.* London : Routledge.

Bolayır, Ali Ekrem. 1991. *Ali Ekrem Bolayır'ın Hatıraları* (The Memoirs of Ali Ekrem Bolayır). Hazırlayan (Ed.) Metin Kayahan Özgül. Ankara: Kültür Bakanlığı.

Brave Bird, Mary. 1990. *Lakota Woman* by Mary Crow Dog and Richard Erdoes. New York: Grove Weidenfeld.

Brodzki, Bella and Celeste Schenck, eds. 1988. *Life Lines: Theorizing Women's Autobiography.* Ithaca: Cornell University Press.

Chatterjee, Partha. 1986. *Nationalist Thought and the Colonial World: A Derivative Discourse?* London: Zed Books for the United Nations University, Totowa, NJ.

—————. 1993. *The Nation and Its Fragments: Colonial and Postcolonial Histories.* Princeton, NJ: Princeton University Press.

Cosslett, Tess, Celia Lury and Penny Summerfield, eds. 2000. *Feminism and Autobiography: Texts, Theories, Methods.* London and New York: Routledge.

Culley, Margo, ed. 1992. *American Women's Autobiography: Fea(s)ts of Memory.* With an introduction by the editor. Madison: University of Wisconsin Press.

Demirtürk, E. Lale. 1986. "The Female Identity in Cross-cultural Perspective: Immigrant Women's Autobiographies." Microfiche (Ph.D. Thesis -University of Iowa).

Dirlik, Arif. 2003. "Reconfiguring Modernity: From Modernization to Globalization." http://www.sidint.org/programmes/politicsplace/politicsDirlik.PDF 10.05.2003.

Ekrem, Selma. 1930. *Unveiled: The Autobiography of a Turkish Girl.* New York: I. Washburn, 1930; London: Geoffrey Bles, 1931; *Peçeye İsyan: Namık Kemal'in Torununun Anıları.* Çev (Trans.). Gül Çağalı Güven. İstanbul: Anahtar Kitaplar, 1998.

————. 1947. *Turkey Old and New.* New York: C. Scribner's Sons.

————. 1964. *Turkish Fairy Tales* collected by Selma Ekrem. Illustrated by Liba Bayrak. Princeton, NJ: Van Nostrand.

Ellerby, Janet Mason. 2001. *Intimate Reading: The Contemporary Women's Memoir.* Syracuse, NY: Syracuse University Press.

Freely, John. 2000. *A History of Robert College: The American College for Girls,* and Boğaziçi University. Istanbul: Yapı Kredi Yayınları.

Gammel, Irene, ed. 1999. *Confessional Politics: Women's Sexual Self-representations in Life Writing and Popular Media.* Carbondale: Southern Illinois University Press.

Gandhi, Leela. 1998. *Postcolonial Theory: A Critical Introduction.* New York: Columbia University Press.

Gilmore, Leigh. 1994. *Autobiographics: A Feminist Theory of Women's Self-representation.* Ithaca: Cornell University Press.

Göle, Nilüfer. 1996. *The Forbidden Modern: Civilization and Veiling.* Ann Arbor, MI: University of Michigan Press.

Greenwood, Keith Maurice. 1965. "Robert College: The American Founders." Typescript (Ph.D. Thesis--Johns Hopkins University), 1965; *Robert College: The American Founders.* Istanbul: Boğaziçi University Press, 2000.

Hagaman, Karin M. 1991. "Beyond the Looking Glass: The Construction of Self in Women's Autobiography." Thesis (A.B., Honors in English and American Literature and Language--Harvard University).

Hoffman, Eva. 1989. *Lost in Translation: A Life in a New Language.* New York: E. P. Dutton.

Jelinek, Estelle C. 1986. *The Tradition of Women's Autobiography from Antiquity to the Present.* Boston: Twayne Publishers.

Kandiyoti, Deniz, ed. 1996. *Gendering the Middle East: Emerging Perspectives.* New York: Syracuse University Press.

Kuran, Aptullah. 2002. *Bir Kurucu Rektörün Anıları: Robert Kolej Yüksek Okulu'ndan Boğaziçi Üniversitesine* (Memoirs of A Founding University President: From Robert College to Boğaziçi University). Istanbul: Boğaziçi University Press.

Loomba, Ania. 1998. *Colonialism/Postcolonialism.* London and New york: Routledge.

Marcus, Julie. 1992. *A World of Difference: Islam and Gender Hierarchy in Turkey.* London: Zed Books.

Mernissi, Fatima. 1975. *Beyond the Veil: Male-Female Dynamics in a Modern Muslim Society.* Cambridge, MA: Schenkman Pub. Co..

Olson, Emilie. "Muslim Identity and Secularism in Contemporary Turkey: 'Headscarf Dispute.'" *Anthropological Quarterly,* 58(4): 161-172.

Özdalga, Elisabeth. 1998. *The Veiling Issue, Official Secularism, and Popular Islam in Modern Turkey.* Richmond, Surrey: NIAS-Curzon Press.

Polkey, Pauline, ed. 1999. *Women's Lives into Print: The Theory, Practice and Writing of Feminist Auto/biography.* New York: St. Martin's Press.

Postma, Kathlene. 1999. "American Women Readers Encounter Turkey in the Shadow of Popular Romance." *Journal of American Studies of Turkey,* 9 (1999) : 71-82.

Pratt, Mary Louise. 1992. *Imperial Eyes: Travel Writing and Transculturation.* London and New York: Routledge.

Pultar, Gönül. 2003. "Moderniteyi Sorgularken (Interrogating Modernity)." *Kültür ve Modernite* (Culture and Modernity). Derleyenler (Eds.) Gönül Pultar, Emine O. İncirlioğlu ve (and) Bahattin Akşit. İstanbul: Tetragon Yayınları ve Türkiye Kültür Araştırmaları Grubu, 2003. 25-62.

Rodriguez, Richard. 1983. *Hunger of Memory: The Education of Richard Rodriguez. An Autobiography.* New York and Toronto: Bantam Books.

Said, Edward. 1994. *Orientalism*. 1978. New York: Vintage Books.

——. 2000. *Out of Place. A Memoir. 1999*. New York: Vintage Books.

Siegel, Kristi. 1999. *Women's Autobiographies, Culture, Feminism*. New York: Peter Lang.

Smith, Sidonie. 1993. *Subjectivity, Identity, and the Body: Women's* Autobiographical Practices in the Twentieth Century. Bloomington, IN: Indiana University Press.

Smith, Sidonie and Julia Watson, eds. 1992. *De/colonizing the Subject: The Politics of Gender in Women's Autobiography*. Minneapolis: University of Minnesota Press.

——. 1998. *Women, Autobiography, Theory: A Reader*. Madison: University of Wisconsin Press.

The Spivak Reader: Selected Works of Gayatri Chakravorty Spivak. Eds. Donna Landry and Gerald MacLean. New York and London: Routledge, 1996.

Stavans, Ilan. 2001. *On Borrowed Words: A Memoir of Language*. New York: Viking.

Trinh T. Minh-ha. 1989. *Woman, Native, Other*. Bloomington, IN: Indiana university Press.

Vaka, Demetra. 1911. *In the Shadow of Islam*. Boston: Houghton Mifflin.

Yeğenoğlu, Meyda. 1998. *Colonial Fantasies*. Cambridge, U.K.: Cambridge University Press.

Damnosa Hereditas: Sorting the National Will in Fuentes' *La Muerte de Artemio Cruz*, and Pynchon's *The Crying of Lot 49*

The University of Leiden was founded in the winter of 1575 under the auspices of the liberator of the city, Prince William of Orange, who asserted in a letter to the Dutch States the character of the university as much as the ideology of its Protestant founders: it was to be an "onder-houdt der vryheyt" (defence of liberty). This early modern paean to national liberation—which in 1917 would be elegantly turned into the "Libertatis Praesidium"[1] that we can all see on its seal—was in keeping with the feeling of liberation from Habsburg-Spanish rule that the city has experienced the previous Autumn. This Protestant rhetoric of national "Libertas," emanating from the classical readings of the renaissance was in direct contrast with the apparently senseless fight by Philip II of Spain—and his two successors—to re-establish the "universal

---

[1] "In zijn diesrede van dat jaar wees hij als oorsprong van de term op de woorden van prins Willem van Oranje in een brief aan de Staten van Holland van 28 december 1574. De prins stelde daarin voor een universiteit op te richten 'tot een vast stuensel ende onderhoudt der vryheyt'." In http://dutchrevolt.leidenuniv.nl/Nederlands/spreuken/libertatis%20praesidium.htm 12/05/2003 21:38. From H.J. de Jonge, 'Ouderdom en herkomst van het devies der Leidse universiteit', *Jaarboekje voor geschiedenis en oudheidkunde van Leiden en omstreken* 70 (1978) 143-146.

religion" over an inherited land he had obtained from his father the Emperor Charles. Historians now agree that the Low Countries were a *damnosa hereditas*, a burdensome inheritance, for the Spanish Habsburgs: not only did it harm their prestige through the muscular propaganda that came to be known as the Spanish black legend, most of which was printed north of the Rhine, but it also bankrupted their Mediterranean and American kingdoms, while it radicalised the politics of the Counter Reformation.[2]

To conjure up these memories may seem a far cry from the contemporary literature that I will be discussing in this essay. Nonetheless, I will use them as the framework for my discussion of nationalism, and the critique of the nation as an inherited commodity in post-modern American literature. It may also help to address the question "how far is America from here?". From Leiden, we can easily point to the Protestant-Catholic boundary that was also projected onto the "cultural geography" of America from very early on. The rhetoric of national liberation used by the Dutch freedom fighters, with its associated cultural, and perhaps even racial, hatred of the Spaniards, would surely have rung in the ears of their guests here in Leiden, the Pilgrim Fathers, as they set off for America.

In his recent remarkable study on the *Dutch Imagination and the New World*, Benjamin Schmidt points to the intimate relation between a nascent Dutch nationalism and its representation of Spanish tyrannies in America:

> From the earliest years of their revolt against the Habsburgs, the Dutch formulated an image of rapacious Spanish "tyranny" in America committed at the expense of "innocent" natives. With enormous polemical energy, the rebels exploited this image to blacken the reputation of Habsburg Spain. With still greater geographic ingenuity, their heirs extrapolated from it a projected "alliance" with the Indians [...] to create a moral basis for overseas commerce.[3]

Interestingly, Schmidt proposes here a critique of the "cultural geogra-

---

[2]   Charles Petrie, *Don John of Austria*. London: Eyre & Spottiswoode, 1967, p. 26, 256. See also John H. Elliott, *Imperial Spain, 1469-1716*. London: Penguin, 2002.

[3]   Benjamin Schmidt, *Innocence Abroad, the Dutch Imagination and the New World, 1570-1670*. Cambridge: Cambridge University Press, 2001, p. xix.

phies" drafted by the Dutch rebels not only as a way of countering the Spaniards at home but also as a strategic move to colonise America in order to "liberate" it. The imagined geographies of America, in Schmidt's words, "helped [...] to establish the 'imagined community' of the nascent Dutch Republic."[4] Nationalism at home and colonialism abroad were only two of the many issues at stake in the configuration of European ideas about America at the time, both in Holland and in Spain. In the two novels that I will analyse here, Anderson's concept of the "imagined community" is underscored insofar as there is no real "community" out there, only its "imagining." It is in both novels an evacuated nation, and as in the time of the Habsburgs, a commodified article that can be passed on, auctioned or inherited. In *The Death of Artemio Cruz*, this inheritance is explored by the conscience of the dying man. In *The Crying of Lot 49*, the legacy of the nation is perceived as a composite ideological narrative that falls apart as it is comprehended. It is the duplicitous nature of the "nation" and "nationalism" as both agents and enemies of uneven development that I intend to explore in these novels by Fuentes and Pynchon. In both novels we encounter a critique of American and Mexican nationalist discourses and in particular, a critique of their hijacking by the amorphous international corporate state in order to encourage consent. This critique does not promote a return to a mystified unadulterated agrarian nation but rather underscores and denounces the conflation of earlier nationalist discourses with narratives of technological prowess.

In *The Crying of Lot 49,* the image of the electronic "printed circuit" is ascertained by the main character, Oedipa Maas, on the San Narciso landscape. Its image is indeed a metaphor for the economic system whose assets the character has to chart as she executes Pierce Inverarity's will. And yet, I detect in Oedipa's search a failure to defy the perceptual predisposition imposed by the educational programming to which she has been subjected. Therefore, the novel aims at unveiling the mechanisms by which national cultures replicate the message of social conformity and compliance to the capitalist mega-machine of internationalised production, aided by the pervasive nationalist consensus. Its conclusion, or apparent lack of it, signifies a pessimistic reaffirmation of the inescapability of such a closed system by any single individual.

---

[4]   p. xxiii.

Artemio Cruz, the dying revolutionary whose fragmented memories are spread throughout the novel, carries the nation on his shoulders or, rather, the nation hangs around his neck. One of the many lengthy catalogues in the novel exotically summarises the things "Mexican" carried by Artemio: "the red deserts, the hills of prickly pear and maguey, the world of day cactus, the lava belt of frozen craters, the walls of golden domes and rock thrones, the limestone and sandstone cities, the tezontle stone cities, the adobe pueblos, the reed-grass hamlets ...."[5] This stereotyped Mexican landscape suitably incorporated into the post-revolutionary representation of Mexico, as Sergei Eisenstein's celebratory film *¡Que Viva Mexico!* (1932) and other contemporary productions amply demonstrate, is constantly contradicted in the novel by the country's heterogeneity. Mexico, which "is not one; there are a thousand countries, with a single name" (232/365), is a fragmentary reality on which such homogenising narratives of nation have often been forced. The national project of the Revolution is identified with the dying Artemio Cruz by the interpolative narrative voice that says to the character: "you will carry these with you and they are leaden, they are stone heavy for one man: they have never moved and you have them bound to your neck; they weigh you down, they have entered your guts, they are your bacilli, your parasites, your amoebas. . ." (232/366). The Mexican national discourse breaths and lives *in* and *through* the figure of Artemio Cruz. It colonises the character as would a micro-organism, in one of the most striking images of nationalist assimilation in Mexican literature.

Thus, the novel is not only "the first literary attempt to integrate the social, ethnic and geographic totality of the nation,"[6] as the Mexican writer Rosario Castellanos suggested, but also a successful attempt to integrate the homogenising discourse of that idealised community called Mexico in order to defy its political appropriation by a class. As the "motherland" he inherits—"heredarás la tierra" [you will inherit the earth/land] (233/367)—comes to be identified with Artemio Cruz himself, his death becomes that of the nation. The fragments of the nation are amalgamated in a crucible inside the dying Cruz. It is around this

---

[5] *La muerte de Artemio Cruz*, José Carlos González Boixo, ed., Madrid: Cátedra, 1998 [1962], p. 232; *The Death of Artemio Cruz*, trans. by Sam Hileman, London: Penguin, 1978 [1964], p. 366.

[6] Rosario Castellanos, *Juicios Sumarios. Ensayos.* Xalapa: Universidad Veracruzana, 1966, p. 125.

identification, this symbolic treatment of the nation, that I want to build my discussion of the novel.[7]

Artemio Cruz stands for that entire class of Mexican revolutionaries who institutionalised the Revolution through the constant use of nationalist symbols in order to cement a political consensus and to become the new ruling class. Thus, Artemio's heritage is, among other things, this new social position: "They will accept your legacy: the decency that you acquired for them: they will offer up thanks to bare-foot Artemio Cruz because he made them people of position..." (233/367) And yet "they," Artemio's heirs, will not be able to take refuge in the revolutionary discourse to carry on with the "sanctioned greed": "they will not be able to speak of their battles and captains, as you can, and shield themselves behind glory to justify rapine in the name of the Revolution, self-aggrandizement in the name of the Revolution." (234/367) As Artemio wonders "what justification will they find?" (234/367), it becomes clear that the institutionalised revolutionary discourse is Fuentes's main object of satire.

In the novel, the Mexican Revolution re-establishes the nation as an expression of a *mestizaje* whose epicentre is Artemio Cruz. His duplicity can be seen as one more avatar of the duplicitous nature of the Mexican, a *malinchismo* that cuts both ways: *Malinche* as the originator of the Mexican *mestizo*, the new race, and as the female traitor of the community, both the tyrant and the saviour. The sense that history repeats itself and that the nation continuously betrays its believers and those who sacrificed themselves for its inception is patent in the generation born during and after the Revolution, to which Carlos Fuentes and Octavio Paz belong. In *The Labyrinth of Solitude* Paz analysed the major contradiction of revolutionary nationalism:

> ...in a certain sense, the Revolution has recreated the nation; in another sense, it has extended the nation to races and classes that neither the colony nor the XIX century were able to incorporate. [...] [But] the Revolution has not turned our

---

[7] There have been some important critical contributions which have already established Artemio's symbolic role, among others Lanin Gyurko in his *"La Muerte de Artemio Cruz* and *Citizen Kane"*, in *Carlos Fuentes, A Critical View*, ed. by Robert Brody and Charles Rossman, Austin: University of Texas, 1982, pp. 64-94. In that article Gyurko compares Welles and Fuentes in this particular use of "characters who function not only as individuals but as national symbols." (66)

country into a community, or even into a hope of a community: a world in which men can see themselves in other men, and where the "principle of authority" –that is, force, whatever its origin and justification- cedes its place to responsible freedom.[8]

The painful realisation of the frustrated attempt of the Revolution at creating a community goes hand in hand with the even more excruciating fact that "nationalist capitalism," as Paz calls it,[9] is based on the old patriarchal structure of *caudillos* and *caciques*.[10] At this point Paz's and Fuentes's analysis of the Revolution seem to merge with Orwell's cynical look at revolution as a replacement of one oppressive elite by another in *Animal Farm* (1945): Mexican nationalism re-enacts a cycle of social and discursive renewal that ultimately fails to empower the community.

The *chingada* (literally, the "fucked one"), a national "destiny," is described by Fuentes with the image of a chain that joins all Mexicans in the interplay of power politics. This interplay is also applicable to gender relations, as the first "chingada," La Malinche, is both the symbolic ravished mother of the *mestizo* at the time of the European conquest and, by the same token, the first traitor to an impossible indigenous sense of national purity. The general inclusion of all Mexicans inside this pyramidal and patriarchal system becomes contested in the novel through the questioning of the frozen temporal structures, linear or circular, on which it is based. At the centre of the authorial preoccupations behind or inside *The Death of Artemio Cruz* is the subversion of the "unity of destiny," Anderson's "empty time," which characterises the unity of the national state. Such breaking up of the chronological unity of the nation is accompanied by a critique of the patriarchal location of the national discourse. Both the critique of time and gender structures become central themes that give the text its parodic focus.

---

[8] All extracts from Paz's works are my own translation unless otherwise indicated. Octavio Paz, *El laberinto de la soledad*, Mexico City: FCE, 1998 [1950], p. 210.

[9] See p. 217-9.

[10] *Caudillos, caciques:* both words in Mexican Spanish refer to political bosses; the second word comes from the Nahuatl meaning chieftain. In her monograph on the novel, María Stoopen has advanced a reading of the novel as the "possibility of making valid, in a fictional universe, the theoretical postulates offered by Paz." María Stoopen, *La muerte de Artemio Cruz: una novela de denuncia y traición*. México: Universidad Nacional Autónoma de México, 1982, p. 11.

Time, in particular the narration of linear time, has been linked with the construction of the narration of the nation. The much celebrated book by Benedict Anderson, *Imagined Communities*, focuses on four nineteenth-century novels, among them the first Mexican novel, *El Periquillo Sarniento* by José Joaquín Fernández de Lizardi, published in 1816, which he uses to test his theory of the novel as a "device for the representation of simultaneity in 'homogeneous, empty time.'" (25) Anderson is referring here to nineteenth-century realist novels with their temporal linearity that, together with the newspaper, "provided the technical means for 're-presenting' the *kind* of imagined community that is the nation." (25) This "empty time" understood by Anderson as the projection of the "calendric time" in which such fictions were inscribed, is the companion of the nation that also moves linearly towards its destiny, its fulfilment: "the idea of a sociological organism moving calendrically through homogenous, empty time is a precise analogue of the idea of the nation, which is also conceived as a solid community moving down (or up) in history." (26) The fragmented narration in *The Death of Artemio Cruz*, as in the case of its modernist predecessors in the English-speaking world, breaks away from that homogenous, empty time to which nations and traditional novels alike are destined, according to Anderson.[11] The fragmentation of the temporal flow in *The Death of Artemio Cruz* has been accurately described by Edna Aizenberg as "a means of interrogating the nation,"[12] but as I argue here, it can also be seen as a means of interrupting the nation's flow into the future empty time of progress.

In *The Death of Artemio Cruz,* the Mexican nation is imagined as a fractured community with the times of the losers, the *chingados* being continuously denied and erased by the official linear times of the *chingones*. Two competing times that conform the Janus-faced failed community as the character's conscience realises: "Always the two times in this double-faced Janus community, so far from what it was, so far

---

[11] Time can be perceived as a gendered metaphor. Even the temporal definition of the imagined community of the nation raises issues of gender and sexuality as Andrew Parker has pointed out in his introduction to *Nationalisms and Sexualities*, London: Routledge, 1992, p. 5.

[12] Edna Aizenberg, 'The Untruths of the Nation: *Petals of Blood* and Fuentes's *The Death of Artemio Cruz*' in *Research in African Literatures*, 1:4 (Winter, 1990), 85-104 (p. 91). However, I agree with Aizenberg's main thesis, namely that "the novel now combats the very thing it once sought to constitute [the nation]." (86)

from what it wanted to be."[13] (128) From the outset, there is a distance that both reifies and fragments Cruz into factions and features. Artemio is that "Someone else. Someone in a mirror in front of his sickbed." (12/118) He is always someone else, "another," in a mercurial succession of identities that foregrounds his symbolic status as the Janus-like nation. One of the many indications of Artemio's duplicitous morality in his relationship with American capital. Not just an agent of American colonisation in Mexico through business deals such as his biased newspapers, Artemio himself is said to be colonised by a metropolitan perspective on Mexico: "Forever since you began to be what you are, to learn to appreciate the feel of fine cloth, the taste of good liquor, the scent of rich lotions, all those things [...] You admire their efficiency, their comforts, their hygiene, their power, their strength of will..." (30/138) This stereotypical opposition between the *chingado* Mexican "us" and the triumphal Yankee "them," confirms not only that the new ruling class represented by Artemio has successfully managed to negate the Revolution through its alliance with American capital, but that it has also corroborated through its nationalist discourse of relative inferiority a view of the Mexican self that justifies the imposed, uneven development. Artemio suffers physically from the process of cultural appropriation: "You ache because you know that no matter how hard you try, you can never be what they are but become at most only a pale copy, a near approximation." (30/183)

Faced with the realisation that the future identity of Mexico would be "at most only a pale copy, a near approximation," Artemio's conscience points once again to the benefits of *malinchismo* and the *comunidad jánica*, one that can be cruel and tender at once, permanently fragmented.[14] As many critics and readers have noted, the novel is

---

[13] My translation. "Siempre los dos tiempos, en esta comunidad jánica, de rostro doble, tan lejana de lo que fue, y tan lejana de lo que quiere ser." (250) Note the standard translation excludes the reference to the two times represented by the double face. Also "comunidad" is translated for the less fortunate "town".

[14] In the lines of Brushwood's evaluation: "...it does seem that the life of Cruz can be understood as one way of looking at the attitudes of the nation and why they are as they are. If my assumption is correct, Fuentes sees Mexico as having deceived herself by accepting values that will not allow her to realise her potential." John S. Brushwood, *Mexico in its Novel: A Nation's Search for Identity*. Austin: University of Texas Press, 1966, p. 41. Sandra Messinger Cypess also reads Artemio Cruz as a *malinchista* character "in the way he sells out his ideals in order to reap material gain", see

essentially a collection of fragments, a novel *about* fragmentation that is itself fragmented: its temporal structure, its syntax, and the narrating voices of the protagonist himself.[15]

In *Artemio Cruz* the nation is constituted as a purely male foundation that cannot be inherited by his only daughter, Teresa, who continuously expresses her derision for Cruz at his deathbed: "even what he loved, he destroyed" (186/301).[16] Their mutual hatred is also an "incestuous intercourse" of sorts that secures the family bond through a chain of *chingados*. Although Teresa's attack is confirmed by Artemio—" my only love has been material possessions, sensual acquisition" (118/239)—she in turn is seen by him as wingless bat waiting for her inheritance by his bedside. As they prey on each other, Teresa for Artemio's will and Artemio on her unfitness as an heir to his media empire, they confirm the pyramidal system of power whose upper places are only reserved for males.[17] Cruz's history is a story of constant duplicity that runs parallel to the nation's flow. After surviving the firing squad at a Villista camp and sacrificing his military honour for his life, he is able to use his acquaintance with the idealist Gonzalo Bernal in order to enter the Bernal family.

Like the lawyers to whom Gonzalo Bernal alludes in his cell, who "want only a half-revolution, compatible with what interests them, their only interest, getting on in the world, living well, replacing Don Porfirio's elite" (164/291), so does Artemio Cruz, whose revolutionary ideals are increasingly blurred in order to survive. His evolution from revolutionary to social climber separates him from "those who wanted a true revolution, radical and uncompromising," and those who "are unfortunately ignorant and bloody men" (164/291), as Gonzalo Bernal laments before his death.

---

her *La Malinche in Mexican Literature* Austin: U. of Texas P., 1991, p. 153.

[15] See for instance Wendy B. Faris, *Carlos Fuentes*. NY: Frederick Ungar, 1983, p. 47, and Jonathan Tittler's chapter in *Narrative Irony in the Contemporary Spanish-American Novel,* Ithaca: Cornell UP, 1984.

[16] See also p. 301, 316.

[17] Irvin D. Solomon wrongly misses the criticism of the novel by summarising it as "based on the notion that females are lesser beings who need to be controlled and dominated." (74) 'A Feminist Perspective of the Latin American Novel: Carlos Fuentes' *The Death of Artemio Cruz'*, *Hispanófila* 33, no. 1 (97) (1989 Sept.): p. 69-75.

Gamaliel Bernal, father of Catalina and Gonzalo, an aristocratic liberal who stands for the old regime of the Porfiriato, passes his inheritance on to Cruz symbolically by allowing him to marrying his own daughter Catalina ,once he realises that his time is up and that Artemio represents the new order: "So that was the name of the newcomers who had appeared to dispossess the old order. Unfortunate land, said the old man to himself as he walked slowly back to the library, unfortunate land where each generation must destroy its masters and replace them with new masters equally ambitious and rapacious." (44/155)

In this judgment on the failure of the Mexican Revolution, we can also hear an authorial judgment on the nation, whose "children" have to be destroyed with the coming of a new generation. By symbolically sacrificing Gonzalo Bernal and the Indian Tobías at the Villista camp, Cruz becomes identified with the nation in its latest devouring frenzy. His duplicity *is* the form of the novel with its constant shifting voices, but it is also the constituting moment of the nation, its "reassuring fratricide," to use Benedict Anderson's terminology. Anderson has pointed to the fact that the nation, that imagined community, is necessarily built on the common fusion through an "emblema ancestral" of the "asesinos" and the "asesinados."[18] The nation is built on a foundational fratricide, the Revolution imagined as the re-birth, the regeneration of the community, but also as the impossible drama of cyclical destruction: "There you have Mexico's drama" (164/291).[19] The absorption of the idealist Gonzalo by Artemio in this symbolic anthropophagic process makes Cruz feel he is: "Not one man but two, with Gonzalo Bernal's life added to his own, as if Bernal when he died had transferred to him the possibilities of his own interrupted existence. Maybe, he thought to himself, the deaths of others is what lengthens our own life. But he had not come to Puebla to think." (39/149) He only came to Puebla to inherit the land, we could add. Cruz's communion with Gonzalo, or rather his symbolic devouring of him, resembles his assimilation of successive women—Regina, Catalina, Laura. Catalina, Gonzalo's sister, is perhaps the clearest example of a

---

[18]   See Anderson's article mentioned above, p. 99.

[19]   As Emir Rodríguez Monegal has noted, Fuentes finds in this Kainite tradition "the key to Mexico", see his article 'El México alucinado de Carlos Fuentes', in *Narradores de esta América*, Buenos Aires: Alfa, 1974, vol II, p. 259.

sacrificial female in the novel, as she becomes part of the *patrimony*, the bridge between the old and the new Mexican nation.[20]

In the novel, the author's subversion of patriarchy and linear time recasts the official discourses of the nation in a critical, parodic mode. The highly experimental time frame of the novel allows Linda Glanze to describe it as a literary instance of cinematic montage in the style of Eisenstein, a montage that foregrounds the conflict between "recit"—the action of the novel, Artemio's agony and death takes place on the 10th of April of 1959—and the "diegesis" of the dispersed memories spanning seventy years of the character's life, which reach back further still, to his grandmother's birth in the auspicious year of 1821.[21]

México, "un país incapaz de tranquilidad, enamorado de la convulsión," (147) is not then the abstract entity in search of the complacent self-identification suggested by the sacred text of the American Constitution—the site of another imagined community that consecrates the fiction of its plural-unified self from its official birth: "We the people of the United States of America." Such a mirage, eroded in the semiotic excavation of *The Crying of Lot 49*, is the background noise from the North against which Mexican intellectuals have eagerly searched for the defining moment, an origin, while traditions and communities were submitted to a permanent and continuous overhaul in the name of the nation to come. Octavio Paz, perhaps the last in the long line of such intellectuals, timidly announced at the end of his major meditation on Mexico the need for an international or "universal" conscience as the result of the long post-revolutionary introspection: "our nationalism, if it is not a mental illness or idolatry, must culminate into a universal search. We have to start with the awareness that our situation of alienation is that of the majority of the other nations."[22] As Mexican nationalism is stripped bare of its many deceiving masks, the essentialist vision of the nation is put into perspective, and even denounced as the colonising

---

[20] Due to this duplicity Catalina Bernal is read by Messinger Cypess as an avatar of the Malinche herself, see op. cit. p. 150 ff.

[21] Linda Glanze, "La distorsión temporal y las técnicas cinematográficas en *La muerte de Artemio Cruz*", *Hispamérica*, 14 (40), April 1985, 115-120: 116.

[22] *El laberinto de la soledad*, p. 233-4.

discourse of the dominant class. Artemio's slow and painful death, rather than announcing the challenges of "yet-to-be nations," as Aizenberg has put it, attests to the contradictions and even the impossibility of such a creation. In his subsequent novel, *A Change of Skin*, Fuentes revisits the dead body of the nation in order not so much to mourn it as try and defuse its resurrection.

In Thomas Pynchon's novel, the commodification of the Californian landscape becomes the obsessive reminder of the social and political cost of undemocratic developmental policies, and the nation is thus presented as a burdensome inheritance, as a will that has to be executed. The quest through this "infected" landscape is based on an extended parody, a direct though subverting textual reference to Sophocles' Theban tragedies: Oedipa Maas, a Republican housewife in her early thirties, has to make sense of the will of a former lover and land tycoon, Pierce Inverarity. As in *Oedipus Rex*, the tragic character has to ascertain the causes of the plague devastating her city as she starts to make sense of her own identity. Her name is an early index that facilitates the decoding of the apparently chaotic network of cultural signs that clutter the text. The classical reference participates in the wholesale carnivalisation of cultural codes, from thermodynamics to philately, in a move to desautomatise their positioning in society. Contrary to Theodore Kharpertian, who maintains that "Oedipa, like her ancient namesake, does come to recognize that the responsibility for the political plague is hers,"[23] I will argue that Pynchon's deviation from the Greek myth does not just rest on his feminisation of the classical character but also on the character's inability to assume the responsibility that might commence a new political epoch.

In her quest Oedipa ventures into her everyday world of commodities, parenthetically identified as "This One" in the title to the *Esquire* story. Although it is indeed a familiar world for her, throughout her quest she is exposed to what had, until then, seemed irrelevant, and which slowly becomes a central issue: the social and moral bankruptcy of the US. Exactly how relevant this theme should be for a critical reading of the text is made clear by the swift change in the wording of the magazine

---

[23]   Theodore D. Kharpertian, *A Hand to Turn the Time: The Menippean Satires of Thomas Pynchon*, London and Toronto: Associated University Presses, 1990, p. 95.

version, revealing some interesting departures from the text of *The Crying of Lot 49* published four months later. In the 1966 Lippincott edition, as in all others after that, the narrator announces early into the novel that "[a]s things developed, she [Oedipa] was to have all manner of revelations. Hardly about Pierce Inverarity, or herself; but about what remained yet had somehow, before this, stayed away." Yet in the *Esquire* version, the same narrator appears to be more punning in the first sentence and finally too explicit: "[a]s things developed, she was to find out a lot. Hardly anything about Pierce Inverarity, or herself; but all manner of revelations about what remained: their Republic."[24] The two sentences have undergone a drastic rephrasing in order to defer the disclosure of the US as the revealed truth. In the final version, "it" literally stays away from the readers, not because the quest varies its course, but rather because we are spared such an early announcement. Additionally, multiple layers of meaning arise behind the word "lot," creating a pun in which the serious sense of "way of life," and the simpler synonym "manifold," obviously referring to the saturation of cultural references awaiting the reader, are mixed with the specific allusion to both the novella's title and the "lot" number 49. The entire joke is lost in the rewriting of the paragraph. Oedipa is indeed haunted by a "lot" throughout the novel, which seems to materialise in the "lot 49"–a collection of subversive stamps that demonstrate the existence of the Trystero, an underground anti-establishment organisation—to be auctioned as a "lot" at the close of the novel.

The traumatic distress at the car lot suffered by Oedipa's husband, Mucho Maas parallels Oedipa's later encounter with the American disinherited during her quest to execute Inverarity's will, and in both cases it points to the Maas as archetypes of the American "little man"[25] of which Pynchon had bitterly written in his "A Journey into the Mind of Watts." His description there of the gap between the two "very different

---

[24]   Thomas R. Pynchon, 'The World, This One, and Oedipa Maas', *Esquire Magazine*, 64 (December 1965), p. 173.

[25]   Ganter has also studied the relation between these two contemporary texts "Pynchon's description of what lay behind the Watts riots suggests a new reading of one of his most enigmatic novels, *The Crying of Lot 49*, and in particular, a new reading of the novel's mysterious WASTE/Trystero conspiracy." G. Ganter, "Rioting, Textuality and *The Crying of Lot 49*", in *Found Object* (1993), Fall: 2, 67-81: 67.

cultures" used to explain the "mind of Watts" parallels the image of the "two worlds" suggested to Oedipa by the Mexican anarchist Jesús Arrabal in *Lot 49*. For Arrabal, Pierce Inverarity represented "the oligarchist, the miracle" (119) that is, "another world's intrusion into this one" as terrifying "as a Virgin appearing to an Indian." (120) Our lady of Guadalupe, Mexico's national icon is set side by side with another American national icon: the tycoon, Pierce Inverarity who, like Cruz, proves to be the owner of the nation.

Arrabal, like so many of Pynchon's characters, bears a name immediately significant for its many connotations.[26] Fernando Arrabal, the Spanish surrealist playwright had successfully staged his *Cementerio de automóviles* from 1959 in Spain, Mexico, and France (as *Cemetière de Voitures*).[27] In it, people live in abandoned cars—literally in a scrap yard—, their attachment to the machine being even more extreme than that witnessed by Mucho at the lot, and under the constant fear of repressive forces, reminiscent of Franco's police state. The central character in the play is a young trumpeter called Emanu, aged thirty-three, whose defiant act is to play his trumpet in the open air, but also to have been sharing his bread and fish with the others. The Christian iconography is consistently kept into his foreseeable punishment—towards the end of the play the police measure his arm width. But Arrabal's play reworks the ideological tenets of Christian peaceful subversion in order to parody it, as Emanu repeats a phrase that can be read as a mantra for social adjustment: "Porque cuando se es bueno se siente una alegría interior que proviene de la tranquilidad en que se halla el espíritu al sentirse semejante a la imagen ideal del hombre." [Because when one is good one feels an inner happiness that derives from the peace of the spirit as it feels to be similar to the ideal image of man.] In Pynchon's Jesús Arrabal, both the Christian allegory and its recent theatrical author are conflated in the Mexican anarchist who perceives things about Pierce that Oedipa hadn't, "as if he were, in some unsexual way, competition." (120) The image of the trumpeter muted by the repressive order is adopted by Pynchon and transformed into the Tristero's muted post-horn through which the disinherited try to

---

[26]   Coincidentally, *arrabal* in Spanish means "ghetto" or "poor urban periphery."

[27]   Fernando Arrabal, *Cementerio de automóviles*. Madrid: Cátedra, 1984.

communicate with Oedipa. This is obviously the novel's clearest irony.

At this point, the title given to the *Esquire* piece becomes significant again: it openly hints at the "world" in which it is published, in the same way that Arrabal refers to his. Arrabal's definition of a miracle works in both directions, and thus the anarchist miracle consists of "revolutions [that] break out spontaneous and leaderless" (120), reminiscent of the Watts violence described by Pynchon: "far from a sickness, violence may be an attempt to communicate, or to be who you really are." Violence is not, then, that threatening social ill perceived by the middleclass social workers, but perhaps the only way out for a muted population.

In their study of race riots in the US during the 1960s, Joe R. Fagin and Hahn Harlan maintain a similar position when they suggest that the "spreading riot ideology often viewed rioting not only as a method of protest but also as a tactic that might bring actual structural and political change to the cities."[28] A structural change to the urban space is seen as the key to breaking through the patterns of racial divide and guettoisation.[29] Watts' blacks live in a space where the rule of law is suspended—i.e. you can be executed at any time—and where life becomes "nuda vita" or "bare life", in Agamben's definition, a life "which dwells in the no-man's-land between the home and the city."[30] A Watts black is indeed the epitome of the *homo sacer*, a "human victim who may be killed but not sacrificed," (83) whose death can go unpunished. Watts is an emblem of the political space inhabited by the blacks elsewhere in the US, whom Norman Mailer described as "living in the margin between

[28] Joe R. Fagin, Hahn Harlan, *Ghetto Revolts: The Politics of Violence in American Cities*. New York: The Macmillan Company, 1973, p. 117.

[29] Terry Anderson in his *The Sixties*. New York: Longman, 1999, points out the make up of this *de facto* apartheid in the American mid-sixties: "Over 40 percent of nonwhites were below the poverty line, and another study demonstrated that the average combined underemployed and unemployed rate for blacks was almost nine times that of whites. The contrast with white America was startling. A black Watts resident told a white from Los Angeles: 'You've got it made. Some nights on the roof of our rotten falling-down buildings we can actually see your lights shining in the distance. So near and yet so far. We want to reach out and grab it and punch it on the nose.' [...] 95 percent of suburban residents were white, and 80 percent of northern blacks lived in segregated ghettos." p. 75.

[30] Giorgio Agamben, *Homo Sacer, Sovereign Power and Bare Life*, Stanford: Stanford U.P., 1998, p. 90.

totalitarianism and democracy."[31] It is not coincidental that Mailer and Pynchon, both white Northeasterners, turn to the discourse of the Civil Rights movement with its critique of WASP values as leaning towards totalitarianism, in search of a response to the "Square" conformity of the fifties against which they also react. But their responses differ. While Mailer identifies his intellectual posture, the Hipster, with the Negro's "existentialist synapses" (341), thus claiming the birth of the White Negro, Pynchon promotes a radical critique of the cultural homogenisation at work in American culture. Like Mailer, Pynchon perceives rioting and revolution as an inevitable form of social exchange between two worlds that have become culturally incompatible, but he does not dwell much on this inevitability. Rather, Pynchon is more troubled by the colonization of the black neighbourhood by a white "unreality" obsessed with averting any future destruction of the status quo, a colonization that would soon be contested by armed movements such as the Black Panthers during the second half of the Sixties.

For Pynchon in "A Journey..." the issue of violence becomes a source of ironic reflection on the hypocritical positioning of dominant values: "among so much well-behaved unreality, it is next to impossible to understand how Watts may truly feel about violence." White residents of Los Angeles are determined to "put the area under a siege of persuasion: to coax the Negro poor into taking on certain white values. Give them a little property, and they will be less tolerant of arson; get them to go in hock for a car or collor TV, and they'll be more likely to hold down a steady job." This act of offering a minimal share of white consumer folly in order to appease an enraged black vitality, part of the process of internal colonisation, is carried out through television, here seen as mainly a political medium, whose counter-image is waste, the other contact point between the two communities. Pynchon notes how in Watts "[i]t's part of their landscape, both the real and the emotional one: busted glass, busted crockery, nails, tin cans, all kinds of scrap and waste." These images of the debris in which the California pariah are immersed, but also of the ways in which their illusorily expectations are raised by TV's dreamy displays appear in the novel as muted messages that undermine

---

[31] Norman Mailer, 'The White Negro,' in *Advertisements for Myself*. (Cambridge: Harvard U.P., 1992), originally published in 1959, p. 340.

the conscience of the white "little man," and of the "little woman," Mucho and Oedipa Maas.

Throughout the years before his marriage to Oedipa, Mucho's unconscious has been cluttered with the image of the waste he had unveiled at the lot: the material remainder of countless disempowered lives. As the car is recycled back into the market, it is cleansed of personal and human waste, "the actual residue of these lives" (13) that can neither be incorporated into Mucho's cognitive system nor into the market place. They have become immersed in Mucho's unconscious in a formless catalogue:

> clipped coupons promising savings of 5 or 10, trading stamps, pink flyers advertising specials at the markets, butts, tooth-shy combs, help-wanted ads, Yellow Pages torn from the phone book, rags of old underwear or dresses that already were period costumes, for wiping your own breath off the inside of a windshield with so you could see whatever it was, a movie, a woman or car you coveted, a cop who might pull you over just for drill, all the bits and pieces coated uniformly, like a salad of despair, in a gray dressing of ash, condensed exhaust, dust, body wastes-it made him sick to look, but he had to look. (13-14)

Once characterised as a "salad of despair" by the narrator, the residue of these lives becomes immediately politicised: it signals the entropic tendency of closed systems such as the American Republic.[32] Beyond the existential sense of exitlessness pervading this imagery, there is a calculated satire of the middle-class observer, whose job forces him to "look" but who remains incapable of understanding the nature of the waste. The choice between the violent reality of the black ghetto and the unreal conformity of the suburb are not, then, those "meaningless binary choices"[33] confronting Oedipa in the words of Frank Kermode and other critics. Some of these critics transfer the emphasis from the political contradictions underscored throughout Pynchon's writings, which they come to deem "meaningless," to "the normal hermeneutic activity in

---

[32] A point extensively developed by some critics, among the earliest is Peter L. Abernethy, 'Entropy in Pynchon's *The Crying of Lot 49.' Critique: Studies in Modern Fiction* 14:2 (1972): 18-33.

[33] Frank Kermode, 'Decoding the Trystero," in Mendelson, E. *Pynchon, A Collection of Critical Essays*, New Jersey, Prentice Hall, 1978, p. 164.

disease."[34] It is precisely in the movement out of the "normal" activity of gazing at the everyday that the conscience of these political contradictions becomes conspicuous but also traumatic and unbearable.

This compulsory viewing of the other world that has tortured Mucho's guilty conscience signifies the breaking down of the physical boundary that had hitherto separated his world, and the world of waste, "the reality of Watts" and "the unreality of Los Angeles." Michael Harrington observes in his *The Other America: Poverty in the United States*, that "[t]he problem, then, is to a great extent one of vision. The nation of the well-off must be able to see through the wall of affluence and recognise the alien citizens on the other side."[35] For Pynchon, too, the breaking of the visual boundary is a first act that would allow white Americans to cross over to the other side. The need for a change of perspective in order to be able to see and perceive the other side of the country is pointed out in his journey to Watts: the panoramic sense of black impoverishment is hard to miss from atop the Harbor Freeway, which so many whites must drive at least twice every working day. Somehow it occurs to very few of them to leave at the Imperial Highway exit for a change, go east instead of west only a few blocks, and take a look at Watts. A quick look.

Mucho's act of looking has to be read not as a deliberate act ("he had to look") and therefore not as the "beginning" to which Pynchon alludes here, but as a traumatic miracle, an incursion from another world into "his one." In a parallel move, Oedipa's quest can also be said to have an "immediate and important residual effect: the revelation of the disinherited," as Kharpertian has pointed out.[36] As in the case of Mucho, the key point stressed by the narrator is Oedipa's incapacity to make any sense of such revelation as she drifts into "some paranoia" (182). Oedipa is, like her husband Mucho, unable to process and sort out a meaning behind the human waste that she perceives. As she unveils Pierce Inverarity's awesome legacy, she confronts a reality habitually unnoticed by her. In order for her to see, she would have to deroutinise her sight,

---

[34]   Kermode, 163.

[35]   Michael Harrington, *The Other America: Poverty in the United States*, New York, 1962, 159.

[36]   T. Kharpertian, p. 88.

and much of the novel is devoted to this process of breaking through the patterns of vision to which she has been culturally conditioned.

In *The Invisible Man*, Ralph Ellison extensively articulates the image of the invisibility of American blacks. The narrator states: "That invisibility to which I refer occurs because of a peculiar disposition in the eyes of those with whom I come in contact. A matter of the construction of their *inner* eyes, those eyes with which they look through their physical eyes upon reality."[37] Ellison's much celebrated equation of marginality and invisibility has also been recreated recently by a Chicana, Gloria Anzaldúa in her *The Borderlands / La Frontera* (1987). In her manifesto "La conciencia de la mestiza: Towards a New Consciousness" she claims: "I am visible—see this Indian face—yet I am invisible. I both blind them with my beak nose and am their blind spot. But I exist, we exist. They'd like to think I have melted in the pot. But I haven't, we haven't."[38] The use of invisibility to disparage the inclusive image of the melting pot—the ur-narrative of the racial inclusiveness of the post-Civil War American nation—succeeds in bringing it down and exposing it as just a myth. It is not that in the sixties "[t]he country discovered, in short, that its citizens were not all white and prosperous."[39] as David Cowart has claimed in his commentary of Pynchon in the sixties. This would imply the existence of a country, a nation, who is by definition white and prosperous, and which all of a sudden realises it is actually not. The use of invisibility is addressed to counter such an argument by emphasising the permanent blindness, the racial "blind spot" of the WASP, but also of those incorporated into the national pot. This is a reminder that race, as language and religion—markedly in the case of Muslims, thus the wave of conversions to Islam among blacks in the sixties and beyond—are closely related in the US to nationhood, and that often citizens who are neither white nor prosperous are not in practice citizens at all.

Oedipa's sight is described at the outset of the novel as faulty, "as if watching a movie, just perceptibly out of focus, that the projectionist refused to fix." (20) Indeed the narrator declines to "fix" the character's

---

[37] Ralph Ellison, *Invisible Man*, London: Penguin, 1995 [1952], p. 7.

[38] Gloria Anzaldúa, *The Borderlands / La Frontera*. San Francisco: Aunt Lute Books, 1987 p. 84.

[39] David Cowart, 'Pynchon and the Sixties' in *Critique*, 41:1 (1999), p. 3-13 (p. 9).

perception of "reality" in order to stress her deficient sight. Most of the apparent ambiguities highlighted by certain critics can be explained by paying attention to Oedipa's perceptual problems. Her quest puts into action some of the epistemological themes and devices distinctive of modernist fiction and identified by Brian McHale in his *Postmodernist Fiction*:

> ... the accessibility and circulation of knowledge, the different restructuring imposed on the "same" knowledge by different minds, and the problem of "unknowability" or the limits of knowledge [...], the multiplication of and juxtaposition of perspectives, the focalization of all the evidence through a single "centre of consciousness"...[40]

The paintings of another exiled Spanish surrealist, Remedios Varo, serve as a sort of iconic manifesto at the start of the novel, which addresses the character's defective eyesight. Her wish to be perpetually saddened by the vision of Remedio Varo's "Bordando el manto terrestre" ("Embroidering the Terrestrial Mantle")[41] lurks over the whole narration. In a flashback to her trip to Mexico City with Pierce Inverarity, Oedipa remembers her wish to "see the world refracted through those tears" provoked by the vision of the prisoners in the tower, embroidering the surface of the world. Oedipa's viewing of the painting saddens her as she realises that she has not escaped from her own tower:

> Oedipa, perverse, had stood in front of the painting and cried. No one had noticed; she wore dark green bubble shades. For a moment she'd wondered if the seal around her sockets were tight enough to allow the tears simply to go on and fill up the entire lens space and never dry. She could carry the sadness of the moment with her that way forever, see the world refracted through those tears, as if indices as yet unfound varied in important ways from cry to cry. (21)

This first act of crying is directly related to the perspective provided by

---

[40] Brian McHale, *Postmodernity Fiction*, London: Routledge, 1987, p. 9.

[41] A painting exhibited at the Galería Copenhagen, Mexico City, in Oct-Nov 1963. See Janet A. Kaplan, *Unexpected Journeys: The Art and Life of Remedios Varo*. New York: Abbeeville Press, 1988.

the water-tight glasses filled up with tears: as she cries, she also consciously stages a first reaffirmation of her blurred eyesight. Pynchon's use of the green coloured glasses through which to look at the world is reminiscent of Adorno's reference to the use of "stereotypes" that are increasingly "reified and rigid in the present set-up of the culture industry" and that become "clichés that seem to bring some order into the otherwise ununderstandable." Through these clichés "people may not only lose true insight into reality, but ultimately their very capacity for life experience may be dulled by the constant wearing of blue and pink spectacles." (171) In the case of Oedipa Maas her glasses as well as her crying are two primary ways of dealing with the inescapability of her tower, her manner of circumventing her own responsibility towards the poisonous inheritance that she has to execute.

Oedipa's quest can be said to have an "immediate and important residual effect: the revelation of the disinherited" as Kharpertian has pointed out.[42] But as in her husband's case, the key point stressed by the narrator is Oedipa's incapacity to make any sense of such revelation as she drifts into "some paranoia" (182). Oedipa is, like Mucho, unable to process and sort out a meaning behind the human waste she perceives. As she unveils Pierce Inverarity's awesome legacy, she confronts a reality habitually ignored by her. In order for her to see, she would have to deroutinise her sight, and much of the novel is devoted to this impossible process of breaking through the patterns of vision to which she has been culturally conditioned.

It is in this context that the Oedipus story becomes immediately useful as a code against which to read hers. The Greek king inadvertently kills his father, marries his own mother, thus fulfilling an old prophecy. Therefore, it is revealed that he is the actual cause behind the plague devastating his city. When he finds out, the reality is overwhelming and Oedipus blinds himself. This act of piercing his own eyes defines Oedipus' moment of awareness as literally blinding, emphasising the character's permanent inability to see: metaphorically first, Tiresias warns him "I say you see and still are blind,"[43] and bodily as his face becomes "an eyeless

---

[42] T. Kharpertian, p. 88.

[43] *Oedipus Rex* in *The Oedipus Plays of Sophocles,* trans. by Paul Roche, New York: Penguin, 1991, p. 23.

mask." (78) Pynchon's version of the tragic character is devoid of the gruesome mutilation, but it contains a more paining defacement as Oedipa is never delivered of her uncertainties. In a move from tragedy to parody, this Oedipa is incapable of ever reaching "the central truth." As Oedipa's memory is emptied of the "central truth," the reader becomes ever keener to understand what this means. For most of the "compiled memories of clues" refer to the possibility of connections pointing to the network of assets belonging to Inverarity's will, and lurking behind his estate, the hidden meaning of the Tristero stamp collection, the apparent lot 49, unveiling an encyclopaedic history of treason and fight over the delivery of messages. This whole history can be read as the "signal, really dross," the historical waste, the "secular announcement," "destroying its own message irreversibly," and therefore leaving her once again blind to the truth, always unable to realise her own involvement in the plague. At a certain point in her search she concludes that "everything she saw, smelled, dreamed, remembered, would somehow come to be woven into The Tristero" (81). Like Oedipus, she is unable to see the real connections, her parentage with the inheritors, and therefore unable to ascertain her moral burden, her burdensome inheritance.

The ubiquitous muted post horn, the emblem of the Tristero, is a simulacrum, the "[i]nformation that devours its own content,"[44] some sort of historical detritus whose escalation brings the loss of communication, confirming *avant la lettre* Baudrillard's third hypothesis about the implosion of meaning in the media: "information is directly destructive of meaning." (79) And what is even more relevant to the truth escaping Oedipa, information "devours communication and the social." (80) It is not then that all Oedipa finds is simulacra but that she is not able to see beyond the simulacra, partly because its connection to reality appears to have collapsed into "unreality," partly because her own perception is culturally jammed. Pynchon's satire of the McLuhanite identification of the medium with the message uses the proliferation of Tristero post horns as an index of the social downfalls of such an equation. His is not so much "a parable of the failure of the humanist desire for 'meaningful communication' and for inter-subjective communion through symbols" as Ganter

---

[44] Baudrillard, *Simulacra and Simulation*, trans. by Sheila Faria Glaser, Ann Arbour: University of Michigan Press, 1994 [1981], p. 80.

suggests,[45] but rather a caricature of the new era of information. And as a caricature, this paranoia is not Pynchon's alternative political mode but a key to understanding his critique.

My reading of the two novels thus proposes that in Oedipa's and Cruz's exploration of their burdensome inheritance, the republican individual freedoms inscribed in the nation's foundational narratives, have collapsed and reverted to a quasi-feudal time when a community could be passed on, and the will of the nation could be simply executed.

Pedro García-Caro

---

[45]   Ganter, 68.

American Culture Meets Post-Colonial Insight:
Visions of the United States in Salman Rushdie's *Fury*

Aspects of American culture hold a key place in the *oeuvre* of Salman Rushdie. His first excursion into fiction was inspired by *The Wizard of Oz* and includes a "talking pianola whose personality is an improbable hybrid of Judy Garland, Elvis Presley, and the 'playback singers' of the Hindi movies" (2002: 3). Later works point to someone who is a trenchant observer of the United States. *Midnight's Children* (1995) has an American character and involves a consideration of US foreign policy towards the subcontinent. *The Ground Beneath Her Feet* (1999) and "The Firebird's Nest" (1997) both have American characters, and they engage in extensive critiques of American literature and history. Rushdie has also struggled with events within the United States. In "How the Grinch Stole America" (2001), he takes aim at the dubious election of President George Bush: "so they Grinched the election" (2002: 362). He has also written articles in *The New York Times* deriding a lack of common sense on the part of religious fundamentalist and a lack of artistic standards in Hollywood. His pen has further been involved in an analysis of the terrorist attacks in New York and Washington DC on September 11, 2001. In "The Attacks on America"(2001), he lashes out at terrorism and implores the United States to "stop making enemies and start making friends" (2002: 293). He also spells out a world view "worth dying for [...]: We must agree on what matters: kissing in public places, bacon sandwiches, disagreement, cutting-edge fashion, literature, generosity, water, a more equitable distribution of the world's resources, movies, music, freedom of thought, beauty, love. These will be our weapon" (2002: 393). It is in this spirit that *Fury* (2001) serves as a commentary on America in days leading up to the terrorist attacks and as a means of re-imagining America's place in the world. A close reading of the novel's intra-textual fable "Let the Fittest Survive: The Coming of the Puppet Kings" elucidates Rushdie's creative use of Old World metaphors about the New World, his assessment of classes of oppression within the United States, and his vision of a revolt in the name of those aspects of tolerance and freedom that matter most.

The Old World Meets the New World

Some of Rushdie's earlier works deal with the way America is viewed in India. For instance, the American protagonist of "The Firebird's Nest" arrives in India to a host of contradictory stereotypes: "She is rich and fertile, say some [....] She is poor [...] and the drought is in her body" say others (1997: 123). *The Ground beneath Her Feet* also views the United States from shores of Bombay. As the narrator observes, "his dream ocean led to America" (1999: 59). However, the metaphorical language in *Fury* is given its fullest expression in European literature. In some ways this is no surprise. After all, the protagonist of the novel, Malik Solanka, has been educated in British universities and he has spent most of his life in England. Additionally, this use of European myths of other countries is in keeping with much of Rushdie's fiction. In fact, one of his major offerings to post-colonial literature has been to challenge British and European views of the subcontinent. With *Fury*, Rushdie creates a protagonist with a promising analytical stance; coming from a country that has been misrepresented by Europe he is able to interrogate Old World images of America.

Three metaphors emerge, which are central to the parable's vision of the United States: America as a beacon of the future, the US as the New Rome, and America as the golden land. Each one of these has a central role in mythmaking about the United States. In *Not Like Us*, Richard Pells argues that Europeans have tended to think of "America as the harbinger of the future whether the rest of the world liked it or not" (Pells 1997: 154). C. Vann Woodward, in *The Old World's New World,* contends that, "soon after the Americans had planted their flag on the Pacific coast a new metaphor for America appeared: the United States as 'The New Rome'" (p.75). And in *The New Golden Land,* Hugh Honour observes that Columbus's discoveries "were pictured as idyllic, as the earthly paradise of a golden age—all the Old World yearned for and lacked" (p.3). Federico García Lorca's *Poet in New York* (1940) gives symbolic vision to these metaphors. In his poetry, the golden age and the New Rome meet on Wall Street, which is represented in *"Cry to Rome, From the Chrysler Building"* as "the white-suited man" who "goes his way / with no thought of the corn-tassel's mystery/ [. . .] unmindful how money burns off the miraculous kiss" (lines 30-34). Augmenting the power of gold in Lorca's New Rome is the corruption of a city, which is run by "perverts of the world, dove-killers" (line 84). The figure trying to create an alternative future is the poet. In *"Ode to Walt Whitman,"* Lorca writes, "Not for one moment, Walt Whitman, comely old man, / have I ceased to envision your beard full of butterflies" (lines 29-30). However, the image of the poet never succeeds in defeating the forces of the mechanical world. In "Navidad en el Hudson" (Christmas on the Hudson), the poet stands "on the gangplanks of suburbs, / letting blood on the stucco of blueprints" (lines 24-25) or he is decapitated: "the neck newly severed: which is mine" (line 36). Around every corner Lorca sees a battleground on which the ethics of business are defeating the visions of poetry.

Although Solanka comes to New York steeped in these metaphors, he does not merely accept them. Instead, he measures them against the America that he finds, leading him to alter, modify, or adapt them for a new time. *Fury*'s Internet fable, "The Coming of the Puppet Kings," updates the Land of the Future for the 21st Century. The placement of the fable on the Internet becomes a central part of its contribution to this study. As Solanka observes:

> The new communications medium was finally paying off. After a summer of skepticism about the potential of many massively unprofitable Internet companies, here at last was the prophe-sied brave new world. Professor Solanka's surprisingly smooth beast, its hour come around at last, was slouching toward Bethlehem to be born. (2001: 224-225)

Although images of the Internet as the future have become commonplace, the way in which Rushdie casts this vision rescues it from banality. Building on W.B. Yeats' "The Second Coming," Solanka links the tale to the study of imperialism. The Internet, as both the "brave new electronic world" and the "surprisingly smooth beast," becomes the setting for new empires, as well as a centre of power in its own right. By incorporating Huxley and Yeats' language, Rushdie hints at dangers and anxieties, while resuscitating a myth that points towards the future of empires, on the one hand, and to the future of American power, on the other.

The New Rome metaphor is also appropriated for this novel. America is described as a place with "circuses as well as bread" and leaders who are "petulant, lethal Caesars" (p.6-7). The narrator uses this metaphor to capture the consequences of a nation given over to an imperial mentality. "Might this new Rome," asks Solanaka, "actually be more provincial than its provinces; might these new Romans have forgotten what and how to value [...] Was nobody in all this bustling endeavour and material plenitude engaged, any longer, on the deep quarry-work of the mind and heart? O Dream-America, was civilization's quest to end in obesity and trivia" (p.87). As an observer who has seen the workings of empire from the other side, Solanka is keenly attuned to the cultural devastation wrought by a New Rome world view. Hence, Solanka breathes life into a metaphor meant to capture the link between America's domestic life and its foreign policy" (p.68).

The story also uses the New Rome metaphor to place America in a cycle of empires. "The Coming of the Puppet Kings" ostensibly deals with the collapse of the Rijk, a place described in terms exactly like that of the United States. Hence, the story of Rijk's decline becomes a tale of America's eclipse. Despite the building of dikes to stave off the flood, Rushdie writes, "the moment was not far off when the glory of the Rijk [...] would be washed away" (p.161). This is the same language that Rushdie uses to describe America at the turn of the 21st Century: "this golden age, too, must end [...] as do all such periods in the human chronicle" (p.114). Hence, in the parable, art and science fail to come to terms with the impending flood: "the economy collapsed. Lawlessness increased. People stayed home and waited for the end" (p.161-2). Rushdie's New York is identical. It is a "Gotham in which Jokers and Penguins were running riot" (p.86). With its impending destruction, Rijk becomes a country waiting for the flood and the New Rome is presented in the twilight of its hegemony.

"The Coming of the Puppet Kings" also challenges Europe's golden age fantasies about America. The Rijk civilization is "enjoying the richest and most prolonged golden age in its history" (p.161). Indeed, the novel opens with Solanka finding "himself living in a golden age" (p.3). The US is described as "boom America, the real-life manifestation of Keat's fabulous realms of gold" (p.184). Yet Rushdie's golden age is anything but Columbus's earthly paradise. The novel, in the spirit of Lorca's New York, is awash in wealth as a defining feature of American life. And Rushdie's reference to Keats points to the irony of America's golden age. As J. Martin Evans contends, "In Keats' imagination, America seems to have been a dreadful kind of anti-paradise, an infernal prison which had more in common with the nightmarish scenery of Dante's underworld than with Ovid's vision of the Golden Age" (Evans 1976:26). The narrator turns this European fantasy about America on its head. Overall, golden age images are only used to highlight materialism and to capture the ways in which America has failed to become "the best of all possible worlds."

The parable includes four main battles that capture the role of these metaphors in Rushdie's America:

> Revolt of the Living Dolls I: The Fall of Kronos, Revolt of the Living Dolls II (This Time It's War), The Humanization of the Machines vs. The Mechanization of the Humans, [...] and the grand finale, Revolt of the Living Dolls III: The Fall of the Mogol Empire. (p.187)

While Rushdie does not flesh out each one of the conflicts, his clues about them indicate that they all deal with battles against New Rome power and Lorca's "dove killers." In Revolt of the Living Dolls I, Kronos is trying to perpetuate a golden age built on the back of slave labour. Other conflicts deal with visions of the future. For instance, "The Humanization of the Machines vs. the Mechanization of the Humans" struggles with issues of authenticity in the computer era. In fact, almost all of the battles in the parable seem to be about oppressed puppets battling against "petulant and lethal Caesars." Overall, Rushdie's rendering of Old World metaphors creates the setting for the battles of the puppet kings. These are wars fought against the way the Golden Age, the New Rome, and the land of the future are manifested in the United States.

Classes of Oppression

The parable's metaphors are augmented by Solanka's encounter with various Americans. These people appear in the fable as puppets from all walks of life. They represent different social classes and distinct American myths. Through these individuals, Rushdie offers a symbolic portrait of the legacies of the frontier, the limits of social mobility, the idea of a collor-blind nation, and the promises of technological progress. By exploring what Rushdie calls the "back story" of these puppet kings, the parable captures the way in which this Golden Age creates its own classes of oppression. On the surface, Rushdie's Americans may seem content. However, the parable presents a host of individuals poised for revolt.

The legacies of the frontier are present throughout this book. It is filled with passages about crossing frontiers and pop culture references to Western movies. However, the savage war aspects of the frontier are most explicitly explored by attacks on three women in the novel, who are murdered and then scalped with tomahawks. As Rushdie writes:

> These living dolls [...] Sky, Bindy, and Ren thus represented the final step in the transformation of the cultural history of the doll. Having conspired in their own dehumanization, they ended up as mere totems of their class, the class that ran America, which in turn ran the world, so that an attack on them was also, if you cared to see it that way, an attack on the great American empire, *Pax Americana*, itself. (p.74)

These women become puppets and they generate the titles for the various battles that fall under the heading of "The Revolt of the Living Dolls." Their presence among this rebellion goes to the heart of this parable's critique of a golden age born of New Rome imperialism. Not only are they wealthy, but their murderers are also members of upper class families. These murderers, then, embody a twisted variation of Theodore Roosevelt's American elite. They are men who have immersed themselves in the savage war conduct of the frontier in an effort to "regenerated through violence." As victims of wealth, the attack on *Pax Americana* serves as an implosion within the upper class. As Rushdie writes, "people were stressed out, cracking up, and talking about it all day long [...] it didn't make any difference that everybody was rich" (p.115). In short, the frontier conquest that created America's utopia brings its history of dehumanization into the 21st Century.

The Revolt of the Living Dolls also addresses the promise of social mobility. Eddie Ford appears in the parable as "The Traumatized Quarterback," where he serves as the voice of the working class. He comes from "Nowheresville" and flees to New York after his father murders his uncle. His past includes an impoverished rural childhood, an emotionally scared Vietnam Vet uncle, and an alcoholic father. In some ways, Rushdie's portrayal of Ford embodies what Gael Sweeney calls the "white trash aesthetic" (Sweeney 2001:1). Beyond a link to social class, Sweeney argues that those labelled "white trash" are also "our repressed Other" (Sweeney 2001:2). In this role, Ford slips into Solanaka's bedroom to kill him. As Rushdie writes, "In his mind's eye he was Samuel L. Jackson, about to waste some punk (p.230). This link to movies builds on frontier violence. As Jean Baudrillard writes, "in America cinema is true because it is the whole of space, the whole way of life that are cinematic. The break between the two [...] does not exist: life is cinema" (Baudrillard 1988: 100-101). Ford brings the murderous legacy of movies, domestic violence, and Vietnam into the realm of Puppet Kings. As a facet of the "white trash" culture, Rushdie creates a figure trapped in violence, unable to experience the promise of social mobility.

In addition to issues of class, this parable also challenges the claim that America has created a collor-blind society. One of the Puppet Kings, "The Blackballed Golfer," is based on Jack Rhineheart, who serves as a key political voice. He is a journalist who has covered numerous wars, and he has written extensively about upper class Americans. While he has a six-figure income, he still confronts a variety of racial barriers. As his title suggests, he is kept out of many of the bastions of privilege in the United States. In fact, his effort to join the group responsible for the murder of Sky, Bindy, and Ren only leads to his own murder. Overall, the experiences of "the Blackballed Golfer" explore the continued manifestations of racism in America.

The final American-born puppets come from the technology revolution. "The Human Spiders" are the architects of the Land of the Future; they are the computer scientists and Internet technicians who create the web page where all the battles take place. They are described as:

> The most fashion-forward geek posse in New York, [...] You see before you the kind of surfer boys and girls the Evil Emperor is really scared of, disguised as Gen X slackers for their own safety

[....] These are like hobbits I'm hiding from Sauron the Dark
Lord [....] Until the time comes and we take him down and burn
his power in Mount Doom. (p.118)

Their technological skills allow the puppets to defeat the Rijk forces,
ending the reign of a New Rome superpower. The hero myths of *The Lord
of the Rings* are updated for the battles of the Dot.Com Era. In "The
Coming of the Puppet Kings" science is put in the service of a revolution.
With this group, Rushdie points to the radical potential introduced by the
Internet era and broadens an ethic of revolt to include even those at the
forefront of technological innovation.

No matter what their class, all the puppets experience what
Rushdie calls "the crushing of dreams in a land where the right to dream
was the national ideological cornerstone" (p.184). Hence, the rebellion
against Rijk is not limited to those left behind or excluded from progress.
As Rushdie writes:

In the tormented flames and anguished bullets Malik Solanka
heard a crucial, ignored, unanswered, perhaps unanswerable
question—the same question, loud and life-shattering as a
Munch scream [. . .]: is this all there is? (p.184)

With these puppets, Rushdie indicates that even those most adroit with
computer advancements experience a golden age discontent that sends
them into a revolt against the "Saurons" of the world.

Overall, this parable brings European metaphors and American
myths together. Rushdie's Americans experience a form of oppression
born of what Jean Baudrillard calls "the tragedy of utopian dream made
reality" (Baudrillard 1988: 32). The land of the future is haunted by a past
of frontier violence, racial prejudice, and broken promises. As a vision of
Rushdie's America, "The Coming of the Puppet Kings" presents an ironic
golden age tainted by a New Rome mentality. The metaphors of American
life create a rationale for revolt. Therefore, the end of the America's
hegemony comes at the hands of American-born puppets. Whether these
puppets can create an alternative land of the future is something the
novel leaves open. "The beast slouching towards Bethlehem" is a site
about possible futures: different alternatives with distinct dilemmas.
More than anything, the novel's "Munch scream" can be heard as a
challenge. As Rushdie writes:

America, the closest thing we have to a new imperial power [...] is battling to understand its new, post-frontier self. Beneath the surface of the American century, with its many triumphs, we may discern something unsettled, a disquiet about identity, a recurring uncertainty about the role America should play in the world, and how it should play it. (2002: 224-225)

In light of the terrorist attacks against America, Rushdie offers the vision of an America which hears the "Munch" scream of the world and refuses to act as a New Rome tyrant. Instead, relying on stealth aircraft and smart bombs, he urges the America to engage in a "public, political, and diplomatic offensive whose aim must be the early resolution of some of the world's thorniest problems" (2002: 392).

Rodney Stephens

Works Cited

Baudrillard, Jean. 1988. *America.* Trans. Chris Turner. London: Verso Press.

Evans, J. Martin. 1976. *America: The View from Europe.* Stanford: Stanford University Press.

Honour, Hugh. 1975. *The New Golden Land.* New York: Pantheon Books.

Lorca, Federico Garcia. 1940. *Poeta en Nueva York.* Trans. Ben Belitt. New York: Evergreen Books.

Pells, Richard. 1997. *Not Like Us: How Europeans have Loved, Hated, and Transformed American Culture since World War II.* New York: Basic Books.

Rushdie, Salman. 1997. "The Firebird's Nest." *The New Yorker* 23 June 1997: 123-30.

————. 1999. *The Ground Beneath Her Feet.* London: Jonathan Cape.

————. 2001. *Fury.* New York: Random House.

————. 2002. *Step Across This Line.* London: Jonathan Cape.

Sweeney, Gael. 2001. "The Trashing of White Trash: Natural Born Killers and the Appropriation of the White Trash Aesthetic." *Quarterly Review of Film & Video* 18 (2001): 1-7.

Woodward, C. Vann. 1991. *The Old World's New World.* Oxford: Oxford University Press.

AMERICAN IDENTITIES

Juan de Velasco's (S.J.) *Natural History:* Differentiating the Kingdom of Quito

The *History of the Kingdom of Quito in Meridional America,*[1] written by the "quiteño"[2] Juan de Velasco (1727-1792), is one of a number of histories written by expelled Spanish American Jesuits[3] that show the beginning of a pre-nationalist consciousness. The *Natural History* is the first of the three parts of Velasco's *History,* the other two being an *Old History* and a *Modern History.* The *Natural History* is not the most overtly patriotic part of the work. However, patriotic feelings do show up in it, and are significant precisely because the work is not a political tract but a study of the natural environment. This presentation examines Velasco's patriotism in his *Natural History of the Kingdom of Quito.*

It is important to bear in mind that this small group of expelled American-born Jesuits—Velasco among them; others being the Mexican

---

[1]   The first history ever written of what we know as Ecuador nowadays.

[2]   I use the term "quiteño" (Quitean) in this paper, to mean "being from, or belonging to the Kingdom of Quito," as Velasco called the region currently known as Ecuador.

[3]   The expulsion of the Jesuits from all Spanish territories took place by royal decree in 1767.

Francisco Javier Clavijero or the Chilean Juan Ignacio de Molina[4]—do not develop their historiographical projects with a political agenda calling for independence. The origin of their patriotic feelings and their need to express them arises from two main circumstances: their expulsion from their native lands and their confrontation, upon their arrival in Europe, with the anti-Americanist ideas held by some European intellectuals[5]. The exile strengthens their love for their native lands and the need, not only to defend "their" America from those anti-Americanist attacks, but also to define a feeling of identity and belonging that, due to the separation from their "patrias," is growing clearer and stronger in them. We are not dealing with a set of unconscious patriotic feelings that happen to show up in their works: these Jesuits set off to write their histories with the determination to define an identity that they know is shared by a wider community of people. They want to make that community conscious of their unique identity, as belonging to a very specific geography, history and culture. It is here that the work of these expelled Spanish American Jesuits plays a pioneer role: it constitutes one of the first attempts to create a regional consciousness with respect to a historical-cultural identity different from that of other American regions, and different from that of Spain. This conscience-creating process is of crucial importance, as it is the step prior to the design of any political program of independence. Hans Kohn has pointed out that even though there are some objective factors that distinguish some nationalisms from others—common origin, language, land, customs, tradition or religion,—the essential element is a "living and active corporate will:"

> It is this will which we call nationalism, a state of mind inspiring the large majority of a people and claiming to inspire all its members. It asserts that the nation-state is the ideal and

---

[4]   Francisco Javier Clavijero, *Storia antica del Messico* (Cesena1780-81); Juan Ignacio de Molina, *Compendio della storia geografica, naturale e civile del regno de Chile* (Bolonia 1776); Juan de Velasco Historia del Reino de Quito en la América meridional, finished in 1789, not published until 1841. Other expelled Spanish American Jesuits were Francisco Javier Alegre, Andrés Cavo and Juan Pablo Viscardo y Guzmán, among others.

[5]   The main European anti-Americanist philosophers were: Count Buffon, *The Epochs of Nature* (1778) and *Natural History* (1749); Cornelius De Pauw, *Recherches Philosophiques sur les Américains* (1768-69); Abbé Raynal, *L'Historie Philosophique et politique des establissements des Européens dans les Indes* (1770); and the Scottish historian William Robertson. *History of America* (1777).

the only legitimate form of political organization and that the nationality is the source of all cultural creative energy and economic well-being (10).

The regionalist, patriotic or pre-nationalistic feelings that appear in the works of these ex-Jesuits, rather than conveying a call for independence, aim at the creation of a particular state of mind, that of the "living and active corporate will" identified by Kohn.

In the "Preface" to the *Natural History*, Velasco explains the reasons behind his *History*: to serve the nation and the native land (patria). We find in Velasco, as well as in his fellow Spanish American Jesuits, an ambivalent double loyalty both to the Mother Land, Spain, as well as to his native land, the Kingdom of Quito. In the same "Preface" he expresses the need to define an identity in which both Europe and America come together but without exactly identifying himself with either: "ni soy Europeo, por haber nacido en América, ni soy americano, siendo por todos lados originario de Europa," ["I am not European having been born in America, nor American being in every respect a native of Europe"]. This is the kind of mixed feelings that show up in the works of this generation of Spanish American creoles who already start to feel and articulate a clear attachment to their native lands. We could even say that this ambivalent loyalty comes into conflict with their clear "Quitean," "Chilean" or "Mexican" identities. But the independentist ideology will not clearly develop and emerge until the creole Spanish American intellectuals get rid of that remaining loyalty to the Spanish crown.

Anthony Higgins talks about a *"criollo* archive," or "source of intellectual authority for criollos" that the creole subjectivity creates in a progressive and changing way according to the shifting political and economic contingencies. Higgins uses this concept of "archive" as "a means to theorize the process of the constitution of a network of intellectuals and institutional formations articulating authoritative texts and statements about Mexico's history and natural environment" (9). Higgins is dealing with Mexican texts, but this concept of "archive" could be equally applied to any other region of America. In this sense, we can also consider Velasco's work a contribution to the creation of that *criollo* archive, since it is the product of a creole subjectivity to serve a creole community that he wants to invest with the power that the knowledge and conscience of itself conveys.

Velasco's patriotic feelings towards the Kingdom of Quito show not only in his *History*; they constitute the theme inspiring the totality of his works, literary as well as historical. His determination to write his *History* in Spanish rather than in Italian (as his fellow Jesuits did) and his firm intention to publish it are clear symptoms of his project: to bestow the Kingdom of Quito with its own and legitimate geographical, natural, historical and cultural identity, different from that of the surrounding regions as well as from that of the Spanish Empire. He aims to make his fellow countrymen conscious of their specific identity.

It is in the *Old History of the Kingdom of Quito* where Velasco's patriotic intentions are more clearly stated. Velasco manipulates his sources and the information available to him in order to vindicate the Kingdom of Quito's legitimate autonomous existence. Velasco wants to assert Quito's independence from the Inca Empire. He does it on the basis of the pre-Inca historical period and through a revision and recreation of the actions, personality and figure of Atahualpa.[6] Velasco's version of the history of the Kingdom of Quito, in particular his account of the Scyris or first inhabitants of Quito, became the object of great controversy among the Ecuadorean critics of the late nineteenth and early twentieth centuries. This controversy reflects the important role Velaco's *History* has had in the formation of an Ecuadorian national conscience.[7]

Even though the *Old History* is the part that more clearly reflects Velasco's incipient patriotic consciousness, the alter is also present in the *Natural History*. The *Natural History of the Kingdom of Quito* constitutes Velasco's "defence of America."[8] It is a direct critical response to European defamatory theories about America, and it must be read as such.

---

[6]   In the *Historia antigua del reino de Quito*, Velasco re-creates the figure of Atahualpa, mythicising and presenting him as a hero and model of virtues. This is quite an interesting image, when we compare him to the horrible and cruel personality of Inca Garcilaso and other earlier chroniclers' Atahualpa. Not only does Velasco argue for the legitimacy of Atahualpa as Huaynacapac's successor and heir but, when Huaynacapac dies, he gives Atahualpa the Kingdom of Quito as part of Atahualpa's mother inheritance, which is seen as an act of restitution of something that had been usurped by force from the "Quitus."

[7]   The result of this controversy, ironically, started by a Spaniard (Marcos Jiménez de la Espada, 1897) working for Peru and followed by some very important Ecuadorean critics, was that Velasco's *History,* previously read and learnt in schools, was eliminated from history books until today.

[8]   For information on this topic see Antonello Gerbi, *La disputa del Nuevo Mundo.*

However, Velasco makes it very clear from the beginning that he articulates his defence of America through the America he knows well, that is, the Kingdom of Quito. The *Natural History* thus becomes a detailed description of Quito's natural world. Velasco makes use of the rhetoric and discourse of natural history to articulate a physical, natural and human geography of the Kingdom of Quito.

Pamela Regis, talking about the early descriptions of the nature of the newly born United States written by contemporaries of these expelled Jesuits—Bartram, Jefferson, Crévecoeur—says:

> But this list of topics— plant, mineral, animal, native people (discovered through travel in the wilderness)— comprises an agenda for one more form of self-creation and self-definition to stand alongside the political documents that promoted these two aims. The creators of the new nation had to consider not only the political justification and foundation of the new country but also the description of the territory or ground on which such politics would hold sway. (4)

In this way, natural history provided the writers of the young North-American nation "with a way of looking at the world, with a way of describing what they saw, and with an overarching scheme in which to fit what they had seen. It provided them with method, rhetoric, and context in their descriptions of the new land" (5).

Velasco's *Natural History* describes a land that is not yet an independent nation but that he already conceives of as an entity of its own, with a well defined historico-cultural identity[9]. He defines in great detail the physical extension of the Kingdom of Quito and describes and historicizes its geography, nature and native inhabitants.

Of the four books that constitute Velasco's *Natural History*, he devotes the first three to describe Quito's geography, mineral wealth, its fauna and flora. Though much of Quito's nature is shared by many other American regions, Velasco talks exclusively about the geography and the nature he personally knows, i.e. those of Quito. Besides describing, Velasco also historicizes Quito's natural world. In this way, many of the components of Quito's nature acquire a local character from the micro-

---

[9] Mind that Velasco, as well as his fellow historian Jesuits, are writing some fifty years before the Spanish American wars for independence.

histories the author supplies them with. Mixed into his descriptions of nature and the criticism of the anti-Americanists, Velasco has inserted anecdotes and local cases that he has seen or has been told, and that illustrate the topic he is dealing with. He makes extensive use of the autochthonous quichua names and one of his main sources of information for the phenomena he describes is indian lore and tradition. This would explain also the fantastic traits present in many of those natural phenomena he describes.[10] In short, Velasco articulates his defence of America specifically through the natural world of the Kingdom of Quito.

Velasco dedicates the fourth book of the *Natural History* to the "rational world" of the Kingdom of Quito, that is, to the Quitean native American. Velasco's description of the indian and of his situation could also be that of the native of any other part of America. However, he focuses his descriptions and argumentations on the people he knows, the natives from the Quito region. Thus, when talking about the origin of American man, he fixes his attention on the west coast of South America in order to talk about the first inhabitants of the Ecuadorean coast. When he deals with the myths of the conquest, he mentions only those that concern the Kingdom of Quito,[11] paying attention to local traits and features. Only in what concerns the degree of civilization of the Quito region, he is forced to resort to the Inca contributions since the latter certainly introduced a higher level of civilization into Quito. However, even in this case he keeps focussing on how these Inca contributions took root and developed in the Quito area.

The Quitean native American man constitutes one of Velasco's main concerns. Rather than isolating him as an object, as merely one more species within the natural world he describes, Velasco looks at him as a human being, and he places him in relation to the rest of humanity. Velasco gives him a specific history and culture different from those of other American peoples and, when describing his situation in the eighteenth century, presents him as a victim of the socio-economic circumstances in

---

[10] It is my belief that Velasco decided to include a series of fantastic descriptions, auchthoctonous folklore and traditions, not necessarily because he believed them to be true but because they are part of the cultural background and identity of Quito. If he did not record those elements of the native tradition, they would probably be lost forever.

[11] The preaching of the Apostles Saint Thomas and Saint Bartholomew in pre-Columbian times, the existence of the Amazons, and the past existence of a race of giants.

which he has been forced to live. Nonetheless, Velasco defends the fundamental equality between the American and the European. The difference between them rests on an inequality of opportunities, the indian being deprived of the instruction and education the European enjoys.

In the four books that constitute the main body of the *Natural History*, Velasco quite frequently gets carried away by his refutations of European philosophers' defamations of the Americas. His most blatantly patriotic reaction can be found in the appendix devoted to the criticism of Salvador Gilij's[12] *Essay on the History of America*. In this appendix Velasco reviews many of the topics he has already dealt with in the previous books, although more briefly and in a more excited tone. Velasco is bothered by the fact that an Italian who only knows the Orinoco area pretends to pass judgment on the nature of the whole American continent. This tendency to generalize from particular or isolated cases was a common device used by the anti-Americanist philosophers. From this kind of logic, they derived many of their derogatory statements about America. Velasco continues to fight this habit in Gilij. But worse, for Velasco, is the fact that Gilij doesn't seem to know where the boundaries between "Tierra Firme"[13] and the Quito territory stand. Gilij freely crosses regional boundaries in his descriptions, discursively appropriating for Tierra Firme some of Quito's land. Besides, Gilij modifies the course of certain rivers within Quitean territory so that even the origin of the Orinoco river is removed from the Quito region.[14] These are but small details that compromise the integrity of the Kingdom of Quito according to Velasco's view, and that could only annoy someone who deeply identifies with that land, feeling it as his. Clavijero and Molina did not notice these details in their criticism of Gilij. Velasco's criticism of Gilij is inspired by a profound need to protect one's possessions against the aggressive deformations and appropriation of outsiders ignorant of the reality they describe.

The defamatory generalizations made by Gilij and the European anti-

---

[12] Salvador Gilij was an Italian Jesuit who spent some thirty years in the Orinoco region. His experience there was not easy, suffering a lot of illnesses and hardships and, consequently, his vision of America was not very positive either.

[13] Approximately the northern coast of Meridional America.

[14] Time would show that Gilij was right in this respect, since the origin of the Orinoco river is south of Venezuela in the Mountains of Parima.

Americanists also provoked the critical responses of Clavijero and Molina. Besides being inaccurate and misleading, those general conclusions directly contradicted the specific identity of the different regions described by these Jesuits. One of these generalizations attracts Velasco's irritated attention: the homogeneous view of American man. Gilij states, together with the anti-Americanists, that, having seen one indian, one has seen them all. As a response to this judgement, Velasco tells us a couple of significant anecdotes which clearly illustrate how man's national identity is not in his physical appearance. It is not something innate or inherent in human nature but something artificial and learnt, shared by a particular community: it is a set of habits, customs, manners, ways of being and behaving. As human beings, the indians differ among themselves as much as one European from another. As members of a particular community, the generally servile situation in which they find themselves, as a consequence of colonization, prevents them from developing and showing their historical and cultural identity.

Finally, the second of the appendixes that Velasco adds to *his Natural History* is a "Catalogue of Writers" who wrote about Perú and the Quito region. Velasco's selection of writers is guided by his genuine interest in the Kingdom of Quito. This catalogue constitutes an interesting archive of sources, and the beginning of a history of the historiography of Ecuador. The Kingdom of Quito lacked an autochthonous history. This catalogue records the main sources of Velasco's *History* and so becomes the historiographical authority that legitimates the existence of a Kingdom of Quito proper. The possession of a common historical past is of vital importance when it comes to defining the identity of a given community. Two important aspects regarding the construction, definition and legitimation of a Quitean identity stand out in this catalogue. On the one hand, it shows the actual existence of historical records for the Kingdom of Quito. Velasco has traced all mentions and references to Quito in those historiographical authorities. On the other hand, out of the fifty five entries that compose the catalogue, there is not a single one specifically about the Kingdom of Quito. The most specific works about Quito are some lost texts—if they ever existed— by Fray Marcos de Niza. Therefore, the first history, dealing specifically with this region, from its remote origins up to the eighteenth century is, precisely, Juan de Velasco's *History of the Kingdom of Quito in Meridional America*. Maybe this is the best proof of Velasco's patriotic love for his native land.

Silvia Navia Méndez-Bonito

Cited Bibliography

Gerbi, Antonello. 1993. *La disputa del Nuevo Mundo*. México: FCE.

Higgins, Anthony. 2000. *Constructing the Criollo Archive. Subjects of Knowledge in the Mexican Bibliotheca Mexicana and the Rusticatio Mexicana*. Indiana: Purdue UP.

Kohn, Hans. 1965. *Nationalism. Its Meaning and History*. New York: D. Van Nostrand Company.

Regis, Pamela. 1992. *Describing Early America. Bartram, Jefferson, Crèvecoeur, and the Rhetoric of Natural History*. DeKalb: Northern Illinois UP.

Velasco, Juan de. 1989. *Historia del reino de Quito en la América Meridional*. 3 vols. Quito: Casa de la Cultura Ecuatoriana.

Creole Identity in Eighteenth-Century Peru: Race and Ethnicity

> Fuera de esto, habiendo reconocido las historias escritas hasta aquí en lengua vulgar, he observado que unas comprehenden muy poco, ... Y así me pareció que haría un singular servicio a la nación y al orbe político si acertase a escribir una historia de España comprehensiva, corregida y corriente, en la cual sola tuviese cualquiera las de todos, y en fin una historia vindicada de aquellos agravios que hace el amor tan bien como la emulación.
>
> — Peralta, *Historia de España vindicada*, prologue

In 1874, Juan María Gutiérrez remarked that Peralta Barnuevo's 1730 *Historia de España vindicada* seldom appeared for sale in European book catalogs, despite its importance as a provocative affront to the Spanish crown on the part of a Creole, whose erudition embodied a contradictory modernity in philosophy, style, and politics.[1] I have recently published a critical edition of Peralta's *Historia*, which now makes the text accessible to students, scholars, and the general public for the first time in more than 275 years. (Re)surging international interest in Peralta occurs at a time when extant approaches to Latin American Studies are undergoing yet another revision by a new group of Hispanic, European, and North American scholars. These scholars, in shifting focus away from postcolonial theory in favor of alternative methods that explore the overall effect of decolonization and Creolization, have introduced Peralta's works into undergraduate and graduate programs as required reading. Despite this growing interest in Peralta, and notwithstanding my own efforts to make him more prominent within the canon of Latin American colonial letters, most of his works remain obscure for today's readers.[2]

I was drawn to the *Historia* not so much by reason of it being one of two major works that had yet to be fully appreciated, but rather by evidence of what critics had failed to see in it: its intimate conceptual link with *Lima fundada* (1732). The historical-scientific course that Peralta espoused in 1730 in the *Historia* gave rise two years later to the poetic notion of conquest found in *Lima fundada*, where models of French neoclassicism predominate. The ambitious plan for the *Historia*, frustrated by a number of factors, paved the groundwork two years later for a more successful and fundamentally poetic account of conquest in *Lima fundada*, a work which affirmed Creole identity through an examination of the history of new-world cultural and political formations. In the *Historia* Peralta championed history as an art, discoursed on his unique "historical method," and attempted to chronicle the complex history of Spain's conquest. His cast of nations, empires, rulers, and diverse peoples—with their attendant ambitions, triumphs and losses in

---

[1]   Juan María Gutiérrez, "Don Pedro de Peralta," *El correo del Perú*, num. XX (Lima, domingo 23 de mayo de 1875). Reprinted in 1874-75 as "Doctor don Pedro de Peralta, peruano," *Revista del Río de la Plata* (Buenos Aires) 8:194-211, 331-67; 9:61-101, 441-78, 553-626; 10: 329-81.

[2]   See my *Historia de España vindicada by Pedro Peralta Barnuevo* (Newark, DE: Juan de la Cuesta Hispanic Monographs, 2003); *Peralta Barnuevo and the Art of Propaganda: Politics, Poetry, and Religion in Eighteenth-Century Lima* (Newark, DE: Juan de la Cuesta Press-Hispanic Monographs, 2001); *Peralta Barnuevo and the Discourse of Loyalty: A Critical Edition of Four Selected Texts* (Arizona: Arizona State University Press. Centre for Latin American Studies, 1996), and *Censorship and Art in Pre-Enlightenment Lima. Pedro de Peralta Barnuevo's 'Diálogo de los muertos: la causa académica,'* (Maryland: Scripta Humanistica, 1994).

war and genealogy—participated to create the "modern" Spain responsible for discovering and conquering the New World.

The advent of postcolonial studies opened the door to my examining the process by which Creoles—the offspring of Spaniards born in the New World—reinvented themselves vis-a-vis their peninsular counterparts. The debates of the eighteenth century were the ideal focal point for answering a series of perplexing questions: How did Peralta, who, under the patronage of seven viceroys, extolled the greatness of the Spanish monarchy, respond to the question of his own "invention"? How did this enlightened Creole engage issues of race, class, and group identification in publications that brought him the admiration of some of Europe's leading thinkers? How reliable was Peralta as spokesperson for the subaltern, for the disenfranchised class to which he belonged? I have studied and edited selected texts by Peralta in order to answer these questions, and have been able to conclude that when Peralta and other Creole writers referred to themselves, at times openly and defiantly, as "Spanish Americans," and to "our America" and "our Creole nation," they were not merely contesting their old-world detractors. They were also confronting their invention by Europe and planting the seeds of a distinct intellectual separation, thus introducing a sociopolitical identity that was as expressive as it was conceptual and ideological. I have come to find in Peralta's writings a shift from an early loyalist expression which, by the end of his career, became discouraged by the mantle of colonialism, in favour of a distinct sociopolitical identity. His early writings have the European readership in mind, whereas in his later works, starting with *Historia de España vindicada*, and followed by *Lima fundada*, he shifts focus to his "criolla nación."

Peralta's unique view of history and conquest was shaped by Bourbon precepts that favoured revisionist notions of conquest; by Cartesian thought and French neoclassicist science, philosophy, and poetics; and by divine providence, tradition, geography, climate, and by human will. In the *Historia* Peralta does not base history on the themes of adventure and glory, nor does he limit himself to the territorial notion of conquest. His goals are to consider ways of rewriting and revisiting conquest, and to render those criteria intelligible to a readership. Through a rationalized and systematized philosophy of conquest, Peralta—within his Creole situation and contradictory modernity vis-a-vis French neoclassicism—acknowledged epic models of conquerors, but shifted emphasis from a European to a Creole interpretation of the conquest. The latter was defined by governance, service, and development over arms, and by the concept of political discourse authorizing religious discourse (conquest of providentialism and an invitation to conquest). Conquest achieved by military means in order to affirm imperialism was of no less consequence than conquest occasioned by love of liberty and peace. A nation's tranquillity was achieved through its ability to resist configuring peace in the face of ambition, and by allowing itself to be disarmed by nature. In the *Historia* this concept demarcated a nation's ultimate valour, as attested to by the alliances forged between the mix of Gauls and Greeks, Goths and Alans, and Celts and Iberians in regions inhabited by the Ausetani, Arevaci and others who comprised part of Cataluña, much of Aragón, the Rioja, and all of Soria, and whose peoples—later called Celtiberians—became the strength of Spain. In the *Historia* nationhood that reflects imperial ties is linked to blood lines ("privilegios de la sangre"), whereas Pruvian nationhood is defined by the soil ("nuestro suelo," "patrio suelo," "la nobleza del primitivo suelo").

By targeting the *Historia* to a peninsular and Peruvian audience which, by inference, would come to understand Spain's complicated conquest of Peru, Peralta saw himself as serving both the monarchy and its American colony, and defending the political and religious entity of nation (*nación*) or group-identification. At the time of Spain's patent military decline, when "sceptres and sciences" had displaced arms, Peralta argued, as he had done in 1714 in *Imagen política*, that letters formed an integral presence in the tripartite relationship of sceptres, sciences, and letters. As Ruth Hill has stated, the rise of men-of-letters and the decline of men-of-arms led in part Hispanic humanists to promote a dynamic definition of heroism and conquest, which nevertheless helped to maintain political and religious institutions and defend a stratified society.[3] Peralta conceived of himself as a modern warrior of the state, whose weapon—the pen—defended the *nación* as valiantly as had any captain or soldier. In the words of his brother José, Peralta's "... arte para persuadir ... es una fortaleza y vivacidad de entendimiento que, aunque pacífica, no es menor y puede ser más útil al público que la fuerza de los

---

[3]   Ruth Hill, *Sceptres and Sciences in the Spains: Four Humanists and the New Philosophy (ca.1680-1740)* (Liverpool: Liverpool University Press, 2000), 4.

espíritus guerreros; y la posteridad conocerá que sirvió Vmd. a la gloria
de la nación con la pluma, como los valerosos capitanes con la espada."[4]
Within Peralta's conceptualization of history, he was a literary conqueror
now forced to wage war and investigate truth on the battlefield of history,
to which peninsular historians had laid waste and left the origin of
Spain's language, towns, rulers, saints, and triumphs and losses confused
and injured. Spain—its provinces and colonies—were to find vindication
in this work. References abound in the *Historia* to the fertility and force
of the pen and its ability to persuade, influence, injure, correct, beautify,
and serve: "Por esto podré decir que si he acertado a consagrar mi anhelo,
la mayor parte de las provincias de España quedarán gloriosamente
servidas de mi pluma" (Prologue). The *Historia* filled a void in Spain's
history at a time when the peninsula was in transition from practising the
sword and the art of war to defending its colonial politics through the
efforts of men-of-letters.

The *Historia* was to have modelled a scientific inquiry, a work in
which fiction, myth, and legend had no place. Peralta's objective was to
correct historians who "angered truth" by stretching it with digressions
into fabulous accounts. The motives for writing the history were many,
but were guided by a search for truth and a desire to see Spain reflected
in a clearer light by which she could be defended for the good of the
nation.

> Ver padecer a España unos despojos de historia y unos atenta-
> dos de discursos; el derecho de su primera población quitado a
> Tubal; su originaria lengua a fuerza de disputarla, oscurecida;
> la presente a fuerza de engrandecerla, trastornada; sus anti-
> guos reyes por quererlos verificados, confundidos, y en los que
> se subrogan en lugar de los que se repelen, mudada la fábula,
> no desvanecida; las primitivas glorias de sus patronos y sus
> santos, destruidas; introduciéndose no sólo el error en el trono
> sino el agravio en al altar; y, lo que es más doloroso, ver mucho
> de esto ejecutado por mano de los más obligados a su culto; la
> firmeza de las épocas y los tiempos vacilantes; la pérdida y
> recuperación de España tan confusas que parece quedó más
> arruinada a la memoria que al dominio; y en fin la fijeza de
> muchos sucesos desquiciada: han sido todos poderosos impulsos

---

[4]   José Peralta in front matter to *Historia de España vindicada*; unnumbered folio.

que, haciéndoseme compasión en la noticia, se me formaron violencia en el trabajo. (Prologue)

Since Peralta's stated desire was to avoid the errors other historians had committed, he would comment less on the ancient centuries in favour of "modern" times, thus focussing on emperors whose governments were connected to Spain in some meaningful way. History, in its broadest application, was to be measured by its excellence as a moralizing, didactic teacher who furthered the cause of learning. Its purity resided in the particular style of eminent historians, their choice of words, clarity of narration, the brilliance of their aphorisms, the force of their clauses, their sense of judgment or presentation of a character's dilemma, and the discreteness of their praise. A well composed history based on truth would inspire or persuade readers to action, for they would see in it models of conduct and a variety of human experiences. An expert writer's appeal lay in the ability to rework history for mass consumption by making it more palatable, as evidenced in the successes enjoyed by ancient authors.

Inasmuch as Peralta was writing for the general public, reading the *Historia* did not presuppose knowledge of the complex history of Spain's origins. In retelling history, his job was to make it come alive, as in narrating the collective suicide of the inhabitants of Saguntum against the impulses of Hannibal (bk. 1, cols. 285-95), or the sacrifice of the inhabitants of Numantia. By seducing the imagination, establishing an affinity between the readership and the text, and following the Cartesian model of making unencumbered transitions from one narration to the next, he sought to have readers invest in the foundation of their own history. History profited from adornment and embellishment as "un animado viviente de razón. El fin de ésta es la instrucción y así fue preciso que en ella sirviese al entendimiento la memoria" (Prologue). Yet Peralta owned that, in exceeding the limits of historian to become an apologist, his zeal exposed him to censorship.

> Si se jugaze que he excedido en estos capítulos los términos de historiador y he pasado a los de apologista, perdónese esto a la naturaleza de un asunto en que va el celo de la verdad histórica tan al lado de el de la nación, considerando que cuando la sinrazón discurre ofensas, es preciso que la razón pronuncie desagravios. En lo demás ni carecen semejantes digresiones de ejemplares ni estos tiempos de la historia de España ofrece más sucesos que los sagrados, siendo mucho más notable divertirse,

como otros, para llenar los años por no hallar los propios a los
que son extraños, y en fin créase la defensa y sufro la censura.
(bk. 3, cols. 799-800)

To controvert the authority of peninsular historians was considered
unpatriotic and a transgression against truth and verisimilitude, because
it too diminished the "paradoja de historia" (bk. 1, 27) of those who stated,
for example, that the peninsula was the cradle of humanity and the seat
of Eden. When Peralta refuted ancient and modern historians, he
acknowledged the difficulty in remaining unbiased: "Bien quisiera mi
genio poder aplicarse al partido de los modernos bien afectos pero esto
sería no ser historiador sino abogado, y hacer sospechoso lo ínclito
justamente alabado con lo perverso falsamente defendido" (bk. 5, col.
1544).

In outlining his historical method, or "order," Peralta accused
peninsular historians of presenting historical facts as if they were
anecdotes and of not having followed the commendable models of
Salustius, Livy, and Florus. the *Historia*'s historical-scientific method
entailed: studying in detail the physical and political geography of the
Iberian peninsula; establishing and measuring positions, longitude and
latitude by using procedures agreed on by the Royal Academy of Paris;
consulting ancient and modern maps published in Paris and Amsterdam;
and following observations and tables from the royal Spanish observatory.
Those "modern" instruments allowed him to challenge historians,
theologians, and astronomical calculations in order to pinpoint the exact
date, hour and age of Christ at the time of his death (bk. 3, cols. 869-75),
to favour Cassiodorus' over Idacio's calculation for computing the
beginning of Thurismundo's reign and the death of Theodoric (bk. 5, col.
1378), and to reject speculative conclusions and errors advanced by
Tertulian and Riccioli, amongst others, regarding the coming of the
apostle Saint James to Spain. In the nomenclature of cities and places, he
surpassed Morales and Moret by employing Pliny, Ptolomy, Strabo,
Pomponius Mela, Livy, and Polybius.

The principal faults of Peralta's "retrospective patriotism" are his
insistence on a pious adherence to the glories that false traditions and
ecclesiastical history promoted within the Spanish church (bk. 1, ch. 28):
quimeric bishops, saints, and martyrs, and his credulous attitude toward
legends and myths. In his religious zeal he accepts without questioning

the tenet held by St. Isidore, Ocampo, Ferreras, and Mariana that Thubal, son of Japhet and grandson of Noah, was a primitive inhabitant of Spain; against Pellicer, he recreates the travels of Bacchus and Pan throughout Spain; he accords recognition to the travels of St. James and the transfer of his body from Jerusalem to Galicia (bk. 5, chs. 1-8); he accedes to the miraculous apparition of the Virgin in the Pilar de Zaragoza (bk. 3, chs. 5-7); he puts a sense upon the monotheism of ancient Iberians (Galicians, Asturians, Cantabrians); against Ferreras and Pellicer he avows the presence in Spain of the warrior-legislator Egyptian Hercules—who predated the Theban son of Alcmene and Amphitryon and was succeeded by king Hispalo or Hispano—in fights with the Geryons during the struggle of the Tartessians against the Phoenicians. In addition, he distorts the history of Hermenegild and argues for Leogivild's public retraction of Arrianism (bk. 1, ch. 31); he rejects that the Arian Visigoths, as Spain's enemy, could have ever been favoured in battle against Chlodoveoch (Clovis II), king of the Franks from 634-57 (bk. 5, ch. 12); he applauds the arrival and the havoc of the Barbers as a providential salvation; and, in accepting Spain as a Visigothic monarchy, excuses the Goths of all errors, such as the sacking of Rome. Lastly, his credulity leads him to see the fall of imperial Rome only as divine retribution for ancient persecutions against Christianity.

Peralta's discourse of loyalty was a continuation of the discourse of commentary found in the body of sixteenth- and seventeenth-century chronicles of South America and histories of Spain by peninsular authors. His design was similar in nature to the work of his compatriot, the Inca Garcilaso de la Vega, who preceded him by two centuries and challenged conventional historiography by writing a corrective history of the Inca empire. In view of his role as spokesperson and chronicler on whom viceroys and dignitaries relied for writing the(ir) official view of history, and in deference to the Spanish Crown, Peralta asked that the history of Spain be shaped by the uniqueness of his mature Creole voice. On repeated occasions he had proven himself adept at using the written discourse of loyalty to control, order, and influence public opinion, as reflected in themes found in numerous festive, religious, and political works. At the forefront of Peralta's discourse of loyalty to the Bourbon monarchy was the ever-present image of Peru and his beloved Lima.

Peralta regarded America as prospering under the same relationship with Spain that Spain once enjoyed with Rome. Peru was better off than other Spanish colonies because it thrived under the largesse of the Bourbon era. In effect, Spain, he thought, had inherited not only the history of Rome but also its majesty and power as head of an American empire. This scheme promoted monarchical sovereignty over territorial possessions as justifiable within the framework of history and the *Historia*. Spain's colonies were, if not the head of its government, at least the heart of its wealth.

The *Historia* was as much a tribute to the glory of Spain as it was to the role that Peru had played in furthering Spain's greatness. Comparisons between Spain and Peru are founded in three basic areas: (1) their shared status as former and present colonies, (2) linguistic dominance, and (3) the early religious systems of each country. America's relationship to Spain was a mirror image of the close ties that Spain once enjoyed as a territory of the Roman empire, a political affiliation that had produced distinguished literary figures.

> No hay duda que el América ha dado a España y a sí misma grandes varones que la han ilustrado, y que cada día la ilustran caminando por aquellas dos grandes calles de la gloria que han formado a un nivel armas y letras. No digo esto por blasonar la paridad sino por defender absoluta la aptitud con que debe cesar cualquiera preocupación, quedándonos sin diferencia alguna, y como a un plan de honor en ambos mundos, siendo el mayor de la nación española haber extendido tan bien como el imperio la virtud. (Prologue 1-2)

In the same fashion that Spain had once enriched Rome's coffers, now too did America enrich Spain's, providing human and material riches: "Era entonces la España la América de los romanos semejante en las riquezas y en la extracción de las riquezas. Desdichada provincia donde dos veces se sacaba la sangre de sus habitadores a cuyos males sólo les servía la muerte que tomaban de remedio" (bk. 2, cols. 411-12).

There is merit to probing the representation of Creole identity in a work that was to be a corrective and current history of Spain, composed in the spirit of—and obeying the historiographic mission of—early chroniclers and historians of the New World. The *Historia* was to address a dual purpose: (1) to establish truth by correcting the "grave errors" of (peninsular) historians and, (2) to be of service to the *nación* and to the political sphere. Peralta asserted that he was the best historian to write of Spain's greatness because he had less to gain as new-world subject.

> Y así, de la manera que un grande orador dijo de sí, que
> ninguno era más conveniente que alabase a príncipe que el que
> era menos necesario, puedo decir que ninguno es más propio
> para escribir de una nación que el que es menos preciso, como
> para la nuestra lo soy yo sin que esta libertad diminuya el
> mérito del amor, ni éste haya embarazado el deseo de la
> exactitud, sabiendo que su legítima gloria consiste en la pureza
> de ésta y que no vive tan escasa de fama su grandeza que
> necesite de pedirla prestada al afecto de los propios, ni tema que
> se la gaste el odio de los extraños. (Prologue)

Unlike other historians, Peralta strives for impartiality based on insignificance, disenfranchisement, and self-effacement. Since Peralta was born in a distant land and was an extended "native" of Spain's provinces, he considered himself to be less passionate and less compelled than peninsular historians to defend and engage Spain's history in an objective manner. In order to make history come alive for readers by having them recognize the historical ties that all Peruvians shared with Spain, Peralta positioned himself as did peninsular historians who wrote passionately—but with degrees of inaccuracy—about the New World, often without having visited it; instead, those historians viewed the new continent more through their soul than with their eyes. Peralta owned that he was writing about a country he had never visited except in his imagination, for despite having achieved international recognition he never left the confines of his native Peru. He conceded the inherent danger in writing about a land he had never seen.

> Si para escribir las historias de los reinos fuese siempre
> inviolable requisito el verlos, negaríamos la fe a Tito Livio en lo
> que habla de España y de Grecia, a Tácito en lo que habla de
> Alemania y Asia y, sin entendernos a otros tan antiguos, a
> Herrera y a Solís en lo que refieren del América. Debiendo
> decirse lo mismo de las descripciones porque ninguno de los que
> las reducen a la línea en cartas, ni a la pluma en libros, han
> necesitado ver todas las regiones que han copiado, pues a
> ninguno ha dado el sol su carro para andarlo todo. (Prologue)

It is ironic and yet a fitting tribute to new-world prowess that an enlightened Creole and subaltern should be the one to attempt to write the definitive history of the Spanish empire.

In vindicating Croele identity and rejecting pseudo-scientific theories about Creole aptitude, Peralta's response to his colonial situation is framed by political and cultural considerations that take centre stage in the *Historia*.[5] In the prologue Peralta shot his first volley at the Crown when he reasoned that the American colonies and their peoples enjoyed the same relationship with Spain as did Spain with Rome when the former was a colony of the Roman empire: "Es innegable que aquella proporción que antiguamente tuvo con Roma España cuando fue la provincia más noble de su imperio es la misma que hoy tiene con España el América ..." (Prologue). This echoes the tone that Peralta used to broach the question of race and class in America: that in the hegemonic battle Spain was the loser, that it did itself a disservice in promoting and maintaining class and race distinctions, and that Spain too suffered when Creoles were divested of rights and opportunities for growth. He used the case of Seneca to illustrate this point: "Era Séneca extranjero y de provincia conquistada. Vergüenza es de aquellas cortes en que no se premian aun los mismos proprios por distantes" (bk. 4, col. 948).

This initial volley was followed by yet another in bk. 1, where Peralta subverted the notion of "natural deficiency" by refuting the fact that the accidental American climate was responsible for influencing the virtue of its subjects. To the contrary, American soil nurtured their roots and spirit, producing enriched talents. America and Peru were home to "unas regiones ennoblecidas de más rica materia, de fecundidad más singular" (bk. 1, cols. 2-3). In essence, from American soil was mined the rich Creole ingenuity that contributed to Spain's economic and spiritual fortune. Within Cañizares-Esguerra's notion of how epistemologies and identities in the eighteenth-century influenced the writing of history, Peralta's patriotic epistemology and defence of Creole aptitude would

---

[5] Pseudo-scientific theories about climatic determinism promoted Creoles to be victims of a form of *capitis diminutio*, where laws of humoral pathology and detrimental effects of geography were forces that impacted negatively on the rational faculties of Creoles. Peralta embedded between the lines of HEV—and oftentimes presented as digressions or asides—his rejection of such theories, bristling at the errant science behind such a concept: "Siempre ha sido el primer honor de los mortales la nobleza del primitivo suelo donde nacen la cual, como si el temperamento del clima fuese influencia de la virtud y las propriedades del terreno fuesen privilegios de la sangre, les sirve como de una alcuña universal de la nación en que tiene por estirpe común la patria" (bk. 1, cols. 1-2). This and similar remarks point to a geographical determinism that was expressed in advance of Buffon and Montesquieu's systematically formulated ideas about the influence of climate and geography on human psychology and intellectual capacity.

have contributed to having "exposed the shortcomings and limitations of Europeans who sought to write natural histories of the New World ... and reflected the longings of the Creole upper classes in Spanish America to have 'kingdoms' of their own."[6] From a pre-enlightened perspective, and within the confines of an evolving academic and political world in which ideological aggression was a mainstay, Peralta beheld his acceptance by European thinkers as a confirmation of "nuestra América" and "nuestra criolla nación." With this confirmation he confronted his invention by Europe, sought to reverse disparaging opinions about Creoles, and reinvented himself.

The historic-literary vindication of Spain was more than a defence of Spain's glories and excellent qualities. At the core of Peralta's thesis, framed by Spain's architecture of conquest, was the vindication of Peru as a nation or *patria*. According to Kahiluoto Rudat, "A clear concept of patria and of nation consisting of people with a common origin, born on the same soil" appears in the *Historia*.[7] This strong sentiment of American regionalism is expressed in the prologue, where Peru, compared to Rome's colonies, was painted as the target of two-fold victimization: "Era el gobierno de los pretores otra guerra de paz que se hacía a los sujetos con que el robo civil no era menos valiente que el saco militar, y la codicia sucedía a la ambición. Era entonces la España la América de los romanos: semejante en las riquezas y en la extracción de las riquezas. Desdichada provincia donde dos veces se sacaba la sangre de sus habitadores a cuyos males sólo les servía la muerte que tomaban de remedio" (bk. 2, cols. 411-12). From a moralizing perspective, Spain and Peru were the subjects of conquest because they allowed their prosperity and riches to lull them into a sense of ambition, false security, and tranquillity.

> Error es de torpe ocio o de necio descuido tener en las riquezas el incentivo que provoca la invasión sin la defensa que asegura la quietud . . . . Los españoles,

---

[6]   Jorge Cañizares-Esguerra, *How to Write the History of the New World: Histories, Epistemologies and Identities in the Eighteenth-Century Atlantic World* (Stanford: Stanford University Press, 2001), 4.

[7]   Eva M. Kahiluoto Rudat, "The Spirit of Intellectual Independence in the Writings of Enlightened Creoles," *Dieciocho: Hispanic Enlightenment, Aesthetics and Literary Theory* 14:80-91 (1991), 85.

que tenían como presente de la naturaleza dentro de
su casa las riquezas, ni las estimaban como solicita-
das ni las buscaban fuera; y las que pudieran servir-
les para adquirir extranjeros dominios, les servían
para perder los propios, siendo señuelo de la ambición
ajena lo que pudiera ser instrumento de la propia
gloria. Causa porque ha sido carácter de la España
estar expuesta siempre a la dominación de otras
naciones, no por defecto de un valor que ha mostrado
aun a favor de sus conquistadores sino por exceso del
ocio o del contento que induce la abundancia. (bk. 1,
cols. 227-29)

This critique seemed to foreshadow Spain's impending transatlantic
losses.

The temporal concept of nation, which had paved the way for
Spain's providential rise, also defined Peru and other historic and cultural
entities with deep roots (Celts, Greeks, Carthaginians, Romans, Goths,
and Muslim Arabs). Within Peralta's discourse, the articulation of
"nuestra España" and "nuestra criolla nación" were far from contradictory
terms: they were affirmative declarations of the continuous political and
religious history that framed his new-world identity.

Jerry M. Williams

Locating the American Voice: Space Relation as Self-Identification in Henry David Thoreau's *Vision*

"I do not propose to write an Ode to Dejection, but to brag as lustily as chanticleer in the morning, standing on his roost, if only to wake my neighbours up" (Thoreau 1963: 62). This statement from Henry David Thoreau's *Walden*, usually taken out as a motto for the book, clearly hints at a cultural dialogue, involving opposite sides. Thoreau would not indicate that it is Samuel Taylor Coleridge's "Ode to Dejection" he has in mind; he makes it quite clear, though, that what he intends is exactly the opposite. His "bragging" is supposed to contradict a whole cultural context which he takes Coleridge's title to symbolize.

Although Thoreau is most often being placed in the context of international Romanticism, the fact remains that in his writings there is only the occasional reference to his European counterparts. (Miller 1961:147-159). Shared dispositions and artistic views with mainly the English Romantics led Thoreau, just like Emerson some time before, to wrestle with the very power of this influence that made it difficult for him to be an authentic New Englander in himself (McIntosh 1974: 59). But an authentic New Englander he wanted to be, always insisted on being. In his transcendental vision, America and Europe formed a complete contrast which he fully internalized in terms of his own self-identity.

What I would suggest here, then, is that the Atlantic for Thoreau turned out to be a psychologically needed physical remoteness overloaded with existential importance, an importance that only grew with the years. Thoreau would always stick to his preoccupation with the "genius loci" of America as his one and only means for self-preservation. He would gladly go to Oregon, but not to London. Place was so crucial to him that he never crossed the Atlantic like his fellow Emerson, never made the return journey from New England to England. Place relation with him existentially equalled self-identification. Therefore, whenever it was threatened, a fervent zeal was needed for its defence. The safety of "I am America" should never turn for Thoreau into the insecurity of "How far is America from me?"; he would not let that happen. Yet as time passed there was an increasing tendency for this to occur, the way from *Walden* to "Walking", from 1845 to 1862, being marked by a gradually deepening discrepancy between the me and the not-me. As a result, the emotional degree of Thoreau's speaking about the American West as opposed to the European East rises considerably towards his older age, proportionally counterbalancing the enhanced disturbance of his relationship with nature. And nature was, for him, entirely American. "Eastward I go only by force; but westward I go free," Thoreau states in "Walking" (Thoreau 1990: 125). Although he fights some of the same battles as Wordsworth, Coleridge or Carlyle, he generally prefers not to exhibit his acquaintance with their works and seeks consciously to avoid European influence. Instead, he locates his human and poetical voice in America, as distinctively American. This is not simply echoing Emerson who had already proclaimed that "here, here in America, is the home of Man" (Emerson 1903-1904: XI, 540); it is not just following Emerson in his search of a poetic which would embody the energy and space of the American continent and the recalcitrance of the American's break from Europe. It is all very personal here, truly existential, the core of a lived philosophy of living. The "genius loci" of America is personified to the utmost extremity. And I would go further here in suggesting that in the course of time this self-identification, so seriously taken as it was, did not turn out to be an easy one and had to be specially cherished. Thus, when experiencing an undisturbed harmony between himself and America's Nature, Thoreau effortlessly outlines the physical and creative hiatus between the West and the East in terms of advantages and, respectively, disadvantages. When, though, his harmony with nature becomes threatened later on, he starts to painfully feel he is going "eastward," closer to the European disposition, closer to an Ode to Dejection. He would never allow that happen, would eagerly defend his New-Englishness, that is to say his very self-identity, would therefore glorify the West zealously, enthusiastically, desperately. If, in other words, in the essay "Thomas Carlyle and his Works," written at Walden Pond in 1845, at the time of his famous experiment, Thoreau had only blamed London for Carlyle's incapacity to create a transcendental hero, almost twenty years later, in "Walking," he would exhilaratingly magnify America's wilderness (as opposed to Europe's tameness) as the world's preservation and future. So let me now draw your attention to these two essays and the deep personal drama of dis/location painfully unfolding itself inbetween them. The essay "Thomas Carlyle and his Works" was written when Thoreau was in the process of composing *Walden*, and simultaneously followed for a while the same creative impulse. Beside the fact that these two works trace the steps of Thoreau's acquiring his own literary voice, they share another distinctive feature: both are preoccupied with the notion of the "genius loci." Though Walden Pond is never mentioned in the essay, it obviously provides Thoreau's perspective towards Carlyle and his works. Thoreau was at the time entirely devoted to his experiment in living. He had gone to the woods, because he "wished to live deliberately, to front only the essential facts of life" and not to live "what was not life" (Thoreau 1963: 67). Walden Pond was his place for true living, his transcendentalist art-life choice, his vision from the midst of Nature. Therefore Thoreau could not but be a Waldener then. And in the vision of this Waldener Thomas Carlyle could not but be justified as a Londoner. Thoreau had left his hometown Concord wishing to experiment with his own life. He had moved from the distractions of the city to the concentration provided by Nature. He had realized the need for changing the place in order for him to fulfil his intention. Such a disposition clearly outlines the choice of place as the only ground for Thoreau's dissatisfactions with Carlyle, because London was the place chosen by the Scotsman, Carlyle, and Thoreau was thinking about this choice after having made the right choice for himself. Thoreau's perspective towards Carlyle always tends towards comparisons in terms of place and relation to place, thus drawing a kind of a topical borderline between the two otherwise alike transcendental minds. "As we read his books here," writes Thoreau, "in New England, where there are potatoes enough, and every man can get his living peacefully and sportively as the birds and bees, and need think no more of that, it seems to us as if by the world he often meant London, at the head of the tide upon the Thames, the sorest place on the face of the earth, the very citadel of conservatism" (Thoreau 1989: 1610). Obviously, this passage is both a comparison and a comment, leaving no hesitation on the part of the reader as to which is the place preferred. Moreover, both transcendental space and Carlyle's transcendental vision are considered in the essay in terms of limitations, those imposed by the walled-in physical space of London. "Carlyle in London ... sees no occasion for minstrels and rhapsodists there," Thoreau observes. And the explanation comes right away: "He lives in Chelsea, not ... on the prairies of the West" (p.1608). The distinction between the East and the West, between closed spaces and open spaces is drawn clearly enough. And Thoreau would never ever separate the spiritual from the physical.

Spiritual spaciousness for Thoreau, as for all the American transcendentalists, is a synonym of poetry. Therefore it is always associated with vision, the true Poet being necessarily a Seer. Thoreau did not simply share Emerson's idea, but took it upon himself to actually live as a Poet and make Poetry out of his own life. Such was the motivation for his Walden Pond enterprise. Not unexpectedly then comes Thoreau's estimation that "Carlyle is not a seer, but a brave looker-on and reviewer" (p.1609). Thoreau's major concern seems to be that Carlyle is not the Poet he could have been, since for Thoreau he "indicates a depth, which he neglects to fathom" and therefore should not speak "to a London ... audience merely" (p.1611).He should finally produce a transcendent hero, but obviously for Thoreau to do that in London is a contradiction in itself. If Carlyle is to fulfil such an expectation he should definitely set himself free from the "genius loci" of London. So, following the general impulse of his essay, Thoreau comes up with the suggestion, that "possibly ... in the silence of the wilderness and the desert he might have addressed himself more entirely to his true audience, posterity" (p.1611). The topical opposition is clearly outlined here in terms of impossibility against possibility, provided respectively by London and the Wilderness, of acquiring the true poetic vision. Though critical on certain grounds, Thoreau never fails to express his reverence and admiration for Carlyle's style and language. And, interestingly enough, this attitude provides another example of the spatial dichotomy that runs throughout the essay. "Such a style—so diversified and variegated!," exclaims Thoreau as if under a spell: "It is like the face of a country; it is like a New England landscape, with farm-houses and villages, and cultivated spots, and belts of forests and blueberry-swamps round about it, with the fragrance of shad-blossoms and violets on certain winds" (p.1600). This passage clearly indicates at least two things. First, that while writing the Carlyle essay Thoreau had reached the point of turning into one of America's masters of style. And secondly, that when considering beauty, he can take his comparisons from nowhere else but Nature. And Thoreau's nature is never any nature; it is essentially American, always the nature of his native New England.

The essay "Thomas Carlyle and his Works" was written at a time when Thoreau was experiencing perfect harmony with nature. He was enjoying his favoured "simplicity," having turned Emerson's idea of "correspondence" into a reality of living; nature for him then really was "a grand collection of metaphors for human actions and relations," that is to say, for his own actions and relations (Emerson 1990: 29). Hence Thoreau's conviction in estimating Carlyle in no other terms but his "genius loci" attachments. There is not a sign yet here of that painful though mostly subdued feeling of separation from nature, that will only deepen with the years into an unrelievable existential drama. That feeling will creep into his Journal a few years after the Carlyle essay, leading him to quite a memorable lament: "We soon get through with Nature. She excites an expectation which she cannot satisfy. The merest child which has rambled into a copsewood dreams of a wilderness so wild and strange and inexhaustible as Nature can never show him" (Thoreau 1906: VI, 293). And in the essay "Walking," written in the year of his death, 1862, Thoreau's isolation crisis persists throughout, expressed as if in compensatory forms through an over exaggerated enthusiasm about the Wilderness, or America's nature. So I would argue here that when secure in his imaginative balance between mind and nature, Thoreau would in the main talk freely about the differences between himself and his transatlantic counterparts: such is the case of the Carlyle essay and the implicit objection to Coleridge. When, though, this balance is disturbed, or even lost, the need for its restoration becomes more and more tormenting, Thoreau starts feeling himself closer to the European (Romantic) disposition of his time, which in its turn makes his situation worse. He would never ever admit this enhancing closeness, nor consider writing another "English" essay. Quite the contrary: in his later years he desperately sticks to his being an authentic New Englander, and therefore passionately glorifies the West as the World, as the only place for humankind. But mainly for the self, of course. In other words, self-location in America becomes for Thoreau emotionally overloaded as existentially indispensable when self-isolation from nature enters. And this is exactly what happens on the way to "Walking." "Methinks my present experience is nothing; my past experience is all in all," Thoreau notes in his Journal of the early 1850s: "Formely, methought, nature developed as I developed, and grew up with me. My life was ecstasy. In youth, before I lost any of my senses, I can remember that I was all alive ..." (Thoreau 1906: II, 306). This sad recognition is followed up in another Journal passage of the same period: "I fear that the character of my knowledge is from year to year becoming more distinct and scientific," Thoreau writes, "that, in exchange for views as wide as heaven's scope, I am being narrowed down to the field of the microscope. I see details, not wholes nor the shadow of the whole ..." (Thoreau 1906: II, 406). Obviously, what Thoreau was already missing was the transcendental knowledge, or the capability of seeing wholes. And it had always been the wholes he had been aiming at seeing, be they called visibilities beyond the visible or transcendental realities. Emerson was the first to notice in him the ability to infer the "universal law from the single fact" (Emerson 1903-1904: X, 474). So, what had happened in the early 1850s with the already aging Thoreau was that single fact and universal law no longer formed an immediate metaphor in his imagination; they were split, and a great effort was needed towards securing their combination (to use Coleridge's term). With Thoreau, this was not merely an intellectual or artistic problem. Since for him the transcendentalist formula of an Art-Life equation had long ago swept from aesthetics to reality and he had been successfully experiencing it in his actual life, the Walden enterprise was nothing but that. This is why, having lost the harmonious whole of self and Nature, he not only grieved. He felt threatened; indeed, his whole world was threatened. And he had to defend both his own self and the world that had made it possible. So the Self became the Walker, "born into the family of the Walkers" and experiencing the art, or the profession of Walking, while the World emerged as the West, as the Wild, as America transcending into the Holy Land—the final destination of the noble Walker (Thoreau 1990: 118).

I would argue that it was at this point that Thoreau overemphasized the two poles of his lost harmony: the scientific and the transcendental, the single fact and the universal law, the detail and the whole, thus providing himself with what Leo Marx called "a token of individual survival" (Marx 1967: 364). In other words, in the last decade of his life Thoreau went further into the thoroughness of his scientific knowledge on the one hand and, on the other hand, gradually directed his transcendental knowledge towards a millenarian vision of his own country. My point is that, undergoing his inner crisis, Thoreau attempted at over exaggerating both the "detail" and the "whole" in order to achieve a global, somewhat titanic balance of the two in his already troubled vision. The classical scholar in him and his romantic disposition reached simultaneously a status of extremity—the very extremity of the contrast being in itself romantic too—leading him altogether to an exceptional image of the wilderness. Both directions he followed with extraordinary zeal, and both directions led him to enthusiastic reconfigurations of America, be they scholarly or transcendental. This was no more Thoreau who used to be at ease to infer the universal law from the single fact; this was already Thoreau, innerly split into extremities and therefore forming a romantically globalized picture of his home country. So it turned out that in the last fifteen years of his life his attachment to the "detail" made him dive into whatever documentation concerning America's past he could come across and thus, "scientifically" as he put it, rediscover his native roots. On the other hand, his painful detachment from the "whole" took him to a revival of the old European myth of America as the New Jerusalem and to his inspired glorification of the West. If he was no more to derive directly from America's wilderness, he would derive from the documentary lore of native and early American history. This was no more the tendency to see the waters of Walden as the waters of the Ganges or the pond's pebbly bottom as the starry sky; it was already "the westward tendency," as he called it in "Walking," to transcend documentary knowledge about America into transcendental knowledge about America and thus to place himself there. It was no more the small pond in the neighbourhood of Concord transcending into the whole universe; it was already the scientifically certified knowledge of America transcending into a glorification, into a hymn of America's wilderness. It probably needed a greater imaginative leap to reach at such a metaphor.

"I live a sort of border life," Thoreau confesses in "Walking" (Thoreau 1990: 139). Between dimensions, suitable for a moss-trooper, and the natural life he's lost the causeway to—this is how he finds himself to be. To reach this "natural life," as he calls it, he would go through "bogs and sloughs unimaginable." Or to counterbalance the "detail" with a global image of the "whole." So, where the "westward impulse" gradually leads him to, is a purely apocalyptic (as Geoffrey Hartman would have called it) vision of America as "the new land and the new sky" of John's Revelation. Thus the light of a New England November sunset is beautifully made to figure forth the light of paradise restored at the end of "Walking":

> We walked in so pure and bright a light, gilding with withered grass and leaves, so softly and serenely bright, I thought I had never bathed in such a golden flood, without a ripple or murmur to it. The west side of every wood and rising ground gleamed like the boundary of Elysium, and the sun on our backs seemed like a gentle herdsman driving us home at evening. So we saunter toward the Holy Land, till one day the sun shall shine more brightly than ever he has done, shall perchance shine into our minds and hearts, and light up our whole lives with a great awakening light, as warm and serene and golden as on a bankside in autumn. (Thoreau 1990: 142-143)

Such was Thoreau's global vision of America. This was his way to preserve both the self and the world, his own world. If in earlier days he had easily turned the local into global, he had now gone a step further, turning the utmost global into local by envisioning the New Jerusalem on the actual soil of his native New England. He would not let himself step "behind the Eastern horizon" and would eagerly struggle with that threat. He would always insist on the location of his American voice as distinctively American, crisis or not. And this process worked, especially, because of the crisis, since his transcendental vision equalized space relation with self-identification and since it was all justified in existential terms.

Albena Bakratcheva

Works Cited

Baym, Nina, and others, ed. 1989. *The Norton Anthology of American Literature*. 3rd. Ed. Vol. I. New York: W.W.Norton & Company.

Emerson, Ralph Waldo. 1990. *Selected Essays, Lectures, and Poems*. Ed. Robert D. Richardson, Jr. New York: Bantam Books.

————. 1903-1904. *The Complete Works*. Boston and New York: Houghton-Mifflin.

Marx, Leo. 1967. *The Machine in the Garden: Technology and the Pastoral Ideal in America*. New York: Oxford University Press.

McIntosh, James. 1974. *Thoreau as Romantic Naturalist: His Shifting Stance toward Nature*. Ithaca, NY: Cornell University Press.

Miller, Perry. 1961. "Thoreau in the Context of International Romanticism." *New England Quarterly*, 34 (1961): 147-59.

Thoreau, H. D. 1906. *The Journal of Henry David Thoreau*. Ed. Bradford Torrey and Francis H. Allen, 14 Vols. Boston: Houghton-Mifflin.

————. 1963. *Walden*. New York: Washington Square Press.

————. 1990. *The Essays of Henry David Thoreau*. Ed. Richard Dillman. Albany, NY: NCUP.

Home away from Home: The Construction of Germany and America in Elsie Singmaster's *The Lèse-Majesté of Hans Heckendorn* (1905)

1. Introduction

Enclave/Exclave and Diaspora

With the terms "enclave/exclave," used in the context of German-American relations, a constellation is portrayed that implies on the one hand a linear movement of migration, the crossing of borders, and settlement, and on the other hand a constant and non-linear repetition of this movement by people who have settled in this "enclave/exclave" construct. Historically, this movement suggests a fixed origin, usually a nation-state, and a new place of settlement in a different country. Contacts between these two places are upheld and thus, in a way, break the definition of "enclave/exclave" as enclosed territories with clearly defined borders. What this word pair nicely illustrates is that although it describes one space only it does so from two perspectives. For example, Germans migrating to and settling in the United States live in an enclave when compared to the rest of the United States; but they live in an exclave from the perspective of their home country.

A term that, in my opinion, contains both meanings of ex- and enclave and easily allows for border-crossing and inner-American and inter-national relationships is diaspora. While Robin Cohen distinguishes between four types of diaspora, namely "victim, labour, trade, imperial and cultural diasporas" (x), all types share that they can only exist with reference to a homeland (cf. Lehmann), an "imaginary homeland," as Salman Rushdie claims. Stuart Hall argues that

> [t]he homeland is not waiting back there for the new ethnics to rediscover it. There is a past to be learned about, but the past is now seen, and has to be grasped as a history, as something that has to be told. It is narrated. It is grasped through memory. It is grasped through desire. It is grasped through reconstruction. It is not just a fact that has been waiting to ground our identities. ("The Local and the Global" 38)

Yet, as Cohen's term "cultural diaspora," which describes any kind of migratory settlements which are motivated by reasons other than expulsion or deportation, shows, original motifs for emigration do not lose validity although the prerequisites for cultural diaspora are "cultural retention or affirmations" of the original identity (144). Although original identity is indeed carefully preserved in many cases, America is gradually approached, albeit in various and numerous ways. Both enclave/exclave and diaspora geographically situate (im)migrants within the United States, so that America becomes an immediately experienced reality on the one hand but remains an ideological and imagined construct from the perspective of the country of origin. However, from the (im)migrants' perspectives, America—although physically present—remains culturally, socially, and politically distant.

Another important aspect of cultural diaspora is language. What happens to the German language in the encounter with not only American English but other languages as well? In this context, Marc Shell uses the term Germerican which he defines as "a lexically and syntactically polyglot mixture of the English and German languages" (261). Consequently, the idea of German American literature assumes at least three dimensions: it is literature written in German in the United States, but it is also literature written in English by German Americans, i.e., Americans of German descent or with German ancestry. Eventually, it is literature written in any mixture thereof. Additionally, for Stuart Hall, diaspora is defined by "the recognition of a necessary heterogeneity and diversity; by a conception of 'identity' which lives with and through, not despite, difference; by *hybridity*. Diaspora identities are those which are constantly producing and reproducing themselves anew, through transformation and difference" ("Cultural Identity and Diaspora" 402). While "[c]ultures, as well as identities, are constantly being remade," "[d]iasporic cultural identity" (Boyarin/Boyarin 721), as the product of "travelling cultures" (Clifford), implies a mixture of cultures as the only possibility for a continued existence (cf. Boyarin/Boyarin 721). The degree to which literature reflects the exposure of the German language and culture to their new surroundings is an indicator of a process that I suggest to call transculturation. Thus, diaspora is both a geographical and cultural contact zone in which home- and host-countries meet and transculturate on linguistic and cultural levels.

Transculturation

According to Mary Louise Pratt, the term transculturation was originally coined by the Cuban sociologist Fernando Ortíz in the 1940s and was meant to "replace overly reductive concepts of acculturation and assimilation" ("Arts of the Contact Zone" 533) and to ascribe agency to the dominated culture(s). An example of this process of transculturation is the writing of autoethnographic texts, which, according to Pratt, are not "autochthonous forms of expression or self-representation ... Rather they involve a selective collaboration with and appropriation of idioms of the metropolis or the conqueror" ("Arts of the Contact Zone" 531). According to Diana Taylor, transculturation is a process in which all participating cultures are transformed into something new. Françoise Lionnet agrees with the Cuban poet Nancy Morejón who wrote in 1982 that

> *"[t]ransculturation* means the constant interaction, the transmutation between two or more cultural components with the unconscious goal of creating a third cultural entity—in other words, a culture—that is new and independent even though rooted in the preceding elements. Reciprocal influence is the determining factor here, for no single element superimposes itself on another; on the contrary, each one changes into the other so that both can be transformed into a third." (15-16)

This ongoing process of transculturation prevents cultures from ever being clearly defined cultural entities. Germerican is an example of linguistic transculturation. Rather, the *mélange* and interpenetration of cultures leads to transculturality because they go beyond and across traditional cultural boundaries:

> Unsere Kulturen haben de facto längst nicht mehr die Form der Homogenität und Separiertheit, sondern sind weitgehend durch Mischungen und Durchdringungen gekennzeichnet. Diese neue Struktur der Kulturen bezeichne ich, da sie über den traditionellen Kulturbegriff *hinaus-* und durch die traditionellen Kulturgrenzen wie selbstverständlich *hindurchgeht*, als *transkulturell*. (Welsch 51)

This transculturality cannot be referred back to exclusively national or geographical identities or boundaries, but follows for the first time purely cultural processes of exchange (59). Not only does Wolfgang Welsch deny the preservation of an authentic self (52), his transcultural or transculturated self is something completely new, different from, and at some point unaware of its components.

My argument is that as a product of diasporic life, German American literature, with as my example here a short story by Elsie Singmaster, by definition engages with concepts of (inter)nationality and ethnicity, self and other, home and exile, and homeland and host-country, and thus constitutes an attempt at overcoming binary oppositions. Elsie Singmaster's life as a German American in Pennsylvania, and her short story "The Lèse-Majesté of Hans Heckendorn," reveal the movement from an ethnically marginalised position as German immigrants toward a form of transculturation that does not require assimilation and a homogenization of cultures, and that breaks apart the fixed notions of the enclave/exclave dichotomy.

2. Elsie Singmaster (1879-1958)

Elsie Singmaster was born in Schuylkill Haven, Pennsylvania, on August 29, 1879, as the daughter of Dr. John Alden Singmaster, a founder of the local United Lutheran Church and for many years president of the Lutheran Theological Seminary, and Caroline Hoopes Singmaster. Her great-great-great (the number of "greats" varies in the sources) grand-father was the first Lutheran minister ordained in America. "On her mother's side she inherited English, Irish and French traditions; on her father's side, Dutch and German. One of her father's ancestors was a pupil of Martin Luther" (anon.). The language spoken in the family must have been English, but her father's German and religious backgrounds influenced Singmaster strongly. At the age of four, Elsie Singmaster moved with her parents to Macungie, Pennsylvania, then to Brooklyn, New York, and finally, the Singmaster family settled in Allentown, Pennsylvania, where Elsie Singmaster graduated from high school. She earned a B.A. in English from Radcliffe in 1907 and began to publish stories in *Scribner's Magazine*. In 1912, she married the musician Harold Lewars and moved to Harrisburg, Pennsylvania. After the death of her husband in 1915, Singmaster then moved permanently to Gettysburg where she soon began to write about her "eastern Pennsylvania roots" (Gordon xv) and "the German immigrants of her home state" (Gordon xvi). National acclaim for her fiction did not come until the 1920s when several of the most prestigious magazines carried her stories. For her fiction, she received "honorary Litt.D. degrees from Pennsylvania State College, Muhlenberg College, and Gettysburg College (she was the first woman to be so honoured there)" (Kribbs 33). She was very productive up until a few years before her death on September 30, 1958, at a Gettysburg convalescent home. By then, she had "published thirty-eight books and nearly three hundred short stories" (Gordon xiii) which magazines such as the *Atlantic Monthly, Harper's, Century, Scribner's, McClure's, Lippincott's*, and the *Saturday Evening Post* had accepted for print (cf. Overton). These stories were collected in four volumes as *Gettysburg: Stories of the Red Harvest and the Aftermath* (1907, 1913), *Bred in the Bone, and Other Stories* (1925), *Stories of Pennsylvania* (1937), and *Stories to Read at Christmas* (1940).

3. "The Lèse-Majesté of Hans Heckendorn" (1905)

As the many German towns and the concentration of Germans in particular areas such as Pennsylvania and Minnesota show, in the nineteenth century Germans in the United States tended to flock together in communities and tried to preserve ethnic customs and markers such as language, festivities, professions, food, and clothing. Many Germans intended to stay and therefore tried to import, implant, and preserve their culture(s) in newly created (diasporic) little Germanies. Instead of in such a German enclave, Elsie Singmaster situates a recently (im)migrated German family in a multicultural context in her story "The Lèse-Majesté of Hans Heckendorn" (1905). This story was published in the mainstream magazine *Scribner's*, a company which also published some of her other writings such as *Gettysburg* (1907), subsequently republished by Houghton Mifflin Company. While America is only geographically present in the beginning, it is transformed into a political and cultural presence in the course of the story and conflates enclave and exclave perspectives. My claim is that in this story transculturation takes place on the linguistic level in the creation of a form of Germerican and on the cultural level in the symbolic salutation of the American flag by the German immigrant children.

(Im)Migrant America
In "The Lèse-Majesté of Hans Heckendorn," Elsie Singmaster introduces Margaretta and Hans Heckendorn along with their children Elsa, Karl, Ernst, and Hans, who come to the United States from Germany. The family's ethnic German background is manifest in their German language and constant references to their home country which the mother views rather realistically whereas her husband cultivates nostalgic feelings as the homeland-oriented elements of a diasporic imagination and refuses to accept their new life. The Heckendorns, in contrast to many of their fellow country people, do not live in a German community, but have Italian, Irish, and Jewish neighbours. The story is set on "Elliger Street" in an unspecified town or city, populated mostly by immigrants whose names tellingly indicate their places of origin: the Maniagos come from Italy; the Goldsteins must be Jewish; the Haggartys are probably Irish; the Smiths sound American, and their store exhibits "a dozen tiny flags ..." (618).

As in much minority and particularly immigrant literature, education is posited as one of the highest values and also a means of Americanization: "There was little that was German about Hans" (625). Little Hans represents second-generation German Americans whose Germanness has transformed under American influences. But what is American about him? What is American about the community in which the Heckendorns live? It is a multicultural community without a single member who is not from somewhere else. None of these people are originally American, but they all seem to have agreed upon a common language, a common political and national system, as well as common cultural activities without, however, neglecting their respective cultural heritages. Therefore, in Singmaster's story Americanization is not so much adaptation to a pre-given system, but acceptance of a new system to which each member can equally contribute. Father Heckendorn, his views coloured by his nostalgia, sees his neighbours in all their separate ethnicities which they have not given up, but does not see what they all share, namely a new country, a new language, and a new—to some degree—transculturated culture. O'Malley, the "American" policeman and representative of the law, for Heckendorn, is "the august representative of the law" (625), but he is also an Irish immigrant. As in much of women's writing about (im)migration (cf. Willa Cather's *My Ántonia* [1918] and Anzia Yezierska's *The Bread Givers* [1925]), it is the father who is the most resistant to the transition from the old German to the new American life and in the mind constantly performs a nostalgic migration back to an imaginary homeland, linguistically rendered in "Germerican."

Nostalgic Back Migration

Hans Heckendorn, the father of the family, regrets their transplantation and keeps up his national pride in his "'Vaterland'" (618) which he does not want his children to forget, although all of them were born in the United States and they are thus, legally, American citizens. But for Hans Heckendorn "'[d]at makes nosing out. My Vaterland iss also der Vaterland from my children'" (618). He repeats several times his "'It iss no place like der Vaterland'" and "'it iss no country like der Vaterland'" (619). In his nostalgia for the home country, he even includes the emperor: "'It iss no one like der Kaiser'" (619) against whom the President of the United States "'iss nosing worth'" (619), a comment which the policeman O'Malley overhears. The few lines quoted here by Hans Heckendorn reveal his insistence on the preservation of ethnic German traits but also the changes his German has undergone.[1]

---

[1]   Generally, except for the fact that they own a bakery, the family does not give the impression of a ten-year residence in the United States. The fact that they believe that the father has to go to prison because of his derogatory remarks about the president – the lèse-majesté of the title –, which

Heckendorn's language linguistically reveals his strong resistance to the family's new life. Singmaster graphically represents Heckendorn's retention of the German language as interferences with English, which results in a mixture of both languages on the levels of pronunciation, vocabulary, and syntax, thus Germerican. Yet, there are minor inconsistencies in the representation of this mixture. While Heckendorn changes the voiceless /the/ in "nothing" to a voiced /s/, he keeps the /th/ in "worth." Also, why does he use "der Vaterland" instead of the correct neutral article "das Vaterland"? It may be either Heckendorn or Singmaster deriving the article "der" from "der Vater" instead of "das Land." These inconsistencies may point to Singmaster's loss of fluency in German as well as to the fact that an English-speaking readership—which was predominantly that of the mainstream magazines—would not notice the difference.

Heckendorn admits that his wife was the driving force behind their emigration to the United States: "'Ach, it wass de Frau. She was talking always United Shtates, United Shtates. I had no rest, only to come'" (619). Whenever she uses a certain tone with him, he obediently follows. While Hans Heckendorn believes in freedom of speech, she fears that he will go to prison because of his refusal to let his children participate in the Memorial Day parade. In her grief, she speaks German to him "instead of the broken English which she usually spoke" (620). But her speech is given in English, which probably is Singmaster's compromise for her English-speaking readers. Thus, both speak broken English, but her husband's Germerican is clearly a satiric means on the part of the author to poke fun at him because of his resistance. The wife chooses German to scold him, which, rendered in perfect English (although at times old-fashioned even for early twentieth-century standards), leaves the impression of her superior linguistic competence.

Margaretta Heckendorn is stronger and more determined than her husband, but linguistically and culturally she also lacks intercultural

---

he, surely, must have made hundreds of times over the years, or the idea that the police have sent him a warning before taking him away, rather suggest that the family has only recently arrived in the United States or has completely kept apart from any interactions with anyone else except their immediate neighbours. It seems to me that there are slight inconsistencies in the story, which, however, do not prevent Singmaster from making strong and critical statements about an illusionary and nostalgic memory of a Germany of the past, about a strong desire for reverse migration, but also – since the latter is impossible – about Americanization and an American multicultural society.

understanding. She establishes a hierarchy with Americans on top and immigrants on the bottom and freedom of speech only for Americans. Nevertheless, she wants to live in the United States because she knows that her husband's nostalgia is based on illusions only:

> "Thou talkest always of home. What hadst thou there? We could save nothing. In eight years poor little Hans must go into the army, as thou didst go into the army, and by and by Karl would also go into the army, and Ernst. Have we not meat three times a day if we want it? There to have it on Sundays and holidays was fortunate. There we ate always the black bread. Here we have whitebread. Fifty-seven people have been in the shop since the morning. At home there came never more in in a day than twenty." (621)

In his crisis, Hans Heckendorn realizes once more that his family has not yet integrated into American society. He sees them "in the midst of strangers. The fruit-seller at the corner came from Italy, the painter next door was an Irishman, the pawn-broker a little farther down the street was a Jew" (622). They have done business together over the years, but friendships have not developed across ethnic lines. Heckendorn exhibits what Caren Kaplan describes as nostalgia for home and a desire to return:

> Various manifestations of nostalgia participate in Euro-American constructions of exile: nostalgia for the past; for home; for a 'mother-tongue'; for the particulars that signify the experience of the familiar once it has been lost. Such nostalgia is rooted in the notion that it is 'natural' to be at 'home' and that separation from that location can never be assuaged by anything but return. (Kaplan 33)

Performing America

The first activity in the story that suggests a political home in the United States is the salutation of the flag as a national symbol of America and the singing of the national hymn, but the action loses its seriousness and value because the salutation turns out to be a game played by the neighbourhood children. They are watched with longing and weeping eyes by the Heckendorn children, who do not understand their father's prohibition, but feel that it excludes them from the other children's company as well as from the game. The game, however, although innocent in its intentions, takes the shape of a military performance because the children march, take their hats off, and salute the flag, and easily becomes a means of indoctrination without their understanding of the game's symbolic value. Here, the reader can watch in a nutshell America in the making held together through rituals. When at the end of the story, the Heckendorn children walk "[a]t the head of the line ... each one, down to tiny Elsa, topped with a soldier cap and bearing over his shoulder a flag" (625), the loyalty of immigrants to America is revealed in a children's game.

When the policeman O'Malley brings a letter, the family believes it is a warrant for the father to go to prison because of his "lèse-majesté." Because Hans and Margaretta Heckendorn are afraid of what the letter might contain, but mostly because they are illiterate in English, they do not even open the letter. When, after having everything in the house in order, no-one has come to fetch Hans and Margaretta, they finally remember that in the midst of all of these strangers their son Hans has learned to read and write English: "'I can read anything'" (625). He then solves the riddle of the letter as an invitation to a festival.[2] In his relief that he is not being thrown into prison and that friendship is actually being offered to him, Hans Heckendorn exclaims: "'Dis United Shtates iss a great place' ... 'Der Vaterland issn't de only pebble on der beach'" (625). This change of attitude, of course, sounds hypocritical, but his "struggle for an American idiom" (625) is serious. Hans Heckendorn has changed and is now willing to fully immerse himself in the new culture without, however, forgetting his German one. Both Germans and Americans equally become valuable "pebbles on the beach." Language is revealed as the key to and reflection of a culture and intercultural understanding. Language is a means of communication, and once communication is established, enclaves open their borders, diasporic imagination loses significance, and thus the distance between here and there, Germany and America, begins to crumble. The story ends with the neighbourhood children's parade and Heckendorn's "'Hoch, de United Shtates!'" (625).

---

[2] Despite the etymological impossibility, I argue that Singmaster plays with the term "lèse-majesté." Although it obviously refers to the father's abuse of the president's name, if pronounced in German "lèse" can allude to the verb "lesen" and thus refers to Hans Heckendorn Jr.'s ability to read the letter which no-one else in the family is capable of doing. He thus achieves equal status with the policeman and his father who are both described as "majestical" (619, 622).

4. Conclusion

In her story, Elsie Singmaster suggests that the distance between here and there, between host- and homecountries, that dominates early (im)migration, can be overcome by linguistic and cultural competence. By portraying Hans Heckendorn's almost stubborn insistence on glorifying his country of origin, Germany, and by contrasting it with his wife's more realistic attitude, Singmaster exposes ethnic and national affiliations as constructed and nostalgic and therefore as replaceable by new affiliations triggered by hospitable and friendly emotions. New affiliations, however, can only be established through linguistic competence. Thus, for Singmaster, writing (the letter of invitation) and reading (this letter) are essential in bridging the gap between here and there, the Old and the New Worlds. Elsie Singmaster and her story, written mostly in English and Germerican, become mediators between past and present, Germany and America, there and here. With the use of German, Singmaster points to the multilingual origins of America and to the need for an inclusion of languages other than English in a definition of American literature. On a cultural level, she reveals both Germany and America as imagined communities (Anderson) based on emotions. Singmaster uses and overcomes the "enclave/exclave" and diasporic point of view, and has her characters enter a linguistic and cultural process of transculturation.

Carmen Birkle

Works Cited

Anderson, Benedict. 1983. *Imagined Communities: Reflections on the Origin and Spread of Nationalism*. London: Verso.

Anonymous. "Elsie Singmaster." *Wilson Bulletin* 4.1 (September 1929). 250.

Boyarin, Daniel, and Jonathan Boyarin. 1993. "Diaspora: Generation and the Ground of Jewish Identity." *Critical Inquiry* 19.4 (Summer 1993): 693-725.

Clifford, James. 1997. "Diaspora." *Routes: Travel and Translation in the Late Twentieth Century*. Cambridge, MA: Harvard University Press. pp.244-77.

Clifford, James. 1992. "Traveling Cultures." *Cultural Studies*. Ed. Lawrence Grossberg, Cary Nelson, and Paula A. Treichler. New York: Routledge. pp.96-112.

Cohen, Robin. 1997. *Global Diasporas: An Introduction*. Seattle: University of Washington Press.

Gordon, Lesley J. 1907. "Introduction." Elsie Singmaster. *Gettysburg: Stories of Memory, Grief, and Greatness*. 1907. Tuscaloosa: The University of Alabama Press, pp. xiii-xxviii.

Hall, Stuart. 1994. "Cultural Identity and Diaspora." *Colonial Discourse and Post-Colonial Theory: A Reader*. Ed. Patrick Williams and Laura Chrisman. 1993. New York: Harvester Wheatsheaf, pp. 392-403.

Hall, Stuart. "The Local and the Global: Globalization and Ethnicity." *Culture, Globalization and the World-System*. Ed. King, pp. 19-39.

Kaplan, Caren. 1996. *Questions of Travel: Postmodern Discourses of Displacement*. Durham: Duke University Press.

Kribbs, Jayne K. 1981. "Elsie Singmaster (29 August 1879-30 September 1958)." *Dictionary of Literary Biography*. Ed. James J. Martine. Vol. 9: *American Novelists, 1910-1945*. Part 3: *Mari Sandoz-Stark Young*. Detroit, MI: A Bruccoli Clark Book, pp. 32-36.

Lehmann, Sophia. 1998. "In Search of a Mother Tongue: Locating Home in Diaspora." *MELUS* 23.4 (Winter 1998): 101-18.

Lionnet, Françoise. 1989. *Autobiographical Voices: Race, Gender, Self-Portraiture*. Ithaca, NY: Cornell University Press.

Overton, Grant. 1928. "Elsie Singmaster." *The Women Who Make Our Novels*. 1918. Rev. Ed. New York: Dodd, Mead and Company, pp. 310-11.

Pratt, Mary Louise. 1996. "Arts of the Contact Zone." *Ways of Reading: An Anthology for Writers*. Ed. David Bartholomae and Anthony Petrosky. Boston: Bedford Books of St. Martin's Press, pp. 528-42.

Rushdie, Salman. 1991. "Imaginary Homelands" (1982). *Imaginary Homelands: Essays and Criticism 1981-1991*. London: Granta Books, pp. 9-21.

Shell, Marc. 1998. "Hyphens: Between Deitsch and American." *Multilingual America: Transnationalism, Ethnicity, and the Languages of American Literature*. Ed. Werner Sollors. New York: New York University Press, pp. 258-71.

Singmaster, Elsie. 1905. "The Lèse-Majesté of Hans Heckendorn." *Scribner's Magazine* 38.5 (November 1905): 618-25.

The In-between Space: Ekphrasis and Translation in the Poems "Objetos y apariciones," by Octavio Paz and "Objects & Apparitions" by Elizabeth Bishop

Through a system of levels analogous to that of medieval allegory, W.J.T. Mitchell (1980) identifies four ways of conceptualizing space in literature. The first level, a literal one, is the spatial form of the text on the page: "The physical text is an 'order of coexistent data,' and the reading process is a conventional procedure for transforming this spatial form into a temporal one" (282). According to him, this process varies depending on the conventions of each particular language and on the nature of the verbal signs (for instance, if we are dealing with ideograms or an alphabetical system). This literal spatial form becomes particularly important in poetry, where the layout of the lines on the page produces and determines meanings that otherwise would not exist. Obvious examples are poems such as those by Herbert, Apollinaire, Tablada or Paz himself.

The second level of Mitchell's system deals with the world represented, imitated or signified in the work. It is a spatial realm that should be reconstructed in the reader's mind and, perhaps, it is space we first think of when reading the title of our panel "American Space in Mexican Perspectives." Although it is a space recreated in our mind and, as such, would seem to be less "real" than "reality," if we think further, as we will do while analysing Paz's and Bishop's poems, we will see that it doesn't have to be less real, or at least not so obviously less real. This is why, for Mitchell, this second level is also literal. Phenomenology has referred to the way we inhabit the world, the way we relate to objects and the possibility of these relations. Why is it that the idea I have of the room I am in, and talk about to somebody else who is also in it, differs from the one produced by a written description of the same room? Mitchell would say that the difference is not significant and this is why he thinks it is still a literal level.

The third spatial level described by Mitchell includes those elements related to blocks of images, to the plot and the story, to the ways that characters and consciousness develop, to historic or thematic subjects that should be grouped during the reading process to produce a kind of textual map. A poem or a novel does not depend simply on the temporal associations we make while reading but also on the way we relate or establish a kind of principle that would order them or that would give them a sequence. Just remember the gaps or indeterminacies that Mukarovsky, following Ingarden, thought we must fill to make the text coherent, and notice how terms such as "gap" and "fill" are related to space (Vid. Bish 1991, 288-290 and Viñas Piquer 2002, 302).

Mitchell's fourth level deals with the complete meaning of the text. It includes the formal principles governing the way the story is told through time, and the "essence" of the story. What lies behind what we are being told? Why is it told this way and not another? The answers to these questions would determine the poetics of the text. For Mitchell, this is a "metaphorical" spatial level because we are not drawing a diagram of the poetics of the text when we read it. However, this does not mean that the supposed "metaphoricity" weakens the level or makes it less valid. Below we will discuss the power of metaphor as a way of acquiring knowledge.

Mitchell's analysis of literary space is inscribed in a tradition that derives from formalism and started with the work of Joseph Frank. Frank opposed those categorizations that considered verbal language—as a consecutive form and thus depending on time—incapable of dealing with the spatial realm. We should remember Lessing's (1766) prescriptions[1] regarding the idea that a poetic text could not generate a visual image because it could not replicate in words its essential simultaneity. Lessing proposed that the poet should leave the representation of space to the painter or sculptor. Frank's work, and those who followed him, including Mitchell, opposed Lessing's ideas and showed that verbal language also depended on spatial forms because these forms are not separable from time. "We cannot understand space without time," writes Mitchell, who emphasizes the "realms" (space itself) objected to by Lessing and his followers. Mitchell's model, then, is located on the "incorrect" side, the forbidden one, the forgotten, the less important, and thereby gives form to a space of in-betweenness where things that we couldn't see before become visible.

This paper follows a similar path. I want to refer to several concepts considered minor (the representation of unimportant things— such as the marbles and buttons in the poems we are going to be referring to—and see what happens when we focus on them, when we are, as Bryson has written, "looking at the overlooked"(Bryson 1990, 7 and ff). Considering Mitchell's four spatial literary levels I will analyse an ekphrastic poem written by Octavio Paz in 1990 that is derived from Joseph Cornell's boxes, and Elizabeth Bishop's 1994 translation of it.

The disposition of a text on the page is included in Mitchell's first spatial level. In the poems we are dealing with, it is evident that we are talking about a title, a dedication, and individual stanzas that look alike. Just consider stanza three of the two versions:

> *Canicas, botones, dedales, dados,*
> *alfileres, timbres, cuentas de vidrio:*
> *cuentos del tiempo.*

And:

> *Marbles, buttons, thimbles, dice,*
> *pins, stamps, and glass beads:*
> *Tales of the time.*

---

[1]   "If it be true that painting employs wholly different signs or means of imitation from poetry, —the one using forms and colours in space, the other articulate sounds in time,—and if signs must unquestionable stand in convenient relation with the thing signified, then signs arranged side by side can represent only objects existing side by side, or whose parts so exist, while consecutive signs can express only objects which succeed each other, or whose parts succeed each other, in time". As quoted by Mitchell 1986, 95.

A bigger difference appears when we look at stanza eleven. While in Paz's version the second line is longer than the others:
Un peine es un harpa
pulsada por la mirada de una niña
muda de nacimiento,
in Bishop's the lines decrease in extension:
A comb is a harp strummed by the glance
of a little girl
born dumb.
We are going to see that this is a very special stanza because it functions differently from the others. For the moment I want to emphasize the way we identify certain textual markers (the title and the dedication above all) that point to Mitchell's second spatial level: they are references to the boxes of Cornell (to whom the poem is dedicated).

When we read Paz's title, "Objetos y apariciones," we may not think immediately that we are dealing with an ekphrasis, that is, with a verbal representation of a visual representation. However, if we remember the dedication, the first stanza becomes a direct reference to Cornell's work ("Hexaedros de madera y de vidrio/ apenas más grandes que una caja de zapatos./ En ellos caben la noche y sus lámparas.") If we look back at the title of the poem, we realize that it is describing the ways in which the boxes work: some are combinations of objects associated by a common subject, others by a specific form, and the result is a weave of affinities that is almost intangible: the "apparitions" of Paz's title.

To clarify how these associations work, let's consider a box by Cornell called "Medici Slot Machine."(Ades, 1990) The box emphasizes the geometrical similarities between a target placed on the circular glass panel at the bottom of the box and the compass located behind it. At the same time we can find a thematic association because both objects are related to the notion of direction or goal: the map located at the back of the box suggests the same idea. The game pieces, the dice and marbles in the lower spaces to the right and left sides of the target and the compass, strengthen the sense of play triggered by the title of the box. The dice have been covered with faces that are repeated throughout the box; identical images that nonetheless vary because they are located at different distances from the frame or from the vertical lines of the target in the glass. But can we be certain of anything else? Do the reproductions of faces have a clearly well defined, unambiguous meaning? Can we do more than simply find some associations among the parts? They are all reproductions of other reproductions, but do the repetitions bring into mind the objects represented in slot machines? Are we being told a specific story? Is there some kind of narration? Or is it that we can only find affinities? Most of Cornell's boxes work through affinities like these ones: marbles, thimbles, dice, stamps, balloons, maps, soap bubbles, constellations and grasshoppers are subtly and intuitively associated; as I have said, the associations are the apparitions mentioned in Paz's title.

The third spatial level described by Mitchell can be seen if we consider that the poem itself may be read as a Cornell's box; each stanza is formed by independent, juxtaposed elements that produce an apparition; memory and the poetic voice weave echoes together; shadowless ladies play hide-and-seek; the fire of a mirror and the water of a stone interact; objects play with the laws of identity and we hear the solos of actresses and singers from the late nineteenth century. However, there is a stanza that deviates from this way of working, stanza eleven. It is a stanza fundamental to understanding the distance between Paz and Cornell; it also emphasizes a kind of progression in the way the previous stanzas function: a comb stops being a comb and becomes a harp ("se aligera de su nombre"). In the following stanzas, "the apparitions are manifest" and become "visible for a moment." Here, we can trace the bigger difference between Cornell's aesthetics and Paz's poetics (the fourth spatial level described by Mitchell).

Cornell shows the fragility of the relations with and among the objects of the world. In his boxes, things are always alienated from each other; they are always other, and the artist tries to convey that alienation, that otherness. His work juxtaposes "worlds" that are scarcely touching, and his intention is related to the expression of such intangibility. But in Paz's poem, something very different happens. The metaphors mentioned before ("agua dormida en el ágata," "fuego enterrado en el espejo," "el teatro de los espíritus") require closer relations; their affinities, though momentary, are made manifest. Paz's metaphors become bridges, means of reconciliation, figures of possibility for the space of Mitchell's second level, that is, of Cornell's boxes. After reading his poem we really feel that it is a representation of the boxes. Paz is searching for control of his language and the world; Cornell, on the contrary, strives to represent the lack of this possibility.

Let's see what we can conclude if we go now to Bishop's translation.

The translation seems to be very close to Paz's original and Bishop herself mentions that "every once in a while something seems to go into English [...] The metre is almost exactly the same. Nothing had to come out different"(As quoted by Starbuck 2003, 1). From this comment we may conclude that what she is looking for in a translation is similarity: the same title, the same dedication, the same number of stanzas, similar images and metaphors and, where they change, a formal reason related to the morphology or the syntax of both languages. For instance, if in Spanish we have, "hechos con los desechos de cada momento," and in English, "refuse of every moment, used," the difference may be explained by looking at the similarity between "hechos" and "desechos" and "refuse" and "used." This similarity reminds us of the "apparitions" that, in the case of the boxes, derives from the subtle relations of their components.

Other times, Bishop changes certain lines to obtain stanzas that function as the ones in Paz's poem and Cornell's boxes. Therefore, as the similarity between "cuentas de vidrio" and "cuentos del tiempo" was impossible to translate literally, she writes "tales of the time" and "beads of glass," and she tries to compensate the lack of similarity in another part of the poem where she uses the ambiguity of "commit" in English: "'One has to commit a painting,' said Degas, / 'the way one commits a crime.'" The Spanish "hacer" seems not such a good choice as "commit"—and more so if we consider some of the associations found in Cornell's boxes. Something very similar happens with the Spanish "vaso de encuentro de las reminiscencias," in a stanza where the other two lines ended with a rhyme between "visiones" y "constelaciones." Bishop compensates for the phonetic difference between "visions" and "constellations" by writing "condensation" and "conversations." The "vase where reminiscences met" becomes a "condensation flask for conversations," an image that can be immediately understood if we consider Cornell's boxes. Here, Bishop emphasizes more the form of the stanza than its meaning. The semantic weight of "memory" and "remains" that makes Paz's "reminiscencias" so touching is lost, but is there another possibility if Bishop's idea was to keep the echo of rhyme?

I am interested in getting to the most noticeable difference between Bishop's translation and Paz's poem. I am referring to stanza six. Writing "Where things hurry away from their names" is not the same as "Donde las cosas se aligeran de su nombre." The wonderful and surrealistic image of things flying, escaping from their names, would contradict what we have just mentioned about the way Cornell includes objects in his boxes. To lighten, to feel that one is not carrying a burden anymore, is different from feeling the need to abandon that burden. If we consider what we have just mentioned about the way the metaphor works in Paz's poetry, we would see that a comb hurried away from its name and becomes the harp of a little girl. In Cornell's work this would never happen[2]; rather, his main goal is to keep the intangibility of the links between things. In Paz' work, according to Bishop's translation, things finally escape from their names and find another one thanks to the power of metaphors. The English version continues the movement started by Paz and shows the distance that separates Bishop's own work from Paz's and Cornell's.

So translation becomes a metatext for Paz's poem: a critical comment that points out several characteristics of Paz's ekphrasis and shows us how it shapes meaning. "Objects and Apparitions" make us notice the very process that produced it, and the selections that Paz makes. Here, and considering Sherry Simon's ideas (1996, 23), translation is a metonymic process (and not metaphoric, as it is usually considered to be) because it is a continuation of the meaning that approximates the "original." In Bishop's translation we discover the way the translator reads what he/she translates, and how he/she sets in motion the previously articulated meanings in a new web of discourses and social texts (a new space) implicit in the very act of translation.

The system of spatial levels described by Mitchell helps us to analyse Paz's and Bishop's poems. The path followed by Mitchell, among others, that focuses on the forbidden realm of space helps him to realize how literature depends on such a realm. In a similar way, the analysis of an ekphrasis, a form often considered to be a mere ornament, helps us to understand the aesthetics of the visual work referred to by the poem, and the poetics of the poem itself. Finally, translation, another overlooked form, shows us the distance between these specific works of art and establishes itself as a critical comment, a continuation of a process already set in motion.

Irena Artigas Albarelli

---

[2] "on way to 9:22 the gulls overhead brought a strong evocation of the house on the hill.. .a "link"—the "reassurance" and "continuity" of a thread so tenuous, so hard at times to keep hold of (or perhaps to communicate to others is what I mean)". Cornell, as quoted by Ades, Dawn, 1990.

Bibliography

Ades, Dawn. 1990. "The Trascendental Surrealism of Joseph Cornell" in McShine Kynaston; *Joseph Cornell.* Munich: The Museum of Modern Art/ Prestel, pp. 15-39.

Bishop, Elizabeth. 1994. *The Complete Poems 1927-1979.* New York: The Noonday Press/ Farrar Straus and Giroux. (Objects & Apparitions, 275-276).

Bryson, Norman. 1990. *Looking at the Overlooked. Four Essays on Still Life Painting.* Cambridge, Massachusetts, Harvard University Press.

Ibsch, Elrud. 1991. "La recepción literaria" in Angento, Marc et al, *Teoría literaria.* México: Siglo veintiuno. (Translated by Isabel Vericot Núé).

Mitchell, W.J.T. 1980. "Spatial Form in Literature: Toward a General Theory" in *The Language of Images.* Mitchell, ed. Chicago and London: The University of Chicago Press, pp.271-300.

————. 1986. "Space and Time. Lessing's *Laocoon* and the Politics of Genre" in *Iconology. Image, Text, Ideology.* Chicago: The University of Chicago Press, p. 95.

Paz, Octavio. 1990. *Obra poética (1935-1988).* México, Seix Barral, pp. 626-628.

Simon Sherry. 1996. *Gender in Translation. Cultural Identity and the Politics of Transmission.* London and New York: Routledge.

Starbuck, George. 2003. "The Work!: A Conversations with Elizabeth Bishop" in *Ploughshares* (10/2/03).

Viñas Piquer, David. 2002. *Historia de la crítica literaria.* Barcelona: Ariel.

Reconfiguring Female Characters of the American West: Marilynne Robinson's *Housekeeping*

"Questing, a woman dares to reinvent herself"
— Dana A. Heller

1. The Framing Argument

In *Housekeeping* (1980), Marilynne Robinson reconfigures the Western female character, taking into account the myths of the American West, the works of the nineteenth century American writers and philosophers, as well as the Biblical tradition.[1] Her text acquires a palimpsestic quality in which various sources are juxtaposed. Such literary themes as loneliness and adventure that have formerly been explored in connection with male heroes are correlated by the author with female protagonists. In this direction, Martha Ravits' analysis of *Housekeeping* points to its double task of responding to the "mainstream of native patriarchal literature and to the swelling current of writing—British and American—by and about women" (644).

---

[1] For a list of bibliographical works, see Lisa Durose "Marilynne Robinson: A Bibliography." *ANQ* 10. 1 (Winter 1997): 31-47.

The framing argument of my discussion is that Robinson writes in and against a literary and cultural tradition so that *Housekeeping* can be interpreted as a postmodern text that self-consciously reflects or destabilizes former concepts institutionalized by the canons of Western literature. Female characters of the American West are reconsidered in a double process that presupposes the displacement of an androcentric literary canon, as much as the repositioning of women's peripheral roles in this canon. Robinson's characters are models of margin empowering, and their transience functions as a form of ontological slipperiness, as a way of subverting any conformist position ascribed to women.

Constructing a world that had "the feeling of femaleness about it," the writer correlates the American West with women's experience, almost to the exclusion of the male heroes in the novel (Robinson, quoted in Schaub, 231).[2] To use Nina Baym's definition, Robinson's story appears as a "melodrama of beset womanhood," since her characters no longer reproduce the model of the woman as a static figure, the pillar around which the whole home gravitates and the refuge for the male hero. The main figures of *Housekeeping*, Ruth and Sylvie,[3] are endowed with transient[4] or polytropic[5] identities revealed by their great propensity to move and challenge the restrictions of their own society. Physical and mental mobility, freedom and nonconformity that have formerly represented basic features of the Western man are now fundamentally related to Robinson's characters who find themselves at odds with their community.

---

[2]   In *Housekeeping* the male and female spheres remain polarized, as the author peoples her fictional world mostly with female characters (except for the grandfather, the owner of a boat, and the sheriff). If male figures appear in the novel, they are present through references to an outstanding literary tradition illustrated by Emerson, Thoreau and Melville.

[3]   Ruth's name has a number of connotation, as Maggie Galehouse observes: "The word *ruth* dates back to Middle English and was used to denote "passion, contrition, sorrow, or regret" (the only form of the word in common language was "ruthless") (120). At the same time, Sylvie's name is also significant, as it comes from the Latin word *silva*, "wood" that draws our attention to her close relationship to nature.

[4]   The etymology of the word "transient" is relevant to our discussion; it comes from Lat. *transire*, "to pass by, to go across".

[5]   In Greek, *poly* + *trepo* means "to turn in a variety of directions." Hence, the polytropic identity presupposes not only an existential mobility, but also the capacity to turn away or deviate from a central axis, i.e. from social, religious and moral standards of behaviour.

The characters' ability to travel in space should be associated with their personal attitudes towards challenging patriarchal ideals. For them, freedom is achieved through distance from the world. This implies shifting away from a general pattern of understanding values and rethinking them in order "to acknowledge that there are really thousands of different ways of thinking about things" (Robinson, in Schaub, 242). Marginality and loneliness attain positive connotations as two protagonists exemplify the independent, unconventional and self-sufficient woman.[6] Thus, the female character that has formerly been represented as "an accessory for the male's heroic adventure" or as the "feminine side of the hero" (Campbell 116), assumes in *Housekeeping* the primary role in the process of initiation.

2. A Palimpsestic Novel

Robinson purposefully uses mythical, literary, philosophical and religious sources incorporating them in a novel about the West. She repeatedly states that one of her intentions is to show to the broad American audience that "the West is not intellectually crippling," having a cultural specificity of its own (1993, 165). At the same time, she has in mind another motivation even broader. She wants to be part of a "cultural conversation," which includes the authors of the nineteenth century—a time which she considers to be underestimated.[7] Significantly, *Housekeeping* was written in accordance with Robinson's model of "an ideal book," which would not only draw on the work of an outstanding tradition, but would also "galvanize all the resources that novels have, the first being language, what languages sounds like and how it's able to create simulations of experience in the reader" (Robinson, in Schaub, 235). The myths of the American West and American authors such as Herman Melville, Ralph Waldo Emerson, Henry David Thoreau, and Emily

---

[6] James Maguire suggests that "whether they are seen as New American Eves or as female versions of traditional male American heroes or as victims of abandonment, Ruth and Sylvie achieve self-reliance, not needing or seeking male assistance, but bearing no ill will toward men, either" (254).

[7] In a 1992 interview, Robinson remarked the existence of "a rupture in the conversation of this culture," since "all sorts of things that were brought up in the early conversation were dropped without being resolved," and "nothing of comparable interest has taken their place" (in Hedrick 1)

Dickinson are reevaluated by the author from the perspective of the main character-narrator, a twelve-year-old girl who grows up in Idaho, in a town symbolically called Fingerbone.

The character's transient identity is deeply correlated with the myth of the American frontier. Frederick Jackson Turner's theory as expounded in his 1893 speech, "The Significance of the Frontier in American History," explains the American development and individuality through their relation to "the existence of an area of free land, its continuous recession, and the advance of the American settlement westward" (81). When this area no longer existed, movement became an interior quest. This is the case of the two protagonists in *Housekeeping*, whose wandering existence indicates an inner fluidity and ability to explore new psychological/geographical zones. Hence, Robinson's task is to reassess the old Western myth of the lone traveller from the female character perspective.

Moreover, the novel can be connected not only with the myth of the frontier, but also with two other types of myths circulating in the American literature. Richard Slotkin points to "the myth of regeneration through violence" and the myth of "the heroic quest" as essential components underlying American cultural mythology (5, 10). The strong interconnection between the two myths appears in *Housekeeping*, where Ruth and Sylvie have to pass through a violent moment of rupture with their social environment in order to accomplish what Slotkin called "the initiation into a higher level of existence and power" (10).

As Robinson confesses in an interview with Thomas Schaub, she is aware of her Western mythological heritage and of the stereotypes that circulate in literature about the American West (231). She stresses that the myths of the old West emphasize the image of the male protagonist, while they distort or exclude the female figures. Two interrelated questions should be raised here. Does Robinson create her female characters simply by transferring upon them the attributes of the male heroes? Or does she undergo an archeology of her own thinking, in which the Western *Weltanschauung* is redefined with a focus on women's existence? More or less explicitly, Robinson offers an answer by constructing female characters whose transience becomes a mode of relatedness to the ever-shifting notion of "home." Unlike most male heroes, her characters do not try to dominate their natural or social milieu, and they discover new ways of self-empowerment by transforming the other space into a home of meanings.[8]

In this light, the best intertextual example is provided by the comparison of *Housekeeping* with *Moby-Dick*—a novel in which Ahab's mesmerizing power aims at controlling external nature.[9] If in Melville's grand opus the forces of the universe embodied in the image of the Leviathan-whale seem to be hostile towards humanity, in Robinson's novel the osmotic relationship with nature becomes an integrating part of the main character's life. Indeed, Robinson admits that she wrote *Housekeeping*, a book with and about women, as a counterpart to Herman Melville's *Moby-Dick*, a novel dominated almost exclusively by male characters (in Schaub 234).[10]

Deeply rooted in the theme of the quest, both *Moby-Dick* and *Housekeeping* have the similar function of a *Bildungsroman*. They present the growth of the heroes by means of an initiating rite of passage, in which characters' spiritual exploration is accomplished in a voyage away from social borders. Still, the two novels differ. On the one hand, Ishmael embodies "the prototype of a new democratic man: exuberant, uncompromised, absurdist, humanitarian; delighting in the speculative play of mind upon fact and redeeming the world from emptiness through his inexhaustible energy" (Elliott 436). On the other hand, Ruth is the epitome of the independent female character, whose playful, explorative, questioning intelligence reshapes not only woman's position in society, but also her perception of nature.

A special merit of Robinson's novel consists in its double affiliation to both the optimist (Emerson, Thoreau) and the negative (Melville)

---

[8]   This idea is advocated by Sheila Ruzychi O'Brien who specifies that Robinson "builds on the foundation of traditional fiction and film Westerns, creating protagonists who are outsiders, yet she makes her central characters female drifters who do not try to dominate other characters or their environment" (173).

[9]   In the interview with Thomas Schaub, Robinson maintains: "The book I admire most in the world is *Moby-Dick*, after the Bible, of course" (234).

[10]   Dana A. Heller argues that "the reinvention of Melville's Ishmael wrests power from the father's sphere and affirms identity in a voice that is at once distinctly American and distinctly female" (96).

tradition of the American Renaissance.[11] She weaves together the threads of this double influence, skilfully re-inscribing women's existence from an innovative perspective, which is connected to the past. Drawing upon what Matthiessen called "the optative mood," Robinson reconsiders the thinking of Emerson and Thoreau by exploring such concepts as experience, nature, independence and personal truth. Singular experience, which is the key to the Emersonian philosophical view, becomes a leitmotif in *Housekeeping*. The transcendentalists' credo in the power of the individual who disobeys social conventions is exemplified by Ruth's deviation from the Procrustean patterns of society.[12]

Through its association with *Walden*, the novel can be circumscribed within a pastoral tradition. This tradition started with Vigil, in his *Eclogues*, but both Thoreau and Robinson made their own American version of the pastoral.[13] The similarity between Robinson's and Thoreau's understanding of nature appears in the episode when the two sisters are caught by night in the forest. The precarious shelter they build near the lake seems to be a parodic, diminished version of Thoreau's cabin built near Walden Pond. As in *Walden*, Robinson creates an in-between topography, a space that is neither real (i.e. Concord, Massachusetts, or Fingerbone, Idaho), nor the ideal Arcadia of Virgil. In this Thoreauvian space, the two sisters interpret the sounds of nature differently. While Lucille can never accept that her physical and mental boundaries may be overrun, Ruth's behaviour is quite opposite, pointing to her sympathetic communication with the surroundings:

> I simply let the darkness in the sky become coextensive with the darkness in my skull and bowels and bones. Everything

---

[11]   Even if F. O. Matthiessen did not include Emily Dickinson as part of his *American Renaissance*, I shall later take her into account in my analysis, as I consider her relevant to Robinson's construction of female subjectivity.

[12]   The novel sends the reader to Emerson's reflections in "Self-Reliance": "Society everywhere is in conspiracy against the manhood of every one of its members. Society is a joint-stock company, in which the members agree, for the better securing of his bread to each shareholder, to surrender the liberty and culture of the eater (450).

[13]   Thoreau succeeds in bringing a new element into this tradition, as he not only writes about nature, but he also lives in nature; he is playing the shepherd's venerable role. As Leo Marx states, Thoreau "refuses to say whether the book is an explicit guide for living or an exercise in imaginative perception... Thoreau had moved to the pond so that he might make a symbol of his life" (380).

that falls upon the eye is apparition, a sheet dropped upon the world's true workings (116).

It is important to notice here that Robinson does more than just re-appropriating the transcendentalist conceptual framework. Not only Emerson's and Thoreau's use of ideas fascinates her, but also their understanding of language and consciousness. In a 1984 *New York Times Book Review*, she discusses the nineteenth century authors: "Nothing in literature appeals to me more than the rigor with which they fasten on problems of language and consciousness—bending form to their purposes, ransacking ordinary speech and common experience... in the act of finding what will suffice" (30). What she admires most in the transcendentalists' work is their capacity to use language to "refresh things," to fabricate new models of understanding reality. This is why, when she writes, she focuses both on Ruth's mental process as a character, and on her own writing process as an author. "What I was doing was testing my method, finding what I could make it yield" (Schaub 241).

The transcendentalists' (lack of) method is employed by Robinson as a means of en-visioning and re-visioning reality. Ruth thinks via associations, linking various aspects of existence by means of an "emotional logic" (Robinson, in Schaub, 242). Her "emotional logic" is not exclusive and does not function according to the pattern "either-or," but to the model "and-and," thus connecting various elements of existence (Miroiu 11). Her thoughts produce the plot of the novel, while she creates analogies or speculates. As the Latin etymology of the word "speculum" (meaning "mirror") suggests, Ruth is the one who holds a mirror in front of diverse aspects of reality, which get interrelated and reflect each other. Therefore, Robinson's style has the poetic quality of melting together—by means of paradox and analogy—different, if not divergent, faces of existence. Making use of the transcendentalist philosophy, she expresses in *Housekeeping* her idea that women may possess a philosophical discourse of their own, one which would not follow a finite number of rules.[14]

Robinson has no anxiety of influence as she rewrites the Western female character by reconsidering the American literary tradition and

---

[14]   In *Philosophy and the Maternal Body*, Michelle Boulous Walker argues that women have a marginal place in philosophy, a place that she defines using Le Doeuff's terms as "enclosed space/interiority" (15).

placing it in connection with the Biblical one. The intertextual beginning of the novel ("My name is Ruth") not only echoes *Moby-Dick*'s opening ("Call me Ishmael"), but also invokes a powerful model of female displacement present in the Biblical story.[15] The novel points to the relationship between Ruth and her mother-in-law, Naomi, as "examples of loyalty, friendship and commitment—to God and to each other."[16] The Biblical key verse contains Ruth's faithful vow, in spite of the fact that she is a Moabite and a stranger to Naomi: "Intreat me not to leave thee, or to return from following after thee: for whither you goest, I will go; and where thou lodgest, I will lodge: thy people shall be my people, and thy God my God" (*King James Version*, Book of Ruth, 1.16).[17] The old story of Ruth is reconfigured in *Housekeeping* in a Western American scenario. The bond between Ruth and Naomi is parallelled by that between Ruth and Sylvie. A Naomi-figure and a substitute of a mother, Sylvie serves also as an initiator for Ruth, just as in the Biblical story. While Ruth remains faithful to her surrogate mother, Lucille reenacts the departure of Or'pah, the other daughter-in-law. Though *Housekeeping* has common points with the Old Testament story, Robinson leaves it open-ended. Whereas the Biblical Ruth settles down (following Naomi's advice and getting married to Boaz), Robinson's Ruth departs with Sylvie and starts a life of transience. Robinson destabilizes the Biblical pattern, reversing it. In the Bible, Ruth leaves behind her homeless status in order to be the wife of one of the most important men in the Jewish community. In contrast, in *Housekeeping*, the initially settled existence of Ruth and

---

[15]   Ruth's and Naomi's story is underscored by loss, as both women are homeless and their beloved ones have recently died. Naomi has lost her sons, while her daughters-in-law (Ruth and Or'pah) have lost their husbands. With no sons to take care of her, Naomi's position as a widow in the ancient world was precarious, since widows had no means of support, and they were almost always poverty stricken. Still, Naomi's attitude shows selflessness and care for her daughters-in-law. While she decides to move to her native country, Israel, she urges Ruth and Or'pah to remain in Moab and get remarried in order to start their lives anew. In spite of the advice given by her mother-in-law, Ruth begs Naomi to take her to Bethlehem.

[16]   See *Life Application Biblie. New International Version*. Tyndale House Publishers, INC. Wheaton, Illinois, 1991, p. 422.

[17]   As Nehama Aschkenasy remarks, "Ruth makes it clear that in choosing to return with Naomi she has not only made a decision about the person with whom she wants to stay, but also about the faith that she wishes to adopt. In her dialogue with Naomi, Ruth also starts a dialogue with Naomi's God" (116).

Sylvie ends abruptly when they burn down their house, depart from Fingerbone, and become wanderers. As the characters are "unhoused," their strong emotional bond operates as an alibi for an absent home whose significance is projected upon a number of unfamiliar spaces. While in the Bible marriage secures a place in the community for both Ruth and her mother-in-law, in *Housekeeping* the emotional attachment between Ruth and Sylvie serves as a catalyst that erodes the stable notion of family, as well as its established place in the social order.

To summarize, Robinson constructs complex female characters by taking into account the mythology of the American West, the works of Melville, Emerson and Thoreau, and the powerful significance of *The Bible*.[18] In consequence, the writer shows the importance of assuming one's past, reshaping and reliving it in connection to her characters' identity, an idea that also appears in her book, *The Death of Adam. Essays on Modern Thought*:

> I propose that we look at the past again, because it matters, and because it has so often been dealt with badly… By definition, it is all the evidence we have about ourselves, to the extent that it is recoverable and interpretable, so surely its complexities should be scrupulously preserved (4).

3. Subverting the Model of the Nuclear Family

Robinson speaks in her article, "The Way We Work, The Way We Live," of the impossibility of imposing a strict definition on such an "elusive" concept as family (1998, 823, b). To prepare the ground for the transient identity that Ruth will assume, the author places her in an unusual family background. The three generations presented in the novel destabilize the patriarchal representation of family, rethinking the concept of motherhood from the perspective of the Western American context. The present analysis of the family connections and the representation of motherhood in *Housekeeping* takes into account a number of

---

[18]   Robinson will make room for other Biblical allusions (the fall from Paradise, the Flood, the story of Noah, and the image of Lot's wife), as well as mythological references (the myth of Carthage and of Orpheus and Eurydice).

critical theories generated by Nancy Chodorow, Dana Heller, and Julia Kristeva. In addition, the characters' transient identity will be further discussed in relation to the mobile structure of the house, an idea present in analyses by Thomas Foster, Paula Geyh, Elizabeth Meese, and others.

From the beginning of *Housekeeping*, the pattern of the nuclear family is disrupted. The succession of women who take care of Ruth and Lucille illustrates a matrilineal genealogy that undermines the patriarchal model, excluding the male figures. Ruth starts recollecting her family memories, initiating a retrospective narrative, a story of events placed in a vague *illo tempore*: "I grew up with my younger sister, Lucille, under the care of my grandmother, Mrs. Sylvia Foster, and when she died, of her sisters-in-law, Misses Lily and Nona Foster, and when they fled, of her daughter, Mrs. Sylvia Fisher" (3).

Bringing several relatives to take care of the two sisters, the writer discloses that the notion of the domestic sphere can be reconsidered and that "the idea of mothering can be shared by several people" (Chodorow 75). Robinson is accordingly aware of the emotional (not necessarily the biological) attachment that makes a family.[19] In *Housekeeping* she dislocates the idea of family and mothering by getting rid of the biological mother and replacing her with a number of surrogate versions. In this way, she suggests that the mother-daughter relationship is socially and personally constructed. She also advocates the mutability of the concept of motherhood, its flexibility and the fact that it can be reshaped by personal criteria.

Ruth gets engaged in a process of searching for her lost mother, "a feminized quest towards a self-naming or self-mapping" (Heller 93). For Ruth, memory is associated with a sense of loss, while recollection represents an attempt to restore the loss through a therapeutic process of anamnesis. Plunging into her family history, blowing the dust off its past effigies, Ruth illuminates disjointed parts of her genealogy, which she attempts to place together in an endless search for her unfathomable roots. One of the few male images in the novel is a tricky figure. Edmund

---

[19]   Robinson remarks: "One's family are those toward whom one feels loyalty, and obligation, and/or from whom one derives identity, and/or to whom one gives identity, and/or with whom one shares habits, tastes, stories, customs, memories. This definition allows for families of circumstance and affinity as well as kinship, and it allows also for the existence of people who are incapable of family, though they may have parents and siblings and spouses and children (Robinson 1998, 823, b).

Foster, the grandfather, is a watchman with the railroad, and therefore connected with the transient identity that his granddaughter will later adopt. He leaves the flat perspective of his "sod house" in the Middle West,[20] and moves to Fingerbone, Idaho, a place that seduces him through its mountains. When he takes the train and descends in Fingerbone, he reaches a world that he has already imagined and copied in his drawings—a realm endowed with an ideal status. In spite of his love for the heights, his sudden death symbolizes a descent into the depths, as the train "slid into the water like a weasel sliding off a rock" (6). Years later, in a journey over the same lake, Ruth meditates upon the imprint her grandfather's travel has left on her destiny: the mountains and the children painted by the grandfather signify for Ruth an ultimate model of understanding the world. From a semiotic perspective, Ruth gets engaged in a quest in which she searches for the real correspondent of the imagined referent established by her ancestor.[21]

Robinson subverts the image of the unitary family not only by excluding the male figures from the novel, but also by fabricating different versions of surrogate mothers. Discussing the three types of mother figures in *Housekeeping*, Thomas Foster observes that they correspond to the three generations of women differentiated by Julia Kristeva. The first type is exemplified by the girl's mother, who is associated with Kristeva's first generation that points to "an entry into history made on masculine terms, an appropriation of the detached position of the male subject" (Foster 88). The girls' mother discards traditional feminine or maternal features; she plays the role of an estranged mother from her own children, so that it seems that the motif of the stranger underlines the family

---

[20] The description of the "sod house" is symbolical: "A house dug out of the ground with windows just at eye level, so that from without, the house was a mere mound, no more a human stronghold than a grave, and from within, the perfect horizontality of the world in that place foreshortened the view so severely that the horizon seemed to circumscribe the sod house and nothing more" (3). The ambivalence of the construction as both house and tomb relates it with both the world of the living that of the dead. Moreover, the house is connected with an element representing the absolute—the horizon—placed in contrast with what is insignificant and earthly. Its paradox appears in the fact that its closeness to the earth also means proximity to the transcendent sphere. For an interesting description of the "sod-house" during the second part of the nineteenth century, see *The Sod-House Frontier 1854-1890*, by Dick Everett.

[21] As in Margaret Atwood's novel, *Surfacing*, the hidden existence of the beloved ones who are dead emerges to the textual surface—a symbolical lake represented by the depth of a page.

relationships in *Housekeeping*.[22]

The second type of femininity represented by the grandmother "performs a narrative function equivalent to the rejection of official history that characterizes the second movement in Kristeva's model" (Foster 88). She is the most stable character in the novel, since she has spent most of her life in Fingerbone. She is apparently the embodiment of "the nineteen century Victorian image of the quiet, obedient mother" (Bernard 14). Nevertheless, her figure becomes *ambivalent* through the tension created between her actual deeds and her thoughts. Even if her existence is circumscribed to the domestic sphere, she thinks of it metaphorically by comparing it to a road, so that her vision of life is akin to a process of accumulation during a cyclical journey.

Finally, the third generation is embodied by Sylvie, who combines the attitudes of the first and the second types. She has a composite personality, as she resembles both the girls' mother and grandmother.[23] Placing Sylvie in *loco parentis*, Robinson challenges the image of the stable mother. Negotiating between past and present, Sylvie serves as an alternative model of motherhood, able to initiate Ruth into her family's past and into her own future. In a double process of displacement and replacement, Ruth's perception of Sylvie undertakes a subtle metamorphosis. Sylvie is gradually associated with a mother figure, so that Ruth reshapes her representation of her mother, dislocating her own memory of motherhood and adopting a new version presented by Sylvie. Nancy Chodorow points that "the infant comes to define itself as a person

---

[22]   Helen's name is also significant, as it sends the reader to the ancient Greek heroine, who was so famous for her beauty that was transformed into an abstraction. Ruth perceives this abstract, remote quality of her mother, who always ignores her daughters and is ready to converse with an invisible presence. In addition, Helen's cold-hearted attitude towards her daughters is symbolically reflected by her family name—Stone—that she took from her husband.

[23]   Sylvie's presence in the novel is prefigured in the conversation between the two aunts, Lily and Nona, who also act as surrogate mothers. A peculiar couple, the aunts can be seen as one entity, a plain character, a parody of the middle class image of spinsterhood. Their hilarious dialogue, their stichomythia functions as an ancient Greek chorus, bringing in the novel the perspective of the commonsensical mind, the gossip circulating in the town about such a strange family history. Thus, they create a horizon of expectation upon which Sylvie's sketchy portrait is projected before her appearance in the story. Their disapproving attitude defines Sylvie as a childless woman, a transient, and a migrant worker: 'Well, how about the little one, Sylvie?' There was a clucking of tongues. 'At least she doesn't have children.' 'So far as we know, at least.' 'An itinerant.' 'A drifter' (31).

through its relationship" to the mother, "by internalizing the most important aspects of their relationship" (78). Taking into account Chodorow's view, Ruth who no longer has a biological mother, perceives Sylvie as a mother and a mediator between herself and the world.

Sylvie enters the novel wearing a mysterious aura. Her first words are symbolically addressed to her dead mother in a note that stresses her itinerant status: "Dear mother, I may still be reached c/o Lost Hills Hotel, Billings, Montana. Write soon. I hope you are well. S" (39). The destination where she wants to be reached, Lost Hills Hotel, bears a significant name that suggests her ubiquity, her elsewhereness. Ruth's first impression of Sylvie associates her with the transient world: "Sylvie had her coat on and appeared to be very transient" (51). Significantly, her favourite means of transportation is the train. For Sylvie, the homeless drifter, the train provides an itinerant refuge, as well as an excellent vehicle of effacement, where she does not have to claim any status or identity among its fluctuant community of passengers.

Robinson envisions Sylvie as "an unredeemed transient" who transforms Ruth into a transient as well.[24] The girl's remarks refer to Sylvie's paradoxical desire to assume a maternal role, while not giving up her drifting mode of existence: "Clearly our aunt was not a stable person" (82); "It seemed to me that if she could remain transient here, she would not have to leave" (103). Sylvie undermines the image of a mother who dominates her children or is dominated by them, as she does not see herself as a "victim," "martyr" or "unfree woman" (Rich, in Bassin, 236). Tension is created between the children's preconceived idea of motherhood and Sylvie's intriguing attitude, between the institution of motherhood and Sylvie's experience of mothering.

At this point, it is essential to remark that in *Housekeeping* not only the model of the patriarchal family disintegrates, but also the stable configuration of the house, which seems to be contaminated by the transient condition of its inhabitant. The mobility of Sylvie's nature lays its imprint on the building whose permeable structure is evident in the trespass-

---

[24] Sylvie not only bears the name of her mother, but also reenacts her mother's almost fatalistic view on life as a road where one's destination is already fixed. Upon arrival, Sylvie assumes the role of her mother, taking her place, while preserving her transient habits. Moreover, just like her sister, she is married to an abstract person, whom she never mentions: "She had simply chosen not to act married," Ruth avows, "though she had a marriage of sufficient legal standing to have changed her name" (43).

ing of the boundaries between the inside and the outside.[25] Nature's invasion of the interior space is parallelled by an "opening up of the outside to the inside" (Meese 59). The narrator eloquently describes how darkness acquires an initiating function, as it effaces all differences, pointing to the original moment of lack of distinction between beings and things:

> Sylvie in a house was more or less like a mermaid in a ship's cabin. She preferred it sunk in the very element it was meant to exclude. We had crickets in the pantry, squirrels in the eaves, sparrows in the attic. Lucille and I stepped through the door from sheer night to sheer night (99).

At the limit between the inside and the outside, the window has a symbolic aspect, referring to the liminal experience that Sylvie reveals to the girl. At night, when the room is flooded by darkness, the window is no longer a boundary, but an instrument of communication between the human and the natural world. Whereas in a room full of light the window is a mirror, a narcissistic instrument of self-reflection, in a dark room the window evades its function of demarcation. A peratologic[26] experience of pushing the limit of one's perception occurs in the dark, where the eye no longer meets its own projection in the glass and plunges into the outside space. Speaking in this almost mystical "brighter darkness," Ruth feels her proximity to nature and the others.

The most powerful example of the invasion of a culturally mapped territory by the natural world appears in the episode of the flood. Not only the configuration of the house changes, but also the boundaries between the realm of the living and that of the dead are trespassed, thus re-drawing a familiar territory and transforming it into an uncanny one. As

---

[25] A number of critics have emphasized Sylvie's itinerant nature, in connection with the idiosyncratic idea of place. Paula Geyh observes that "*Housekeeping* both explores the centrality of the space of the house in the construction of feminine subjectivity and attempts to imagine a new *transient* subjectivity which is located in a place outside all patriarchal structures" (Geyh's italics, 104). In the same direction, In the same direction, Dana Heller compares Sylvie's "flexibility and fluidity of ego boundaries" with the permeable boundaries of the house (98).

[26] The term *peratology* is taken from the Romanian philosopher Gabriel Liiceanu, who explains its etymology and double significance. Derived from the Greek *peras*, meaning "limit," the *peratology* represents "a theory of the limit." It is "an analytical discourse, which refers to the variety of natural limits: the limits that determine the identity of the finite natural bodies (the ontology of the physical limit), and the limits that are part of the field of human experience (the ontology of the limit related to consciousness)" (64).

the cathartic power of the flood changes the appearance of visible reality, Ruth broods on the mutability of all existent things. While she ponders the Biblical motif of *vanitas vanitatum*, she realizes that every spirit leaves its imprint on things, transforms them, and moves on:

> Every spirit passing through the world fingers the tangible and mars the mutable, and finally has come to look and not to buy. So shoes are worn and hassocks are sat upon and finally everything is left where it was and the spirit passes on, just as the wind in the orchard picks up the leaves from the ground (73).

This image suggests that there is a sense of permanence in transience and that, although things remain where they have always been, they are forever changed as the spirit passes over them. The Heraclitean theme of *pantha rhei*, of the universal flow of all things, is connected here with such objects as shoes and hassocks, symbolizing the contact with the earthly realm and with the transcendent sphere. The way the spirit "fingers the tangible" can be finally seen as the only testimony of its passage through the world.

In this light, the name of the town—Fingerbone—becomes representative as it points to the relationship between the spirit and the earthly objects. The representation of the fingerbone binds the world of the living with that of the dead. Disclosing the mutability of the world of flesh and bones, the fingerbone is a *memento mori*, a way of remembering the change inherent in all things. The fictional world that Robinson creates seems to be made of fingerbones: those of the dead people lying at the bottom of her textual universe and those of the characters and readers who take hold of the novel. The fingerbone stands for a relic, a remnant of a past existence made visible to the reader—the only testimony that has survived the flood of time.

To draw a conclusion to this part and link it with the last one, we must remark that the reconfiguration of the female identity as transient is deeply related to the subversion of both the model of the nuclear family and the image of the house with solid boundaries. "Home" is therefore expanded into a flexible concept, operating on multiple levels of significance. As "home" can be translated into its opposite and the spatial meanings of sameness and otherness overlap, Robinson's characters are "unhoused," taken out of their ordinary condition and located in an uncanny situation. In this way, the West is re-envisioned as a topos of the female outcast, where the familiar notion of "housekeeping" is ironically placed under a question mark.

4. At Home with Transience

Strange as it may seem, Robinson chooses to weave together the complementary meanings of "home" and "travel." This peculiar pattern has been explored before by one of the most eccentric figures in American literature—Emily Dickinson. The poet's *modus vivendi*, and especially her *modus scribendi* will be used as a starting point for the present discussion. Robinson acknowledges her indebtedness to Dickinson, who is identified, along with other nineteenth century authors, as one of her guiding influences:

> I think they must have believed everything can be apprehended truly when seen in the light of an aesthetic understanding appropriate to itself, whence their passion of making novel orders of disparate things. I believe they wished to declare the intrinsic dignity of all experience and to declare the senses bathed in revelation—true, serious revelation, the kind that terrifies (1984, 30).

The "terrible revelation" of the world's strangeness enthrals both Dickinson and Robinson.[27] *Housekeeping* resonates with basic motifs present in Dickinson's poetry: the obsession with home and the escape from it, the movement on several existential and metaphoric layers, the seductive power of loneliness and its positive overtones, the refiguration of loss and emptiness as inner growth and fulfilment. To borrow Allen Tate's words, both authors master the world by rejecting it. While Dickinson decided to transform her home into an exemplary topos for her imaginary travels, Robinson seems to suggest that the notion of "home" can be reconsidered and projected upon strange spaces of otherness. Dickinson managed to change an allegoric prison into a friend, the repressive patriarchal home into a free space for her quest, and woman's

---

[27] From Dickinson's "passion of making novel orders of disparate things," Robinson learns that the conventional "House of Prose" may be changed into a "House of Possibility", one of "imaginative, epistemological freedom" (Weisbuch 5).

passive role into a spiritual voyage. In the same direction, Robinson destabilizes binary oppositions by rendering "home" and "otherness" as fictional concepts that can be made and unmade, reshaped in an authorial process of self-reflection.[28]

Either explicitly or implicitly Emily Dickinson is "blessedly unavoidable" in *Housekeeping* (Robinson 1993). Mainly, the poet offers Robinson a possible pattern of constructing "a woman-identified redefinition of the subject" (Braidotti 96). Dickinson's withdrawal from the public scene and her intense preoccupation with her self—which has its most profound roots in the Protestant ethics and the Puritan emphasis on privacy—are also central in Robinson's novel. The author exemplifies in Ruth the personification of the private self, while, in contrast, Lucille is represented as the epitome of the public self, the settled personality who abides by social rules.

Suggestively, Ruth does not feel at home within the restrictive boundaries of school. Ruth has a "cold, visceral dread of school" (77), where she refuses the company of the others. The principal's words addressed to Ruth—"You're going to have to learn to speak for yourself, and think for yourself, that's for sure" (135)—lay stress on the importance of speech as a means of social integration and personal fulfilment. Analysing Ruth's attitude through Luce Irigaray's lens, it becomes obvious that Ruth's effacement reflects "the evasiveness of women's position in society" and "the difficulty to make their voices heard from these positions" (127). Furthermore, Ruth's elusiveness functions as a means of resistance to patriarchy, as a way of refusing to assume a role in this system, of endowing silence and solitude with positive meanings.

In both Robinson's novel and Dickinson's poetry effacement acquires a privileged status. Through Ruth, Robinson suggests that the idea of growth should be seen as an inner achievement that is accomplished in loneliness, as illustrated by one of Dickinson's famous poems:
> Growth of Man - like Growth of Nature –
> Gravitates within –
> Atmosphere, and Sun endorse it –
> But it stirs – alone –

---

[28] Smyth cogently notices: "To posit the home as a continent to be escaped—or, in other words, to posit home as an opposition to vagrancy—is to continue defining vagrancy in domestic terms" (283).

Each – its difficult ideal
Must achieve – Itself -
Through the solitary prowess
Of a Silent Life –
(Poem no. 750)

Both Dickinson and Robinson articulate the quest in terms of inner growth. One may argue that Ruth seems to know that personal accomplishment is achieved only in solitude, where "Transaction—is assisted/ By no Countenance" (Dickinson, poem no. 750). Ruth's depth of perception feeds on silence and invisibility. She is both character and secret witness who considers herself privileged to watch, while the others are unaware of her presence. Being also a narrator, she tries to find ways of voicing the unsayability of her itinerant existence.[29]

Ruth's initiation takes place away from society, in a symbolic setting across the lake, at the site of an abandoned homestead—a parodic version of a mythic home. In Sylvie's maternal company, Ruth begins to perceive a secret world located beyond the normal limits of understanding, while she passes through practices of initiation that presuppose an inner transformation and renewal.[30] As in Dickinson's poem mentioned above, Ruth's spiritual growth is accomplished in solitude. Sylvie, the mediator, leaves the girl alone, in a "situation of unfamiliarity," in which Ruth passes through a "struggle for identity" (Bartkowski viii). At its climax, Ruth's self-discovery is acutely related to her quest for family

---

[29] As Lindsey Tucker points out, there is an inter-connection between women writers' attempt to escape both thematic and the genre restrains and the idea of movement: "When women do write subversive texts, when they do manage escapes from imprisoning, male-identified narrative models, from genre, even from mimesis itself, their discourses often have as a central concern the problem of movement" (4).

[30] The symbolism of death and rebirth that underscores the moment of the quest has been emphasized by Susan Rosowski who stresses that Robinson extends "the metaphor of birth," and the scene at the lake is a "birth meditation" (183). Moreover, Martha Ravits points that Ruth's "quest and choice is always for the missing mother." Ravits compares Ruth's search for her mother with such heroes as Ishmael, Huck Finn, Isaac McCaslin, who "undertook the struggle for maturity by choosing surrogate fathers" (648).

roots, mostly for her lost mother.[31] "Unhoused", taken away from everything that is familiar, Ruth begins her meditation upon the nature of human bonds, and realizes that having a close connection with someone signifies a means of protection, of "housing", of shielding the invisible:

> Having a sister or a friend is like sitting at night in a lighted house. Those outside can watch you if they want, but you need not see them... Anyone with one solid human bond is that smug, and it is the smugness as much as the comfort and safety that lonely people covet and admire. I have been, so to speak, turned out of the house now long enough to have observed this in myself. Now there was neither threshold nor sill between me and these cold, solitary children who almost breathed against my cheek and almost touched my hair (154).

Ruth's thoughts refer to her lack of protection, when confronted with the children—unknown messengers of the ineffable. Attempting to establish contact with these children, Ruth gets engaged in a game with the unseen, in which the element of amusement and recreation is replaced with a deep meditative state of mind. Since the function of the play is "stepping out of common reality into a higher order" (Huizinga 13), Ruth's search for invisible children can be interpreted as a peratological experience situated at the limit of the known and the unknown. However, visual access to the metaphysical realm is denied, while she comprehends the impossibility to grasp an unfathomable essence. As in Dickinson's poem, "Our journey had advanced," Ruth arrives "to that odd Fork in Being's Road – / Eternity – by Term –" (poem no. 615).[32]

In Ruth's quest, Robinson reconsiders the archetypal model of initiation proposed by Jung, in which "the rebirth journey takes the hero beyond social boundaries and back again" (in Pratt 137). A basic difference between

---

[31] Roberta Rubenstein discusses Ruth's initiation in analogy with the Greek myth of Demeter and Persephone—that is subverted. If in the ancient story, Demeter, the mother, is in search for Persephone, her daughter, in *Housekeeping*, it is the daughter who is in quest for her lost mother. Since the seducer, Hades or Pluto, is absent, the author excludes the male figure, but preserves the imagery of death.

[32] The motif of playing with the invisible will be later reiterated by Ruth's game in the orchard, in which she experiences a state of physical apathy, a way of proving her internalization of the knowledge acquired during the initiation trip. Ruth's act of playing reenacts Huizinga's idea that any game is an act of freedom, "a stepping out of 'real' life into a temporary sphere of activity with a disposition of its own" (8).

Jung's and Robinson's understanding of rebirth and inner transformation can be identified. While Jung points that the goal of the journey is the hero's reintegration into society, Robinson does not allow her characters to be later assimilated into their community. Inocculated with the thrill of "otherness," they remain permanent transients, truly faithful to their itinerant condition. Consequently, the sheriff and the honourable citizens of the shallow-rooted Fingerbone, cannot understand Ruth's and Sylvie's eccentric behaviour, as well as Ruth's recognition of Sylvie as a mother figure and her desire to remain with Sylvie.

When they return to society, the two women in *Housekeeping* do not accept the tasks of a housewife, in a figurative act of burning down the house. The destruction of the house and the characters' hurried departure stage a double escape from the boundaries of society and from the limitations of their own home. Ruth's remark—"Now truly we were cast out to wander and there was an end to housekeeping"—implies that they assumed their transient position also as a result of society's attitude towards them.[33] Since the motivation that makes them leave society and assume their migrant existence is their desire not to be separated, the novel advocates the paradoxical idea that female kinship can be preserved through movement.

Ruth's and Sylvie's itinerant existence places in a new perspective "Dickinson's analogy of wandering without an established home" (Gardner 11). The act of crossing the bridge marks their entrance into the world of invisibility. Can their passage be understood as perpetual transience, disquieting madness or ghostly death?[34] The author leaves the question open in the end of the book. Interpreting the proleptic ending, most critics draw attention to the blurring of the boundaries of such antithetic notions as presence and absence, stability and mobility, conformity and non-conformity.

More than that, the end offers an escape from clichés of female identity by dislocating the patterns of domesticity and vagrancy, which

---

[33] As marginal characters, Ruth and Sylvie occupy what Kristeva called "the position of the abject," "that which has been cast off because it disrupts identity, system and order" (26).

[34] Thomas Foster points out that this "proleptic anticipation of the narrator's death" should also be found in Emily Dickinson's poem, "I heard a Fly buzz—when I died," "a poem Ruth was required to recite in school and which she remembers as one of the few events interrupting the tedium of her time there" (97).

are no longer seen as antithetic notions. "Home" becomes a concept that works *in absentia*, as it can be projected upon the space of "otherness," whereas vagrancy may expose that "travelling is a fool's paradise," and that all "journeys discover to us the indifference of all places" (Emerson 150). As Paula Geyh affirms, the characters' options "do not appear to be limited to either vagrancy or inscription within the household," so that "the feminine subjectivity might be constituted... by an interaction between the two" (120).

In this way, Ruth, Sylvie and Lucille no longer occupy antipodean places, but become part of a triangle in which they continuously switch places. As Ruth and Sylvie inhabit marginal social locations, being outcasts who could be arrested for "increasing erratic behaviour" (213), so Lucille seems isolated in the privacy of her own home or in the middle of society. Not only Ruth's and Sylvie's "unredeemed" transience becomes meaningful through their repeated return to an imaginary home, but also Lucille's image as a stereotypical housewife is reconsidered through her perpetual meditation upon her sister's fate.

The last scene in the novel is therefore suggestive as it re-presents Lucille in a new light.[35] Lucille's figurative gesture of completing a circle of water on the table refers to both her circumscribed existence and her wish to complete the broken family ties. The vision in the last sentence, constructed through an accumulation of negations, reveals Lucille's attitude of effacement from the company of others, while her full attention is focussed on Ruth and Sylvie:

> No one watching this woman smear her initials in the steam on her water glass with her first finger, or slip cellophane packets of oyster crackers into her handbag for the sea gulls, could know how her thoughts are thronged by our absence, or know how she does not watch, does not listen, does not wait, does not hope, and always for me and Sylvie" (219).

---

[35] The setting is a restaurant in Boston—a sort of El Dorado, bearing the attributes of a dreamlike place. As Ravits shows, "this final projection of Ruth's imagination means that this novel set in the West ends, ironically, in the East, at the birthplace of American letters" (666).

5. Conclusion: Opening Perspectives

In essence, Robinson's novel is written in accordance with her idea of a general pattern in American writing, in which characters "go through a journey that leads to a kind of realization that is just at the limits of their ability to comprehend or articulate, and after that, there's an openness where earlier experience becomes impossible, and you're abandoned into a new terrain without being able to use your old assumptions about how to find your way" (Robinson quoted in Hedrick 6).

From a feminist perspective, Ruth and Sylvie exemplify the possibility of going beyond the social roles usually ascribed to women by patriarchy. The novel consequently confirms Margaret Hall's argument for the "uniqueness of women," for their integrity which shows that no roles such as "sisterhood, womanhood or motherhood" should be given to them, since roles are restrictive and stereotypical (29). From this point of view, the title of the novel is ironic, since it places a question mark next to women's condition as keepers of the house and points to the "unhousing" of characters that are cast into roles that have previously been credited to male heroes. By juxtaposing the images of Ruth, Sylvie and Lucille, the novel proposes a new type of identity that is created neither by taking into account Ruth's and Sylvie's mobile existence, nor Lucille's static subjectivity, but a combination between the two.

At an intertextual level, Robinson's translation of home-ness into strangeness signifies a process of revisiting former texts. By placing these texts in a new context, she suggests that writing may be a form of appropriating the alterity of the other texts, but also one of distancing from them, of playing them against each other. "Unhousing" the texts of the others, she exposes the strangeness of the American literature. In a palimpsestic reading of the American literature and philosophy as well as of the Biblical motifs, Robinson proposes new versions of identity by reconfiguring through them the attributes that have formerly been given only to male heroes. For these women, transience comes to represent not only physical and mental mobility, but also movement from a marginalised position to an independent literary role.

Through her characters, Robinson discloses to us how to be at home with strangeness.

Corina Anghel

Works Cited

Aschkenasy, Nehama. 1994. "Language as Female Empowerment in Ruth." *Reading Ruth: Contemporary Women Reclaim a Sacred Story.* Ed. Judith A. Kates and Gail Twersky Reimer. New York: Ballantine.

Bassin, Donna, Margaret Honey, Meryle Mahrer Kaplan, eds. 1994. *Representations of Motherhood.* New Haven: London: Yale University Press.

Baym, Nina. 1981. "Melodramas of Beset Manhood: How Theories of American Fiction Exclude Women Authors." *American Quarterly* 33 (Summer 1981): 122-39.

Braidotti, Rosi. 1989. "The Politics of Ontological Difference." *Between Feminism and Psychoanalysis.* Ed. Teresa Brennan. London, New York: Routledge, pp. 89-105.

Bernard, Jessie. 1974. *The Future of Motherhood.* New York: Dial.

Campbell, Joseph. 1949. *The Hero with a Thousand Faces.* Princeton: Princeton University Press.

Chodorow, Nancy. 1978. *The Reproduction of Mothering: Psychoanalysis and the Sociology of Gender.* Berkeley: Los Angeles: London: University of California Press.

Dickinson, Emily. 1951. *The Complete Poems.* Ed. by Thomas H. Johnson. Boston: Toronto: Little, Brown and Company.

Elliott, Emory, ed. 1988. *Columbia Literary History of the United States.* New York: Columbia University Press.

Emerson, Ralph Waldo. 1929. *The Complete Writing of Ralph Waldo Emerson.* New York: Wise and Co. Publishers.

Everett, Dick. 1937. *The Sod-House Frontier 1854-1890: A Social History of the Northern Plains from the Creation of Kansas and Nebraska to the Admissions of the Dakotas.* New York—London: D. Appleton-Century Company.

Foster, Thomas. 1988. "History, Critical Theory, and Women's Social Practices: 'Women's Time' and Housekeeping." *Signs: Journal of Women in Culture and Society* 14. 1 (1988): 73-99.

Galehouse, Maggie. 2000. "Their Own Private Idaho: Transience in Marilynne Robinson's *Housekeeping.*" *Contemporary Literature* 41. 1 (Spring 2000): 117-31.

Gardner, Thomas. 2001. "Enlarging Loneliness: Marilynne Robinson's *Housekeeping* as a Reading of Emily Dickinson." *The Emily Dickinson Journal* 10. 1 (2001): 9-33.

Geyh, Paula E. 1993. "Burning Down the House? Domestic Space and Feminine Subjectivity in Marilynne Robinson's *Housekeeping. Contemporary Literature* XXXIV 1 (1993): 103-22.

Hall, Margaret C. 1979. *Woman Unliberated. Difficulties and Limitations in Changing Self.* Washington: London: Hemisphere Publishing Corporation.

Hedrick, Tace. 1992. "On Influence and Appropriation." *Iowa Review* 22. 1 (1992): 1-7.

Heller, Dana A. 1990. *The Feminization of the Quest Romance: Radical Departures.* Austin: University of Texas.

Huizinga, Johan. 1950. *Homo Ludens: A Study of the Play-Element in Culture.* Boston: The Beacon Press.

Irigaray, Luce. 1985. *This Sex Which Is Not One.* Translated by Caroline Porter with Carolyn Burke, Ithaca, New York: Cornell University Press.

Jung, C. G., Kerényui, C. 1963. *Essays on a Science of Mythology.* Trans. R. F. C. Hull. New York: Evanson: Harper & Row, Publishers.

Kristeva, Julia. 1982. *Powers of Horror.* New York: Columbia University Press.

Liiceanu, Gabriel. 1994. *Despre Limită / About the Limit.* București: Humanitas.

Maguire, James H. 1999. "Marilynne Robinson." *Dictionary of Literary Biography.* Vol. 206. Twentieth Century American Western Writers, First Series. Ed. Richard Cracroft. Detroit: A Bruccoli Clark Layman Book, pp. 251-60.

Marx, Leo. 1992. "*Walden* as a Transcendental Pastoral Design." In *Walden and Resistance to Civil Government*, 2nd edition, ed. by William Rossi. New York and London: W. W. Norton & Company, first edition 1966, pp. 377-90.

Matthiessen, F.O. 1941. *American Renaissance: Art and Expression in the Age of Emerson and Whitman.* London: Toronto: Oxford University Press.

Meese, Elizabeth A. 1986. *Crossing the Double Cross: The Practice of Feminist Criticism.* Chapel Hill: University of North Carolina Press.

Melville, Herman. 1993. *Moby Dick.* Kent: Wordsworth Editions Limited.

Miroiu, Mihaela. 1996. *Convenio. Despre natură, femei și morală/ Convenio. About Nature, Women, and Morals.* București: Alternative.

O'Brien, Sheila Ruzychi. 1993. "*Housekeeping*: New West Novel, Old West Film." *Old West—New West. Centennial Essays.* Ed. Barbara Meldrum Howard. Moscow: Idaho: University of Idaho Press, pp. 173-83.

Pratt, Annis, Barbara White, Andrea Loewenstein, Mary Wyer. 1981. *Archetypal Patterns in Women's Fiction.* Bloomington: Indiana University Press.

Ravits, Martha. 1989. "Extending the American Range: Marilynne Robinson's *Housekeeping*." *American Literature* 61. 4 (December 1989): 644-66.

Rich, Adrienne. 1976. *Of Woman Born.* New York: Norton.

Robinson, Marilynne. 1980. *Housekeeping.* New York: Farrar, Straus & Giroux.

————. 1984. "The Hum Inside the Skull - A Symposium." *New York Times Review* (13 May 1984): 30.

————. 1993. "My Western Roots." *Old West—New West. Centennial Essays.* Ed. Barbara Meldrum Howard. Moscow: Idaho: University of Idaho Press, pp. 165-72.

————. 1998a. *The Death of Adam. Essays on Modern Thought.* Boston and New York: Houghton Mifflin Company.

————. 1998b. "The Way We Work, the Way We Live." *Christian Century* 115. 24 (1998): 823-33.

Rosowski, Susan J. 1999. *Birthing a Nation. Gender, Creativity and the West in American Literature.* Lincoln and London: University of Nebraska Press.

Rubenstein, Roberta. 1987. *Boundaries of the Self.* Urbana and Chicago: University of Illinois.

Schaub, Thomas. 1994. "An Interview with Marilynne Robinson." *Contemporary Literature* XXXV 2 (1994): 231-49.

Slotkin, Richard. 1973. *Regeneration through Violence: The Mythology of the American Frontier, 1600-1860.* Wesleyan University Press.

Smyth, Jacqui. 1999. "Sheltered Vagrancy in Marilynne Robinson's *Housekeeping.*" *Critique* 40. 3 (1999): 281-92.

Tate, Allan. 1963. "Emily Dickinson." *Emily Dickinson. A Collection of Critical Essays.* Ed. by R. B. Sewall. Englewood Cliffs.

Thoreau, Henry David. 1992. *Walden and Resistance to Civil Government,* ed. William Rossi, 2nd edition. New York and London: W. W. Norton & Company.

Tucker, Lindsey. 1994. *Textual Escap(e)ades. Mobility, Maternity, and Textuality in Contemporary Fiction by Women.* Westport: Connecticut: London: Greenwood Press.

Turner, Frederick Jackson. 1989. "The Significance of the Frontier in American History." *A Nineteenth-Century American Reader.* Ed. by M. Thomas Inge. Washington: United States Information Agency, pp. 80-85.

Walker, Michelle Boulous. 1998. *Philosophy and the Maternal Body.* London: New York: Routledge.

Weisbuch, Robert. 1972. *Emily Dickinson's Poetry.* Chicago: University of Chicago Press.

Homing In? —

The Critical/creative Transformation of a Genre

> Nature is "home," then to Native Americans in a
> way exactly opposite to its function for Boone.
> [...] Nature is "house."
> — Bevis, 602

Introduction

William Bevis argues that Native American novels work from a tribal
ontological premise, whereas the western reader prioritizes individualism
and American self-reliance in his (or her) very different ontological
assumptions.

These books suggest that "identity" for a Native American, is not
a matter of finding "one's self," but of finding a "self" that is transpersonal
and includes a society, a past and a place. To be separated from that
transpersonal time and space is to lose identity. These novels are
important, not only because they depict Indian individuals coming home
while white individuals leave but also because they suggest—variously
and subtly and by degrees—a tribal rather than an individual definition
of "being." (585)

Such an identity might be "trans-individual," but the very choice of the novel form militates against the strength of this argument. Techniques of characterization suggest the individuality of the protagonist to the implied reader. Even *Ceremony* combines the ritual elements of Navajo sandpainting and chantways with a Euro-American depiction of character. While it is appropriate to note that individual characters exist within a social context, tribal affiliation and kinship identity are not simple issues easy of resolution in these novels. The variety of post-war Native American fiction indicates that there is not one pan-tribal past, nor is there one pan-tribal identity to be worked out singly and conclusively. I am wary of the synthesizing tendency of Bevis' argument, especially if it leads us to make generalizations about pan-tribal ontology and culture.

It would be a gesture of inappropriate cultural colonialism to assume that mixed-blood novelists are fixed in a static tribalism that has remained unchanged since Edward Curtis' day. Mixed-blood narrators almost by definition find themselves negotiating the untranslatability between cultures. Mixed-blood narratives could be said to educate their implied readers and through diegesis and mimesis tell and show the transformative cultural spaces that they dwell in. Mixed-blood narratives substantiate Homi Bhabha's sense of cultural hybridity as testimony to the "split-space of enunciation" that is "*inter*-national culture." In my opinion Bevis' observations are nearer the mark when we consider the issue of the white *author* of a mixed-blood narration, rather than the presumed inadequacies of a generalized white *reader*.

Frank Waters' *The Man Who Killed the Deer*

Waters 1942 novel seems to fit Bevis's model most neatly. In Homi Bhabha's terms, we might say that Waters subscribes to an ideology of cultural diversity but not of cultural difference. His novel offers a "mirror of representation" of a Pueblo culture that he assumes to be "a homogenizing, unifying force, authenticated by the originary Past, kept alive in the national tradition of the People." In "Cultural Diversity and Cultural Differences" Bhabha argues that "hierarchical claims to the inherent originality or 'purity' of cultures are untenable," since "all cultural statements and systems are constructed in this contradictory and ambivalent space of enunciation," that is the "Third Space." Citing Fanon as the basis of his argument—"it is to the zone of *occult instability* where the people dwell that we must come" (207)—he writes:

> It is that Third Space, though unrepresentable in itself, which constitutes the discursive conditions of enunciation that ensure that the meaning and symbols of culture have no primordial unity or fixity; that even the same signs can be appropriated, translated, rehistoricized, and read anew. (208)

Waters' practice as a novelist is the antithesis of this, since at the levels of characterization, plot, and style he reasserts a sense of Pueblo culture as having a primordial fixity and unity that it is desirable to return to. Repeatedly in *Book of the Hopi* Waters speaks of the "Hopi Road of Life" and even of "evolutionary progress on the Road of Life" (230). This ideological need to reframe the cyclic nature of Pueblo rituals and belief systems into an evolutionary progress or type of religious quest narrative is also evident in *The Man Who Killed the Deer.* Against the backdrop of the Pueblo ceremonial year, Martiniano finds himself in a three-part plot that will end in the re-establishment of his spiritual harmony with the Pueblo. The novel ostensibly fits the structure of the homing-in paradigm by adhering to its characteristic plot, yet misfits it, by othering the tribal identity it purports to sympathize with. Issues of authorial intentionality are always tricky, but I would contend that the author unintentionally translates the tribal and the Pueblo culture, for which he evidently feels great personal and political sympathy, into a westernized and romanti-cized version. Vizenor has theorized this typical move of Western culture, describing it as the production of simulations of the white man's antiselves in *Manifest Manners*.[1] Paradoxically, in attempting to evoke an originary Pueblo culture and tell the story of its continuing relevance and vitality in the twentieth century, Waters produces a manifest simulation, that bespeaks his own spiritual need for the primitive more clearly than it enunciates the transformational continuance of tribal identity.

---

[1] Vizenor's work is crucial to an understanding of the innumerable ways in which the dominant culture and the literature of dominance plays Indian. However, his postmodern, trickster discourse can cause some dismay to readers unfamiliar with his style; and his delight in postmodernist theory can also be confusing for the reader expecting him to counterbalance the simulations of manifest manners with an authentic Native American culture. In his texts the "reality" of indigenous ethnic identity is as elusive and illusive as images of the Indian in Buffalo Bill's Wild West show.

Waters is well intentioned as an author, but several aspects of his
novel undercut his good intentions and graphically illustrate his inability
to move into an ambiguous and dynamic third space in his treatment of
racial and tribal cultural identity. Firstly, his tendency to think of race
categorically and discretely means that at best he might be operating with
a paradigm of cultural diversity, but that he can never overcome his
categorizations to enter the third space where cultural differences
converse on equal terms. Secondly, despite his express sympathy for the
American Indian way of life, whether tribal or mixed blood, he cannot
escape from his own ideological, cultural assumptions, especially in
subscribing to a linear and progressive sense of history as inevitable and
universally applicable. Thirdly, he is unable to enunciate tribal ontology,
specifically tribal ways of perceiving the past, relating to place and
belonging to society, since his authorial and narrative voice can only
speak in a romanticizing discourse. All of these limitations in his analysis,
his imagination and his enunciation contribute to the overwhelming
impression that the novel is a systematic specularization of the Pueblo
and its inhabitants. Sadly, this text does not really advance the People's
cause for it cannot avoid othering them in its advocacy. Thus, the ending
of the novel cannot be read as a real reaffirmation of tribal values and
ways, as Bevis' model of the homing-in plot would advocate.

Although the ending reads superficially as the reintegration of the
alienated, acculturated Indian into his tribal origins, the narrative
represents Martiniano as accepting the dominant myth of the Vanishing
Indian in his decision to give his own son to the kiva for initiation:

> One must not forget one's beginning, thought Martiniano. And
> that was why he had consented to the adoption of his son into
> a kiva, with Palemon for the boy's godfather, his preceptor.
> Times were changing, and his son should know something of the
> old before he was confronted with the new. (215)

I would contend that this is memorialization rather than perpetuation of
tribal presence.[2] It does not challenge the author's social evolutionary
model, and it does not allow Indian writers to begin representing their

---

[2] See Vizenor. *Manifest Manners*: 8: "Those who 'memorialized rather than perpetuated' a tribal
presence and wrote 'Indian history as obituary' were unconsciously collaborating 'with those bent
on physical extermination,' argued Ziff. 'The process of literary annihilation would be checked only
when Indian writers began representing their own culture.'"

own culture or to enter the historical and literary process in order to transform it and perpetuate it. Instead, this version of the homing-in plot, for all its apparent sympathy, relegates the Pueblo Indian and the mixed-blood Indian to the formlessness of alienation or the unreality of simulation. Using *The Man Who Killed the Deer* as a "control" text, we can now turn briefly to Silko's *Ceremony* for an example of cultural synthesis and transformation that genuinely enters that third space of inter-cultural imaginings.

Indian "homing" as healing ceremony

In his article Bevis constructs his argument on the basis of six "canonical" novels.[3] If one extrapolates and applies the points of his argument solely to Silko's *Ceremony*, aspects of Bevis' homing-in paradigm can seem categorical and rather too emphatic.[4] However by doing so one discovers

---

[3]   McNickle's *The Surrounded* and *Wind from an Enemy Sky*, Welch's *The Death of Jim Loney* and *Winter in the Blood*—although *Fool's Crow* also gets a substantial mention—Momaday's *House Made of Dawn* and Silko's *Ceremony*. It is noteworthy that the two latter receive least detailed commentary, possibly because Bevis favours social realist narratives.

[4]   *Ceremony* tells of a wanderer in the white world coming home. In *Ceremony*, an Indian serviceman returns from Japan to the Southwest Laguna tribe, and slowly breaks from a pattern of drinking and madness to participate in a healing ceremony guided by an old medicine man, a ceremony that begins with a quest for cattle and ends with an amended story and rain for the desert land. Indian "homing" is presented as the opposite of competitive individualism, which is white success, characterized in the novel by Rocky.
The protagonist, Tayo, seeks a meaningful relation to a meaningful structure. He becomes a healthy man through accepted social ritual. Self-realization is not accomplished by the individual or by romantic bonding only; that would be incomprehensible.
Tribal reality is profoundly conservative; "progress" and "a fresh start" are not native to America. Most of the Western tribes shared a belief in a "distant past." Old Betonie is in touch with a tradition tracing from the distant past, and extends this connection to the young protagonist. Tayo succeeds because he finds a connected ancestor.
No "free individual" who achieves white success is really admired—not Rocky—and certainly the free "mode of life" he has "chosen" is not preferred to tribal context.
To call Tayo back from the war an "individual", implying all the weight of dignity, promise, and law which is carried by that term in white culture, is misleading.
The protagonist seeks an identity that he can find only in his society, past, and place; unlike whites, he feels no meaningful being, alone. Individuality is not even the scene of success or failure; it is nothing.
Tayo's mythic romance places his acquisition of crucial knowledge in a social [and family] context. The plot is regressive because Native American knowledge is regressive; the traditional elders of *Ceremony* teach the protagonist the only knowledge which proves useful in the book. "I been there before" is a primary virtue. Both meaningful "being" and meaningful "knowledge" are supra-individual aspects of tribe.

that he conducts his argument in terms of: the plot, the protagonist, the novel (or the book), the author Silko, and the themes. Bearing in mind the narrative strategies of Silko's text, including its construction around processes of transition and transformation, I would argue that we cannot simply read *Ceremony* by focussing on the protagonist and the plot. To do so would oversimplify the thinking of the novel, to use Bevis's preferred term, and the thought-creating activities of the implied author. In considering to what extent and in what manner this is a homing-in novel, we need to bear in mind the dialogic nature of the text, where rituals, myths, modernist stream of consciousness, narrative prose, poetic clan stories and chantways and reservation / dirty realism all enter its polyphonic conversation.

Bevis argues that the novel opts for tribal ontology, specifically in its expression of the themes of society, place and history. However he does not discuss tribal or clan cultural formations in any detail. I want briefly to consider how particular tribal cultural formations, with their location in a specific sense of history and of place, inform the narrative strategies and textures of the novel. *Ceremony* is an interesting text to investigate since the mixed-blood narrative deploys European, Laguna Pueblo, Keresan[5] and Navajo cultural elements. Arguably it is *par excellence* the

---

The novel comes from an inland West reservation and from a tribe not drastically displaced from its original territory or ecosystem. Place is not only an aspect of this work; place may have made it possible.

Conversely, white disregard and disrespect for place is crucial in this book.

The novel depicts an Indian coming home and staying home, but "home" is not the "house" of white heaven.

The protagonist succeeds largely to the degree in which he reintegrates into the tribe, and fails largely to the degree in which he remains alone.

The novel is a profound and articulate critique of modern European culture, combined with a persistent refusal to let go of tribal identity.

Silko is not resurrecting archaic rituals for symbolic purposes, but telling of the pull of tribal identity, tribal despair, tribal pride.

Silko is taken with the grand themes of sacredness and place.

[5] I list Laguna and Keres separately to emphasise the complexity of Pueblo cultural identity. Consider the following recent and reliable description of the cultural geography: "Living dispersed among the Tanoan speakers are the *Keresans*. Along the Rio Grande and its tributaries are the Keresan villages of Cochiti, Santo Domingo, San Felipe, Santa Ana and Zia; farther west are Laguna and Acoma. [...] The Pueblos are divided into two main subgroups based on location and ecological adaptation. The Eastern Pueblos (Tanoan and Keresan speakers), who live on the Rio Grande and its tributaries, have a permanent water source enabling them to practice irrigation agriculture. The Western Pueblos (Hopi, Hopi-Tewa, Zuni, Acoma and Laguna), lacking a steady supply of water, rely on dry farming. The difference in water supply affects many aspects of culture from food procurement to religion. [...] The Pueblos share a way of life, a world view and a

exemplary type of a novel generated in the third space of creative, cultural hybridity that Bhabha advocates.

To consider information supplied by A. Lavonne Brown Ruoff in 1978, for example, rather complicates several of Bevis' points, by altering our perception of Laguna Pueblo Indians as a people with their own, pure, tribal history, somehow separate from the history of contact with Europeans.[6] It also confounds any tendency we might have to assume that Pueblo cultures have less "history" than Europeans. We need to take account of their specific and complex history of multiple relocations, inter-tribal mergers and alliances, inter-marriage even with the Navajo —traditionally depicted as marauding bully boys and land grabbers

landscape, but they speak half a dozen languages and live in more than 30 villages. Although several pueblos may share a language, internally they may have different societies and clan structures, so that they are not alike in organization. There are, naturally, several distinct styles of pottery." (Taylor & Sturtevant 73, 75 & 106)

[6] According to their origin legends, the Laguna tribe (in existence since at least 1300), came southward from the Mesa Verde region. Some versions indicate that after pausing at Zia, they were joined by the head of the Parrot clan, who decided to take his people southward with them. After wandering further, first southward from the lake at Laguna and then northward back to the lake, they settled Punyana, probably in the late 1300s. After founding Old Laguna (Kawaik) around 1400, they issued invitations to other pueblos to join them. Those which responded were the Parrot clam from Zia, the Sun clan from Hopi, the Road Runner and Badger clams from Zuni, and the Sun clan from Jemez. The tribe occupied the site of what is now called Laguna by the early 1500s. Additional immigration occurred during the 1690s, when the Lagunas were joined by Indians from the Rio Grande, probably fleeing both drought and the hostility of the Spanish after the Pueblo Rebellion in 1680 and the renewed uprising in 1696. These immigrants came chiefly from Zia, Cochiti, and Domingo, but a few came from Jemez, Zuni, and Hopi. Over the years, a few Navajos intermarried with the tribe, bringing with them the Navajo Sun clan and kachina. The Spanish first entered the area in 1540, when Francesco de Coronado led an expedition to Zuni and two years later passed through the present site of Laguna on his way back to Mexico. Antonio Espejo, who commanded an expedition to New Mexico in 1582, visited the area in 1583. [...] Although the pueblo was not subjected to as many attacks from the Spanish as the Rio Grande pueblos, it was forced to surrender in 1692 after an attack by the troops of Governor Diego de Vargas. Concerning the mixture of people who settled at Laguna, Parsons comments that "it is not surprising that Laguna was the first of the pueblos to Americanize, through intermarriage." Around 1860 and 1870, George H. Pradt [or Pratt] and two Marmon brothers (Walter and Robert) came to the pueblo, married Laguna women, and reared large families. [...] While Robert Marmon served as governor, the two kivas of Laguna were torn down by the progressives and what was left of the sacred objects was surrendered. There were no kachina dances for some time after the Great Split and the laying of the railroad on the edge of the village. When a demand arose later for the revival of the dances, Zuni influences were introduced into Laguna rituals. Parsons closes her description of Laguna with the comment that although the ceremonial disintegration was so marked when she first studied it (around 1920) that it presented an obscure picture of Keresan culture, it now (1939) offered "unrivalled opportunities to study American acculturation and the important role played by miscegenation." (Ruoff 1978: 2-3)

compared with Pueblo inhabitants—contact and conflict with the colonial Spanish, inter-marriage with whites, or, as Parsons could put it, miscegenation from the 1860s onwards, and importation of other tribal cultural influences. Rather than view the implied author of *Ceremony* as favouring a simplistic "return to the blanket" and the kiva, we should view her as the product of a history of hybridization and acculturation that stretches back for generations.

In terms of cultural hybridity within the text, scholars agree on the main contextual sources and their provenance. Silko has repeatedly stressed the importance of oral storytelling traditions in her family, her clan and in Laguna; but she also alludes in interviews to the work of Parsons.[7] Robert Nelson indicates that, contrary to Paula Gunn Allen's accusation that Silko revealed clan secrets, specific materials in *Ceremony* had already been transcribed by Elsie Clews Parsons and edited by Franz Boas. He points out that the Boas and Parsons volumes are now scarce and only to be found in research libraries; thus they have had the effect of taking the stories away from the people. Refuting Allen's criticisms, he argues that Silko performs an act of restitution by embedding the clan stories in her novelistic text. In his reading, *Ceremony* rescues the stories from the mouldering anthropological tomes sitting on museum or library shelves and brings them back home to the people they belong to:

> All that's left to do now, Boas's critical apparatus in *Keresan Texts* tells us, is to pickle as many of these artifacts as we can still find in the preservative of print for future study. It is a telling comment, then, that the Boas book is out of print, impossible to come by except through special interlibrary loan. One is reminded of the boxes and boxes of human bones and "artifacts" in a museum warehouse somewhere, waiting to be sorted and displayed in the museum—or, if they get lucky, repatriated back to Indian Country.
> This, it seems to me, is what Silko's presentation of these same materials amounts to: an act of repatriation, putting those Laguna bones collected by the ethnographers back to their original use—to serve as backbone for a Laguna story about Laguna life in Laguna country. (53)

Thus in relation to the specifically Laguna stories, he suggests that Silko brings the stories back home rather than consigns them to a museum.

---

[7]   See for example, *Conversations* 14 & 19.

Unlike Bevis' model, however, this version of the return of the stories takes account of historical process, including the role of ethnographers and anthropologists. The text becomes a "telling" in more than one way, including its entering into a dialogical relation with cultural anthropology, and its entering historical process to restore balance after the harm done to the stories in the 1920s and 1930s. Although Silko draws on the oral traditions of Laguna storytelling, or gossip, she does so in a postmodern text. I say postmodern, not simply because she follows the modernist paradigm of Eliot's *The Waste Land* but also because she employs a very postmodern technique of combining different styles from different cultural locations: in this case the "Arrow Boy and the Witches" story, as well as other Keres clan stories that are laid out as poetic text, with European narrative techniques of the modern novel. In addition, she draws extensively on Navajo sandpainting and chantways. In fact, Navajo cultural formations seem central to *Ceremony* as ritual and text.

At the heart of the Navajo worldview is the belief that thought is potent and creative:

> Navajos believe strongly in the power of thought. The world was created by it; things are transformed according to it; life is regenerated from it. People are cured and blessed, vegetation is improved and increased, and health and happiness are restored by the power of thought. [...]
> Both order and disorder are first conceived in thought, and then projected on the world through speech and action. In both Navajo language and culture, things are considered to be in a random or an unordered condition unless a thinking, animate being has ordered them into some sort of a pattern. (Witherspoon 29 & 132)

So, the clan stories of Laguna Pueblo intersect with the Navajo Red Antway Chant, and Thought-Creating Woman of Keresan mythopoesis converses with the Navaho belief in the power of thought and the potency of language to neutralize witchery, restore harmony, and cure the disorders of the contemporary, post-atomic world.[8]

---

[8]   We might pause for a moment and ask ourselves: would we be surprised to read the quotation from Witherspoon in a different textual context with the word "Navajos" replaced by the phrase "postmodern theorists" and the phrase "in postmodern language and culture" substituted for his reference to "Navajo language and culture"?

In this imagined "third space" of dynamic hybridity and transformations of gossip, ritual, sandpainting, chantways, storytelling and prior ethnographic texts we needs must also find room for European cultural influences. One of the most eclectic and persuasive essays on transformation in *Ceremony* has to be Shamoon Zamir's. Yet at the point that he introduces the possible influence of *The Waste Land* on the structure and particularly the ending of the novel, he accuses Silko of espousing a European model of transcendence that diminishes the textual politics he discovers in the body of the work. His argument depends on reading the ending as "an ahistorical nostalgia for mythical transcendence" and as her deploying her source materials "as part of a strategy of negotiating historical crisis" through the "abandonment of the historicist literary imagination in favour of the transcendentalism T. S. Eliot termed the 'mythic method.'" (406) But what if European modernism's transcendentalism is actually the Navajo medicine man's curing ritual in creative dialogue with clan stories of Arrow Boy, told by Thought-Creating Woman? Can we as readers assume that the text retreats from the inter-tribal and inter-national third space it has conceived and been conceived in, back to just one element, the European? Or should we attempt to read the ending as an ongoing conversation in a complex, imaginative universe that is stranger to us than we can consciously tell?

Even though the bare bones of the plot fits Bevis' homing-in paradigm, the narrative strategies of *Ceremony* complicate the static, over-simplified, bipolar model of homing in, back to tribal identification that he proposes. Self-evidently, Silko and her protagonist home in on a different kiva from either of the two that were torn down during her paternal ancestor's governorship. Tayo's entering the kiva and telling his story to the elders cannot be read as his deciding to return "to the blanket" in a repetition of the plot resolution of *The Man Who Killed the Deer*. True, he returns with a restored—or in his case a newly acquired—sense of identification with the Pueblo, its people and its traditions. But this restoration of civic and environmental harmony is not a simulation of an Edward Curtis or Reverend Voth image caught in time and framed in perpetuity. This is a conversation of differing cultural elements that will have to function in a historical, contingent, post-atomic world, where the stories, chants and rituals will continue to signify only if they continue to transform traditional formations in renewed, differing cultural patterns.

The half-breed protagonist, Tayo, and, speaking through his actions, the implicit author have moved beyond the static, either/or model of Bevis' argument. Tayo does not choose to retreat into the local and ignore the global situation; Tayo learns that in the post-war, post-atomic situation the global is located in his backyard. Laguna Pueblo is at the complex nexus of Keres and Navajo stories and rituals, but it is also at the advanced capitalist nexus of uranium mining, atomic weapons testing and military strategic defence installations. Tayo is both hero of the "Arrow Boy" stories and patient of the curing "sing" or ceremony, restoring harmony to his environment and transforming post-war, post-traumatic shock syndrome into usable knowledge for his people. When he enters the kiva to tell his story at last he brings with him a complex understanding of the transformational ceremony for a changing world situation. "Earth surface people (Navajos or human beings) can expand their awareness or command of knowledge," (Witherspoon 33) and *Ceremony* is a culturally hybrid multi-stranded telling of why this becomes a matter of life and death post-World War II.

"I have learned to inhabit a hybrid, unpapered, Choctaw-Cherokee-Welsh-Irish-Cajun mixed space in between."

Why would Pushmataha and the other Choctaws have sided with foreigners like the Shawnee warrior Tecumsey, when they at least knew the English and white Americans? Whites never understood that, thinking that all Indians were the same.

In "Mapping the Mixedblood," Owens draws on his own experience to enunciate a definition of mixed-blood cultural identity that, like Bhabha's, is imagined as a spatialized concept. Given the painful and shameful history of contact, colonization, forced assimilation and attempted termination that is American history, his choice of metaphor is particularly appropriate. Owens reclaims the concept of "frontier" and defines it as a creative, transformational, trickster space, similar to Bhabha's sense of the third space. Owens draws on his knowledge of the rich trickster traditions of oral American Indian cultures to propose a specifically American theory of elusive and multifarious cultural hybridity.[9] Despite his self-deprecatory disclaimers that he is not an intellectual—just a writer, Owens' definition strikes me as eloquent and satisfyingly adequate:

> Because the term "frontier" carries with it such a heavy burden of colonial discourse, it can only be conceived of as a space of extreme contestation. Frontier, I would suggest, is the zone of trickster, a shimmering, always changing zone of multifaceted contact within which every utterance is challenged and interrogated, all referents put into question. In taking such a position, I am arguing for an appropriation and transvaluation of this deadly cliché of colonialism—for appropriation, inversion, and abrogation of authority are always trickster's strategies. "Frontier" stands, I would further argue, in neat opposition to the concept of "territory" as territory is imagined and given form by the colonial enterprise in America. Whereas frontier is always unstable, multidirectional, hybridized, characterized by heteroglossia, and indeterminate, territory is clearly mapped, fully imagined as a place of containment, invented to control and subdue the dangerous potentialities of imagined Indians. Territory is conceived and designed to exclude the dangerous presence of that trickster at the heart of the Native American imagination, for the ultimate logic of territory is appropriation and occupation, and trickster defies appropriation and resists colonization. (26)

"Mapping the Mixedblood" is one of the series of linked essays that constitute the non-fiction volume, *Mixedblood Messages*, a volume that enacts cultural hybridity in its blending of autobiography, eco-philosophy, literary theory and criticism as well as reflecting Owens' personal engagement in identity politics. Moreover it is the volume that most clearly indicates the influence of Vizenor on Owens' mature writing. Its preoccupations are further refracted in Owens' last novel, *Dark River*, published the following year (1999). All of his previous novels draw on trickster aesthetics at the level of plot and arguably characterization, but *Dark River* comes closest to the trickster discourse that Owens so admires

---

9   See Owens' essay "As If an Indian Were Really an Indian: Native American Voices and Postcolonial Theory." *I Hear the Train*: 207-226 for an excellent critique of postcolonial critics, including Homi Bhabha and Toni Morrison, who as a general rule ignore the presence of Native American literature and culture in their discourses. Like Owens I turned to Bhabha in the hope of finding a critical discourse that would be adequate to the situation of Native American literature, and found some of his conceptual formulations useful despite his ignorance of the specific canon.

in Vizenor's fiction. The trajectory that leads to the overtly trickster ending of *Dark River* draws the reader away from her prior expectations and strategically leads her to confront the issues that Vizenor raises in *Manifest Manners* and *Fugitive Poses*. It seems to me that Vizenor's postindian, postmodernist thought influences both Owens' late fiction and his final volume of essays.[10]

In his formulation of the notion of frontier space he articulates the confrontational struggle of which it is metonymical:

> From the very beginning of European relations with indigenous Americans, the goal of the colonizer has been to inhabit and erase an ever-moving frontier while shifting "Indian" to static and containable "territory"—both within the trope of the noble and vanishing red man and within the more effective strategy that equated good Indians with dead ones. (27)

While it is true that Native Americans made homelands out of "prisons," i.e. reservations; it is clearly no longer the case that all Native Americans could or would want to return to their tribal homelands and the tribal traditions of previous centuries. When Commissioner John Collier attempted to legislate for a return to such traditional tribalism in 1934, he met with much skepticism and resistance from various groups and factions.[11] Bevis's critical efforts to return all mixed-blood protagonists to the tribal ways of their ancestral past should be countered with similar resistance by writers and readers. And yet, mixed-blood protagonists from Welch's Jim Loney to Owens' Jake Nashoba not only internalize the hybridized frontier, they also play out in their painful psychodramas the anomie of the culturally displaced and dispossessed. While their emotional symptoms are similar to those of the fashionably alienated modernist, existentialist hero, their malaise is deeply rooted in the history of displacement that frequently became genocide and in the paradox that sent (proportionate to the population) twice as many Native American soldiers to fight in US wars as from any other American ethnic group. Welch's Jim Loney, with his unredeemed, self-elected death casts a strong shadow over Jake Nashoba. A comparison of the two novels

---

[10]   The notion of trickster aesthetics is still unfamiliar to many European readers of Native American novels. As well as Vizenor's own writings on the subject, I recommend Jeanne Rosier Smith. *Writing Tricksters*.

[11]   See Wilson 1998: 333-358; Iverson 1998: 77-102.

would suggest that like Jim, Jake doesn't have enough childhood memories to provide resources for self-healing; like Jim, the figure who might be the guiding elder fails to assist him even though living in the near neighbourhood; and like Jim, there is no effective cure or timely "medicine" to purify the returning warrior / soldier.

Home, a bad joke

Owens acknowledges that the raw materials for his novels are drawn from his own experiences and those of his family. In an extended rebuttal of Cook-Lynn's tribalist position, for example, he asserts the obviousness of this and also suggests that while pre-Columbian tribal peoples might not have had a westernized sense of individual identity, the late twentieth-century Native American author inevitably will.[12] In *Mixedblood Messages* and *I Hear the Train* he strives to leave clear evidence of the relationships between his family's complex, marginalised history, their individual characters, their shared experiences and his works of fiction. Most poignant is his acknowledgement in *I Hear the Train* that his elder brother's experiences as a Vietnam veteran and his attempts to deal with the sense of loss this in turn inflicted on himself led to his writing his second novel, *The Sharpest Sight*:

> And then one day, after a quarter of a century of silence, my brother called. He had found a copy of *The Sharpest Sight* [...] he had read it and had known at once that it was about him, had read past layers of metaphor and myth, through a complex "mystery" plot, to see that I'd written a novel about the loss of my own brother. (12)

In this novel not only the missing brother, Attis, but most of the male characters are formed or deformed by their memories of Vietnam. Tom Holm has described the ways in which post-traumatic shock syndrome affects veterans, and the ways in which their experiences of conflict leave them estranged from members of their peer group who haven't experienced warfare. At a point in their lives when they might normally feel the "immortality of youth" they bear instead a heightened sense of their own mortality and the immanence of violent and senseless death. (7) Owens

---

12 *Mixedblood Messages*: 153, 181-183.

returns to the subject more allusively in *Bone Game*—in a trickster twist
of the plot, one of the two murderers is a seriously deranged Vietnam
veteran, a deadly joker in the pack when everyone thinks the game is
over. However, his most mature tribute to his brother Gene and war
veterans like him, who continue to suffer twenty-five years on, is in my
opinion the characterization of Jake Nashoba.

In a moment of reminiscence that touches me all the more deeply
for the simplicity of its utterance, Owens captures the nobility of his
brother's life:

> Sitting there after catfish and fried potatoes, I was able,
> however, to ask the question that had clawed at me for years:
> Why had he re-upped twice? Why had he stayed three years in
> what his letters had described as worse than any hell a person
> could imagine? He looked at me directly when he answered, his
> brown eyes locking on mine for the first time since I'd come to
> his home. "I stayed so that someone wouldn't have to take my
> place," he said. (11)

For all the postmodern games and trickster aesthetics of *Dark River*, Jake
Nashoba is a tragic hero, journeying ineluctably towards the heart of
darkness, playing over and over the pointless futility of America's
apocalypse now. The clues are there from the start, but the implicit
reader is unlikely to take them too seriously, since they are balanced by
a textual playfulness that suggests survivance rather than vanishment.[13]
Paradoxically, this realistic mixed-blood protagonist will get involved in
the deadly hyperreality of Rambo-esque war games.

Despite the superficial similarity to Silko's novel, there are a
number of significant differences. Jake does not return to his tribal
homeland after serving in Vietnam; he reflects the restless motion of late
twentieth-century American culture:

> [H]e'd been driving toward the tilting red cactus like he'd been
> driving toward the tilting red sun every day since being
> discharged in New Jersey. He'd drunk and fought his way
> across from Amarillo to Albuquerque and down to Las Cruces
> and through Silver City, Patagonia, and Tucson before turning
> the Chevy pickup north to Phoenix. Flagstaff was on the other
> side of Phoenix, and he had a Navajo buddy in that patriotic-

---

[13] Neologism intended.

sounding town who said it was full of beautiful women and cheap liquor. (32-33)

Here he gets into another fight and two months later ends up married to the dancer he fought over. Thus he lives on a reservation that is strange to him: he doesn't know its stories and traditions, and although he learns its environmental landscape he can never know its significance in tribal culture. He is a perpetual stranger in this place, even in his own home: He hadn't counted on a couple of things. First, as Tali had explained, the tribe was matrilocal, which basically meant that he and Tali were expected to live with her parents, sisters, unmarried drunken brothers, and anyone else who dropped by. [...] The second thing he hadn't considered was that in the tribe the wife owned the house. The husband was a kind of guest, and in his case not even high on the bathroom waiting list since he was not just a husband but a foreigner. (31-32)

After two years his wife divorces him, matrilocal style, by "setting his few possessions on the porch" (33). Yet he remains on the edge of the reservation geographically and on the edge of the community socially, and is still there after twenty-five years. The allusion to Owens' brother Gene is of course encoded in the quarter century that Jake has existed as a resident stranger at Black Mountain. As is the description of his violent nightmares, focalized in the novel through Jake himself:

> Sometimes he'd fall over the edge of sleep into that other world, a black, tangled place where everything conspired to destroy him, and he'd leap to protect his life. Those were the times he'd awakened to find his wife on the floor or against a far wall of the bedroom, her mouth or nose bleeding and her eyes staring in terror. (36)

In his memoir, Owens recounts the source of this textual reminiscence, in a stripped-down, laconic style:

> In a matter-of-fact way, his wife interrupted to explain that he'd nearly killed her a few months earlier when she moved during the night unexpectedly.
> "Gene still has his problems," she said, looking at him with what struck me as critical love. (10)

Knowing that he draws on personal and family experiences shouldn't lead us to assume that he writes "transparent" texts. Especially in *Dark River* there is a critical creative intelligence at work.[14] Thus he alludes to and deals with the trope of the ceremony early in the narrative. Jake is taken by Tali for counselling at the Phoenix Indian Centre, but is unable to talk to the therapist; Tali suggests that he attend an inter-tribal sweat, but he dismisses the idea; and most ominously Mrs Edwards refuses to help him because she sees straight away that he is beyond healing. I assume that "Black Mountain" is a fictitious and deeply metaphorical tribal name and location, possibly an imaginative synthesis of the Apache White Mountain reservation and a shadowy, colonial, heart of darkness. The point is that Jake doesn't know its beliefs and ceremonies; Mrs Edwards might have the power to help him but feels suspicious and antagonistic towards him as a dislocated, traumatised foreigner. Moreover, in the late twentieth century tribal culture has become a complex modern phenomenon for all the characters who dwell at Black Mountain. In a Vizenor-like paradox, the only "real" traditional tribal member is the New York, Jewish anthropologist: the utter fake is the only hyperreal Indian, recognizable to white perception. As a fake, he is unable to save Jake, despite his deep and accurate, acquired knowledge of the past tribal culture. Thus, the novel enters into a tricky dialogue with its prior text, *Ceremony*, in order to refute Silko's optimistic ending that affirms the curing ceremony can still function, albeit in a radically transformed fashion.

The post-modernism[15] of Owens' protagonist is darker and more fragmented, with no sense that a ritual can be recovered to heal the Fisher King. Early in the novel Jake laconically tells his boss why he enjoys reading Hemingway. He does so partly to wind Sam up, because he intuits that Sam might be withholding information, as indeed he also does. However, the dialogue also reveals to the implicit reader both the kind of novel they are reading and the kind of novel they shouldn't expect to find in the pages that follow:

> "Say, did I ever tell you why I like to read Hemingway? You ever read his stuff?"
> "What the fuck are you talking about?" Sam yelled. "You got blood all over my goddamned floor last night."

---

[14] See Vizenor's comments on the oral story-telling tradition noting that the performing art is also criticism. *The People Named the Chippewa*: 7-8.

[15] I use the hyphenated "post-modern" to imply that the author is working in relation to prior texts from literary modernism.

"It's mostly his language, Sam. It's restful, you know, and honest; it doesn't require some kind of action. His people are all fucked up, just like the rest of us, but there's this sense that he's not trying to hide anything, that nothing's going to change and it's not so great but basically okay. I tried one of those Indian novels, a best-seller supposedly written by a real Indian, but it was nothing but a bunch of stupid skins drinking and beating each other to death and being funny about it. At least the writer was trying to be funny about it."

"Fuck Hemingway and fuck Indian writers and fuck you, Jake. We have a problem here. Have you talked to anybody about this head?" (11)

Unlike the implied author of *Ceremony*, the implied author of *Dark River* signals to his readers that "nothing's going to change and it's not so great but basically okay." The rituals of the healing sing won't be transformed into a hybrid, optimistic literary text this time. But neither will the author fulfil reader expectations of dead-end, self-destructive Indians, vanishing themselves with humour. Trickster-like, the implied author simultaneously announces that the plot might do both of these contradictory things as well, after a fashion.

In a late story about Luther Cole, published in *I Hear the Train*, Owens defines a characteristic of Native American and mixed-blood identity:

> All of his life the old man had balanced two realities, two worlds, a feat that had never struck him as particularly noteworthy or difficult. (195)[16]

Both the implicit author and the protagonist perform this balancing act; and it is also an important feature of the plot. Jake is characterized as Choctaw/Irish, "with only shadowy notions of what it might mean to be Choctaw" (37). The homing-in plot simply is not available to him:

> "*Chahta*," he said. "*Chahta okla*. White people say 'Choctaw.' They have plenty of stories. Stories, in fact that tell me who you are." He knew he was treading on thin ice. He remembered only

---

[16] For another perspective on this phenomenon we can turn to James Wilson's history of Native America: "Almost since the time of Columbus, the Native American ability to syncretize two realities – to accept that different people have different truths or to believe that two apparently contradictory statements can be true in different ways – has baffled and frustrated Europeans brought up with the idea of a single, monolithic truth." (9-10)

the barest fragments—*alikchi*, sorcerers, dream-senders, *isht*-
something or other. There were good ones and bad ones with
different names. His granma's stories had become bits and
pieces like a jigsaw puzzle dumped thoughtlessly on the ground,
some pieces carried off by careless children. [...]
"Then why have you never gone home?" She looked at him
keenly. "Hasn't that old man called you?"
He thought of the cabin in Mississippi, his father, whom he
couldn't visualize in his memory half as well as he could the old
man across the river, his granma talking about blooded earth
as though sacrifice had been made, and his thin, Irish mother
brushing hair from her face in the cabin door. "Look, Grandmother, I'm no Indian. My people have stories of leprechauns,
too, and something called the *sidhe*. You know about those?
Besides, home is where the heart is, and I'd like you to stop
messing with my dreams. I don't know what you're up to, but I
don't like it." (42)

A couple of generations younger than Luther Cole, his knowledge both of
his Irish inheritance and of his Choctaw culture is so fragmented that
they have become part of the unusable past. He remembers just enough
to realize that Mrs. Edwards is some kind of sorcerer or dream-sender,
without having a clear idea what kind she is. He utters "Home is where
the heart is" ironically: as a saying it might still have had resonance for
his Irish mother, but for him it is a clichéd husk of language.

Owens plays tantalizingly with another aspect of the homing-in
plot, namely, the role of the traditional elder to teach the protagonist "the
only knowledge which proves useful" (Bevis 592). Bevis describes such a
figure as "a connected ancestor," commenting:

[A]ll are in touch with a tradition tracing from the distant past,
and all extend this connection to the young protagonists. Only
Loney fails to find a connected ancestor, and only Loney fails.
(588)

Bevis' essentialist certainty has no place in this novel, for the Dark is a
"zone of multifaceted contact within which every utterance is challenged
and interrogated, all referents put into question." The Dark is of course
both the river canyon where nobody is supposed to be, but just about
every character in the novel ends up, and the state of mind that Jake has
existed in all these years on Black Mountain. It also functions as a

mnemonic for Jake, reminding him of the intense but fleeting encounter he had with the connected ancestor, Luther Cole, on that other river in his Mississippi childhood:

> As a very young boy, he'd hidden in the woods once and watched the stringy old Choctaw man haul a mudcat out of the river, the ugly fish longer than the man's arm. The old grandfather had clubbed the fish with a piece of oak and then, unexpectedly, raised his eyes to look directly at where he hid, the eyes so taut that he could feel them go over him like smooth hands. [...] His mother had died on his first tour of duty, and so he was tied to nothing in the whole world except a childhood vision of an old man he never knew. Luther Cole. (108-109, 111)

Owens uses intertextual allusion to his own prior novels, and the implicit reader will only realize the significance of Luther's role in this story if they know the roles he played in prior texts. In *The Sharpest Sight* Luther and Onatima (Old Lady Blue) intervene in the story of Attis' death to guide Cole McCurtain in his task of retrieving his brother's bones and thus freeing his shadows to rest. In *Bone Game* they still play a significant role, knowing when to assist Cole in his encounter with the "Gambler." But already they are not able to control the outcome of the story; they can only help Cole to do that. In this novel, Cole is referred to once as a distant cousin of Jake's. Thus, there is a tenuous connection that serves to highlight the difference. Uncle Luther is Cole's connected ancestor, but is not close enough to be Jake's. Consequently, as a young boy he glimpses what "he never knew," and there seems to be no way the knowledge can be given to him. In Jake's focalized memories Luther denotes absence and loss, a childhood of dislocations and missing pieces of the puzzle:

> He'd asked his granma about the old man. "Luther Cole," was all she'd said, shaking her head and spitting the eternal tobacco juice. And then his mother had taken him away from whatever that dream had meant. He lived with a vague yearning to go home, but he couldn't locate that place on all the maps he bought and hoarded. (50)

Somehow the Dark River and its canyon answer this vague yearning. Jake makes a kind of home in its environment, unaware of its specific tribal traditions and knowledges. This lack of relevant cultural knowledge leads him to make the mistake of constructing a hubristic, marital home that reminds Mrs. Edwards of a US cavalry Fort Apache, rather than an appropriate matrilocal dwelling. Luther and Onatima are unable to act as dream-senders or storytellers; they are unable to intervene to save him. Yet as tenuously related, connected ancestors they do what they can within their Choctaw reality:

> His body was soft, like melting plastic, and he remembered the old Choctaw man across the river. *Chahta*, they said. *Chahta*. With the memory, the old man approached, his broad hat drawn down low over his thin, dark face. "We don't send this dream, Grandson," the old man said. "But the Grandmother and I are watching your shadows." (214)

In *Dark River,* Jake's story is appropriated by Shorty Luke, as indeed are everybody's stories. At the beginning, he appears to be a harmless, comic character; a playful, postmodern characterization of what Hollywood does to real Native Americans who go there to play Indian. The implicit reader interprets him as something of a joke: an Apache who passed as an Italian actor in order to act as an Indian extra, and who is clearly not a contender to be viewed by the *National Geographic* film crew as an authentic Indian. Unfortunately, he is a rather bad joke, as he and Mrs. Edwards emerge as dark and unpredictable parodies of Luther and Onatima. Shorty knows the old tribal stories, having learnt them from the tribal chairman's grandmother, but he has also learnt Hollywood lines and acted in hyperreal screenplays. Like Luther Cole, he balances two realities, two worlds, but unlike Luther he allows them to intersect disastrously. Like Jake, the implicit reader doesn't have enough knowledge to judge whether Mrs Edwards is "a good one or a bad one." Is she belatedly trying to help Tali and to cure Jake, or does she remain convinced that, unlike Domingo Perez, he won't survive? The fact that she has the power to save Domingo Perez, veteran of World War II, but cannot restore Jake to life in the Black Mountain community may tell the reader something about her character. However, I believe it says far more about the difference between the traumas experienced by World War II veterans and the post-traumatic shock syndrome of veterans of the Vietnam Conflict. At the dark heart of this novel is a core sense of the inexpressible and incommunicable nature of that experience.

In "As if an Indian Were Really an Indian,"[17] Owens invokes Bakhtin:

> [F]or Native Americans the only burden of expectation is that he or she put on the constructed mask provided by the colonizer, and the mask is not merely a mirror but more crucially a static death mask. [...] He or she who steps behind the mask becomes the Vanishing American, a savage/noble, mystical, pitiable, romantic fabrication of the Euroamerican psyche fated to play out the epic role defined by Mikhail Bakhtin: "The epic and tragic hero," Bakhtin writes, "is the hero who by his very nature must perish . . . . Outside his destiny the epic and tragic hero is nothing; he is, therefore, a function of the plot fate assigns him; he cannot become the hero of another destiny or another plot. (218)

Owens' sense of the perniciousness of "the absolute fake, the fabricated 'Indian'" (217) pervades this novel, including the darkly comic scenes at the tribal Casino, and the depiction of Jesse's fatal Vision Quest Enterprises. However, even though he quotes Bakhtin as authority, as trickster author of *Dark River* he complicates the Bakhtinian definition of the tragic hero. Despite and/or because of Shorty Luke's and Mrs. Edward's dream-sendings and story tellings, Jake *can* "become the hero of [...] another plot." In the shimmering, multifaceted frontier zone that this text inhabits, Jake becomes the hero of a Spider Woman story:

> There was only a small black hole in the ground between the clumps of grass. He began to walk away, but a voice said, "What are you looking for?"
> He stopped and tried to find the speaker, but no one was there. "I'm looking for my own people," he said. "I've been gone a long time, and I have a long way to go."
> "Don't you realize that no one can go to that place?" The voice said.
> Jake looked down to see a black spider at the top of the hole. "Come into my house, Grandson," the spider said. "Don't be frightened."
> How can I go into such a tiny hole, Jake thought, but he closed his eyes and when he opened them he was in a warm, lighted room [...]

---

[17]   An impressive and mature engagement with post-colonial theorists, including Bhabha, who write as if Native Americans have not only vanished but were invisible throughout American history.

> Jake closed his eyes and found himself in the room of soft earth. He was sitting up with his back straight, a wonderful feeling of life coursing through his body. A great black spider crouched close by. "Welcome home," the spider said. [...]
> "Welcome back, Grandson. *Halito*. It's been a long time."
> *Halito*. Jacob turned toward the smiling old Choctaw man, the flow of a big, dark river in his brown eyes. (235, 271)

A characteristic feature of Spider Woman is that she can change shape and size from tiny spider to beautiful young woman or to wise old grandmother figure. She often helps the hero by perching behind his ear and being a tiny, invisible voice directing him; and when he stumbles upon her home it is a tiny hole in the ground, but at her command he finds he can enter it.

In Owens' previous novels the reader is expected to suspend disbelief. In the first four novels, the implicit author establishes conventions that require the implicit reader to accept various tribal belief systems as well as Western rationalism. So, in the final sequence of this novel the implied reader who has stalwartly suspended disbelief is confounded by the improvisatory turn the dénouement takes. Questioned by Jesse's shadow, Shorty opines: "Well, Jake's not predictable, or hackneyed, as they say. Seems pretty original to have him down in a hole like that. He's the hero, right?" (282) This prompts him to improvise an ending that Hollywood special effects departments would be proud of:

> The earth had opened up, and two enormous mandibles framed by spider legs reached out and seized Jake. In a moment he was gone, dragged into a hole that closed at once.
> "My idea," Shorty said.
> "Good one," Jesse replied admiringly.
> Shorty turned to Alison. "Don't worry, your grandfather has gone home." (284)

Shorty, the tribal storyteller and Hollywood authentic/fake Indian, balances both realities for Jake. At one level, the implied reader recoils at the irresponsible killing off of the hero, when it looked as if a good ceremony might have saved him. However, giving up the struggle to suspend disbelief on this cutting-room floor of an ending, the implied reader realizes that Jake has gone home to the reality he has yearned for all his life. The implicit author, through the improbable character of

Shorty Luke, holds in balance a realistic, existential, Hemingwayesque honesty and a traditional tribal telling. The novel begins with the extra-heterodiegetic narrator invoking the traditional oral framing phrase: "That's what they say" (9). It ends with Shorty, who has usurped the story telling to become the intra-homodiegetic narrator, explaining to a perplexed tribal chief: "It is said that Jacob Nashoba went home" (286).

It's as if the trickster author challenges his implicit white reader: O.K., if you want a regressive plot, I'll give you the ultimate regressive ending; but I don't think you're going to like it! But then Jake's other (or should that be *tribal*) name is "The Lone Ranger." So, Kimo Sabe! *(Que no sabe)* **Qué** *no sabe?*

Helen M. Dennis

Works Cited

Bevis, William. 1987. "Native American Novels: Homing In." Brian Swann & Arnold Krupat, eds. *Recovering the Word: Essays on Native American Literature*. Berkeley: University of California Press, pp. 580-620.

Bhabha, Homi K. 1995. "Cultural Diversity and Cultural Differences." Ashcroft, Bill, Gareth Griffiths and Helen Tiffin, eds. *The Post-Colonial Studies Reader*. London: Routledge, pp. 206-209.

Bhabha, Homi. 1994. *The Location of Culture*. London: Routledge.

Holm, Tom. 1996. *Strong Hearts Wounded Souls: Native American Veterans of the Vietnam War*. Austin: University of Texas Press.

Iverson, Peter. 1998. *"We Are Still Here": American Indians in the Twentieth Century*. Wheeling, Illinois: Harlan Davidson.

Mullet, G. M. 1979. *Spider Woman Stories: Legends of the Hopi Indians*. Tucson: University of Arizona Press.

Nelson, Robert. M. 2001. "Rewriting Ethnography: The Embedded Texts in Leslie Silko's *Ceremony*." Elizabeth Hoffman Nelson & Malcolom A. Nelson, eds. *Telling the Stories: Essays on American Indian Literatures and Cultures*. New York: Peter Lang, pp. 47-58.

Owens, Louis. 1991. *The Sharpest Sight*. Norman: University of Oklahoma Press.

————. 1994. *Bone Game*. Norman: University of Oklahoma Press.

————. 1995. *Wolfsong*. Norman: University of Oklahoma Press.

————. 1997. *Nightland*. New York: Signet.

————. 1998. *Mixedblood Messages: Literature, Film, Family, Place*. Norman: University of Oklahoma Press.

————. 1999. *Dark River*. Norman: University of Oklahoma Press.

————. 2001. *I Hear the Train: Reflections, Inventions, Refractions*. Norman: University of Oklahoma Press.

Ruoff, A. LaVonne. 1978. "Ritual and Renewal: Keres Traditions in the Short Fiction of Leslie Silko." *Melus.* 5: 4. 1978: 2-17.

Silko, Leslie Marmon. 1986. *Ceremony.* New York: Penguin.

—————. 2000. *Conversations with Leslie Marmon Silko.* Ellen L. Arnold, ed. Jackson: University Press of Mississippi.

Smith,Jeanne Rosier. 1997. *Writing Tricksters: Mythic Gambols in American Ethnic Literature.* Berkeley: University of California Press.

Taylor, Colin F. & Sturtevant, William C. *et al.* 1996. *The Native Americans: the Indigenous People of North America.* New York: Salamander Books (Smithmark).

Vizenor, Gerald. 1984. *The People Named the Chippewa: Narrative Histories.* Minneapolis: University of Minnesota Press.

—————. 1993. "Trickster Discourse: Comic Holotropes and Language Games." Gerald Vizenor, ed. *Narrative Chance: Postmodern Discourse on Native American Indian Literatures.* Norman & London: University of Oklahoma Press.

—————. 1994. *Manifest Manners: Narratives on Postindian Survivance.* Lincoln: University of Nebraska Press.

—————. 1998. *Fugitive Poses: Native American Indian Scenes of Absence and Presence.* Lincoln: University of Nebraska Press.

Waters, Frank. 1977. *Book of the Hopi.* Harmondsworth: Penguin Books (1st published 1963).

—————. 1971. *The Man Who Killed the Deer.* New York: Washington Square Press (1st published 1942).

Wilson, James. 1998. *The Earth Shall Weep: A History of Native America.* London: Picador.

Witherspoon, Gary. 2001. *Language and Art in the Navajo Universe.* Ann Arbor: University of Michigan Press (1st published 1977).

Multilingual Narrative and the Refusal of Translation: Theresa Hak Kyung Cha's *Dictee* and R. Zamora Linmark's *Rolling the R's*

United States language politics have come to play a newly prominent role in current neo-imperial policy discussions. In an article titled "Iraq's New English Studies," Joe Lockard points to the trend among some conservative intellectuals to advocate the geopolitical benefits of spreading U.S. English globally. He reviews in detail, for example, one proposal that "advocates the deployment of the English language [in U.S.-occupied Iraq] as a means of ideological acculturation and language education for mass control." In support of this plan, the proponent cited England's ability "to transmit modern and liberal ideas" in colonially ruled India through the English language.[1] As Lockard points out, the substitution of "English-speaking" for the racial category of white (or Anglo) is typical of current discourse and an uncanny echo of late-nineteenth century nationalism. So, too, is the slippery equation of "English-speaking" with "Western values," modernity, and futurity, thus painting non-Euro-American

---

[1] On the colonial institutionalization of English Studies in India as a means of securing political control, see Viswanathan, *Masks of Conquest*.

cultures as "backward" in the uni-directional teleology of progress. In this fashion, old arguments linking colonial administration with language imposition from nineteenth-century England and the early twentieth-century U.S. are being made new again: "The Victorian English that laboured so long to encode a racial order within promissory phrases of civilizational progress has re-emerged as a global English that sugarcoats the political realities of imperial rule with promises of a democratic future. To learn English has become to learn the future again."

What, then, is to be done in the face of a colonialism so deeply ingrained in language itself? As anti-colonial writers have demonstrated in myriad ways throughout the past century, this linguistic domination also provides the means to oppose its power. "English Studies today are equally counter-hegemonic self-defence; learning the Englishes of globalization can provide a paradoxical safety from their more malignant effects. All human languages bear an inherent concept of an empowered speaking subject, the possessor of independent narrative rights," Lockhard explains, "and English serves subversive purposes as well as any language."

In the current context of ongoing international political and cultural conflicts that are intimately intertwined, I would like to add to this conversation of counter-hegemonic linguistic self-defence the political work of contemporary multilingual literatures, particularly the radical multilingualism that rarely provides internal translation for monolingual readers. As a result of 1980s and 1990s multiculturalism debates, the canon of contemporary U.S. literature has grown markedly more multicultural; however, the canon has not become demonstrably more *multilingual*. In fact, given the changing demographics of the nation and recent developments in television and film, a strong case could be made that today popular culture takes multilingual expression more seriously than the academy. Film, newspapers, photography, spoken word performance, and literature currently are being composed in an ever-widening number of linguistic contact zones within the nation—particularly multilingual vernaculars that syncopate the status of dominant languages as normative.

Multilingual works tend to be composed with force and specificity. Knowing that the battle for readers/viewers of multilingual cultures is always uphill, artists whose work is multilingual have devised (and continue to invent) aesthetically compelling and politically exigent modes of expression. Consequently, as critics we must do more than speculate abstractly about linguistic hybridity or other vague and toothless categories while ignoring these works' substantive historical and political contributions. With this in mind, I consider the ideological charge of late twentieth-century U.S. multilingual literature. Is there an affinity between radical multilingualism and radical politics? Considering the English-Only hierarchies governing U.S. history and the language politics of contemporary globalization, strategies now familiar to readers of multi-ethnic literatures, such as internal translation, mistranslation, and translation refusal offer a radical politics of "counter-hegemonic self-defence." As particularly powerful examples of multilingual literature, Theresa Cha's *Dictee* and R. Zamora Linmark's *Rolling the R's* demonstrate the intensified significance of these linguistic strategies in the era of globalization.

The first part of my argument is that the political charge of multilingual U.S. literatures has had a particularly lasting quality. Throughout various eras, from the eighteenth and nineteenth centuries to modernist and postmodern periods, literary works that counter U.S. monolingual expectations remain omnipresent and arrestingly powerful, despite their rarity.[2] Over time, language has functioned as a deeply complex, unsettling site of resistance and submission, consent and dissent. Its effects are neither obvious nor predictable. Relatively recent examples of the unexpected force and surprising (even to participants) outcomes include the Oakland Ebonics debate, California's anti-bilingual education Proposition 227 (charmingly named by its supporters "English for the Children"), and unprecedented numbers of accent discrimination lawsuits. Why does language remain such a politically charged element of mass and avant-garde culture, in both national and global cultures?

To consider the vexed field of multilingual cultural production, I turn to the interdisciplinary methodology of translation theory because it has developed a set of useful analytic concepts for describing the most fraught areas of multilingual cultures. Implicitly and explicitly, transla-tion theorists have outlined a number of suggestive arguments on behalf of the socially transformative inclusivity that a shift from a monolingual culture to a multilingual one might entail.

---

[2] For evidence of the omnipresence of multilingual U.S. cultures, see Sollors and Shell, *The Multilingual Anthology of American Literature*; Sollors, *Multilingual America*; and Shell, *American Babel*.

1990s multiculturalism propounded a vision of a transformative inclusivity, of a restructuring social vision as a positive ideal as well as a basis for critique. But, from the vantage point of the early twenty-first century, one can safely say that 1990s multiculturalism did not deliver that vision.[3] Why not? Among other omissions, multiculturalism did not include a thorough consideration of the importance of national multi-lingualism. I want to suggest that the novels I am identifying as "radically multilingual"—Cha's *Dictee* and Linmark's *Rolling the R's*—clarify crucial points of technique, audience, and ideology in order to challenge monolingualism. Many other recent works bear out these arguments, including films, such as Ang Lee's *The Wedding Banquet*, Wayne Wang's *Eat a Bowl of Tea*, John Sayles's *Lone Star* and *Hombres Armados*, Julian Schnabel's *Before Night Falls* and fiction, such as Junot Díaz's *Drown* and Ernesto Quiñonez's *Bodega Dreams*.

Like these other works, Cha's narrative of a Catholic childhood merged with the Japanese occupation of Korea and Linmark's brilliantly innovative episodic novel of gay Filipino youths defiantly call attention to the everyday lives of U.S. residents as requiring multiple languages. It should (but cannot) go without saying that this critique of monolingual U.S. residents is not a recent development, but a long-standing and historically rooted one. As John Sayles said in discussing his film *Lone Star*, "English-speaking culture is just one of many cultures. It has become the dominant culture or subculture in certain areas, but it's a subculture just like all the others. American culture is not monolingual or monoracial. It's always been a mix" (Carson 212-13).

The most immediate risk—or opportunity—posed by multilingual writing is, of course, audience [in]comprehension. The two works that I'm discussing—*Dictee* and *Rolling the R's*—are richly intertextual and multimedia, as well as multilingual. While both novels are ambitiously experimental in their linguistic strategies and narrative forms, they represent very different kinds of multilingual novels. *Dictee* is a frag-mented, discontinuous, avant-garde meditation on Korean identity and feminist history that challenges readers' comprehension at every turn. By contrast, the episodically structured *Rolling the R's* takes as its context

---

[3]   The scholarly discussions of multiculturalism are too vast to be referenced here exhaustively. Among the many important contributions, see Gordon and Newfield, *Mapping Multiculturalism*; Thomas, "Civic Multiculturalism"; and Rogers Smith's historical overview, *Civic Ideals*.

popular music and queer Filipino/Hawai'ian youth culture. Cha was an experimental video artist, and a visual dimension is crucial to her experimental narrative, illustrated through inventive typography and image-text juxtapositions. Even languages are portrayed visually as well as aurally in *Dictee*. Individual Japanese characters take up whole pages, as do hand-written passages, images of Korean characters, and columns of Latin/English and French/English translations. By not only drawing on but actually *drawing* languages that represent religious ritual, school instruction, imperial conquest, and anti-colonial memory in one narrative, Cha composed *Dictee* as an achronological, associative, anti-didactic retrieval of feminist and Korean immigrant history. She accomplished this retrieval of history by recovering three life-stories of exiled Korean women: the protagonist-speaker's, her mother's, and that of the revolutionary Yu Guan Soon:

> Why resurrect it all now. From the Past. History, the old wound. The past emotions all over again. To confess to relive the same folly. To name it now so as not to repeat history in oblivion. To extract each fragment by each fragment from the word from the image another word another image the reply that will not repeat history in oblivion. (33)

Cha's "resurrect[ed]" revolutionary history does not merely do justice to a woman who organized "the largest collective outcry against the Japanese occupation of the Korean people who willingly gave their lives for independence" (30). Cha tells the story of Guan Soon in order to "extract each fragment by each fragment from the word from the image another word another image" in an appropriately fragmentary composition. By shattering words and images into barely recognizable bits, she "extract[ed] … the reply that will not repeat history in oblivion." It is worth noting that Cha's allusive, flat, repetitive style in English suggests affinities to another enigmatically revolutionary immigrant feminist writer who famously eschewed punctuation marks: Gertrude Stein.

Cha's unapologetically untranslated multilingualism accomplishes more than simply a subversion of U.S. English or of normative language expectations. Born in Korea in 1951 and murdered in New York City in 1982 (tragically and ironically just days after the publication of *Dictee*), Cha implicitly argued that a textual representation of her life required the particular languages that contributed to her sense of self— in flagrant disregard of the deeply ingrained convention that U.S. literature must be written in English and English only.

Dictee challenges the didactic framework of dictation-based language learning from the very outset. The first section begins with the words, "She mimicks the speaking. That might resemble speech. (Anything at all.) Bared noise, groan, bits torn from words" (3). Throughout the work Cha associates the didacticism of language-learning dictations with the rigidity of religious learning (not to mention the force of sexual violence and of imperial conquest), so that such descriptions of enforced verbal acts at once suggest multiple meanings. At the beginning of the book, Cha includes several seemingly literal examples of translation exercises. For example, here is the first set:

> Ecrivez en français:
> 1. If you like this better, tell me so at once.
> 2. The general remained only a little while in this place.
> 3. If you did not speak so quickly, they would understand you better.
> 4. The leaves have not fallen yet nor will they fall for some days.
> 5. It will fit you pretty well.
> 6. The people of this country are less happy then the people of yours.
> 7. Come back on the fifteenth of next month, no sooner and no later.
> 8. I met him downstairs by chance.
> 9. Be industrious: the more one works, the better one succeeds.
> 10. The harder the task, the more honourable the labour.
> 11. The more a man praises himself, the less inclined are others to praise him.
> 12. Go away more quietly next time. (8)

This exercise demonstrates cultural imperatives activated in the process of language imposition. Violence registers beneath the apparently innocuous sentences of the language lessons: the repeated commands to produce honourable labour selflessly (#9, 10, 11), for example, and direct criticism of the speaker/student, who is blamed for her difficulties (#3, 12). The concluding sentence of the exercise is terse and punishing, encouraging the student to disappear "quietly," which neatly negates the speech lesson itself. The sixth sentence expresses a guilty acknowledgement that the people of this new, adopted country are not as happy as those living in the student's previous country, which begs the question of why the student has moved. The implication, perhaps, is that the student did not choose, but rather was forcibly removed from her country.

The following exercise, which requires the student to "traduire" sentences (rather than "écrivez") from French to English, turns a lesson in verb conjugation into an extraordinarily touching haiku-like meditation on articulation and longing:

1. I want you to speak.
2. I wanted him to speak.
3. I shall want you to speak.
4. Are you afraid he will speak?
5. Were you afraid they would speak?
6. It will be better for him to speak to us.
7. Was it necessary for you to write?
8. Wait till I write.
9. Why didn't you wait so that I could write to you? (8-9)

In this poem-exercise, the series of sentences form a plaintive soliloquy exploring the desire, necessity, anxiety, and regret bound up in speech. In both of these exercises, neutral, functionalist, transparent words without underlying meaning or consequence, words that form sentences simply to encourage language acquisition, prove to be impossible. Whether disparaging, poignant, or seductive (or all three), words in *Dictee* disprove functionalist theories of transparent language by demonstrating the underlying emotive and authoritarian impulses lurking within every utterance.

R. Zamora Linmark's episodic novel *Rolling the R's* is composed of a series of short stories, letters, dialogues, articles, reports, and a book review. Through all of the sketches, Linmark shifts the narrative point-of-view among a group of fifth-grade Filipinos growing up in Hawai'i during the 1970s. The novel picks up on the adolescents' sexually-charged, pop music-influenced speech of Hawai'ian Pidgin, English, Spanish, and Tagalog.

Reviewers noted the "eccentric" and "startlingly beautiful" quality of Linmark's idiom, highlighted by the author himself in the title. Instead of focussing on its aesthetics, though, I am arguing that the multilingualism in *Rolling the R's* forms a particular strategy of resistance to linguistic, imperial, and sexual norms. In an interview, Linmark described his inherently multilingual aesthetic: "I wrote in a voice that I was familiar with which is actually a multilingual voice, which is Pidgin English thrown in with Tagalog, standard English with some Spanish. It's a laced-up invented language, but it was a language that was spoken in my physical setting" ("*Rolling*"). Strikingly, Linmark claims his linguistic style as simultaneously invented and already-existing, both imaginary and representative.

Given the educational examples from *Dictee*, I turn here to two textual moments in *Rolling the R's* that bear out this comparison of multilingual literary politics, particularly in the face of imperialism disguised as benevolent, educational assimilation. The chapter titled, "The Sentencing of Lives, Or Why Edgar Almost Failed Mrs. Takemoto's Class," consists entirely of the sentences Edgar Ramirez writes to prove he can use the English words on the forty-five minute exam. Edgar, who "at grade five was already out, a flaming queen, accepting himself as a fag" (Linmark "*Rolling*") artfully defies linguistic and sexual norms in his speech and, in this case, in his writing:

> 4. sobriety, n. When my father drinks and beats the shit out of me, I wish he would be sobriety ...
> 11. clandestine, adj. In this class is a clandestine boy who freaked out after I gave him a torrid kiss.
> 12. transition, n. Exotica is in a state of transition at this moment because he wants to undergo a sex change operation so he can enter the Ms. Fusion-Pacifica pageant, but if he does, Daniel, his Air Force loverboy will leave him.
> 13. maudlin, adj. My maudlin career is taking off so fast that if I don't try and control it, I'm going to have a nervous break-down...
> (*Rolling* 121-23)

In composing these sentences, Edgar followed the all-caps instructions: "NO PIDGIN-ENGLISH ALLOWED" (121). But even within the institutional confines of "standard" English, Edgar reinvents the words through puns and expanded definitions. Many of the sentences defy the power of authority figures in the older generations, particularly priests, teachers, and parents, by showing them to be as sex-crazy, arbitrary, and confused as the children. More provocatively, Edgar's creative punning turns even the most "standard" words, those given by Mrs. Takemoto for the students to learn, into pidgin: "My maudlin career ... she has a lot of vituperative living in her stomach ... my hands get all calamity inside" (122-3). In these cases, as throughout the book, Linmark's characters undermine normative imperatives through the witty inventiveness of their speech.

In the concluding chapter, "F FOR BOOK REPORT," Katrina summarizes the plot, character, and conflicts of Judy Blume's *Forever*. She declares it "one of the bestest bestest books I ever read cuz it's so true-to-life and I know it cuz I lived it. I feel like I know Katherine so well, even though I one local and she live all the way east coast side ... Was kinda scary actually, reading this book, cuz felt like I was reading about myself" (145). Katrina's mature and perceptive reading of Blume's melodramatic, Anglo, middle-class novel of sexual awakening (marking Linmark's post-colonial queering of similar themes) emerges in a reversal. She recommends the novel to her teacher not because of the novel's artistry, but because it might help explain to Mrs. Takemoto why her husband is having an open affair with Katrina's mother: "I also hate for be the one to tell you that there's love between my mother and your husband. That's why they no care what everybody saying about them" (149). The novel concludes in Katrina's book-report voice, wise beyond her years: "As for me, my heart stay with Erwin. Our relationship ain't perfect. He graduating this year, I moving up to sixth [grade]. Now and then, we get into fights. He threaten me with his fist and I kick his balls ... But for now I just gotta make the most of Erwin, cuz for now, Erwin is my forever."

In this welter of narrative experimentation, what is transformative, either formally or politically, about multilingual literary practice? Translation theory is an odd framework within which to consider this question, since multilingual literature often does *not* provide translations. That's precisely its point.

However, the genre or tradition of multilingual writing poses a wide range of fascinating problems that I will only be able to begin outlining here. I want to suggest that we read multilingual literature as an inherently comparative and translational (and untranslational) genre. Multilingual cultures fundamentally challenge the bedrock binaries of translation, beginning with the seemingly unobjectionable categories of native/original/source and foreign/secondary/target languages. By questioning native-foreign distinctions, multilingual authors disrupt what might otherwise be considered the domestication of a foreign text. In this context, the conflation of nationalist and linguistic markers seems inadequate, if not misleading. These works do not participate in the history of translation, stretching back at least to nineteenth-century Romantic theorists (e.g., Schleiermacher and von Humboldt), that considers translation as an instrument for augmenting and expanding national culture.[4]

One of the critical arguments that multilingual U.S. novels (and, increasingly, film) have advanced is that multilingual and vernacular contact zones that depend on (and transform) translation have always existed within the officially (or unofficially) monolingual nation. Or, to mistranslate a line from James Baldwin, one might say that the nation is no longer monolingual, and it will never be monolingual again.[5]

Narratives that include two, three, or five languages hint at the implicit utopianism of universalist translation projects (i.e., Esperanto, cybernetics, or "Global English"). While some multilingual narratives presumably uphold romantic visions of reversing linguistic diffusion, more often these works point to the incommensurability of diverse languages, defamiliarize the repressive force of standard/nonstandard power-language hierarchies, or, more broadly, stage the inadequacy of language itself as a means of representation or communication.[6] In "The Politics of Translation," Gayatri Spivak argues for "a second step" to follow the "great first step" of "humanist universality": "Rather than imagining that women have something identifiable in common, why not say, humbly and practically, my first obligation in understanding solidarity is to learn her mother-tongue ... This is preparation for the intimacy of cultural

---

[4]   "To the same extent that a language is enriched, a nation is also enriched [by translation]. Think how the German language, to cite only one example, has profited since it began imitating Greek metre. And think how well our nation has progressed, not just the well-educated among us but the masses as well—even women and children—since the Greeks have been available to our nation's readers in an authentic and undistorted form. ... It is difficult to imagine a more powerful and beneficial impact on an already highly developed national culture" (von Humboldt 57).

[5]   Baldwin concludes the essay "Stranger in the Village" with the following lines: "The time has come to realize that the interracial drama acted out on the American continent has not only created a new black man, it has created a new white man, too. No road whatever will lead Americans back to the simplicity of this European village where white men still have the luxury of looking on me as a stranger .... It is precisely this black-white experience which may prove of indispensable value to us in the world we face today. This world is white no longer, and it will never be white again" (129).

[6]   On incommensurability in translation, see Hart, "Translating the Untranslatable."

translation ... if you are interested in talking about the other, and/or in making a claim to be the other, it is crucial to learn other languages" (407).

Translation theorists and sociolinguists have provocatively interrogated the political implications of what, in 1937, José Ortega y Gasset called the "false utopianism" of translation, the expectation that because seamless, commensurate translation "is desirable, it is possible" (53). Multilingual cultures accomplish important political work toward similar critiques, by showing various linguistic codes overlapping and colliding in ways that are, if not untranslatable, impossible to render in perfectly commensurate fashion within monolingual translation. *Dictee* and *Rolling the R's*, like many other works, develop strategies by which they translate internally, leave untranslated, purposively mistranslate, and provide contextual clues to the meaning of unfamiliar words in order to bring several forms of speech—state-sanctioned and despised/ stereotyped/illegitimate—into inextricable and intimate combinations.

Translation is an inherently unequal hierarchy, Laurence Venuti argues, because translations "make possible only a domesticated under-standing, however much defamiliarized, however much subversive or supportive of the domestic" (469).[7] Translations attempt to convey a sense of what native readers read, but that sense always can only be partial. This effort at analogy through lexicographical equivalence that can only be partial connects (at least) two readerships as communities that share refracted perspectives on certain ideas, events, plots, characters. This seems even more striking in the case of film, where subtitles make possible the simultaneous shared experience of the film—even by audience members who cannot speak to each other directly.

And yet, through these debates, a modified utopianism survives in the practice of translation; one can view acts of translation as projecting a future multilingual community that will be constituted by and around the intertextual dynamics. A similar spirit motivates multilingual art, but this is an ideal tempered by the acknowledgement of the asymmetrical and partial-at-best, imperialist-at-worst nature of translation.

My contention is, thus, partially a methodological one. The dynamics of multilingual literature and its practices of partial, hidden,

---

[7]   See also Lane-Mercier, "Translating the Untranslatable."

incomplete, and absent translations need to be acknowledged and considered by translation studies—for their transformative innovations. Simultaneously, scholars of ethnic and multilingual cultures would do well to attend to the exciting conceptualizations of translation studies, particular in comparative contexts.

In addition to this methodological point, I contend that contemporary multilingual literatures subvert the concept of "standard" languages and contribute to the ethnic particularist challenge to prescriptive and universalist notions of homogenized national identities. However, in its most optimistic moments, multilingual literatures also seek to constitute new communities of shared—though partial, mediated, and contingent—understandings. As Linmark writes: "No pauses, no hesitations, no tongue too embarrassed to release the right Englishy words. And no need to think American to speak English because, to Mai-Lan, language is not words, but rhythms and sounds" (*Rolling* 49).

Joshua L. Miller

Works Cited

Baldwin, James. 1998. *Collected Essays*. New York: Library of America.

Carson, Diane, ed. 1999. *John Sayles: Interviews*. Jackson: University Press of Mississippi.

Cha, Theresa Hak Kyung. 1995. *Dictee*. Berkeley: Third Woman Press, 1st published 1982.

Gordon, Avery F. and Christopher Newfield, eds. 1996. *Mapping Multiculturalism*. Minneapolis and London: University of Minnesota Press.

Hart, Roger. 1999. "Translating the Untranslatable: From Copula to Incommensurable Worlds." *Tokens of Exchange: The Problem of Translation in Global Circulations*. Ed. Lydia H. Liu. Durham and London: Duke University Press.

Lane-Mercier, Gillian. 1997. "The Translator's Aesthetic, Ideological and Political Responsibility." *Target* 9.1 (1997): 43-68.

Linmark, R. Zamora. 1995. *Rolling the R's*. New York: Kaya.

—————. 2004. "*Rolling the R's* Author R. Zamora Linmark Over a Load of Laundry." *Maganda Magazine* 11 (1998). 5 Aug. 2004. <http://www.magandamagazine.org/11/rolling1.html>.

Lockard, Joe. 2004. "Iraq's New English Studies." *Bad Subjects*. 11 May 2003. 5 Aug. 2004. <http://eserver.org/bs/editors/2003-5-11.html>.

Ortega y Gasset, José. 1992. "The Misery and the Splendor of Translation." Trans. Elizabeth Gamble Miller. *Theories of Translation: An Anthology of Essays from Dryden to Derrida*. Eds. Rainer Schulte and John Biguenet. Chicago and London: University of Chicago Press, pp. 93-112.

Sayles, John. 1999. *John Sayles: Interviews*. Ed. Diane Carson. Jackson: University Press of Mississippi.

Shell, Marc. 2002. *American Babel: Literatures of the United States from Abnaki to Zuni*. Cambridge: Harvard University Press.

Shell, Marc and Werner Sollors. 2000. *The Multilingual Anthology of American Literature: A Reader of Original Texts with English Translations*. New York: New York University Press.

Sollors, Werner. 1998. *Multilingual America: Transnationalism, Ethnicity, and the Languages of American Literature.* New York: New York University Press.

Spivak, Gayatri. 1993. "The Politics of Translation." *Outside in the Teaching Machine.* London and New York: Routledge, pp. 179-200.

Smith, Rogers. 1997. *Civic Ideals: Conflicting Visions of Citizenship in U.S. History.* New Haven and London: Yale University Press.

Thomas, Brook. 2001. "Civic Multiculturalism and the Myth of Liberal Consent." *New Centennial Review* 1.3 (Winter 2001): 1-35.

Venuti, Lawrence. 2000. "Translation, Community, Utopia." *The Translation Studies Reader.* Ed. Lawrence Venuti. London and New York: Routledge, pp. 468-88.

Viswanathan, Gauri. 1989. *Masks of Conquest: Literary Study and British Rule in India.* New York: Columbia University Press.

von Humboldt, Wilhelm. 1992. "From the Introduction to His Translation of *Agamemnon*." Trans. Sharon Sloan. *Theories of Translation: An Anthology of Essays from Dryden to Derrida.* Eds. Rainer Schulte and John Biguenet. Chicago and London: University of Chicago Press, pp. 55-9.

Ty Pak: Korean American Literature as "Guilt Payment"

I. 1. Ty Pak and the Silence of Asian American Studies

Ten years ago Korean Americans were commonly perceived as being well adapted to American culture, a model-minority. It wasn't until the "post-colonial turn" in ethnic studies[1] and the aggression directed at Korean immigrants during the "Los Angeles Riots" that research started focussing on a de-centred diasporic community, held together by collective memories of colonization, war, and post-war dictatorship.[2] Korean American literature, video productions and the visual arts have since challenged the idea of an essentially "ethnic" Korean American enclave[3]. The focus shifted

---

[1]   I refer to new conceptions of culture which focus less on shared experiences of racism, stereotypisation and discrimination but on a "politics of representation" which places questions of power, hybridization and agency centre-stage. See Stuart Hall, "New Ethnicities", *Critical Dialogues in Cultural Studies*, eds. David Morley and Kuan-Hsing Chen (London and NY: Routledge, 1996) 441-444.

[2]   See for example Elaine Kim, „Myth, Memory, and Desire: Homeland and History in Contemporary Korean American Writing and Visual Art", *Holding Their Own: Perspectives on the Multi-Ethnic Literatures of the United States* (Tübingen: Stauffenburg Verlag, 2000) 80, and Min-Jun Kim,"Moments of Danger in the (Dis-) Continuous Relation of Korean Nationalism and Korean American National-ism", *Special Issue: New Formations, New Questions: Asian American Studies. Positions east asia critique 5:2* (Fall 1997), guest eds. Elaine Kim and Lisa Lowe (Durham and London: Duke University Press, 1997) 358. Brenda Kwon Lee, "Beyond Keeamoku: Koreans, Nationalism, and Local Culture in Hawai'i." Diss. U. of California, Los Angeles, 1997. *DAI* A 58/06 (1997): 2210.

[3]   I take my concept of "ethnicity" as a "process of inter-reference between two or more cultures" from Michael M.J. Fischer, "Ethnicity and the Post-Modern Arts of Memory", *Writing Culture: The Poetics and Politics of Ethnography*, eds. James Clifford and G. Marcus (Berkeley: University of

away from notions of a dynamic "tradition"[4] towards postcolonial identity constructions and the paradigm of cultural hybridity. According to Homi Bhabha, cultural hybridity complicates colonial representation and "reverses the effects of the colonialist disavowal, so that other 'denied' knowledges enter upon the dominant discourse and estrange the basis of its authority."[5] Like other postcolonial critics Bhabha aims at pointing out strategies that undermine the authority of the dominant culture.

Elements of postcolonial subversion can certainly be found in *Guilt Payment*, Ty Pak's 1983 collection of short stories[6] which I will discuss in this paper. However, *subversion* is not my focus. What Bhabha and some critics of Korean American literature have tended to ignore is the problem of trauma. In my view Korean American cultural productions[7] point to a collective crisis which keeps the community from constructing a future-oriented ethnic identity.[8] *Guilt Payment* is an early example of this pessimistic tendency. It gives the most radical account of what Pak's writer-colleague Theresa Cha had called the Koreans' legacy of "perpetual exile" just a year before, in 1982.[9]

I.2. Korean America: Enclave or Exclave?

Pak's protagonists have lived in the United States for decades but they continue to be obsessed with what he describes as "the story of the race—the vagabondage that originated from Central Eurasian steppes, trekking and meandering across the mountains and deserts of two

---

California Press, 1986) 194-233.

[4]   I refer to "tradition" in the sense of Michael Fischer's use of the term as a dynamic concept.

[5]   Homi K. Bhabha, *The Location of Culture* (London and New York: Routledge, 1994) 114.

[6]   (Honolulu: Bamboo Ridge Press and the Hawai'i Ethnic Resources Centre, 1983).

[7]   Examples of this are Yong-Soon Min's works of art and videos such as *Sa-I-Gu* (1993 by Elaine Kim, Christine Choy and Dai Sil Kim-Gibson) or Wonsun Choy's *Forgotten Yesterdays* (1994).

[8]   See Michael Fischer, "Ethnicity..." 196 and 201.

[9]   *Dictee* (New York: Tanam Press)

continents, the persecutions, discriminations, genocides that hounded them everywhere they went" (115). In this construction of a collective identity there is not even a homeland to return to. Like in Theresa Hak Kyung Cha's *Dictee,* "Korea" is a cultural space that has always already been defined by enemy powers. It refers not so much to the national geography of the divided Korean nation but to a desired place of origin, a memory of something never had.

My initial reluctance to use the proposed term "exclave" had to do with this presumed lack of a "real" homeland as a point of reference. Somewhat ironically, however, the factual existence of Korea as a divided nation allows for an interesting approach to this spatial concept of the exclave. As Elaine Kim has pointed out, the historical separation of families has gained the status of a central cultural memory shared by Koreans both within and outside the country of origin.[10] We can thus safely assume that there must be a strong sense of connectedness between "homeland" and "exclave." This sense of connectedness can certainly be found in the Korean American community in the United States whose artists often lament the division of the country. The transferral of South Korean nationalism is another example of this identification.[11]

The homeland's condescending attitude towards what many South Koreans perceived as an "Americanized" exclave[12] changed quite radically

---

[10] "Geographical displacement and separation from family members" due to the division of the Korean peninsula "are the rule rather than the exception [...] touching even those born long after the armistice or living on distant continents" (Myth 79).

[11] As Min-Jun Kim has pointed out, many Korean Americans identify with South Korean nationalist ideology. It is, however, a romanticizing discourse which helps construct an ethnic Korean American identity. Min-Jun Kim argues in a similar way when she compares Korean nationalist identity constructions with romanticizing accounts of a Korean American „ethnic" identity „that alludes to the discursive forms of an earlier Korean ‚nationalist' identity." Min-Jun Kim, 358. In my discussion of the „Los Angeles Riots" I have shown how historical events in the „host country" become meaningful when they are appropriated to a Korean discourse of national destiny. See my Ph.D. thesis *No Korean is Whole—Wherever He or She May Be: Erfindungen von Korean America seit 1965* (Frankfurt a.M.: Peter Lang, 2002). Another instance which shows the sense of connectedness was when Korean Americans supported a South Korean worker's protest against a transnational American firm in 1990. See Ramsay Liem and Jinsoo Kim, "The Pico Workers' Struggle: Korean Americans and the Lessons of Solidarity, *Amerasia Journal* 18:1 (1992): 49-68.

[12] For an example see Elaine Kim's autobiographical account in *Writing Self Writing Nation* (Berkeley: Third Woman Press, 1994), Theresa Cha's description of the hostile reactions of some South Koreans when a Korean American comes to visit (*Dictee* 56-57). In the 1950s the Korean American director Peter Hyun became a celebrity in post-war Korea while in America he had

when people in Seoul or Pusan witnessed the looting of Korean American stores during the "Los Angeles Riots" via television. The growing awareness of the Korean American situation is mirrored by the interest South Korea's cultural institutions take in the art and literature of the exclave. Korean American Literature has been translated into Korean within a very short time. According to Ki-han Lee from Myonji-University in Seoul, Korean American authors are often seen as "heroes or even patriots, advancing Korea's image and prestige in the United States."[13] This has not been true for the three books[14] published by Ty Pak. His work does not attract the South Korean publishing business, probably because stories about male guilt abound in that country.[15] An additional reason may be that his books do not offer a positive image of the exclave. Of course, the author's decision to write in English must be interpreted as a move *away* from both the exclave and the "enclave" towards the American mainstream.[16] When in 1996 I interviewed a Korean American bookseller in Los Angeles, she had never even heard of any of the Korean American books which I mentioned, all of them written in English. At least at that time and place Korean American bookstores presented themselves as "linguistic and literary exclaves."[17] The store was literally *marked* by difference. The shelves were overflowing with books and journals covered with the Korean writing system known as *hangul*.[18]

---

suffered severe exclusion as an artist. See his autobiography *In the New World: The Making of a Korean American* (Honolulu: University of Hawai'I Press, 1995).

[13]   http://kn.koreaherald.co.kr/SITE/data/html_dir2002/05/18/200205180027.asp

[14]   The second collection of short stories, *Moonbay* and Pak's first novel, *Cry Korea Cry* were both published by The Woodhouse Press, New York, in 1999.

[15]   I thank Professor Kun Jong Lee from Korea University for pointing this out.

[16]   Lawrence Venuti. "Introduction". *Rethinking Translation: Discourse, Subjectivity, Ideology*. London and NY: Routledge, 1992, 5.

[17]   I thank Armin Paul Frank for the terminology.

[18]   For a discussion of „oriental stores" see Enrique Bonus. "Marking and Marketing 'Difference': Filipino Oriental Stores in Southern California". *Positions...*, eds Elaine Kim and Lisa Lowe, 643-696. It would be worth investigating whether these bookstores are by now selling Korean translations of Korean American texts. In 1996 there were still only a few translations available.

We should be wary, however, toward reducing the community to an extension of the "homeland" connected via satellite, Korean language newspapers, and a network of personal and business relations. Trying to help, the bookseller handed me a Korean American success story written by a politician in the Midwest—in Korean, of course. This linguistic exclave may not have a high command of English, but it clearly shows an interest in the American myth that brought many of its members to the US in the first place. In addition to *this* variety of Korean American literature (which is written in *hangul*), the community also has access to translations of American literature into Korean.

I.3. Torn between Cultures: Ty Pak

This immigrant community is certainly not the readership Pak had in mind when he wrote his overall pessimistic stories of failed assimilation. However, he is widely known in academic circles, especially among Asian American scholars. But while he is "known," he has not been receiving much critical attention.[19] I believe this is due to *Guilt Payment*'s "failure" to assimilate to dominant academic discourses. Unlike Cha, who used to be dismissed as an "elite" author in the 1980s and who now is among the most celebrated Asian American writers, Pak's work is not primarily concerned with hybrid identity constructions, successful postcolonial strategies of subversion, or other preferred topics in contemporary debates.

In what follows, I will discuss Pak's "failure" as a meaningful phenomenon. My argument is that Pak's reaching out to the general American public is a highly ambivalent move. He deliberately chooses to write in the language of the superpower whose name is connected to the bloody war of 1950-1953, the division of the country, and a succession of authoritarian regimes in the "democratic" South. While the stories are written in the language of the liberator/colonizer, they also keep up an extraordinarily strong connection to the Korean cultural tradition. As I understand the title of the book, it could be seen, at least on one level, as a tribute to Korea, an emigrant's "Guilt Payment."

---

[19] See Seiwoong Oh on Ty Pak in a forthcoming reference book on Asian American short stories.

Furthermore, the book mirrors an opinion which is rather wide-spread in immigrant enclaves: While Pak pragmatically supports translation as a means of survival, he has strong doubts about its ability to communicate across *cultural* borders. "Possession Sickness," one of the best stories in the collection, helps to illustrate this: It centres on George Kahn, a Korean American who even changed his name to an American one. Years ago he had abandoned his wife in order to start a new life. When he finds his daughter watching an interview with a Korean shaman on American television, he recognizes his wife Moonhee. In the middle of her interview with "Western specialists," she "departs from the agreed-upon text" and directly addresses her ex-husband in front of the TV, calling him a "son of a bitch" in Korean. Ironically, the narrator translates her "strong Cholla vernacular" into an entirely different and somehow ill-fitting *American* vernacular ("son of a bitch"), thus emphasizing the impossibility of finding a cultural equivalent to her verbal attack (27). Consistent with this scepticism Pak refuses to serve as a "cultural translator" in a very substantial way which effects not only the structure of the stories but their overall narrative pattern as well.

Without a doubt Pak and his protagonists have a lot in common. Their histories of immigration are products of international power relations and post-colonialism. Ty Pak was born during the Japanese occupation of Korea in 1938, he lost his father during the Korean War, and came to the United States in 1965 to eventually settle down in Hawaii. Like many Korean Americans, including the second generation, Pak never severed his ties with his native country. In the 1990s he even returned and attempted to establish a business in South Korea. He now lives in the United States again.[20] The transferral of Korean cultural codes to the American context is a direct symptom of this concept of migration.

The following discussion is concerned with translation as a multi-layered process of cultural textualization. Although commonly labelled an "author," Ty Pak is also a translator: In *Guilt Payment* he translates a Korean cultural discourse into the American cultural context. Or is it the other way around? Pak relates two stories simultaneously yet separately, thereby ignoring the traditional hierarchy between the "original" and the "translation".

---

[20] I thank Seiwoong Oh and Myung Ja Kim for the biographical information.

There are of course limits to my "translation" of *Guilt Payment*. I am myself a "Western specialist" with limited access to the dynamic concept of Korean culture. I do not even speak Korean. The "canon" of Korean literary tradition is scarcely available in English. The same it true for academic discussions about Korean literature. Translations from Korean are still fewer than those from Japanese or Chinese.[21] Although more recent Korean fiction often deals with the peninsula's post-colonial experience and its connectedness to American foreign policy, few authors have found major publishers in the English-speaking world.[22] Of course, I don't want to uncritically celebrate translations as I am aware of the element of domestication implicit in "fluent" translations.[23] But I am equally sceptical of Esther Ghymn's proclamation that "a study of ethnic literature is best done by someone with a background in that culture".[24] What we need is an open-minded, self-reflective, interdisciplinary, and intercultural collaboration. We live in an age where the ideas of "home" and "abroad," "self" and "other" seem less clearly opposed. "On six continents" says James Clifford "foreign populations have come to stay—mixing in but often in partial, specific fashions."[25] I think we should at least try to exchange ideas about this "new diversity." We are all a part of it. This paper is a contribution to this kind of exchange.

First I will outline some general implications of Pak's strategy. Second, I will introduce the Korean background of *Guilt Payment*. In my concluding remarks, I will make a preliminary assessment of Pak's strategy.

---

[21] The only data I could find about this were in *Publisher's* Weekly, July 5, 1990: C.B. Grannis. "Balancing the Books", pp. 21-23.

[22] See Bruce Fulton's list in "Selected Readings in Modern Korean Fiction in English Translation", 1-9

[23] Koskinen, 132

[24] Esther Mikyung Ghymn, *The Shapes and Styles of Asian American Prose Fiction* (New York: Peter Lang, 1992) 9.

[25] *The Predicament of* Culture. (Cambridge: Harvard UP, 1988) 13

II. 1. Ty Pak's *Guilt Payment:* General implications

Guilt Payment is concerned with questions about cultural identity in the face of trauma. As I will demonstrate in the rest of my remarks, trauma not only prevents successful identity formation but also the construction of a meaningful text.

Guilt Payment includes thirteen short stories set in various countries, including America, Korea, Vietnam, and Saudi Arabia. Together these spacial configurations form what Mary Louise Pratt has called a "contact zone," spaces where cultures meet "in contexts of highly asymmetrical relations of power."[26] Most of the protagonists are male immigrants who left Korea at a time of personal or political crisis.

In order to tell us more about their past, Pak uses the patterns of *trauma* and the "return of the repressed"[27] as a narrative structure: In the first part of each story we are introduced to a model minority Korean American who leads a very ordinary "American" life. In the story, "Possession Sickness," for example, the Korean American protagonist is pestered by his daughter to let her go to Italy, where she pretends she wants to study music. Triggered by this conversation (in many other stories a surprise encounter serves the same purpose) the protagonist is overcome by memories he has denied successfully until that point. Through flashback the story then relates an individualized account of the protagonist's past. The "Korea" of the 1950s emerges as an earlier version of a more familiar "Vietnam." In other words, Pak appropriates a pattern known from the 1970s TV series M*A*S*H. But while in M*A*S*H "Korea" had become the fictional Ersatz-setting for the war in Southeast Asia, *Guilt Payment* re-focuses the reader's attention to the devastating reality of the Korean War itself.[28]

As Than Nguyen Viet has pointed out in *Race and Resistance,* "Vietnam" has introduced a new Asian stereotype to American society: the

---

[26] "I use this term to refer to social spaces where cultures meet, clash, and grapple with each other, often in contexts of highly asymmetrical relations of power, such as colonialism, slavery, or their aftermaths as they are lived out in many parts of the world today." Mary Louise Pratt. "Arts of the Contact Zone". http://web.new.ufl.edu/ ~stripp/2504pratt.html. April 30, 2003.

[27] Psychologically the two concepts are linked but not similar. Pak uses them interchangeably.

[28] For an in-depth analysis see chapter I.2 in the second part of my dissertation.

victim.[29] In comparing Vietnamese and Filipino literatures, he argues that "the discourse of victimization and the status of the Vietnam War in the American imagination allow Vietnamese voices to attain a certain limited stature in American discourse" making them much more "visible" than other Asian minorities. By introducing the Korean as victim, Pak shifts the readers attention from an imaginary "Vietnam" to an equally devastated Korea, a place where "many were simply shot on the streets and left there to be trampled. Whole families, including the very young and old, were executed" (12).

Like all the other stories "Guilt Payment" ends by returning to the original time setting, where the father finally agrees to send his daughter to Italy. The reader's initial impression of an "assimilated" immigrant seems superficial after he/she has learned about the psychological motivation of the father's consent. He turns out *not* to be the liberal, "Americanized" model-minority father but a guilt-ridden, traumatized immigrant who feels an urgent need to atone for abandoning his daughter's mother during the war.

In order to bring across the suffering of Koreans during the War Pak uses a narrative pattern derived from what we have come to know as "the return of the repressed" and "trauma." The protagonist suffers from memories of the past, which are triggered by everyday encounters. He then—in flashback—lives through the past experience. When he "returns" to his present life, he has difficulties orienting himself.[30] Closely linked to "the return of the repressed," "trauma" is a Western psychoanalytic concept that includes the inability of body and mind to forget or overcome past experiences. As a historical phenomenon, "trauma" was redefined by American psychiatrists after the Vietnam War.[31] Especially in

---

[29] (Oxford UP, 2002) 27-28

[30] In Pak's story "The Grateful Korean" e.g., the protagonist's surprise encounter with a "tall woman" with "blonde hair", a "high nose" and other attributes of American beauty triggers the feelings of guilt linked to memories of the past. He mistakes the woman for his former wife, "the avenging Fury herself" (195). He abandoned Moonhee in the aftermath of the Korean war, the memory of which "still returned with the vividness of a nightmare" (189).

[31] What we know as "trauma" today was called "homesickness" after the American Civil War, in the First World War Germans would speak of "Granatenschock", after the Second World War it became known as "Gefechtserschöpfung". See Ronald J. Comer, *Klinische Psychologie* (Heidelberg: Spektrum Akademischer Verlag, 1995) 232-237.

the pluralist society of the US, the concept has gained the status of a very powerful cultural narrative. In the feminist discourse on rape and also in connection with African American, Native American, or Jewish American identities, "trauma" has become an important marker of individual and historical *difference*. By inscribing Korean Americans into this cultural discourse and narrative pattern, *Guilt Payment* produces acceptable meanings for the cultural community of "American" readers.[32] In other words, Pak seems to *accept* the dominance of American cultural codes.[33]

The fact that like the English language itself the discourse of trauma has become part of post-colonial South Korea adds to, rather than weakens this point. But, as I previously suggested, the narrator is also a translator, a code-switcher. While he skilfully adapts to the language of assimilation, he erodes what may be called the American cultural hegemony. Pak establishes a very powerful cultural subtext. This subtext proposes a distinctly "Korean" approach to what we call "trauma." As Christina Schäffer and Beverly Adab have pointed out, "[c]ultures not only express *ideas* differently, they shape *concepts* and *texts* differently."[34] Further complicating the matter, Pak employs a cultural doubling with a twist because he does not openly *thematize* his strategy.[35]

II.2. Double Telling

For the Western reader it is not easy to identify this subtext. How *did* I experience a sense of "cultural difference" in *Guilt Payment*? I found what

---

[32]   See Renate Resch. "Ein kohärentes Translat – was ist das? Die Kulturspezifik der Texterwartungen" and Michaela Wolf, „Translation as a Process of Power: Aspects of Cultural Anthropology in Translation". *Translation as Intercultural Communication* (Amsterdam/Philadelphia: John Benjamins Publishing Company, 1995) 271-281 and 123-133.

[33]   About questions of power in language use see Venuti "Introduction", *Rethinking Translation* 5. I would like to add that not all of the stories relate directely to the war. They do, however, relate *memory* as a "traumatic" one, preventing the individual's participation in American society.

[34]   Christina Schäffer and Beverly Adab. "Translation as intercultural communication – Contact as Conflict", *Translation as Intercultural Translation*, 327. Emphasis mine.

[35]   In this he differs from his writer colleague Theresa Cha. Her *Dictee* is a highly subversive post-colonial exercise which constantly attunes its readers to implicit cultural differences, reminding him/her of "narrative shifts" (145) and "second shroudings" (145).

Schäffer and Adab have called "features that somehow seem 'out of place/strange, unusual'" for the American "receiving culture."[36] However "fluent"[37] each short story seemed to be, there still was a sense of irritation disrupting the narratives. The apparent ritualistic narrative pattern disturbed me as much as the obsessive preoccupation with a similar set of characters. *All* of the stories focus on a male protagonist who, like the narrator in "Nostalgia," feels "like a man on vacation away from home," "a prince travelling incognito" (85). Although "the new country had opened her arms wide to receive" them ("The Grateful Korean, 188), they remain in a state of mental exile for decades. Their life in America is devoid of meaning until the Korean woman whom they once left behind intrudes into their existence. Could this gendered pattern be a specifically "Korean" version of survivor guilt?

According to Sheila Miyoshi Jager "[t]he figure of the anguished, lonely female, unduly separated from family and friends" shows an "ubiquitous presence in Korea."[38] The concept exists at least since the Koryo dynasty (19th century). It is a popular discourse rather than an "original story." Rooted in an oral tradition, which is still popular today, it was spread over the country by travelling singers and storytellers. The "Story of Ch'unhyang" is the most popular of these stories. While her lover leaves her behind in order to accomplish a carreer, *Ch'unhyang* resists the approaches of an evil governor. While she is tortured, she practices *jeoljo* (absolute chastity for women), a concept based on Confucian beliefs. During her torture she quotes basic concepts from Confucian thought, accusing the evil governor of offending against the principles of responsibility. In the course of Korean literature the story around "Korea's most cherished heroine" has become something of a genre.

In the 20th century the emphasis shifted from Confucianism toward the symbol of *woman as nation*. As Jager points out, the ontological concept of "woman" entered Korea around the turn of the 19th century,

---

[36] "Translation as intercultural communication – Contact as Conflict" 325.

[37] About "fluency" as a central feature of a "good" translation see Venuti, "Introduction", *Rethinking...*, 5.

[38] "Women, Resistance, and the Divided Nation: The Romantic Rhetoric of Korean Reunification". *The Journal of Asian Studies*, 55.1 (February 1996): 4.

when American missionaries began to settle in Korea. The figure of the oppressed female came to symbolize Korean class conflict and colonization.[39] This ideological re-framing also resulted in a body of pro-feminist writing. In Kwang-Su Yi's[40] classical modernist novel *Mujông* (1917), the female hero refuses to suffer while his male protagonist "consoles himself in the way of many male protagonists of Korean fiction, in the 'dream-world' of irrationality: his future life in America."[41] Does that sound familiar?

In Pak's stories the "master narrative" *Ch'unhyang* continues to shape the immigrants' thinking about history in terms that are strictly gendered. Akin to Yi's pro-feminist stance, Pak's "deserted women" have emancipated themselves after they were left behind.[42] Using the means of modern transport and communication they ignore geographical borders and enter the United States.[43] They are looking for their husbands, whom they want to call to account. Since their guilt-ridden husbands are already waiting, they all succeed. As one of Pak's *Ch'unhyangs*, another woman named Moonhee remarks that her husband still keeps some "primitive fetishism" about Korea. He never changed his name "to an Anglo-sounding one like Richard Taylor" (105). When Moonhee claims to "forgive" her husband's unfaithfulness, the story resonates with a mocking commentary on the *Ch'unhyang* legacy.

All of the encounters in *Guilt Payment* are characterized by the theme of affliction. The German word "Heimsuchung" is even more apt. It contains both a sense of hauntedness and the idea of a "familiar"

---

[39]   Jager, "Women and the Promise of Modernity: Signs of Love for the Nation in Korea", *New Literary History* 29:1 (Winter 1998): 124

[40]   Sometimes also spelled „Lee".

[41]   Jager, 1998, 128.

[42]   While Pak's male figures undoubtedly conform to Western stereotypes of Asian men, the women are no longer "the Oriental wife men dream of: understanding, forever yielding, obedient, self-effacing, and yet a rock of strength and wisdom" (Jager 91).

[43]   As Seiwoong Oh has pointed out to me there also exists a whole tradition of ghost stories about abandoned women who come back to haunt the men. These stories are very popular and have been interpreted as cautionary tales about why men should not abandon their women. This genre cannot be separated from the *Ch'unhyang* tradition.

cultural origin. "A Second Chance" is one of the few stories with a happy ending, with the male protagonist regaining his sexual potency. But Pak gives prominence to the point that most of his protagonists *fail* in solving their problem with the past. In his story "Possession Sickness" the protagonist is not able to accept the "second chance" a life in America offers him. Overwhelmed by sudden guilt and superstition, he returns to Korea, dragging his "Americanized" daughter along with him.

III. Concluding Remarks

Drawing on the narrative patterns of "trauma," the "return of the repressed," and on the concept of "survivor's guilt," Pak adopts a style for which there is a model in the target culture. Like his use of English, this is clearly a signal of assimilation. By using these familiar discourses he is able to convey to Americans the Korean experience of what has been called "the forgotten war." At the same time he employs a distinctively Korean cultural narrative and introduces it to the American context. This strong connection to the "homeland" shows that not only the protagonists, but the author himself embraces an exclave identity.

As the title to the collection indicates, *Guilt Payment* is a tribute to Korea. At the same time many of the stories are full of praise for "the new country" that "had opened her arms wide to receive him" (187). Pak not only picks out the potential dilemmas of immigrant identities as a central theme, but *Guilt Payment* actually *mirrors* these difficulties on the textual level itself.

By emphasizing the *cultural* aspect of trauma and memory, *Guilt Payment* highlights differences which on another level it attempts to bridge. While these stories actively support the belief in the human capacity to share grief, they remain pessimistic when it comes to intercultural mimesis. Ty Pak does not take the stance of a "radical" narrator/translator who refuses to "share his culture with an all-absorbing America"[44] in an act of "faithfulness" to his mother tongue. After all, he uses the English language without ever discussing its role in the postcolonial Korean scenario.

---

[44] James Clifford, *The Predicament...,* 217.

Pak is a difficult case when one tries to categorize him in the context of "Korean American literature." He uses the language of the dominant culture to cross the border between the exclave and the more general American public. Unlike other Korean American literature, *Guilt Payment* largely resists the label of an "ethnic" or "hybrid" text. By using a narrative derived from the home country, the collection constructs a fictional exclave/enclave based on a *continuation* of Korean literary history. Somewhat paradoxically, however, *Guilt Payment* turns its back to "Korea." Pak's criticism of immigrant nostalgia echoes through the book. The use of the English language , thus, marks the *will* to break with the past. But since this break is never realized on the story level itself, the English language remains a very isolated yet powerful gesture of assimilation. Pak's protagonists themselves rarely succeed in integrating/translating "Korea" into their American lives. Some leave the United States and find themselves out of place in modern Seoul, some remain alienated from both the community and the larger society, some commit suicide.

Pak clearly supports the idea of a collective cultural memory, but he approaches the concept of a Korean-American identity by breaking it up into radically different fictional "case histories." While every one of these individuals suffers from a strong "cultural trauma," Pak refuses to offer any *collective* solutions to help them define a meaningful cultural identity in the complex field of an enclave/exclave immigrant situation. I am usually very careful with biographical analogies. Minority authors are easily dismissed on this basis as writers of autobiographical non-fiction. In the case of Ty Pak, however, I'll make an exception: His stories resonate almost desperately with the search for a "home." In the end, *Guilt Payment* itself is presented as a fictional site for the author's own shifting identities, shifting between "assimilation" and "exile," between the "ethnic" and "diasporic subject."

Kirsten Twelbeck

Bibliography

Arteaga, Alfred, ed. 1994. *An Other Tongue: Nation and Ethnicity in the Linguistic Borderlands.* Durham and London: Duke University Press.

Bonus, Enrique. 1997. "Marking and Marketing 'Difference': Filipino Oriental Stores in Southern California". *positions east asia cultures critique.* Ed. by Elaine Kim and Lisa Lowe. Durham: Duke University Press, pp. 643-696.

Brigham Young University Research Team (directed by Mark Peterson at the David M. Kennedy-Center). *Coverage of Korea in American Textbooks and Reference Works.* http://kennedy.byu.edu/ staff/ peterson/ over.htm (2004.07.07).

Cha, Theresa Hak Kyung. 1995. *Dictee* (1982). Berkeley: Third Woman Press.

Clifford, James. 1988. *The Predicament of Culture: Twentieth-Century Ethnogreaphy, Literatur, and Art.* Cambridge: Harvard University Press.

Comer, Ronald J. 1995. *Klinische* Psychologie. Heidelberg: Spektrum Akademischer Verlag, pp. 232-237.

Fisher, Michael M.J. 1986. "Ethnicity and the Post-Modern Arts of Memory." *Writing Culture: The Poetics and Politics of Ethnography.* Ed. by James Clifford and G. Marcus. Berkeley: University of California Press, pp. 194-233.

Fulton, Bruce. 2004. "Selected Readings in Modern Korean Fiction in English Translation." 1-9. http://www.kahs.org/downloads/99KoreanFic.pdf. (July 08, 2004).

Ghymn, Esther Mikyung. 1992. *The Shapes and Styles of Asian American Prose Fiction.* New York: Peter Lang.

Grannis, C.B. 1990. "Balancing the Books, *Publishers Weekly,* 5 July 1990, pp. 21-23.

Hall, Stuart. 1996. "New Ethnicities". *Stuart Hall. Critical Dialogues in Cultural Studies.* Ed. by David Morley and Kuan-Hsing Chen. London and New York: Routledge, pp. 441-449.

Hammerschmid, Beata and Hermann Krapoth, eds. 1998. *Übersetzung als kultureller Prozeß: Rezeption, Projektion und Konstruktion des Fremden.* Berlin: Erich Schmidt Verlag.

Haverkamp, Anselm, ed. 1997. *Die Sprache der Anderen*. Frankfurt a.M.: Suhrkamp Verlag.

Hyun, Peter. 1995. *In The New World: The Making of a Korean American*. Honolulu: University of Hawaii Press.

Jager, Sheila Miyoshi. 1998. "Women and the Promise of Modernity: Signs of Love for the Nation in Korea". New Literary History 29:1 (Winter 1998): 121-134.

Jager, Sheila Miyoshi. 1996. "Women, Resistance, and the Divided Nation: The Romantic Rhetoric of Korean Reunification". The Journal of Asian Studies, 55.1 (February 1996): 3-21.

Kim, Elaine and Norma Alarcón, eds. 1994. *Writing Self Writing Nation*. Berkeley: Third Woman Press.

Kim, Elaine. 2000. "Myth, Memory, and Desire: Homeland and History in Contemporary Korean American Writing and Visual Art." *Holding Their Own: Perspectives on the Multi-Ethnic Literatures of the United States*. Tübingen: Stauffenburg Verlag.

Kim, Jin. 2002. "Blooming Where They're Planted: Korean American Writers Make their Mark in American Literature." *Digital Korea Herald* 2002.04.26. http://kn.koreaherald.co.kr/SITE/data/html_dir2002/05/18/200205180027.asp (2004.07.07)

Kim, Min-Jun. 1997. "Moments of Danger in the (Dis)continuous Relation of Korean Nationalism and Korean American Nationalism." *positions east asia cultures critique*. Ed. by Elaine Kim and Lisa Lowe. Durham: Duke University Press, pp. 357-389.

Kupsch-Losereit, Sigrid. 1997. "Übersetzen als transkultureller Verstehens- und Produktionsprozess." In Snell-Hornby pp. 249-259.

Oh, Seiwoong Oh. 2003. "Ty Pak." *Asian American Short Story Writers: An A-to-Z Guide*. Ed. by Guiyou Huang. Westport, Cn. and London: Greenwood Press, pp. 251-255.

Pak, Ty. 1999. "The Court Interpreter". *Moonbay*. New York: The Woodhouse Press, pp. 89-118.

Pak, Ty. 1999. *Cry Korea Cry*. New York: The Woodhouse Press.

Pratt, Mary Louise. 1999. "Arts of the Contact Zone," *Ways of Reading: An Anthology for Writers*. 5th edition. Ed. David Bartholomae and Anthony Petroksky. New York: Bedford/St. Martin's, pp. 528-42.

Resch, Renate. 1997. "Ein kohärentes Translat – was ist das? Die Kulturspezifik der Texterwartungen." In Snell-Hornby pp. 271-281.

Roth, Klaus. 1996. *Mit der Differenz leben: Europäische Ethnologie und Interkulturelle Kommunikation*. Münster, Munich, and New York: Waxmann.

Schäffer, Christina and Beverly Adab. 1997. "Translation as intercultural communication – Contact as Conflict." In Snell-Hornby pp. 325-337.

Snell-Hornby, Mary et.al., eds. 1997. *Translation as Intercultural Communication: Selected Papers from the EST-Congress, Prague 1995*. Amsterdam/Philadelphia: John Benjamins Publishing Company.

Sollors, Werner, ed. 1998. *Multilingual America: Transnationalism, Ethnicity, and the Languages of American Literature*. New York: New York University Press.

Sollors, Werner. 1986. *Beyond Ethnicity*. New York: Oxford University Press.

Twelbeck, Kirsten. 2002. *No Korean is Whole—Wherever He or She May Be. Erfindungen von Korean America seit 1965*. Frankfurt a.M.: Peter Lang.

Venuti, Lawrence, ed. 1992. *Rethinking Translation: Discourse, Subjectivity, Ideology*. London and New York: Routledge.

Venuti, Lawrence. 1995. *The Translator's Invisibility: The History of Translation*. London and New York: Routledge.

Wolf, Michaela. 1997. "Translation as a Process of Power: Aspects of Cultural Anthropology in Translation." In Snell-Hornby pp. 271-281.

"Buried Alive in the Blues":
Janis Joplin and the Souls of White Folk

In 1968 the fame of hippie rock star Janis Joplin had begun to seep out of San Francisco and into the broader cultural landscape. One measure of this awakening was the decision to interview her for the popular television news magazine *60 Minutes*. As the crew set up the cameras and equipment, Joplin told reporter Mike Wallace "Listen, man, if I start saying something you don't like, just scream 'Fuck' because they'll have to take it out of the TV thing." She then explained that if she considered his a stupid question she'd use the same code. The interview proceeded without incident until Wallace asked, "can a white man sing the blues?" Joplin just looked at the camera and said, "'Fuck.'"[1]

The product of a Cold War suburban childhood, Joplin was raised to inherit all the privileges of her white skin: economic affluence, social prestige, and cultural authority. And, indeed, by the time Mike Wallace interviewed her, she appeared to have come fully into the promised reward. It was precisely this incongruity – a rich white woman singing the music of poor blacks – that compelled him to ask if this was entirely appropriate. After all, he no doubt reasoned, Cold War-era prosperity had

---

[1]   "Janis, the Judy Garland of Rock?" *Rolling Stone* March 15, 1969, 6.

eliminated grief, misery, and heartache for whites altogether, and allowed them to claim in full what George Lipsitz has called the "possessive investment in whiteness."[2] Janis Joplin and her numerous fans, however, suggests that this narrative needs some revision.

Scholars working in the field of music and race relations have frequently answered Mike Wallace's question with an emphatic "no!" They have dismissed Joplin as a blackface minstrel in hippie beads, a performer whose blues-inflected psychedelic rock one writer has rather typically described as "mongrel blues."[3] In this telling Janis Joplin, like innumerable white musicians from Elvis to Eminem, exploited black creativity, making a fortune off the efforts of more talented African American artists.[4] To put it plainly, hers is the sadly familiar tale of an interracial cultural exchange that Eric Lott has pithily characterized as "love and theft."[5]

Joplin's brusque response to Wallace's question, however, offers another way of studying this relationship. What if the blues—or *any*

---

[2] George Lipsitz, *The Possessive Investment in Whiteness: How White People Profit From Identity Politics* (Philadelphia: Temple University Press, 1998). The post-war climate of cultural optimism is expertly discussed in Elaine Tyler May, *Homeward Bound: American Families in the Cold War Era* (NY: Basic Books, 1988), 162-82. For an examination from the perspective of whiteness see Catherine Jurca, *White Diaspora: The Suburb and the Twentieth-century American Novel* (Princeton: Princeton University Press, 2001).

[3] Brian Ward, *Just My Soul Responding: Rhythm and Blues, Black Consciousness, and Race Relations* (Berkeley: University of California Press, 1998), 248. Nelson George concurs in his assessment of Joplin labelling her a "white Negro." Nelson George, *The Death of Rhythm and Blues* (NY: Pantheon Books, 1988), 110; see also Craig Werner, *A Change is Gonna Come: Music, Race and the Soul of America* (NY: Plume, 1998), 92. For other works examining Joplin's career within the context of race, see David Emblidge, "I Feel, Therefore I Am," *Southwest Review* 61 (Fall 1976): 341-53; Gayle Wald, "One of the Boys?: Whiteness, Gender and Popular Music Studies," in Mike Hill, ed., *Whiteness: A Critical Reader* (NY: New York University Press, 1997), 151-67; Alice Echols, *Scars of Sweet Paradise: The Life and Times of Janis Joplin* (NY: Metropolitan Books, 1999), esp. 229-240.

[4] See, for instance, Margo Jefferson, "Ripping off Black Music From Thomas 'Daddy' Rice to Jimi Hendrix," *Harper's Magazine* 246 (January 1973): 40-45; Steve Chapple and Reebee Garofalo, *Rock 'n Roll is Here to Pay: The History and Politics of the Music Industry* (Chicago: Nelson Hall, 1977), 231-267.

[5] Eric Lott, *Love and Theft: Blackface Minstrelsy and the American Working Class* (NY: Oxford University Press, 1993). See also his "White Like Me: Racial Cross-Dressing and the Construction of American Whiteness," in Amy Kaplan and Donald E. Pease, eds., *Cultures of United States Imperialism* (Durham: Duke University Press, 1993), 474-495.

cultural product—is not the property of a race? I tentatively advance this question because it seems to me that though American Studies as a field has largely embraced the proposition that race is an ideological construct, we continue to use the "love and theft" model, which re-essentializes race as a form of cultural identity. We try to have it both ways—race is real; race is fiction—and politely paper over the resulting logical inconsistencies by saying that race's *effects* are real.

Perhaps Janis Joplin can help us escape this rather unsatisfactory resolution. She reminds us that within those categories we call "white" and "black" there are significant dissents, conflicts, and contestations. All whites don't understand what it means to be white in the same ways, and they don't experience their whiteness in identical ways. In fact, Janis Joplin, along with the Beats and the hippies with whom she identified, launched a sustained attack against a particular *kind* of suburban whiteness that, to them, lead to spiritual and emotional impoverishment. The response was, of course, a "silent majority" style of working class whiteness exploited by the Nixon-era Republicans. Thus, neither whiteness nor blackness had monolithic meanings that were closed to internal contestation. Joplin helps us tune our ears more finely to catch the multiple strains of "whiteness" wafting through the late 1960s and early 1970s, and reminds us how racial identities are created, contested, consumed, and performed.

* * *

From every early indication, Janis Joplin seemed destined to join her parents in the normal round of segregated suburban, east-Texas life. Born in 1943 in Port Arthur, Texas, her childhood social activities revolved around memberships in the Junior Reading Circle for Culture, the Glee Club, and the church choir. Though anxious to cultivate independent minds in their children, the Joplin parents did little to encourage attempts at subverting reigning orthodoxies. They did nothing, for example, to bring down Port Arthur's system of racial segregation. Joplin's sister Laura defensively depicted her parents as "quiet rebels who recognized the authority of the larger society." What this meant in practice, she explains, was that her folks paid their African American cleaning ladies "a fair wage" and gave them "our cast-off furniture when we bought new."[6] Despite whatever private misgivings the Joplin parents may have harbored about segregation, they, like countless whites throughout the Cold War South, accepted Jim Crow as an unalterable social reality. Laura Joplin explained that "there wasn't much opportunity to do anything anyway, beyond trying to smile and be kind to a black person on the street."[7] In a land where only one generation ago whites lynched black people, whites considered the stance of benevolent courtesy expected of the Joplin children a great stride in racial reconciliation. But it obviously did little to make them question existing racial hierarchies.

Indeed, though considering herself a liberal when it came to the status of blacks in America, Joplin's later career confirms a rather temperate interest in the political upheaval sparked by the civil rights movement, and a willingness to indulge in familiar stereotypes and racial fantasies. As a youth in Port Arthur she had advocated school integration and subsequently endured the familiar taunt of "Nigger lover."[8] She even took her preference for blues and jazz as a stand against the values of white Port Arthur that she'd been taught to embrace.[9] Yet she also endorsed long-standing "White Negro" stereotypes of black people as more hip, sexually liberated, and soulful than whites, spouting ideas fervently embraced by the generation of white Beat writers and poets with whom she became enamoured as a teenager.[10]

It was the Beat generation's envy of some mythic black soul that drew Joplin so powerfully to the 1920s generation of blues queens like Bessie Smith, Memphis Minnie, and Ma Rainey. Her admiration for Smith was particularly intense, so much so that one friend recalled that

---

[6]   Laura Joplin, *Love, Janis* (Petaluma, CA: Acid Test Productions, 1992), 56.

[7]   Laura Joplin, *Love, Janis* (Petaluma, CA: Acid Test Productions, 1992), 44.

[8]   Laura Joplin, *Love, Janis* (Petaluma, CA: Acid Test Productions, 1992), 56; Myra Friedman, *Buried Alive: The Biography of Janis Joplin*, rev. ed (NY: Harmony Books, 1992), 14; Ellis Amburn, *Pearl: The Obsessions and Passions of Janis Joplin* (NY: Warner Books, 1992), 25-6.

[9]   Her sister Laura remembers that Janis ripped classical works off her parents' record player and put on R & B and blues artists instead. Laura Joplin, *Love, Janis* (Petaluma, CA: Acid Test Productions, 1992), 61-2.

[10]   For the Beats' fascination with aspects of black culture, see Andrew Ross, *No Respect: Intellectuals and Popular Culture* (NY: Routledge, 1989), 65-101.

early in her career Joplin could "almost [imitate] the scratches in [Bessie Smith's] records."[11] Though done as a loving tribute to Smith, her 1968 song "Turtle Blues" comes across as an almost full-blown minstrel performance, complete with barroom chatter, patented Bessie Smith vocal lines, and stereotypical black dialect. In 1969 she made another odd step by forming an integrated soul band, certain that all she needed to make things complete was, as she said, a "great big ugly spade cat" to blow baritone.[12] In short, her understanding of black life and culture—even if admiring—was profoundly skewed.

This short catalogue of insensitivities and half-baked racial caricatures, which of course could be extended with additional examples, adds up to a seemingly inescapable conclusion—the very "love and theft" conclusion that I rejected in the first place. Joplin would seem a classic case of reaping the financial benefits and the industry's plaudits for a repertoire hopeless mired in fantasies of racial primitivism.

But to halt our analysis here is to overlook some pretty significant variations in the meanings and in the definitions of whiteness. In Joplin's case, eliding race and gender is an understandable since, for any girl growing up in the segregated South, race and gender expectations were so tightly bound together that it's impossible to pull them apart. But we risk simplifying our understanding of whiteness by our inability to discern the difference. Altering the perspective allows us to see that Joplin's embrace of what she saw as black culture was not merely an escapist fantasy from tasteless "whiteness." It was the most effective means in her cultural repertoire to attack the particular *kind* of whiteness to which she was heir: the "southern lady."

This brand of whiteness had maintained its talismanic power over the South since the end of Reconstruction, and it had yet to loosen its grip on the Port Arthur of Joplin's childhood. Coming of age in the 1940s and 1950s, Joplin's sister recalled that "Port Arthur could be a very proper place, offering a clear idea of what young ladies should be like."[13] Though initially conforming to those dictates, from the time Joplin began high

---

[11] Interview with Sam Andrew at http://www.bbhc.com/sam-interview-1.htm

[12] "Janis, the Judy Garland of Rock?" *Rolling Stone* March 15, 1969, 6.

[13] Laura Joplin, *Love, Janis* (Petaluma, CA: Acid Test Productions, 1992), 43.

school she flamboyantly rejected the propriety that governed the southern lady's life. She abandoned the panty girdle and poodle skirt for jeans and workshirts, ditched the bridge club for the Cajun bars, and embroidered elaborate tales of manic drinking and sexual marathons. "I was one of the girls who always wanted to do things that my mother said I couldn't because only boys get to do those things," she said many years later.[14]

By embracing the blues, Joplin added to her repertoire of dissent. "Back in Port Arthur," she explained, "I'd heard some Leadbelly records, and, well, if the blues syndrome is true, I guess it's true about me."[15] Joplin arrived at the blues not merely out of an interest in racial exoticism, but because it gave her a rhetorical strategy to express her sense of alienation in a system that provided no sanctioned means of dissent. Blues was, as she said, a *syndrome*, the devastating effects of which were not the property of any one race. "I keep trying to tell people that whites have soul, too," Joplin pleaded with one reporter in 1968. "There's no patent on soul."[16] As Joplin's tone concedes, however, there *was* a racial patent on soul, at least popularly conceived, and it belonged to blacks. She aimed at breaking that particular monopoly, and she did so by quietly embracing the one established form of musical dissent for whites: country.

Joplin's ostentatious embrace of the blues overshadowed the potent influence country music on her own artistic development. A member of Joplin's first San Francisco band recalled that initially her voice "had a real country influence,"[17] and Joplin began her singing career in what she

[14] Quoted in Alice Echols, *Scars of Sweet Paradise: The Life and Times of Janis Joplin* (NY: Metropolitan Books, 1999), 14; see also Ellis Amburn, *Pearl: The Obsessions and Passions of Janis Joplin* (NY: Warner Books, 1992), 17.

[15] David Dalton, *Piece of My Heart: A Portrait of Janis Joplin* (NY: Da Capo Press, 1985), 123. For more of her thoughts on these early black artists she encountered see "Janis Reunes at Jefferson High School," *Rolling Stone* Sept. 17, 1970: 8.

[16] Quoted in Alice Echols, *Scars of Sweet Paradise: The Life and Times of Janis Joplin* (NY: Metropolitan Books, 1999), 236.

[17] Interview with Sam Andrew at http://web.wt.net/%7Eduane/ bigbro.html

called a "hillbilly band."[18] Indeed, her best known song—"Me and Bobby McGee"—has firm roots in country music, and its vocal inflections remind us of Joplin's keen interest in white folk-revival performers like the Appalachian ballad singer Jean Ritchie. She could meld country music with the blues because both had their roots in identical soil: the loam of southern poverty and cultural alienation. Country and the blues were "countercultural" before the radicals of the 1960s assumed that label for themselves. They contradicted the American Dream and mocked narratives of affluence, power, and optimism with sad tales that dwelt on restrictions and constraints.[19] Country and folk revival music were, then, white complements to the mythic black soul that she wished to emulate.

Country and the blues were not identical, of course, because the racial suffering that gave rise to them were not identical. Joplin acknowledged this in a moment of remarkable candour. Each race, she asserted, had its own particular *kind* of blues. "I don't know if this is grossly insensitive of me, and it well may be," she explained, "but the black man's blues is based on the 'have not'—I got the blues because I don't have this, I got the blues because I don't have my baby," and so on. Because of their numerous privileges, she said, whites rarely experienced that kind of blues. But that didn't spare them from the blues syndrome. They suffered from what she called the "Kozmic Blues." These addressed the implicit promise made to her to and to countless others of her generation that if they obeyed the rules their lives would be void of pain and difficulty. "I remember when I was a kid," she continued, "they always told me, 'oh you're unhappy because you're going through adolescence. As soon as you grow up everything's going to be cool.' I really believed that, you know." But, she explained, "one day I finally realized it ain't all right and it ain't never gonna be all right, there's always something going wrong." When the reporter responded by musing

[18]   Alice Echols, *Scars of Sweet Paradise: The Life and Times of Janis Joplin* (NY: Metropolitan Books, 1999), 50; 53-56; 74; David Dalton, *Piece of My Heart: A Portrait of Janis Joplin* (NY: Da Capo Press, 1985), 95.

[19]   Country music is at heart, writes Trent Hill, "intensely fatalistic and sceptical about the possibilities of solving the tensions articulated in country songs by individual action or fiat." Trent Hill, "Why Isn't Country Music 'Youth' Culture?" in Roger Beebe, Denise Fulbrook, and Ben Saunders, *Rock Over the Edge: Transformations in Popular Music Culture* (Durham, NC: Duke University Press, 2002), 161-190 (quote 163); Barbara Ching, *Wrong's What I Do Best: Hard Country Music and Contemporary Culture* (NY: Oxford University Press, 2001).

that "the world is a really sad place," Joplin shot back angrily, "I know but they never told me that when I was young!"[20]

* * *

Writing about her sister in retrospect, Laura Joplin muses that Joplin's early enthusiasm for black music allowed her "to move beyond race."[21] I would argue precisely the opposite. Joplin devoted her considerable talents to understanding just what it meant to be human, but because of the time and place of her living, it was a quest that she had to take through race. That is, race was so fundamental to how she understood the world's possibilities and limits that she had difficulty describing herself in any other way. She told one reporter in 1970, for instance, "well, you know, I'm a middle-class white chick from a family that would love to send me to college and I didn't wanna. I had a job, I didn't dig it. I had a car, I didn't dig it. I had it real easy."[22] Janis Joplin did not—and nor should we—do away with race as a useful category of inquiry. But we should use it more carefully, to take less comfort in sweeping generalizations about "blacks" and "whites," and to remember that racial identity is an evolving series of understandings, influenced by time, place, gender, class, and so on. As Joplin herself said "a ... *middle class ... white ... chick.*" None of those terms alone circumscribed her understanding of herself and of her whiteness.

Thus, though it would seem that Eric Lott's pithy phrase "love and theft" would apply in Janis Joplin's case, it proves an awfully inflexible scholarly tool. For one thing, it only works in one direction. That is, if culture is racially determined and, consequently, "owned" so that other races may steal it, we must consequently coffle Marian Anderson, and Kathleen Battle, and Yo Yo Ma together and send them to ideological prison as cultural criminals, for they are no less guilty than Joplin of profiting from music not racially "their own." Obviously this is patently absurd, for whites have no privileged claim on opera or any musical form.

[20] David Dalton, *Piece of My Heart: A Portrait of Janis Joplin* (NY: Da Capo Press, 1985), 181-82.

[21] Laura Joplin, *Love, Janis* (Petaluma, CA: Acid Test Productions, 1992), 61.

[22] David Dalton, *Piece of My Heart: A Portrait of Janis Joplin* (NY: Da Capo Press, 1985), 182.

By extension, then, blacks cannot "own" rap or the blues. Moreover, using "love and theft" necessitates a belief in air-tight racial cultures that must be constantly monitored for their level of purity or corruption based upon a series of maddeningly vague and shifting standards. Scholars working on Jimi Hendrix, for example, have seen him simultaneously as a "psychedelic Uncle Tom," and as the bearer of the "tradition from which [African] voodoshi derives."[23] The problem obviously stems from a struggle over defining and measuring just what "black culture" is. That we cannot arrive at a definition should make us more cautious about launching ourselves into the logical morass of "love and theft." In short, Joplin reminds us that we must not replace biological definitions of race with cultural ones.[24]

Gavin James Campbell

[23] Samuel A. Floyd, Jr., *The Power of Black Music: Interpreting its History from Africa to the United States* (NY: Oxford University Press, 1995), 203. Floyd is particularly interested, as his title suggests, in the "African" elements in black song, connecting both classical and rock formations to the central principle of the African (and African American) ring shout, or what he calls the "ring impulse." (161). For other opinions on the matter of Hendrix's "blackness" see Lauren Onkey, "Voodoo Child: Jimi Hendrix and the Politics of Race in the Sixties," in Peter Braunstein and Michael William Doyle, eds., *Imagine Nation: The American Counterculture of the 1960s and 1970s* (NY: Routledge, 2002): 189-214; Ward, *Just My Soul Responding*, 244-48.

[24] In the field of music, scholars who have attempted to combat this problem include Philip Tagg, "Open Letter: 'Black Music,' 'Afro-American Music' and 'European Music'" *Popular Music* 8 (October 1989): 285-298; Keith Negus, *Popular Music in Theory: An Introduction* (Cambridge: Polity Press, 1996), 99-113; Les Back, "Out of Sight: Southern Music and the Coloring of Sound," in Vron Ware and Les Back, *Out of Whiteness: Collor, Politics, and Culture* (University of Chicago Press, 2002), 227-270; Christopher A. Waterman, "Race Music: Bo Chatmon, 'Corrine Corrina,' and the Excluded Middle," in Ronald Radano and Philip V. Bohlman, eds., *Music and the Racial Imagination* (Chicago: University of Chicago Press, 2000), 167-205. In the field or race theory more generally the hallmark works include Kwame Anthony Appiah, *In My Father's House: Africa in the Philosophy of Culture* (NY: Oxford University Press, 1992); Whiteness has largely gone ignored by music scholars. An interesting exception is Bryan K. Carman, *A Race of Singers: Whitman's Working-Class Hero From Guthrie to Springsteen* (Chapel Hill: University of North Carolina Press, 2000).

How Far is the Canadian Border from America?: A Case Study in Racial Profiling

Introduction

On September 11, 2001,[1] the world changed for Americans. Suddenly, the prevailing view of the United States as safe, strong, and impenetrable was no longer accurate. Due to experiencing a major terrorist attack in their own land, Americans had to begin to view their own country, its foreign policy, and its borders in a whole new light. The new homeland security initiatives that have been put in place since then are aimed at keeping the nation safe. But what constitutes safety? This paper looks at some of the changes the U.S. has undergone since 9/11 to try to ensure its safety, and what this has changed about the U.S. relationship with Canada, especially where race is concerned. The U.S.-Canada border is used as a convenient way to symbolize the interaction of these two countries and the distance that has grown between them.

---

[1] September 11, 2001 was the day two airplanes struck the World Trade Centre, one struck the Pentagon, and one was downed in a field before it could hit a major target. 9/11 has become a conventional way of referring to this in the U.S., and will be used in this paper hereafter.

Where is Here?

Talking about the changes to U.S. policy and the institution of "homeland security" assumes that we have an idea of the extent of the U.S. We can see it on a map, and armed officials will tell us when we are about to encroach on the boundaries, but what does it really mean to be American? Where is America and who is American?

One way that the U.S. is asserting its "here-ness" is through things like the Container Security Initiative (CSI). This is a new program that inspects the large containers ships typically carry before they leave their port of origin rather than after they arrive in the U.S.[2] By sending U.S. Customs agents to foreign posts to assist the ports of origin with the inspection, the U.S. is asserting its extraterritorial location. Therefore, the U.S. no longer starts at the geographical boundaries on a map, but extends outward to claim rights and privileges far beyond its physical borders.

The U.S. is also extending its reach in a metaterritorial way. If the CSI symbolizes "here is where we are," the War on Terrorism and Operation Iraqi Freedom symbolize "there is where we want to be." These two military operations speak to metaterritory. "Extra-" is defined as "outside;" "meta-" means in this context "beyond."[3] Thus, "extraterritorial" refers to a nation-state acting outside its territory as it does inside its territory, while I am using "metaterritorial" to refer more to an attitude or mindset in which a nation-state *mentally* or *philosophically* extends its territory either to protect or enrich itself without the goal of either annexing physical territory or acting in a extraterritorial manner. Embassies are accepted examples of extraterritoriality; spying is an age-old example of metaterritoriality. While extraterritoriality extends a state's reach, it has the cache of being legitimate. Metaterritoriality has the aura of moral necessity for the state engaging in it, but it is not necessarily seen as legitimate in the international arena. Because of a basic fear that ascribes evil's point of origin to the caves of Afghanistan

---

[2] Robert C. Bonner, Remarks at the Centre for Strategic and International Studies, Washington, DC, 26 August 2002. Available at http://www.csis.org/features/bonner.pdf.

[3] *Webster's Unabridged Dictionary of the English Language*, New York: Random House, 2001, pp. 685, 1206.

and the presidential palaces of Iraq, the U.S. has unilaterally decided[4] to invade in order to preemptively protect itself, or perhaps to punish those who (are perceived to) have done it harm. Thus the mental borders of the state have been pushed out quite far, while the physical borders are subject to increased securitization.

One of the things that 9/11 has made the U.S. aware of is that the borders are never completely secure, and they are always porous. Before 9/11, the focus was on the porosity of the Mexican border, primarily in regards to illegal immigration, but also for drugs. Post-9/11, much of the focus has shifted to the Canadian border's potential for leaking in terrorists. Ideologically, borders are an insecure area until a true Fortress USA is created, where everyone and everything is checked as it enters, and there are no unguarded or undefended areas where evil could slip in. The other option is a Fortress North America, commonly known as "perimeter security," which the U.S. has been trying to sell to its North American Free Trade Agreement (NAFTA) partners, especially Canada. Under perimeter security, Canada would change its immigration policies to jibe with the U.S.'s, and then the need for a secure U.S.-Canada border would be eliminated.[5]

The discourse about the vulnerability of U.S. borders has also changed. Illegal immigrants are still talked about to some degree as Mexicans seeking low wage jobs, but Mexicans are no longer discussed as a significant threat. The new discourse deals with the coasts and the Canadian border, which are all now dangerous due to illegal-immigrant terrorists' ability to enter. The old moniker of Canada as a "Club Med for terrorists"[6] is also continuing to be tossed around. Canada is no longer

---

[4] The *actions* taken may have been multilateral, but I would argue that the decisions to invade were made almost entirely by the U.S., which then convinced other countries to join the action.

[5] For a good, unbiased overview of perimeter security and Fortress North America, see Mapleleafweb.com: Education – Spotlight: Fortress North America at http://www.mapleleafweb.com/education/spotlight/issue_3/printable.html accessed 11 May 2003.

[6] This phrase was initially uttered by Claude Pacquette, a Montreal police investigator. It was made famous by U.S. Representative Lamar Smith in his statement to the Subcommittee on Immigration and Claims (Lamar Smith (R-TX), Statement of the Honourable Lamar Smith, Chairman, Subcommittee on Immigration and Claims, House Committee on the Judiciary, Hearing on Terrorist Threats to the United States, 25 January 2000, http://www.house.gov/judiciary/smit0125.htm accessed 1 October 2002).

described as the nation next door with whom the U.S. is proud to boast the longest undefended border in the world. Instead, it is a country full of false-asylum-seeker-terrorist-semi-Canadians who represent potential security breaches for the U.S.

The implications for U.S. policy of this "triple play" of blithely increased extraterritorial activity, a panic-driven metaterritoriality, and the isolationist streak of increasingly securitised borders are wide. Extraterritoriality can lead to increased impositions of U.S. rules on other countries, and a resultant change in the nature of trade with the U.S. Rather than declaring items unfit to enter the U.S., they can be declared unfit to leave their port of origin if bound for the U.S. This could potentially lead to uncomfortable situations with foreign governments. Taken to its logical conclusion, the current trend in metaterritoriality could lead to the U.S. invading virtually everywhere to rout out potential and actual terrorists. The U.S.'s increased isolationism can lead to two things: a curtailment or end of immigration, and a decrease in civil rights for some or all groups.

Who Belongs Here?

Historically, America was defined as a white country. Though there have always been non-whites, the overarching racial project[7] has been one of denying the full rights, privileges, and identity of being American to non-whites. That has been slowly changing, and now is more de facto than de jure. In an interesting contrast to this, the U.S.'s current propagandistic self-image is multiethnic/multiracial. For example, television shows now have token minorities and textbooks have been changed so that the people mentioned do not all have WASPy[8] names.

True acceptance (whether or not as equals) into the polity seems to take some time. African Americans have finally been grudgingly accepted, as have Native Americans (American Indians), and neither of those groups significantly antedates WASPs. Ethnic white groups (such as

---

[7]   Racial projects are defined and explained in more detail below.

[8]   WASP stands for White Anglo-Saxon Protestant, the original settlers and traditionally the most privileged segment of U.S. society.

Jews, Irish, Italians, etc.) have slowly gained acceptance over the past more than a century, and Asians and Latinos are becoming more and more integrated. It was not that long ago, however, that people who were neither white nor black could not become naturalized citizens.[9]

Just a few generations ago, people of Japanese descent in the U.S.—citizens and non-citizens alike—were demonized to the point of being put in internment camps. Though they were grudgingly accepted before World War II (WWII), as soon as Pearl Harbor was bombed, they were seen as inherently un-American. That situation is somewhat of a parallel to today's situation for Arab Americans, which will be explored in more detail below. Luckily, since the nation went through this situation not that long ago with the Japanese, it seems unlikely that Arabs will be rounded up and interned wholesale. The treatment of legal immigrants from the Middle East by authorities and the public leaves something to be desired, however.

The Racial State and the Anti-Arab Racial Project

One of the less-discussed side-effects of the newly emerging American view of the world is the disruption of an unstable racial equilibrium and the creation of a new racial project. Omi and Winant explain racial formation theory.[10] Basically, it begins with a racial state[11] and a racial movement (a movement to change the racial status quo). The racial state and racial movement are at an unstable equilibrium. The interaction causes tension and friction, and the conflict slowly simmers. At some point the conflict boils over, and the result is a "crisis phase," in which a disequilibrium is created and the racial order can be changed.

---

[9] The law changed to allow naturalization regardless of race in 1952 (Ian F. Haney López, *White By Law: The Legal Construction of Race,* New York: New York University Press, 1996, p. 1). People of any race (with the partial exception of blacks under slavery) have always been granted citizenship if they were born on U.S. soil.

[10] Michael Omi and Howard Winant, *Racial Formation in the United States: From the 1960s to the 1990s,* 2nd ed., New York: Routledge, 1994, pp. 84-8.

[11] "The state is composed of *institutions,* the *policies* they carry out, the *conditions and rules* which support and justify them, and the *social relations* in which they are imbedded" (Omi and Winant, p. 83, emphasis in original).

Crisis phases can occur because a more liberal racial movement is challenging a more conservative racial state, or because a more conservative racial movement is challenging a more liberal racial state. An example of the former is the Civil Rights Movement of the 1960s. An example of the latter is the "backlash" (repealing of Civil Rights laws) that occurred in the Reagan era.

Omi and Winant do not really address what creates that "certain level of intensity"[12] that the conflict has to reach to initiate the crisis phase. In fact, they imply that crisis is reached through a steady, almost predictable, increase in tensions. I contend that sometimes there are specific historic events that act as catalysts, tipping points, or the straw that broke the camel's back. History shows us these points—we remember events that might otherwise not be considered very significant. In fact, there would be no other reason to remember these points if they were not significant. A perfect example from U.S. history is Rosa Parks. Her actions are considered by many to have started what became the Civil Rights Movement by initiating the Montgomery bus boycott, though all she did was refuse to move to the back of the bus.[13] It is unclear why the actions of one woman one day would have taken the situation out of equilibrium. Another, more recent, example is Rodney King.[14] Other African American men had been beaten up by other white police officers before him, yet somehow his beating set off an outcry, and the acquittal of the officers touched off riots. The fact that the beating was videotaped and shown on the news probably helped, but it is not a complete explanation. In fact, part of the explanation has to include why the media agreed to show it, not just in Los Angeles, where it happened, but in the

---

[12] Ibid., p. 86.

[13] For Rosa Parks's story, see Kira Albin, "Rosa Parks: The Woman Who Changed a Nation," http://www.grandtimes.com/rosa.html accessed 11 May 2003. Rosa Parks's actions took place during segregation (or "Jim Crow") in the U.S., where the society in the southern U.S. was by law "separate but equal," which in practice meant that whites and blacks had separate facilities, and the facilities for blacks were of poorer quality. In Montgomery, Alabama, blacks had to sit in the back of the bus if whites were on the bus.

[14] For a brief synopsis of Rodney King's story, see "Hate Motivated Violence: The Rodney King Case and Possible Implications for Canada" http://www2.ca.nizkor.org/ftp.cgi/orgs/canadian/canada/justice/hate-motivated-violence/hmv-006-00 accessed 11 May 2003.

rest of the U.S., and internationally, as well. The time was right, and just one more event was needed to push the equilibrium into a crisis phase that I believe we have yet to completely emerge from. That phase is one in which we are reexamining the way the state polices racial minorities. It began with the Rodney King-inspired examination of police brutality and moved to an examination of racial profiling, which had been a topic not very many people discussed until just a few years ago.

In the middle of this crisis phase, another simmering conflict was pushed to the boiling point: the place of Arabs[15] in U.S. society. The crisis sparked by Rodney King was one in which a more liberal racial movement challenged a more conservative racial state. Our most recent crisis phase, however, sparked by the events of 9/11, is one in which the somewhat more liberalized (thanks to the King-sparked crisis) racial state is challenged by a more conservative racial movement before the equilibrium can even be reestablished.

The new way Arabs are being viewed in the U.S. is part of a process known as racial formation, which is "the sociohistorical process by which racial categories are created, inhabited, transformed, and destroyed."[16] Racial formation processes link structure and representation, and "[r]acial *projects* do the ideological 'work' of making these links."[17] Racial projects thus connect the meaning of race in a given situation with the organization of social structures and everyday experiences based on that meaning. Using this theory, we can begin to understand what is happening in the U.S.: 9/11 served as a catalyst to initiate a new crisis phase which is resulting in a new racial project in which Arabs are demonized in the name of national security.[18]

---

[15] I am using "Arab" throughout this paper as a shorthand and for the most part in its commonsense meaning of people of Middle Eastern descent (excluding Jewish Israelis), both immigrants and descendants of immigrants. There are some gray areas, such as whether Iranians are categorized thusly, but for the most part, the group is relatively evident.

[16] Omi and Winant, p. 55.

[17] Ibid., p. 56, emphasis in original.

[18] For examples of often nationally-sponsored and socially-acceptable racial profiling of Arabs (and people who appear to be Arab), see the American Civil Liberty Union's racial profiling page: http://www.aclu.org/RacialEquality/RacialEqualitylist.cfm?c=133 accessed 11 May 2003.

In this newest racial project, both the meanings and structures of race in the U.S. have changed. Before 9/11, "Arab" was not a racial classification for the most part. It definitely had not entered societal structures to a deep degree, as it was not an option on the 2000 census.[19] In most parts of the country, "Arab" was a vague ethnic classification—Arabs were considered white (though "ethnic white", like Jews and Italians). The category "Arab" (similar to the category "Latino") has slowly been going through a process of racialization—the redefinition of a group as a race. In the Detroit area, which boasts the largest Middle Eastern population outside the Middle East,[20] this process was further along than in the rest of the country, though I contend that 9/11 caused the rest of the country to catch up.

The new racial project that is racializing Arabs across the country has a number of aspects. The meaning of "Arab" is beginning to solidify. It tends to refer now to people from (or people whose ancestors were from) the Middle East, usually only Muslims (though at times Christians and other minority religions are included—Jews are specifically excluded). People who would not normally self-identify as Arab are becoming identified as such, because "Arab" and "Muslim" are being conflated. This process began earlier, and recent events serve to help along the equation of terrorist=Islamic fundamentalist=Muslim=Arab=Middle Eastern. The new racial project demonizes this still in-flux category of "Arab."[21] Arabs become anyone who poses a threat to the U.S., and that becomes any

---

[19]   The options were White, Black/African American/Negro, American Indian/Alaskan Native (write in tribe), a choice of Asian specific identities (lumped into Asian in the statistics), a choice of Native Hawaiian or Other Pacific Islander specific identities (lumped into Asian/Native Hawaiian or Other Pacific Islander in the statistics), and Some Other Race. Hispanic origin was a separate question. People were able to select as many as applied. (U.S. 2000 Census, "Overview of Race and Hispanic Origin 2000", http://www.census.gov/prod/2001pubs/c2kbr01-1.pdf accessed 11 May 2003.)

[20]   "ADC's Imad Hamad is Detroit News' Michiganian of the Year" http://www.adc.org/index.php?id=1802 accessed 11 May 2003.

[21]   Most racial categories at most times are in flux to some degree. Probably one of the most stable in the U.S. has been black/Negro/African American, because of the historical one-drop rule (F. James Davis, "Who is Black? One Nation's Definition," University Park, PA: Pennsylvania State University Press, 1991, pp. 4-6.). Whiteness has been continuously contested, as seen in Haney López. In fact, the American-Arab Anti-Discrimination Committee (ADC) treats the identity as if it is completely not in flux, and everyone knows what "Arab" means. See their site: http://www.adc.org.

Muslim, as Islam is seen as antithetical to the U.S. way of life.[22]

This new crisis phase, and its concomitant racial project, has come out of fear. 9/11, as many have said, showed Americans how vulnerable they were to attack at home. Previous events, such as the attacks on U.S. embassies, the Oklahoma City bombing, and the earlier attempt on the World Trade Centre scared Americans, but not as much. The U.S. embassies were elsewhere, so Americans at home did not feel like they were in danger. Oklahoma City had a domestic source, so Americans took it as an isolated criminal incident, rather than part of organized terrorism. The earlier attack on the World Trade Centre was so minor that people put it out of their minds.[23] 9/11, however, was qualitatively different, as it was an attack that originated outside of the country, took place on U.S. soil, and resulted in a large loss of life and destruction of property. Handily, the perpetrators came from the then-nebulous "Arab" group, which was already associated with extreme Islamic fundamentalism (seen as inherently un-American) and terrorism.

The fear of more terrorism has led to increased security measures. Some of these security measures are just that: aimed—non-racially—at protecting the borders and easing communication among the various agencies involved in keeping the country safe. Other measures are part of the social structures of the racial project. Since "Arab" has come to be synonymous with "terrorist," or at least "potential terrorist," logic says that Arabs and Muslims are naturally a threat to security. Hence, the U.S. has instituted a registration system for nonimmigrant male visitors who are citizens or nationals of particular countries only.[24] "From" has

---

[22] For example, the ADC's warnings of possible hate crimes tend to be directed at "Arab Americans and Muslims". See http://www.adc.org/index.php?id=1751 (accessed 11 May 2003).

[23] Only six people died and 1,000 were injured; over 50,000 people were evacuated safely (Dave Williams, "The Bombing of the World Trade Centre in New York City," International Criminal Police Review, No. 469-471 (1998), http://www.interpol.int/Public/Publications/ICPR/ICPR469_3.asp accessed 11 May 2003).

[24] These countries are: Afghanistan, Algeria, Bahrain, Bangladesh, Egypt, Eritrea, Indonesia, Iran, Iraq, Jordan, Kuwait, Lebanon, Libya, Morocco, North Korea, Oman, Pakistan, Qatar, Saudi Arabia, Somalia, Sudan, Syria, Tunisia, United Arab Emirates, and Yemen. "Special Registration," Department of Homeland Security, http://www.immigration.gov/graphics/shared/lawenfor/specialreg/ index.htm (accessed 11 May 2003). Note that all but North Korea are either Arab or predominantly Muslim or both.

also been redefined. Citizenship aside, the U.S. wants people to register if they were born in one of those countries, regardless of what country (other than the U.S.) they are now permanent residents of.[25]

This racial project can be seen to stem to some degree from the tendency of enemies to be strictly categorized during wartime. As Neufeldt explains:[26]

> The demarcation of friend is critical for [individuals in] groups who are in some way identified with the enemy, whether by language, heritage, or marriage. If they are categorized as an enemy they run the risk of losing political, civic and social rights and freedoms and becoming targets of public derision and violence. ... If the group on the periphery is categorized as friends and loyal compatriots they are able to continue living within the same parameters of freedom as their fellow citizens.

To make it even more difficult to be identified as a "friend," during wartime "the borders of identity groups become more rigid and more actively patrolled."[27] The fear of a fifth column springs up, and "[o]fficial government structures and unofficial community members who seek to ensure national security heavily police civic and ethnic ... boundaries."[28] The current situation looks on the surface to be simply another example of this, and one might assume that treatment of Arabs will return to normal again after the end of the war on terrorism, as it has for the Germans, Italians, and Japanese categorized as enemies in WWII. However, this neglects the way this enemy has been socially constructed, and the racialization that is taking place. In September 2001, George W.

---

[25] At this point, U.S. citizens born in one of the countries on the list do not have to register, though U.S. permanent residents do.

[26] Reina C. Neufeldt, "Boxed In: Expanding the Constricted Narratives of Wartime Nationalism," Paper presented at the 44th Annual International Studies Association Convention, Portland, Oregon, 26 February 2003, p. 1.

[27] Ibid., pp. 3-4.

[28] Neufeldt, p. 4. She defines "fifth column" as "internal subversive agents who attempt to undermine a nation's solidarity during wartime" (p. 3).

Bush declared this "war on terrorism."[29] However, "terrorism" is not a nation-state, nor is it an ethnic group. The fact that a group of people has been singled out as members of the fictitious national group Terrorism belies the racialized nature of the new anti-Arabism in the U.S. Thus, the equation Terrorist=Arab can be seen as part of the new racial project.

Much like with the internment of people of Japanese descent in the early 1940s, this current racial project constructs who is and is not "truly" an American, and thus who does and does not belong. Terrorists cannot be Americans, because our country is at war with terrorism. Thus, since Arab=Terrorist, we begin to question if Arabs can ever really be truly American. The current U.S. racial project also constructs who is and is not "truly" a Canadian, as I discuss below.

Canada=There?

If the U.S. is "here," and has become very specific about who belongs "here," then perhaps Canada is now part of "there," along with Iraq, Afghanistan, etc. Canada's race relations are strikingly different from the U.S.'s, based on different histories and a different overall attitude toward the integration of minorities and immigrants. The U.S. philosophy is the "melting pot"—everyone should assimilate as much as possible to the status quo, and all melt together into one people. The Canadian philosophy—in fact official policy since the Trudeau era[30]—is multiculturalism. This means that attitudes toward Arabs and Muslims are different in Canada. With this different attitude, Canada has a hard time understanding and acceding to the U.S.'s treatment of such a disparate group in the name of secure borders.

---

[29] He first mentioned it in his address to the nation on the evening of 11 September. See George W. Bush, "Statement by the President in His Address to the Nation," 11 September 2001, http://www.whitehouse.gov/news/releases/2001/09/20010911-16.html (accessed 12 May 2003).

[30] Multiculturalism became official policy in 1971 (R. Breton, "Ethnicity and Race in Social Organization: Recent Developments in Canadian Society," in *The Vertical Mosaic Revisited,* ed. Rick Helmes-Hayes and James Curtis, Toronto: University of Toronto Press, 1998, pp. 60-115; Will Kymlicka, *Finding Our Way: Rethinking Ethnocultural Relations in Canada,* Don Mills, Ontario, Canada: Oxford University Press, 1998).

One example of the treatment Canada does not understand is the new National Security Entry-Exit Registration System (NSEERS) system described above, which requires people to register based on place of birth. This has Canadian officials up in arms. Canada accepts a larger number of immigrants as a proportion of its population than the U.S. does.[31]

Thus, naturally, many of the people who cross the Canada-U.S. border were not born in Canada. Canada believes that it has a perfectly acceptable set of criteria for granting permanent resident status. The U.S., on the other hand, has lumped Canada in with all other countries (ignoring the fact that that border hosts about 200 million crossings annually, and very few end in problems) and has demanded that Canadian permanent residents born in one of the "bad" countries register upon entering the U.S.

Canada is not pleased with the new U.S. securitization. It has been fighting for years its image as a "Club Med for terrorists," and has pointed out that none of the 9/11 hijackers entered the U.S. via Canada. One point of leverage that Canada has is its position as the U.S.'s largest trading partner, and the international agreements it has with the U.S. to ease the flow of goods (and thus the people who transport those goods, at least) across the border. The current agreement is NAFTA, but the goodwill began with the Canada-United States Free Trade Agreement (CUSFTA), and Canada tries to point out that it does not like being treated as a valuable trading partner yet an untrustworthy exporter of people.

Similarly, Canada has been having a hard time with George W. Bush's blanket statements. It feels it has a unique relationship with the

---

[31] Canada accepts an average of 221,000 immigrants and refugees a year, with a population of 30,007,094, thus 0.7% of the population; the U.S. accepts an average of 800,000 per year, with a population of 281,421,906, thus 0.2% of their population
(Citizenship and Immigration Canada, "Serving Canada and the World,"
http://www.cic.gc.ca/english/department/brochure/service.html accessed 14 May 2003;
Canada 2001 Census,
http://www12.statcan.ca/english/census01/products/standard/popdwell/Table-PR.cfm accessed 14 May 2003; Immigration and Naturalization Service, "The Triennial Comprehensive Report on Immigration: Executive Summary,"
http://www.immigration.gov/graphics/aboutus/repsstudies/ExSum.pdf accessed 14 May 2003; United States 2000 Census,
http://www.census.gov/main/www/cen2000.html accessed 14 May 2003).

U.S. and should not be subjected to the same kinds of rules and ultimatums as other countries. In response to Bush's statements along the lines of "you're either with us or you're against us," Canada shook its collective head in puzzlement—could the U.S. really think Canada was "against" it just because Canada refused to help invade Iraq, along with most of the rest of the world? Bush's discourse, combined with security policies that do not treat Canada preferentially, pushes Canada further away, moving the border metaphorically further away from America.

Conclusion

It appears that the events of 9/11 set off a chain reaction that caused the United States to become both more insular and act more extraterritorially and metaterritorially. The U.S. securitized its borders and has worked on alienating Canada. This is partly due to the newly emerging racial project on the place of Arabs in U.S. society and partly due to recent foreign policy moves. As both Arabs and Canadians become a frightening other to the "real" America, and "here" becomes more and more circumscribed, discourse and policy move the new site of racial profiling of people of Middle Eastern descent—the Canadian border—far, far away from America.

Helen McClure

Works Cited

"ADC Advisory Statement to Arab Americans and Muslims."
http://www.adc.org/index.php?id=1751. Accessed 11 May 2003.

"ADC's Imad Hamad is Detroit News' Michiganian of the Year."
http://www.adc.org/index.php?id=1802. Accessed 11 May 2003.

Albin, Kira. "Rosa Parks: The Woman Who Changed a Nation."
http://www.grandtimes.com/rosa.html. Accessed 11 May 2003.

American Civil Liberty Union. "Racial Equality: Racial Profiling."
http://www.aclu.org/RacialEquality/RacialEqualitylist.cfm?c=133. Accessed 11 May 2003.

Bonner, Robert C. Remarks at the Center for Strategic and International Studies. Washington, DC, 26 August 2002. http://www.csis.org/features/bonner.pdf. Accessed 11 May 2003.

Breton, R. 1998. "Ethnicity and Race in Social Organization: Recent Developments in Canadian Society." *The Vertical Mosaic Revisited.* Ed. Rick Helmes-Hayes and James Curtis. Toronto: University of Toronto Press, pp. 60-115.

Bush, George W. "Statement by the President in His Address to the Nation." 11 September 2001. http://www.whitehouse.gov/news/releases/2001/09/20010911-16.html. Accessed 12 May 2003.

Canada 2001 Census.
http://www12.statcan.ca/english/census01/products/standard/popdwell/Table-PR.cfm. Accessed 14 May 2003.

Citizenship and Immigration Canada. "Serving Canada and the World."
http://www.cic.gc.ca/english/department/brochure/service.html. Accessed 14 May 2003.

Davis, F. James. 1991. *"Who is Black? One Nation's Definition."* University Park, PA: Pennsylvania State University Press, 1991.

Haney López, Ian F. 1996. *White By Law: The Legal Construction of Race.* New York: New York University Press.

"Hate Motivated Violence: The Rodney King Case and Possible Implications for Canada." http://www2.ca.nizkor.org/ftp.cgi/orgs/canadian/canada/justice/hate-motivated-violence/hmv-006-00. Accessed 11 May 2003.

Immigration and Naturalization Service. "The Triennial Comprehensive Report on Immigration: Executive Summary." http://www.immigration.gov/graphics/aboutus/repsstudies/ExSum.pdf. Accessed 14 May 2003.

Kymlicka, Will. 1998. *Finding Our Way: Rethinking Ethnocultural Relations in Canada.* Don Mills, Ontario, Canada: Oxford University Press.

Mapleleafweb.com: Education – Spotlight: Fortress North America. http://www.mapleleafweb.com/education/spotlight/issue_3/printable.html. Accessed 11 May 2003.

Neufeldt, Reina C. "Boxed In: Expanding the Constricted Narratives of Wartime Nationalism." Paper presented at the 44th Annual International Studies Association Convention. Portland, Oregon. 26 February 2003.

Omi Michael, and Howard Winant. 1994. *Racial Formation in the United States: From the 1960s to the 1990s.* 2nd ed. New York: Routledge.

Smith Lamar. Statement of the Honorable Lamar Smith, Chairman, Subcommittee on Immigration and Claims, House Committee on the Judiciary. Hearing on Terrorist Threats to the United States. 25 January 2000. http://www.house.gov/judiciary/smit0125.htm. Accessed 1 October 2002.

"Special Registration." Department of Homeland Security. http://www.immigration.gov/ graphics/shared/lawenfor/specialreg/index.htm. Accessed 11 May 2003.

United States 2000 Census. http://www.census.gov/main/www/cen2000.html. Accessed 14 May 2003.

United States 2000 Census. "Overview of Race and Hispanic Origin 2000." http://www.census.gov/prod/2001pubs/c2kbr01-1.pdf. Accessed 11 May 2003.

Webster's Unabridged Dictionary of the English Language. New York: Random House, 2001.

Williams, Dave. 1998. "The Bombing of the World Trade Center in New York City." *International Criminal Police Review.* No. 469-471 (1998).
http://www.interpol.int/Public/Publications/ICPR/ICPR469_3.asp. Accessed 11 May 2003.

SPACE AND PLACE
IN
AMERICAN STUDIES

Space and Place in Geography and American Studies

This paper grew out of a panel of three linked papers designed to address one of the four central themes of the First IASA Congress: where is here? From what position is here articulated? Focussing particularly on geographer Doreen Massey's book *Space, Place and Gender*, the panel collectively set out to suggest ways in which the concepts of 'hereness' and of place as they have been articulated in the theory and practice of social and critical geographers could be folded into work in American studies. Our various experiences on the ground at the IASA Congress confirmed for us our sense that the theoretical work of critical social and cultural geographers can make a vital contribution to the conceptualization of 'international' American studies itself, particularly to the critique and renegotiation of its normative terms and practices. In our panel, however, we focussed on the usefulness of geographical theory for Americanists on a different scale, with each of the papers exploring the potential of geographical theory for American studies practice through case-study discussions of particular texts in US cinema or literature. While assuming a broadly geographical understanding of and approach to American studies itself, in other words, we concentrated on this occasion on a demonstration of some of the specific ways in which the terminology, concepts, and theories of contemporary critical geography can be used to frame textual analysis. In submitting these papers to the proceedings we decided to keep the three presentations in their original compressed conference format, presenting the joint work of the panel as a co-authored paper, not only because we want to highlight their interdependence but also in order to make a collective argument for the usefulness and relevance of geographical theory to American studies in general.

Doreen Massey's book *Space, Place and Gender*, first published in 1994, has had a powerful impact on her own field as well as on many areas of the humanities, including American studies. Her work has allowed scholars across the disciplines to better theorize the centrality of space in the twentieth century, whether the frame of reference is postmodernism, transnationality, postcoloniality, or globalization. Across changes in scale, too, Massey's work has helped to theorize the local as well as global, looking at the power relations in the home as well as in the workplace. Using concepts developed in Massey's essays on space, place, globalization, gender, and home, our papers engage specifically with the power relations created by networks of US racial and ethnic identities. The first section takes up Massey's fundamental redefinition of geographical place in order to rethink the relationship of 'local' to 'national' to 'international' in US literature, through a discussion of Toshio Mori's *Yokohama, California*. The second section then brings into play the concept of geographical scale, thus further complicating the concept of place in a close reading of Judith Ortiz Cofer's short story "American History." The third section focuses on Edward Zwick's 1998 movie about Arab terrorism in the US, *The Siege*, taking the concept of place as the basis for a discussion of the film's production of safe and unsafe cinematic spaces and its projection of a particular ideologically-loaded interpretation of time-space compression.[1]

'Here' in *Yokohama, California*: Toshio Mori's Place in American Literature

Yokohama, California is the title of a collection of short stories by the American writer Toshio Mori, published in 1949, forgotten for decades,

---

[1] The panel consisted of the following linked papers: "'Here' in *Yokohama, California*: Toshio Mori's Place in American Literature" by Sheila Hones, "The Social Construction of Geographical Scale in 'American History'" by Julia Leyda, and "Locating Terrorism: Safe and Unsafe Space in *The Siege*" by Khadija El Alaoui-Fritsch.

and rediscovered in the 1970s.[2] "Yokohama, California," is also, of course, a place name. The title and the place name both position Mori's stories in an American context. "Yokohama, California" is an American place like "Boston, Massachusetts." *"Yokohama, California"* is an American book like *Winesburg, Ohio*.[3] When the stories are put together and named, Mori's text becomes a book, and his "Lil' Yokohama" becomes a place. The stories have a strong sense of "here," and, as the geographer Michael Curry has pointed out, "hereness" provides a powerful frame for normativity. The normative idea that "that's how we do things" is very often place-related: "that's how we do things *here.*" But where is "here" in *Yokohama, California*? And who are "we?"

Because we are usually in more than one place at the same time, the normative "that's how we do things here" effect generates ethical dilemmas, Curry argues. Here, for instance, we are in a public space, at an international meeting, in Leiden, in an English-speaking environment, in the Netherlands, in Europe, at an American studies conference. How do we figure out how we do things "here?" The characters (and the readers) who find themselves "here" in Yokohama, California have to negotiate similarly complex geographies. *Yokohama, California* is not only the name of a book and the name of a place; it is also, in fact, the names of two places, "Yokohama" and "California," two names and two places separated and linked by a comma. Let's say they are two American places: Lil' Yokohama, the neighbourhood, and California, the state. As there is no part of Yokohama that is not also California, and as all the stories take place in Yokohama, this means that all the stories happen in two places at the same time—or three, in fact, if we add the implied "America."

But yet another way to read the title and understand the "here" of the text appears when we imagine Yokohama and California as two places which exist in *different* locations, distinguished in this case not by scale but by distance. That version of the title of the book (and the name of Mori's fictional community) juxtaposes the Yokohama of a remembered

---

[2]   The collection had been accepted by Caxton Publishers and scheduled for printing when publication was stopped by the events of December 1941. After a gap of nearly eight years—which Mori spent mostly in an internment camp in Utah—the collection was revised by the addition of two strongly pro-American stories set in the post-war era and finally published.

[3]   As Lawson Fusao Inada notes, Mori consciously modelled his collection on Sherwood Anderson's *Winesburg, Ohio*.

Japan and the California of a present America. When the comma separating and linking the two places represents an ocean, then we can see how the title, like the stories, generates a folded space of physical distance and relational proximity, and the geographical "here" of the text starts to look very complicated indeed.[4]

So, Mori's stories are about one specific place: Yokohama, California. They are about two American places of different relative sizes spatially co-present in one American location: Yokohama, and California. And they are about two places which despite being physically distant are nonetheless relationally co-present in a spatial network of journeys and communications and memories: Yokohama over there and Yokohama over here, Japan and America.

Mori's title in this way not only presents the reader with a place (or places); it also raises the question of how place in general (and American place in particular) is defined. The stories of *Yokohama, California* are quite commonly read as descriptions of a unique, bordered community: an insular Japanese inside sharply defined by its difference from the surrounding American outside. But as the very title *Yokohama, California* suggests, and as Doreen Massey has clearly shown, it is not a comprehensive definition of 'place' to see it as a bordered space with a fixed and static location and a unitary identity, a simple inside with an outside, a centre with a margin (155). As Massey and others have argued, there is nothing in the nature of place itself which means it has to be understood this way, as a self-evident and self-contained combination of community and location. Places can equally usefully be understood as "localized knots in wider webs of social practice" (Gregory 321), and their specificity grasped as the result of the "juxtaposition and co-presence of ... sets of social interrelations and by the effects which that juxtaposition and co-presence produce" (Massey 169). Places, in this geography, are not static, not possessed of any single, unique identity, not the products of an internalized history, and not defined by internal coherence. Instead, their "inside," their uniqueness, is always the product of a combination of particular unfixed and dynamic connections to, and exchanges with, a variety of "outsides."

---

[4]   I take the concept of physical distance and relational proximity from the work of John Allen, Doreen Massey and Michael Pryke in *Unsettling Cities: Movement / Settlement*.

Places cannot easily be purified of these links and exchanges and complex interactions, despite the fact that it's relatively common to identify a place in a particular way and then ignore the aspects which do not appear to fit. I once read a book review, for example, which character-ized a novel set in Japan as being "more a story of the English in Tokyo than of Tokyo itself." This separation of the city "itself" from one type of resident seemed to me puzzling. Was it based on the assumption that "the English in Tokyo" were somehow not really a part of Tokyo "itself," not really there?[5]

Toshio Mori is best known today as a Japanese American writer, a pioneer in the writing of Japanese America. His books, we might say, are commonly read as records of the Japanese in America, not expressions of "America itself." At the time of the book's rediscovery, the first generation of self-consciously Asian American writers and critics read the book in this way, as a specifically Japanese American text, for good reason. They were looking for a forgotten tradition, and engaged in a collective and specifically Asian American "act of recovery" (Wong 12). Mori's stories were so important to them because they "remain the only collection of Japanese American stories to faithfully describe the pre-World War II Japanese American community nestled in the East Bay Cities of Oakland and San Leandro" (Wong 11-12). For Lawson Fusao Inada, writing an introduction to the reprint edition of the newly rediscovered Yokohama, California in 1985, it was simply "the book,"—"the first real Japanese-American book" by "the first real Japanese-American writer." It was the "legacy, tradition ... the embodiment of a people." "This *is* Japanese America," he wrote (v). Shawn Wong positioned the book similarly as a specifically Japanese American text about a Japanese American community, ascribing its relative lack of early success to the fact that in the post-war years when it was originally published "it was still the wrong time for a Japanese American to be the first of anything, including the first author to show how remarkable and unique Japanese American communities were in the East Bay of the San Francisco Bay area" (75).

---

[5]   An Amazon.com customer review of Gavin Kramer's 1998 novel *Shopping* calls it "an English novel set in Japan," adding that although "there are great scenes of the well known parts of Tokyo" it is still "more a story of the English in Tokyo than of Tokyo itself." Review accessed June 22, 2003 at <http://www.amazon.com/exec/obidos/tg/detail/-/1569472297/qid=1056367716/sr=12-1/103-8874468-7830230?v=glance&s=books>

I read these stories at a different time, in a different place, from a different perspective. And my impression of the stories is rather different; to me, their point is not only that they show "how remarkable and unique" those Japanese American communities were at all, but also that they show how normal and ordinary they were. In this alternative reading, the stories are not only emphasizing the uniqueness, the Japanese-ness of this way of life, but also presenting it to the reader as an everyday American normality, a normative part of America itself.

Reading the stories in this way, the "here" of Yokohama, California functions on many layers at the same time. Reading the book, we are here in Lil' Yokohama, here in California, here in a web of networks linking Japan and the USA, here in America. And who are "we?" Critics writing about Mori's work in the context of Asian American literature have sometimes implied that his natural readership is Japanese American. But I think it's useful here to make a distinction between Mori's apparently intended reader and his implied reader, because it seems clear that although the stories read as if their "here" is grounded firmly in the community of Lil' Yokohama, Mori's primary target audience was the broad American "white reading public" (Yamamoto 8; Kim 163).

It is true that, as Stan Yogi has remarked, not only are all the characters in the stories Japanese American, but "the narrative voice speaks with confidence to a familiar community" (131). And this means that, as Inada puts it, "the reader is allowed to experience the people and situations directly, immediately. In effect [Mori] allows each reader to *be* a Japanese American and to experience that life, from the inside out." (xvii-xviii). But none of this means that Mori wrote the stories for Japanese Americans, or intended the textual "here" of the fictional Lil' Yokohama to be inaccessible to readers who in real life inhabited different kinds of neighbourhoods. For me, Mori's stories put Yokohama firmly 'here' in America. "The people of Lil' Yokohama are here," Mori writes. "*Here, here,* they cry with their presence just as the youngsters when the teacher calls the roll" (71).

In fact, the way in which Mori puts the intended (distant) reader in the position of the implied (local) reader actually allows them to experience Yokohama, California as a part of the "we," on the inside, as normal–even, indeed, as typical. Mori seems to make no concessions in creating this inclusive voice, writing as if everybody understands everything: the author, the narrator, the characters, and the reader are in positions of equal linguistic power and equal local knowledge. And he reinforces this sense of the local by the constant use of inclusive plural first-person pronouns–"we," "our", "us"–so that any reader is as a result included, is temporarily hailed as Japanese American. As Inada emphasizes, in Lil' Yokohama, "the people do not define themselves as non-white," and the fact that Ayako Saito, the "All-American Girl" of the story of the same name, is incidentally Japanese is not surprising at all but just "fitting and natural" (xvii). In "The Woman Who Makes Swell Donuts," the donut-making woman is known as "Mama." Mori writes: "I suppose there is in every block of every city in America a woman who can be called Mama by her friends and the strangers meeting her." Strangers and friends, we (readers) are both. In the same way that we read Mori's stories, he eats Mama's donuts: we "drop in and taste the flavour; her flavour, which is everyone's and all flavour" (25). My point is that the normative "here" of Mori's text is inclusive, not exclusive; the stories are set in a complex "here" that is at the same time and in the same place specific and generic, Yokohama, California, America, Japanese America, an old women's Yokohama, a young man's Yokohama, Yokohama's baseball ground, baseball grounds in general.

What Mori has created, I think, is a collection of stories that present the Californian Yokohama as a place with a unique flavour, a specifically local flavour, but nonetheless a flavour that has been produced out of national and transnational connections. And I think it's important to notice that although the flavour really is unique, the way in which the flavour is produced is not unique at all. The existence of a unique local flavour produced within the frame of national and transnational networks can be read, in fact, as typical not of *Japanese* American fiction, but of American fiction in general. When the narrator drops by to visit the woman he calls 'Mama,' to sit with her and taste the flavour of her donuts, he understands that even while she is, uniquely, the Mama of Yokohama, California, there is still "in every block of every city in America a woman who can be called Mama by her friends and the strangers meeting her" (23). She is both unique and typical, and, visiting her for both these reasons, he likes to "drop in and taste the flavour; her flavour, which is everyone's and all flavour" (25). Yokohama's Ayako Saito is both a particular girl and an "All-American Girl," (91) just as "morning, noon, and night roll on regularly" in Yokohama both uniquely and just as they do "in Boston, Cincinnati, Birmingham, Kansas City, Minneapolis, and Emeryville" (71). Yokohama, too, has a flavour which is both *its* flavour and everyone's flavour. So Toshio Mori's Yokohama, California is in this sense not only a unique American community but also a typical American community—typical, in fact, in its uniqueness, typical precisely in the way in which it comes uniquely into being at the meeting place of a complex interwoven set of spatial and social networks. Similarly, Mori's *Yokohama, California* is both a unique text and yet a representative text, coming into being as a textual 'here' at a particular crosspoint in a complex interwoven set of networks of social and textual reference.

The geographer Marc Brosseau has called for a geographical approach to text that asks how it "generates norms, particular models of readability, that produce a particular type of geography" (349). In Brosseau's terms, I think, Toshio Mori's texts generate a normative geography in which relational proximity is as socially and spatially significant as physical distance. This is a geography so familiar when it links, for example, Boston with Rome, or New York and Chicago with Oxford and Montenegro, that it has often gone unmarked. Transatlantic Euro-American links have routinely been taken as so foundationally American as to not really seem transnational at all. But in our newly transnational American studies more and more networks are coming into view: *nuestro America*, for example; the Black Atlantic. Read as a part of transnational America, and understood in terms of the geographical articulation of place offered by geographers like Doreen Massey, in other words, *Yokohama, California* becomes a typical as well as a unique American text. To be "here" in Yokohama, California, it turns out, is to be no further distant from the authentic centre of American literature than to be "here" on Walden pond, "here" on *Mango Street,* or "here" in *The House of the Seven Gables.*

The Social Construction of Geographical Scale in "American History"

This section explores a method of reading literature that draws on theoretical work in cultural geography to show that the concept of geographical scale is useful in reading a short story, "American History" by Judith Ortiz Cofer. First, the term scale needs some explanation. In geography, scale refers to the level of analysis; for example, geographers might conduct their research at the regional scale, or the national scale.

We probably all use the concept of scale without naming it, as in the global and the local. But as critical geographers are careful to remind us, there is nothing natural about the scales we are accustomed to in contemporary life. Indeed, although in recent history the nation-state has been a "powerful scale of social organization," it wasn't before the seventeenth century in Europe; then the city-state and regional scales were more relevant to political and economic systems (Smith 725). So one of the most important things to remember about scale is that there is nothing natural or inescapable about the division of scales into global and local, national and regional; rather scale, like place, is socially constructed through human interactions, movements, and relationships (Marston 220). And as with many products of social interaction, "scale-making is not only a rhetorical practice; its consequences are inscribed in, and are the outcome of, both everyday life and macro-level social structures" (Marston 221).

Recent discussions in geography have called attention to the way in which analyses that confine themselves to one scale can ignore the frequent interpenetration of scales, and to how often the bigger scales are more privileged (i.e., global as more important than local). Critical geographers today, for example, recognize a "loose hierarchy of geographical scales, from that of the body, the home and the community, through the local, regional, national and global" (Smith 725). For feminist geographers, as Robyn Longhurst argues, this hierarchy has meant that women's experiences, traditionally lived at the scale of the home and community, have been deemed less important than events operating at the national and global scales, in which men are often the main actors. But as Massey's conception of 'place' points out, recognizing the uniqueness of a particular "local" place does not mean we must ignore social and political activity occurring at a national or global scale that has direct connections with that local place (Duncan 583). This key term, place, challenges any potential oversimplification in the hierarchy of scales. As Massey argues, place can be theorized as a web of interconnections that shifts over time and that complicates any effort to separate out social relations according to scales such as global and local. Her concept of place reveals the many links of identity and location, so that it is no longer possible to characterize places as homogeneous and fixed. Rather, "the geography of social relations forces us to recognize our interconnectedness, and underscores the fact that both personal identity and the identity of those envelopes of space-time in which and between which we live and move ... are constructed precisely through that interconnectedness" (Massey 122). Even in extremes such as segregation or apartheid, places are generated and defined not only by the majority or the powerful, but also by the very maze of power relations that operate there, including forms of resistance and conflict. Like Mary Louise Pratt's "contact zones," places encompass both battles and alliances. Places are constituted by encounters at every imaginable scale, forming a kind of hub that stretches out beyond the local, folding various geographical locations into one place.

Thus, place is not confined by physical or cartographic boundaries; it also includes connections with "outside" places, at multiple scales, as for example in urban areas with immigrant populations (the setting of Cofer's story discussed below). Certainly the urban scale is important, yet the national and global scales are also factors in defining places such as, to take this story as an example, Puerto Rican neighbourhoods in New Jersey cities. Geographer Neil Smith has written about what he calls "simultaneity of scales" in which the "interflow between bodily, global and intervening scales is neither smooth nor regular, and specific events may embody destructions and reconstructions of various scales at the same time" (726). In a similar vein, scholars in American studies and women's studies have argued that the separation of public and private spheres, while initially a useful hermeneutic tool, can lead to the mistaken notion that the spheres ever really were separate (Kaplan 1998). I'm trying to argue here that like those inseparable separate spheres, scales are also a useful hermeneutic as long as we examine them in their place-based contexts in all their simultaneity.

The story "American History" by Judith Ortiz Cofer describes a New Jersey teenage girl's crush on her neighbour and classmate, culminating in a visit to his house to study for an American history test on a cold November day in 1963. But the boy's mother turns her away at the front door, trying to discourage a relationship that she disapproves of: her son Eugene is white and the narrator, Elena, is Puerto Rican. The story operates on several significant scales, each of which I'd like to examine in the process of explicating the spatial allegories and relations of power at work in the story. What follows is a brief gloss of the story, moving from the most intimate to the widest scale and then back again to argue that the story demonstrates that the scales cannot be success- fully separated. In this sense, the story illustrates Massey's notion of place, where there are multiple and contradictory relationships of power, scale, and identity.

The story's most intimate scale is the family and community of an individual young woman in Paterson, New Jersey. From her window in a high-rise tenement, she observes the occupants of the only house on her block that has a yard, first an elderly Jewish couple and then a white family from the South. Elena badly wants to enter that family home as a partner to her classmate, Eugene: "to sit at the kitchen table with Eugene like two adults, like the old man and his wife had done, maybe drink some coffee and talk about books" (Cofer 97). But her crush on Eugene is only the most recent reason she wants to go inside; before, when the older couple lived there, she had "become part of their family, without their knowing it, of course" and when they were gone, she "had to resist the temptation to climb down into the yard and water the flowers the old lady had taken such good care of" (94-5). In her relationship with her next-door neighbours, Elena experiences feelings of exclusion and longing that she directs toward both the space—the house itself—and its occupants, the older couple and then Eugene.

Zooming out slightly to the urban scale, the story narrates the transformations occurring in many US cities in the 1960s, for example, shifting urban populations and suburbanization. The history of American immigration is legible in Elena's neighbourhood geography: she describes how incongruous the little house and yard appear next to her home, the tenement they call El Building. As she ponders how "Paterson, the inner core of the city, had no apparent logic to its architecture," she realizes that "the little houses had been there first, then the immigrants had come in droves, and the monstrosities had been raised for them—the Italians, the Irish, the Jews, and now us, the Puerto Ricans, and the blacks" (101). The haphazard urban landscape of tenements and single-family homes is also heavily inflected by class and race: Eugene's family, recently arrived from the South, insist that they "won't be in this place much longer" (101) and El Building is inhabited by working-class Puerto Rican families, including Elena's, who dream of the suburbs "where people mowed grass on Sundays in the summer and where children made snowmen in the winter from pure white snow, not like the gray slush of Paterson" (97). Despite similar strivings for middle-class suburban life, the neighbours are divided by racial and ethnic differences.

At the national scale, Elena's position as outsider looking in on the

family house can be read as a spatial allegory of segregation, a microcosm
where the tenement and the little house represent both the geographical
proximity and the social divisions between white Americans and people
of collor in the US. But it also, at the same time, echoes the international
scale of migration and immigration, resembling successive generations of
immigrants who preceded the Puerto Ricans in the urban enclave where
Elena lives. The ugly El Building comes to stand for the "other" presence
in Paterson, a place everyone dislikes and longs to leave behind. In this
way the story illustrates the way in which there is no easy way to
separate out one scale from another without losing something in the
process.

Elena's perspective, literally suspended, unnoticed, on the fire
escape or gazing out the window into the house's backyard and kitchen
window, also reproduces on a smaller scale the geopolitical relations
between the US and Puerto Rico. She has a kind of double consciousness,
a privileged view into the lives of the "Americans" in the house, yet they
seem not to notice her. Although Eugene's house is next door to El
Building, an invisible boundary separates them; although the teenagers
may not notice it or choose to ignore it, both mothers know it exists.
Elena's mother sees her watching Eugene's house from the window and
warns her not to forget the way ethnicity limits social relationships: "You
are forgetting who you are, Niña. ... You are heading for humiliation and
pain" (100). When Elena arrives to study American history with Eugene,
his mother asks if she lives in El Building and turns her away at the door,
explaining that they will be moving soon and her son won't need help
studying. "Run back home now," she says (101).

The friendship with Eugene complicates Elena's own sense of place
as she identifies both with her tenement and with the home she yearns
for: she sees the world not only from her own perspective, peering down
from the fire escape into the windows of the house, but she also realizes
the impact El Building has on the lives of the family who live in the
house: "It was not until Eugene moved into that house that I noticed that
El Building blocked most of the sun" (96). After befriending him, she is
able to perceive not only the enviable advantages of living in the house,
but also the drawbacks that result from its proximity to her own building.
Her identification with El Building conflicts with her sympathy and desire
for the house-dwellers: "El Building blocked the sun to such an extent
that they had to turn lights on in the middle of the day. I felt ashamed

about it." (100). In this city block, each building affects the neighbour-hood; Elena recognizes the way in which El Building's presence impacts Eugene's quality of life and vice versa.

One of the most striking ways in which the story exemplifies the simultaneity of scales, the interweaving of personal, neighbourhood events with events of national and global significance, is the fact that it takes place on November 23, 1963, the day President Kennedy was assassinated. This day is usually recounted in literature and memoirs as a traumatic national event that was experienced as a personal loss by millions of individual Americans. Narrated through Elena's eyes, the assassination is a vague, disturbing event that causes shocking emotional behaviour in all the adults she encounters. She recognizes the pain in her community, where her parents "talk sadly about the young widow and her two children, as if they were family" (102). But for her, the trauma of that day is more immediately personal: she is refused entry into a house she has wanted for years to see, and refused friendship with Eugene on the basis of her ethnicity. The irony isn't lost on her: she lies crying in bed, "trying to feel the right thing for our dead president. But the tears that came up from a deep source inside me were strictly for me" (102). Although she recognizes that today the national scale "should" take precedence over the personal, Elena cannot adjust her sense of loss and realizes that for her, on this day, Kennedy's death was overshadowed by her own traumatic experiences.

To conclude, this story illustrates the way in which the interconnec-tion of scales defines place in Doreen Massey's conception of the term. Even a quick gloss of the story such as this shows the usefulness of geographical theory to Americanists interested in power, identity, and space. The "American History" of the story's title is ironic in its multiple and contradictory meanings: a high school class to study for, the assassination of a US president, the layers of urban history of Paterson, and the long history in the US of spatialized power relations.

Locating Terrorism: Safe and Unsafe Space in The Siege

This section analyses the cinematic representation of space in Edward Zwick's *The Siege* (1998), a film that deals with terrorism in New York City. The story involves Arab Muslims who blow up buses and buildings in the city thereby generating fear among the citizens. The FBI team headed by Anthony Hubbard, played by Denzel Washington, takes up the role of tracking down the terrorists and restoring peace and security to the city. The movie's plot is about an enemy who is an insider and lives in the midst of New York, so first I consider why it has the title of *The Siege*, a concept that implies a bounded area, such as a fortress, which identifies the outsiders and enemies as those people living outside its boundaries. The siege recalls medieval imagery of wars and invasions and evokes a nostalgic yearning for "the old days" when it was possible to set up spatial barriers to prevent somebody from entering one's space. At another level, in Hollywood cinema the imagery of the siege has become a stable topos in American Westerns, where the scene of the besieged wagon train or fort has provided the justification for the annihilation of Native Americans in the course of fulfilling teleological notions of national progress and manifest destiny.[6] Now looking at the title of Zwick's film, the question that comes to mind is "who is besieging whom?" And since the film narrative shows that it is the Arab Muslims who are laying siege to the public space of New York, then what facets of manifest-destiny agenda are involved here? And since *The Siege* seeks to justify the expulsion of Arab Muslims from the US, how can that be possible in a time of globalization and a new and violent phase of "time-space compression?" (Massey 157).

Yet, as Massey rightly points out time-space compression is not a recent phenomenon, one of the outcomes of our era of globalization. Indeed, colonialism, as Massey and a lot of other postcolonial critics argue, was a form of time-space compression in which the colonized people's lives were disrupted by a colonizer who brought not only his civilization but also his short-term project of turning the colony to a supplier of natural resources and/or markets to his products. Yet, as she writes, "[t]hose who today worry about a sense of disorientation and a loss of control must once have felt they knew exactly where they were, and that they *had* control. For who is it in these times who feels dislocated/placeless/invaded? To what extent ... is this a predominantly white/First World take on things?" (165). Given the visibility of the

---

[6] See Shohat and Stam's analysis of the action of the siege as a crucial cinematic trope in the Hollywood western, 114-21.

conflict over geography, space, and identity within the film's narrative, it is productive to work with Massey's idea in relation to the eurocentrism involved in the belief that time-space compression constitutes a threat. At first glance, New York City in *The Siege* appears to be a place with a multicultural identity; yet, as I will prove, the film insidiously locates the presence of the Arab Muslim community as a source of deadly threat. And as Doreen Massey argues: "When time-space compression is seen as disorienting, and as threatening to fracture personal identities (as well as those of place) then a recourse to place as a source of authenticity and stability may be one of the responses" (122). Certainly the film's movement from the desert somewhere in the Middle East to a mosque in a Brooklyn street then to the FBI headquarters in New York folds together different spaces that produce a frightening sense of fragmentation. Later in the film, Brooklyn's multicultural communities will be in danger because they include this other place/culture/identity which is marked as exclusively Middle Eastern and Islamic. The film's narrative then enlists these several "minor" and "major" communities, represented by no less than the multicultural FBI team, in the crusade to purge their city of the enemy whose identity is conveniently established in an Arab street in Brooklyn. So in a sense *The Siege*'s liberal gesture in foregrounding the multi ethnicity of contemporary New York becomes all the more mischievous, because the Arab American community, which should have been considered as one, certainly heterogeneous, element of the several minority cultures in New York, is cast out as evil. Arabs, precisely male Middle-Easterners, are the only deadly threat which will destroy the happily-living-together communities. In this regard, terrorism, which understandably raises fear and anxiety in the people afflicted by it, provides the justification for lumping all Arab Muslims together into stereotypes as intruders in and destroyers of an idealized space of New York City.

In *The Siege*, the pre-credit sequence resorts to stock footage showing the explosion of the US military barracks in Dhahran, Saudi Arabia, onto which it juxtaposes the voices of well-known American news announcers whose comments serve to introduce the alleged terrorist Sheikh Ahmed Bin Talal, a clearly fictionalized version of Bin Laden. Right after this, we are given a scene that shows the Sheik roaming freely in the desert; yet, his hiding in what he thought as his impenetrable space, as highlighted by his satisfactory grin, will be only short-lived.

Indeed, the shots of President Clinton's condemnation of the terrorist act and his promise of punishment are instantly gratified via a cut-away scene to CIA agents and/or Israelis whom we will see laying a trap for the Sheik and then successfully capturing their "package."

This sequence, actually, represents time-space compression *par excellence,* for the US military presence in Dhahran, as such, is there not only to secure the flow of the oil with all the neocolonial implications of that mission but also to maintain control over global energy supplies. Here the US, via its oil multinationals and military bases in Dhahran, represents what Massey terms "the power geometry of time-space compression.... [which is] about power in relation *to* the flows and the movement . ... [which involves] the groups who are really in charge of time-space compression, who can really use it and turn it to advantage, whose power and influence it very definitely increases" (149). Significantly, too, this opening sequence portrays the presence of the US mainstream media in close connection with US global control over oil, reflecting the US media's power as a tool that reinforces and is reinforced by US economic and military dominance over time-space compression.

Yet, the pre-credit sequence in the film narrative does not explain and contextualize how the differential mobility and control of time-space compression by the US oil multinationals supported by the US government as well as the Saudi oligarchy severely undermine the powers of the others. Instead, the sequence creates a dichotomous relation in space that honours the long perpetuated binary images of "their" barbarism and "our" burden to defend the world. This simplistic construct echoes the concept of the title with its insiders/outsiders as mutually exclusive. This is why in the texture of the film, the bearded and robed Sheikh Ahmed bin Talal makes an appearance only after the blast, is approached by a camera that catches his profile *a la* police photography, and is ushered into a US prison without ever being given the chance to reveal his perspective on the attacks on the US military in Dhahran.

Accordingly, the pre-credit sequence, instead of showing Dhahran as a product of the complex interrelationships between the US and the Saudi royal family, and among military, oil, and media interests, simply establishes the enemy as an evil Arab Muslim man. In my view, this sequence exercises what Stuart Hall terms "symbolic violence" in the way it relentlessly perpetuates a eurocentric view that recognizes threat only if "our" mobility is at stake and "our" control of time-space compression is under attack (259). The devastating effects of "our" political and economic power on weak nations or oppressed people is elided in exchange for a simpler good/evil binary represented by the long-established Orientalist construct of a degenerate and fanatic Muslim mentality. In this scheme only the threat lurking for the US oil giant industries and USAF is recognized; there is no space for recognizing how these giants' mobility and power undermines the freedom and well-being of other groups.

Since the pre-credit sequence pursues an essentialist encoding of the innocent, righteous "us" vs. the irrational, criminal "them," the siege as a medieval strategy to keep out and eliminate the undesirable community will prove to be feasible even in a global city like New York, one of the centres of the world economy. In fact, from the very beginning of the film, our recognition of New York will be welded with our apprehension of the lurking threat embodied in the presence of the Arab Muslims via the minaret shot, as will be explained below. The argument is that the film succeeds in achieving this effect by manipulating its use of the cinematic technique of safe/unsafe space. Richard Maltby explains that classical Hollywood cinema, which sought to engage the viewers' emotions, paid special attention to the camera's movements in order to create a sense of safe space. Hence, movies tend to begin with an establishing long shot and move smoothly to a medium shot after which it might move to a close up creating thereby what Maltby designates as a safe space inside which "we [the audience] can direct our attention to engaging emotionally with the characters, confident that the movie's image stream will avoid any sudden shocks that may abruptly disrupt our involvement in the action" (204-06).

Dealing with "their" terrorism (equated with Islam and Arabs) and "our" forced response to punish, as foreshadowed by the pre-credit sequence, *The Siege* consciously produces two different kinds of cinematic space: safe and unsafe. On the one hand, the unsafe space created by abrupt cuts and swift changes in camera movement and placement flings at us images of a Muezzin in a minaret, and people praying in a mosque and another group praying at home. More importantly when the camera starts tracking out of the mosque and we start realizing that the mosque in question is in New York, twilight-like colours fall upon the screen and ominous non-diegetic music blends into the *Muezzin*'s call, all of which serve to trigger a feeling of uneasiness, a foreboding of coming threat.

Certainly the *mise-en-scène* at that level seeks to convey incongruity in the juxtaposition of the mosque and the New York skylines. Right after that the camera reverts to the safe space technique and comfortable measured editing for the introduction of the FBI agent Anthony Hubbard and his multicultural team.

Unsurprisingly the first battle that will take place between the "evil" Arab Muslims and the "good" FBI will take us back to the same street where we spotted the mosque before. This Arab street, which is in Brooklyn, also provides the background for a chase scene between an Arab suspect and the FBI. That Brooklyn or an Arab street should harbor an Arab terrorist is not the issue being contested here, but the fact that *The Siege* insists on building up a space of terrorism that is exclusively Arab and Muslim. Indeed, the following violent scenes that show us the terrorists in action juxtapose the Arab Muslims as faceless hijackers of the city's public spaces with fear-stricken people who are fleeing for their lives. Significantly we are directed to identify some of these attacked people as particular minorities, such as Jewish Orthodox men. By cynically pitting New York's diverse communities against the Arabs, *The Siege* does not allow these latter to be seen as simply inhabiting the domestic space of their unthreatening daily lives, or for that matter as also being threatened by the terrorists' actions.

Indeed, the film makes the city derive its specificity in its obsession to ostracize the aberrant street in Brooklyn. Yet, as Massey argues "what gives a place its specificity is not some long internalized history but the fact that it is constructed out of a particular constellation of social relations, meeting and weaving together at a particular locus... the specificity of place... derives from the fact that each place is the focus of a distinct *mixture* of wider and more local social relations...." (154-56). Yet, via its manipulation of the safe/unsafe space technique, the film succeeds in collapsing the Arab Muslims into a dangerous community which is bent on destroying New York and by extension American civilization. The film achieves this effect because it is clearly seeking the elimination of the Arabs from the space of New York. And only by portraying "them" as members of a foreign culture that brings terrorism to the US home can the film justify that "they" pose an apocalyptic threat and thereby deserve death. Indeed, the Arab characters reinforce the film's spatial representation, for they are enlisted to plead guilty and support the decontextuali-

zation and political disinformation the film pursues.[7]
If we turn again to the title and look at it in relation to the film's plot, it seems that *The Siege* is actually about the fantasy of creating a purified space where the siege, or secure divisions of space along patterns of medieval times, would be possible. At the same time, *The Siege*'s narrative is encoded around the siege as a cinematic trope that perpetuates the myth of the innocent American under attack.

Sheila Hones
Julia Leyda
Khadija Fritsch - El Alaoui

---

[7]   For example, the character of the Palestinian professor of Arabic studies in New York who recounts that his brother and other young men strap themselves with bombs and explode themselves in Israel in order to obtain the seventy virgins promised to them by the Sheiks. He doesn't mention any political commitment on the part of the Palestinians, only their primitive patriarchal religious fanaticism.

Works Cited

Allen, John, Doreen Massey, and Michael Pryke, eds. 1999. *Unsettling Cities: Movement/Settlement.* London: Routledge/The Open University.

Brosseau, Marc. 1994. "Geography's Literature." *Progress in Human Geography* 18 (1994): 333-353.

Cofer, Judith Ortiz. 1993. "American History." *Growing Up Ethnic in America: Contemporary Fiction About Learning to Be American.* Ed. Maria Mazziotti Gillan and Jennifer Gillan. New York: Penguin, pp. 93-102.

Curry, Michael. 1999. "'Hereness' and the Normativity of Place." *Geography and Ethics: Journeys in a Moral Terrain.* Eds. James D. Proctor and David M. Smith. London: Routledge, pp. 95-105.

Duncan, James. 2000. "Place" in Johnston, et al. pp. 582-84.

Gregory, Derek. 2000. "Edward Said's Imaginative Geographies." *Thinking Space.* Eds. Mike Crang and Nigel Thrift. London: Routledge, pp. 302-48.

Hall, Stuart, ed. 1997. *Representation: Cultural Representations and Signifying Practices.* London: Sage.

Inada, Lawson Fusao. 1985. Introduction. *Yokohama, California.* By Toshio Mori. Seattle: University of Washington P, v-xxvii.

Johnston, R. J., Derek Gregory, Geraldine Pratt, and Michael Watts, eds. 2000. *Dictionary of Human Geography.* 4th ed. London: Blackwell.

Kaplan, Amy. 1998. "Manifest Domesticity." *American Literature* 70.3 (1998): 581-606.

Kim, Elaine H. 1982. *Asian American Literature: An Introduction to the Writings and their Social Context.* Philadelphia: Temple University Press.

Longhurst, Robyn. 1995. "The Body and Geography." *Gender, Place and Culture* 2.1 (1995): 97-103.

Maltby, Richard. 1995. *Hollywood Cinema: An Introduction.* Malden, MA: Blackwell.

Marston, Sallie. 2000. "The Social Construction of Scale." *Progress in Human Geography* 24.2 (2000): 219-242.

Massey, Doreen. 1994. *Space, Place, and Gender.* Cambridge: Polity.

Mori, Toshio. 1985. *Yokohama, California.* 1949. Seattle: University of Washington Press.

Pratt, Mary Louise. 1991. "The Arts of the Contact Zone." *Profession* 91 (1991): 33-40.

Shohat, Ella and Robert Stam. 1994. *Unthinking Eurocentrism: Multiculturalism and the Media.* London: Routledge.

Smith, Neil. 2000. "Scale" in Johnston, et al. pp. 724-27.

Wong, Shawn. 1996. *Asian American Literature: A Brief Introduction and Anthology.* New York: HarperCollins College.

Yamamoto, Hisaye. 1979. Introduction. *The Chauvinist and Other Stories.* By Toshio Mori. Los Angeles: UCLA Asian American Studies Center, pp. 1-14.

Yogi, Stan. 1997. "Japanese American Literature." *An Interethnic Companion to Asian American Literature.* Ed. King-Kok Cheung. Cambridge: Cambridge University Press.

Innocents Abroad?
The U.S. and the World in *National Geographic*

The bright, yellow frame, the breathtaking photographs, and the detailed maps are factors which make *National Geographic* easily recognizable and conspicuous. It is a magazine with pages enough to accommodate a spine, whose title is clearly seen, if you put it like a book in a shelf. Each issue comprises 140 to 150 pages, and thus spans the length of a short book. One issue contains a collection of texts: a feature article and six or seven shorter texts. Every article is made up of a combination of text, photos, maps, drawings, captions, and legends, and in this way it sticks to a well-defined code of presentation. Format and presentation appeal to reader recognition. The reader is invited to look at the world with the eyes of the photographers and the reporters. Once readers return to *National Geographic*, they will recognize features and formulas which add a sense of safety and snugness to the recognition, and in this way they will feel familiar with the world, or rather, the way the world is depicted in *National Geographic*.

In the magazine there is an ethos of open-eyed wonder at the marvels of the world which could very well be described as innocence: an innocent human being, the reporter, meets and discovers the world and finds that it is a good and wonderful world. This is the moral story presented to the reader. Notwithstanding its title, *National Geographic* describes the world—originally for a national audience, which is the reason for its title. Nowadays, however, the magazine is spread worldwide. It also has its own TV channel, whose programs, according to the website, "are available in 135 countries. With broadcasts in 23 languages, the Channel reaches more than one hundred and ten million households." Such spread blurs the interpretation of the word "national," and it can be argued that what *National Geographic* provides is an interpretation of the world, which is nationally filtered. That interpretation is distributed, not only nationally, but also globally. It is this redistributed national/international world view which is my topic here. To refer to the title of my talk, the modes of presentation in *National Geographic* may look innocent, but to my mind they are part of a national strategy to conventionalize and frame the world. According to Anders Stephansson, Columbia University, there are two asymmetries governing the relation between the U.S. and the world: 1. The U.S. is the world, but the world is not the U.S.; 2. The U.S. means more to the world than the world means to the U.S. I think both these asymmetries are relevant to the relation between the U.S. and the world the way it is portrayed in *National Geographic.*

To illustrate how the relation is expressed in *National Geographic* I will use examples mainly from the issues of 2001 and 2002. First of all, I will describe how the world is covered and what parts of the world are covered, to find out to what extent *National Geographic* really is abroad. Then I will illustrate the attitude with which the reporters of the magazine describe the relation between the U.S. and the world.

Before I go into that exploration, there are, however, two comprehensive aspects I would like to present as points of departure: the legitimacy of *National Geographic Society*, and the code in which the magazine is composed and written.

The popular texts comprising the issues of *National Geographic* are framed by the legitimacy and the authority which the link between the magazine and the *National Geographic Society* provides. The society, we learn from one of the first pages of each issue, was founded in 1888 and works "for the increase and diffusion of geographic knowledge." It is a "non-profit scientific and educational organization," which has "supported more than 7,000 explorations and research projects." This information is connected to a list of present and former trustees, members of the research and exploration committee, the names of explorers-in-residence, and the listing of ten mission programs with their managers. Thus readers are reminded that the *National Geographic* magazine is part of an organization of considerable age and a long history of explorations and research.

These references position *National Geographic* in an academic, philanthropic, and positivist late nineteenth-century tradition. It is part of a society whose history originates in the same decades as other embodiments of late nineteenth-century U.S. ideals, for instance the Library of Congress building, opened 1897, where George W. Maynard's paintings can summarize ideals relevant to *National Geographic*. I quote the description of them in the information brochure: "The paintings here are the work of George W. Maynard, and the subjects, beginning on the east side, to your left as you enter the pavilion, and proceeding around to your right are: *Adventure, Discovery, Conquest,* and *Civilization.* The spirit of *Adventure* leads to *Discovery,* which in turn leads to *Conquest* and then *Civilization.* At the centre of the dome, Mr. Maynard has selected the four qualities he finds are the most appropriate to these four stages of a nation's development: *Courage, Valour, Fortitude* and *Achievement.*" This legacy, conflating transcendent nationalism and Americanization, are present also in the *National Geographic Society* and its magazine.

The information about the society provided in the magazine makes clear that the organization and management are national. No name provided in the many lists comes from another country than the United States. What is true of the organization is also true of the magazine. The exploration and research in various parts of the world are undertaken by Americans or by the society's support of research groups in which other nationalities may be members but which are headed by Americans and linked to universities in the U. S. Such information is so clearly underlined and so often repeated that the reader, without any further references, may get the impression that, in fact, there is no geographical research, which does not originate in the U. S. The link between the society and the magazine provides a qualitative, national assurance.

Such assurance the Society underlines by more commercial interests than the magazine. To return to the information about the society, it also contains a title called "National Geographic Ventures," and the information also lists the presidents for "Television," "National Geographic Channel," "nationalgeographics.com," "Maps," and other "Enterprises." In the magazine, references to more relevant material on the website abound. The reader thus becomes part of two nets, wider than the magazine itself: one related to ongoing research and explorations which the society supports, and another which is related to a commercial network to be encountered through TV and the Internet.

The intersection of legitimacy and commercialism makes up the frame in which *National Geographic* is set. This frame delimits the code for the publication of the magazine or the contract which the editors draw with the readers. There are more obvious signs of that contract: a repeated outer appearance, a selection of letters from readers about previous articles, a set layout, and set parts like short, introductory sections called "Geographica" or "Behind the Scenes" which take the readers behind the curtain of the completed texts and present anecdotes and fragmented information about the composition process of individual texts.

There are two reappearing sections at the end of each number: one is called "Flash back," and it publishes a black-and-white photo with the assertion that "[t]his photograph was never before published in the magazine." It is from way back, taken for a specific purpose in relation to some previous expedition or exploration and with some reference, spatial or topical, to one of the texts in the issue where it is published. The publication of hitherto unpublished material reinforces the historical tradition of the society and the magazine, and it also presents the richness of the archives.

The other end section is called "ZipUSA," and it takes the reader to an inconspicuous spot of the U. S., hardly besieged by tourists or generally known for a specific reason. This short section functions as a snapshot of U. S. diversity, be it geographical, social, or cultural, at the same time that the section confirms national virtues, because of its position at the end of the magazine: Wherever you are in the world—and the magazine takes you in large loops—you will always return to the United States at the end of the journey.

The code of the magazine relies heavily on the long-standing reader: with special offers and gifts to subscribers, with map supplements of geographically or historically interesting territories, with files in which to collect your years of the magazine, etc. The letters to the editor also comprise a running commentary on previous articles to remind readers of the sequencing of the texts. Furthermore, some texts are published in two or three parts. In this way, the editor and the reader share the world of *National Geographic*. The reader knows what to anticipate, and the individual reporters are the interpreters and definers of the world within the frame and code of the magazine.

It is the subscriber or the returning reader that *National Geographic* aims at in a strategy to create a sense of belonging. The world is there for the reader's enjoyment and the reader's recognition. It is easily identifiable and easily recognizable according to the rules and conventions set up: it is portrayed in exquisite photographs of landscape and animals, people and flowers, it is clad in the golden light which is the trade mark of *National Geographic* photography; it is drawn in clear and detailed maps for the eye to follow; it is described in a combination of texts— captions, short, informative notices, and articles. This is the world as home entertainment, a world which exists inside the covers of the magazine. Both texts and photos demonstrate the clear detail—something said in an interview or the reporter's observation of people, animals, and sceneries. In the code of *National Geographic* the clear detail becomes a metonymy of a transparent world, easy to understand and easy to handle.

There is a certain naivety or innocence behind the code, and from repetition the editors of *National Geographic* have made it the invented tradition with which the magazine observes and explores the world. For the well-accustomed reader, lulled by the magazine's soothing and entertaining description, the code may well become a story taken for granted: this is the world! Under the cover of the contract the ideological transmission of national virtues forms the unnoticed part of the invented tradition. Thus, *National Geographic* relies on an undefined nationalism, where the U. S. becomes the prism through which the world is observed. If the reader abides by that code, he or she fits into the picture of the "innocents abroad." The world becomes a free space, a background, which you visit, and through which you are guided by *National Geographic*.

My point is that under an ethos of looking at the world with wide-eyed wonder, there is a transmission of a world picture in which the U. S. constitutes the undisputed centre, and in this way *National Geographic* provides an heuristic example of the U. S. and the world, a two-party relationship which may even give the impression that the U. S. and the world are distinct parts.

The national presence I have described so far is related to the long history of the *National Geographic Society* and the long, invented tradition of the magazine. There are two more visible aspects of the national presence I would like to cover with recent examples: one quantitative and one qualitative. The first will consider which countries are represented in the magazine, and the place which the U. S. takes amongst them. The second will consider the attitudes with which writers look at the world.

In all, the monthly issues of 2001 and 2000 contain about 180 texts. Some texts deal with topics that are not immediately connected to a defined part of the world. They can be about physical or biological phenomena and more general topics. The remaining texts are all spatially located. Most texts are about a limited geographic location, but some are related to the world at large, like a text about the flower trade; or a part of the world, dealing with, for instance, a particular animal species, be it the grizzly bears, the leopards, the Asian lions, or the jaguars.

The distribution of texts between the different countries and parts of the world shows that about two texts out of the seven which most issues contain, are located in the U.S., that is slightly more than 25%. A few of the U.S. texts cover processes that are relevant for the entire country—urban sprawl, public lands, nuclear waste. Other texts are set in a distinct state. Those states cover the outer boundaries of the country rather than the middle parts: Hawaii, California, Washington, Alaska, Maine, Georgia, Florida. Reasons for this distribution could be many: to show geographic diversity, the largeness of the whole, particularly scenic beauty, etc. It is a curious fact, however, that there is a hole in the middle.

Most texts, however, are more definitely located in one place: Paradise in Arizona; Rico in Colorado; Jamestown in New Mexico; Murfreesboro in Arkansas; Delacroix in Louisiana; Steelville in Missouri; Pickstown in South Dakota; Cary in North Carolina; Adjuntas on Puerto Rico; Ocean Grove in New Jersey; Monhegan Island in Maine; Philadelphia in Pennsylvania; Harlem, New York; Falls Church in Virginia; Dayton in Tennessee. Again, the central parts of the country are less visible, and if they are, an angle out of the common is chosen as the point of observation. It is as if the magazine wanted to present the boundaries and the extension of the nation in a movement from the known to the unknown, from a tacit centre of knowledge and values, a shared ethos that in a way is confirmed by the exploration of the outskirts of the country.

The world outside the U. S. is better suited to the society's objectives of research and exploration. It is the unknown and distant which is explored. There are far more articles set in Asia and Africa than in Europe or parts of the Americas outside the U.S..[1] This makes a world picture where the U. S. dominates. On the other hand, the national and the global coverage are symmetrical in the sense that the U. S. is represented by areas away from the national centre, and the same is true for the rest of the world. Thus, Distant parts are observed from a national and global centre. Explorations and research projects supported by the society reach far, to the frontiers of the known. The concern with peripheral areas presupposes a centre and therefore indirectly confirms and corroborates the existence and location of that centre, be it seen in a national or in an international context.

To illustrate the attitudes with which the world is observed and described, I would like to consider the concept of "exploration." In *National Geographic*, exploration is subject-oriented, or territorial. Subjects explored are related to the future, "Beyond Gravity," or to age, "How Old Is It? Solving the Riddle of Ages"; they are physical and deal with light, "Power of Light" or with auroras, "Earth's Grand Light Show"; they are biological: "Spider Webs: Deadly Silks," "Evolution of Whales," "Asia's Last Lions," etc. The vast majority of the explorations are territorial, however. They are territorial in the good, old colonial sense: one American man, or a group of men, explores a hitherto unknown, forgotten, or rarely visited part of the world and reports home.

The years 2001 and 2002 cover several explorations to unknown lands: one takes place in central Africa. In an article called "Mega-transect," presented in three instalments, J. Michael Fay explores the interior of central Africa on foot. It is a third-person narrative told by the author David Quammen, a story of endurance and hardship, where the hero finally, after 15 months and 2,000 miles of walking, reaches the Atlantic Ocean: "At 12.39 p.m. on December 18, 2000, J. Michael Fay and his support team broke through the forest onto the beach at the Atlantic Ocean. 'Wow,' he said, 'Wow.' Then, matter-of-factly, 'This is just where I wanted to come out.' It was Day 456 of the 2,000-mile Megatransect, an exploration of historic proportions" (August 2001, 97). Before that time the author has met the protagonist regularly in his struggle, but at long intervals, and he has described the gradual, physical traces of the

---

[1]   There are three articles located in Canada and Alaska, two in Mexico, seven in Central America, and eight in South America. 18 articles are, directly or indirectly, related to Europe; 30 to Asia and 24 to Africa.

hardships that the explorer has endured. It is also a story of leadership and the protagonist's relations to the differing members of his native crew: "I need to ship these boys home ... They are haggard, totally worn out. No matter how good they were they are just going to go down one by one" (March 2001, 28). Thus the text maintains a paternal relationship between the protagonist and his native crew, and the expedition resembles the 19th-century tradition of white colonial encounters, or, why not, *Indiana Jones*?

The second territorial exploration traces the present-day vestiges of a historical journey. In a three-part series of articles, Mike Edwards retraces the journey of Marco Polo. With Polo's writings in his hand Edwards travels from Italy, through Iran and Afghanistan, to China, and back again along the coast of South East Asia and India. This is not a story of endurance; it is rather a story of identification and recognition. In the first person, Mike Edwards tells the story about what he sees of what Marco Polo saw: "Half of Saveh consists of concrete boxes and half of loaf-domed buildings made of soft brick, such as Marco must have seen. I went looking for someone familiar with local history and soon was drinking tea with Professor Ahmad Nemati, who believes Marco's account is correct" (May 2001, 13). In this way, the text describes the tension between continuity and change.

The story demonstrates recognition originating in the comparison of two periods of time, 1271-1295, the period of Marco Polo's account, and the four years during which the author gathered his material, 1997-2001: this makes an exploration of the present time from the perspective of the past. The attitude of the writer is not paternal; he rather impersonates an inventive Yankee ideal and is very wrapped up in himself as an American observer. Like an "innocent abroad," he recognizes a friendly world: "I was mindful of these words [that members of the caravan of the Polos were sold, and others killed] as I regarded my rifle-toting escort. Relations between my country and Iran had been sour for years. Would they really protect an American? A burly sergeant named Reza assured me: 'If the smugglers try to kidnap you, they'll have to kill us first.' I decided I believed him'" (May 2001, 19).

Another category of explorations pursues one single topic in many parts of the world. "Gypsies—The Outsiders" is an example of this category. The title refers to Peter Godwin's exploration of the fate of the gypsies. He traces them in poverty-stricken Eastern Europe, in mundane

European settings, and among migrants in North and South America. This is a text about stereotyping. In Slovakia, the author visits the Gypsy quarter of a village, and he finds, as he writes, "a scene of medieval squalor," where the man in charge has "a walrus mustache, and a blurred amateur tattoo of a cowgirl on his right bicep," and where his family watches "their favourite Mexican soap opera, dubbed into Slovak" (April 2001, 85). The selection of material illustrates unfavourable impressions of gypsies: "The week before they get their social security is always the worst; that's when they're short of money. They just want to drink and smoke and make babies" (85). We learn that they eat dogs, that they marry at twelve, and that the individual clans disdain each other deeply. Admittedly, the information transmitted comes from named or described persons in the text, but still it is the author who has selected the information, and it is not set in a context of discussion or comment.

The presentation of gypsies closer to home is different and compares two ways of life. As Joe Mark's son Kelly, who lives in Philadelphia, says to the author: "'We may look modern and adapted on the outside, but on the inside we're pure Rom. We're naturally secretive because we have such a long history of persecution'" (101). The change of attitude and mode of presentation can illustrate a relation between the U. S. and the world: the closer to home, the more nuanced the picture, and vice versa.

In conclusion I doubt if "innocents abroad" is an appropriate description of how the world is presented in *National Geographic*. This doubt is of course evident from the way the gypsies are presented in Peter Godwin's article, but there are subtler ways in which the relation between the U. S. and the world in *National Geographic* may look innocent, but in fact is not. The magazine presents a world picture with the U.S. solidly in the centre. This picture is reinforced by the legitimacy which the *National Geographic Society* offers and spreads by means of its magazine, its television channel and its websites. Furthermore, *National Geographic* establishes and maintains an invented tradition of describing the world as recognition and entertainment. Also in the concrete sense, the U. S. takes a conspicuous position in that world, to judge from the 2001 and 2002 texts. It occupies a position of power which is reinforced by the concern for the national and international periphery rather than the centre. Attitudes and stereotypes in individual texts add to that impression and thus maintain an official, nationalist mythology of the U.S. This is the same transcendent, national goodness as that which makes even the hardworking and critical civil servants in *West Wing* relish in a "God bless America" salute to each other as they empty their beer bottles on the porch steps after a long, exhausting day; the absolute, nationalist foundation of faith.

In reference to *National Geographic*, Benedict Anderson's "imagined communities" come to mind. With the example of *National Geographic*, the entire world becomes an "imagined community," described and drawn in fascinating detail. But whose world is it? That is the inevitable, ideological question. The answer to that question can be discussed in terms of global nationalism, but what then becomes of the word "international" or "transnational"? In this respect, the world in *National Geographic* is a world of statements rather than questions.

Anders Olsson

"Is it down on any map?" Space Symbols and American Ideology in Melville's *Typee*[1]

By the middle of the nineteenth century, the South Seas were still a blurred geography, a region where to veer off course could lead to the discovery of new archipelagoes.[2] As Melville wrote:

> From obvious prudential considerations the Pacific has been principally sailed over in known tracts, and this is the reason why new islands are still occasionally discovered, by exploring ships and adventurous whalers, notwithstanding the great number of vessels of all kinds of late navigating this vast ocean. Indeed, considerable portions still remain wholly unexplored; and there is doubt as to the actual existence of certain shoals, and reefs, and small clusters of islands vaguely laid down in the charts. (*Omoo*: 362)[3]

---

[1]   The paper is part of a larger work in progress, dealing with this theme in Melville's first three novels, *Typee, Omoo*, and *Mardi*.

[2]   See O. H. K. Spate, *Paradise Found and Lost* (Minneapolis: University of Minnesota Press, 1988).

[3]   Herman Melville, *Typee, Omoo, Mardi* (New York: Library of America, 1982).

But what interests us here is not the discovery of the South Seas, but the cultural distortion of that geography. The representation of the encounter between coloniser and colonised is an important trope in the American genesis. The mark of distinction between *self* and *otherness* has often been very blurred as far as American representation is concerned, since American identity needed both to confront itself with otherness and at the same time to read in that otherness the sign of its own traits. As Bruce Harvey notes:

> The nation ads a whole [...] defined itself through hierarchical, racial taxonomies of foreign regions (the Orient, Latin America, Polynesia, and Africa). Comparative geography helped to shape national self-consciousness, and its stereotypical vocabularies and ideologies. [...] In the writers I have selected, idiosyncrasies of identity often becomes projected onto a foreign topography and its inhabitants. One result, to put it bluntly, is that the dialectic of encounter will sometimes seem to lose one of its dialectical sides: when the Non-European world is textually re-created in terms of authorial anxieties.[4]

At a time (1830-40) when the United States perceived the closure of its own space as an approaching and inescapable transition towards a more rigid and institutionalized form of nation, the South Seas came to be the *elsewhere* that the West had been during the previous decades [5]. *Typee* describes and re-enacts the attempt to separate/distinguish the American self from the space/culture of the *other*, and, at the same time, to see in the space of the *other* traits comparable to America's own past, and the mystification that this implies—often with the result "that the dialectic of encounter will sometimes seem to lose one of its dialectical sides: when the Non-European world is textually re-created in terms of authorial anxieties."[6]

---

[4] Bruce A. Harvey, *American Geographics: US National Narratives and the Representation of the Non-European World, 1830-1865* (Stanford: Stanford University Press, 2001), 5-6.

[5] As Bruce Harvey notes, cultures are necessarily comparative entities; and this is particularly true in the case of a culture (the American one) that would become entirely 'solidified' only after the Civil War and with the closing of the frontier. See Harvey, *American Geographics*, 17

[6] Harvey, *American Geographics*, 5-6.

What I here propose is to conceive space as a magnifier, as a lens focussed on social and cultural structures, and to look at the island of Typee as the stage upon which different ideologies and perspectives are simultaneously re-enacted: the native one, the Westerner one, and in particular the American one, torn between the false reminiscence of an idyllic past and the perception of its impending fall into modernity. I will then focus on some spatial and cultural patterns that emerge in *Typee*: the relationship between the self and the landscape in Western and Native cultures, and the concepts of centrality and liminality.

Under Western Eyes

Despite the fact that from the very beginning of the novel the Island of Nukuhiva is not a virgin space any more but a Western outpost, already contaminated by the colonizers' presence, the narrator expects the island to be a "fairy world", wild and innocent.[7] What he wants is a *blank* space onto which to project national expectations.[8] The difference between ideal and real geography is emphasized by Tommo at the very beginning, while the ship is still approaching the bay:

> The reality is very different; bold rock-bound coasts, with the surf beating high against the lofty cliffs, and broken here and there into deep inlets, which open to the view thickly-wooded valleys, separated by the spurs of mountains clothed with tufted grass, and sweeping down towards the sea from an elevated and furrowed interior, form the principal features of these islands.
> (*Typee*: 21)

Tommo's (and Toby's) approach to the island is mainly a self-centred experience,[9] and his voyage toward the Typee valley underlines a sense

---

[7] See Robert K. Martin, *Hero, Captain, and Stranger: Male Friendship, Social Critique, and Literary form in the Sea Novels of Herman Melville* (Chapel Hill: University of North Carolina Press, 1986), 24.

[8] See Robert Roripaugh, "Melville's *Typee* and Frontier Travel Literature of the 1830s and 1840s," *South Dakota Review* 19.4 (1982): 46-64.

[9] Juniper Ellis, "Melville's Literary Cartographies of the South Seas," *Massachusetts Review* 38 (1997): 15.

of personal challenge: the ascent is often difficult, and opposes the self to the landscape. As Mitchell Breitwieser has pointed out, the geographical description of the island underlines the sense of a strong gratification and expression of the explorer's potential:

> He is lord not by the contingency of political entitlement but by imaginative, self-sufficient supremacy. This island's topography is an image of his desire gratified: from this apex, rock spokes to the sea; each valley, seen from the apex, is a rich possibility that culminates at the white beach that stretches between the ends of the spokes. Here, Tommo is a pure, boundless potentiality, distinct from its outcomes.[10]

The two American fugitives look at (or purpose to look at) the island in the same way the first pioneers looked at the West, with the same "imperial eye", as Mary Louise Pratt would define it.[11] South Seas and Western space overlap ideologically in every glance, in every "peep" Tommo takes: the protagonist seeks a frontier, in a clearly marked rite of passage that authenticates his experience. Nukuhiva is compared to a new *wilderness* (*Typee*: 58) that has yet to be mapped, an Eden in which the protagonists feel a certain "disappointment in not finding the various fruits" (*Typee*: 58). When the description shifts from nature to the inhabitants of the valley, more than once Tommo compares the Typees with the Niagaras, one of the first tribes the Europeans met in their journey West.[12] Although it has often been stressed how a specific editorial tendency pointed towards the Americanization of exotic contexts in order

---

[10]   Michael Breitwieser, "False Sympathy in Melville's *Typee*," in Myra Jehlen (ed.), *Herman Melville: A Collection of Critical Essays* (Englewood Cliffs, N. J.: Prentice Hall), 1994, 25.

[11]   Mary Louise Pratt, *Imperial Eyes: Travel Writing and Transculturation* (London: Routledge, 1992).

[12]   Ibidem: 79. This analogy between the South Seas and the American experience has been noted by A. N. Kaul, who writes: "The sojourn among the South Sea Islanders was indeed the nineteenth-century mariner's version of a gesture often celebrated in American life and literature. It was his equivalent of the communitarian experiment at Plymouth, of Crèvecoeur's projected journey to the Indian tribe, and of Coverdale's pilgrimage to Blithedale. Fanciful as these actions are—some looking forward and others back—they all have a serious side to them. In one way or another all of them arise from the background of the given civilization of the time and embody the American theme of rejection and quest." A. N. Kaul, *The American Vision: Actual and Ideal Society in Nineteenth-Century America* (Westport, Connecticut: Greenwood Press, 1963), 216. See also Edwin Fussell, *Frontier: American Literature and the American West* (Princeton: Princeton University Press), 1966.

to make them appealing and understandable to the American reader, it is quite clear that the discourse here is more than an attempt to please the reading public.[13] Through his protagonist, Melville reiterates the forefathers' desire of an empty Promised Land. Tommo perceives the island's geography as a trial, a test for his own potential. The "edenic geography" that he expects indicates that he sees such a space as a blank space onto which to project national expectations.[14] As Juniper Ellis writes:

> Melville attempts to clear a space to present his own creation of identity as an eyewitness to events that have (ostensibly) not been seen or recorded by whites or Pacific Islanders. *Typee* introduces a narrative strategy that Melville relies upon in *Omoo* and *Mardi* as well. All these texts begin with a description of a 'blank' Pacific ocean that awaits mapping. [...] The cartographic void or the 'chartless sea' that Melville refers to here and in *Moby Dick* evidence the empty field that he constructs to inscribe authorial, cultural, and national identity.[15]

If the two Americans (Tommo and Toby) thus attempt to represent that place as a void to be mapped and inscribed with their own cultural grids while ascending the mountains, then a turning point occurs—that changes this perception of place. Again, cultural and geographical journeys converge here. Once arrived at the top of the mountains, the two sailors (injured and frightened) have to stop for the night, and endure a terrible storm while on the edge of a precipice. The "fearful night" spent by the two young sailors also marks an ontological rite of passage. Not only does ascent become descent: geography itself seems inverted and

---

[13] See Fussell, *Frontier*, chapter 5.

[14] As Robert Roripaugh has pointed out, there are many features that link the Typee valley to the definitions advanced by Frederick Jackson Turner decades later: his formulation of the frontier as "the outer edge of the wave, the meeting point between savagery and civilization" is particularly meaningful in regard to Melvillean settings. The island is already crossed by a frontier, and the white man's advance into the interior parts of Nukuhiva moves this line forward. And in moving forward this invisible line, Tommo is both an insider and an outsider: even his desire to escape is a trait that makes him a true representative of the Western spirit. See Roripaugh, "Melville's *Typee* and Frontier Travel Literature of the 1830s and 1840s," passim.

[15] Ellis, "Melville's Literary Cartographies of the South Seas," 15.

transformed into a specular reality where heaven turns into hell, ambrosia into rotten fruits and poisonous water, Adam and Eve into threatening cannibals. This specular reality starts with the metaphorical duplicity of the baobab described when the sailors descend into the valley: its branches which resemble roots (as if it were a tree turned upside down), its roots which must be climbed by the two travellers in order to reach the bottom of the cliff. From this point onward, empirical approach is the only possibility in a world in which reality is the opposite of what was imagined (it should be).[16]

Once the two have arrived in the valley, Tommo's anthropological curiosity pushes him to try and find out more about the Typee society: and so to map its spatial structures and its symbols of power. But the village doesn't even seem to have a centre: the houses are scattered around without a precise order, and don't even follow the axis of the most travelled roads. Moreover, villages are not permanent structures: they are often moved from one place to another for no apparent reason, as Tommo's discovery of several rotten huts in the forest testifies.

Tommo's desire of a progression towards an ontological/geographical centre is frustrated in the end.[17] What Tommo has grasped are fragments of a culture that he is not able to compose into a coherent pattern—chiefly because he cannot conceive a pattern different from his own. There are new geographical and cultural maps that need to be discovered if one wants to penetrate into the native's space—maps that (as the author repeatedly underlines) the two sailors will not be completely able to recognize and understand.

The Geography of the "Other": the *Taboo*

As Rod Edmond writes at the beginning of *Representing the South Pacific*:

> In 1769 Tupaia, a priest from the Tahitian group of islands, drew Cook a map of his world. Taking its centre at Tahiti, the

---

[16] False expectations turn into bitter disappointment (this last a recurrent word) for the protagonist: see Melville, *Typee*, 70.

[17] See Rod Edmond, *Representing the South Pacific. Colonial Discourse from Cook to Gauguin* (Cambridge: Cambridge University Press, 1997), 88.

map showed seventy-four islands scattered across a large oceanic area measuring about three thousand miles from east to west and a thousand miles from north to south. The islands were arranged in concentric circles based on sailing times from the map's centre rather than on linear distance.[18]

There could hardly be a better visual example of how spatial and cultural paradigms are relative concepts. In this map, there is not a clearly marked opposition between land and sea, the two being two elements of the same unified pattern. Moreover, the distance is calculated not according to space but to time, with the social, rather than the geographical, centre being the focal point around which to construct space. It is precisely this connection between culture and space that Tommo is often unable to grasp. Nevertheless, Melville registers not only the way in which Tommo and Toby see the island, but also, more indirectly, the way in which the natives see and *live* in the valley[19]. There are two fundamental elements in the representation of native coordinates that Melville emphasizes: the *taboo* and the *tattoo*.

The *taboo* (prohibition) is the first, clear sign for Tommo of a native organic and coherent cultural map; a pattern that has been long lasting in that community. The *taboo* reveals itself as the "geography of the forbidden", a concept which is particularly difficult to understand, being invisible and sometimes even inexplicable for the Western observer.

In Melville's *Typee* nearly all *taboos* directly concern space and movement: the taboo comes to be the rule that allows or negates a certain action *in a well defined* space. One example is the taboo groves, the place where animals (or perhaps human beings) are sacrificed to pagan gods—a place forbidden to Tommo. Water itself becomes for Tommo a taboo: water equates with movement, being the way through which the protagonist can re-establish a connection with the outer world, more or less in the same way in which water brought the two travellers to the valley.[20]

---

[18]   Edmond, *Representing the South Pacific*, 1.

[19]   According to Malini Johar Schueller, Melville attempts several times to destabilize his American readers' ethnocentric ideas; if this is true, one of the vehicles he uses to reach this goal is also the representation of space. Malini Johar Schueller, "Colonialism and Melville's South Seas Journeys," *Studies in American Fiction* 22 (1994): 7.

[20]   Melville, *Typee*, 73.

The taboo works as an invisible map, since there are often no walls or barriers to protect the sites/symbols of power. The principle of exclusion is determined by *distance from the centre* rather than by proximity to a centre: sacred places are far from the village: the "holla holla ground" are located in the middle of the forest (*Typee*: 112-113), the mausoleum of the old chief (*Typee*: 203) and the "Typee Stonehenge" (*Typee*: 184) are surrounded by trees which protect them both from the sun and from the sight. The presence of an invisible order regulating religious and everyday experience is not opposed to, but combines with, liminality and transiency.

Being a sum of social rules, the *taboo* is relative: it depends on the gender and the class a native belongs to. There are places forbidden to men and places forbidden to women (as Tommo finds out when he tries to persuade Fayaway to follow him onto a small ship on the lake).[21] The *taboo* doesn't only separate feminine and masculine geographies, but it is also strongly linked to sexuality and the body itself. There's one ritual among the Typees which seems to integrate place and body: it is the *tattoo*. With the *tattoo*, the sense of belonging (to a tribe, and so to a place) is inscribed onto the body. It is a native rite of passage that marks the entrance of the individual into the community, but also his "being a part of the place" as well, by way of accepting the social (and spatial) rules that govern that society. As Breitwieser writes:

> Cannibalism and tattooing are thus extreme versions of the lapse of self chronicled in the lazy narrative they interrupt. They usefully terrify Tommo with the thought that freedom as he understands it is among the Typees precarious and subject to reversal in a moment, that each individual is inescapably knower and known, eater and eaten, writer and written upon.[22]

Tommo refuses to be rooted in the community, since this would also mean to cancel the distance between self and the space; the "I/eye" would lose its privileged standpoint, whereas difference and distance are precisely the two main elements of the observer's identity.

---

[21] Being the steadiest social elements, women could move much less than men. The larger number of tattoos seem to underline and to preserve this stability.

[22] Breitwieser, "False Sympathy in Melville's *Typee*," 24. See also Walter Herbert, *Marquesan Encounter: Melville and the Meaning of Civilization* (Cambridge, Mass.: Harvard University Press, 1980), 170.

The connection between *taboo* and *tattoo* is particularly evident in Marnoo's description. Marnoo is himself a *taboo*, since he belongs neither to one tribe nor to one valley. He is a liminal presence in the rigid subdivision of space and cultures, and he has complete freedom of movement. In relation to this, the design that appears on his back is particularly meaningful:

> The tattooing on his back in particular attracted my attention. The artist employed must indeed have excelled in his profession. Traced along the course of the spine was accurately delineated the slender, tapering, and diamond-checkered shaft of the beautiful "artu" tree. Branching from the stem on either side, and disposed alternately, were the graceful branches drooping with leaves all correctly drawn, and elaborately finished. Indeed, this piece of tattooing was the best specimen of the Fine Arts I had yet seen in Typee. A rear view of the stranger might have suggested the idea of a spreading vine tacked against a garden wall. (*Typee*:162)

The image of an artu tree climbing a garden wall underlines Marnoo's border status and mirrors the man's social role: that of a crossroads figure, living at the border of the Garden of Eden. *Taboo* and *tattoo* link the self both to society and to the space one lives in. The taboo does not only draw a cultural geography, but it regulates it, and preserves the borders and division. It is a way to separate one's own space from what stands outside its borders by erasing the "spaces of temporariness": like mountains, like Marnoo, like water. As Breitwieser underlines:

> The taboos circumscribe things that do not fit into categories of classification: women prohibited from canoes, their menstruation a possible pollution of masculine martial implements; animals imported from outside the islands; young men in the process of being tattooed, that is, in transition from boyhood to social manhood; Marnoo, an intertribal diplomat permitted to move from tribe to tribe because he is not a full member of any permitted single tribe; and the alien Tommo himself.[23]

The taboo is thus a system opposed to the changes that may come from both within and without society. Together with the tattoo, it is the way

---

[23] Breitwieser, "False Sympathy in Melville's *Typee*," 25.

native have to perform a system of exclusion (from places) as well as inclusion (within the community). A system that Tommo doesn't seem to understand completely, since the different basis for the native's and the coloniser's mapping also implies different hierarchies of the same spatial elements, and different ways to organize space, power and knowledge. Spatial/power structures differ from one culture to another: the misunderstanding or ethnological failures Tommo experiences are also the result of a lack of geographical insight.

But there are other liminal spaces within the island that the *taboo* will not be able to control and that constitute interesting sites where a common ground between two cultures will be unexpectedly found.

A liminal frontier

Despite Tommo's naive perspective, Nukuhiva is depicted from the very beginning as a heterogeneous setting, being the place where French soldiers are camping:

> At Nukuheva, there were about one hundred soldiers ashore. They were encamped in tents, constructed of the old sails and spare spars of the squadron, within the limits of a redoubt mounted with a few nine-pounders, and surrounded with a fosse. Every other day, these troops were marched out in martial array, to a level piece of ground in the vicinity, and there for hours went through all sorts of military evolutions, surrounded by flocks of the natives, who looked on with savage admiration at the show, and as savage a hatred of the actors. (*Typee*: 26)

The beach is then the contact zone among societies and powers: it is both the place of (un)dialectics between civilizations and the stage on which to perform military superiority and in so doing to establish power relations. Melville depicts them very clearly: the Western soldiers occupy the centre of the stage, while the natives (numerically superior) are confined to the margins.

Whereas the valley is the contact zone between the (American) self and the native tribe, the beach is the liminal space of contact between Native and American societies. This is a "saturated contact zone", in which two different concepts of liminality converge (a confluence that implies inclusion and exclusion, affirmation and erasure).

Liminality is an important characteristic for both Native and American cultures, which nevertheless elaborate it by different patterns: to South Seas cultures, as we have briefly seen, liminality is a founding element through which it is possible to organize power/space relations: it works as a process of exclusion (the distance between the village and sacred spaces) or it turns into a blurred zone which can be suspended (or erased) by recurring to the *taboo*. Liminality is an element that the Native culture tries to incorporate, in order to unarm it, to contrast the subversive force of transiency. At least, as long as no interference comes from the outside.

On the other hand, liminality is also an ambivalent element in the American culture. As opposed to centrality, it becomes the American counter-trait to the European world and culture. It works from both inside and outside, and in so doing it is a potentially subversive force which contrasts strict settings, fixed powers, rigid spaces (the most important example being the mythologization of the frontier, the blurred unsettled space embodying different forms of *dissent*). And in fact, the liminal/peripheral space is the ultimate destination of the Melvillean protagonists' quest—the place where to re-enact American genesis and exploration. In Melville's work, liminality is related both to the past and to the future: it is linked to the myth of the frontier and of the wilderness as a primitive space to map, as well as to the fragmentation and instability of modernity, to the shifting places and times of the colonial encounter—as *Omoo* underlines[24].

As we have already seen, the Typee valley is a sort of time (and space) warp. The mountains surrounding the valley—a *no-man's-land* for the natives, who define them as *taboo*—have to preserve the different spaces of the *otherness*, among the different native tribes. But for Tommo and Toby, this threshold turns first into a personal challenge, then into a bigger time dislocation, that throws them back towards the beginnings of the American experience and its contradictions: what A. N. Kaul defines as "the dialectical movement between a corrupt civilization and an ideal community, or the opposition between the dream and the reality of society

---

[24]   This doesn't mean that liminality can be identified with national borders, since national space isn't necessarily homogeneous and there are "places on the margins." See Rob Shields, *Places on the Margins. Alternative Geographies of Modernity* (London: Routledge, 1991). Melville's *The Confidence Man* clearly shows this as well.

in America".[25] While the natives try to preserve an order through liminality, Americans see it as a subversive element, a barrier waiting only to be torn down. But it is a threshold that, rather than dividing, metaphorically links the island's present to the American past (or to its repetition), even if it becomes clear that the Natives' present is not (and cannot be) the American past, once these two meet and clash on the beach.

And it is precisely the re-enactment of histories and the concept of time the last stage of this spatial unveiling of ideological superimposition which deeply affects the Melvillean characters in their perception of spatial *otherness*.

Clashes of times, dialectics of history

The attempt to preserve space from change, from external forces leading toward modernization and hybridization, is soon doomed to failure: not even the remotest places can be monadic entities disjunct from contingency. Spaces and cultures imply different perceptions of time as well, and since different historical paths converge on the islands, the representation of time and history is necessarily relative.

Nukuhiva is invaded by the Western world: by soldiers, cultures, and—consequently—their concept of time. Their expansion and colonization of the South Seas is the last wave in the sea of history. If history is identified by the Western world with movement and change, the natives perceive time as a cyclical experience, as a repetition of customs and rites: the *taboo* itself, as we have seen, is an attempt to interfere with movement and so with evolution and change. Once the explorers reach the island, the cultural perceptions and representations of time spuriously overlap, according to the degree of hybridization reached by the different zones.

As it has already been underlined, this setting is further complicated by the presence of the narrator, who reads space as well as time with his own ontological/cultural pattern. When Tommo is in the valley, his perception of linear time fades away, and so does his idea of movement. His sense of time emerges only when he remembers that there is a world waiting for him beyond the mountains—in other words, when he

---

25   Kaul, *The American Vision*, 230.

relativizes space. The oblivion of time does not depend only on the Typee culture, but it relates also to the expectations and the false ideology Tommo has projected onto that space: he expects it to be a New Garden of Eden, where nothing should change. This cosmological stasis can be identified by the narrator only with an ancestral past, a moment preceding civilization, untouched by history. At the beginning, he underlines the parallels between natural sceneries and images of ruins and temples. The bay of Nukuhiva is compared to a Roman amphitheatre (*Typee*: 34), while Tommo and Toby's descent into the valley is similar to Belzoni's descent into the Egyptian catacombs:

> Belzoni, worming himself through the subterranean passages of the Egyptian catacombs, could not have met with greater impediments than those we here encountered. But we struggled against them manfully, well knowing our only hope lay in advancing. (*Typee*: 75)

When Tommo finds traces of human work, he tends to attribute them to natural events; when he finds a path leading toward the valley, he affirms that it is the result of natural forces (*Typee*: 60). By doing this, Tommo wants the Nukuhiva landscape to gain the status of an important historical landmark. Moreover, he also wants that space to have its own history—but a natural history, that excludes human elements and a native history. So when he finds a path leading towards the valley, he states that it is the result of natural forces (*Typee*: 60) rather than of human work. Here Tommo repeats the same act of cultural erasure his forefathers had performed with the Native Americans.

Once he has entered the valley, Tommo's perspective gradually changes. By living with the Typees, he realizes that the natives have their own past: he finds impressive ruins of temples and tombs (bigger than those that Typees can create in the present), able to compete with those of the ancient Western cultures. But after the description of amazing stone terraces, which Tommo compares to Stonehenge, he adds:

> These structures bear every indication of a very high antiquity, and Kory-Kory, who was my authority in all matters of scientific research, gave me to understand that they were coeval with the creation of the world; that the great gods themselves were the builders; and that they would endure until time shall be no more. Kory-Kory's prompt explanation, and his attributing the

> work to the divine origin, at once convinced me that neither he
> nor the rest of his countrymen knew anything about them. As
> I gazed upon this monument, doubtless the work of an extinct
> and forgotten race, thus buried in the green nook of an island at
> the ends of the earth, the existence of which was yesterday
> unknown, a stronger feeling of awe came over me than if I had
> stood musing at the mighty base of the Pyramid of Cheops.
> There are no inscriptions, no sculpture, no clue, by which to
> conjecture its history: nothing but the dumb stones. [...] These
> remains naturally suggest many interesting reflections. They
> establish the great age of the island, an opinion which the
> builders of theories concerning the creation of the various
> groups in the South Seas are not always inclined to admit.
> (*Typee*: 184-185)

Although the Typees have their own history, Tommo indirectly tries to push them back into an inferior state for their (real or apparent) cultural nemesis: the Typees do not know anything about their past, and since they ignore it, this does not seem to *belong* to them. Moreover, compared to a monumental era, the Typees' present time appears as a regression, an involution of civilization. In order to negate ultimately a status to the Typee culture, Tommo tries to preserve the monumentality of that ancient time by drawing a gap between the natives' past and their present. Because it is only in the Typee past (like in his own past) that Tommo can find the atemporal "stillness [...] and the calm solitude" (*T*, 203) that he is looking for. And the only place that embodies this feeling is precisely the tomb of the old chief (which the previous quotation refers to). Once again, it is only in the space of the past (and of death) that it is possible to find a historical suspension within geography: or, to paraphrase Marshall Sahlins's words, an island within history.[26]

Cinzia Schiavini

---

[26] See Marshall Sahlins, *Islands of History* (Chicago: University of Chicago Press, 1985).

Willa Cather's Deep Southwest

In his essay, "The Gaze of Orpheus," Maurice Blanchot states that "Orpheus's error seems to lie in the desire which moves him to see and to possess Eurydice, he whose destiny is only to sing of her. He is Orpheus only in the song ... He has life and truth only after the poem and because of it..." (Maurice Blanchot, 1989, 172). One can hardly disagree with Blanchot's contention that literary characters are alive only within the fictional space of literature; however, the reality illusion is often so strong that it grants life to those characters and their world. It is in this sense that Willa Cather can be considered as a great creator of spaces. Certainly Cather's spaces are not limited to the Southwest of the United States; her descriptions of the prairies are also infused with such life that sometimes they become the protagonists in the story.

Although there are obviously many different approaches to the creation of space, I intend to concentrate mainly on Cather's narrative technique, based on the approach of Mexican critic Luz Aurora Pimentel, as well as on Mieke Bal's narrative theory. I intend to discuss one of her prairie novels, but I will focus mainly on her Southwestern spaces because of the role they play in the development of the main characters in the novels. Such spaces are considered "thematized", since they become an acting place rather than a place of action, and they influence the fabula (Bal,95). Nevertheless, in *Death comes for the Archbishop*, a novel without a plot, according to Marcus Klein, the Southwest *is* a place where the action takes place, yet it is also a dynamic space that allows the characters to travel through it. The setting is extremely important for it allows the priests, who are the heroes, to carry on their missionary work in spite of the dangers and discomfort they have to endure.

As Luz Aurora Pimentel mentions, the reality effect is first obtained through references to "real" places. The action takes place mostly in New Mexico, and a series of geographical names such as Santa Fe, Taos and Albuquerque are in themselves potential descriptions. This will, of course, vary according to the cultural encyclopaedia of the reader, but the ensuing details reinforce the original effect. Along their travels the heroes traverse spaces where they endure storms, wind, snow and the scorching sun, thus adding not only to the topographical context but also to the positive image of the characters involved. As descriptions of the landscape keep appearing throughout the narrative, the impression of rugged grandeur accumulates and enhances the merits of the main characters, thus generating an ideological dimension (Pimentel, 2001,28).

Mexican writer Mariano Azuela creates such a dynamic space in his novel *Los de abajo*, where a group of revolutionaries moves through different types of space. Canyons, plains and mountains as well as towns are described, always subjectively related to the events in which the group participates. As a matter of fact, the novel begins and ends in the same canyon, where the main character finds victory and finally death.

In Cather's *The Professor's House*, there is striking contrast between different spatial contexts. Cather's realistic descriptions of domestic and urban spaces mingle with an idealized Lake Michigan and with her evocation of the mythical Blue Mesa.

Actually, the novel begins with a description of the house from which the professor has just moved, which creates a dysphoric isotopy: "almost as ugly as it is possible; ... painted the collor of ashes ... the stairs that were too steep, the halls that were too cramped, ... wobbly stair treads, ... creaky boards ... taps so old that no plumber could ever screw them tight enough to stop the drip" (3). The professor's study on the third floor shares the uncomfortable impression of the house. The only opening for air and light is a single window on the east, the walls and ceiling were covered with a yellow paper "which had once been very ugly, but had faded into inoffensive neutrality" (7). However, Professor St. Peter is unhappy in the new house and is unwilling to abandon "this dark den" (8) in spite of the fact that he shares it with the seamstress. It "was the most inconvenient study a man could possibly have, but it was the one place in the house where he could get isolation, insulation from the engaging drama of domestic life"(16). The professor's frame of mind can be detected in the value granted to these particular qualities—insulation and isolation. This attic increases its value due to the fact that from the window "he could see, far away, just on the horizon, a long blue hazy smear--Lake Michigan, the inland sea of his childhood"(20). The name of a "real" referent triggers the reality effect, and is followed by a description linked to the perception of the professor: "The sun rose out of it, the day began there; it was like an open door that nobody could shut. The land and all its dreariness could never close in on you" (20). Cather herself commented that she had overcrowded the St. Peter's house and opened a window that would let in the fresh air, thus establishing another value contrast. She compared her experiment with those Dutch paintings of a room full of furniture where an open window reveals a view of the landscape (Gilbert & Gubar, 1989, 206).

Tom Outland's story, embedded in the same novel, takes place in the Southwest and the place called the Blue Mesa becomes particularly significant to Outland's process of self-knowledge. It is a place without a "real" referent, although both the name and the description evoke Mesa Verde, in Colorado. Regardless of the referent, the illusion of space is generated both linguistically and culturally, oriented and organized through a system of enforced contiguity (Pimentel,45): "overhanging us, indeed, stood the mesa, a pile of purple rock, all broken out with red sumach and yellow aspens up in the high crevices of the cliffs" (168). Cather projects this space through another narrator, Tom Outland himself, who describes the mesa through his own idealized perception. Once Tom begins ascending the canyon, the perspective changes from a distant view to the actual climbing of the mesa, and the tone operators add an ideological dimension. "The bluish rock and the sun-tanned grass, under the unusual purple-grey of the sky, gave the whole valley a very soft colour, lavender and pale gold... it seemed to me that I had never breathed in anything that tasted so pure as the air in that valley"(178). As the narrator (Tom) continues moving up, the space is organized vertically. Even when he discovers the hidden city there was "in the middle of the group, a round tower" that "held all the jumble of houses together and *made them mean something*"(180, my italics). This discovery adds a mythical dimension to the Blue Mesa, and as has been previously mentioned, enhances its importance as an element in the development of Tom's personality. Iterative descriptions of his successive trips to the Mesa and Tom's "relationship" to its early inhabitants accumulate and infuse this space with strong ideological content. It is one of those "thematized" spaces described by Mieke Bal(95). "I had that glorious feeling that I've never had anywhere else, ... the air, my God, what air! it was like breathing the sun, breathing the colour of the sky." (217). The description is completely subjective, with synesthesia adding to the euphoric effect. Even Tom's teacher, Father Duchene, shares the narrator's perception: "Like you, I feel a reverence for this place ... (it) is a sacred spot"(199). Time and space meet in this relationship with the early dwellers of the Mesa, and the author leads Tom to consciousness and appreciation of his own cultural and historical heritage.

The eventual loss of the Cliff City's relics causes the rupture of Tom's relationship with Roddy, his protector, but at the same time reinforces Tom's consciousness of the meaning of his experience, which could be considered an epiphany: "It all came together in my understanding, ... For me the mesa was no longer an adventure, but a religious emotion"(226).

An equivalent conjunction of time and space appears in *The Song of the Lark*, where Thea Kronborg, the heroine, develops a strong bond with the early dwellers of Panther Cañon and internalizes the site. She detects a dignified sadness emanating from the ancient dwellings, "a voice out of the past, not very loud, that went on saying a few simple things to the solitude eternally" (271). For Thea this space has a life of its own. Time seems to stop in this canyon, where the voice of the past is able to reach the actors and project itself into the future.

As in *The Professor's House*, there is in this novel a significant contiguity of the vast Southwestern landscape with small, protective spaces. As a child in a family of seven children Thea sleeps in a sort of attic room she fitted up herself: "Thea and Tillie papered the room, walls and ceiling in the same paper ... She made white cheesecloth curtains and hung them on a tape" (51). The room is not heated and the ceiling is so low an adult can touch it, it has only one window but it is large and gives Thea a view of the street. She loves this space that she can call her own, "The acquisition of this room was the beginning of a new era in Thea's life. It was one of the most important things that ever happened to her"

(52). During the time Thea spends at Panther Cañon she takes one of the rock-rooms in the dead city for her own and fits it with Navajo blankets for heat and comfort. She enjoys relaxing in this space where, as in her childhood room, she could touch the ceiling with the tips of her fingers. Cather describes minutely both Thea's room at home and the one in the dead city, transmitting a feeling of comfort and security. There is a close relationship between these rooms and Professor St. Peter's crowded attic studio, since all three spaces open into the outer world but at the same time protect the occupants. This protection varies from actual storms in the Cañon to equivalent interference from the family in the other cases. However, the idea of a confined space that opens into the outer world becomes particularly meaningful when it is associated with Cather's simile at the end of *The Song of the Lark* (417). It refers to the waters of the Venetian lagoon, which are renewed every night by the flow of the tide, thus preventing the water from becoming stagnant and establishing a connection with the rest of the world.

Upon Thea's arrival at the Ottenburg ranch the topography of the place is described objectively. It is only when Thea starts her walks through Panther Cañon that the space is linked to the perception of the heroine, and thus, the accumulation of adjectives creates an isotopy. Panther Cañon, a fictional name, (although based on a real canyon) is close to a "real" referent, Walnut Canyon, near Flagstaff, Arizona. The name evokes a geographical context, and the author's description does the rest. This space acquires both mythical and mystical dimensions through its influence on Thea, who perceives the atmosphere of the place as "ritualistic" (273). Bathing in the stream Thea feels "a continuity of life that reached back into the old time ... Thea's bath came to have a ceremonial gravity" (273). The whole canyon becomes an acting space rather than a place of action. The fact that 'this is happening here' is just as important as 'the way it is here', which allows these events to happen" (Bal,96). Space is evoked through an accumulation of collor, sound, light and metaphor. "The cañon twisted and wound like a snake"(268) and between both sides of the cliff there is a "river of blue air" (268). Swallows swam in "that blue gulf" (271). Thea listens to the "whirr of the big locusts and to the light, ironical laughter of the quaking asps" (269). "The thin red clouds ... began to boil and move rapidly, weaving in and out like smoke" ... "the golden light seemed to hang like a wave upon the rim of the cañon ... the frosty piñons were glittering and trembling, swimming in the liquid gold" (281). The presence of the ancient ruin and its dwellers links past and present, space and time.

Basking in the sun, Thea is able to reflect and to experience music as a sensation more than as an idea. The image of the pottery found in the ruins combined with the flowing stream lead her to a sudden conception of art as "an effort to make a sheath, a mould in which to imprison for a moment the shining, elusive element which is life itself" (273). In singing she finds an analogy between her throat and nostrils with one of those vessels for holding water. Cather infuses her heroine with a realization of her own potential, which enables her to decide that she will take her life into her own hands and commit herself to her art. "The Cliff Dwellers had lengthened her past. She had older and higher obligations"(276). Space and time combine to project Thea's future.

Gilbert and Gubar believe that Cather used the Southwest "to reconstruct prehistoric native culture in order to analyse the interaction between civilized and primitive societies" (1989,208). Although this interaction definitely exists, I believe Cather goes farther than that when she attaches such importance to historical sites set in isolated geographical spaces. These spaces suggest an identification of the new generations with their mythical past or at least with part of it, since most of Cather's characters have European origins.

Such originatory moments -and spaces- permeate Cather's "prairie" fictions as well. As a matter of fact, *The Song of the Lark* begins and ends in Moonstone, Colorado, a small town in the plains east of Denver. The neighbouring desert and sand hills fascinate Thea as a child and Cather, as in other cases, generates a positive isotopy—"a line of many-coloured hills; rich, sun-baked yellow, glowing turquoise, lavender, purple; all the open, pastel colours of the desert" (43). On the other hand, Moonstone shares some of the unpleasant characteristics of Hanover, the town in *O Pioneers!* It is quite likely that both these towns were modelled after Red Cloud, Nebraska, where Cather grew up.

Cather's distaste for cluttered interiors is evident in *O Pioneers!* when she describes the heroine's new dining room "where highly varnished wood and coloured glass and useless pieces of china were conspicuous enough to satisfy the standards of the new prosperity" (66). We learn that this is not Alexandra's taste but that of the Hanover furniture dealer who did "his best to make her dining-room look like his display window" (66). The picture is completed when Alexandra states "the conviction that the more useless and utterly unusable objects were, the greater their virtue as ornament". This is ideologically charged with Alexandra's (and therefore the author's) distaste of social pretensions, and makes the company dining room an unpleasant area where friction eventually takes place.

Mieke Bal mentions the relations between space and event in certain stereotypical combinations (96). In this regard it is interesting to note how Cather relies on this tradition only to subvert it later. The orchard where Emil finds Marie sleeping under the white mulberry tree, is the classical *locus amoenus* for the consummation of love, in a scene with strong Ovidian echoes. However, such a site also becomes the setting for a crime, when her jealous husband kills the lovers. A number of symbolic meanings have been read into this tragedy; some critics, like Blanche H. Gelfant, read into it references to Paolo and Francesca in Dante's *Inferno*; nevertheless, the idyllic orchard setting where danger lurks seems closer to the Garden of Eden. This impression is reinforced by Ivar's words: "sin and death" applied to the tragedy and later on by Carl's explanation that "there are women who spread ruin around them" (207).

One could say that natural elements play one of the leading roles in *O Pioneers!* Something similar appears in Mexican writer Juan Rulfo, although frequently with negative connotations. In his short story "Luvina," for example, the atmosphere destroys the people, not only physically but psychologically as well. In "Luvina" the wind becomes a character that "scratches as if with nails"; it recalls the erosion caused upon the land, its constant sound parallelling the murmur of people.

It is the land that interests the author in *O Pioneers!* and thus becomes an actor in the novel. There is repeated personalization of the land in terms suggesting power as well as beauty. The author repeatedly endows it with the power of will, "the last struggle of a wild soil against the encroaching plowshare" (32). In most cases the land is seen through the perception of Alexandra, the heroine. Instead of a detailed description, what the author provides is a subjective picture. Alexandra looks at the land with love and yearning. "It seemed beautiful to her, rich and strong and glorious. Her eyes drank in the breadth of it (the land), until her tears blinded her" (44). Throughout the narrative the author builds the "personality" of the prairie by means of an accumulation of odour, collor and metaphor: "the furrows of a single field often lie a mile in length, and the brown earth, with such a strong, clean smell, and such a power of growth and fertility in it, yields itself eagerly to the plow ... with a soft, deep sigh of happiness" (52).

Cather implies that the pioneers have finally succeeded in conquering the land, thus becoming part of the history of the country. As in her Southwest novels, space becomes one with history and there is a sense of mythic origins. The diversity in the composition of the human groups in this space-time context and the qualities they represent suggests the author's consciousness of a collective culture at a particular historical period. In spite of the fictional nature of these novels, Cather's projection of space is not merely ornamental, it is an ideological position through which she conveys the importance of the past that built the multi-ethnic mosaic that covers the wide territory of the western United States.

Perhaps Orpheus is not mistaken when he breaks the law that binds him for, once more with Blanchot, his gaze is "the extreme moment of liberty" (175). Writing begins with Orpheus' gaze, "but in order to descend toward this instant, Orpheus has to possess the power of art already"(176). This is the power that I believe Cather possessed.

Rosario Faraudo

Bibliography

Azuela, Mariano (1916) 1988. *Los de abajo*. México: Fondo de Cultura Económica.

Bal, Mieke. 1994. *Narratology: Introduction to the Theory of Narrative*. Toronto: U. of Toronto Press.

Blanchot, Maurice. 1989. *The Space of Literature*. Lincoln: U. of Nebraska Press.

Cather, Willa. (1915) 1988. *The Song of the Lark*. Boston: Houghton Mifflin Co.

——————. (1925) 1990. *The Professor's House*. New York: Random House.

——————. (1927) 1990. *Death comes for the Archbishop*. New York: Random House.

——————. (1913) 1994. *O Pioneers!* New York. Penguin Books.

Gubar, Susan & Gilbert, Sandra.1989. *No Man's Land, Vol. 2, Sexchanges*. New Haven: Yale U. Press.

Pimentel, Luz Aurora. 2001. *El espacio en la ficción*. México: Siglo XXI.

Rulfo, Juan. (1953) 2000. "Luvina." In *El llano en llamas*. México: Plaza y Janés.

Zamora, Lois Parkinson. 1990. "The Usable Past: The Idea of History in Modern U.S. and Latin American Fiction". In *Do the Americas have a Common Literature?* Ed. Gustavo Pérez Firmat. Durham: Duke U. Press. Pp. 7-41.

The Transitional in the American Cities: Introduction

The following four articles deal with two U.S. American cities—Los Angeles and New York—as material and imaginary sites of transit. Under this aspect, the following papers address different notions of what is "traversed": political and topographical borders, cultural and national boundaries, those of class and ethnicity, the boundaries between the material and the imagined city, as well as cityspace itself, which is traversed both in the wanderings of its inhabitants and visitors, and in its conceptualization from various perspectives.

Different views on the city evolve here:
• socially defined perspectives that ask questions of how Los Angeles and New York are represented as contact zones, and how their ethnic and social heterogeneity is negotiated,
• political/ideological perspectives that ask questions about the cultural and political meanings of American cities in a globalized world, and
• aesthetic perspectives that ask questions about the representational forms that guide the perceptions of the city.

The articles address as diverse topics as the filmic representations of Los Angeles across the Mexican-American border; the construction and representation of ethnic diversity in Los Angeles' music festivals; the redefinition of New York since the "global impact" of September 11; and concepts of New York's cityspace from the perspective of tourism and homelessness. This section, then, will touch on a variety of issues that analyse the global cities of Los Angeles and New York from a perspective of cultural diversity and transnationalism.

The idea of the "global city" goes back to Saskia Sassen's analysis of world cities as crossroads of international financial flows, which connect the corporate elites of New York and Los Angeles more tightly with the corporate elites of Tokyo and Hong Kong than with local neighbourhoods like the Bronx or South Central (*The Global City*, 2nd ed. 2001). Closely related to the economic perspective is that of the social and cultural consequences of migration and its impact on ethnic and national identities. In contrast to the term immigration, which stems from a pre-globalized economic system, migration stresses the movements in and out of the United States, and the close cultural, economic and social contact that migrants keep with their places of origin. The idea of cities as sites of assimilation and homogeneity is thus replaced by one that calls for the acceptance of diversity and heterogeneity. The global city, then, renegotiates ideas of "America"; equally, the global city is renegotiated in terms of its meaning for "America." Considering the wide-spread anti-urbanism that has characterized U.S. American culture in the 20th century, it is important to call for a vision of urbanity not in the sense of homogenous communities, but as "a vision of social relations affirming group differences," "an openness to unassimilable otherness" (Iris Marion Young, see also Doreen Massey on "hybrid spaces"[1]). However, globalization has not only led to a diversification of American cities, but also (and actually, this is how globalization is discussed in the first place) to a homogenisation where urban spaces are produced for tourist and corporate consumption. Within this tension between the global and the local, the terrorist assaults of September 11 have not only brought "home" the conflicts of globalization, but they have also led to a renegotiation of New York as a national symbol. Negotiations of nationality, then, take place not only within the ethnically diverse set-up of urban space, but they also concern the national and spatial imaginary of the United States.

The global city has found many forms of representation. It is important to realize that urban space does not precede representation. Rather, I

---

[1]   Young, "City Life and Difference," in: *Justice and the Politics of Difference* (Princeton, 1990) 226-41; Massey, "Power-geometry and a progressive sense of place," in: *Mapping the Futures: Local Cultures, Global Change*, ed. Jon Bird et al. (London, 1993) 59-69.

would like to draw attention to Henri Lefebvre's idea of the "production of space" that takes place simultaneously on three levels: according to Lefebvre, space is produced as a material reality that is perceived through the body and through spatial practice; as a discursive field that is conceived in ideologies; and as a symbolic space that is expressed in cultural representations (*The Production of Space*, English translation: 1991). Edward Soja, who has adapted Lefebvre's theory to an analysis of the American postmodern city (especially Los Angeles) has boiled this down to the triad: real, imagined, and "realandimagined" space (*Thirdspace*, 1996). This breaking up of the dichotomies of real vs. imagined space introduces a new platform of agency for cultural studies: urban space is not already "there" waiting to be described, but it is also the product of cultural concepts. Urban space, then, is "produced" in the various representations that the following papers will address: in cultural practices and systems of intercultural and transnational infrastructures such as world music concerts and tourism, as well as in specific media such as film, music, literature (both fictional and essayistic), and in maps. It is from this perspective that this section contributes both to a transnational notion of American cities, and to the discourse of urbanism.

Dorothea Löbbermann

Schizopolis:

Border Cinema and the Global City (of Angels)

There is no greater global city of dreams, fictions, and fantasies than the city with no centre, than Los Angeles. The globalism of Los Angeles has much to do with its production of images and fantasies, where many of the films, television shows and commercials of the popular cultural landscape are generated. Its status as a global city is exceptional, not only an effect of its emplotment in the shadow of Hollywood, but in its proximity to another mythological construction, the border between the United States and Mexico. Many critics have described L.A. as a border city; a city that harbors the border as part of the experience of its topography (Davis, 2000; Fox, 1999; Guillermo Gómez Peña, 1996). This is not to diminish the trauma of border crossing, the disorienting experience of entering a new territory or a new nation-state, but rather to explore the various real and symbolic effects of the arbitrary designation of borders and boundaries. The border emerges in the city as a symbolic boundary and a complex of operations, especially in the technologies of surveillance that reach northward and link up to the policing agencies within the city. Border policies are directed against areas of the city that have their own economies and mythos of sovereignty, that are abandoned by the city proper and have become a separate national entity; as in the collection of short stories by Luis J. Rodriguez, *The Republic of East L.A.*

The border had become an impasse of national politics by the early eighties, giving rise to a wave of border films that dramatize and work through anxieties about immigration in the popular imaginary. Though there are a number of such films from this period, I turn attention to a classic of major independent cinema, Nava's *El Norte,* for its depiction of border crossing and the subsequent everyday experience of the border in the global city. *El Norte* explores the hidden workings of split economies. Moreover, it reveals the real political, socio-economic as well as psychic costs of divided cities by bringing the simulated realities of mass media to their logical end, which means sacrificing each character to the disorder of the city.

By the nineties, immigration policy had become increasingly phobic from the 1993 "Operation Blockade" in El Paso, which served as protocol for other border cities to California's "Save Our State" proposition 187 in 1994, and the passing of a bill into law in 1996 that would lead to increased sanctions on trade of undocumented immigrants, and regulation on legal immigration (Maciel and García-Acevedo 1998, 4). Border ideology had shifted into a more intensely polarized and complex debate at the same time that Latinos were struggling for equitable and fair representation in film and television after years of being typecast negatively; also known as the "Hispanic Hollywood" boom of the late eighties (Noriega and López, 1996). This double reality of immigration and representation is reflexively analysed in *Star Maps*. Like *El Norte,* it depicts the alluring images of North American media as they come to bear on the spatialization of Los Angeles; the title alludes to the tourist maps of stars' homes while the story takes place beyond the exclusive neigh-bourhoods of the movie stars. In *Star Maps,* Carlos dreams of becoming the next major Latin star, but this dream is rendered delusional within the racist ideology of the corporate studio system. The main characters of both films are depicted crossing the border with dreams of a better life only to be borderlined and broken down by Los Angeles. The experience of Los Angeles by the immigrant and racialized population is uniquely deranging; L.A. doubly bi-polarizes: literally in *El Norte* in the split economy of the city, and symbolically in *Star Maps* through the mass mediation of Los Angeles' most dominant industry, Hollywood. Each character is traumatized and tyrannized by the culture of the city, and each depiction reveals how the global schizopolis divides and destroys psyches.

Our expectations of major global cities are guided in part by their media-induced mythos. Cities shape and transform you through various kinds of interactions and designations contingent upon where you live, work, play, shop, belong, and feel safe or unsafe. Mike Davis describes post-liberal Los Angeles as a militarized space of permanent surveillance riddled with barricades protecting the well-to-do against the dangerously invidious underclass (Davis, 1992). Imagine coming to the city with the dream of free mobility only to find that your presence is the subject of security measures, that parts of the city are off-limits to you—from gated communities to shopping malls and other semi-public and public spaces—or that you are under permanent surveillance and profiled as part of a criminal class. You risk a deranging alienation of self-conception to social being. For recent arrivals to the city, the disturbing effects of the urban experience are intensified by the disorienting transitions inherent to immigration. In a study of the psychic effects of immigration, Carola and Marcelo Suárez-Orozco describe the process of displacement as isolating and alienating since immigrants are bereft of resources and typical coping strategies. In the shift from a "predictable contexts" to unpredictable contexts, immigrants are often stripped of social and extended familial relationships, a sense of social status and belonging, and cultural competence and control. The distress of the new context can be intensified by traumas left behind in origin countries—war, famine, poverty, violence—along with the trauma of migration for those who, undocumented, cross the highly militarized border zone separating the U.S. and Mexico.

In *El Norte*, we begin our itinerary in Guatemala with a series of images of the idyllic Guatemalan landscape where mist partly veils mountains against a lush verdant valley. The Guatemalan landscape, frozen as this picturesque scene of untouched mountainsides, is initially offered as a tourist's postcard of life before the onslaught of industrial capitalism. Suddenly the ideological gloss of the postcard image is destroyed with the irruption of a surprising and even shocking element across its smooth surface. The dream-like imagery is violently cut-off by the image of hands picking coffee and to a close-up of mountain sides revealing the toil of workers stooped over coffee, depersonalized and visible only by their straw hats. The scene registers as violent with the sound of a gun firing, signalling the end of a work day, followed by a shot of the procession of disembodied feet. The fantasy scene is ruptured by the reality of native subjugation to an export-oriented economy, a reality that stains the otherwise picturesque scene. The stain, the sullying element, is that piece of the real that irrupts into and destroys the cohesive and hermetic form of the fantasy, the beautiful and untouched countryside that satisfies the tourists' gaze. The tacit critique registers as an irritation, in the sense that the image would be captivating if it weren't for the presence of the workers. The abject toil of the workers reminds the viewer of the irksome labour that generates the products of leisure—these workers are not the Juan Valdez that joyfully selects every bean for the enjoyment of the North American consumer. As we watch, the coffee will travel, unhindered, from the countryside of Guatemala to the restaurant in Los Angeles. This displacement also marks the transformation of Enrique, the movie's protagonist, from agrarian to industrial worker, from labouring on the coffee plantation to serving coffee in the city. However, unlike the coffee, his presence in the city is not welcome.

The opening scene sets up the critical structure of the film in which the critique of globalization is transmitted in the form of the negative kernel, the piece of reality that upsets the flow of the viewer-as-tourist expectation set by the initial series of images. This scene and others like it constitute the bad dream of ideology, the slip in meaning that makes the viewer realize that the dream is not a dream, but real. The film is both an entertaining suspension from reality and a reminder that there is no wholesale escape from this reality. Reality is the support of the fiction, labour of leisure, and urban ghettos and outskirts maintain the sanctity and serenity of the centres of power and wealth of the global city. In this way, *El norte* destroys even the most familiar and comforting skylines, landscapes and cityscapes, an effect that deters the viewer from falling into a numbing Hollywoodesque haze.

The story exposes the centripetal forces of late capitalism that draw people to the global city, it is a story about the forced mobility of globalization. Zygmunt Bauman describes globalization in terms of the split status of mobility determined by whether you can travel or not and why you travel. Globalization "divides as much as it unites," as it presents the world as a global village, as a single place, it deepens divisions between, quite simply, the haves and the have-nots (1998, 2). Bauman asserts that movement is inevitable even if you stay put, since even the landscape of home is in constant flux. Whether movement is cybernetic, intellectual or supersonic, it signals the expansive possibilities of globalization from above. Yet, there is movement that is constraining and unfree, an economic exile that is both cause and symptom of freedom. This movement is paradoxically never fully globalized, but is a continued localization-in-movement. The border-crossing immigrant so often depicted in the eighties represented this terrifying unfreedom created by globalized wealth. Hollywood border films fence off this engulfing and shaming other from the US psyche with renewed borders and boundaries. *El Norte* refuses such happy oblivion.

The Los Angeles of *El norte* is initially cast as a global and hospitable city, but its globalism is one of concentrated wealth and criminalized and persecuted immigrant workers. This is conveyed in the split images of each place and the class-conditioned experience of urban space. The presentation of the underrepresented space or image is the other-side, the stain, of the normative viewing expectation. The restaurant in which Enrique initially takes a job conveys this splitting in the image-ing of the worker-space of the frantic kitchen against the serene and sombre dining room. This division of labour from leisure has racial, ethnic and temporal implications; the Anglo patrons leisurely enjoy a slow-paced meal while the Latino workers sweat in the kitchen. Likewise, the space of the city is divided between zones of labour and leisure. The Mexican American neighbourhood is characterized by a hustle-bustle atmosphere, while the Hollywoodesque neighbourhoods are tranquil. The split scenes in the city visually accord with the establishing shot in Guatemala. *El Norte* reveals the hidden secret of ideology, the labour behind the commodity. The North American audience of coffee drinkers get full exposure to the workers picking coffee beans on the Guatemalan countryside and restaurant diners see the workers in the kitchen. The products of labour emerge as a fragment of some other reality that persists in another narrative frame, another part of the city and another national economy.

El Norte sacrifices Enrique and Rosa to the schizopolis to make its critique legible. After the northern progression through various polarizations and contradictions, each character is rendered "crazy" by diverse standards. Both are given over to the effects of late capitalism, but each deteriorates differently. Enrique, driven from his job by INS, is given an opportunity for employment in Chicago, which seems ideal except that it means leaving Rosa ill with typhus behind in the hospital. Enrique initially decides to leave, a surprising decision that is deemed outrageous within the narrative. Yet Enrique's careerism would be endorsed by an Anglo urban norm that values individual success over family or community ties. Though momentarily redeemed by choosing to remain, he lapses back into the lunacies of capitalism by enacting a willful amnesia of his father's warning not to be reduced to the disembodied arms of labour. In the end Enrique has capitulated to the borderlining economies of the city by aggressively competing for work as a day labourer.

New Despair-ities

Like Nava, Miguel Arteta often thematizes Los Angeles in his work, using the city not just as a backdrop, but as a significant and signifying space. Both filmmakers, Nava and Arteta, can be located within the same political continuum; both made distribution deals with Fox Searchlights' president Lindsay Law because of his commitment to Latino cinema. Yet, Miguel Arteta's *Star Maps* works the schizopolis from its symbolic and mythological landscape, from Hollywood. The border reemerges in the city as a *cinematic* border that corresponds to the actual split within the city, of centre to periphery, but also the boundary and barrier that keeps Latinos and other racialized groups from emigrating to the centre of the city-based, but globally impacting, media production.

 Star Maps is a film about a severely dysfunctional Mexican-American family whose father works for a large prostitution ring of Mexican-American kids into which he has drawn one of his sons, Carlos. The father is abusive and cruel and his tyranny is the source of the family dysfunction. The mother has suffered a nervous breakdown and hallucinates the presence of Mexican comedian Cantinflas; one of the sons is mentally disturbed, and the daughter, Maria, is the only seemingly stable person. Carlos has delusions of Hollywood stardom, yet this fantasy will remain just that, since the city, like the industry, has already mapped him out of its coveted spaces.

 Star Maps opens with the familiar image of the northbound bus from Mexico to L.A. full of Mexican nationals, though in the case of Carlos, he is returning home. He is returning from a stint doing community theatre in Mexico, where he was sent to be out of the clutches on his pimping father. The small taste of recognition sparks a desire for fame that is complicit with an immigrant desire for a "better life." We see the bus on the cusp of the city moving in from the south with the city centre just beyond. Though the bus is in transit, this is the fixed perspective of L.A. for Carlos, a perspective from below and outside. Carlos dreams that he is swamped by the adoration of fans asking for his autograph. We realize this is a fantasy when we see Carlos open his eyes to a quiet bus and the camera fixes on the article that inspired the reverie. The article proclaims Antonio Banderas as "el nuevo Valentino" installing Banderas as a symbolic point of departure in the story within a legacy inherited from Rudolph Valentino, the Italian immigrant actor first associated with the idea of the Latin lover. Banderas, now well-known in the U.S., is an immigrant from Spain where his career began as part of the main repertoire of actors in Pedro Almodóvar's gender-bending camp classics. He was often cast as a clueless character whose youth, inexperience and pretty boy looks mark him as an object of male and female desire —reminiscent of the rumours of bi-sexuality attributed to Valentino. When Carlos casts an identificatory gaze on Banderas, we immediately form the symbolic connection, a connection that links Carlos with a visual legacy of imported Latin lover and boy toy.

Behind the city map is a story about the cartography of history, of the micro-legacies of family and the larger legacies of culture. Carlos works under a double patrimony, corresponding to two controlling fathers, that of his sadistic father, Pepe, and the legend of classical Hollywood, Valentino. Pepe guides the economic logic of Carlos' quest for fame; he consents to introduce his son to the "right" people only if he works for him as a prostitute. Carlos is forced to trade his body for a shot at stardom, and yet, in the legacy of Valentino, even stardom requires that he traffic in his body; if he can attain it. The results of Carlos' quest are dissonant with his expectations. He lands a walk-on part on a major soap opera, an opportunity provided by his soap star john, Jennifer. Yet, he plays an undocumented worker who says things like "I am like a matador with my leaf-blower" before being seduced by the older Anglo female lead, Jennifer. He plays the part of the sexually available "hired help" though he had aspired to be a leading man Latin lover. Disenfranchised labour in the city is cast into its symbolic counterpart, is made telegenic and cinematic as these supporting and typecasting roles that add sexuality to stereotype—not a far cry from the prostitution ring Carlos abandons for the soap role. In an impasse reminiscent of Enrique's fate as disembodied labour, Carlos can't seem to transcend his fate as fetishized and prostituted object. He is sacrificed to the schizoid split of the Hollywood system, the immigrant fantasy that anyone can become a star against the reality of racial denigration.

Carlos is deeply disturbed; his deep family trauma, in the form of a memory of a scene of paternal violence, keeps returning and interrupting his life. The family trauma reverberates as a racial trauma induced by the fetishizing sex-work and media-work. When he has a traumatic block, he stops whatever he is doing. These momentary lapses stop the film from moving forward smoothly while bringing the flow of images to a traumatic impasse. The film ends on this kind of gridlock: Carlos walks away from a violent confrontation with his father to wander in the city. We are left wondering what kind of future he might have and what kind of future Hollywood might map for him and other minorities of mass media.

Los Angeles is considered a global city for its media-induced circuit of international trade and, in the case of *El Norte* and *Star Maps,* the object of trade is the body of the immigrant. These films end pessimistically to expose the unhappy contradictions of urban late capitalism and the trauma it induces. The Latin American immigrant and Latino alike experience the global city in the discomfiture and derangement of being-temporary and extraneous rather than integrated and integral to the city. These films reveal the continual disenfranchisement of immigrant labour as guest worker, surplus labour, sex worker and day-labourer continually cast into informal and deeply promiscuous flexible economies.

The experience of Los Angeles by the immigrant and racialized population is uniquely deranging. L.A. doubly bi-polarizes: literally in the split economy of the city, and symbolically in the deceptive images of a global city that is open and hospitable to the world, or where the global city is a "melting pot." Instead, in *El Norte* and *Star Maps*, the immigrant urban experience is depicted as a transnational disenfranchisement that cuts deeply into the operations of the city. This is the paradox of the global city; it is a major world centre of economic and cultural power and yet as this power becomes more centralized, the socio-economic structure of the city becomes more intensely bifurcated. The centre of the city not only becomes more opposed to the periphery, the periphery becomes more and more exiled from the city proper. Moreover, the global aspect of the city refers more to the economy of a world system than a cultural inclusivity or a cosmopolitan embrace of the other, the stranger or the immigrant. Rather, the globalism of the city is spatially exclusionary, the city is re-borderized in a way that polices the boundaries of the nation ever more stringently. These large cities are places that are thought to diminish the presence and importance of national self-definition, yet the symbolic border is intrinsic to the city and thrown into relief with the presence of the immigrant. The immigrant, having just crossed the border, is suddenly faced with a new border within the city.

Camilla Fojas

All the World's in L.A.: Public Concerts in the Global City

Last November, the Mayor of Los Angeles went to China. According to the *Los Angeles Times*, the mayor was "touring China to promote business and tourism at home" (Shuster 2002: B4). To this end, he hoped to obtain a pair of giant pandas for the Los Angeles Zoo. He thought "Los Angeles would be a natural place for giant pandas because it has a large Chinese community and is a gateway for Asian tourists" (Shuster 2002: B4).

While the mayor was trying to get pandas for the Los Angeles Zoo, Grand Performances' Director and Director of Programming were travelling in China looking for performing groups to present in their 2003 season. They travelled to Hong Kong and mainland cities that included Beijing, Shanghai and Zhengzhou. The Director of Programming travelled alone to the Hunan province. Their trip was organized through the Chinese Consul General in Los Angeles and all hospitality and activities were arranged by local Chinese Friendship Associations. They were taken to tourist oriented performances of Peking opera and acrobats. In an effort to find out about the art forms they were interested in presenting in Los Angeles, such as rock, hip hop, electronic music, or modern dance, they asked young people about their favourite artists and purchased recordings to bring home. In Hunan province, the Director of Programming was shown four performances of what she described as "commodified, Disneyfied" versions of traditional music and dance. When, upon hearing three old men playing percussion and vocalizing at a reconstructed Tujen village who were, as she said, "folk" and not "slick," she told her tour guides that was what she wanted to hear, they were surprised.

The trip to China was intended to help fulfill part of a three year grant to present performing artists creating contemporary art forms from so-called developing countries that have had major immigration to Southern California in the last twenty-five years. The goals of this project, as outlined in the application to the Irvine Foundation, are to "1) present these arts to a broader community in order to promote better understanding between communities, 2) make recent immigrants become more engaged in the Los Angeles society by presenting arts from their home countries on an established stage, and 3) to broaden images of what types of art are being created in various countries." To support these goals, the artists presented should "use a contemporary genre to address their societies' current issues and/or tell their 'stories,'" and "be considered among the best in their countries for artistic merit and excellence." Ultimately, with this grant Grand Performances hopes to "challenge audiences and break stereotypes."

The first year of this project focussed on Mexico. Two modern dance companies from Mexico City were presented at Friday and Saturday evening concerts and a Friday noontime concert. In presenting these companies much emphasis was placed on working against stereotypes, especially, in this case, the idea that Mexican performances would only be mariachi or folklorico dance. Audience responses affirmed the existence of these stereotypes. Before the performance, an older man in the audience stated that he was looking forward to the performance as he liked mariachi, adding, "at least I think it will be mariachi." At a facilitated discussion after the performance, school children, mostly Latino, were asked what kind of dance they had seen previously, to which many responded "folklorico." They expressed their surprise at seeing modern dance, as they had not known that such dance was being done in Mexico. The second year of the grant features artists from China, and the third will likely be Iran (although it is stated that the Iranian artists will probably have to be expatriates living in Paris or elsewhere).

Grand Performances presents free summer concerts in a corporate plaza on Bunker Hill in downtown Los Angeles. Its goal is to provide access to high quality performing arts for everyone, present free performances that reflect the city's diverse ethnic groups, provide a place for groups to perform outside of their ethnic communities, and allow Angelenos to see the performing arts of nationalities other than their own. Its slogan "Celebrate the World...Celebrate L.A.!" reflects a new imagining of urban diversity as something that helps to constitute the city as global. This new imagining is realized through its work of presenting performing arts from around the world in order to showcase the diversity of the city. The Irvine project highlights a connection made by the presenters between local immigrant groups and art forms from their home country that is reflected in world music and dance programming throughout the season. This connection helps produce the global city through public concerts, marking the intersection of cosmopolitanism, multiculturalism, and transnationalism.

Los Angeles as a cosmopolitan city

According to the Oxford English Dictionary, cosmopolitan means to belong "to all parts of the world; not restricted to any one country or its inhabitants." It is derived from the Greek "cosmopolite", meaning "citizen of the world." A person who is cosmopolitan is at home in many countries. A cosmopolitan city is one with people from many countries. Los Angeles is undoubtedly a cosmopolitan city. Its cosmopolitanness is based on active transnational personal and business connections, current migration in and out of the city, and the presence of large numbers of recent immigrants from Mexico, Central America, China, the Philippines, Syria, Vietnam, Europe, Africa, and elsewhere. Los Angeles is cosmopolitan because of the presence of people from different countries, who, to make the city cosmopolitan, are recognized for their non-local backgrounds. That they often live and run businesses in neighbourhoods with other immigrants from those countries has lent to the demarcation and labelling of areas such as Little Ethiopia, Historic Filipinotown, Little Tokyo, and Chinatown.

Who though, in the cosmopolitan city of Los Angeles, is a cosmopolitan? And for whom is the city cosmopolitan? If a cosmopolitan is one who belongs to many countries, can immigrants from specific countries who, in maintaining many of the practices from those countries (including food and festivities) that create the cosmopolitan city, be cosmopolitans? Those who constitute the cosmopolitan city are expected to stay in a designated area of the city and to be marked by their country of origin. Because they are marked by particularity rather than universality, they are not cosmopolitan. Who, then, is the cosmopolitan (or should it be "cultural tourist"?) who experiences the cosmopolitan city, travelling from neighbourhood to neighbourhood to eat unfamiliar food, to attend the Chinese New Year Parade and Cinco de Mayo events in East Los Angeles, to listen to jazz at Leimert Park, and have dinner at the French Café in the garment district in downtown L.A.; who might live in Los Angeles, but is never rooted there, travelling the world in the same way she tours the city?

There is a qualitative difference between the producer and consumer of the cosmopolitan city: the former is particular, the latter universal. The cosmopolitan city depends on both. Cosmopolitanism is not inherently exclusive in regard to specific social categories of ethnicity, race, and nationality; rather, it excludes the particular in the abstract. At the heart of the meaning of cosmopolitan is an idea of universality. Being cosmopolitan entails a process of abstraction to universalism. Multiculturalism also depends on abstraction. The multicultural city is based on local differences related, like the cosmopolitan city, through an abstraction. The abstraction of multiculturalism is culture. Culture is the universal, but for multiculturalism to be *multi,* culture also has to be particular and based in some kind of difference. The cosmopolitan city helps link multiculturalism and transnationalism. It allows for local multiculturalism to be based on the presence of people from other nations, and for multiculturalism to help constitute the global city through the transnational connections of the city's residents. Multiculturalism, however, presents cosmopolitanism with the problem of difference.

The editors of a special issue of *Public Culture* on Cosmopolitanism raise the conundrum of relating contemporary multiculturalism to cosmopolitanism. "Refugees, peoples of the diaspora, and migrants and exiles represent the spirit of the cosmopolitical community. Too often, in the West, these peoples are grouped together in a vocabulary of victimage and come to be recognized as constituting the 'problem' of multiculturalism to which late liberalism extends its generous promise of a pluralist existence. Cultural pluralism recognizes difference so long as the general category of the people is still fundamentally understood within a national frame" (Pollock, Bhabha, Breckenridge, and Chakrabarty 2000: 582).

When Grand Performances presents performing artists from around the world, there is often a pop element to the music, or movements are recognizable as the language of modern dance. In other words, there is a common element to the performance that makes it accessible for a public to which it might be unfamiliar (although some would say that just by being music it is universal). However, these performances also draw audiences connected to the music by race, ethnicity, and nationality, in other words, those categories upon which multicultural notions of difference are based. Here, the abstract universal consumer of the multicultural qua cosmopolitan city is marked by difference. The question, though, is what constitutes difference, what kinds of difference are part of multiculturalism, and what the limits to difference are for multiculturalism.

Mapping the multicultural city

Like many cities, the diversity of Los Angeles is mapped geographically through statistics based on census figures, news features with journalists reporting from the scene of the crime, and in the imaginations of the city's residents. The racialization of urban space inspires feelings of safety and fear, of familiarity and the unknown, motivating residents' activities and travels around the city. Often, the names of geographic areas are used as euphemisms to describe ethnic or racial groups. In Los Angeles at the present moment, East L.A. stands for Latino, South Central (recently officially renamed "South Los Angeles" by the City Council) for African-American, the West Side for white.[1] Demographic shifts, such as the influx of Mexican and Central American immigrants to the area originally called South Central, are used by those with more firsthand experience as "evidence" against stereotypes, yet the stereotypes remain. Reflecting the strong association of area name with demographics rather than geography, the term "South Central" refers not to a geographic area but to the area with the highest African-American population. As the *Los*

---

[1]   The racialization of urban geography has a history based in racial and economic segregation enacted through, among other things, zoning and housing policies such as redlining and restrictive covenants, white flight, gentrification, and the formation of ethnic enclaves based on shared language and background.

Angeles Times reported, the name "originally applied to the black community that flourished along South Central Avenue from the 1920s to 1940s. As African Americans moved west, the name South-Central followed them" (Gold and Braxton, 2003, p. B3).

Public concerts take place in cities that, like Los Angeles, are mapped ethnically and racially. However, public concert programming, as exemplified by Grand Performances, marks a new perception of the residents of the ethnicized or racialized city, who are now understood to be connected to traditions and homelands they might have left a few years before or generations ago. This awareness is realized through programming and marketing. In keeping with its mission, an effort is made to program music and dance each summer that will attract the range of racial, ethnic, and national groups that are present in Los Angeles. Artists are programmed that, along with a general audience, will also attract a particular ethnic group. This programming, that helps constitute the diversity of the audience, is influenced by how the presenters imagine the diversity of the city. Musical genres and dance are programmed that are coded by race (such as jazz), ethnicity (rock en español), nationality (Indian dance), or age (hip hop). These performances are presented to draw audiences connected to that music because of their shared social category as well as help others not in that category better understand and tolerate those whose art form is presented.

Marketing helps draw the audiences connected to the featured performers through race, ethnicity, nationality, and age. In addition to its general season marketing that includes distribution of 35.000 season brochures to their mailing list, others distributed through libraries, cultural organizations and at concerts, and advertisements in the mainstream press such as the *Los Angeles Times* and the *L.A. Weekly*, Grand Performances target markets some of its events to ethnic communities with the same background as the performer. A performance of a modern dance company from Mexico City in 2001 was marketed heavily to the city's Latino population. The Spanish-language newspaper donated advertisement space, the Mexican consulate was involved in the planning and organization of the event, and Latino businesspeople and politicians were solicited for support. In 2002, to advertise a concert of jarocho music from Veracruz, the mailing list was queried to find addresses with zip codes in areas known to have many Latino residents. This summer, the Director of Marketing will work with the Chinese

American Museum to distribute information to the Chinese communities in Los Angeles about performances of Chinese artists.

The success of the aims of Grand Performances depends on the attendance and recognition of audiences. Audience demographics are determined by mailing list zip codes, staff estimations based on observing audiences, self-reports on mailing list sign-ups, and occasional surveys. Performances often draw significant numbers of people with the same ethnic or racial background as the performer. According to those who reported their ethnicity on mailing list sign-ups, in 2002 the audience for a Latino comedy group was 73% Latino; the audience for an African-American jazz singer was 50% African-American two nights in a row; and the audience for the Los Angeles Baroque Orchestra was 66% Caucasian. Exceptions to these patterns are seen at concerts of artists that are more established as part of a general "world music" genre, where audiences are predominantly Caucasian. However, at these events, the ethnic group that shares the background of the performer is present in larger numbers than at other performances, such as Hawaiians and Pacific Islanders at hula performances, Middle Easterners (especially self identifying Persians) at the Central Asian Festival, Indians at an Indian dance performance, and so forth.

The fact that audiences usually have a large number of people of the same ethnic background as the performers shows not only that target marketing is effective, but that many ethnic communities pay attention to the media, whether mainstream or ethnic specific, and go to see groups from their home country. Many audience members state that they heard about a concert from an ethnic-specific media source. Chinese audience members at a Chinese opera performance noted that they had been informed about the event from the local Chinese media. At the Central Asian Festival, many audience members of Middle Eastern descent reported that they had heard about the event on AM670, an Iranian radio station that is broadcast in Farsi. (This station was later the source of information about INS detentions after a registration process instigated by the newly formed Department of Homeland Security. Iranians rallied in front of the Federal Building to protest these detentions after hearing about them on AM670, indicating the significance of the station as a news source for and about the Iranian community as well as a motivator of activities, whether protesting or attending a public concert.)

As the marketing of jarocho music to residents in zip code areas with a high percentage of Latinos reflects, non-homogeneous ethnic groups are often collapsed into more regimented categories (Dávila 2001). Jarocho is from a specific part of Mexico, yet the concert was marketed to anyone with a Latin background. While there might be some connections to that music for everyone categorized as Latino, it would not be the same affiliation expressed by the audience member who wrote, "Thank you for playing my music. I'm from Veracruz." Hence, celebrating Los Angeles by celebrating the world is also about celebrating the world through the lens of Los Angeles, the ethnic formations particular to the United States, and the meanings that world music has outside its countries of origin.

Marking the threshold of the limits to difference for presenters, class is not a category used in relation to programming. Class diversity is, however, touted in relation to audience demographics. The example often given is of janitors who, after watching open rehearsals, return the night of the performance with their children. Audience surveys conducted last summer for the first time asked about income level, and thus provide "evidence" that the ethnically diverse audiences also have a range of incomes. These stories and statistics further obscure the fact of who is excluded. A significant effect of American multiculturalism is the exclusion of class as a category of diversity. At Grand Performances, showing that audiences consist of people of different racial and ethnic backgrounds and all income levels allows them to obscure their exclusions. Apparent from a variety of discussions and practices by those at Grand Performances as well as other downtown institutions and individuals is the fact that those who are fully excluded from Grand Performances, and the public of Los Angeles, are the homeless: those who "don't look like you and me," who make class distinctions apparent by the way they look, who raise the issue of the politics of class when they are visible. Thus, by keeping the homeless invisible by not allowing them to participate as members of the public, presenters and other downtown residents and power brokers exclude class as a category of multicultural diversity.

Conclusion: Golden monkeys and modern dancers

The mayor of Los Angeles was unsuccessful in his attempt to acquire pandas for the Los Angeles zoo. He was, however, promised two endangered golden monkeys, which would make Los Angeles the first North American city to have the opportunity to exhibit these "acrobatic monkeys with rusty gold fur and distinctive blue faces" (Gold 2002).

After their trip to China, Grand Performances' Director and Director of Programming settled on the Beijing Modern Dance Company, which they will present in August, 2003. This performance will be the company's premiere in the Americas. The dancers will present a work based on Stravinsky's Rite of Spring, thus fusing their Chinese roots with a "sophisticated" European art form, defying stereotypes (and meeting the terms of the grant that is funding their performance) in the process.

Grand Performances has already begun to consult with local Chinese community organizations, politicians, and media about how to market the programs. A partnership was made with a pan-Asian television network that programs in 14 languages that include Korean, Mandarin, Japanese, Tagalog, and Farsi. This network does extensive community outreach, much of which is oriented around the basic needs of recent immigrants. The director of community relations said that she is interested in doing more with the arts, something, she stated, in which immigrants participated in their home country. The Chinese American Museum will also help promote the event, and, reciprocating, Grand Performances will place information about the Chinese American Museum at its information booth. There is talk of encouraging local Chinese business people to sponsor the event. As part of these outreach activities, efforts are made to be culturally aware and sensitive; proper pronunciations will be practised, and Grand Performances' staff will research the variances of Los Angeles' Chinese communities in terms of regional background, language, and cultural participation.

The presentation of the Beijing Modern Dance Company reflects how Grand Performances inscribes the global in the local at downtown public concerts: Plans are made to present a group from China to reflect the large Chinese population of Southern California. The directors travel to China to find a group to present and work with the Chinese Embassy and local Chinese-American cultural organizations and media to fund and promote the performance. On the three nights of the performances, the staff will comment on the higher than usual number of Chinese in the audience. Those Chinese will be understood as connected to China through national origin, feelings of belonging, and ongoing personal and business connections. And on those nights they will help constitute Grand

Performances' diverse audience, reflecting the ideal multicultural, and cosmopolitan, city.

Postscript

At this moment, SARS makes the presentation of the Beijing Modern Dance Company uncertain. If they are unable to travel to the United States, local Chinese artists will be presented.

Marina Peterson

References

Dávila, Arlene. 2001. *Latinos, Inc.: The Marketing and Making of a People*. Berkeley, University of California Press.

Gold, Matea. 2002. L.A. Ponies Up Funds for Golden Monkeys. *Los Angeles Times*.

Gold, Matea and Greg Braxton. 2003. Considering South-Central by Another Name. *Los Angeles Times* April 10: B3.

Pollock, Sheldon, Homi K. Bhabha, Carol A. Breckenridge, and Dipesh Chakrabarty. 2000. Cosmopolitanisms. *Public Culture* 12(3): 577-89.

Shuster, Beth. 2002. Hahn's China Visit Yields Golden Monkeys for L.A. Zoo. *Los Angeles Times* November 20: B4.

New York City as America:
Examples from Auster and DeLillo

To account for the kind of comparative approach I am taking, let me mention a few things authors Don DeLillo and Paul Auster have in common, besides being friends and colleagues: both were born and grew up in or near New York City, both are huge fans of baseball, and what is still more significant for my analysis, both reacted in writing to the notorious events known as 9/11—although DeLillo's response was admittedly a far more immediate and elaborate than Auster's. DeLillo published his essay "In the Ruins of the Future" in December 2001, Auster his little pamphlet-like article "The City and the Country" in September 2002.[1]

Throughout his career, Auster has written in and about New York; a large part of his literary reputation still rests on the *New York Trilogy* (1985-86), three books in which the city thoroughly intertwines with textual and thematic concerns. Later he dedicated the novel *Leviathan* (1992) to Don DeLillo and, one might argue, for a good reason, since it

---

[1]   Don DeLillo, "In the Ruins of the Future: Reflections on terror and loss in the shadow of September." *Harper's* Dec. 2001: 33-40. Repr. *The Guardian* (Manchester), 22 Dec. 2001: <http://www.guardian.co.uk/Archive/Article/-0,4273,4324579,00.html>; Paul Auster, "The City and the Country", *New York Times*, 9 Sept. 2002, late ed., A23.

seems to be the one among Auster's books that best conforms with DeLillo's self-proclaimed literary objective of depicting and using "the whole picture, the whole culture", of the United States.[2] DeLillo, who returned the compliment by dedicating his latest novel *Cosmopolis* to Auster, has also written extensively on New York. Although a number of texts by both authors would have considerable relevance to the topic at hand, what follows concerns mainly the two short pieces mentioned.

In the wake of 9/11, these are both transitional essays in the sense that they attest either a need for a profound change or such a change already taking place. The 1990s, writes DeLillo, belonged to the discourse of capital markets. Now, he declares, this "narrative ends in the rubble and it is left to us to create the counternarrative". A counternarrative is precisely what DeLillo is constructing in his essay by personalising the tragedy, by watching human nature appear from the ruins, by pointing out how imagined memories tend to replace real ones. Auster, on the other hand, calls for a more concrete change: an acknowledgement of New York City as the new American heartland on the basis of its success in the realisation of democratic cultural pluralism.

There is a certain—characteristically Western if not American—patriotic element in DeLillo's musings: he sees the ongoing conflict as a struggle between "two forces in the world, past and future"; he talks about "us" and "them"; he connects violence and religion; and he suggests that "the blessings of our technology", if shared by "less scientifically advanced cultures", might erase the need for terrorism altogether. The emphasis, however, is not on political statements as such. Instead, DeLillo fully applies his distinctive literary style to create a stream of observations, visions, and arresting one-sentence paragraphs. In his own way, he contributes to the intensification of the tragic (televisual) spectacle of 9/11 by providing high-pitched descriptive language to accompany the well-known images ("... and there was the huge antenna falling out of the sky, straight down, blunt end first, like an arrow moving backwards in time"). This might be compared with the way in which his fiction has repeatedly added to the aura of certain events from collective cultural memory, whether they are mass weddings or famous baseball

---

[2]   Begley, Adam. "Don DeLillo: The Art of Fiction CXXXV," Interview, *Paris Review* 128 (Fall 1993): 274-306. Quoted in *Don DeLillo's America* <http://perival.com/delillo/delillo.html>.

games.[3] Here, above all, the aura is constructed around (American) technology:

> The World Trade towers were not only an emblem of advanced technology but a justification, in a sense, for technology's irresistible will to realise in solid form what ever becomes theoretically allowable. Once defined, every limit must be reached.
>
> ...
>
> Think of a future in which the components of a microchip are the size of atoms. The devices that pace our lives will operate from the smart quantum spaces of pure information.

This is a continuation of DeLillo's still growing preoccupation with the psychology of technology; more recently he has argued in various interviews that technology itself, its never-ending urge to find outlets for its (destructive) potential, may have partly contributed to, if not directly caused, the war in Iraq. In the essay, there are two distinct conclusions related to technology (the first explicit, the second a result of the first). Firstly, technology owns the future, it equals the future—the two words are virtually interchangeable. Secondly, technology (i.e. the future) belongs to "us", not to "them". It is practically impossible to know whether DeLillo's "we" refers to New Yorkers, Americans, or western civilisation in general, but in this context one could claim that it hardly matters. The WTC was a landmark of New York and a symbol of American capitalism but, as a functional unit, also very much part of international flows of people and capital. DeLillo's New York is the Technological Metropolis, or Technopolis, a city upon a hill in a nation bent on the future.

A different American reality (and myth) appears at the climax of the essay, when the author describes an evening walk he took in August, 2001. Among the "panethnic swarm" of Canal Street, DeLillo came across a young woman on a prayer rug, bowing towards Mecca in front of a store. He experienced something of an epiphany: "it was clearer to me than ever, the daily sweeping taken-for-granted greatness of New York. The city will accommodate every language, ritual, belief and opinion". That ideal of

---

[3]   For a thorough analysis on the concept of aura in relation to DeLillo's "Pafko at the Wall", a novella that later became the first chapter of *Underworld*, see John N. Duvall, "Baseball as Aesthetic Ideology: Cold War History, Race, and DeLillo's 'Pafko at the Wall'", *Modern Fiction Studies* 41.2 (1995): 285-313.

tolerance of difference may have been compromised by 9/11 and the aftermath, but DeLillo clearly maintains his belief in the image of the young Islamic woman as emblematic of New York. The essay ends with the image of ultimate equality: Muslim pilgrims on their way to Mecca, stripped of all signs of status—perhaps an implicit reference to New Yorkers in the wake of the tragedy, perhaps also a reminder that different cultures have different holy cities.

If in DeLillo's case it is difficult to determine who the "we" refers to, Paul Auster is different in this respect. In his short article, he attempts to summarise the relationship between New York City and the whole United States. What he sets out to prove is that "as a laboratory of human contradictions" New York continues to embody democracy, respect for the individual, and other values Americans generally consider characteristic of their country. He concludes the essay with a tongue-in-cheek suggestion that George W. Bush move to New York from Washington DC, a city the president so clearly dislikes. In the process, as Auster writes with full seriousness, Bush "might learn something about the country he is trying to govern. He might learn, in spite of his reservations, that *we* are the true heartland". The choice of the pronoun underlines the sense of community and togetherness Auster seems to feel in his city. Although he acknowledges New York's ethnic essence as a cross-section of the whole human world, he evidently feels comfortable enough with that heterogeneity to give a voice to the entire population of the metropolis, to write his central statement with the first person plural. In this brief two-sheet essay, he uses the pronoun *we* in its various forms thirty-one times, twenty-five of which clearly in the meaning "we, New Yorkers". An expression such as "my fellow New Yorkers", although not used as a salutation, creates a sense of equal belonging and establishes the speaker as one of the many. This image of a seamless, close-knit community receives even more emphasis when he refers to the attacks on the twin towers as "a family tragedy". From one point of view, there is an inherent paradox in the position Auster assumes as a spokesman of New Yorkers: while insisting that the city primarily expresses *American* values (rather than qualities specific to itself), he also maintains that these very values are what sets New York apart from the rest of the country. The underlying argument seems to be that the other parts of the nation are not democratic enough, a reproach he also explicitly aims at the president. In other words, to adopt the widely used equation between the USA and democratic values, the rest of America is not American enough.

At first glance, what all this seems to amount to is little more than an unconditional celebration of the city as the centre of all things American. However, behind these statements there is some interesting empirical material, which leads to a more thorough analysis of the bond between the city and the nation. On the basis of the over four thousand short narratives written by Americans for the National Story Project, Auster claims New York is the only city that lives as an idea, not as a mere place, in the minds of ordinary people. It tends to assume a role as the subject of a story rather than simply providing the setting in the background. And this, according to these stories from the grassroots, seems a systematic tendency in the American imagination: New York was "the only city anyone ever wanted to talk about". If this is true, the strong association between the city and the country's ideals immediately seems more solidly grounded in reality. But the mere fact that people see New York as a significant centre of national consciousness does not necessarily mean that this foregrounding is based on the heterogeneity of the city's ethnic composition or the democracy of its institutions. There are certainly several other fundamental reasons deriving from history, popular culture, art, and architecture; reasons that hardly need to be explicated here (those that made Marshall Berman call the city "a multimedia presentation whose audience is the whole world"[4]).

By naming New York as the heartland, Auster is promoting a specific image of U.S. society. What we see here—and, to some extent, in the concluding passage of DeLillo's essay—is, in the words of Richard Slotkin, "a myth of American nationality that remains vital in ... political and cultural life: the idealized self-image of a multiethnic, multiracial democracy, hospitable to difference but united by a common sense of national belonging".[5] According to Slotkin, this vision, although appearing to be as old as the country itself, in fact came to the fore in popular culture as late as the Second World War and has since then increasingly competed with the earlier, WASP-based myth of American nationality in

---

[4]   Marshall Berman, *All That Is Solid Melts into Air: The Experience of Modernity* (New York, 1988), 288.

[5]   Richard Slotkin, "Unit Pride: Ethnic Platoons and the Myths of American Nationality", *American Literary History* 13.3 (2001): 469.

public discourse. The old vision of a homogenous American culture has gradually given more space to a way of representation based on an emphasis on difference. In American Studies, of course, there has been a similar movement away from a holistic paradigm. Nevertheless, a certain terminology, exemplified by the word *heartland*, continues to rest on the old self-ideal of sameness, and to support it.

It should be made clear that in underlining the image of New York as a centre of difference, these writers are neither alone nor pioneers of the cause. To take one example, sixteen years ago Thomas Bender wrote an article on precisely that topic, with the subtitle "How America's Metropolis Counters American Myth".[6] His purpose was to show the incompatibility of the myths cherished by the dominant American culture, namely Puritanism and Jeffersonianism, with the conditions of modern urban life. The reason for this incongruity, according to Bender, is that both these traditional ideologies—in their own specific ways—reject the idea of difference, the very principle of culture and politics in a metropolis like New York. In his article, Auster connects this principle with the city's immigrant history and contends that the Statue of Liberty, evidently his favourite icon, is the best imaginable embodiment of the ideal.

The image of New York as an ideal centre of heterogeneity is certainly not in the foreground in Auster's novels, which rarely attempt to depict any kind of cross section of society but instead often convey a type of urban nothingness, a sense of being lost in a maze, with a solitary individual struggling for survival. The representation of Brooklyn in Auster's film *Smoke* (1995), with its celebration of community and local colour, serves as a better model for the salad bowl utopia. Presumably, the real-life model here is Park Slope in Brooklyn, Auster's home and a place he has described as "one of the most democratic and tolerant places on earth."[7]

A short section at the start of the last chapter of the novel *Leviathan* seems to contain several main ideas of the article Auster wrote

---

[6] Thomas Bender, "New York as a Centre of 'Difference': How America's Metropolis Counters American Myth", *Dissent* 34.4 (1987): 429-435.

[7] Quoted in Nicola Caleffi, "Paul Auster's Urban Nothingness", Stillman's Maze <http://www.blue-cricket. com/ auster/ articles/ nothing.html> 20 Apr 2003. Originally published in Italian: *Alfa Zeta* 54 (April 1996): 18-23.

ten years later. Even the phrasing is at times strikingly similar. In *Leviathan*, the use of weighty symbolism—especially a focus on the Statue of Liberty—contributes to a discussion of national ideals that ends with a model New Yorker, protagonist Benjamin Sachs, blowing up replicas of the statue and delivering straightforward moral messages to the public: "Wake up, America . ... It's time to start practising what you preach".[8] Here we come across the same principle that Auster advocates in his article, viz. that the adjective "American" should equal "tolerant and democratic," and that the USA as a whole is therefore not American enough. It is also useful to note the political background of these two statements: that Benjamin Sachs's protest in the novel stems from the *Zeitgeist* of the Reagan era—what the narrator describes as a climate of "moronic, chest-pounding Americanism"—and that Auster's recent critique is directly aimed at the present project for national unity and security, which inevitably produces fertile soil for intolerance.[9]

The primary value Auster discusses in relation to both the city and the whole country is democracy; for DeLillo, it is technology. Both, however, attach their key concepts to iconic New York landmarks and thus participate in a discourse that could be said to produce an excess of signification in the space of the city. This discourse tends to boil down the ideological meanings of both "New York" and "the USA" somewhat in an effort to bring them closer to each other (or, if the meanings of these two entities were conceived graphically as two circles, to render them concentric).

Markku Salmela

---

[8]   Paul Auster, *Leviathan* (London: Faber & Faber, 1992), 216.

[9]   Leviathan, 104.

Transient Figures in New York:
Tourists and Street People

I want to talk about two figures of postmodernity, the tourist and the homeless person, and their relationship to concepts of cityspace. In the first part of my paper, I will describe these figures and their place in the cultural imagination; in the second part, I will sketch out their different movements in the city, as well as the different maps and concepts of urban space that they produce from their different perspectives. Both the tourist and the homeless person in my talk are symbolic characters rather than social realities: I am interested in their representations of two ways of being out-of-place. As such, they have heavily stimulated the cultural imagination, in theory (this relates especially to the tourist) as well as in literature, film, and the visual arts (this relates especially to the homeless person).

1. Tourist and Homeless Person as Figures of (Post)Modernity

Both the phenomenon of tourism and that of homelessness have shaped the cultural imagination of New York. As outsiders in the eyes of the city's inhabitants, tourist and street person form an oppositional pair, whose perspectives on the city I want to utilize for questions about cultural conceptions of urban space. As transients, they cut through the urban topography, they repeat the city's plan, transgress and rewrite it; they interact with the city's system. With their status as "other" users of the city they produce "other" urban spaces.

The figures of tourist and homeless person are closely connected to a postmodernist imagination, from which their cultural significance stems and into which it feeds back. As Caren Kaplan writes, in *Questions of Travel*, "(the) prevalence of metaphors of travel and displacement in [recent cultural criticism] suggests that the modern era is fascinated by the experience of distance and estrangement, reproducing these notions through articulations of subjectivity and poetics."[1] It is this translation of migrancy from social experience to cultural articulations that interests me here. Although they move in different social spaces, the figures of tourist and homeless person are connected in the postmodern discourse that invests their existence with a symbolic meaning. I want to inquire into this symbolic meaning less with the aim to confront the figures with their social reality, but rather to analyse them as "building blocks" of the cultural imaginary.

Tourists and street people represent two poles of migrancy, both of which are significant for modern homelessness and postmodern mobility. In an "emergent dialectic (...) between two ways of being-out-of-place," as Dean MacCannell puts it,[2] they take up an important position within the cultural imaginary. I want to introduce the tourist and the homeless person as a pair of figures that represents the dychotomies inherent in postmodernity, and as an oppositional pair that acts within a discursive field in which a variety of competitions is acted out: the competition of visibility vs. invisibility, of gaze vs. practice, of security vs. flexibility, of economic vs. symbolic power, of various ways of agency, and of simulation and authenticity.

Theory connects tourism with simulation, aesthetization, play and pastiche. The tourist finds everything equally "interesting": the Statue of Liberty's presence and the World Trade Centre's absence, the dancers in

---

[1] Caren Kaplan, *Questions of Travel: Postmodern Discourses of Displacement* (Durham:Duke UP, 1996) 1.

[2] MacCannell, "Introduction," *Empty Meeting Grounds: The Tourist Papers* (London: Routledge, 1992) 5.

a Broadway musical and the panhandlers in the street, Kandinsky paintings in the Guggenheim and graffiti on the walls. The categories of "fake" and "real" merge in tourism.[3] The foreign is domesticated, and a world arises that seems to comply with the tourist's desires. In Zygmunt Bauman's words, this "makes the world seem infinitely gentle, obedient to the tourist's wishes and whims, ready to oblige." This world has one objective only: "to excite, please and amuse."[4]

Tourists are the producers of urban fictions: they construct coherent images from an otherwise contingent urban reality. These touristic images create a closed semiotic circle: everything in New York becomes a sign of "New York."[5] The tourists (re)produce that image of the city which they have booked at home. Their categorizing and "knowing" gaze stems from guide book informations or the descriptions of a tour guide; with this gaze they seem to "control" the city they perceive. At the same time they are painfully aware that they move on the city's surface. Therefore, they desire to see behind the "front stage," in order to catch a glimpse of the city's authenticity.[6]

The site of authenticity, on the symbolic map, is the site of the homeless. In the cultural imagination, the homeless exist in the last space behind the last stageset. Theirs is a position neither of control nor of economic or political power. However, the homeless seem to see beyond the surface, as they dwell in the "bowels" of the city, in its "bare streets" and subterranean tunnels. Even if their world is characterized by harsh ambiguities, even if—or because—it is marked by lack, trauma, addiction or madness, their world seems to become the last "true" world. According to Dean MacCannell, the homeless are "the souls of postmodernity." If they push their shopping carts filled with scavenged materials through

[3] See e.g. Umberto Eco, *Travels in Hyperreality* (London: Picador, 1987); Jean Baudrillard, *America* (New York: Verso, 1989); John Frow, "Tourism and the Semiotics of Nostalgia" (October 56, 1991): 123-151.

[4] Zygmunt Bauman, "From Pilgrim to Tourist – or a Short History of Identity," *Questions of Cultural Identity*, eds. Stuart Hall and Pau du Gay (London: Sage, 1996) 30.

[5] Cf. Jonathan Culler, "Semiotics of Tourism" (*American Journal of Semiotics* 1.1-2, 1981): 127-140.

[6] MacCannell, *The Tourist: A New Theory of the Leisure Class* (1976; Berkeley: Univ. of Calif. Press, 1999) 91-102, where Erving Goffman's *The Presentation of Self in Everyday Life* is appropriated for an analysis of tourism.

public space, they parody the tourists's activity of souvenir-hunting.[7] But while the homeless collect material fragments of the city, the tourists collect its representations: images, postcards, reproductions of attractions.

While the discourse on the tourist is omnipresent in postmodern theory as well as in the vernacular, the symbolic appropriation of homelessness develops mainly in contemporary literary texts, in film, and in the visual arts.[8] Both figures are affectively marked. The tourist has become a figure of ridicule, of which the speaker seeks distance (this is part of the touristic discourse, in which the tourists are always the "others"). Homeless people, contrarily, are often romanticized and mythicised in fictional representation. They are portrayed as resistant, self-reliant individuals, not as the masses that are dependent on a dysfunctional city administration, and relegated to overcrowded shelters. Equally, the homeless person in American literature is predominantly male and single, calling up topoi of American outlaw heroes; and thus clearly fails to work as representation of the growing numbers of homeless women and families. This myth-building is not unproblematic. However, it is not the only achievement of literary representation. It also enables a view on the cultural fantasies and anxieties that are expressed through figures of homelessness. Specifically in contrast with the tourist, the homeless person discloses a view on the postmodern city that addresses fears of loss: the middle-class's feeling of a loss of authenticity, and its anxiety about a material and conceptual home in a globalized world.

Tourists and street people open up specific modern spaces, not only through their opposed social status, but through their specific movements and through their outside perspective. These spaces are fundamentally different from each other. They depend on different relations to the cultural system. Dean MacCannell argues that "the tourist weaves together all the various attractions (...). His movements are a binding

---

[7]   MacCannell, *Empty Meeting Grounds* 111.

[8]   This is only a selection of recent representations of homelessness in fiction: Paul Auster: *City of Glass* (1985), *In the Country of Last Things* (1987), *Moon Palace* (1989); T.Coraghessan Boyle: *The Tortilla Curtain* (1996); Samuel R. Delany: *The Mad Man* (1994); Don DeLillo: *Mao II* (1991); Bret Easton Ellis: *American Psycho* (1991); George Dawes Green: *The Caveman's Valentine* (1995); Colum McCann: *This Side of Brightness* (1998); Sara Paretsky: *Tunnel Vision* (1995), *Ghost Country* (1999); Hubert Selby: *The Willow Tree* (1998).

together of the high points of his culture. The movements themselves are merely necessary to the reconstruction of culture."[9] These acts of confirmation are opposed by the practices of the homeless who, with all their restrictions as agents, mis/appropriate the culture and its places in more or less subversive acts. I quote MacCannell again:

> The movements of the homeless have nothing to do with the official definition of social spaces. Their movements and passages are the grounds for their very existence. If there is a stop along the way to watch television in a store window, to piss in the privacy of a stairwell, to sleep next to the hot lights of a billboard, it is because these places have been forgotten, at least temporarily, by the official marking and policy apparatus. (111-112)

In using these forgotten spaces, the homeless, according to MacCannell, produce "temporal interstices in the postmodern" (112), that is, they interrupt the immanence of postmodernity.

While the tourists reconfirm the immanence of the postmodern urban space, while they walk the main streets and never really leave the proverbial beaten track, the homeless refunctionalize the streets, using them for something other besides transit, for instance, as MacCannell writes, "to harvest (them) for aluminum cans" (112). Equally, the sidewalks are refunctionalized as short-time dwelling sites, in which a building's outer wall may become the inner wall of a temporary card-board home. The space of the homeless, then, is full of paradoxes. Inside and outside lose their definitions when public space is momentarily privatized, and when the private takes place in public. Boundaries are marked only to be given up or transgressed. This flexibility, however, is not only understood as a sign of insecurity and loss. In the cultural imagination, it satisfies desires for adventure and play in those people who feel their lives are excessively organized—tourist desires, in short, that to a large extent frame the perception of the everyday.[10]

---

[9]   MacCannell, *Empty Meeting Grounds* 111.

[10]   See MacCannell, *The Tourist*, passim.

2. Itineraries

In consequence to their different movements, tourists and street people produce different maps of the city. I want to compare two maps of New York City, a commercial tourist map, and a set of maps from Paul Auster's *City of Glass*, which I will read as the itineraries of a homeless person.

Tourist Map[11]

This tourist map, with its suggestion of perspective, is reminiscent of the panoramic view on which Michel de Certeau elaborates in his influential essay "Walking in the City," where he describes the "voluptuous pleasure" of the god-like observer who seems to possess the city and be possessed by it in his gaze from above.[12] In comparison with non-tourist maps, this map demonstrates the city's transformation in the tourist gaze. It is not ruled by topographic abstraction, but by the suggestion of concretion. The inserted representations of concrete attractions recall images that are already present in the viewer's imagination and localize them in the topography. The attractions rise up from the ground towards the viewer as an enticing, clear and manageable ensemble. This ensemble negates the chaos of skyscrapers that block each other from view, in favour of a bright plane, from which single buildings emerge in all visibility.

The selected attractions are connected with red lines—these represent the itineraries of the sight-seeing buses. The buses themselves are visible, too, in oversize representations. The vehicles and their marked itineraries introduce the idea of story into the map, and thus of narrative.[13] The map does not limit itself to a representation of urban space as an object of the viewer's gaze, but it also produces a space of agency and experience. This space, however, is subjected to the same rules as the observed space: even as participants in the urban web, the tourists remain in possession of the general view that is guaranteed by

---

[11]   New York Apple Tours brochure (7/2000).

[12]   Michel de Certeau, "Walking in the City," *The Practice of Everyday Life* (Berkeley: University of California Press, 1988) 92.

[13]   Cf. Jurij Lotman, *The Structure of the Artistic Text* (German transl: p. 340).

the map.[14] The city's meaning results from the sum of its attractions. It is not even necessary to "read" the city, since the map's icons suggest that the city imprints itself in its reproduction. Taking up MacCannell's metaphor cited above, the buses "weave" the city's attractions together into a seemingly closed text. The space hereby represented is a striated space, in which the lines and trajectories of the New York Apple Tour are subordinated to the points, the attractions: "one moves from one point to the next," as Deleuze and Guattari describe striated space.[15]

However, the itineraries and their markers, the arrows, refer also to the nomad quality of smooth space, in which the points are subordinated to the trajectory. On bus tours, then, both spaces have the same value, as have journey and arrival, the trip and its destination. Insofar, tourist New York is a commodified simultaneity of smooth and striated space.

"Homeless Map"

With their resistance to reglementation, the homeless' world defies mapping. While the tourist map represents the tourist's privileged position of control, homeless persons have hard work to do to explore the topographies and schedules of soup kitchens and shelters that are not cartographed.[16] Yet the impossibility to map the homeless is translated into symbolic capital, for instance in journalist Jennifer Toth's book *The Mole People*, where the absence of maps of the uncountable subway tunnels of New York are part of the myth of the subterranean homeless individuals and communities.[17]

The itineraries of the homeless have fascinated many writers. And even maps have entered the imagination of homelessness, as is the case

---

[14]   Cf. Dorothea Löbbermann, "Productions of Ethnic Space: Tourism's Narrations," *Postmodern New York City: Transfiguring Spaces / Raum-Transformationen.* Eds. Günter H. Lenz and Utz Riese (Heidelberg: Winter, 2003).

[15]   Deleuze/Guattari, *A Thousand Plateaus* (German transl: p.663).

[16]   See, e.g. Lee Stringer's account of his early periods of homelessness in *Grand Central Winter: Stories From the Street* (New York: Seven Stories Press, 1998).

[17]   Jennifer Toth, *The Mole People. Life in the Tunnels Beneath New York City* (Chicago: Chicago Review Press, 1993).

in Colum McCann's novel *This Side of Brightness*.[18] But the best mapped itinerary of a homeless person can be found in Paul Auster's *City of Glass*.[19] True, Stillman, the character whom protagonist Quinn follows on his ways through the city, is not explicitly homeless, he resides in a hotel. However, his seemingly aimless wanderings and his activities of collecting objects from the streets are strongly reminiscent of a street person, especially if one considers the importance of homelessness not only in *City of Glass* but also in Auster's larger body of work.[20]

Auster is equally fascinated with spatial practices as is Michel de Certeau. Like de Certeau he favours the practitioners of the city, the pedestrians, "whose bodies follow the thicks and thins of an urban 'text' they write without being able to read it."[21] Auster overwinds the metaphor of 'reading the city': First in his protagonist's attempt to make sense of Stillman's wanderings by drawing maps of his walks, and second, in his discovery of letters in this urban text which *could* be elements of a word or sentence (yet they might not be letters at all; the meaning of Stillman's walks depends entirely on Quinn's interpretations).

In contrast to the tourist map, Auster's maps are entirely schematic and abstract. No perspective invites the integration of an observer's gaze into the map's text. While the tourist map marks points and itineraries, these maps register nothing but paths. Thus they represent a radical subjectivity—the imprint of Stillman's wanderings into the city's topography. Stillman's space, then, is a smooth nomad space, which is meant to be striated by Quinn's mapping. Yet through the ambiguity of the marks on the map—we are reminded that the "W" might just as well be a bird's icon—the attempts to make the space legible seem quite futile.

Stillman's name refers to the refusal of his itineraries to speak to Quinn. In real life, street people do not so much refuse to speak, they are not heard in the public debate, their paths are unaccounted for. Yet in Auster's imagination, they become language. Or rather, their paths and

---

[18]   Colum McCann, *This Side of Brightness* (London: Phoenix, 1998).

[19]   Paul Auster, *City of Glass. The New York Trilogy* (London: Faber, 1999). 66-69.

[20]   Paul Auster, *Moon Palace, In the Country of Last Things, Tumbuktu*.

[21]   de Certeau 93.

their alleged message express a longing for the city's meaning, which is impenetrable to the observing subject.

It is here that the homeless person becomes a sign for the particularity of the city's signification, for its opacity and refusal to be read as a whole, through one reading subject. Clearly, homeless people make a lot of sense of the urban space they inhabit; however, the frame of their sign system is radically different from the sign system in which the city is normally held to make sense. In contrast, the tourist's gaze reconfirms the "normal" view of the city; and more than that: as cities are increasingly restructured for tourist consumption[22], tourists not only gaze at the city, but shape it as well. This agency is denied to homeless people. Their acts of shaping the city (through their undesired presence; through erections of shanty-towns) never make it into the city's plan.

As an oppositional pair, then, tourist and street person mark two extreme views of the city and of interaction with urban space, unfolding an imaginary map of New York that leads from the tourist's privileged ownership of the city to the homeless subversive appropriation. Clearly, tourist and homeless person meet in more spaces than in the cultural imaginary. In every-day practice, each searches for the other, either as a spectacle or as a possible source of income. Furthermore, to some extend, tourist and street person are causally linked through processes of gentrification, which make the city inviting to tourists, and which have repeatedly been identified as a main factor for contemporary homelessness.[23] There is much more to be said, for instance, about the different ethnicities and nationalities that interact in the urban space of tourism and homelessness. Yet the focus of my paper has been the spatial imagination and the postmodern consciousness. Here, tourist and homeless person evolve as key figures, as they negotiate the extremes of visibility and invisibility, of gaze and practice, of presence and absence, of inclusion and exclusion. In their contrariness they not only express different practices to make the city's text readable, but they also point to the gaps that open up within and behind this text.

Dorothea Löbbermann

---

[22] For New York, see e.g. the developments of Times Square.

[23] See e.g. Neil Smith, *The New Urban Frontier: Gentrification and the Revanchist City* (London: Routledge, 1996).

Corina Anghel is an assistant professor at the English Department, Faculty of Foreign Languages, University of Bucharest, where she teaches American literature and philosophy, and creative writing. Her past awards include an O.S.I. - Chevening Fellowship at Oxford University (2000-2001) and a Fulbright Fellowship at Oregon State University (2001-2002). She has participated int conferences and projects in Germany, Great Britain, Finland, Hungary, the Netherlands, Romania, Serbia, and the U.S., and her academic papers have been published in international journals and books. She is also the author of two volumes of poetry: *Fugue in a Minor Age* (Paideia, 2002) and *Triptych* (Paralela 45, 2004).

Irene Artigas Albarelli teaches at the Universidad Autónoma of Mexico, Mexico City.

Kousar Jabeen Azam retired recently as a Professor of Political Science from Osmania University Hyderabad, and presently is a member of the Public Service Commission of the Government of Andhra Pradesh in Hyderabad, India. Apart from American Studies, her research interests include International Relations, US Foreign Policy and South Asian Security Issues. A recipient of Ford, Fulbright, and Rockefeller Fellowships, she served the American Studies Research Centre at Hyderabad for five years till 2000.

Albena Bakratcheva is Associate Professor of American Studies at the New Bulgarian University of Sofia, Bulgaria, and the Chair of the American and British Studies Program. She is author of "Similarities in Divergences. Realistic Narrative Characteristics in the Eighteenth-Century British Novel and Late Nineteenth-Century Bulgarian Fiction" (Sofia, 1995) and "Potentialities of Discourse. Bulgarian/British-American Cross-cultural Dialogues" (Sofia, 1997). Her book-in-progress is on American Transcendentalism. Dr. Bakratcheva is member of the International American Studies Association (IASA) and the Swedish Association for American Studies (SAAS). Albena Bakratcheva's international experience includes: Fellowship of the John F. Kennedy Institute for North American Studies at the Freie Universität Berlin, Germany, 1992; Fulbright Grant in the SUNY USA, 1993-1994; USIA Fellowship - Summer Institute on Contemporary American Literature at the University of Louisville, Kentucky, USA, 1999. E-mail: abakratcheva@nbu.bg

Carmen Birkle is Associate Professor of American Studies at the Johannes Gütenberg-Universität Mainz. She has taught as a guest professor at the University of Vienna and at Columbia University in New York City. She received the degrees of Dr. phil. and Dr. phil. habil. in American Studies from the University of Mainz. Her publications and research focus on American women's literature and culture, travel writing, postcolonialism, ethnic writers, popular culture, and detective fiction. She is the author of *Women's Stories of the Looking Glass: Autobiographical Reflections and Self-Representations in the Poetry of Sylvia Plath, Adrienne Rich, and Audre Lorde* (1996) and *Migration — Miscegenation — Transculturation: Writing Multicultural America into the Twentieth Century* (2004) and co-editor of *(Trans)Formations of Cultural Identity in the English-Speaking World* (1998), *Frauen auf der Spur: Kriminalautorinnen aus Deutschland, Großbritannien und den USA* (2001), and *Sites of Ethnicity: Europe and the Americas* (2004).

Allison Blakely is Professor of European and Comparative History, and George and Joyce Wein Professor of African American Studies, at Boston University. He moved to Boston University in 2001 after teaching for thirty years at Howard University. He is the author of *Blacks in the Dutch World: the Evolution of Racial Imagery in a Modern Society* (Indiana University Press, 1994); *Russia and the Negro: Blacks in Russian History and Thought* (Howard University Press, 1986 - a winner of an American Book Award in 1988); several articles on Russian populism; and others on various European aspects of the Black Diaspora. His interest in comparative history has centred on comparative populism and on the historical evolution of collor prejudice. Among the awards he has received are Woodrow Wilson, Mellon, Fulbright-Hays, and Ford Foundation Fellowships. He is an elected Senator at Large of the Phi Beta Kappa Society and serves on the editorial board of its journal, *The American Scholar.*

Jacob Brits is professor of history at the University of South Africa (Unisa). His main field of research and teaching is modern South African history and his publications include *Tielman Roos: Political prophet or opportunist?* (Pretoria, 1987); three chapters in *South Africa in the twentieth century*, edited by B.J. Liebenberg and S.B. Spies (Pretoria, 1993); *Doing history: 'A practical guide to improving your study skills* (Cape Town, 1993); *Op die vooraand van apartheid: Die rassevraagstuk en die blanke politiek in Suid-Afrika, 1939-1948* (Pretoria, 1994); *The Penguin concise dictionary of historical and political terms* (London, 1995). In addition he produced numerous articles on modern South African history, including South African relations with the USA.

Helena Carvalhão Buescu is full professor of Comparative Literature in Universidade de Lisboa. Her main areas of interest centre on the 19th and 20th centuries, as well as theoretical issues in comparative literature. She regularly collaborates with foreign Universities, as a Visiting Professor or Researcher (Universities of Köln, Indiana/Bloomington, Harvard, Porto Alegre, Belo Horizonte, Rio de Janeiro, Madison/Wisconsin, Stanford, Princeton) and she has more than one hundred essays published, in both Portuguese and international periodicals. She founded and directs the research Centre of Comparative Studies (Universidade de Lisboa). Main books include: *Incidências do Olhar. Percepção e Representação* (1990); *A Lua, a Literatura e o Mundo* (1995); editor of *Dicionário do Romantismo Literário Português* (1997); *Em Busca do Autor*

Perdido (1998); editor (with M. Tamen) of *A Revisionary History of Portuguese Literature* (Garland, 1999); *Chiaroscuro. Modernidade e Literatura* (2001); *Grande Angular. Comparatismo e Práticas de Comparação* (2001). Member of Academia Europaea.

Gavin James Campbell is associate professor of American history and culture in the Graduate School of American Studies at Doshisha University in Kyoto, Japan. The author of *Music and the Making of a New South* (University of North Carolina Press, 2004), he has also written numerous articles on American music and cultural history, and is currently working on a study of the relationship between music and the contemporary South in the American imagination.

Mary Kupiec Cayton is Professor of History and American Studies at Miami University. She is the author of *Emerson's Emergence: Self and Society in the Transformation of New England, 1800-1845* and co-editor of two prize-winning reference works, *The Encyclopedia of American Social History* and *The Encyclopedia of American Cultural and Intellectual History*. Her published essays include contributions to the *American Historical Review*, the *Journal of Social History*, *American Quarterly*, and *Reviews in American History* (among others).

Amaryll Chanady is Professor of comparative literature and departmental chair at the Université de Montréal, Canada. She has published mainly on marginalization, the constitution of national identity, the question of the Other, multiculturalism, postcolonialism, and Latin American literature and culture. Her articles have appeared in *The International Journal of Politics, Culture, and Society*, *Revista de crítica literaria latinoamericana*, *Diogenes*, *Sociocriticism*, *Revista de estudios hispánicos*, *Impréévue*, *Espace caraïbe*, *Río de la Plata*, *Semiotica*, *Études françaises* and *Terceira Margem*, as well as in various collective volumes. Her books include *Entre inclusion et exclusion: la symbolisation de l'autre dans les Amériques* (Paris: Honoré Champion, 1999 and (as editor) *Latin American Identity and Constructions of Difference* (Minneapolis: University of Minnesota Press, 1994).

Helen M. Dennis is a Senior Lecturer in the Department of English and Comparative Literary at the University of Warwick. She has published on Ezra Pound and Medieval Provençal, Gender in American Literature and Culture, Elizabeth Bishop, Willa Cather and Adrienne Rich. Most recent publications include an edited volume on *Ezra Pound and Poetic Influence* with Rodopi Press, Amsterdam, an essay on modernist memoirs in a volume published by Presses de l'Université de Paris Sorbonne, and an essay on desiring space in the writings of Native American women authors in a volume published by Universitätsverlag Winter Heidelberg. She is currently working on European readings of Native American Literature.

Theo D'haen is Professor of American Literature at Leuven University (The Catholic University of Louvain) in Belgium, and emeritus Professor of English and American Literature at Leyden University, in The Netherlands. He has published widely on modern literatures in European languages, particularly on Modernism and Postmodernism, Colonialism and Postcolonialism, and popular literature. His most recent publications include *Contemporary American Crime Fiction* (London and New York: Palgrave/Macmillan, 2001, with Hans Bertens), *Europa Buitengaats: Koloniale en Postkoloniale literaturen in Europese talen* (Amsterdam: Bert Bakker, 2002), and *Configuring Romanticism* (Amsterdam and New York: Rodopi, 2003). He served as Executive Director of IASA 2000-2003, and as General Organizer of the First IASA Congress, at Leyden University, in 2003.

Rosario Faraudo is professor of English Literature at the Universidad Nacional Autónoma de México, and at the Colegio de México. She holds a Master's Degree in Comparative Literature from UNAM, and a Bachelor of Arts in English from London University. Her main areas of interest include Medieval Literature, Nineteenth-Century Literature by women in North America and Europe, Mexican modernism, and Literature and the visual arts.

Camilla Fojas is an Assistant Professor in Latin American and Latino Studies at DePaul University. Her main areas of research are cultural, film, and media studies of the Americas within a comparative postcolonial frame that includes Latin America, the Caribbean, the United States, Hawai', and the Philippines. Her book *Cosmopolitanism in the Americas* is forthcoming from the Comparative Cultural Studies Series at Purdue University Press in early 2005. She has work forthcoming from *Comparative Literature Studies*, *Comparative Literature and Culture*, and *Aztlán*.

Khadija Fritsch-El Alaoui is an Instructor, Part-time, at the Institute for North American Studies, T.U. Dresden. She holds a Ph.D. in American Studies from T.U. Dresden, and a B.A. in English Literature from Hassan II University in Casablanca.

Pedro García-Caro has recently gained his PhD at the Department of American Studies, King's College London with a thesis entitled "Dismantling the Nation: History as Satire in the Works of Thomas Pynchon and Carlos Fuentes." He researches on nationalism and the historical novel, the construction and critique of nationalist discourses in the Americas, and in particular the relations between Mexican and American literary reactions to hegemonic cultural and political discourses. He has taught Spanish at the University of Oxford and is currently working at the Foreign Languages and Literatures Department at MIT.

Paul Giles is Reader in American Literature and Director of the Rothermere American Institute at the University of Oxford, U.K. He is also Vice-President of the International American Studies Association. Among his books are *Virtual Americas: Transnational Fictions and the Transatlantic Imaginary* (2002), *Transatlantic Insurrections: British Culture and the Formation of American Literature, 1730-1860* (2001), and *American Catholic Arts and Fictions: Culture, Ideology, Aesthetics* (1992).

Kathleen Haney teaches at the University of Houston, Downtown.

Sheila Hones is an Associate Professor at the University of Tokyo, where she teaches in the Area Studies department of the Graduate School of Arts and Sciences, and the English section and the North American studies division of the College of Arts and Sciences. In her research she works with English-language texts in the contexts of critical/cultural geography, literary theory, and American studies.

Djelal Kadir is the Founding President of the International American Studies Association. He holds the Edwin Erle Sparks Professorship of Comparative Literature at the Pennsylvania State University, University Park, PA, USA. Former Editor of the international quarterly *World Literature Today,* he has also served on the editorial board of *PMLA* and continues to serve on the editorial board of a number of scholarly journals, including *Comparative American Studies, Comparative Literature Studies, Variaciones Borges,* and *Modern Fiction Studies, CR: Centennial Review, Revue Française d'Études Américaines,* and *Dedalus.* He is Co-Editor of the *Literary Cultures of Latin America: A Comparative History,* 3 vols. (Oxford UP, 2004), of the *Longman Anthology of World Literature,* 6 vols. (2003), of *Other Modernisms in An Age of Globalization* (Heidelberg: Universitätsverlag C. Winter, 2002), and editor of a special issue of *PMLA* on "America: The Idea, the Literature" (January 2003). Some of his previous book publications include: *Columbus and the Ends of the Earth: Europe's Prophetic Rhetoric As Conquering Ideology* (University of California Press, 1992); *The Other Writing: Postcolonial Essays in Latin America's Writing Culture* (Purdue University Press, 1993); *Questing Fictions: Latin America's Family Romance.* (University of Minnesota Press, 1987); He has authored numerous articles, essays, and reviews in the field of American Studies, globalization, and comparative cultural studies. He is a Senior Fellow of SYNAPSIS: The European School of Comparative Studies, and an active member of the Accademia Equestre Italiana Monta da Lavoro.

Amy Kaplan is the Edmund J. and Louise W. Kahn Endowed Term Professor in the Humanities at the University of Pennsylvania. She is the author of *The Anarchy of Empire in the Making of U.S. Culture* (Harvard, 2002) and *The Social Construction of American Realism* (Chicago, 1989), and coeditor of *Cultures of U.S. Imperialism* (Duke, 1993). She was the president of the American Studies Association in 2003.

Bernd Klähn studied Physics, Philosophy and English Philology. He is Associate Professor at the University of Bochum (Germany) and Guest Professor at the University of Dortmund (Germany), teaching English Philology and American Studies. His book publications include *Materialistic Theories of Art and Dialectical Models* and *Postmodernist Prose: Pynchon, Hawkes, Coover* (Munich 1999). He has published in international journals in the area of English and American Studies, especially in the field of postmodernism, aesthetics, and the history of science and is focusing his attention on interdisciplinary studies, including literature and ethics, and narrative constructions of body and nature.

Julia Leyda teaches in the Department of English Literature at Sophia University in Tokyo.] Her research interests include US literature and culture, critical geography, and the construction of class identities in literature. She has published articles in *Arizona Quarterly, Cinema Journal, The Japanese Journal of American Studies*, and *Comparative American Studies*. She is currently writing a book with Sheila Hones tentatively entitled *Geographies of American Studies*.

Dorothea Löbbermann teaches American literature at Humboldt-University, Berlin, and has been associated with the Zentrum für Literaturforschung, Berlin (Center for Literary Studies) for a number of years. Her book publications are *Memories of Harlem: Fiktionale (Re)Konstruktionen eines Mythos der zwanziger Jahre* (Frankfurt: Campus, 2002) and *Other Modernisms in an Age of Globalization*, coedited with Djelal Kadir (Heidelberg: Winter, 2002). In 2004, she was a Fulbright research fellow at The Graduate Center, The City University of New York, where she worked on her forthcoming book about figurations of homelessness.

Helen R. McClure is a Ph.D. candidate in International Relations at the School of International Service of American University in Washington, D.C. Her concentrations include International Peace and Conflict Resolution and Comparative and International Race Relations. Her dissertation compares the discourse surrounding Arabs/Muslims in the United States and Canada post-September 11.

Silvia Navia Méndez-Bonito is Assistant Professor of Spanish at Webster University (Saint Louis MO, USA). She holds a doctoral degree from the University of Massachusetts, Amherst. For her dissertation she has worked on Juan de Velasco´s *Historia natural del Reino de Quito*. Her current research focuses on the presence of a national consciousness in the histories written by eighteenth-century Spanish American ex-Jesuits. Her article "Las Historias Naturales de Francisco Javier Clavijero, Juan Ignacio de Molina y Juan de Velasco" is forthcoming in the volume *Jesuit Knowledge, Natural Histories and the New World, El saber de los jesuitas, historias naturales y el Nuevo Mundo*, to be published by Iberoamericana-Vervuert.

Joshua L. Miller is assistant professor of English at the University of Michigan. He has published essays on James Baldwin and Richard Avedon, John Sayles, and Carlos Bulosan. He is currently completing a book-length study titled *Lingual Politics: The Syncopated Accents of Multilingual Modernism*.

Tatsushi Narita is Professor of American Literature and American Culture at the Graduate School of Humanities and Social Sciences, Nagoya City University, Nagoya City, Japan. He has published over 40 articles, three books, two edited books, two co-authored books, and others. He was a Visiting Scholar at Harvard University on several different occasions, working with Walter J. Bate and Ronald Bush. His current interest is in the conceptualization of Transpacific American Studies; his particular concern is with resituating T.S. Eliot's American period based on new materials. He serves on the Executive Council, International American Studies Association (IASA); he is also President, Nagoya Comparative Culture Forum (NCCF).

Anders Olsson is senior lecturer of English at Mid-Sweden University with a Ph.D. in American Literature from Uppsala University. He has published two books: *Studies in American Literature* (1996) and *Managing Diversity: The Anthologization of "American Literature"* (2000) and is at the moment one of the scholars in the project *Literary Generations and Social Authority: A Prosopographical Study of U.S. Prose-Fiction Debut Writers 1940-2000*. He is the secretary of The Swedish Association of American Studies and has written numerous essays on topics related to American Studies and American Literature, most recently as a part of The Futures of American Studies Institute at Dartmouth College 2004.

Marina Peterson is a Ph.D. candidate in Anthropology at the University of Chicago. She is currently completing her dissertation "Sounding the City: Public Concerts and Civic Belonging in Los Angeles."

Gönül Ayda Pultar teaches at Boğgaziççi (Bosphorus) University (Istanbul, Turkey), and taught previously at Bilkent University and Middle East Technical University. She was a research fellow at the Longfellow Institute of Harvard University. She is the Chair of the Group for Cultural Studies in Turkey, a charter member of IASA, and a member of the International Advisory Board of MELUS-India. She was the Vice-President of the American Studies Association of Turkey; the chair of the Executive Committee of the Discussion Group on American Literature in Languages Other than English at the MLA; a member of the International Committee, and of the Sakakabira International Prize Committee of the ASA; and a member of the Advisory Board of MESEA. The founding editor of *Journal of American Studies of Turkey*, she is currently an Editorial Advisory Board member of *Journal of Popular Culture*. Her published works include the monograph *Technique and Tradition in Beckett's Trilogy of Novels* (1996); and two original novels, *Düünya Bir Atlikar ınca* (The

World is a Merry-go-round, 1979); and *Ellerimden Su Iççsinler* (Let Them Drink Water from My Hands, 1999); as well as numerous entries, articles and chapters in encyclopedias, journals and books. The collection of essays she edited, *On the Road to Baghdad or Traveling Biculturalism: Theorizing a Bicultural Approach to Contemporary World Fiction* is forthcoming.

Cecilia Enjuto Rangel is finishing her Ph.D., *Cities in Ruins in Modern Poetry*, in the Department of Comparative Literature at Yale University. She is currently teaching Spanish and Latin American poetry at Harvard University. She has published on Octavio Paz and Pablo Neruda.

Justin Read is Assistant Professor of Spanish and Portuguese in the Department of Romance Languages at the State University of New York at Buffalo. His areas of interest are twentieth-century poetry, architecture, and popular music of the Americas. He is currently completing a book manuscript on modernist/avant-garde poetry entitled, *Inter:America (The Cultural Poetics of Inter-American Studies)*.

Janice L. Reiff is an Associate Professor of History at the University of California, Los Angeles. Co-editor with James R. Grossman and Ann Durkin Keating of the *Encyclopedia of Chicago* (2004), she is author of *Structuring the Past: The Use of Computers in History* (1992), co-editor with Helen Hornbeck Tanner, Dirk Hoerder, John Long, and Henry Dobyns of *The Settling of North America: The Atlas of the Great Migrations into North America from the Ice Age to the Present* (1995), and numerous articles in urban and social history. She is currently at work on a book tentatively titled *Industrial Towns, Suburban Dreams, and Urban Realities: Pullman's Communities, 1880-1981*.

Markku Salmela is a Ph.D. student of English in the University of Tampere, Finland. As a member of the Finnish Graduate School of the Americas, he is completing a dissertation on Paul Auster. He spent the academic year 2003-04 as a Fulbright grantee at Case Western Reserve University in Cleveland, Ohio.

Cinzia Schiavini holds a research appointment at the University of Milan, Italy. She has published articles and essays on Jerome David Salinger, Henry Roth, Edgar Allan Poe and Herman Melville. The essay included in this volume is part of a broader study on the representation of space and the definition of American national identity in Melville's novels. She is currently working on travel writing and the rediscovery of the past in contemporary American culture.

Amporn Srisermbhok is a former Fulbright scholar, specialized in American Literature. For the past ten years she has been a graduate studies administrator and curriculum designer at the Department of Western Languages of Srinakharinwirot University, Thailand. She has been Director of the American Studies program since 1995. She is also Chair of the new Graduate Program in

Business English for International Communication. Her publications include essays on Henry James' major works, and on Toni Morrison. Her new book on feminism is currently in press.

Werner Sollors, the author of *Beyond Ethnicity: Consent and Descent in American Culture* and of *Neither Black Nor White Yet Both: Thematic Explorations of Interracial Literature*, received the Dr. phil. degree from the Freie Universität Berlin and teaches African American Studies, English, and Comparative Literature at Harvard University.

Rodney Stephens is Assistant Professor of English at Howard Payne University. His publications include "Shattered Windows, German Spies, and Zigzag Trenches: World War I through the Eyes of Richard Harding Davis" and "Rape, Writing, and Recovery in Bao Ninh's *The Sorrow of War.*" He lived in Spain for six years, where he taught post-colonial literature at Saint Louis University (Madrid) and European images of America at Syracuse University (Madrid). He received a Ph.D. in American Studies from Saint Louis University in 2001.

Kirsten Twelbeck currently teaches American culture and literature at the University of Hannover. She studied American Studies and Theater and Drama at the University of Erlangen-Nürnberg, the Freie Universität Berlin, and at Indiana University in Bloomington, USA. She is especially interested in questions related to ethnicity and cultural contact in the postcolonial context. Her dissertation on Korean American culture and literature was published in 2002. She is currently working on a book on concepts of the American nation during the Civil War and Reconstruction.

Jerry Varsava is a Professor of Comparative Literature and English at the University of Alberta (Canada) where he also serves as Associate Dean in the Faculty of Graduate Studies and Research. He has published extensively on contemporary fiction, and is currently working on a monograph on the contemporary American social novel.

Roland Walter is Associate Professor of English and Comparative Literature at the Federal University of Pernambuco (UFPE), Recife, Brazil. He is the author of *Magical Realism in Contemporary Chicano Fiction* (1993) and *Narrative Identities: (Inter)Cultural In-Betweenness in the Americas* (2003) and has published widely in journals throughout the Americas on diverse aspects of inter-Amercan literatures. He is currently writing on African cultural expressions in the Americas. E-mail: walter_roland@hotmail.com

Jerry M. Williams is chair of Foreign Languages and professor of Spanish and Latin American Studies at West Chester University of Pennsylvania. His books include an edition of *Historia de España vindicada by Peralta Barnuevo* (2003), *Peralta Barnuevo and the Art of Propaganda: Politics, Poetry, and Religion*

(2001), *Peralta Barnuevo and the Discourse of Loyalty: A Critical Edition of Four Selected Texts* (1996), *Censorship and Art in Pre-Enlightenment Lima* (1994), *Early Images of the Americas: Transfer and Invention* (with Robert Lewis, 1993), and *El teatro del México colonial: época misionera* (1992). He has published critical essays on sixteenth-century Spanish-American historiography, theatre, religious iconography, and censorship in journals such as *Colonial Latin American Review, Revista de Estudios Hispánicos, Luso-Brazilian Review, Revista Canadiense de Estudios Hispánicos, Dieciocho*, and *Hispania*.

Lois Parkinson Zamora is Professor at the University of Houston in the Departments of English, History, and Art. Her area of specialization is contemporary fiction in the Americas. Her books include *Writing the Apocalypse: Historical Vision in Contemporary U.S. and Latin American Fiction* (Cambridge University, 1989), *Magical Realism: Theory, History, Community*, co-edited with Wendy B. Faris (Duke University, 1995), *The Usable Past: The Imagination of History in Recent Fiction of the Americas* (Cambridge University, 1997), and *Image and Memory: Photography from Latin America 1866-1994* (University of Texas, 1998). *The Inordinate Eye: Reflections on the New World Baroque and Recent Latin American Fiction*, a study of the visual arts and their relation to Latin American literature, will be published by the University of Chicago Press in 2006, and a collection of essays, *Baroque New Worlds: Representation, Transculturation, Counterconquest*, co-edited with Monika Kaup, is forthcoming from Duke University Press.